FEMINIST INTERPRETATION OF THE HEBREW BIBLE, III

Recent Research in Biblical Studies, 9

Series Editor
Alan J. Hauser

General Editors
Scot McKnight and Jonathan Klawans

Feminist Interpretation of the Hebrew Bible in Retrospect

III. Methods

Edited by
Susanne Scholz

Sheffield Phoenix Press

2017

Copyright © 2016, 2017 Sheffield Phoenix Press
First published in hardback, 2016
First published in paperback, 2017

Published by Sheffield Phoenix Press
Department of Biblical Studies, University of Sheffield
Sheffield S3 7QB

www.sheffieldphoenix.com

All rights reserved.
No part of this publication may be reproduced or transmitted in any form or by any means, electronic or mechanical, including photocopying, recording or any information storage or retrieval system, without the publisher's permission in writing.

A CIP catalogue record for this book
is available from the British Library

Typeset by CA Typesetting Ltd
Printed on acid-free paper by Lightning Source

ISBN-13 978-1-910928-11-0 (hardback)
ISBN 978-1-910928-29-5 (paperback)

Contents

Preface	ix
Abbreviations	xii
About the Contributors	xv

INTRODUCTION:
METHODS AND FEMINIST INTERPRETATION OF THE HEBREW BIBLE
   Susanne Scholz ... 1

PROLEGOMENA: METHODS AS HERMENEUTICAL CONSTRUCTS

1
ON METHODS AND METHODOLOGY IN FEMINIST BIBLICAL STUDIES:
A CONVERSATION
   Pamela J. Milne and Susanne Scholz ... 19

2
SEXUAL BIBLICAL POLITICS AS AN INTERVENTIONIST INTERROGATION:
THE ISRAELITE AND FOREIGN WOMAN IN FEMINIST LITERARY
APPROACHES
   Esther Fuchs ... 35

Part I
FEMINIST READINGS BEHIND THE TEXT

3
BACK TO THE PAST:
AN OVERVIEW OF FEMINIST HISTORICAL CRITICISM
   Sarah Shectman ... 55

4
BEYOND THE BIBLE: ARCHAEOLOGY, ETHNOHISTORY, AND
THE STUDY OF ISRAELITE WOMEN
   Carol L. Meyers ... 74

5
ADVANTAGES AND CHALLENGES: COMPARATIVE HISTORICAL CRITICISM AND FEMINIST BIBLICAL STUDIES
Rebecca Hancock   91

6
WITHIN AND WITHOUT PURITY, DANGER, HONOUR, AND SHAME: ANTHROPOLOGICAL APPROACHES IN FEMINIST HEBREW BIBLE STUDIES
Johanna Stiebert   111

7
THE GOD OF THE FATHERS ENCOUNTERS FEMINISM: OVERTURE FOR A FEMINIST OLD TESTAMENT THEOLOGY
Phyllis A. Bird   136

Part II
FEMINIST READINGS WITHIN THE TEXT

8
DISCOVERING HER STORY IN THE TEXT: LITERARY CRITICISM IN FEMINIST HEBREW BIBLE STUDIES
Beth LaNeel Tanner   161

9
PATRIARCH ON THE COUCH: PSYCHOLOGY IN FEMINIST EXEGESIS
Serge Frolov   181

10
TRACING DIFFERANCE, POWER, AND THE DISCOURSE OF GENDER: DECONSTRUCTION IN FEMINIST HEBREW BIBLE STUDIES
Susanne Scholz   199

Part III
FEMINIST READINGS IN FRONT OF THE TEXT

11
SEEKING OUR SURVIVAL, OUR QUALITY OF LIFE, AND WISDOM: WOMANIST APPROACHES TO THE HEBREW BIBLE
Karen Baker-Fletcher   225

12
WHEN WOMEN AREN'T ENOUGH:
GENDER CRITICISM IN FEMINIST HEBREW BIBLE INTERPRETATION
Nicole J. Ruane 243

13
BIBLICAL WOMEN AS IDEOLOGICAL CONSTRUCTS TOWARD JUSTICE:
IDEOLOGICAL CRITICISM AS A FEMINIST/WOMANIST METHOD
Tina Pippin 261

14
DEALING WITH EMPIRE AND NEGOTIATING HEGEMONY:
DEVELOPMENTS IN POSTCOLONIAL
FEMINIST HEBREW BIBLE CRITICISM
Jeremy Punt 278

15
SURPASSING THE LOVE OF WOMEN:
FROM FEMINISM TO QUEER THEORY IN BIBLICAL STUDIES
Rhiannon Graybill 304

16
MODES OF PRODUCTIONS AND READING LABORS ON THE MARGINS:
MARXIST FEMINIST CRITICISM OF THE HEBREW BIBLE
Roland Boer 326

17
SPACE FOR WOMEN AND MEN:
MASCULINITY STUDIES IN FEMINIST BIBLICAL INTERPRETATION
Katherine Low 345

18
ENGAGING WITH CULTURAL DISCOURSES:
CULTURAL FEMINIST CRITICISM IN HEBREW BIBLE STUDIES
Caroline Blyth 364

Index of References 380
Index of Authors 383

Preface

Susanne Scholz

Thus the three volumes on the feminist interpretation of the Hebrew Bible in retrospect are finished. This third volume, only slightly delayed from the expected schedule mentioned in the preface of Volume 2, is the largest volume of the three. Like the previous two books, this third volume offers a comprehensive but selective survey on feminist Hebrew Bible scholarship; it centers on exegetical methods. The eighteen essays cover considerable ground and indicate the maturity, depth, and extend of feminist biblical exegesis as it has emerged since the 1970s. Again, I want to thank the mothers, aunts, sisters, and some brothers of feminist biblical studies. We studied with you, read your work, and joined you in your effort to theorize gender justice in the context of the field of the Hebrew Bible. We cherish your feminist scholarship, interpretative insight, and hermeneutical boldness. All of us are grateful to our feminist foremothers for starting to pave the way for us, and this three-volume series aims to keep paving the way for the next generation.

The series as a whole contributes to the present task of describing, explaining, and evaluating what has been done in feminist biblical exegesis. All three volumes intend to assist feminist exegetes in building upon the feminist achievements as they stand today. Gratitude for the feminist accomplishments is thus in order, as well as the recognition that after forty years the field of feminist biblical studies finds itself in a consolidation phase. Interestingly, no other volume currently exists that reviews, discusses, and evaluates the significance of exegetical methods in feminist Hebrew Bible exegesis. There is certainly no lack of books on exegetical methods in biblical studies, but no other volume examines how feminist biblical scholars have used the wide spectrum of exegetical methods in their work. It is thus with great pleasure that I present the eighteen essays to the scholarly and interested public in this third volume of *Feminist Interpretation of the Hebrew Bible in Retrospect*.

I thank the contributors for their willingness to submit their essays in a speedy fashion and to work with me, as the editor, in preparing a unified manuscript. I also thank Sheffield Phoenix's publisher and director, David J.A. Clines, for his encouragement and advice while I worked on this volume. Thanks also to Alan J. Hauser for including the book in the

'Recent Research in Biblical Studies' series of Sheffield Phoenix Press. I am grateful to Sheffield Phoenix's publishing team for their professional care with which they turned the manuscript into this book.

I am most grateful to my employing institution for granting me a research leave in spring 2015 during which I feverishly worked on Volume 3. Time away from teaching and committee obligations gave me concentrated focus to complete the editing of the manuscript, as well as to research and write my introduction essay as well as my own contribution to the volume. I thank the various reference librarians of Bridwell Library at Perkins School of Theology/Southern Methodist University for their generous and reliable support. I thank my research assistant, David A. Schones, for his professional help in identifying missing information in countless footnotes, in making sure that interlibrary loans get to my office, and in assisting me to proofread the manuscript in its entirety. I am most grateful to the Associate Dean for Academic Affairs at Perkins School of Theology, Evelyn L. Parker, for her support in granting me ongoing research assistance while I prepared this volume for publication.

At the finishing-line of this multi-volume project I admit: I am relieved that it is finished. Yet there is no seventh day and hence no rest in sight. Too much remains to be done in feminist Hebrew Bible studies, and so neither complacency nor contentment about feminist accomplishments are in order. Too much continues to be at stake. The ongoing efforts to sideline feminist and other theologically progressive scholarship are not new, as becomes immediately clear when we remember past or present women theologians. Let us remember their names, for instance, Marguerite Porete who was murdered by the Church in 1310. Intersectional relationships also continue to be crucial, really life-giving, in the centuries-long struggle for gender justice in its manifold manifestations, including in biblical studies. Frederick Douglas, the African American social reformer, abolitionist, and writer of the nineteenth-century, made the following powerful statement on his biblical hermeneutics that, in my view, is also relevant for feminist readers even today. His sentiment about the significance of the Bible illustrates the significance of this sacred text in many communities. He states:

> They have declared that the Bible sanctions slavery. What do we do in such a case? What do you do when you are told by the slaveholders of America that the Bible sanctions slavery? Do you go and throw your Bible into the fire? Do you sing out, 'No Union with the Bible'? Do you declare that a thing is bad because it has been misused, abused, and made bad use of? Do you throw it away on that account? No! You press it to your bosom all the more closely; you read it all the more diligently; and prove from its pages that it is on the side of liberty—and not on the side of slavery.[1]

---

1. Frederick Douglass in a speech in Glasgow, Scotland, on March 26, 1860; cited in

So what have contemporary feminists done when it was declared the Bible sanctions androcentrism, sexism, and gender injustice in its various manifestations? This three-volume retrospective on feminist Hebrew Bible interpretation traces the scholarly responses of the past few decades. Sometimes they 'prove' that some biblical texts are on the side of 'liberty', and sometimes their responses are less optimistic, showing the muddle in which biblical literature played and continues to play a considerable role in gendered structures of domination. All in all, however, the three volumes demonstrate that feminist biblical studies is a burgeoning field and there are many different responses, perspectives, approaches, and directions chosen by feminist exegetes since the 1970s. Feminist biblical exegesis is far from being finished.

J. Albert Harrill, *Slaves in the New Testament: Literary, Social, and Moral Dimensions* (Minneapolis: Fortress Press, 2006), pp. 177-78.

ABBREVIATIONS

AB	Anchor Bible
ABD	David Noel Freedman (ed.), *The Anchor Bible Dictionary* (New York: Doubleday, 1992)
ANQ	*Andover Newton Quarterly*
AOAT	Alter Orient und Altes Testament
Bib	*Biblica*
BibInt	*Biblical Interpretation*
BR	*Biblical Research*
BRev	*Bible Review*
BTB	*Biblical Theology Bulletin*
BWANT	Beiträge zur Wissenschaft vom Alten und Neuen Testament
CBQ	*Catholic Biblical Quarterlyy*
CBR	*Currents in Biblical Research*
ETR	*Evangelical Theological Review*
FAT	Forschungen zum Alten Testament
FCB	Feminist Companion to the Bible
FemTh	*Feminist Theology*
GCT	Gender, Culture, Theory
HBT	*Horizons in Biblical Theology*
HeyJ	*Heythrop Journal*
HTR	*Harvard Theological Review*
HUCA	*Hebrew Union College Annual*
Int	*Interpretation*
JAAR	*Journal of the American Academy of Religion*
JBL	*Journal of Biblical Literature*
JBQ	*Jewish Bible Quarterly*
JBTh	*Jahrbuch für biblische Theologie*
JFSR	*Journal of Feminist Studies in Religion*
JHS	*Journal of Hellenic Studies*
JRT	*The Journal of Religious Thought*
JSOT	*Journal for the Study of the Old Testament*
JSOTSup	Journal for the Study of the Old Testament: Supplement Series
LHBOTS	Library of the Hebrew Bible/Old Testament Studies
NRSV	New Revised Standard Version
OBO	Orbis biblicus et orientalis
OBT	Overtures to Biblical Theology
OTE	*Old Testament Essays*
OTL	Old Testament Library
OTS	Oudtestamentische studiën
RIBLA	*Revista de Interpretación Bíblica Latino-Americana*
SBLSS	Society of Biblical Literature Semeia Studies
SBLSymS	Society of Biblical Literature Symposium Series

SJOT	*Scandinavian Journal of the Old Testament*
SJT	*Scottish Journal of Theology*
StBL	Studies in Biblical Literature
TheolSex	*Theology & Sexuality*
TTod	*Theology Today*
USQR	*Union Seminary Quarterly Review*
VT	*Vetus Testamentum*
VTSup	Supplements to Vetus Testamentum
WW	*Word and World*
ZAW	*Zeitschrift für die alttestamentliche Wissenschaft*

About the Contributors

Karen Baker-Fletcher, PhD, is Professor of Systematic Theology, Perkins School of Theology at Southern Methodist University in Dallas, Texas, USA. Her research areas include historical and constructive theology, theology and literature, womanist scholarship in religion, womanist and feminist theology, feminist theory, ecology and theology, theology and culture. Her publications include *Dancing With God: A Womanist Perspective on the Trinity* (2006), *Sisters of Dust, Sisters of Spirit,* (1998); (with Garth Baker-Fletcher) *My Sister, My Brother: Womanist and Xodus God-Talk* (1997); *A Singing Something: Womanist Reflections on the Writings of Anna Julia Cooper* (1994).

Phyllis A. Bird, PhD, is Professor Emerita of Old Testament Interpretation at Garrett-Evangelical Theological Seminary in Evanston, Illinois, USA. Her research interests center on the social world of ancient Israel, with particular attention to women and gender, and biblical theology, with a current focus on creation theology and environmental ethics. Her publications include *Faith, Feminism, and the Forum of Scripture: Essays on Biblical Theology and Hermeneutics* (2015), *Missing Persons and Mistaken Identities: Women and Gender in Ancient Israel* (1997), *Feminism and the Bible: A Critical and Constructive Encounter* (1994), and *The Bible as the Church's Book* (1982).

Caroline Blyth, PhD, is lecturer in Biblical Studies and Religious Studies at the University of Auckland, New Zealand. Her research interests include gender violence and religion, feminist and queer readings of the Bible, the Bible and gender in popular culture, and spirituality and gender in the medical humanities. Her recent publications include *The Narrative of Rape in Genesis 34: Interpreting Dinah's Silence* (2010), *Sexuality, Ideology and the Bible: Antipodean Engagements* (co-editor, 2015), and *Spirituality and Cancer* (co-editor, 2015). She is current co-editor of the *Bible and Critical Theory* journal.

Roland Boer, PhD, is Research Professor in Philosophy of Religion at the University of Newcastle in Australia, and Professor of Literary Theory at Renmin University of China, Beijing. His main research focus is on

Marxism and religion in its many manifestations. Among many works, he has recently published *The Sacred Economy of Ancient Israel* (2015), *In the Vale of Tears: On Marxism and Theology* (vol. 5; 2014) and, with Christina Petterson, *Idols of Nations* (2014).

Serge Frolov, PhD, is Professor of Religious Studies and the Nate and Ann Levine Endowed Chair in Jewish Studies at Southern Methodist University in Dallas, Texas, USA. His areas of research include biblical hermeneutics and theology, history and religions of the ancient Near East, and Jewish history and thought. He is the author of *The Turn of the Cycle: 1 Samuel 1–8 in Synchronic and Diachronic Perspectives* (2004) and *Judges* (2013).

Esther Fuchs, PhD, is Professor of Judaic Studies at the University of Arizona in Tucson, Arizona, USA. She published numerous pioneering essays in feminist critical theory and the Bible since the 1980s, as well as *Sexual Politics in the Biblical Narrative: Reading the Hebrew Bible as a Woman* (2000) and *Feminist Theory of the Bible: Interrogating the Sources* (2016). She is the co-editor of *On the Cutting Edge: The Study of Women in Biblical Worlds* (1994).

Rhiannon Graybill, PhD, is Assistant Professor of Religious Studies at Rhodes College in Memphis, Tennessee, USA. Her research interests include prophecy, gender and sexuality, psychoanalysis, and contemporary theory. She is the author of *Unstable Masculinity in Hebrew Prophets: Reading the Prophetic Body* (2016).

Rebecca S. Hancock, PhD, teaches biblical studies at the Ecumenical Institute of St Mary's Seminary and University in Baltimore, Maryland, USA. Her research interests focus on the Hebrew Bible and its ancient Near Eastern context, ancient and modern historiography, and gender and ethnicity in the Hebrew Bible. She is the author of *Esther and the Politics of Negotiation: Public and Private Spaces and the Figure of the Female Royal Counselor* (2013).

Katherine Low, PhD, is Assistant Professor of Religious Studies and Chaplain to the College at Mary Baldwin College in Staunton, Virginia, USA. She has published numerous articles that reflect her research interest in tracking the intersections and interactions between gender studies, cultural studies, and biblical studies. Her book is *The Bible, Gender, and Reception History: The Case of Job's Wife* (2013).

Carol Meyers, PhD, is the Mary Grace Wilson Professor Emerita of Religious Studies at Duke University in Durham, North Carolina, USA, and past president of the Society of Biblical Literature. Her research interests include Hebrew Bible studies, Syro-Palestinian archaeology, and gender in the biblical world. Among her published books are the edited reference work *Women in Scripture* (2001), *Exodus* (2005), *Households and Holiness: The Religious Culture of Israelite Women* (2005), *Excavations at Ancient Nabratein: Synagogue and Environs* (co-author, 2009), *Rediscovering Eve: Ancient Israelite Women in Context* (2013), and *The Bible in the Public Square: Its Enduring Influence in American Life* (co-editor, 2014).

Pamela J. Milne, PhD, is Professor Emeritus of the University of Windsor in Ontario, Canada. Her research focuses on secular literary analyses of the Hebrew bible and on employment equity in the Canadian university context. Her only book, *Vladimir Propp and the Study of Structure in Hebrew Biblical Narrative* (1988), used the work of a dead, white male folklorist to examine the good old boy hero stories in Daniel 1–6. Such was the state of biblical criticism and academia in Canada in the 1980s. Subsequently, after gaining tenure, she utilized this type of narrative surface structure analysis for feminist purposes in studies of texts such as Genesis 2–3, Ruth, and Judith. Now in retirement, her pursuits are equestrian rather than academic because the manure is more palatable in the former than the latter.

Tina Pippin, PhD, is the Wallace M. Alston Professor of Bible and Religion at Agnes Scott College in Decatur, Georgia, USA. Her research interests are in bible and cultural studies, the politics of apocalypse, feminist theory, ethics, human rights, and pedagogical theories and practices. She was a member of The Bible and Culture Collective (*The Postmodern Bible* (1995), and among her publications are *Apocalyptic Bodies: The Biblical End of the World in Text and Image* (1999).

Jeremy Punt, PhD, is Professor of New Testament at Stellenbosch University, South Africa. His work focusses on the New Testament and hermeneutics, past and present, and on cultural studies and critical theory in particular. He has published widely in academic journals, contributed to various books, and his published books include *The New Testament interpreted. Essays in honour of Bernard C. Lategan* (co-editor, 2006) and *Postcolonial Biblical Interpretation. Reframing Paul* (2015).

Nicole J. Ruane, PhD, is a lecturer in the department of Classics, Humanities, and Italian at the University of New Hampshire in Durham, New Hampshire, USA. Her research interests include biblical law, ritual theory, feminist thought, anthropology of religion and violence, and comparative Semitic linguistics. She is the author of *Sacrifice and Gender in Biblical Law* (2013).

Susanne Scholz, PhD, is Professor of Old Testament at Perkins School of Theology at Southern Methodist University in Dallas, Texas, USA. Her research engages feminist biblical hermeneutics, epistemologies and sociologies of biblical interpretation, and cultural and literary methodologies. Among her books are *La Violencia and the Hebrew Bible: Politics and Histories of Biblical Hermeneutics on the American Continent* (co-editor, 2016); *Feminist Interpretation of the Hebrew Bible in Retrospect (Volume 1 and 2)* (ed., 2013, 2014); *Hidden Truths from Eden: Esoteric Readings of Genesis 1–3* (co-editor, 2014); *God Loves Diversity & Justice: Progressive Scholars Speak about Faith, Politics, and the World* (ed., 2013); S*acred Witness: Rape in the Hebrew Bible* (2010); *Introducing the Women's Hebrew Bible* (2007); *Rape Plots: A Feminist Cultural Study of Genesis 34* (2000).

Sarah Shectman, PhD, is an independent scholar living in San Francisco, California, USA. Her research interests include the composition history of the Pentateuch, the history of women in ancient Israel, social roles and status, and the Priestly cult. Her publications include *Women in the Pentateuch: A Feminist and Source-Critical Analysis* (2009) and *The Strata of the Priestly Writings: Contemporary Debate and Future Directions* (co-editor, 2009).

Johanna Stiebert, PhD, is Associate Professor of Hebrew Bible at the University of Leeds in the UK. Her research interests include biblical Hebrew terminology of self-conscious emotions, African-centered approaches to biblical texts, ideological-critical and social-scientific methods of interpretation, and family structures in Hebrew Bible laws and narratives. Her published books are *Fathers and Daughters in the Hebrew Bible* (2013), *The Exile and the Prophet's Wife: Historic Events and Marginal Perspectives* (2005), and *The Construction of Shame in the Hebrew Bible: The Prophetic Contribution* (2002).

Beth LaNeel Tanner, PhD, is the Norman and Mary Kansfield Chair of Old Testament Interpretation at New Brunswick Theological Seminary in New Jersey, USA. Her areas of research include biblical poetry, feminist hermeneutics, and the history and religion of the Afro-Asiatic region. Her publications include *The Psalms for Today* (2008) and *The Book of Psalms* (NICOT; with Rolf Jacobson and Nancy deClaissé-Walford; 2014).

INTRODUCTION:
METHODS AND FEMINIST INTERPRETATION OF THE HEBREW BIBLE

Susanne Scholz

Explorations on method have been an integral and central intellectual activity in the modern scientific quest for knowledge, truth, and the understanding of the universe and humanity's place in it. René Descartes' *Discourse on Method*, first published in 1637, set in stone the centrality of reason and doubt in this quest that he summed up with his famous statement: 'Je pense, donc je suis', or in Latin: 'Cogito ergo sum'.[1] Ever since, no project has been accepted as scholarly if it was not grounded in the scientific method. It is thus unsurprising that biblical interpreters conformed to this standard rather than risk being characterized as unscientific and passé. In 1677, Baruch Spinoza ensured the future of biblical interpretation under the changed intellectual-academic circumstances with his *Tractatus Theologico-Politicus*.[2] Challenging religious doctrine, he criticized the traditional authorship of the Pentateuch and brought reason and critical analysis to biblical interpretation. His work contributed to biblical exegesis attaining and keeping academic credibility by implementing scientifically defined procedures that rejected religious obligations, traditions, and doctrines.

These efforts led to what we today call historical criticism, locating biblical truth in the historical origins and meanings of biblical texts. The development of exegetical methods has thus unquestionably been linked to the modern epistemological belief that scientific procedures and methods guarantee the production of objective, universal, and value-neutral knowledge. Yet, in the last few decades, the identification and implementation of the scientifically correct method have come under scrutiny, as it has become clear that claims of objectivity, universality, and value-neutrality invariably come from Western-European, Christian-Protestant, white, male, and upper-class locatedness. Even when objective claims are made from somewhere else,

---

1. René Descartes, *Discourse on Method, and Other Writings* (trans. with an introduction by Arthur Wollaston; Baltimore: Penguin Books, 1962, 1960).
2. Benedictus de Spinoza, *Theological-Political Treatise* (trans. by Michael Silverthorne and Jonathan Israel; Cambridge/New York: Cambridge University Press, 2007).

they are always indebted to this initial context. In the last five-hundred years, the scientific claim of objectivity, universality, and value-neutrality has been powerful, and it continues to dominate academic discourses and aspirations in many places, despite challenges articulated by the philosophical, scientific, artistic, and literary avant-garde.

About the Lack of Theoretical Debate on Method in Feminist Exegesis

Perhaps predictably, feminist Bible interpreters have accepted and participated in scientifically endorsed exegesis. For instance, Elizabeth Cady Stanton proudly grounded her innovative volume *The Woman's Bible* in the new and, at that point, still controversial method of historical criticism when she stated in 1895: 'To women still believing in the plenary inspiration of the Scriptures, we say give us by all means your exegesis in the light of the higher criticism learned men are now making, and illumine the Woman's Bible, with your inspiration'.[3] Another more contemporary feminist exegetical appreciation for scientifically endorsed exegesis comes from Peggy L. Day who, in 1989, explains that '[a]s social and social science historians of the biblical world, one of our fundamental tasks is to generate a reliable body of knowledge about that world and specifically about gender-related roles and structures that comprised that world'.[4] She also acknowledges that '[w]e need to ask feminist questions, but we must be prepared to obtain answers that do not directly confirm the values we hold in the modern world'.[5] In short, the quest for a scientific method has played a prominent role in gaining and keeping scholarly credibility in biblical studies, including in feminist biblical studies. It has perhaps even contributed to the very invention of the field,[6] and so this third volume of *Feminist Interpretation of the Hebrew Bible in Retrospect* investigates how feminist Hebrew Bible exegetes have used various exegetical methods in their readings of the Bible. The volume presents a wide array of methods, as they have emerged in the field of biblical studies; it surveys how feminist scholars have taken advantage of the scientifically legitimated methods of biblical interpretation.

It has become clear in putting this volume together that feminist Bible exegetes have not been particularly interested in debating rationale, purpose, or

---

3. Elizabeth Cady Stanton, *The Woman's Bible* (Seattle, WA: Coalition Task Force on Women and Religion, 6th edn, 1978), p. 12.

4. Peggy L. Day, 'Introduction', in Peggy L. Day (ed.), *Gender and Difference in Ancient Israel* (Minneapolis: Fortress Press, 1989), pp. 1-11 (4).

5. Day, 'Introduction', in Day (ed.), *Gender and Difference in Ancient Israel*, p. 3.

6. Stephen D. Moore and Yvonne Sherwood, *The Invention of the Biblical Scholar* (Minneapolis, MN: Fortress Press, 2011).

reason for using this or that method. Rather, they have mostly accepted standard exegetical methods as an inheritance from the field and adopted them for feminist biblical commentaries, feminist historical reconstructions of ancient Israelite society, and feminist cultural analyses of gender, androcentrism, and issues of sexuality. Consequently, some critics suggest that 'feminist criticism' does not constitute a separate method, and they do not clearly distinguish between method and hermeneutical interests.[7] A case in point are the positions of three pioneering feminist scholars in Hebrew Bible interpretation. One position comes from Phyllis Bird who differentiates between her use of historical criticism and her hermeneutical interests when she writes: '[M]y own approach to the Bible, as a feminist and as a Christian believer, is fundamentally dialogical, requiring as its first step an attempt to formulate the sense of the text in its ancient social and literary context—viewing the text as itself a response to a conversation in the author's own time, an effort to persuade an ancient audience of a new or alternative view. My response to the text comes only after I have clarified its terms—just as my response to a modern dialogue partner demands that I first attempt with all the means at my disposal to hear as accurately and as sympathetically as possible what he or she means to say... Thus I want to separate analytically and operationally the horizons of production and reception, even as I acknowledge their inevitable interpenetration'.[8] Similarly, though grounded in literary criticism, and more specifically in rhetorical criticism, Phyllis Trible affirms the distinction between the method she employs and her hermeneutics when she explains that '[a]s the total process of understanding, hermeneutics employs many acceptable methodologies, though a particular interpreter may prefer one over another. My choice is rhetorical, a discipline I place under the general rubric of literary criticism'.[9]

Yet another position is advanced by Esther Fuchs who does not so much focus on method in difference to hermeneutics, but on the general lack of theoretical consideration in feminist exegesis. Specifically, she sees great need for increasing the critical analysis of feminist exegesis 'by category, discipline, focus, theory, and *method*'[10] [emphasis added]. In her view, the

---

7. See, e.g., J. Cheryl Exum, 'Feminist Criticism: Whose Interests Are Being Served?', in Gale A. Yee (ed.), *Judges & Method: New Approaches in Biblical Studies* (Minneapolis: Fortress Press, 1995), pp. 65-90.

8. Phyllis A. Bird, 'What Makes a Feminist Reading Feminist? A Qualified Answer', in Harold C. Washington, Susan L. Graham, and Pamela L. Thimmes (eds.), *Escaping Eden: New Feminist Perspectives on the Bible* (New York: New York University Press, 1998), pp. 123-31 (126-27).

9. Phyllis Trible, *God and the Rhetoric of Sexuality* (Philadelphia: Fortress Press, 1978), p. 8.

10. Esther Fuchs, 'Feminist Approaches to the Hebrew Bible' (unpublished article made available to me by the author on October 1, 2014), pp. 1-28 (2).

lacuna of theoretical debate in feminist exegesis has led to serious deficiency in methodological and epistemological clarity. Fuchs acknowledges that the lack of theoretical erudition is not limited to feminist biblical scholarship; it is a general condition of biblical studies. She asks feminist exegetes to engage with each other on theoretical, methodological, and epistemological levels and not to limit our works to textual interpretation, no matter how innovative and creative it may be.

Fuchs also models what she finds lacking in the works of her colleagues. She 'begins from the premise that the Bible is not merely an androcentric literature, namely composed, edited, transmitted and canonized by men, but it is also a patriarchal compilation, namely a collection of writings that textualizes patriarchal institutional practices and one that inscribes and endorses a discourse of sexual dissymmetry and hierarchy'.[11] Consequently, in her own work, Fuchs emphasizes theoretical and methodological considerations when interpreting biblical texts. For instance, in an essay on female prophets in the Hebrew Bible, she posits that '[p]rophecy is the core and culmination of the monotheistic paradigm. The discursive intermingling of God's words and those of the male prophets represents the apotheosis of the andro-theistic relationship infrastructure of monotheistic ideology. This andro-theistic relationship must preclude female discourse'.[12] She substantiates her thesis by studying the various references to female prophecy in the Hebrew Bible. In other words, Fuchs is a feminist critic who promotes resistance to biblical ideology because she dismantles it as political ideology in service of women's subordination and presents evidence available in the text. However, while grounding her exegetical work in feminist theoretical analysis, Fuchs still does not focus her theoretical discussion on method itself. She, too, does not discuss why she prefers this or that method but seems to take her method of choice for granted, as if it were a given and not a deliberate choice coming with a considerable set of assumptions and conventions.

In short, feminist Hebrew Bible scholars have not been particularly engaged in conversations about method. As Pamela J. Milne notes perceptively in her essay in this volume, feminist exegesis shows a considerable terminological indifference, perhaps even confusion and ignorance, about method and certainly about methodology, epistemology, and theory. Consequently, when feminist Bible scholars gain academic credentials from historical critics, their future work will most likely employ historical criticism. When they study with literary critics, they will probably read biblical texts

---

11. Fuchs, 'Feminist Approaches', p. 5.
12. Esther Fuchs, 'Prophecy and the Construction of Women: Inscription and Erasure', in Athalya Brenner (ed.), *Prophets and Daniel: A Feminist Companion to the Bible (Second Series)* (Sheffield: Sheffield Academic Press, 2001), pp. 54-69 (68).

with literary approaches. When they study with cultural critics, they will almost certainly produce cultural biblical readings throughout their careers. Some exceptions exist, but many feminist exegetes prefer the exegetical method of their doctoral-studies years throughout their careers and rarely engage in meta-level discussions about the reasons for their choices.[13]

In a sense, then, this volume brings to our attention how feminist Hebrew Bible exegetes employ a wide spectrum of methods. Further, it shows that very few methodological debates exist about these choices and what they entail. To date, there simply are no substantive and extensive reflections on method among feminist Hebrew Bible exegetes. Too often, we assume to employ this or that method in service of feminist meanings while not explaining what makes our readings 'feminist'.[14] Perhaps this situation is slightly different for womanist biblical scholars, although they, too, emphasize the biblical texts.[15] In fact, some exegetes may believe that an interpretation is feminist when it focuses on women as neglected subjects of study, and many different methods have been used to serve this purpose.[16] Yet such an understanding of feminist exegesis as a historical, literary, or cultural recovery project is naïve and narrow. It adheres to a liberal ideology that assumes the feminist job is done when the recovery of biblical women is complete. Conceptualized accordingly, it does not offer in-depth meta-level discussions on feminist methodologies as they have evolved in other fields of feminist inquiry such as sociology, anthropology, or feminist theories in general. This deficiency is pervasive in feminist biblical exegesis. Perhaps this is a reason why feminist Hebrew Bible exegesis has mostly remained confined to the field of biblical studies. As sometimes noted, few scholars and Bible readers outside the guild of biblical studies have actually heard of the existence of feminist biblical interpretation.

---

13. An exception is Phyllis Trible who published an entire book on her method of choice, rhetorical criticism. Yet her book does not center on feminist rhetorical interpretation when she elaborates on this method's history from ancient Greek literature to the twentieth century as well as on its application to the book of Jonah. See Phyllis Trible, *Rhetorical Criticism: Context, Method, and the Book of Jonah* (Minneapolis: Fortress Press, 1994).

14. For a beginning conversation, see Bird, 'What Makes a Feminist Reading Feminist?', pp. 123-31; Pamela Thimmes, 'What Makes a Feminist Reading Feminist? Another Perspective', in Harold C. Washington, Susan L. Graham, and Pamela L. Thimmes (eds.), *Escaping Eden: New Feminist Perspectives on the Bible* (New York: New York University Press, 1998), pp. 132-40.

15. For an analysis of this and other issues as they relate to womanist Hebrew Bible hermeneutics, see the essay by Karen Baker-Fletcher in this volume.

16. For the prevalence of this assumption, see the various discussions in Susanne Scholz, *Feminist Interpretation of the Hebrew Bible in Retrospect* (vols. 1 and 2) (Sheffield: Sheffield Phoenix Press, 2013, 2014).

Defining Feminist Methodologies in Feminist Research

Feminist methodologies emerged because feminist scholars in various academic disciplines, most prominently in sociology and anthropology, realized that 'traditional' methodologies did not examine experiences, thoughts, and practices of women and 'other' marginalized people. They critiqued the prevailing positivist scientism and began questioning epistemological assumptions of 'traditional' methodologies. They also asked what makes a feminist research project feminist. An extensive and many decades lasting conversation has evolved ever since. An early publication in this conversation is Sandra Harding's 1987 essay entitled 'Introduction: Is There a Feminist Method'.[17] Harding argues that a feminist method of research does not exist because '[a] research *method* is a technique for (or way of proceeding in) gathering evidence'.[18] In contrast, so Harding, '[a] methodology is a theory and analysis of how research does or should proceed; it includes accounts of how "the general structure of theory finds its application in particular scientific disciplines"'.[19]

Accordingly, feminist research is not defined by the methods it uses but by its methodologies that recognize the importance of using women's experiences 'in the plural'[20] as resources for the investigations. Women's experiences are always in the plural because they are related to differences in classes, races, and cultures. Feminist methodologies are also invested in social, political, economic, and cultural changes. As such, 'feminist inquiry joins other "underclass" approaches'.[21] Furthermore, feminist methodologies imply that feminist scholars place themselves 'in the same critical plane as the overt subject matter',[22] and are accountable to the groups of people under investigation. In short, Harding maintains that, at its best, feminist research 'can be thought of as methodological features because they show us how to apply the general structure of scientific theory to research on women and gender'.[23] Thus, methodologies, including feminist ones, shape 'how we approach and conduct research'.[24] Feminist works

---

17. Sandra Harding, 'Introduction: Is There a Feminist Method', in *Feminism and Methodology: Social Science Issues* (Bloomington and Indianapolis: Indiana University Press; Milton Keynes: Open University Press, 1987), pp. 1-15.
18. Harding, 'Introduction', p. 2
19. Harding, 'Introduction', p. 3.
20. Harding, 'Introduction', p. 7.
21. Harding, 'Introduction', p. 8.
22. Harding, 'Introduction', p. 9.
23. Harding, 'Introduction', p. 9.
24. Sharlene Nagy Hesse-Biber and Deborah Piatelli, 'From Theory to Method and Back Again: The Synergistic Praxis of Theory and Method', in Sharlene Nagy Hesse-Biber (ed.), *Handbook of Feminist Research: Theory and Praxis* (Thousand Oaks, CA: Sage, 2007), pp. 143-53 (143).

demonstrate that '[w]hether one's epistemology is rooted in empiricism, standpoint, postmodernism, or postcolonial critique, a feminist methodology challenges status quo forms of research by linking theory and method in a synergistic relationship that brings epistemology, methodology, and method into dynamic interaction across the research process'.[25]

In other words, feminist researchers question androcentric bias, 'critique the hierarchical, deductive approach to knowledge building', call attention 'to the partiality, fluidity, and situatedness of knowledge', and seek 'new ways to approach knowledge building'.[26] Among the central feminist concerns are questions such as '*[w]ho* can know, *what* can be known, and *how*...can [we] construct the most authentic view of the social world'.[27] A 'heightened attention'[28] to power plays a significant role in feminist methodological conceptualizations of knowledge, as it promotes a participatory research strategy.

Another emphasis on the nature and purpose of feminist methodologies comes from Caroline Ramazanogly and Janet Holland. They explain that there are different methodologies in social research because they are 'different responses to how, or whether, the knowledge people produce about social life can be connected to any actual reality'.[29] Ramazangly and Holland stress that, first, a '[f]eminist methodology is not distinguished by female researchers studying women'; second, '[t]here is no research technique that is distinctively feminist'; third, '[t]here is no ontological or epistemological position that is distinctively feminist'; and fourth, '[f]eminist methodology is distinctive to the extent that it is shaped by feminist theory'.[30] They note that the 'particular political positioning of theory, epistemology, and ethics'[31] ensures that feminist scholars produce research as a challenge to the unjust, silencing, and oppressive gendered status quo. Only when these criteria are fulfilled can 'something distinctively feminist...be claimed for diverse approaches to methodology'.[32]

---

25. Hesse-Biber and Piatelli, 'From Theory to Method and Back Again', p. 143.
26. Hesse-Biber and Piatelli, 'From Theory to Method and Back Again', p. 144.
27. Hesse-Biber and Piatelli, 'From Theory to Method and Back Again', p. 144 [italics in the original].
28. Sharlene Nagy Hesse-Biber, 'Feminist Research: Exploring the Interconnections of Epistemology, Methodology, and Method', in Sharlene Nagy Hesse-Biber (ed.), *Handbook of Feminist Research: Theory and Praxis* (Thousand Oaks, CA: Sage, 2007), pp. 1-26 (13).
29. Caroline Ramazanogly and Janet Holland, *Feminist Methodology: Challenges and Choices* (London: Sage, 2002), p. 9.
30. Ramazanogly and Holland, *Feminist Methodology*, pp. 15-16.
31. Ramazanogly and Holland, *Feminist Methodology*, p. 16.
32. Ramazanogly and Holland, *Feminist Methodology*, p. 16.

Three particular areas of feminist methodological concern have emerged in feminist thought over the past forty years. Nancy A. Naples identifies them as 'reflexivity', 'postcolonial and postmodern challenges', and 'research for social change'.[33] Although Naples talks about the specifics of developing feminist methodological considerations in sociology, I suggest that her remarks apply to feminist Hebrew Bible exegesis as well, providing valuable guidelines for methodological discussions on feminist exegesis. More specifically, the first area of 'reflexivity' directs feminist researchers to adopt reflective strategies regarding the inequalities and processes of domination involved in research, including institutional forms and procedures, informal organizational processes, and discursive frames that define, shape, and construct research goals and targets. A feminist researcher must be self-reflective throughout the research project and acknowledge 'the partial and situated nature of all knowledge production'. Reflexivity helps researchers to be 'aware of…domination and repression…produced in the course of [the] research and in the products of this work'.[34] Naples maintains that '[t]his approach ensures that a commitment to the political goals of the women's movement remains central to feminist research by foregrounding how ruling relations work to organize everyday life'.[35] A reflective stance takes seriously 'how problems are defined, which knowers are identified and are given credibility, how interactions are interpreted, and how ethnographic narratives are constructed'.[36]

The second methodological concern, 'postcolonial and postmodern challenges', urges feminist scholars to disclose 'assumptions and politics involved in the process of knowledge production in order to avoid exploitative research practices'.[37] Naples emphasizes that it is necessary to recognize 'disciplinary metanarratives' so that feminist scholars face the embedded power relations in their research.[38] In the effort of negotiating and countering the pervasiveness of power relations inherent in every scholarly encounter and discourse, postmodern and postcolonial feminist theorists suggest grounding feminist research in 'particular, local feminist praxis' and understanding 'the local in relation to larger cross-national processes'.[39] Intersectional analyses that build on class-conscious and anti-racist methodological approaches aim to connect feminist studies to women

---

33. Nancy A. Naples, 'feminist methodology', in George Ritzer (ed.), *The Blackwell Encyclopedia of Sociology (vol. iv)* (Malden, MA: Blackwell, 2007), pp. 1701-706.
34. Naples, 'feminist methodology', pp. 1701-706.
35. Naples, 'feminist methodology', p. 1703.
36. Naples, 'feminist methodology', p. 1702.
37. Naples, 'feminist methodology', pp. 1703-704.
38. Naples, 'feminist methodology', p. 1704.
39. Naples, 'feminist methodology', p. 1704.

from around the world, especially the most impoverished and exploited ones among them.

The third area of concern in feminist methodological discussions deals with the purpose of feminist knowledge as a contribution toward social change, and it informs the selection of methods to be used in feminist work. Admittedly, the range of methods available to social scientists is considerably more diverse than in biblical studies. The methods include 'participatory research, ethnography, discourse analysis, comparative case study, cross-culture analysis, conversation analysis, oral history, participant observation, and personal narrative'.[40] Yet this list also begs the question why feminist Hebrew Bible exegetes have mainly limited ourselves to text-based methods dominant in the field of biblical studies. Why have feminist biblical scholars not developed participatory research methods for the interpretation of the Bible? Why have we not relied on comparative case studies or cross-cultural analysis of Bible readings? Asked differently, why has feminist Hebrew Bible exegesis remained within the range of methods traditionally defined by the field of biblical studies and not attempted to boldly go where few Bible exegetes have gone before? Although some feminist Bible scholars have worked hard 'to democratize the research process'[41] in biblical studies, overall feminist exegetes have a long way to go in articulating 'linkages with activists and policy arenas in such a way as to effectively bridge the so-called activist/scholar divide'.[42]

Perhaps feminist exegetes ought to remember that feminist exegesis is always implicated in 'processes of politicization, diversity and continuity in political struggles over time'.[43] This insight helps reduce an increasingly recognizable tendency to assimilate into the status quo of the field, and it might also assist in contesting the viability of kyriarchal ideologies in biblical research and interpretation. Put differently, the question is whether feminist exegetes develop biblical studies as a site of struggle over meaning-making, authorization, and symbolic power, to paraphrase

---

40. Naples, 'feminist methodology', p. 1702.
41. See most prominently the tireless work of Elisabeth Schüssler Fiorenza, *Democratizing Biblical Studies* (Louisville, KY: Westminster/John Knox Press, 2009); *The Power of the Word: Scripture and the Rhetoric of Empire* (Minneapolis, MN: Augsburg Fortress Press, 2007). Most recently, she published an anthology of her various essays and writings, some previously published, in *Empowering Memory and Movement: Thinking and Working Across Borders* (Minneapolis, MN: Fortress Press, 2014). Perhaps the work of Renita Weems should also be mentioned in this third area of feminist methodological deliberation; see her most well-known book entitled *Just a Sister Away: Understanding the Timeless Connection Between Women of Today and Women in the Bible* (West Bloomfield, MI: Walk Worthy Press, 1988, 2005).
42. Naples, 'feminist methodology', p. 1705.
43. Naples, 'feminist methodology', p. 1705.

Elisabeth Schüssler Fiorenza's powerful framework, or, to lean on the conceptual articulations of Vincent L. Wimbush, whether feminist exegetes critically investigate socio-political, religious, economic, and cultural relations produced in the multiple meanings of 'Scriptures' in society and culture, and excavate the Bible's social textures and critical histories to map and model critical orientations of the exegetical enterprise that are different from the field's text-focused conventions.

The debate about feminist method and methodology is far from unambiguous or resolved, and can even be 'confusing because feminists have been arguing for feminist methodology from differing political and epistemological positions'.[44] After all, not every feminist researcher is critical of Cartesian positivism and the scientific-empiricist epistemology of modernity. This insight also pertains to biblical scholars and some feminist biblical scholars. As Elisabeth Schüssler Firoenza expresses it so well: 'From the nineteenth into the twentieth and now twenty-first centuries, the Bible has been used both as a weapon against emancipatory struggles for equal citizenship in society and church and as a resource for emancipatory struggles for liberation'.[45] Not every biblical scholar writing on women, gender, or sexuality claims to be part of 'the struggle of committed participants' who want to unmask power and delegitimize the intersectional structures of gendered domination in the world and in the text. Yet it would be advantageous to feminist and gender-studying exegetes to engage in feminist meta-level discussions on methodology and to openly debate why a particular method is chosen, what purpose it serves, and how the choice relates to the political goals of the women's movement with its intersectional analyses about gendered oppression in the world.

The considerable lacuna of these kinds of conversations within the field of feminist biblical studies indicates considerable theoretical deficiency. This volume aims to make a contribution toward remedying this shortcoming, and so the eighteen chapters survey some of the exegetical methods as they have been employed by feminist exegetes in the past forty years. It is high time to engage feminist theories about method and methodology, as well as epistemology, in relation to the feminist interpretation of the Hebrew Bible so that feminist biblical scholarship will grow in theoretical sophistication, methodological awareness, and strength of exegetical argumentation.

---

44. Ramazanogly and Holland, *Feminist Methodology*, p. 16. For a discussion on the various and even contradictory positions taken by feminist theorists in discussions on methodology, see also Marjorie L. DeVault, *Liberating Method: Feminism and Social Research* (Philadelphia: Temple Press, 1999), esp. pp. 25-45.

45. Schüssler Fiorenza, *Democratizing Biblical Studies*, p. 12.

Yet certainly, a hegemonic positioning of feminist methodological discourse is never a goal under any circumstances. Rather, what is needed is the promotion of 'academic feminist pluralism'.[46] In the case of feminist biblical studies, attention to feminist methodologies promises to nurture conversations about the particular characteristics of feminist biblical scholarship and its adherence to modern, postmodern, and perhaps even post-postmodern epistemologies. After all, not every reading of biblical women and gender in the Bible is 'feminist' in itself. As J. Cheryl Exum clearly explains, it is the political positioning of feminist interpreters that challenges gendered hierarchies in their various intersections with other forms of oppression, such as race, class, disability, or geopolitics. The political positioning makes interpretations feminist or not.[47] Already in 1995, the Bible and Culture Collective expresses this fact clearly when its members explain: 'What has come to be called "feminist interpretation of the Bible" is not parallel to the other interpretive strategies...insofar as *feminism* is itself not a method of reading, but rather both a set of political positions and strategies and a contested intellectual terrain'.[48] Yet the discussion about what makes a feminist reading feminist is far from resolved.

Part of the difficulty of this term relates to the many different ways of defining feminism. For instance, Susan Brayford, listing five definitions in a single paragraph, states that some feminist exegetes characterize 'feminism as "a determined movement of women seeking to break free of the judicial and economic predominance of 'father' and from the psychic and ideological tutelage of men"'.[49] She also mentions other interpreters who refuse to limit themselves to any particular definition; while still others define feminism as 'a critical and constructive stance that claims for women the full humanity accorded to men...'. She refers to Pamela Thimmes who regards feminism as 'a political term describing a "liberation movement that not only critiques the oppressive structures of society but,

---

46. Liz Stanley and Sue Wise, 'Method, Methodology and Epistemology in Feminist Research Processes', in Liz Stanley (ed.), *Feminist Praxis: Research, Theory and Epistemology in Feminist Sociology* (London/New York: Routledge, 1990), pp. 20-60 (47).

47. For this characteristic of a feminist positioning, see, e.g., J. Cheryl Exum, *Fragmented Women: Feminist Sub(versions) of Biblical Narratives* (London: Bloomsbury, 2nd edn, 2016), p. x: 'I continue to call myself a feminist critic because the term declares a political position, a commitment to feminism as a worldview and political enterprise'.

48. The Bible and Culture Collective, *The Postmodern Bible* (New Haven, CT: Yale University Press, 1995), p. 234.

49. Susan Brayford, 'Feminist Criticism: Sarah Laughs Last', in Joel M. LeMon and Kent Harold Richards (eds.), *Method Matters: Essays on the Interpretation of the Hebrew Bible in Honor of David L. Petersen* (Resources for Biblical Studies, 56; Atlanta, GA: Society of Biblical Literature, 2009), pp. 311-31 (312-13).

by its various voices and approaches, works for transformation'".[50] Finally, Brayford acknowledges that she has developed her own definition of feminism. She believes feminism to be 'an intellectual commitment and a political movement that seeks justice and equal rights for women and the end not just of sexism but of any type of discrimination'.[51] That feminist theorists have developed historically and politically located characterizations of feminism remains unaddressed in any and all of these definitions. After all, as The Bible and Culture Collective recognizes, there 'are various feminist modulations that generally express rather different and perhaps incompatible political positions',[52] such as liberal feminism, radical feminism, Black feminism, French feminism, Materialist feminism, Queer feminism, Marxist and Socialist feminism, postmodern feminism, Mujerista and Chicana feminism, and Womanism.[53] Why is it that in feminist biblical studies few, if any, of the secular feminist theoretical frameworks are used to define, characterize, and analyze feminist exegetical positions? It is urgent that we have sustained conversations on these matters, and this volume seeks to contribute to them.

This Volume's Structure

Since no single book on exegetical methods in feminist Hebrew Bible studies can be expected to cover all possible varieties of established and emerging 'methods' in the field, this volume includes a selection of them as they have been productively, substantively, and creatively applied in feminist interpretations of the Hebrew Bible. Hence, the eighteen essays cover a wide spectrum but they do not cover every possibility.

Four sections organize the included methods. The book begins with a section entitled 'Prolegomena: Methods as Hermeneutical Constructs' that presents the essays by Pamela J. Mine and Susanne Scholz, and Esther Fuchs. Both contributions address general concerns on feminist biblical hermeneutics featuring a conversation on the distinction between method and methodology in feminist biblical studies as well as a discussion on essentialist notions about the Israelite 'woman'.

The following three sections are structured according to the three corners of the so-called hermeneutical triangle. Part One, which focuses on 'Feminist Readings Behind the Text', contains five essays on reading biblical texts

---

50. All three positions appear in Brayford, 'Feminist Criticism', p. 313.
51. Brayford, 'Feminist Criticism', p. 313.
52. The Bible and Culture Collective, *Postmodern Bible*, p. 236.
53. See, e.g., Jennifer Rich, *Modern Feminist Theory: An Introduction* (Penrith: Humanities-Ebooks, 2nd edn, 2010); Valierie Bryson, *Feminist Political Theory: An Introduction* (New York: Palgrave Macmillan, 2nd edn, 2003).

with variously flavored historical methods. Sarah Shectman surveys how feminist exegetes employ historical criticism. Carol L. Meyers discusses archaeological and ethnohistorical methods for studying Israelite women's lives beyond the biblical record. Rebecca Hancock offers an evaluative essay on comparative historical criticism and feminist exegesis. Johanna Stiebert outlines anthropological approaches that emphasize issues of purity, danger, honor, and shame. Phyllis Bird elaborates on the merits of relying on historical methods in the development of a feminist Old Testament theology.

The subsequent section, 'Feminist Readings Within the Text', covers feminist exegetical works grounded in literary methods with which scholars have read the Hebrew Bible as literature or as a literary document whose scope is not limited to the historical communities, authors, or redactors behind the text. Beth LaNeel Tanner sketches the disciplinary developments of literary criticism and its application in feminist works on the Bible. Serge Frolov considers feminist biblical interpretations that engage psychological criticism. My own essay examines what is generally known as 'deconstruction' and how this approach has shaped feminist Hebrew Bible exegesis.

The final section, 'Feminist Readings In Front of the Text', consists of eight contributions. It is the most extensive section, perhaps indicating that feminist exegetes have tended to read biblical literature from various reader-positioned approaches. Unsurprisingly, then, this section covers a lot of ground. Karen Baker-Fletcher evaluates the accomplishments of womanist Hebrew Bible scholarship. Nicole J. Ruane describes the emergence of gender criticism. Tina Pippin reviews the status of ideological criticism in feminist exegetical works. Jeremy Punt offers an extensive assessment of postcolonial feminist Hebrew Bible studies. Rhiannon Graybill outlines the developments from feminist to queer readings. Roland Boer portrays the accomplishments of feminist biblical scholarship on gender and class analysis. Katherine Low outlines the recent move toward masculinity studies and its significance for feminist interpretation. Caroline Blyth elaborates on feminist biblical publications that interrogate representations of prominent biblical women characters and themes in popular culture and media.

Some methods are not included in this book, mainly because not enough feminist exegetical work has been produced to merit an individual chapter or feminist exegetical interpretations are currently at an early stage of development. For instance, very few, if any, feminist interpreters work with form, tradition, or redaction critical approaches. The same is true for other methods, such as iconographic approaches, even though individual feminist scholars have employed them.[54] Feminist exegesis on ordinary readers is also only in an emerging stage, and so no individual chapter is included

---

54. See, e.g., Silvia Schroer, 'Gender and Iconography from the Viewpoint of a Feminist Biblical Scholar', *lectio difficilior: European Electronic Journal for Femi-*

in this volume. On occasion, methods have been grouped together; for instance, the chapter on literary criticism comprises discussions on narrative, rhetorical, and poetic criticisms.

Method as Epistemé: Final Thoughts

Perhaps the entire idea to differentiate feminist Hebrew Bible exegesis into various exegetical methods is debatable. Although such differentiations are regularly made in the mainstream of biblical studies, perhaps most famously by John Barton,[55] biblical scholars usually talk about methods as if they were tools independent of larger socio-political, cultural, religious, and intellectual interests and historical developments. Yet methods always come from somewhere: emerging, climaxing in significance, and then disappearing again. It should, in fact, be argued that methods direct interpreters to do their biblical interpretations on the basis of those methods. In other words, perhaps it could be said that methods shape human subjectivity. Methods are thus not neutral tools but carriers of ideologies. They are heavy with cultural expectations and assumptions, even if their users believe otherwise. Such is the power of methods: to facilitate their own invisibility and their own posturing as tools. Meanwhile, they conform to and participate in the epistemic discourses within which they operate.

For this reason, it is important to think about methods and how feminist exegetes have used them rather casually and seemingly unconscious of their power. Indeed, the power of exegetical methods is so pervasive that most feminist exegetes have yet to venture beyond the classical canon of methods in the academic field of biblical studies. As already stated above, the spectrum of methods available in feminist anthropological and sociological studies is impressive and unparalleled to the field of biblical studies. Why is that, and why do feminist exegetes not discuss this considerable difference to feminist use of methods in other fields? This observation alone should make us suspicious about the power of biblical methods to keep us in our various exegetical places. In this sense, Stephen D. Moore and Yvonne Sherwood are absolutely right when they observe: 'Method is our madness', as biblical scholars turn everything into a 'long assembly line of critical "-isms"' that are 'at the centre of the biblical studies enterprise'.[56] Symptomatic for

---

nist Exegesis 2 (2008), available at: http://www.lectio.unibe.ch/08_2/Silvia_Schroer_Gender_and_Iconography.html.

55. John Barton, *Reading the Old Testament: Method in Biblical Study* (rev. and expanded edn; Louisville, KY: Westminster Press, 1996).

56. Stephen D. Moore and Yvonne Sherwood, 'Biblical Studies "after" Theory: Onwards Towards the Past: Part One: After "after Theory", and Other Apocalyptic Conceits', *BibInt* 18 (2010), pp. 1-27 (23, 22).

our 'methodolatry' is that we—feminist or not—do not like to talk about it. What does it mean that collectively, as feminist Hebrew Bible scholars, we have yet to recognize that methods are part of an entire network of discursive formations and practices, an episteme—to use the classic Foucauldian concept,[57] grounded in particular epistemologies that are not easy to transgress, expand, or modify? Is it simply that feminist biblical interpretations have to come clean that they, too, participate 'merely' in the project of the 'Enlightenment Bible'?[58] Even the very thought about these meta-critical issues seems transgressive, dangerous, daring, and 'hardly comfortable'.[59]

Yet it is obvious that an accepted set of methods and the popularity of this or that method at various moments in time and space are situated within powerful epistemological and methodological structures that have their roots in vast arrays of historical, political, economic, social, and religious factors. They shape our readerly worldviews, assumptions, and belief systems. Methods are not abstract tools waiting to be used by variously located readers of the Bible. Rather, they powerfully shape how readers see themselves, what they want from the Bible, and how they go about reading biblical texts. For instance, it was certainly no accident that the Garden Story in Genesis 2–3 gained such prominence in early modern approaches to the Bible. Julius Wellhausen utilized this narrative so convincingly in his Documentary Hypothesis of the Pentateuch toward the latter part of the nineteenth century because it was at that moment when Christian-dominated imperial societies of the European continent correlated their geopolitical and geo-economic explorations around the globe. Exegetes felt immensely compelled to resolve intellectual, religious, and political contradictions that had developed between the Bible and the 'discoveries' in the world. They turned to the biblical creation accounts and studied them perhaps more than any other text in the Hebrew Bible,[60] as the quest for historical origins had come to define the epistemological and methodological convictions of the 'Enlightenment' era.

We are only now starting to shift beyond this quest as we are moving further into the post-postmodern era,[61] and the question is what this most

57. For more information, see, e.g., http://www.michel-foucault.com/concepts/.
58. Stephen D. Moore and Yvonne Sherwood, 'Biblical Studies "after" Theory: Onwards Towards the Past: Part Two: The Secret Vices of the Biblical God', *BibInt* 18 (2010), pp. 87-113 (90).
59. Stephen D. Moore and Yvonne Sherwood, 'Biblical Studies "after" Theory: Onwards Towards the Past: Part Three: Theory in the First and Second Waves', *BibInt* 18 (2010), pp. 191-225 (225).
60. For a survey on these developments, see, e.g., Philip C. Almond, *Adam and Eve in Seventeenth-Century Thought* (Cambridge: Cambridge University Press, 1999).
61. See, e.g., Jeffrey T. Nealon, *Post-Postmodernism: Or, The Cultural Logic of Just-in-Time Capitalism* (Stanford, CA: Stanford University Press, 2012).

recent development will mean for the interpretation of the Hebrew Bible. It has already become clear that feminist biblical exegesis is moving beyond the impressive accomplishments of feminist biblical scholarship, as it has emerged since the 1970s. We will need to chart a future that is not merely accountable to the modernist past. What will be the feminist exegetical questions in light of contemporary culture, politics, and religion, and how will our methods, methodologies, and epistemologies help in articulating our responses? Yet before we can go there, we have to understand what has been achieved. This volume, like the other two volumes of *Feminist Interpretation of the Hebrew Bible in Retrospect*, aims to contribute to such an understanding and to offer ideas where to go next.

Prolegomena: Methods as Hermeneutical Constructs

1

ON METHODS AND METHODOLOGY IN FEMINIST BIBLICAL STUDIES: A CONVERSATION

Pamela J. Milne and Susanne Scholz

s2: Hi, Pam. Thanks for talking with me about method and methodology in feminist biblical studies.

Pam: It is a subject I think needs much more careful consideration within feminist biblical studies. I have long been frustrated by how many works I have read that use the terms 'method' and 'methodology' without making any effort to clarify what is meant by them. Even worse is the frequency with which the two terms are used interchangeably with no distinction between them. One recent example can be found in the published report on a panel discussion held at the 2013 annual meeting of the American Academy of Religion.[1] The focus of the panel was on the English translation of a major feminist biblical commentary originally published in German in 1998.[2] Contributors to the panel were asked to offer constructive criticisms as well as appreciative evaluations of the commentary. In his contribution to the report, Robert Wafawanaka notes that some of the book's commentators 'engage historical-critical methods or even chapter-by-chapter analysis', but then he goes on to say that 'their insights are "sharpened with a specifically feminist perspective"'. This comment suggests to me that Wafawanaka sees feminism as a perspective and not a method and that he sees a clear distinction between the two though he does not tell us exactly what that distinction is. Although he does not employ the term 'methodology',

---

1. Susanne Scholz (ed.), 'Feminist Commentary upon Feminist Commentary: A Report from the Feminist Biblical Trenches', *lectio difficilor: European Electronic Journal for Feminist Exegesis* 1 (2014), online: http://lectio.unibe.ch/14_1/scholz_susanne_feminist_commentary_upon_feminist_commentary.html (accessed September 20, 2014).

2. Luise Schottroff and Marie-Theres Wacker (eds.), *Feminist Biblical Interpretation: A Compendium of Critical Commentary on the Books of the Bible and Related Literature* (trans. Lisa E Danhill, Everett R. Kalin, Nancy Lukens, Linda M. Maloney, Barbara Rumscheidt, Martin Rumscheidt, and Tina Steiner; Grand Rapids, MI/Cambridge, UK: Eerdmans, 2013).

Wafawanaka appears to draw a distinction between a 'feminist perspective' and various 'methods' of biblical criticism.

Deborah Rooke, on the other hand, uses both 'method' and 'methodology' interchangeably without discussion or definition. Her work focuses on four aspects of the commentary: scope, coverage, methodology, and outlook. In her discussion of methodology, she notes that many contributors to the book use 'historical-critical methodologies'. In the next sentence, she explains that these historical-critical 'tools' are sometimes used 'together with other more ideologically based methodologies'. Later in the same paragraph, she comments that 'historical-critical methods' are not invalid but that 'in feminist biblical interpretation as a whole there are plenty of non-historical methodologies that provide equally insightful results for those who use them'. It is apparent that Rooke equates the terms, 'method', 'tool', and 'methodologies'. She also uses terms such as 'outlook' and 'perspective' interchangeably but in distinction from method and methodology when she writes:

> However, in view of its relative uniformity of outlook and methodology, I cannot help feeling that there is something disingenuous about the claim that the title makes. It promises without qualification to offer feminist biblical interpretation, and yes, it is feminist biblical interpretation but with the methodological and perspectival limitations noted above.[3]

One could also page through Volume 2 of *Feminist Interpretation of the Hebrew Bible in Retrospect* and find many authors employing these terms in very loose ways.[4]

s2: I agree with you that there is a considerable degree of terminological confusion about these concepts in feminist Hebrew Bible studies on many levels. In this Volume 3, the goal is to pay attention to various 'methods' as they have been used in feminist Hebrew Bible studies. Yet what to include as a method is highly debatable and unclear. Other books, for instance the *Postmodern Bible*, include 'feminist criticism'[5] as a method, but is feminism

---

3. Scholz (ed.), 'Feminist Commentary upon Feminist Commentary'.

4. For example, Wong states that Archie C.C. Lee 'establishes a methodology of "cross-texutal interpretation"...' (p. 29), and her essay includes a section on 'Asia as Method' (pp. 43-48) but she does not discuss any of the terms. Melanchthon talks about male interpreters who apply 'feminist hermeneutics and methods...' (p. 60) without telling us what those methods might be. Rooke's chapter again seems to use method and methodology interchangeably along with the term 'perspective' (pp. 74-75, 78, 81-82, 85-86); all of them are in Susanne Scholz (ed.), *Feminist Interpretation of the Hebrew Bible in Retrospect: Social Locations* (vol. 2; Sheffield: Sheffield Phoenix Press, 2014).

5. Bible & Culture Collective, *The Postmodern Bible: The Bible and Culture Collective* (New Haven, CT: Yale University Press, 1995), pp. 225-71.

a 'method'? For the purpose of this volume, I define 'methods' as various tools that feminist exegetes have used to interpret biblical literature. Each chapter also outlines how a particular method has developed outside of feminist usage. And not every method is included for a variety of reasons. In fact, when one starts looking at how feminist interpreters have used various methods, it is clear that each scholar has come to rely on this or that method in her (or his) particular or 'quirky' way. Hence, a reflection on the difference between methodology and method is a good idea and you have thought about this distinction quite a bit. In my view, another concept needs to be introduced into the discussion of this dissimilarity—epistemology. This is because the distinction between method and methodology relates to the modernist worldview and the so-called postmodern worldview. When we learn to think about modern and postmodern epistemologies,[6] we learn to deconstruct the assumption that we can create any kind of reconstruction, whether history, the meaning of a novel, the morning news, or the Bible, in an objective, universal, and value-neutral fashion. Rather, we have the postmodern worldview in which readers are implicated and part and parcel of the meaning-making process. How method figures into this dynamic is the interesting task at hand.

Pam: This discussion of concepts like epistemology is important but let me be clear: it is not a distinction that I want to discuss. Before anything meaningful can be said about the relationship between methodology and method, it is necessary to explain how each term is being used. I do not see methodology and method as subcategories of theory, nor do I regard them as interchangeable terms. I concur with your comment that feminist criticism should not be called a method. Instead, I see it as methodology for reasons that I will try to explain.

The reason you are having problems deciding what to include as methods is precisely because there has been so little effort put into clarifying what is meant by the concept in our discipline. In the social sciences, it is typical for research studies to have sections devoted specifically to the method being employed as well as the methodology guiding the use of the method. I believe such clarity would also benefit our field. Being able to distinguish method from methodology is helpful, I think, for appreciating what distinguishes feminist research from non-feminist research. It is also helpful in allowing us to understand the ways in which various studies differ from one another or how they are similar. It provides us with a comparative basis for assessment.

s2: How would you differentiate them?

6. That is how we know what we know.

Pam: Frankly, I find it puzzling that the conflation of the words 'method' and 'methodology' is so widespread. Other English words ending in 'ology' are not typically conflated with the noun embedded in them. 'Criminology' is never used interchangeably with 'crime' nor is 'psychology' with 'psyche' or 'sociology' with 'society'. The suffix 'ology' generally denotes 'an academic discipline or field of knowledge'.[7] In most dictionaries, 'method' and 'methodology' have distinct definitions. 'Method' is typically defined as 'a procedure for attaining an object',[8] or 'a systematic procedure or mode of inquiry'.[9] Definitions of 'methodology' include 'a system of methods used in a particular area of study or activity',[10] and 'a set or system of methods, principles, and rules for regulating a given discipline'.[11]

There has been much discussion among feminists in the social sciences about method and methodology and about what makes feminist research feminist. I want to draw on their work because I find it useful. One of the key debates among feminists in other disciplines has been on the question of whether or not there are methods that are feminist.

Catherine MacKinnon, a feminist legal theorist, takes the position that 'method organizes the apprehension of truth. It determines what counts as evidence and defines what is taken as verification'.[12] Method, for MacKinnon, is not neutral. She identifies 'consciousness raising' as the one distinctively feminist method: 'As Marxist method is dialectical materialism, feminist method is consciousness raising: the collective critical reconstruction of the meaning of women's social experience, as women live through it'.[13]

Another, different understanding of method is found in the work of Sandra Harding, a feminist philosopher of science. She makes a clear distinction between and among the terms 'method', 'methodology', and 'epistemology'. In her view, conflating or using these three terms interchangeably has made it difficult to find a satisfactory answer to the question of what is distinctive about feminist research. To overcome this problem, Harding sets out her understanding of each concept. For Harding, a research method is

---

7. *Oxford Dictionaries*: online: http://www.oxforddictionaries.com/us/definition/american_english/ology.

8. *Oxford Dictionaries:* online: http://www.oxforddictionaries.com/us/definition/american_english/method.

9. *Merriam-Webster Dictionary* online: http://www.merriam-webster.com/method.

10. *Oxford Dictionaries:* online: http://www.oxforddictionaries.com/us/definition/american_english/methodology.

11. *Webster's New Universal Unabridged Dictionary* (New York: Barnes and Noble, 1996), p. 1209.

12. Catherine MacKinnon, *Toward a Feminist Theory of the State* (Cambridge and London: Harvard University Press, 1989), p. 106.

13. MacKinnon, *Toward a Feminist Theory of the State*, p. 83.

simply a technique for gathering evidence. All techniques fall into one of just three basic categories: listening to informants, observing behaviour, or examining historical traces and records. Methods may be given other names but they all belong to one of these three categories.

Harding describes methodology as a theory or analysis of how research does or should proceed. In other words, methodology determines how the research methods are used. Epistemology is a theory of knowledge that addresses the issues of who can be a 'knower' and what counts as 'knowledge'.[14] For Harding, there are no feminist research methods. Methods are simply tools. The same tools can be used by feminist and non-feminist researchers. It is the way various methods are used and the purpose for which they are used that determine whether or not research is feminist. What is distinctive about feminist research for Harding is that it generates its problematics from women's experiences and answers questions of interest to women. It is research that places the researcher on the same critical plane as the subject matter, revealing the researcher as a 'real, historical individual with concrete, specific desires and interests'.[15] This process introduces the subjectivity of the researcher and in so doing creates what Harding refers to as 'strong objectivity' because it produces knowledge that is fully socially situated.[16]

If MacKinnon's 'consciousness raising' is examined on the basis of Harding's distinctions, it becomes clear that consciousness raising uses as the evidence-gathering tool or method of 'listening to informants'. How we use consciousness raising as a tool makes it feminist. Consciousness raising can be a feminist form of research because it involves women listening to other women about their lived experiences. The underlying epistemology is one that identifies and values women as knowers and producers of knowledge. This knowledge is the purpose for which the listening is done. Further, it is the subjects who are listening and those listened to, rather than the listening itself, that makes this form of listening feminist. In other words, consciousness raising, as MacKinnon describes it, is a form of research that uses the

---

14. Sandra Harding, 'Introduction', in Sandra Harding (ed.), *Feminism and Methodology* (Bloomington and Indianapolis: Indiana University Press, 1987), pp. 1-14 (2-3). Sandra Kirby, Lorraine Greaves, and Colleen Reid offer a similar distinction. They describe research methods as 'tools in the toolbox' that are 'specific data collection and analysis procedures and techniques' while methodology is 'a set of rules and procedures that indicates how research is to be conducted'; see Sandra Kirby, Lorraine Greaves, and Colleen Reid, *Experience Research Social Change: Methods Beyond the Mainstream* (Peterborough Ontario: Broadview Press, 2nd edn, 2006), pp. 12-13.

15. Harding, 'Introduction', p. 9.

16. Sandra Harding, 'Rethinking Standpoint Epistemology: What is "Strong Objectivity"', in Linda Alcoff and Elizabeth Potter (eds.), *Feminist Epistemologies* (New York: Routledge, 1993), pp. 49-82 (69, 74).

method or tool of listening to informants which is, in turn, directed by a feminist methodology. The utilization of this method is for the purpose of exploring and valuing women's lived experiences. It is not the act of listening per se that makes her research feminist, but rather how MacKinnon uses this particular method of listening to women and of valuing what they say.

Many other social scientists share Harding's view that methodology makes feminist research feminist.[17] Methodology governs the choices a researcher makes about what data to gather with the method or methods being used, why those data are being gathered, and how such information will be analyzed. The assumptions from which research proceeds, the purpose for which it is done, the interests and needs it serves, and the impact it has on the lives of people are all matters of methodology, not method. Feminist research can utilize any number of methods or tools for gathering data in order to place women (and other marginalized groups) at the center of inquiry, to expose embedded power relations, and to promote positive social change. Feminism, however the individual researcher chooses to define it, provides the methodology from which the research is carried out.

s2: So how does this apply to biblical criticism?

Pam: Biblical criticism has always been a discipline that has borrowed its basic research tools from other disciplines. With the rise of modern critical approaches to the study of the bible, scholars primarily focused on examining the historical processes by which the text reached is final form. Early researchers asked questions about authorship and the origins and development of various parts of the text. This gave us source, form, and tradition-historical critical methods. But if you think about these kinds of investigations, they all have to begin with the text as we have it in order to go behind the text to its earlier stages. So, we can say that even in historical critical studies, the tools for gathering evidence are primarily literary. Source criticism, for example, gathers clues from the text about different vocabulary, different orthography, different literary

---

17. See, e.g., Gayle Letherby, *Feminist Research in Theory and Practice* (Buckingham and Philadephia: Open University Press, 2003), pp. 4-6, 87-88. Letherby makes clear distinctions among method, methodology, and epistemology and cites several other researchers who regard methods as neutral tools and who look to methodology as the locus of what makes research feminist. See also Sharlene Nagy Hesse-Biber, 'Feminist Research: Exploring the Interconnections of Epistemology, Methodology and Method', in Sharlene Nagy Hesse-Biber (ed.), *Handbook of Feminist Research: Theory and Praxis* (Thousand Oaks, CA: Sage, 2012), pp. 2-26. Hesse-Biber provides an extensive survey of the development of feminist research and the complex relationships between theory and praxis as well as among method, methodology, and epistemology.

styles, different thematic foci, contradictions, or duplications. In Harding's terms, historical critics examine historical records. Their goal or purpose is not to interpret the text itself but to use the text as a window to look back into the world that produced it, to gain insight into the authors, and their circumstances and processes that led to the production of the texts as we have them now.

More recently, biblical scholars have put more emphasis on the final form of text. We generally think of this as literary criticism within which there is a wide range of elements that an analysis may examine (e.g., narrative surface structure, rhetorical devices, deep structures, themes, characterization, or plot). But in actuality, the data-collecting tools of the historical critic and the literary critic are essentially the same. It is how they use the tools, the purposes for which they collect the data that ultimately separate historical from literary analyses. Literary critics are only interested in what the text itself reflects in its final form. Both the form critic and the literary critic might examine type scenes in a group of texts but they would do so for different reasons.

And this is true for several other critical approaches in biblical studies. Sociological or anthropological criticisms must also gather literary data from the text itself. A sociological study of kinship or inheritance patterns in ancient Israel uses a literary tool to pull data from such things as genealogical texts or narratives that contain references to family relationships. Anthropological studies of intermediation in ancient Israel examine those texts that speak about prophecy or contain prophetic oracles. Yet the purpose for gathering sociological or anthropological data is different from that of the historian or the literary critic. In short, the methodology of the historical critic is different from that of the literary critic and that of the scholar interested in sociological or anthropological questions.

In the same way, a feminist critic employs the same evidence-gathering tools as the non-feminist exegete but for a different purpose. To be sure, the feminist critic may also be a literary critic or a historical critic. There may be many factors informing the use of the method to gather evidence so the methodology may be complex. A feminist researcher in our discipline is much more likely to tell us which theory informs her or his research than to tell us why the research is being done. This omission, in my view, is a serious deficiency. In sociology, if a feminist researcher does research on domestic violence, there will almost certainly be a stated purpose for that research. Yet the articulation of the purpose is far less common in feminist biblical criticism. In our discipline, readers usually need to infer the motivation that led to an interpretation.

Having said this, I do want to recognize that there have been some feminist biblical scholars who have discussed what makes feminist research feminist and who have made the distinction between method and methodology.

For instance, Phyllis Bird and Pamela Thimmes have both supported the view that it is methodology which is the determinative aspect.[18]

s2: Okay, I would like to expand it a little bit and say that some feminist critics also investigate how biblical texts have been used in the history of interpretation.

Pam: I see this as the same situation. Those feminists who investigate the history of interpretation, rather than the text itself, still examine a historical record. Like a historical critic, they examine interpretive texts diachronically but for feminist purposes. Here, too, there is a need for more explicit discussion of methodology. What motivates such studies? Why does the researcher choose a particular tool to gather data and why those data? These are the underlying questions that so often are not asked or answered.

s2: So do you want feminist interpreters to be explicit and open about our underlying commitments?

Pam: Yes. Let me try to illustrate this point with some examples. The first example shows how methodology is the key factor in determining whether or not a particular research study is feminist. It is an example from the late 1970s, but it is useful because it shows so vividly the difference methodology makes to research.

Jerome T. Walsh and Phyllis Trible each published studies of Genesis 2–3 in 1977 and 1978, respectively.[19] Both analyzed this narrative using a method called rhetorical criticism that focuses on formal structures or patterns on the surface of a text along with various other rhetorical devices. The type of rhetorical data they gathered differed slightly but, remarkably, they both concluded that the story's surface structure is patterned concentrically. In other words, they both maintained that the text has sets of parallel rings working down to a center section that stands alone as the focal point

---

18. Phyllis Bird, 'What Makes a Feminist Reading Feminist? A Qualified Answer', in Harold Washington, Susan Lochrie Graham and Pamela Thimmes (eds.), *Escaping Eden: New Feminist Perspectives on the Bible* (Sheffield: Sheffield Academic Press, 1998), pp. 124-31; Pamela Thimmes, 'What Makes a Feminist Reading Feminist? Another Perspective', in Harold Washington, Susan Lochrie Graham and Pamela Thimmes (eds.), *Escaping Eden: New Feminist Perspectives on the Bible* (Sheffield: Sheffield Academic Press, 1998), pp. 132-40.

19. Jerome T. Walsh, 'Genesis 2:4b–3:24: A Synchronic Approach', *JBL* 96 (1977), pp. 161-77. In the very last paragraph of his article, Walsh refers to his study as 'an experiment in methodology'. However, in terms of the distinctions I have introduced above, he is talking about his tool for collecting data, i.e., his method. Phyllis Trible, *God and the Rhetoric of Sexuality* (Philadelphia: Fortress Press, 1978), pp. 72-143.

of the story. For Walsh, the story center is found in Gen. 3.6-8 whereas for Trible, the center is to be found in Gen. 3.2-3.

Both scholars are conscious of and discuss their analytical method although Walsh calls it methodology. However, only Trible tells the reader anything about the methodology informing her use of the rhetorical method even though she uses different terms to do so. Like Walsh, she calls her research tool 'methodology' but she explains that she is working with two methodological perspectives in her use of rhetorical criticism: one is theological (the biblical text is sacred scripture for her) and the other is feminist.[20] She also reveals that, to her, feminism is 'a critique of culture in light of misogyny'.[21] Even though Trible does not always use the term 'methodology' in the sense I advocate here, she is very perceptive insofar as she tells her readers that 'all methodologies are subject to the guiding interests of individual users…'.[22] Here, she has put her finger on exactly why her conclusion differs so strikingly from Walsh's.

Walsh's interpretation regards Genesis 2–3 as an etiology of the human condition. That condition is one of a divinely created social hierarchy in which man is above woman. The woman overturns that hierarchy (the center of the story) but the deity reestablishes it in the end and all is as it should be with woman back in her place of subordination. Trible's interpretation comes to a different position despite some initial agreement. Trible agrees with Walsh insofar as she sees a social hierarchy at the end of the story, one in which the man dominates the woman. Yet she disagrees with him that such a hierarchy appears at the story's beginning. Rather, she maintains, *ha'adam* is an earth creature, not yet gender differentiated, and not the fully formed Adam, as Walsh asserts. Trible's well-known argument is that human creation begins and ends Genesis 2 and woman and man are equal in creation. In her reading, the center of the story, the conversation between woman and serpent, reveals the woman to be an intelligent, informed, and perceptive theologian, ethicist, hermeneut, and rabbi. Thus, to Trible, the end of the story represents the very corruption of the divine order, the triumph of Death over Life.

So the question that begs an answer is how could these two scholars arrive at such opposite conclusions when their analyses used the same method and when both of them identify very similar concentric patterns? The answer is that their methodologies are different, and so their conclusions are polarized. Simply stated, Trible's methodology is feminist and Walsh's is not. Thus, their motivations for studying this text are very different. I do not think Walsh was at all conscious of his motivations. He believed that he experimented by

20. Trible, *God and the Rhetoric of Sexuality*, pp. 1-23.
21. Trible, *God and the Rhetoric of Sexuality*, p. 7.
22. Trible, *God and the Rhetoric of Sexuality*, p. 11.

applying the relatively new tool of rhetorical criticism. Yet when we look at the social locations of the two exegetes, we can understand why they reach their conclusions. The standpoints from which they analyze the biblical narrative are vastly different although, as Christians, they both work within the assumption that the text is sacred. Walsh approached his study from his perspective of a male and Roman Catholic priest. He stands in a hierarchical tradition in which women are restricted to the lowest hierarchical levels and so, unsurprisingly he identifies a social hierarchy as divinely ordained in which a male deity and a male human rank higher than the woman and the animals. Although the snake and the woman challenge this hierarchy in the narrative, in the end the social hierarchy is restored. More importantly, since Walsh assigns a positive value to social hierarchy, his interpretation bolsters androcentric conventions of reading Genesis 2–3 that have damaged women for millennia. Trible, on the other hand, is a woman and a lay Christian of a Protestant denomination which does not value such a hierarchy. She tackles the Adam/Eve story because it has long been used by men, including scholars such as Walsh, to justify male domination over women. As a feminist, she challenges readings that have justified such gender domination. Thus, neither Walsh nor Trible are unbiased or neutral in their approach to the text. No one is. That is part of the point I want to make. It is not that bias can be avoided or that objectivity in the traditional sense can be achieved but rather that researchers need to discuss assumptions and motivations, the standpoints that influence their research choices.

In other words, methodology is just as important for understanding the differences between and among feminist analyses of the bible. Not only are there many ways to understand feminism, there are also many other factors that motivate the kind of works undertaken by researchers. For instance, Trible and Esther Fuchs are both feminist interpreters of the Hebrew bible, but their respective understandings of feminism and other key factors of their standpoints are markedly different. Both of them interpret the story of Jephthah and his daughter in Judges 11 by employing basically the same method, literary criticism, for gathering data. Yet their methodologies for using this particular method are so dissimilar that their conclusions are vastly different.

Trible's wants to analyze Judges 11 to recount a tale of 'terror *in memoriam*'. She offers a sympathetic reading of an abused woman and searches for a remnant theology 'that challenges the sexism of scripture'.[23] Her feminist methodology thus seeks 'to redeem the time' by telling sad stories such as this.[24] As a committed Christian, Trible undertakes all of her research on Hebrew biblical texts by searching for 'lost tokens of faith—for the remnant

---

23. Trible, *Texts of Terror*, p. 3.
24. Trible, *Texts of Terror*, p. 3.

that makes the difference' despite acknowledging the fact that the 'patriarchal stamp of scripture is permanent'.[25] This search for the 'remnant' is the driving force behind her method of choice, rhetorical criticism. It is her methodology.

Accordingly, Trible characterizes Jephthah as a faithless father who sacrifices his young daughter to fulfill an unnecessary vow. The narrator, rather than leaving the daughter a forgotten victim, adds a postscript in which the sacrificed daughter is memorialized by the women with whom she spent her last days. According to Trible, this turn in the story is the redeeming aspect of the story: the focus shifts from the father's vow to the victimized daughter, from death to life so that Jephthah's daughter 'becomes an unmistakable symbol for all the courageous daughters of faithless fathers'.[26] Hence, Trible sees this story as Scripture, troubling to be sure, but with a female character who is a courageous heroine, presented in sharp contrast to her faithless father. Trible's methodology is to lament, mourn, and eulogize the daughter while blaming the father for the daughter's fate. Trible's methodology identifies a path for feminists to accept the story as divinely inspired.

Esther Fuchs also sees Jephthah's daughter as a victim of male violence. Her interpretation, however, is significantly different from Trible's.[27] Like Trible, Fuchs gathers rhetorical data, but it is not the same data gathered by Trible. Fuchs argues that the author uses literary strategies to create ambiguity in the text so that readers marginalize and silence the daughter. To Fuchs, therefore, the story is an ideological construct that has the effect of understating the culpability of the father at the expense of his daughter.[28] Accordingly, Fuchs emphasizes that Judges 11 both inscribes and erases the story of Jephthah's daughter.[29] For instance, the daughter does not have a name because she is only relevant to the story in her role as a daughter. As a literary construct, she is presented as completely obedient to her father, 'a quality that in the final analysis has elevated her into an institutionalized heroine'.[30] Consequently, the narrator makes her responsible for her own fate by depicting her as actively participating 'in the process of her own demise' while the father is not depicted as a 'brutal sacrificer of his daughter'.[31] When the daughter speaks, her words echo her father;

---

25. Trible, *God and the Rhetoric of Sexuality*, p. 202.
26. Trible, *Texts of Terror*, p. 108.
27. Esther Fuchs, 'Marginalization, Ambiguity, Silencing: The Story of Jephthah's Daughter', in Athalya Brenner (ed.), *A Feminist Companion to Judges* (FCB, 4; Sheffield: Sheffield Academic Press, 1993), pp. 116-30.
28. Fuchs, 'Marginalization', p. 117.
29. Fuchs, *Sexual Politics in the Biblical Narrative: Reading the Hebrew Bible as a Woman* (Sheffield: Sheffield Phoenix Press, 2000), p. 178.
30. Fuchs, *Sexual Politics*, p. 182.
31. Fuchs, *Sexual Politics*, p. 182.

her words simply serve the purpose of expressing her compliance.[32] To Fuchs, identification with the daughter, as advocated by Trible, is dangerous because the daughter is constructed to be complicit and self-effacing in order to create sympathy for Jephthah her father.

In other words, the feminist methodology guiding Fuchs's use of her literary method does not identify with the victim; certainly it does not exonerate or redeem the text. Instead, Fuchs identifies how the androcentric narrator employs certain literary strategies to promote the text's ideology of male supremacy. When readers understand how this ideology is promoted in Judges 11, they can resist it.[33]

Fuchs provides extensive discussions on the assumptions and the methodology she brings to her reading of biblical texts.[34] She explains that the Hebrew bible is a cultural-literary text that is androcentric by virtue of being male authored. As such, it is a political text that does not only portray women as marginal and subordinate to men but also advocates and fosters this politics of male domination.[35] Furthermore, Fuchs also asserts that the 'sexual politics' of biblical narratives not only 'describe a male-dominated social order but justify it as morally requisite and sanctioned by God'.[36] Biblical theology is inherently misogynist and Fuchs has made it her exegetical task to expose it as such.

Fuchs acknowledges her standpoint as an Israeli born Jew but she clarifies that she does not approach the biblical text as a religious reader. She identifies herself as a Jewish feminist post-secular literary critic of the Hebrew bible who assumes that the biblical text is an ideological construct that justifies and legitimates patriarchal hierarchies.[37] She has no interest in redeeming or defending the bible, rather she seeks to deconstruct it. She describes her task as resisting and challenging the bible's sexual politics because it has had such a negative impact on women by virtue of the fact that the bible is 'inscribed in Western culture and its consumers' leaving no woman free of 'the myth of male supremacy'.[38] Thus to Fuchs, the text is a cultural artifact of both past and present significance within Western cultures. Precisely because the bible is a foundational cultural script, Fuchs

---

32. Fuchs, *Sexual Politics*, p. 187.
33. Fuchs, 'Marginalization', p. 130.
34. Fuchs, *Sexual Politics*, pp. 177-99.
35. Fuchs, *Sexual Politics*, p. 11.
36. Fuchs, *Sexual Politics*, p. 14.
37. Esther Fuchs, 'A Feminist Hermeneutics of Resistance: A Jewish Response to Interpretive Hegemony', in Susanne Scholz (ed.), *Feminist Interpretation of the Hebrew Bible in Retrospect: Social Locations* (vol. 2; Sheffield: Sheffield Phoenix Press, 2014), pp. 151-87. In this article, Fuchs provides an extensive discussion of her social location and the methodological assumptions she brings to her work.
38. Fuchs, *Sexual Politics*, p. 17.

thinks there is an urgent need for a political critique.[39] Such critique will disrupt the process of male empowerment[40] that biblical narratives have fostered in Western culture.

Fuchs articulates clearly her methodology that underlies her work, as well as the methodologies characteristic of the works of traditionalist feminist critics who seek to rehabilitate the bible or to find its liberating message for women. She also highlights the differences between her interpretation and the readings of literary critics who are reluctant to raise questions about 'the political implications of the Bible's patriarchal ideology' because 'the biblical narrative is too complex, or heterogeneous' or because reading is 'an endless process of approximation'.[41] In short, Fuchs is quite open about her methodology and the reasons for her analysis. Readers get a clear sense of the purpose of her exegetical interests and how the data she collects, grounded in rhetorical criticism, enable her to reach her analytical goals.

I, too, have worked on Judges 11 to find out how ordinary readers interpret this biblical tale.[42] I find Fuchs's interpretation much more convincing than Trible's, mainly because I do not accord the text any sacred status. In my view, lay readers do not know Trible's reading strategies and do not come up with them on their own unless they had been taught to read in this way. In contrast, Fuchs's argument that the narrator constructed the text to encourage readers to accept the embedded patriarchal ideology is very plausible. Unless readers are taught to recognize and resist the literary strategies that convey the embedded patriarchal ideology, they will likely be influenced by it. Thus, in my own work on Judges 11, I hypothesized that ordinary readers do not recognize and resist the embedded patriarchal ideology. The story leads them to empathize with Jephthah and to see the daughter as a willing victim.

In order to find out how ordinary readers interpret the story, I had to use a method that would collect a different kind of data than collected by Trible or Fuchs. The data that I sought to collect was in Harding's category of 'listening to informants'. Hence, I used a qualitative method that required me to interview a group of university-educated reader-participants. Although the results cannot be generalized, my qualitative study showed that none of the participants knew any feminist interpretations and none

39. Fuchs, *Sexual Politics*, p. 24.
40. Fuchs, *Sexual Politics*, p. 19 n. 26. Fuchs borrows this term from Patrocinio Schweickart who defines it as 'the process by which male-authored and male-centered texts produce in the female reader an identification that obliterates her sense of herself as a woman'.
41. Fuchs, *Sexual Politics*, p. 20.
42. Pamela J. Milne, 'Son of a Prostitute and Daughter of a Warrior: What Do You Think the Story in Judges 11 Means?', *lectio difficilior* (2009), http://www.lectio.unibe.ch/09_2/milne_son_of_a_prostitute.html.

read the story as suggested by Trible. Most of them read the story in ways that support Fuchs's claims. They tended to see Jephthah as a man of great faith who should be respected for making and keeping his vow. Only one participant was even critical of Jephthah's murder of his daughter. None of the interviewees raised the issue of male violence. In other words, the literary strategies of the biblical narrator, as identified by Fuchs, were effective and made most of them adopt the patriarchal ideology of the text. I find this result rather depressing though not surprising, as feminist biblical criticism is little known outside the small circle of feminist biblical scholars. For the most part, we debate amongst ourselves, and so our work has had little impact on the street, outside academia.

s2: So how does the distinction between method and methodology help in getting feminist work out there into the world?

Pam: That is a difficult question. On the one hand, as Fuchs points out, the bible is a cultural artifact that has ongoing significance in Western culture. On the other hand, as you have pointed out, the influence of biblical literature on contemporary society has diminished greatly.[43] Perhaps, if the bible's influence continues to decline, there will not be any need for feminist studies to explore how the bible should be used to limit its harm on women's lives.

Personally, I am glad to see the bible's influence decline in Western countries, but I do not think the bible is already completely irrelevant. One only needs to think of contentious social issues like same-sex marriage or women's reproductive rights to find people, some of whom exercise political power, turning to the bible to support religious fundamentalist or socially traditionalist positions. Perhaps, if the work of Fuchs and other feminist exegetes were more widely known today, I would not be so concerned about the bible's influence on contemporary society. This is not to say that others have not used the bible for more positive and equitable goals in mind, but their interpretations often lack visibility and do not succeed in overriding sexist readings.

You regard the bible's decline as regrettable. In your work on biblical rape texts you even assert that biblical rape texts are a sacred witness to the past and present prevalence of rape and that by naming those texts, they will 'signify the Hebrew Bible's ongoing theo-ethical relevance, sociopolitical meaningfulness, and cultural-religious significance in our contemporary rape culture'.[44] You think that, by naming rape in biblical literature, feminist

---

43. Susanne Scholz, *Sacred Witness: Rape in the Hebrew Bible* (Minneapolis: Fortress Press, 2010), p. 1.

44. Scholz, *Sacred Witness*, p. 211.

interpreters destabilize, subvert and deconstruct traditional interpretations in such a way that religious and secular readers will be less able to remain silent about rape.[45]

While I do not share your assessment of these texts as sacred witness and I am not optimistic about them being helpful in breaking the silence, I do think there is value in the kind of project you have undertaken because you have set out a methodology that clearly identifies why you are doing the kind of analysis you do and I have a sense of the assumptions you bring to your work. You have connected your analysis to a significant problem for women in the contemporary world. Making feminist biblical criticism relevant in this way will be necessary, I think, if our work is to attract a wider audience.

s2: So you want us to get to this kind of meta-level discussion at all times which enables us to become conscious of why we do what we do and how we do it?

Pam: Indeed, I think the lack of clarity about why we do feminist biblical criticism has contributed in a significant way to its irrelevancy. If our work is feminist, we need to say why and how it is feminist. We need to show how it will contribute to improving the lives of women and how it contributes to the feminist movement in general. We need to articulate the feminist point of our work. We have to ask what the expected feminist outcome is when we choose this or that method to collect a particular type of data about a given text or about the history of its interpretation. This is the kind of methodological discussion that would make feminist exegesis more readily appreciated by those outside the field of biblical studies.

For instance, in one of your articles on Genesis 34,[46] you characterize your analysis of the rape of Dinah as a 'right' reading because it openly acknowledges that you interpret this biblical text from a feminist perspective. You also explain that other 'right' readings can emerge when interpreters clarify their interests and stances.[47] You make this point even more clearly in your book when you state that your goal in studying rape texts in the Hebrew bible is not just intellectual but practical: it is to contribute to the task of ending rape.[48] Historically, rape is one of the most serious issues of violation that women have endured and, thus, your effort to address this

---

45. Scholz, *Sacred Witness*, p. 210.
46. Susanne Scholz, 'Through Whose Eyes? A "Right" Reading of Genesis 34', in Athalya Brenner (ed.), *Genesis: A Feminist Companion to the Bible* (Second Series; Sheffield: Sheffield Academic Press, 1998), pp. 150-71.
47. Scholz, 'Through Whose Eyes?', p. 171.
48. Scholz, *Sacred Witness*, p. 3.

through a critical analysis of biblical texts speaks to an experience of profound relevance to many women.

By contrast, Lyn Bechtel argues that Genesis 34 does not portray a rape of Dinah.[49] To make her argument, she employs a method that is based in anthropology. Yet neither does she reveal what motivates her to do this kind of study nor does she support many of her key assumptions. What does she want to accomplish by using this method? Why does she make the assumptions she does? Who benefits from such an argument? Is it feminist or not, and why? In other words, I do not find a clear discussion of methodology in her work. When I get to the end of her article, I know what she argues but I am not at all sure why she argues for it or to what end. Whether explicitly stated or not, every researcher has a standpoint from which she or he approaches biblical texts. In this sense, all research is ideological because it emerges from a set of ideas held by researchers and shapes the research. All researchers bring biases that impact the works they do. If we as biblical exegetes want to be taken seriously by feminist scholars in other fields, we need to be transparent about our assumptions and motivations.

This is particularly important, in my view, because scholars who study religious traditions and texts are often also confessionally committed to those traditions. Often those commitments allow or compel them to work with assumptions that would be outside the boundaries of scholarship in other disciplines. Not all feminist scholars in biblical studies work from a confessional context so a clarification of the rules with which we interpret and whose interests we serve with our scholarship is essential if we want to connect our work to the wider feminist movement. The clear articulation of the purpose of our research, the assumptions we bring to that research and the kind of data we seek to collect will make the results of our work more transparent and will make it possible for others to assess our research on its academic merit in the context of feminist scholarship more generally. In my view, feminist biblical scholarship can only be enriched by such clarity.

---

49. Lyn M. Bechtel, 'What If Dinah Is Not Raped? (Genesis 34)', *JSOT* 62 (1994), pp. 19-36.

2

Sexual Biblical Politics as an Interventionist Interrogation: The Israelite and Foreign Woman in Feminist Literary Approaches

Esther Fuchs

The Israelite woman as a specifically nationalized configuration of a collective gendered identity has recently been both marginalized and neglected in biblical feminist criticism. Viewed as the binary opposite of the non-Israelite woman, she has been pitted against the ethnically and racially 'other' woman as a collaborator with the male elite leadership of the nation, and a privileged subject with self-evident class advantages. Whether indicted as a bitter and vindictive Naomi out to humiliate the Moabite Ruth, a punitive Sarah out to oppress the Egyptian Hagar, an idealized symbol of Wisdom over against the 'Strange' woman, the conquering Israelite over against the oppressed Canaanite—the Israelite woman has come to embody her nation in its most nefarious aspects.[1]

The Israelite woman has not enjoyed much scrutiny because recent postcolonial interpretations tend to identify her as a representative of the oppressor nation over against the stigmatized 'foreign' nations of the Bible. The ironic result is a critical consensus that recapitulates rather than deconstructs the biblical prophetic trope that already represents the nation and the land in feminized terms. Moreover, this critical consensus tends to uphold a Christian theology that condemns in the 'Old Testament' what has apparently been repaired in the New Testament, namely, the inclusion of all

---

1. Danna Nolan Fewell and David M. Gunn, *Gender, Power and Promise: The Subject of the Bible's First Story* (Nashville: Abingdon Press, 1993); Claudia V. Camp, *Wise, Strange and Holy: The Strange Woman and the Making of the Bible* (Sheffield: Sheffield Academic Press, 2000); Gale A. Yee, *Poor Banished Children of Eve: Woman as Evil in the Hebrew Bible* (Minneapolis: Augsburg Press, 2003); Musa S. Dube, *Postcolonial Feminist Interpretation of the Bible* (St. Louis: Chalice Press, 2000); Caroline Vander Stichele and Todd Penner (eds.), *Her Master's Tools? Feminist and Postcolonial Engagements of Historical Critical Discourse* (Atlanta: Society of Biblical Literature, 2005), pp. 211-32; Judith E. McKinlay, *Reframing Her: Biblical Women in Postcolonial Focus* (Sheffield: Sheffield Phoenix Press, 2006).

'foreign' nations in the new covenant.[2] By singling out the 'Hebrew Bible' as a model of colonial ideology, they uphold a Christian paradigm of difference. So-called postcolonial feminist readings of the Bible identify the oppressor as the Israelites (and by extension, the Jews), thus bolstering a Christian imaginary. Current so-called feminist postcolonial criticism of the Bible accept as self evident what are in essence biblical constructions, and invert the binary 'Israelite' 'foreigner' rather than subvert it.

Judith Butler warns against precisely such inversions and exclusions as the inevitable outcome of any essentialist approach to gender.[3] Gender is not an essence but rather a relationship to power; it is discursive and unstable and must be analyzed in each context in such a way as to question previous consensual and hegemonic definitions. Feminist criticism is most effective at the level of discourse and knowledge or at the level of the representations of gender. Gayatri C. Spivak who introduced postcolonial perspectives into feminist theory also insists on the mediation of texts and the need for self consciousness on the part of any critics who claim a 'subaltern' or oppressed and silenced position by identifying with a self-evident cultural identity, be it Third World, indigenous, or racial.[4] Recent feminist postcolonial theory questions the tendency to essentialize native, immigrant, or previously colonized women as a homogenized collective of oppressed victims.[5] Increasingly, feminist theorists make the point that previous binary polarizations of colonizer and colonized are too simplistic and often romanticize a complex web of relationships of collusion, resistance, and mutual transformation. Thus, for example, Chandra T. Mohanty who criticized feminist scholarship for its Eurocentric and ethnocentric bias, more recently rejected an exclusive focus on non-Western women as emblems of victimization and calls for a transnational scholarship based on a politics of materialist support and intellectual alliance.[6]

The best way to approach the Israelite woman is thus not by reconstructing an essence that is presumably already present either in history, in a retrievable past, or 'in' the text, but to expose the textual politics of her

---

2. Jon D. Levenson, *The Hebrew Bible, the Old Testament and Historical Criticism* (Louisville, KY: John Knox Press, 1993).

3. Judith Butler, *Gender Trouble: Feminism and the Subversion of Identity* (New York: Routledge, 1990).

4. Gayatri C. Spivak, *In Other Worlds: Essays in Cultural Politics* (New York: Routledge, 1988).

5. Rosemary M. George, 'Feminists Theorize Colonial/Postcolonial', in Ellen Rooney (ed.), *The Cambridge Companion to Feminist Literary Theory* (Cambridge: Cambridge University Press, 2006), pp. 211-31. See also Leela Gandhi, *Postcolonial Theory: A Critical Introduction* (New York: Columbia University Press, 1998).

6. Chandra T. Monhanty, *Feminism Without Borders: Decolonizing Theory, Practicing Solidarity* (Durham, NC and London: Duke University Press, 2003).

constructions. Textual politics refers to the ways in which literary configurations signify and promote relationships of power.⁷ What a textual politics then exposes are the functions of the suppressions, exclusions, and erasures that are operative in the representation of Israelite femininity as a national ideal. To the extent that the representation of Israelite womanhood is relational, that is depends on a double distinction from Israelite manhood on the one hand and foreign womanhood on the other, it must be identified along the fluctuating textual borders between and among these cultural identities. In other words, the representation of Israelite womanhood cannot be examined independently from representations of Israelite manhood or foreign womanhood.

My purpose in this essay is not merely to offer an objective description of these representations, but rather to provide a critical inquiry of the nation, femininity, and heterosexism as discourses of propriety. The nation refers here to an imaginary community, a distinct collective identity, constituted by a memory of common origins and a consciousness of difference based on 'other' often inimical collectivities. National identity is always already implicated in an awareness of violent conflict with and separation from foreign imagined communities.⁸ Violence both representational and discursive characterizes the emergence of the Israelite nation, as a consecrated collective. Discourses of clashing collective identities, tribal, monarchic, and prophetic are equal in their violent zeal to national discourses seeking to differentiate the ideal nation as a whole from a host of foreign nations.⁹ The narration of the nation in the Hebrew Bible consists of idealized representations, or pedagogic discourses on the one hand and performative discourses on the other hand, detailing the numerous deviations from and violations of the pedagogic code.¹⁰ Idealized representations focus on the nation's distinct separation from foreigners, and internal cohesion, peace and prosperity, and collective adherence to laws and regulations divinely produced. In this context women are likely to be constructed as mothers of sons, as virtuous wives, or idealized representatives of the nation's interests. Performative representations describe the various deviations from the pedagogic code. The nation is shown to indulge in 'foreign' behavior, in violations of the ideal code, and as a consequence it suffers upheaval, famine, exile, or subjugation to foreign powers. In such a paradigm national foreignness

---

7. Toril Moi, *Sexual/Textual Politics: Feminist Literary Theory* (London: Methuen: 1985). See also Ghandhi, *Postcolonial Theory*, pp. 141-66.

8. Benedict Anderson, *Imagined Communities: Reflections on the Origin and Spread of Nationalism* (London: Verso, 1991).

9. Regina M. Schwartz, *The Curse of Cain: The Violent Legacy of Monotheism* (Chicago: University of Chicago Press, 1997).

10. Homi K. Bhabha, *Nation and Narration* (New York: Routledge, 1990).

is encoded in sexual terms, especially in prophetic literature, which often feminizes the nation as a sexually vulnerable female body, victimized and oppressed by its enemies, or as an adulterous wife deserving her demise.

As a secular dislocated Israeli immigrant employed by an American university, I claim a hybrid identity of two nationalities. As a native speaker of Hebrew, nurtured by Zionist pedagogic discourses up to mature adulthood, I claim a diasporic location in my adopted country.[11] As a feminist critic, I take ambivalent solace in my homelessness, recognizing that nations are constructed by multiple exclusions of the feminine. As a literary critic, I am aware of the textuality and constructedness of all identity, personal and collective.[12] As an Israeli citizen, I recognize the privileges that were granted to me while denied to my Palestinian and Mizrahi sisters. As a daughter of Holocaust survivors, I am constantly aware of the inherited traumas of victims of genocidal anti-Semitism.[13] As a feminist Bible scholar, I am aware of the colonial violence both material and epistemic that has been perpetrated in the name of Eurocentric Christian empire building against natives of the Third World.[14] As a Jew, I share with non-Christian Third World scholarship an awareness of the colonial use and abuse of the English Bible both by missionaries and by modern and contemporary Bible scholars who encode in their 'Old Testament' scholarship Christian biases against Jewish identity.[15] At the same time, however, I am aware of the political abuse and essentialist interpretations of the Hebrew Bible by right-wing extremists in contemporary Israel. I seek to interrupt this enterprise through my scholarship. My present critical reading of biblical national discourses then is informed by my own politics of location and dislocation. It is invested in a radical vision

---

11. See my essay 'Exile, Memory, Subjectivity: A *Yoredet* Reflects on National Identity and Gender', in Nahla Abdo and Ronit Lentin (eds.), *Women and the Politics of Military Confrontation: Palestinian and Israeli Gendered Narratives of Dislocation* (Oxford and New York: Berghahn Books, 2002), pp. 279-94.

12. Ellen Rooney (ed.), *The Cambridge Companion to Feminist Literary Theory* (Cambridge: Cambridge University Press, 2006); Stuart Hall, 'Cultural Identity and Diaspora', in Patrick Williams and Laura Chrisman (eds.), *Colonial Discourse and Postcolonial Theory: A Reader* (New York: Columbia University Press, 1994), pp. 392-403.

13. Esther Fuchs, 'Exile, Daughterhood, Writing: Representing the Shoah as Personal Memory', in Ronit Lentin (ed.), *Representing the Shoah for the 21st Century* (Oxford and New York: Berghahn Books, 2004), pp. 253-68; Ronit Lentin, *Israel and the Daughters of the Shoah: Reoccupying the Territories of Silence* (New York: Berghahn Books, 2000).

14. R.S. Sugirtharajah, *The Bible and the Third World: Precolonial, Colonial and Postcolonial Encounters* (Cambridge: Cambridge University Press, 2001); R.S. Sugirtharajah, *Postcolonial Criticism and Biblical Interpretation* (Oxford: Oxford University Press, 2002).

15. Jon D. Levenson, *The Hebrew Bible, the Old Testament, and Historical Criticism* (Louisville, KY: Westminster/John Knox Press, 1993).

of scholarly knowledge as a mechanism for transformation and the performance of solidarity with the marginalized and the oppressed.[16]

In short, the invention of ancient Israel is mediated through legal, historical, and prophetic discourses which suppress the feminine as discursive subject, and repress feminine sexuality as discourses of appropriate desire. In this regard, then, ancient Israel exemplifies the multiple exclusions of the feminine that construct the nation as such. All national narratives promote motherhood as woman's highest mission, and they extol sexual 'virtuousness' or repression in married and unmarried women.[17] In the Hebrew Bible the repression of feminine sexuality is encoded as virginity for daughters under the authority of their fathers, and as purity for wives under the authority of their husbands. The mission of wives is to become mothers and to give birth to sons, who will insure patrilineal continuity.[18] While historically the oppression of women and the repression of femininity is not unique to Israelite nationhood, as it was broadly practiced throughout the ancient Near East, the biblical narration of the nation represents foreign femininity as more autonomous, free, and even aggressive. While Israelite women are represented as virtuous mothers and victims of sexual violence, foreign women are often described as sexually autonomous subjects using their sexuality for political purposes. In sum, the narration of the nation projects on foreign women the sexuality it denies the nation's women. The derogation of 'foreign' sexuality cannot be understood without its corollary because both of them construct Israelite womanhood. As the narration of the nation is doubled, many feminist critics do not assume the dichotomization of these imaginary identities as much as they ought to.

The Construction of the Israelite and Foreign Woman in Legal Discourses

As texts that prescribe proper conduct biblical law codes are best understood as pedagogic discourses whose goal is to delineate the borders of the nation and this nation's desired difference from other nations. The laws are often framed by covenantal formulas that link national exclusivity to proper sexual conduct. Proper sexual conduct is defined in procreative terms, especially for

---

16. Esther Fuchs (ed.), *Israeli Women's Studies. A Reader* (New Brunswick: Rutgers University Press, 2005).

17. Anne McClintock, *Imperial Leather: Race, Gender, and Sexuality in the Colonial Contest* (New York: Routledge, 1995); Anne McClintock, Aamir Mufti and Ella Shohat (eds.), *Gender, Nation and Postcolonial Perspectives* (Minneapolis: University of Minnesota Press, 1997); Nira Yuval-Davis, *Gender and Nation* (London: Sage, 1997); Tamar Mayer, *Gender Ironies of Nationalism: Sexing the Nation* (New York: Routledge, 2000).

18. Esther Fuchs, *Sexual Politics in the Biblical Narrative: Reading the Hebrew Bible as a Woman* (Sheffield: Sheffield Academic Press, 2000).

women, in line with the priorities of national viability and survival. Motherhood, notably of sons, is the ultimate desideratum for the Israelite woman. This motherhood, however, is proscribed by strict laws of adultery insuring male control of the family's progeny, and thus emerges as a means to an end, always contingent on male authority.[19] The family is the basic unit biblical law regulates by insuring proper gender subordination and sexual restriction. Recent readings of biblical law seek to expose the ideology and textual politics of legal discourse as masculine discourse, in the sense that it privileges men over women and authorizes male exploitation, control and even violence against women's bodies.[20] Marital laws construct the patriarchal family as the nation's fundamental heterosexual unit, a microcosmic paradigm for the nation whose 'father' is none other than a masculine God who is presented as the source and origin of these laws.[21] Laws governing sexuality define Israel's distinctive nationhood. For instance, Lev. 18.24-28 states: 'Do not defile yourselves in any of those ways, for it is by such that the nations that I am casting out before you defiled themselves. Thus the land became defiled; and I called it to account for its iniquity, and the land spewed out its inhabitants. But you must keep my laws and my rules, and you must not do any of those abhorrent things (*to'evot*), neither the citizen nor the stranger who resides among you; for all those abhorrent things (*to'evot*) were done by the people who were in the land before you, and the land became defiled. So let not the land spew you out for defiling it, as it spewed out the nation (goy) that came before you'.

Howard Eilberg-Schwartz links the representation of the deity as masculine and as asexual to a symbolic ambiguity about human sexuality.[22] On the one hand men are instructed to procreate, but on the other hand they are said to have been created in the image of an asexual God who does not procreate nor indulge in any sexual activity. According to Eilberg-Schwartz,

---

19. Carolyn Pressler, *The View of Women Found in the Deuteronomic Family Laws* (Berlin: W. de Gruyter, 1993).

20. Harold C. Washington, '"Lest He Die in the Battle and Another Man Take Her": Violence and the Construction of Gender in the Laws of Deuteronomy 20–22', in Victor H. Matthews, Bernard M. Levinson and Tikva Frymer-Kensky (eds.), *Gender and Law in the Hebrew Bible and the Ancient Near East* (Sheffield: Sheffield Academic Press, 1998); Cheryl B. Anderson, *Women, Ideology, and Violence* (New York: T. & T. Clark, 2004).

21. Julia Kristeva, *New Maladies of the Soul* (trans. Ross Guberman; New York: Columbia University Press, 1995). See also Julia Kristeva, *Powers of Horror: An Essay on Abjection* (trans. Leon S. Roudiez; New York: Columbia University Press, 1982).

22. Howard Eilberg-Schwartz, 'The Problem of the Body for the People of the Book', in Timothy K. Beal and David M. Gunn (eds.), *Reading Bibles, Writing Bodies: Identity and the Book* (London and New York: Routledge, 1996), pp. 34-55. Also see Howard Eilberg-Schwartz, *God's Phallus and Other Problems for Men in Monotheism* (Boston: Beacon Press, 1994).

the multiple laws governing sexuality in particular and the body in general reflect an obsessive attempt to resolve this basic ambiguity. For instance, the law of circumcision marks the masculine sexual organ as the locus of procreative generation; it is the symbolic link to priestly distinction. At the same time, incest laws and other taboos are restrictive; they imply that sexuality is an undesirable activity. Yet Eilberg-Schwartz's analysis does not recognize the symbolic connection between circumcision and the formation of national identity. It also does not recognize the privileging of the phallus as the locus of active procreation. Eilberg-Schwartz merely implies that God's sexuality is phallic rather than clitoral or vaginal, and that sexual pleasure is identical with procreativity. In this sense, he repeats the phallogocentric representation of human desire as the same rather than multiple and as locatable rather than ubiquitous.[23]

While far more aware of the national implications of biblical sexual legislation, Tikva Frymer-Kensky also subscribes to a general theory of sexuality as a biological fact unmarked by gender.[24] Like Eilberg-Schwartz, she detects in biblical sexual law a fundamental ambivalence, promoting sexuality as a positive social force on the one hand, and restricting its manifestation as potentially chaotic and dangerous on the other hand. Frymer-Kensky maintains that the ancient Israelites approved of sexual activity within the limits of the authorized heterosexual nuclear family for purposes of procreation, and sought to restrict and control it as measures of national self-protection through legislation. She explains: 'The power of sex to cross over the lines between households or blur distinctions between units of a family is an example of sex's power to dissolve categories. This is problematic on a national scale'.[25] Drawing on Mary Douglas's theory of the binary oppositions implied by biblical purity laws and the prohibition to transgress the categorical boundaries between them (e.g. male/female, god/man, law/chaos), Frymer-Kensky asserts that sexual laws set up boundaries between appropriate and inappropriate conduct. According to Frymer-Kensky, the law of the suspected adulteress exemplifies the national proportions of a wife's alleged violation of marital commitment, as well as the legal logic that requires a husband to subject his wife to this ritual (Num. 5.11-31). Frymer-Kensky compares this law to the law of the decapitated heifer which requires the community to respond ritually to a case of unresolved murder. The inability to ascertain the woman's guilt requires extreme measures, and

---

23. Luce Irigaray, *This Sex Which Is Not One* (trans. Catherine Porter; Ithaca, NY: Cornell University Press, 1985).

24. Tikva Frymer-Kensky, 'Law and Philosophy: The Case of Sex in the Bible', in *Studies in Bible and Feminist Criticism* (Philadelphia: The Jewish Publication Society, 2006), pp. 239-54.

25. Frymer-Kensky, 'Law and Philosophy', p. 246.

the participation of the entire community to insure that the nation remain guiltless. Frymer-Kensky concludes that the law of the suspected adulteress makes sense both symbolically and philosophically. In her view, it does not manifest patriarchal oppression or any vindictive or unjust collective punishment.

This approach to biblical laws on sexuality is contested by Alice Bach who rejects both its descriptive tone and its objective comparisons to ancient Near Eastern precedents.[26] According to Bach, such approaches fail to question the violence, traumatic impact, and profound stigmatic implications of the ordeal imposed on the suspected adulteress. While most scholars work with the premise that the suspected adulteress is guilty, Bach assumes that the wife in question is innocent, and that the priestly authorities should not have taken seriously the husband's irrational jealousy. Whereas previous scholarship begins with a general perspective of what is best for the heterosexual family, or the community, Bach outlines the perspective of an innocent wife whose husband is seized with a 'fit of jealousy' (Num. 5.14). Marital law grants the husband a priori complete control over his wife's sexuality, and so the innocent wife has no recourse but to follow the law. Yet that law, rather than investigating the husband's bizarre accusations, puts the wife on trial exposing her to shame. Bach emphasizes the hypothetical situation, and the lack of evidence, the trial imposed on the woman to highlight the law's prevarication of justice and the infliction of physical and psychological violence on the woman. In addition, the mysterious concoction the woman is made to drink, made up of holy water, soil from the floor of the tabernacle, and the dissolved curse words, adds a national dimension to a ritual that is presented as a familial and communal affair. The soil from the floor of the tabernacle symbolizes the holy center of the nation, the temple itself. Since the woman apparently refused to absorb the familial and national injunction mentally, she is now made to ingest it physically. The curse words used by the priest also involve an explicit reference to the woman's having 'defiled' (*tm'*) herself and thus having become an 'imprecation' (*alah*) 'among your people' (*amekh*) (Num. 5.21). The association of adultery with national symbols is not accidental because even a hypothetical or potential commitment of adultery is viewed in the law as a transgression against the nation.

The pedagogic construction of the ideal Israelite woman as a virgin-daughter, a virtuous and 'pure' wife and as a mother is mediated through violent legal discourses that casuistically or apodictically stipulate what would happen to women daring to violate the laws of sexual propriety.

---

26. Alice Bach, 'Good to the Last Drop: Viewing the Sotah (Numbers 5:11-31) as the Glass Empty and Wondering How to View It Half Full', in Alice Bach (ed.), *Women in the Hebrew Bible* (New York: Routledge, 1999), pp. 503-22.

Whether and to what extent these laws were followed is less material than the lasting effect of the epistemic violence perpetrated in the legal authoritative definitions of appropriate womanhood. The ordeal of the suspected adulteress highlights the silencing of the culprit and the dictation to her of a formula of acceptance she is made to utter in response to the priest's imprecation (Num. 5.22). It thus exemplifies the essence of biblical sexual codes that legitimate male control of female sexuality while penalizing women's attempt to violate this control.

The Israelite and Foreign Woman in Biblical History

The Deuteronomic history, or the narration of Israel's rise and fall, is replete with images of masculine aggression and violence. Non-Israelite or foreign leaders and commanders are portrayed as cowardly or ineffective warriors (e.g. Eglon, Sisera, Goliath). National victory and survival are shown to be contingent on appropriate masculinity, one that is both confrontational and honorable. Internally, honor and power codes represent as an intricate system of multiple homosocial systems (families, clans, tribes) whose relationships are determined through the proper, i.e. marital, circulation and exchange of women.[27] The construction of Israelite femininity is determined by their position within the patriarchal family and by their filial, uxorial, or maternal affiliations. Appropriate femininity is defined as subordinate in social terms and submissive in sexual terms. Honor codes require sexual purity or avoidance of sexual relations that are not meant for legitimate marital procreation. The Israelite woman's connection to the nation is thus usually mediated through her familial role, but in times of crisis her familial role may be suspended for the sake of national interest. For example, the first phase in the national story is the conquest of the land of Canaan which includes a brief narrative about a woman who won direct access to a piece of land. It is the story of Achsah which appears both in the book of Joshua and in the book of Judges (Josh. 15.16-18; Judg. 1.12-15). The access to land, however, is mediated through her father, Caleb, the warrior who conquered the entire region and through her husband, Othniel, who conquered the city of Devir, or Kiriath Sepher.[28] Achsah is presented as the prize for which Othniel fights and conquers the city. 'And Caleb announced: I will give my daughter Achsah in marriage to the man who attacks and captures Kiriath Sepher' (Josh. 15.16). Achsah appears here as an object of

---

27. Ken Stone, *Sex, Honor, and Power in the Deuteronomistic History* (Sheffield: Sheffield Academic Press, 1996).

28. Danna Nolan Fewell, 'Deconstructive Criticism: Achsah and the (E)razed City of Writing', in Gale A. Yee (ed.), *Judges and Method: New Approaches in Biblical Studies* (Minneapolis: Augsburg Fortress, 1995), pp. 119-45.

exchange between Caleb and Othniel, his younger brother. She is given by Caleb as a reward, and the text implies that she was the only reward Othniel received in exchange for his response to his elder brother's challenge. This female character emerges from objectification to subject position by exhorting Orthniel to ask her father for a piece of land, and by eventually approaching her father directly with her request for arable land, a request that is granted (Josh. 15.19). In other words, Achsah is both object and subject within the economy of the family unit, but her access is made possible through a request, a speech act which connotes an awareness of her own subordinate station both vis-à-vis her father and her husband.

In contrast, autonomy from male control and the non-procreative use of sex are clearly attributes that mark foreign femininity. In the book of Joshua, Rahab the Canaanite is defined as a *zonah*, a prostitute (Josh. 2.1). While *zonah* is a stigmatic label, the biblical narrative representation of female prostitution is ambiguous.[29] In this regard, Rahab is no exception. She is said to have provided safe haven to the Israelite spies sent by Joshua to 'see the land and Jericho' and to report about its military preparedness and morale. Not only is Rahab said to shelter the two spies, she is also reported to mislead the king of Jericho, who is shown to believe her and chase after the spies in the wrong direction.

In addition, she is shown to be a shrewd diplomat in her own right. A long and detailed speech act is attributed to her, demonstrating her ability to communicate with her potential enemies in their own conceptual language, or perhaps indeed in their own (Hebrew?) language, unless the spies have learnt the indigenous vernacular (Josh. 2.8-12). Shrewd and practical she requests a verbal commitment and a sign that will assure her that the spies will spare her and her family's life during the onslaught on the city (Josh. 2.13). Recent feminist criticism has indicted the story about Rahab's collaboration and eventual cooptation as a colonial script.[30] To the extent that Rahab represents the foreign enemy nation, she symbolically stands for Canaanite sexual iniquities that in turn justify the conquest of the land and the purported annihilation of its inhabitants. Rahab is promoted by the text for having betrayed her own people and for supporting the colonial invaders. The stigmatization of Rahab and the colonial use of her services should not, however, be interpreted only in terms of opposition but also in terms of co-construction. The narration of the nation reveals that the detailed attention to military exploits and confrontation with the collective enemy or competitor, indeed to the discursive performance of masculinity, further

---

29. Phyllis Bird, 'The Prostitute as Heroine', in Bach (ed.), *Women in the Bible*, pp. 3-20.

30. See, e.g., Dube, *Postcolonial Feminist Interpretation of the Bible*.

marginalizes Israelite women who have already played a subordinate role within the family stories of the nation's origins.

An exceptional case in this regard is the book of Judges, the story of tribal settlement in the land. Not only are women more visible here than in most other texts, they appear in diverse and heterogeneous roles.[31] Despite this heterogeneity, a juxtaposition of Israelite and foreign figurations of femininity reveals remarkable consistencies in line with the figurations that emerge from the book of Joshua. Like Rahab, Jael the Kenite is portrayed as collaborating with and supporting the national cause of the Israelites, and like Rahab she offers her own domestic space as shelter. Unlike Rahab, the man she deceptively invites into her tent is the enemy: 'Jael came out to greet Sisera and said to him: "Come in, my lord, come in here, do not be afraid"' (Judg. 4.18). Though the text refrains from explicit sexual descriptions, the textual gaps leave sufficient room for speculation. Did Sisera go into the tent because he sought shelter or because of Jael's sexual attraction? Did Jael cover Sisera with a blanket (*smikha*) as a gesture of hospitality or as sexual seduction? Did he fall asleep as a result of physical exhaustion or sexual satiation? The poetic version describing Sisera falling 'between her legs' (*bein ragleha*) is even more suggestive (Judg. 5.27). Such speculation is rendered impossible in the case of Deborah, whose leadership is mostly rhetorical. It consists of imperative speech acts directed at Barak, the military commander, and of a long poetic description of the war and its victorious outcome. While national crisis justifies the release of Deborah from the usual familial frame, the sexual code continues to be enforced. It is Jael who is shown to be capable of using her sexuality for political purposes and to use violence against a stronger man. This conduct will only later be attributed to an Israelite woman (Esther, Judith) although the former will be shown to follow the male guidance of her male relative, and the latter will be described as a chaste pious widow.

The use of sex for political purposes is again attributed to foreign women in the case of Delilah. However, this time deceptive manipulation of a mighty warrior is aimed not against the enemy but against an Israelite leader. Samson's masculinity is constructed as both violent and sexually unconstrained. His sexual entanglements with his Timnite bride, the Gazaite prostitute, and finally with Delilah lead him to wreak havoc on Israel's mortal enemies. Masculine sexuality is thus constructed as an unusual but legitimate national resource. This legitimization is framed by an appeal to divine authority: 'His father and mother did not realize that this was the Lord's doing: He was seeking a pretext (*to'ana*) against the Philistines, for

---

31. Susan Ackerman, *Warrior, Dancer, Seductress, Queen: Women in Judges and Biblical Israel* (New York: Doubleday, 1998); Marc Zvi Brettler, *The Book of Judges* (New York: Routledge, 2002).

the Philistines were ruling over Israel at the time' (Judg. 14.4). Yet this time the foreign woman is shown to manipulate an Israelite man, and so she is characterized in terms that are less ambiguous than those who frame Rahab and Jael. While in the cases of Rahab and Jael sexual autonomy and lack of male control is encoded as foreign, only Delilah is shown to be motivated by greed. Delilah betrays the man who loves her for eleven hundred shekels of silver (Judg. 16.4-5). Foreign feminine sexuality is shown to outdo the enormous muscular strength of Israelite masculinity in the detailed description of Samson's emasculation and humiliation at the hands of the Philistines (Judg. 16.18-22).

This representation of foreign women contrasts dramatically with the representation of Israelite women as victims of male violence. The story of Delilah is preceded by the story of the sacrifice of Jephthah's daughter (Judges 11) and followed by the story of the nameless wife who is gang raped, murdered, and dismembered (Judges 19). Neither Jephthah's daughter nor the nameless victim appear to resist the violence directed at them. The violent aggression at the heart of these and other narratives in the book of Judges led Mieke Bal to conclude that the victimization of young innocent Israelite daughters reveals a social and institutional transformation in Israelite society, a shift from patrilocal to virilocal marriage.[32] Bal suggests that the frequent representation of the violent demise of Israelite daughters reflects a historical increase in the authority of the husband in marital relationships; young brides were the victims of this social transformation. The dramatic contrast between one group of violent women and another group of passive victims led her to a psychoanalytic interpretation according to which the repressed mother figures emerge in the guise of violent women to avenge the murders of young innocent daughters.[33] J. Cheryl Exum argues similarly that the violent deaths of victimized daughters serve the purposes of the patriarchal family order; they are meant to inculcate appropriate behavior by describing the demise of young women who dared venture out of their proper domestic space.[34] The negative portrayal of openly sexual women on the other hand reveals a deep seated fear of female sexuality. Either way, such narratives work as discursive justifications for the continued male control of female sexuality. While I agree with both Bal and Exum that the stories work as discursive controls on female sexuality, I would emphasize that they also promote ideals of self-sacrifice and the family.

---

32. Mieke Bal, *Death and Dissymmetry: The Politics of Coherence in the Book of Judges* (Chicago and London: The University of Chicago Press, 1988), p. 1.

33. Bal, *Death and Dissymmetry*, pp. 197-230.

34. J. Cheryl Exum, 'Feminist Criticism: Whose Interests Are Being Served?', in Gale A. Yee (ed.), *Judges and Method: New Approaches in Biblical Studies* (Minneapolis: Fortress Press, 1989), pp. 65-90.

The juxtaposition of national and foreign femininities constructs a national ethos of propriety that justifies the collective violence directed at outsiders and collective others who do not adhere to such an ethos. Thus war and sexuality emerge from the book of Judges as inevitably linked in the process of narrating the nation.

Both Israelite and foreign women are less visible in the story of the monarchy, as narrated in the books of Samuel and Kings, and for the most part seem to embody the usual dichotomy between appropriate and inappropriate models of femininity. Motherhood is promoted through detailed narratives about barren women who are eventually rewarded for their tenacious and eager pursuit of this national ideal. Thus Hannah, despite her struggles as a barren co-wife is rewarded with the birth of Samuel, the prophet who will establish the monarchy (1 Samuel 1–2). The barren woman of Shunem, though anonymous, is defined as 'gedolah', which means great, and described as a devout supporter of the prophet Elisha (2 Kgs 4.8-37). The most profound violation of the nation's sexual code is described in the narrative about David's 'adulterous affair' with Bathsheba, Uriah's wife (2 Samuel 11–12). The violation of sexual boundaries is emblematic of national turmoil and political vulnerability.[35] Amnon's violation and humiliation of Tamar, David's daughter, is defined by the victim as a national outrage (*nebala*): 'Such things are not done in Israel. Do not commit this outrage (nebala)? Where will I carry my shame? And you will be like any of the scoundrels in Israel' (2 Sam. 13.12-13). Tamar embodies Israelite femininity, and the story of her outrageous humiliation leads to a rebellion within the monarchy. The narrator implies that the violation of national codes of sexuality may very well explain the eventual split of the Davidic monarchy. Toward the end of his life, like his father the son who was born to David and Bathsheba violates a sexual code of conduct with clear national implications: 'King Solomon loved many foreign women in addition to Pharaoh's daughter—Moabite, Ammonite, Edomite, Phoenician, and Hittite women (1 Kgs 11.1). Solomon's foreign wives are said to have enticed him to indulge in idolatrous cultic practices, blamed by the narrator for the demise of the nation.

Foreign femininity is linked most spectacularly to idolatrous cultic practices in the characterization of Jezebel the Phoenician wife of Ahab. There is no reference to her motherhood, and like Delilah, she exerts power over the man in her life. Like Delilah she uses her sexuality for political purposes, but unlike Delilah she possesses political power and persecutes the nation's most cherished leaders, its prophets (1 Kgs 19.2). Jezebel embodies

---

35. Regina Schwartz, 'Adultery in the House of David: The Metanarrative of Biblical Scholarship and the Narratives of the Bible', in Bach (ed.), *Women in the Hebrew Bible*, pp. 335-50.

an intensified model of the foreign woman already adumbrated in the characterization of Delilah. Foreign femininity is stigmatized through associations to economic gain. The story about the illegitimate expropriation of Naboth's vineyard presents her as greedy, ambitious, deceptive, and unscrupulous ruthless (1 Kings 21). Aware of her imminent death, Jezebel does not hesitate to taunt Jehu, the warrior who eventually murders her (2 Kings 30–37). The text notes in this context that shortly before her death, Jezebel attends to her appearance and cosmetics. The reference to her make up and coiffure is satirical, aimed at foreign sexuality as seduction, as precisely the kind of sexuality that is not of the nation. In both cases references to sexuality are oblique and muffled.

Feminist criticism has deconstructed the biblical representation of Jezebel, reconstructing her point of view as a devoted wife, as a proud Phoenician queen, as a devotee of the Goddess Asherah, as a rebel who stood up to Elijah's Jahwistic rejection of the Goddess.[36] Both Delilah and Jezebel embody a warning against exogamy and personify the danger of trusting other nations. It is not merely the flaunted sexuality that the narrative rejects; it is rather its dangerous combination with political power that seems to trouble the narrator. Despite recent historical critical reconstructions of the *gevirah*, or so-called queen-mother, the narrative itself condemns the association of Israelite women and power, notably monarchic power.[37] The construction of the foreign woman thus enforces that of the Israelite woman. The approbation of the anonymous Israelite mother complements the derogation of the named, known, and powerful foreign woman. I would go as far as suggesting that the erasure of Israelite women's names from the historical record is itself a discursive enactment of the principle of chastity or the covering up of their bodies.

The Construction of the Israelite and Foreign Woman in Prophetic Literature

The process of inscription and erasure of the Israelite woman as subject is most apparent in the latter prophets.[38] There are no references to women's names as signifiers of individual identities, and the few references to women as subjects present them as the wives or lovers of prophets (Hosea 1–3; Isa.

---

36. Tina Pippin, 'Jezebel Re-Vamped', in Athalya Brenner (ed.), *A Feminist Companion to Samuel and Kings* (Sheffield: Sheffield Academic Press, 1994), pp. 196-206. See also McKinlay, *Reframing Her*.

37. Susan Ackerman, 'Queen Mother in Israel', in Bach (ed.), *Women in the Bible*, pp. 21-32.

38. Esther Fuchs, 'Prophecy and the Construction of Women: Inscription and Erasure', in Athalya Brenner (ed.), *Prophets and Daniel: A Feminist Companion to the Bible (Second Series)* (Sheffield: Sheffield Academic Press, 2001), pp. 54-69.

8.3). The few references to women prophets in the historical narrative are replaced by associations of the *nebi'ah* with uxorial and maternal functions. Women prophets appear as cynical and deceptive (Ezek. 13.17-22). In other words, the prophetic literature transforms the Israelite woman into a figure of speech, a metaphor that embodies the nation. The prophetic interpretation of the fragmentation and eventual expulsion of Israel and Judah by the colonial powers of Assyria and Babylon provides for the most part a performative discourse which deconstructs the body of the Israelite woman. While erased from the narrative as national subject, the Israelite woman resurfaces as a figure of speech, as a metaphor. Poems of consolation depict her as a virginal bride or grieving mother, while poems of recrimination present her as a lascivious young woman, prostitute, or an adulterous wife. The elaborate descriptions of inappropriate feminine sexuality associate the woman's body with foreignness. The metaphoric woman either enjoys orgiastic encounters with foreign lovers, or she conducts herself in ways that have previously been attributed to foreign women. The Israelite woman's body is no longer distinguishable from the foreign woman's body; both are portrayed in terms of deviant sexuality and both are constructed as objects of male violence.

The justification of male violence as punishment for feminine deviancy, and the detailed poetic descriptions of inappropriate female sexuality have been analyzed as a genre of ancient pornography. Though pornography is a post-Victorian phenomenon, in response to post-Enlightenment restrictions on the language of the body, feminist scholars criticized prophetic language as 'pornoprophetics' for its stigmatization of the woman's body.[39] Feminist criticism decried the implications of prophetic discourse on male violence and the female body for women in contemporary societies.[40] Through tantalizing representations of feminine debauchery the prophets sought to attract attention to their oracles. But by portraying God as a punitive husband and the nation as an adulterous wife, prophets like Hosea, Jeremiah, and Ezekiel reinforce a sexual ideology of female subjugation. More recently, however, feminist critics have begun to focus on the textual politics of prophetic literature. However, in my view, it is more effective to attend to the ways in which the prophetic text negates itself. By turning Gomer, the prostitute, from the margin to the center and by providing her with a voice, the feminist critic challenges the prophets valuation.[41] Alice Keefe, by contrast,

---

39. Athalya Brenner, *The Intercourse of Knowledge: On Gendering Desire and 'Sexuality' in the Hebrew Bible* (Leiden: E.J. Brill, 1997).

40. Renita Weems, *Battered Love: Marriage, Sex, and Violence in the Hebrew Prophets* (Minneapolis: Fortress Press, 1995).

41. Yvonne Sherwood, *The Prostitute and the Prophet: Hosea's Marriage in Literary–Theoretical Perspective* (Sheffield: Sheffield Academic Press, 1996).

argues that any excessive focus on the metaphoric representation obscures the fact that prophetic discourse is concerned with Israel's 'social body' and uses the woman's body as a figure of speech.[42] The woman's body is 'a locus of sacred meaning' and its violation symbolizes the breakdown of social order.[43] Focusing on the social body, Gale Yee argues that the marital metaphor decries the monarchic regime which pursued a cultic and foreign policy that was exploitive and oppressive. The lovers with whom Gomer consorts are the foreign nations with whom the elite are economically and politically entangled.[44]

The efforts to decode the use of feminine sexuality in the context of prophetic literature stem from the jarring combination of such different discourses. My argument here is that femininity determines the making of the nation. It is indeed one of the discourses that define and represent national difference. It should therefore come as no surprise that the nation is often represented as a woman. While feminine sexuality is used to satirize and derogate foreign national cultures in other biblical contexts, it surfaces in prophetic literature with special force. The prophets castigate the nation for failing to live up to its ideals by representing it as a fornicating woman, thus suggesting that the nation has become foreign. As a foreign nation, then, Israel deserves the political collapse which is figured as divine punishment. Since the nation has been overpowered by stronger nations, masculine codes of representation can no longer serve as appropriate means of representation. Prophetic discourse therefore makes more extensive use of feminine codes of national representation. Masculinity, the code of hierarchical order and control, is deified in the figure of a cuckolded husband disciplining his wife. The other nations are represented as male lovers but true masculinity in the sense of legitimate power is transposed to its national God, Yhwh. True masculinity is the discourse of law and order, morality, and strict discipline of sexuality, which in the prophetic literature becomes encoded in the woman's body.

The Future of Biblical Sexual Politics in Postcolonial Studies: A Conclusion

My intervention in this essay is meant to move the feminist discussion of biblical texts from sexual to textual politics, namely, to questions of purpose, investment and orientation of the nation as narration. The hermetic

---

42. Alice A. Keefe, *Woman's Body and the Social Body in Hosea* (Sheffield: Sheffield Academic Press, 2001).
43. Keefe, *Woman's Body and the Social Body in Hosea*, p. 12.
44. Gale A. Yee, *Poor Banished Children of Eve: Woman as Evil in the Hebrew Bible* (Minneapolis: Fortress Press, 2003), pp. 81-110.

analysis of the 'foreign' woman versus the normative 'Israelite' woman ignores the fact that both representations create idealized constructions of desirability that necessarily depend on the textual politics of the nation. Recent discussions of the 'foreign' woman presume a historical factuality that is rarely substantiated on the one hand, or a sacral eternality that all but ignores the national parameters of the biblical text. Recent discussions have become increasingly emulative of conventional paradigms of hair-splitting details and the construction of feminist biblical scholarship as a form of specialized knowledge rather than as an interventionist interrogation of prevalent scholarly assumptions. It is time to consider the fact that the nation is as contingent on gender as it is on narrative mediations, and therefore simplistic reversals of the Israelite/foreign binary will not do. While the focus on this binary construction is an excellent starting point for feminist analysis, it will not do without a consideration of the textual politics of the nation.

Part I
FEMINIST READINGS BEHIND THE TEXT

3

BACK TO THE PAST:
AN OVERVIEW OF FEMINIST HISTORICAL CRITICISM[1]

Sarah Shectman

In feminist Hebrew Bible studies, historical-critical methods have generally taken a back seat to literary approaches. This methodological situation parallels trends within the field of biblical studies as a whole during the past several decades. Although feminist interpretation has become an important and influential element of biblical scholarship, it has not been integrated so much as it has simply been accepted. Historical-critical methods, a mainstay of biblical exegesis, have remained generally isolated from feminism. In part this situation is likely a result of the dearth of historically reliable information about women in the Bible and of the overall invisibility of women in many biblical texts. Feminists have focused especially on biblical books such as Genesis and Judges that feature women much more prominently than other books. Yet these books are historically problematic because of their mythological nature, although this does not prevent their use in many historical treatments of women in ancient Israel. The books of Samuel and Kings, which are often considered to contain a more reliable historical framework, include much less material about women. Other books feature women of a definite literary rather than historical stripe, such as Proverbs, Ruth, Esther, and the Song of Songs. Women are even less visible in the prophetic books despite the frequent personification of Israel in feminine terms. All of this material may be used for historical analysis of one kind or another, but it must be carefully examined and a variety of tools must be applied to see behind the literary constructs.

Because much women's history is about women's social roles construed broadly, social-scientific models are especially useful in feminist historiography. Feminist historians thus rely frequently on anthropological,

---

1. This essay is a revised and updated version of a chapter of my doctoral dissertation, entitled 'Women as Looking Glasses: Reflections in the Pentateuchal Sources' (PhD dissertation, Brandeis University, 2007), which appears in a revised form as *Women in the Pentateuch: A Feminist and Source-Critical Analysis* (HBM, 23; Sheffield: Sheffield Phoenix Press, 2009). I am grateful to Sheffield Phoenix Press for the permission to reuse the material.

sociological, and ethnographic tools and on archaeological evidence, generally preferring these approaches to traditional historical-critical tools, such as source and redaction criticism, textual criticism, and form criticism. And as with all biblical interpretation—all textual interpretation—such readings are also always literary readings and to some extent must use literary methods.

From Theology to History

As a Western philosophical movement, feminism has to deal with the Bible's role in the secondary status of women throughout history. Feminism from its inception thus involved biblical interpretation of both a literary and a historical nature. Early biblical feminism, however, was largely a theological movement concerned with freeing women from a status derived from traditional biblical theology. In this vein, one of the first feminist Hebrew Bible scholars, Phyllis Trible, sought to 'depatriarchalize' the Bible and to overturn misogynistic tendencies thought to be inherent in biblical texts, allowing scholars to move beyond androcentric biblical meanings and to identify positive aspects of the Bible for women.[2]

Trible's work was methodologically, exegetically, and theologically groundbreaking. Most notably, she argued that male and female are originally equals in the creation stories of Genesis, and God is no more male than female.[3] Many of her conclusions have become part of the canon of feminist biblical interpretation.[4] Although she was primarily concerned with the theological implications of her analysis and the 'journey' of the Bible through time,[5] historians and literary critics alike have felt the impact of her work, as Trible has overturned many long-standing suppositions about the Bible that endorse the inferior status of women.[6]

In difference, Phyllis Bird, also interested in biblical theology from a feminist perspective, has relied on historical criticism in her work. She has been critical of Trible, for instance arguing that Gen. 1.27 has to be understood not only within the context of Gen. 1.26-28 but also within the entire

---

2. Phyllis Trible, 'Depatriarchalizing in Biblical Interpretation', *JAAR* 41 (1973), pp. 30-48.

3. Phyllis Trible, *God and the Rhetoric of Sexuality* (OBT, 2; Philadelphia: Fortress Press, 1978), p. 17.

4. See, for instance, the treatment of the verse in Susan Niditch, 'Genesis', in Carol A. Newsom and Sharon H. Ringe (eds.), *Women's Bible Commentary* (Louisville, KY: Westminster/John Knox Press, 1998), pp. 13-29 (16).

5. See, for example, Phyllis Trible, 'Eve and Miriam: From the Margins to the Center', in Phyllis Trible *et al.* (eds.), *Feminist Approaches to the Bible* (Washington, DC: Biblical Archaeology Society, 1995), pp. 5-24.

6. See also her useful list of these suppositions in Trible, *Rhetoric*, p. 73.

Priestly creation story (Gen. 1.1–2.4), which aims to depict creation's connection with God.[7] Hence, Bird writes that both male and female are 'mentioned here only out of necessity';[8] arguing that the verse reflects the Priestly author's alleged concern with equality of the sexes, as Trible claims, goes beyond the evidence.

Bird thus bridges the work of earlier feminist biblical theologians and feminist biblical historians. She approaches theology 'in historical and descriptive terms' and places biblical theologies within their historical contexts.[9] She also keeps historical development in mind, for example, when she notes the impact of centralization on women. She suggests that with the advent of the monarchy and the increased centralization of both the government and the cult, women's status and role in the ancient Israelite cult was increasingly diminished, although there remains a countermove (notably in Deuteronomy) to include women within the 'religious assembly'.[10]

Looking back at the progress of feminist biblical criticism from the early works of Trible and Bird, Susan Ackerman notes:

> [D]espite the fact that Trible's and Bird's articles were published almost simultaneously, and despite the fact that both of them, in my estimation, presented equally provocative and programmatic descriptions about how issues concerning women and gender might be considered in Hebrew Bible studies, it seems fair to say that the majority of subsequent feminist biblical scholars have taken their cues from Trible and not from Bird. Which is to say that, rather than offer, like Bird, a historically-oriented analysis, asking basically what we can ascertain from Hebrew Bible texts regarding the actual lives and experiences of ancient Israelite women, feminist critics of the Hebrew Bible have tended to focus, like Trible, on the role literary-critical methodologies might play in illuminating issues concerning women and gender, describing especially the means and techniques by which biblical stories are told and the impact of these means and techniques upon the stories' depictions of women.[11]

In part, this trend is owing to the links between feminist studies and literary studies, especially in the formative period of feminism in the 1960s and

---

7. Trible, *Rhetoric*, pp. 128, 131.
8. Trible, *Rhetoric*, p. 143 n. 50.
9. Phyllis Bird, *Missing Persons and Mistaken Identities: Women and Gender in Ancient Israel* (OBT; Minneapolis: Fortress Press, 1997), p. 6. See also the discussion of Bird's method in Susanne Scholz, '"Tandoori Reindeer" and the Limitations of Historical Criticism', in Caroline Vander Stichele and Todd Penner (eds.), *Her Master's Tools? Feminist and Postcolonial Engagements of Historical-Critical Discourse* (GPBS, 9; Atlanta: Scholars Press, 2005), pp. 47-69 (57).
10. Bird, *Missing Persons*, pp. 93, 102.
11. Susan Ackerman, 'Digging Up Deborah: Recent Hebrew Bible Scholarship on Gender and the Contribution of Archaeology', *Near Eastern Archaeology* 66.4 (2003), pp. 172-85 (172).

1970s; but in part it is also owing to the difficulty in finding reliable historical evidence about women in ancient Israel.[12] As Ackerman notes, much of the difficulty arises from the fact that most biblical texts are written from an androcentric perspective and are thus frequently dismissed by feminists as meaningless for the reconstruction of women's historical reality. This has led to a marked tendency among feminist exegetes to focus on literary rather than historical approaches.[13]

It was not until the late 1970s, and especially the early 1980s, that a feminist biblical historiography took hold. The nature and dearth of the material is a primary obstacle in writing about the history of women in ancient Israel. Most of the usable biblical texts are not concerned with women's history and are 'often shrouded in ambiguity or limited in scope and value'.[14] Theological and literary interpreters are free to question the texts and to fill in the gaps, but historians, filling the gaps as well, are further constrained by the limits of historical methodology. In addition, feminist historians are often caught between feminism's rejection of the notion of objectivity and a historian's desire to chronicle historical reality. Whereas the rejection of objectivity is central to feminist theological arguments, 'for feminist historians...absolute rejection of objectivity has not been a central plank in the platform... The challenge for feminist historians has been to find ways of insisting upon the importance of female experience that are appropriate to historical inquiry'.[15] Yet as Ackerman observes, though it is difficult to rely on the biblical text for historical accuracy, this difficulty does not mean that biblical texts have no value for reconstructing women's lives in ancient Israel:

> [W]hile I will not assume a historical reality for any of the stories or characters I will be discussing, I do believe it is crucial to assume a historical reality for the authors who wrote these stories and for the audience for whom these authors wrote. I further believe it is crucial to assume that this historical reality matters, that the biblical authors shaped their stories about various 'types' of women in a certain way and that the biblical redactors preserved certain versions of tales about women because these narratives somehow 'worked' within the context—the mind-set and the worldview—of the authors' and redactors' day.[16]

12. Ackerman, 'Digging Up Deborah', pp. 173-74.
13. Susan Ackerman, *Warrior, Dancer, Seductress, Queen: Women in Judges and Biblical Israel* (ABRL; New York: Doubleday, 1998), p. 12.
14. Carole R. Fontaine, 'A Heifer from Thy Stable: On Goddesses and the Status of Women in the Ancient Near East', in Alice Bach (ed.), *Women in the Hebrew Bible: A Reader* (New York: Routledge, 1999), pp. 159-78 (159).
15. Peggy L. Day, 'Introduction', in Peggy L. Day (ed.), *Gender and Difference in Ancient Israel* (Minneapolis: Fortress Press, 1989), pp. 1-11 (2-3).
16. Ackerman, *Warrior*, pp. 14-15.

In short, Bird's work marked the beginning of the historical examination of women in the Hebrew Bible, which in other scholarly works often became a reconstruction of the history of women in ancient Israel. Such reconstructions have relied on evidence from a wide variety of biblical texts, in addition to social-science methods and archaeology. The work of Carol Meyers has been on the forefront of this type of research. Meyers has especially examined the historical circumstance of women in early Israel of the Late Bronze and Iron I periods (c. 1550–1000 BCE).[17] Using anthropological and ethnographic tools, along with archaeological evidence, Meyers argues that in early Iron Age Palestine women had to be indispensable contributors to the subsistence economy of the family. She grounds her historical work in comparative evidence about women in subsistence economies, and she also uses sociological models and archaeological evidence. Women in early Israel 'would have had to perform certain regular productive tasks that otherwise might have been relegated to males alone'. A focus on family life emphasized women's roles and thus resulted in higher social status for women, drawing as near to equality as is generally possible in subsistence societies.[18] Meyers thus maintains that early Israel was 'a community in which the "myth" of male control is superimposed on a condition of functional nonhierarchy',[19] with both the myth and the reality represented in the biblical text. Yet even in Meyers's subsistence world of near equality, men predominate. She acknowledges that even when women achieve relatively high social status, the myth of male domination is still part of the social structure in ancient Israel.

On the Difficulty of Reading the Hebrew Bible as Women's History

One issue that feminist historians must address is how to use the biblical material in light of the problem that it was not intended to be read as history

---

17. See Carol Meyers, *Discovering Eve: Ancient Israelite Women in Context* (New York: Oxford University Press, 1988); Carol Meyers, 'Procreation, Production, and Protection: Male-Female Balance in Early Israel', *JAAR* 51 (1983), pp. 569-93; Carol Meyers, 'Of Drums and Damsels: Women's Performance in Ancient Israel', *BA* 54 (March 1991), pp. 16-27; Carol Meyers, 'Miriam the Musician', in Athalya Brenner (ed.), *A Feminist Companion to Exodus to Deuteronomy* (FCB, 6; Sheffield: Sheffield Academic Press, 1994), pp. 207-30; Carol Meyers, *Households and Holiness: The Religious Culture of Israelite Women* (Facets; Minneapolis: Fortress Press, 2005).

18. Meyers, 'Procreation', p. 580; Meyers, *Discovering Eve*, p. 56.

19. Meyers, *Discovering Eve*, p. 43. Meyers enumerates a list of features found in this type of society, which she believes also apply to early Israel. The key feature of such a social structure is a closer affiliation between the public and private spheres, with male dominance in the former and female in the latter but with 'interdependence' between the two. Although men may have more legal rights, women have a relatively high degree of informal power.

in the modern sense. Much of it is in fact historically unreliable. The extent to which the material contains historical echoes or reveals the historical setting of its authors (rather than its characters) is a matter of debate which lacks scholarly agreement. Feminist historians must look for clues in the text that fit particular historical settings and for clues that stand out as anachronistic in the various literary settings. Thus, for instance, Meyers can take the etiological tale of Genesis 2–3 and examine it for clues as they pertain to the early Israelite period. This procedure requires the use of corroborating external evidence from the archaeological record and from sociological studies of the kinds of cultures that share the early Israelite material culture reflected in the record. Although Meyers uses textual evidence such as Genesis 2–3, she is wary of using other texts, including the ancestral narratives of Genesis, because they are 'instructional, sacred literature'.[20] However, rather than discarding these narratives in their entirety, she notes that they do contain some historical importance regarding the status of women:

> The Genesis ancestor traditions combine two features relevant to our methodological perspective: first, they are oriented to the domestic or household world, with the interaction between the Hebrews and other peoples taking place through a single, eponymous 'family' (Abraham, Isaac, and Jacob) over several telescoped generations; second, women play an especially prominent role in these narratives, with the outcome of critical family decisions determined by female activity and initiative. These observations imply that this literature reveals women exerting power in charting the course of family and, by extension, national well-being.[21]

Meyers sees these female-centered values embedded in the text (that is, the texts' domestic orientation, along with the fact that women play an important role in domestic activity) as evidence for the status of women at the time the texts were composed. According to this analysis, the authors provide a backdrop for their narratives that reflects women's position at that time in history.

Meyers's most recent book, *Rediscovering Eve*, is a new edition of her groundbreaking volume entitled *Discovering Eve*.[22] Expanding the scope of the original study, Meyers argues that for the majority of Israelites who did not live in cities the condition of functional nonhierarchy of the early

---

20. Meyers, *Discovering Eve*, p. 138.
21. Meyers, *Discovering Eve*, p. 176. See also Meyers's discussion of the phrase 'mother's house' in Carol Meyers, '"To Her Mother's House": Considering a Counterpart to the Israelite *Bêt 'ab*', in David Jobling, Peggy L. Day and Gerald T. Sheppard (eds.), *The Bible and the Politics of Exegesis: Essays in Honor of Norman K. Gottwald on His Sixty-Fifth Birthday* (Cleveland: Pilgrim, 1991), pp. 39-51.
22. Carol Meyers, *Rediscovering Eve: Ancient Israelite Women in Context* (Oxford: Oxford University Press, 2012), pp. 196-99. See also her SBL presidential address: Carol Meyers, 'Was Ancient Israel a Patriarchal Society?', *JBL* 133 (2014), pp. 8-27.

Iron Age extended through the entire Iron Age and even encompassed the monarchic period. Meyers takes on the notion of patriarchy with particular force. She maintains that especially nonurban/agrarian aspects of Israelite society were not part of a hierarchically structured patriarchy. Instead, these aspects followed structures that ought to be characterized as 'heterarchy', a system in which power was not always vertically or hierarchically aligned. Accordingly, women's contributions, especially to the household, were understood to be essential to the welfare of everybody. In other words, Meyers emphasizes that ancient Israelite society is mischaracterized with the term 'patriarchy' because Israelite women had considerable decision-making power and were not the property of men, especially during the pre-monarchical era.

Another historian, Jennie Ebeling, makes a similar argument. Ebeling, who like Meyers is a field archaeologist, has published a book on women's daily life in early Iron Age Israel using a similar methodological approach. Her study provides a hypothetical reconstruction of one woman's life that traces the various stages and roles of women in Israelite villages.[23] Ebeling intersperses creative accounts of this hypothetical woman's life with a scholarly discussion of the historical settings and textual evidence. She notes that the use of a variety of types of evidence in reconstructing women's history is a corrective to the 'incomplete and androcentric perspective of life in ancient Israel that is still presented to the public in popular publications…and scholarly works'.[24]

Many other feminists have followed in this vein, using archaeological and anthropological analysis to reconstruct the social history of Israelite women. Their studies vary in focus. Sometimes they consider particular social roles and sometimes they look at particular literary genres. A few examples must suffice here. For instance, Susan Niditch investigates oral traditions and folklore[25] in a study that uses comparative models to excavate evidence for characters, themes, and genre.[26] Niditch observes that certain narratives may not offer specific historical evidence, but they do depict certain attitudes that help define the text's date and authorship. This data, in turn, can be used to place the text's depiction of women in historical context and discern changes

---

23. Jennie R. Ebeling, *Women's Lives in Biblical Times* (New York: T. & T. Clark, 2010).

24. Ebeling, *Women's Lives*, p. 147.

25. Susan Niditch, *Chaos to Cosmos: Studies in Biblical Patterns of Creation* (SIH, 6; Chico, CA: Scholars Press, 1985); Susan Niditch, *Folklore and the Hebrew Bible* (GBS; Minneapolis: Fortress Press, 1993); Susan Niditch, *A Prelude to Biblical Folklore: Underdogs and Tricksters* (Urbana: University of Illinois Press, 2000); see also Susan Niditch, 'The Wronged Woman Righted: An Analysis of Genesis 38', *HTR* 72 (1979), pp. 143-49.

26. See, e.g., Niditch, *Chaos to Cosmos*.

in women's status over the course of Israelite history.[27] Another feminist historian, Jo Ann Hackett, suggests that biblical texts dated to the early Israelite period reflect a more egalitarian status for women than later texts in which women's status is often lower and women's roles more limited in comparison to their earlier counterparts. Hackett links this social development to increased political-economic centralization[28] that is based on the observation that women's status increases when there is less centralization and when centralized institutions break down or are temporarily disabled.[29]

Another historical critic, Susan Ackerman, combines historical criticism with social-scientific models and archaeology to reconstruct the history of Israelite women's religion.[30] Like Hackett, Ackerman maintains that times of political instability result in a higher status for women. Thus the Babylonian exile had positive implications for women, as the rise of female prophets suggests.[31] In general then, in periods of social liminality, and even in fictive accounts of such periods, gender roles become increasingly fluid, which results in women assuming leadership positions that they were previously denied.[32] Interestingly, much of Ackerman's work focuses on the preexilic period in Israelite history, as this is generally seen as a period when women had more autonomy and higher status than during later times.

Whereas some feminist historians argue that premonarchic social structures like the extended clan gave way to smaller, and thus less individually powerful, nuclear families in the period of the monarchy (see below, on the legal material), Hennie Marsman argues that the clan persisted in the monarchic period, though its influence lessened as a result of economic and political factors.[33] This decrease in autonomy would have influenced the

---

27. Susan Niditch, 'Portrayals of Women in the Hebrew Bible', in Judith R. Baskin (ed.), *Jewish Women in Historical Perspective* (Detroit: Wayne State University Press, 2nd edn, 1998), pp. 25-45 (26-27); Niditch, *Oral World*, p. 18.

28. Jo Ann Hackett, 'In the Days of Jael: Reclaiming the History of Women in Ancient Israel', in Clarissa W. Atkinson, Constance H. Buchanan and Margaret R. Miles (eds.), *Immaculate and Powerful: The Female in Sacred Image and Social Reality* (HWSR; Boston: Beacon Press, 1985), pp. 15-38 (17).

29. Hackett, 'In the Days of Jael', p. 19.

30. Ackerman, *Warrior*, p. 10. In part, at least, this is owing to her view that the biblical text may not be historically reliable enough to reconstruct 'what really happened' (p. 11). See also Susan Ackerman, 'And the Women Knead Dough: The Worship of the Queen of Heaven in Sixth-Century Judah', in Peggy L. Day (ed.), *Gender and Difference in Ancient Israel* (Minneapolis: Fortress Press, 1989), pp. 109-24; Susan Ackerman, 'The Queen Mother and the Cult in Ancient Israel', *JBL* 112 (1993), pp. 385-401.

31. Susan Ackerman, 'Why Is Miriam Also among the Prophets? (And Is Zipporah among the Priests?)', *JBL* 121 (2002), pp. 47-80 (57).

32. Ackerman, 'Why Is Miriam Also among the Prophets?', p. 71.

33. Hennie J. Marsman, *Women in Ugarit and Israel: Their Social and Religious Position in the Context of the Ancient Near East* (OtSt; Leiden: Brill, 2003), pp. 62-63.

role of women in the family. The situation became particularly acute in the exilic and postexilic periods, according to Marsman, when the rise of the nuclear family unit caused further restrictions on women's roles, especially as the division between public and private became more entrenched—the less fluidity of movement between the two spheres women have, the less social status and autonomy they generally have held as well.[34]

This division between public and private is particularly important for women because one of the primary social institutions governing women's lives—marriage—bridges these two spheres. Women's place in this institution takes place mostly in the private household sphere, but the transaction of marriage itself takes place in the public sphere, usually between men (fathers/brothers on the one side and husbands on the other). Restriction to the private sphere, and therefore dependence on men for the public transaction of marriage, may make it appear that women are essentially property, private goods being traded between public (male) operators. But Marsman argues that young women in ancient Israel were not treated as property.[35] Rather, she claims that laws governing penalties for the sexual violation of a woman were part of family law and not property law.[36] Though this meant that fathers had considerable power over the sexual disposition of their daughters, it is not tantamount to treating them as property. Likewise, Tracy Lemos contends that women should not be regarded as property in ancient Israel, although they were certainly subordinate to men.[37] Lemos's comprehensive historical study about marriage gifts in Israelite and early Jewish history traces the development of these institutions and their relationship to women's status.[38] Her work demonstrates that differences in types of marriage gifts—bride wealth versus dowry—were related to changes in social stratification. This study is one of the few recent in-depth treatments of marriage in ancient Israel, and it makes an important contribution to understanding women's status in ancient Israel.[39]

---

34. Marsman, *Women in Ugarit and Israel*, pp. 162-63.

35. Marsman, *Women in Ugarit and Israel*, pp. 69, 106. See Judith Romney Wegner, *Chattel or Person: The Status of Women in the Mishnah* (New York: Oxford University Press, 1988).

36. Marsman, *Women in Ugarit and Israel*, p. 69.

37. Tracy M. Lemos, 'Were Israelite Women Chattel? Shedding New Light on an Old Question', paper presented at the Annual Meeting of the Society of Biblical Literature in Baltimore, Maryland, on November 24, 2013.

38. Tracy M. Lemos, *Marriage Gifts and Social Change in Ancient Palestine, 1200 BCE to 200 CE* (Cambridge: Cambridge University Press, 2010).

39. There is no recent book-length treatment of marriage more generally, which leaves a bit of a hole in our understanding of women's social position in ancient Israel; see Sarah Shectman, 'What Do We Know about Marriage in Ancient Israel?', in Marvin L. Chaney, Uriah Y. Kim and Annette Schellenberg (eds.), *Reading a Tendentious Bible:*

Other feminist historians investigate women's lives beyond the private sphere and the social institution of marriage. For instance, Mercedes García Bachmann explores numerous occupations held by women in ancient Israel.[40] Although some of these professions are based on single biblical references, Bachmann excavates how women, especially of lower social status, faced relatively few restrictions regarding their work choices. It seems likely that they were involved in public life, although some of their occupations are invisible. Often their work is mentioned in conjunction with unnamed women who serve prominent characters.[41] Bachmann's study is important because it deconstructs textual ideologies, looking between the lines of the text itself to write women's history.

So far, relatively few feminist historians have examined the postexilic period, perhaps because little historical material relating to women can be firmly dated to this period. A few studies are available. For instance, Lemos's study includes marriage contracts from this period, concluding that the increase in dowry in the later period was tied to increased social stratification and an accompanying decrease in women's status and rights.[42] Tamara Eskenazi analyzes the prohibitions against foreign marriages in Ezra-Nehemiah, which she connects to the evidence from marriage contracts at Elephantine to argue that women continued to have rights and status in the exilic period.[43] These divergent conclusions illustrate the difficulty of analyzing the sparse material available; evaluations of what constitutes an increase or decrease in status may also depend on the standard against which one is measuring: the pre-exilic period (in Lemos's case) or prior scholarly opinion about the same period (in Eskenazi's case).

Women and Law

Feminist historical studies include texts from various books and genres, but most of them are prose texts. Several feminist scholars have, however, analyzed legal materials about women. For instance, law codes are central for the reconstruction of women's status in ancient Israel. They provide insight into women's religious obligations, women's presumed access to the cult, and women's status and rights in society. Carolyn Pressler was among the first feminist exegetes to study Deuteronomic laws and analyze women's

---

Essays in Honor of Robert B. Coote (HBM, 66; Sheffield: Sheffield Phoenix Press, 2014), pp. 166-75.

40. Mercedes L. García Bachman, *Women at Work in the Deuteronomistic History* (IVBS, 4; Atlanta: Society of Biblical Literature, 2013).

41. García Bachman, *Women at Work*, pp. 342-44.

42. Lemos, *Marriage Gifts*, pp. 233-36.

43. Tamara Eskenazi, 'Out from the Shadows: Biblical Women in the Postexilic Era', *JSOT* 54 (1992), pp. 25-43.

rights in various situations. Pressler maintains in her work that in Deuteronomy the family is hierarchically structured and protected women's interests only in certain cases.[44]

Another feminist historian who worked with biblical law, Naomi Steinberg, argues the opposite in her sociopolitical analysis of the effects of the monarchy on family structures in Israel and its impact on other institutions, including ancient Israelite legal systems. Steinberg observes that Deuteronomic law moves the locus of legal activity from the family to the centralized monarchy. The premonarchic Covenant Collection (Exodus 20–23) granted more authority to the father (*paterfamilias*) and protected the extended family whereas Deuteronomy gave more authority to the elders to enforce monarchic law.[45] Thus laws ostensibly protecting women's rights, like the levirate (Deut. 25.5-10), were developed to protect the nuclear family and to strengthen state authority. Furthermore, some of the sex and rape laws put women 'at a social disadvantage vis-à-vis men' and so indicate that women's interests were not as important to the legal authors of Deuteronomy as some historians have maintained.[46] According to Steinberg, the political beginnings of this shift appear in the move to a strengthened governance structure in the early monarchic period, which decreased the power of clan or extended-family structures and emphasized the importance of smaller nuclear-family units. Such a move meant that the monarchy and its cultic and legal arm might appear to be safeguarding the rights of women within individual families, but it was in fact more interested in minimizing local authority and the power of the *paterfamilias*.[47]

---

44. See, e.g., Carolyn Pressler, *The View of Women Found in the Deuteronomic Family Law* (BZAW, 215; Berlin: W. de Gruyter, 1993), pp. 95-114. Eckart Otto concludes that women are treated well and their rights protected in D family law. However, he also argues that D's view is probably utopian and did not reflect reality; D (and Dtr) continued to battle for centralization, meaning it was not actually achieved; see Eckart Otto, 'False Weights in the Scales of Biblical Justice? Different Views of Women from Patriarchal Hierarchy to Religious Equality in the Book of Deuteronomy', in Victor H. Matthews, Bernard M. Levinson and Tikva Frymer-Kensky (eds.), *Gender and Law in the Hebrew Bible and the Ancient Near East* (JSOTSup, 262; Sheffield: Sheffield Academic Press, 1998), pp. 128-46 (143).

45. Naomi Steinberg, 'The Deuteronomic Law Code and the Politics of State Centralization', in David Jobling, Peggy L. Day and Gerald T. Sheppard (eds.), *The Bible and the Politics of Exegesis: Essays in Honor of Norman Gottwald on His Sixty-Fifth Birthday* (Cleveland: Pilgrim, 1991), pp. 161-70 (166). For a summary of Steinberg's argument, see also David Jobling, 'Feminism and "Mode of Production" in Ancient Israel: Search for a Method', in David Jobling, Peggy L. Day and Gerald T. Sheppard (eds.), *The Bible and the Politics of Exegesis: Essays in Honor of Norman Gottwald on His Sixty-Fifth Birthday* (Cleveland: Pilgrim, 1991), pp. 239-51 (245-46).

46. Steinberg, 'Deuteronomic Law Code', p. 168.

47. Steinberg, 'Deuteronomic Law Code', pp. 165-69. See also Bernard M. Levinson,

The other large body of biblical law, the Priestly materials from Exodus through Numbers, has also been the subject of study in feminist historical exegesis. An early treatment of the topic by Mayer Gruber focuses on women's opportunities to participate in the Israelite cult.[48] Gruber suggested that women were allowed to bring sacrifices and to make vows, and although a woman's vow might be effectively annulled under certain circumstances, she had to fulfill her vows if they were not annulled.[49] Phyllis Bird also discussed women's roles in the Israelite cult although she focused on other texts than the Priestly legal texts and developed several categories for women's cultic participation, not just as worshipers but also as prophets, singers, dancers, and sanctuary attendants.[50]

Other feminist historians have turned their attention to sexuality and law. For instance, Deborah Ellens examines laws about sexual behavior in Leviticus and Deuteronomy. She discerns differences between the two law codes and sees them grounded in different understandings of women's status.[51] Leviticus focuses on categorization—that is, it is concerned with fitting things into their proper categories (such as clean/unclean, holy/profane, and also male/female)—whereas Deuteronomy stresses property rights. Thus in Leviticus women have more agency than in Deuteronomy because in Leviticus women are responsible for maintaining the purity laws that apply to them.[52] Several additional volumes reveal a growing interest in gender and the laws that governed the Israelite cult.[53] Though not all of the essays in these books approach the topic from a historical perspective, many of them do. For example, Tarja Philip argues that regulations about impurity do not single women out as inherently more impure or as more morally guilty than

---

Deuteronomy and the Hermeneutics of Legal Innovation (New York: Oxford University Press, 1997), pp. 138-43, and Gary N. Knoppers, 'Rethinking the Relationship between Deuteronomy and the Deuteronomistic History: The Case of Kings', *CBQ* 63 (2001), pp. 393-415.

48. Mayer I. Gruber, 'Women in the Cult according to the Priestly Code', in Jacob Neusner, Baruch A. Levine and Ernst Frerichs (eds.), *Judaic Perspectives on Ancient Israel* (Philadelphia: Fortress Press, 1987), pp. 35-48.

49. Gruber, 'Women in the Cult', pp. 39-40.

50. Bird, *Missing Persons*, pp. 81-102.

51. Deborah L. Ellens, *Women in the Sex Texts of Leviticus and Deuteronomy: A Comparative Conceptual Analysis* (LHB/OTS, 458; New York: T. & T. Clark, 2008).

52. This rule applies to laws related to menstruation and childbirth and to those related to pure and impure foods and contact to which men are also subject.

53. See, e.g., Kristin De Troyer *et al.* (eds.), *Wholly Woman, Holy Blood: A Feminist Critique of Purity and Impurity* (Studies in Antiquity and Christianity; Harrisburg, PA: Trinity Press, 2003); Deborah W. Rooke (ed.), *A Question of Sex? Gender and Difference in the Hebrew Bible and Beyond* (HBM, 14; Sheffield: Sheffield Phoenix Press, 2007); Deborah W. Rooke (ed.), *Embroidered Garments: Priests and Gender in Biblical Israel* (HBM, 25; KCLSBG, 2; Sheffield: Sheffield Phoenix Press, 2009).

men because of their impurity.⁵⁴ Eve Levavi Feinstein examines the intersection of cultic pollution and sexuality, arguing that the Priestly laws on sexual pollution see women as the sexual property of men. This idea has ramifications for understanding transgressive male sex as well, and it also illuminates ideas about collective impurity and responsibility in later biblical books influenced by the Priestly authors.⁵⁵ Such works add to our understanding of the role of gender—for men as well as women—in the history of Israelite religion and worship.

Historians and Goddesses

A popular topic in feminist historical criticism is goddess worship and the role that women, as the keepers of household religious traditions, played in it. For instance, Meyers maintains that the presence of female figurines at many Israelite archaeological sites denotes the prevalence of goddess worship. It was accompanied by both a greater role in the family-oriented religious cult and higher overall status for women.⁵⁶ Another feminist historian, Tikva Frymer-Kensky, devotes particular attention to the study of goddesses and how goddess religion affected Israelite religion.⁵⁷ Her work shows that the Bible was the product of a post-goddess gap that left early Judaism (and Christianity) open to misogynist influences from Greek/Hellenistic culture. Yet to Frymer-Kensky, the Hebrew Bible itself is not sexist but sexless, as the loss of goddess worship created an inability to adequately include sexual characteristics in Israelite theology. Thus, Israelite religion, in moving to worship Yhwh exclusively, was left with aspects of goddess worship that could not entirely be incorporated into the image of the male deity.⁵⁸ This gap resulted in a biblical view of Yhwh's power over fertility in which fertility was a natural property of the earth. To Frymer-Kensky, therefore, 'the Bible offers an alternative system that does not fully answer human needs'.⁵⁹ It integrates both female and male aspects into the depiction of YHWH but in so doing creates a deity that is not fully either one.

---

54. See Tarja Philip, 'Gender Matters: Priestly Writing on Impurity', in Deborah W Rooke (ed.), *Embroidered Garments*, pp. 40-59.

55. Eve Levavi Feinstein, *Sexual Pollution in the Hebrew Bible* (New York: Oxford University Press, 2014).

56. Meyers, 'Roots of Restriction', p. 93.

57. Tikva Frymer-Kensky, *In the Wake of the Goddesses: Women, Culture and the Biblical Transformation of Pagan Myth* (New York: Fawcett Columbine, 1992).

58. Frymer-Kensky, *In the Wake of the Goddesses*, p. 92.

59. Frymer-Kensky, *In the Wake of the Goddesses*, p. 212. For a counterpoint, see Alice Bach, who criticizes Frymer-Kensky's simplified presentation of the goddesses' loss of power; Alice Bach, 'Introduction: Man's World, Women's Place; Sexual Politics

In contrast to Frymer-Kensky's treatment of goddess worship as something of an ideal, the absence of which left a hole in the spiritual life of ancient Israel and contributed to women's secondary status, Jo Ann Hackett offers a counterpoint.[60] She suggests that feminists reclaimed 'fertility cults' and 'fertility goddesses', partly in connection with the rise of Neopaganism, but in reality both are based on mostly fictional creations of male scholars. They are primarily an attempt to deal with the 'scary' feminine aspects of cult and deity by pigeonholing. Hackett notes the tendency of many studies, even those by feminists, to treat women as though 'we are all alike and we are most easily described in terms of biological functions'.[61] However, as Hackett goes on to point out, the evidence for fertility cults of the type most scholars describe—centered on the worship of a robust mother-goddess cult, embodied in the classic figurine with pronounced sexual features that was a regular item of women's household worship—is largely lacking. Though Hackett's work undoes some earlier feminist history, stripping away the goddess cult that was a key feature of reconstructions of women's religious worship in early Israel, it nevertheless increases the accuracy of our historical understanding of women in ancient Israel.

Like Hackett, Hennie Marsman questions long-held notions about goddess worship and its relationship to women's status. Marsman's study on the social and religious status of women in ancient Israel and Ugarit is a specific response to allegations that women had higher status in polytheistic cultures with goddess worship than they did in the monotheistic culture of ancient Israel.[62] Marsman assumes that ancient Israelites primarily worshiped YHWH and that Asherah played a minor and diminished role as Israelite religion moved toward monolatry and monotheism.[63] The latter assumption is well supported in biblical scholarship.[64] Marsman posits that Israelite women had roughly the same social status as women in polytheistic Ugarit but that their religious status was lower, especially as the Yahwistic religion became more firmly monotheistic.[65] These studies all question

in the Hebrew Bible', in Alice Bach (ed.), *Women in the Hebrew Bible: A Reader* (New York: Routledge, 1999), pp. xiii-xxvi (xvii-xviii).

60. Hackett, 'Sexist Model', pp. 65-76.
61. Hackett, 'Sexist Model', p. 66.
62. Marsman, *Women in Ugarit and Israel*, p. ix.
63. Marsman, *Women in Ugarit and Israel*, pp. 736-37.
64. See, e.g., Robert K. Gnuse, 'The Emergence of Monotheism in Ancient Israel: A Survey of Recent Scholarship', *Religion* 29 (1999), pp. 315-36. For a different view, see Stephen L. Cook, *The Social Roots of Biblical Yahwism* (SBLStBL; Atlanta: Society of Biblical Literature, 2004). That Asherah worship was commonplace before the exile is amply attested in the diatribes of Deuteronomy and DtrH against it; see, e.g., Deut. 7.5; 12.3; 16.21; Judg. 3.7; 1 Kgs 15.13; 18.19; 2 Kgs 21.7; 23.4.
65. Marsman, *Women in Ugarit and Israel*, p. 737.

whether the shape of the Israelite pantheon—specifically the presence or absence of a goddess in it—is directly related to women's social and religious history. What they differ on is the extent to which they believe such goddess worship existed and whether its existence had any kind of beneficial effects for women.

Feminism and the Historical-Critical Method

Most feminist historians discussed thus far depend on social-scientific tools and do not use what are considered to be the methods of historical-criticism, such as text criticism, source criticism, and redaction criticism. In other words, feminist historians are less interested in the composition history of the Bible, a primary concern of historical-critical scholarship, even when their works are diachronic in nature, focused on a particular author, or uplifting a particular biblical genre such as the Priestly laws. Only a small number of feminists advocate the use of traditional historical-critical tools and they are frequently trained by historical critics.

One of them is Monika Fander, who explains why feminists have largely avoided traditional historical-critical interpretation: 'The historical-critical method may be and is suspected of serving masculine interests'.[66] Nonetheless, she argues that historical-critical methods are not only suitable for feminist criticism but may also help in 'working through a number of deficiencies in feminist readings of the Bible and in giving precision to some statements'.[67] Thus, for instance, Fander suggests that historical criticism may aid in distinguishing between older traditions and later redactional elements. Despite the usefulness of the historical-critical method, Fander notes that there are still 'tensions' between it and feminism, most notably the suspicion with which proponents of one regard the other. Fander insists that this tension is hermeneutic, resting 'on the preunderstanding that consciously or unconsciously shapes the treatment of the texts, and on the question of the authority that is to be attributed to those texts'.[68] Elisabeth Schüssler Fiorenza, who like Fander is a New Testament scholar, has made similar observations about the apparent incompatibility between feminist and historical-critical methodology, particularly because the latter tends to take a positivist stance.[69] However, Schüssler Fiorenza argues that 'it is not

---

66. Monika Fander, 'Historical-Critical Methods', in Elisabeth Schüssler Fiorenza (ed.), *Searching the Scriptures: A Feminist Introduction* (2 vols.; New York: Crossroad, 1992), pp. 205-24 (206). Although Fander, like other feminist exegetes who address such methodological issues, is a New Testament scholar, her comments are also relevant for the study of the Hebrew Bible.

67. Fander, 'Historical-Critical Methods', p. 212.

68. Fander, 'Historical-Critical Methods', p. 214.

69. Elisabeth Schüssler Fiorenza, 'Remembering the Past in Creating the Future:

the search for early Christian origins, agency, memory, and history...but the rhetoric of exclusivist Christian uniqueness, negative boundary drawing, and claims to *sui generis* status that feminists must reject'.[70] Feminists interested in historiography must look for other voices in the text, using a variety of methods (for example, liberation theology) to question androcentric or kyriocentric (elite-male centered) interpretations and incorporate those other voices into the cultural record.

In the introduction to a volume on historical-critical and feminist scholarship, Caroline Vander Stichele and Todd Penner note the indebtedness of approaches like feminism to historical-critical work, which is itself a product of Enlightenment thinking.[71] Feminist biblical scholars are still interested in reconstructing the past,[72] they argue, and so feminist work often makes positivistic statements about women in history, even when those feminist exegetes are not specifically writing histories. Modern methods such as historical criticism and postmodernist ones, including many types of feminist interpretation, are more closely related than many scholars would have it appear.[73] Rather than reject historical-critical discourse and its methods outright, Vander Stichele and Penner thus suggest that feminists reject 'the ways in which they have been used' and instead 'use them to serve different ends'.[74] In the same volume, Hanna Stenström also explains that historical-critical analysis, like feminism, began as a radical, even subversive approach to biblical study but that 'historical-critical approaches did not live up to the potential for liberation that they promised at the beginning'.[75] Instead it became the traditional method of the androcentric

---

Historical-Critical Scholarship and Feminist Biblical Interpretation', in Adela Yarbro Collins (ed.), *Feminist Perspectives on Biblical Scholarship* (SBLCP; SBLBSNA, 10; Chico, CA: Scholars Press, 1985), pp. 43-63 (47).

70. Elisabeth Schüssler Fiorenza, '"What She Has Done Will Be Told...": Reflections on Writing Feminist History', in Holly E. Hearon (ed.), *Distant Voices Drawing Near: Essays in Honor of Antoinette Clark Wire* (Collegeville, MN: Michael Glazier, 2004), pp. 3-18 (6).

71. Caroline Vander Stichele and Todd Penner, 'Mastering the Tools or Retooling the Masters? The Legacy of Historical-Critical Discourse', in Caroline Vander Stichele and Todd Penner (eds.), *Her Master's Tools? Feminist and Postcolonial Engagements of Historical-Critical Discourse* (GPBS, 9; Atlanta: Scholars Press, 2005), pp. 1-29 (12).

72. Vander Stichele and Penner, 'Mastering the Tools', p. 15.

73. Vander Stichele and Penner, 'Mastering the Tools', p. 27.

74. Vander Stichele and Penner, 'Mastering the Tools', p. 14.

75. Hanna Stenström, 'Historical-Critical Approaches and the Emancipation of Women: Unfulfilled Promises and Remaining Possibilities', in Caroline Vander Stichele and Todd Penner (eds.), *Her Master's Tools? Feminist and Postcolonial Engagements of Historical-Critical Discourse* (GPBS, 9; Atlanta: Scholars Press, 2005), pp. 31-45 (39). Schüssler Fiorenza notes likewise that as a student she 'experienced historical-critical

status quo.⁷⁶ This is not to say, however, that the historical-critical method is therefore valueless where feminism is concerned. That radical potential is still there; it has simply remained mostly unused.

This has begun to change incrementally in recent years, as a few feminist scholars have taken up traditional historical-critical methods like textual, source, and redaction criticism. In the same volume just discussed, Kristin De Troyer uses the Septuagint text of Joshua to make a text-critical argument that during the Maccabean period (to further the military and political goals of the Maccabean revolt) there was a concern with showing the importance of obeying orders. De Troyer concludes that in order '[t]o show that the commandments of God or the orders of important characters...were obeyed, second-century BCE editors of some of the stories added phrases or sentences in order to indicate that the commandments or orders given in the text were in fact followed'.⁷⁷ Though this example does not concern women, De Troyer argues for its relevance to feminist criticism, as it supports questioning textual authority and sheds new light on the connection between authorship and power, questions that are also fundamental to feminist inquiry.⁷⁸ Roland Boer likewise proposes a means of entry for feminists into texts with little or no material about women. He observes that there is almost no feminist discussion of Ezra–Nehemiah since there are almost no women present in the text. What little discussion there is focuses on the rules concerning foreign wives in Ezra 9–10 and Nehemiah 13. Rather than skipping the remaining material, however, Boer argues that feminists need to look at the broader themes of the books and see how they might relate to the inclusion or exclusion of women in the text.⁷⁹ Although Boer is not necessarily advocating the use of historical-critical methods, his argument is valuable for those who are interested in historical analysis and reconstruction.

Source criticism, a mainstay of mainstream historical research, has received only limited attention from feminists. Irmtraud Fischer is one of a

---

scholarship as liberating, setting [her] free from outdated doctrinal frameworks and literalist prejudices' (Schüssler Fiorenza, 'Remembering the Past', p. 43).

76. Stenström, 'Historical-Critical Approaches', p. 40.

77. Kristin De Troyer, '"And They Did So"· Following Orders Given by Old Joshua', in Caroline Vander Stichele and Todd Penner (eds.), *Her Master's Tools? Feminist and Postcolonial Engagements of Historical-Critical Discourse* (GPBS, 9; Atlanta: Scholars Press, 2005), pp. 145-57 (156).

78. De Troyer, 'And They Did So', pp. 156-57; De Troyer's essay also highlights the fact that it can be difficult to find sufficient material about women to which to apply such traditional methods, especially textual criticism.

79. Roland Boer, 'No Road: On the Absence of Feminist Criticism of Ezra–Nehemiah', in Caroline Vander Stichele and Todd Penner (eds.), *Her Master's Tools? Feminist and Postcolonial Engagements of Historical-Critical Discourse* (GPBS, 9; Atlanta: Scholars Press, 2005), pp. 233-52 (249).

very small number of feminist Bible scholars to do so, arguing that material about women was integral to the narratives found in Genesis 12–36 from the outset.[80] Fischer points out that although traditions about women have been important for source criticism, the meaning and importance of women in the texts has largely been ignored.[81] The prominence of women in the text is striking: Sarah is just as important as Abraham, and Gen. 25.22-26a is told from Rebekah's perspective while Genesis 29–30 highlights women's emotions.[82] The story is a 'family history'[83] that stresses the continuation of the family through childbirth. However, the older traditions portray women in central roles whereas the Priestly materials shift the focus to men. Yet the Priestly texts do not entirely displace the female presence.[84] Like Meyers, Fischer suggests that the prominent role of women in the traditions indicates that Israelite society may have been patriarchal but it did not lead to the 'exclusive dominance' of men.[85]

My own work builds upon Fischer's to argue that the trends in Genesis are in evidence throughout the Pentateuch.[86] Disentangling the narrative threads reveals a marked tendency of the non-Priestly material to include women where the P material does not. This difference represents a diachronic development, with the earlier non-Priestly material likely deriving from a period when women had more autonomy. As other feminists also maintain, I claim that religious and political centralization led to a curtailing of women's rights, and the text reflects this development. To my knowledge, my book is the only attempt to bring feminist analysis to bear on the composition history of the Pentateuchal stories. No similar treatments of other biblical books or narrative collections exist so far.

The Historical Endeavor as Corrective: Conclusions

Most feminist historians agree that the Bible is the result of a patriarchal society. Yet rather than rejecting the text as too focused on men to reliably relate any historical experiences of women, feminist biblical historians push through the layers of ideology to recover ancient Israelite women's history. For some, the recovery project entails using various methods and models to determine what kinds of social roles women may have occupied, what women's status was in different periods, and what effects religious and

---

80. Irmtraud Fischer, *Erzeltern Israels: Feministisch-theologische Studien zu Genesis 12–36* (BZAW, 222; Berlin: W. de Gruyter, 1994).
81. Fischer, *Erzeltern*, p. 338.
82. Fischer, *Erzeltern*, pp. 10, 26-28.
83. Fischer, *Erzeltern*, pp. 9, 378.
84. Fischer, *Erzeltern*, pp. 11-14.
85. Fischer, *Erzeltern*, p. 377.
86. Shectman, *Women in the Pentateuch*.

political institutions may have had on women. For others, feminist history means identifying and interpreting the ideologies of biblical authors. Where the former seeks to strip authors away in some sense, relying on social-scientific approaches, the latter keeps authors at the center of the analysis, relying on traditional historical-critical methods.

The Hebrew Bible is the work of a small and select group of people from long ago. The evidence contained in the biblical books is not necessarily indicative of the experience of most, or even many, Israelites. It is thus difficult to reconstruct the history of women in ancient Israel. Likewise, as a piece of literature with a long and important influence, it is critical to understand the context out of which biblical literature arose and the selectiveness of the opinions it contains. When we study how women are depicted by the various authors, we recognize that we may be unable to reconstruct the full history of Israelite women in every period and place from the fragmentary evidence. Yet we can reconstruct certain attitudes and developments in women's status, at least among certain groups. We can provide a corrective to long-held assumptions about the place of women in the Bible and in ancient Israel.

4

Beyond the Bible:
Archaeology, Ethnohistory,
and the Study of Israelite Women

Carol Meyers

Archaeology is often heralded as an indispensable source for studying the Bible and its world. After all, material remains from the biblical period are plentiful and constantly increasing whereas, especially when it comes to information about women, the Bible is a limited, closed source. Also, archaeological data represent the lives of all groups of people—women and men, villagers and city-dwellers, average people and national figures, rich and poor—whereas most biblical texts were probably produced by one group: urban, male, political or literary elites. Moreover, as an independent witness to the context of the Bible, material remains are free of the theological and cultural biases of biblical texts. And archaeological discoveries date from the actual time periods mentioned in the Bible, whereas most texts referring to those epochs date to centuries later, at least in their final form. It is no wonder that some extol the virtues of archaeology as a 'primary source' for Israelite history and religion.[1] It seems simple—but is it? Do the methods and results of archaeology provide a useful resource for feminist hermeneutics?

As the subtitle of this essay indicates, archaeology is directly relevant to the study of Israelite women rather than to biblical texts mentioning them. Only by reconstructing the social reality of their lives can the relationship between Israelite women and their portrayal in the text be considered. For, as feminist biblical scholars have long noted, there is a disconnect between the lived experience of women and the textual representation of female figures. Peggy Day, for instance, stressed the importance of making a 'distinction between the biblical text and Israelite culture' in an essay published in 1989, the same year Katherine Sakenfeld advocated the study of material culture in order to 'construct a clearer and more reliable picture of women in ancient Israel.'[2] Similarly, classicists recognize that the exceptional nature

---

1. E.g., William G. Dever, *Did God Have a Wife? Archaeology and Folk Religion in Ancient Israel* (Grand Rapids: Eerdmans, 2005), pp. 74-76.
2. Peggy L. Day, 'Introduction', in Peggy L. Day (ed.), *Gender and Difference in*

of what has survived in ancient literary sources hardly reveals the 'normal'.³ Anthropologists too note that aspects of the everyday life of both women and men in traditional societies differ from gender images in the conventional notions or folk literature of those societies.⁴ Indeed, a recent study of Middle Eastern women bemoans the fact that, for studying the past, scholars must rely on texts reflecting the views of elite men rather than on 'direct material about how women lived and thought'.⁵

Given the many problems of using the Bible alone as a source of information about women,⁶ going beyond the Bible is essential; archaeology thus should have become a major resource for reconstructing women's daily reality and assessing its relationship to biblical representations. Yet archaeological discoveries have had little influence on the feminist biblical scholarship of the last four decades. There are several reasons for this, and I begin this essay by explaining two problems in using archaeology to study Israelite women: the availability of relatively little relevant data, and the complexities of data interpretation. Next I propose that the term *ethnohistory* represents the essential interdisciplinary aspect of an engendered archaeology concerned with understanding women's lives, and I then provide two examples: the reconstruction of women's roles in household economy and household religion. Finally, I conclude the ethnohistorical analysis of these roles by looking at their personal and social correlates, which in turn inform the question of how the lived experiences of Israelite women relate to biblical perspectives.

*Problem 1: Availability of Materials for the Archaeology of Gender*⁷

Archaeological materials are indeed plentiful, but those useful for studying women's lives are less abundant because of the traditional agendas of

Ancient Israel (Minneapolis: Fortress Press, 1989), pp. 1-11 (5); and Katharine Doob Sakenfeld, 'Feminist Biblical Interpretation', *TTod* 46 (1989), pp. 154-68 (161-62).

3. Keith Hopkins, *Death and Renewal* (Sociological Studies in Roman History, 2; Cambridge: Cambridge University Press, 1983), p. 41.

4. A classic study is Susan Carol Rogers, 'Female Forms of Power and the Myth of Male Dominance: A Model of Female/Male Interaction in Peasant Society', *American Ethnologist* 2 (1975), pp. 727-56. For a more recent and nuanced discussion, see Roberta Gilchrist, *Gender and Archaeology* (London: Routledge, 1999), pp. 32-36.

5. Nikki R. Keddie, *Women in the Middle East: Past and Present* (Princeton, NJ: Princeton University Press, 2007), p. 9.

6. For a detailed list of these problems, see Carol Meyers, 'Archaeology: A Window to the Lives of Israelite Women', in Mercedes Navarro Puerto and Irmtraud Fischer with Andrea Taschl-Erber (eds.), *Torah* (The Bible and Women: An Encyclopedia of Exegesis and Cultural History, 1.1; Atlanta, SBL, 2011), pp. 61-108 (62-66).

7. This essay considers only non-epigraphic archaeological materials; for a summary of inscriptional evidence, see Meyers, 'Archaeology', pp. 91-98.

Syro-Palestinian archaeology and the accompanying modes of collecting, recording, and publishing the data. From its inception, archaeology in the land of the Bible has focused on excavating sites with a biblical connection.[8] Nationalist and theologically conservative archaeologists often seek discoveries that might verify the Bible's historicity. But even for other archaeologists, the urge to correlate 'facts' from the ground with details in the text has been irresistible. Consequently, large urban sites have drawn the greatest attention even though most people were agrarians living in walled agricultural towns and small villages. Site selection itself has thus precluded the collection of data relevant to the lives of ordinary agrarian women.

Moreover, excavations at those large sites have focused on the monumental structures—palaces, fortifications, and temples or shrines—that are prominent in the Bible's narrative and poetic landscapes and are associated with male leaders: kings, generals, and priests. The domestic buildings in which most women (and men!) lived are usually of secondary interest; relatively few projects concentrate on household archaeology, which would be most likely to recover materials pertinent to the women's lives.

Associating archaeological discoveries with the Bible's overarching interest in the people Israel and their national story is also manifest in the digging strategies that serve diachronic interests. Excavation design is preoccupied with dating structures and related artifacts. Thus field work often favors digging deep trenches to determine the chronological sequence of a site's history rather than exposing entire dwelling units of a single period so that the artifacts and organization of domestic space, crucial for understanding women's lives, can be recovered. Again, household archaeology suffers. To be fair, although chronological concerns are still dominant, field projects since the 1970s have been influenced by the 'new archaeology' and are more comprehensive in collecting data.

Chronological concerns and possible biblical associations also impact the way data are recorded. Because pottery, which changes over time, is the key to dating strata in the absence of epigraphic materials, the find spots of potsherds are carefully noted so that the excavator can establish the sequence of pottery forms and thereby date the strata of a typical *tel* (mound). Dated destruction layers can then be linked, for example, to biblical passages about military events that supposedly affected that site. Because of this biblically driven preoccupation with ceramic typologies, other household objects used by women are sometimes treated less carefully, especially in many older archaeological publications. Final reports do not always indicate the find

---

8. See Carol Meyers, 'Recovering Objects Re-visioning Subjects: Archaeology and Feminist Biblical Study', in Athalya Brenner and Carole Fontaine (eds.), *A Feminist Companion to Reading the Bible: Approaches, Methods, and Strategies* (Sheffield: Sheffield Academic Press, 1997), pp. 270-84.

spots of household objects—perhaps because they were not recorded in the first place—nor the number of examples of each artifact type. They thus limit access to information about the spatial distribution and quantity of artifacts that is essential for studying gendered activities and the social relations and meanings embedded in them. The failure to provide a full record of household remains has deprived us of much crucial data.

These problems can be termed a failure to 'engender archaeology.' *Engender* means 'create' or 'incite,' but it has a new connotation in feminist hermeneutics: it denotes work in which gender is an analytical concept that 'creates' new ways of understanding humans and their communities.[9] Engendered research is part of a paradigm shift that has brought gender into mainstream scholarly discourse in the social sciences and humanities disciplines. This shift has had little impact on Syro-Palestinian archaeology.[10] Still, several projects have developed excavation strategies and publication designs amenable to gender concerns, and some of the work described below draws on their published data.[11]

The relative dearth of archaeological materials useful for recovering women's lives is, however, not always the fault of the excavators. Often these materials are missing because people abandoned their homes and took their tools with them; or the materials are not in their original use locations because later settlers cleared or jumbled the ruins if earlier buildings. Only when sites are destroyed before the inhabitants can remove their possessions and when destruction debris seals those artifacts in place so that rebuilding activities do not greatly disturb them, do the building and its artifacts contribute to understanding the gendered use of space by its ancient inhabitants. Because this situation does not always obtain, the possibilities for engendered archaeology at Israelite sites are often limited.[12]

---

9. See Margaret W. Conkey and Joan M. Gero, 'Tensions, Pluralities, and Engendering Archaeology: An Introduction to Women and Prehistory', in Joan M. Gero and Margaret W. Conkey (eds.), *Engendering Archaeology: Women and Prehistory* (Oxford: Blackwell, 1991), pp. 3-30.

10. Carol Meyers, 'Engendering Syro-Palestinian Archaeology: Reasons and Resources', *Near Eastern Archaeology* 66 (2003), pp. 185-97.

11. See, e.g., the work at Tell Halif: James Walker Hardin, *Households and the Use of Domestic Space at Iron II Tell Halif: An Archaeology of Destruction* (Reports of the Lahav Research Project: Excavations at Tell Halif, Israel, II; Winona Lake, IN: Eisenbrauns, 2010). Another example is the work at Beth Shean: Amihai Mazar, *Excavations at Tel Beth-Shean 1989–1996. I. From the Late Bronze AGE IIB to the Medieval Period* (Jerusalem: The Israel Exploration Society and The Institute of Archaeology/The Hebrew University of Jerusalem, 2006). See also Assaf Yasur-Landau, Jennie Ebeling, and Laura Maslow (eds.), *Household Archaeology in Ancient Israel and Beyond* (Leiden: Brill, 2011).

12. In this essay 'Israelite sites' refers to settlements that were within the likely boundaries of Israel and Judah in the Iron Age (ca. 1200–587 BCE).

Problem 2:
Complexities of Interpreting Archaeological Data

Archaeological data alone do not tell the whole story. Material culture provides information about structures and artifacts, not about the people who used them and the social units and dynamics they represent.[13] That is, they do not reveal directly what Israelite women did, what kind of social relationships were related to their activities, and what impact their activities had on their households and community. Well-excavated and properly published domestic structures and artifacts must be subjected to three interpretative processes in order to become useful for assessing women's lives. These processes draw upon a variety of sources and methodologies, making feminist interpretation of archaeological data a truly interdisciplinary task.

The first process is not a gender-specific one; it involves establishing the function of artifacts. Most archaeologists do this intuitively, unaware of the analogic process involved. Take, for example, the ubiquitous ceramic remains that are fundamental for dating structures and their contents, as mentioned above. Pottery vessels are characteristically designated by terms like 'cooking pot', 'storage jar', 'water jug', 'chalice', etc. But those designations are not inscribed on the vessels. Rather, they are based on *ethnographic* evidence—on analogies with the way similarly shaped pots are used in still-existing traditional cultures that produce their own pottery. This identification of an object and its use by ethnographic analogy is called *ethnoarchaeology*, the study of data from observable premodern societies in order to understand the function of ancient artifacts and structures.[14]

A word about ethnographic analogy is in order, for it figures in the other two interpretive processes. Although some scholars believe that contemporary traditional cultures differ too much from ancient ones for comparisons to be valid, most insist that ethnographic analogies are indispensable as long as certain precautions—such as seeking data from cultures in the same geographic area and at the same level of social complexity as the ancient one—are taken.[15] The extensive study of several sites in rural Iran has been particularly helpful in this regard,[16] as have smaller projects in Israel, Cyprus, Jordan, and Syria.

---

13. Penelope M. Allison, 'Introduction', *The Archaeology of Household Activities* (ed. Penelope M. Allison; London: Routledge, 1999), pp. 1-18 (2).

14. See Charles E. Carter, 'Ethnoarchaeology', in Eric M. Meyers (ed.), *Oxford Encyclopedia of Archaeology in the Near East* II (New York: Oxford University Press, 1997), pp. 280-84.

15. See ibid. and also Carol Kramer, *Ethnoarchaeology: Implications of Ethnography for Archaeology* (New York: Columbia University Press, 1979).

16. Patty Jo Watson, *Archaeological Ethnography in Western Iran* (Tucson: University of Arizona Press, 1979); Carol Kramer, *Village Ethnoarchaeology: Rural Iran in*

The second interpretive process is identifying the gender of those who used household artifacts. Artifacts are not 'gender noisy'; they lack not only labels denoting their function but also information about who used them. The division of labor by gender is nearly universal; but there is virtually no universal pattern to that division.[17] For example, one cannot be certain, a priori, that objects identified as weaving tools, are women's tools. Identifying women's activities and their setting thus requires attributing gender to artifacts. Iconographic depictions, information from other ancient Near Eastern cultures, and ethnographic analogies are useful in gender identification. Biblical references too are helpful; despite the Bible's biases, many texts contain reliable details about quotidian features of daily life. Once identified as tools or installations used mainly by women, their location in household space must be noted.

The third interpretive process, determining the personal and social correlates of women's household roles, is perhaps the most difficult. The dynamics of gendered activities can be suggested by *ethnology*, which uses comparative data from observable traditional cultures to identify general patterns and also to attribute meaning to social phenomena.[18] Although they cannot be fully verified, these paradigms are arguably closer to the social reality of antiquity than to our contemporary experience in an industrialized society.

Engendering Syro-Palestinian Archaeology: Ethnohistory

Clearly, engendering archaeological remains from Israelite sites depends on interdisciplinary research. The term *ethnohistory* is an appropriate designation for this enterprise, for it represents its interdisciplinary methodology in several ways.[19] First, the hallmark of ethnohistory is that it integrates and

---

Archaeological Perspective (New York: New York Academic Press, 1982). An excellent example of Syro-Palestinian ethnoarchaeology is John S. Holladay, Jr, 'House, Israelite', *ABD* III (New York: Doubleday, 1992), pp. 308-18.

17. The classic cross-cultural study of the range of female and male domination of basic economic tasks is George P. Murdock and Catherine Provost, 'Factors in the Division of Labor by Sex: A Cross-Cultural Analysis', *Ethnology* 12 (1973), pp. 203-25. However, the gendered division of labor is rarely absolute, and there is usually some crossover or sharing of tasks; see Sarah Milledge Nelson, *Gender in Archeology: Analyzing Power and Prestige* (Walnut Creek, CA: AltaMira Press, 2nd edn, 2004), pp. 64-87.

18. For a recent summary of theoretical advances and case studies, see Sarah Milledge Nelson (ed.), *Handbook of Gender in Archaeology* (Lanham, MD: AltaMira Press, 2006). Note that 'ethnology' is also called 'cultural anthropology' (in the USA) or 'social anthropology' (in the UK).

19. Two review articles provide information about ethnohistory: Robert M. Carmack, 'Ethnohistory: A Review of Its Development, Definitions, Methods, and Aims', *Annual*

analyzes data from a variety of sources. Second, because it insists on using every possible source, it provides more accurate and complete information about a group of people than would otherwise be possible. Third, it assumes that cultures of living peoples can provide insights into past cultures.[20]

Two other features of ethnohistory make it an especially apt designation for the study of Israelite women. First, it insists on an emic evaluative perspective and resists judging a traditional culture in relation to Western (American or European) notions or values.[21] That is, it avoids 'presentism', in which current values and ideas affect our interpretation of past events or conditions.[22] Second, ethnohistory developed specifically to study groups that are invisible or marginalized in traditional written sources and have been relegated to the sidelines of conventional inquiry. This resonates with the study of Israelite women because of their low visibility and often marginal role in the Hebrew Bible.

As an interdisciplinary enterprise with archaeological data as an essential component, ethnohistory is an appropriate methodological label for the task of investigating women's lives in biblical antiquity. However, because it requires proficiency in the methods of several disciplines, it has not been embraced by feminist biblical scholarship. As Ackerman notes, the difficulty in engaging all the methodologies necessary for ethnohistorical research has proved daunting. She also suggests that the current popularity of literary-critical approaches in feminist scholarship contributes to the lack of feminist ethnohistorical studies.[23] It is no wonder, then, that feminist ethnohistorical research focused on Israelite women has drawn relatively few researchers. Nevertheless, this interdisciplinary work has attracted some scholars and has produced excellent results. The section on 'The World of Women: Gender and Archaeology' was instituted at the American Schools of Oriental Research annual meeting in 2000 and

---

Review of Anthropology 1 (1972), pp. 227-46, and Shepard Krech III, 'The State of Ethnohistory', *Annual Review of Anthropology* 20 (1991), pp. 345-75. See also Kelly K. Chaves, 'Ethnohistory: From Inception to Postmodernism and Betyond', *Historian* 70 (2008), pp. 486-513. Note that some anthropologists use the term ethnohistory more narrowly to refer to anthropology that uses written sources of various kinds and that strives to interpret them emically.

20. See William S. Simmons, 'Culture Theory in Contemporary Ethnohistory', *Ethnohistory* 35 (1988), pp. 1-14 (10).

21. For a classic discussion of the emic (as opposed to etic) perspective, see Marvin Harris, *Cultural Materialism: The Struggle for a Science of Culture* (New York: Vintage, 1979), pp. 32-41.

22. See Carol Meyers, *Rediscovering Eve: Ancient Israelite Women in Context* (New York: Oxford University Press, 2013), pp. 117-24.

23. Susan Ackerman, 'Digging Up Deborah: Recent Hebrew Bible Scholarship on Gender and the Contribution of Archaeology', *Near Eastern Archaeology* 66 (2003), pp. 172-84.

generated some important papers.[24] They inform the discussion below of women and the household economy.

Ethnohistorical recovery of women's lives means examining the agrarian household life of the Israelites. The term *household* is used here in the comprehensive way advocated by anthropologists.[25] In a traditional agrarian society it has three main components: material culture including the dwelling itself and associated land holdings, livestock, installations, and tools; people, both family members and sometimes servants or unrelated persons; and the activities that sustain existence. As a task-oriented unit, an Israelite household was the primary economic, social, and religious unit of society. It was probably roughly equivalent to the biblical 'father's house/household' (*bêt 'āb*) and also 'mother's house/household' (*bêt 'ēm*), which appears in a few passages[26]; and its dwelling is represented archaeologically by the architectural form known as the 'pillared house'.[27]

Women and the Household Economy
As in nearly all traditional agrarian societies, Israelite women performed most of the household's maintenance activities, a term referring to practices providing for the welfare of the household.[28] Several of the major maintenance activities, especially the transformation of crops and animals into food and fabrics, leave traces in the archaeological record. As noted above, a feminist ethnohistorical hermeneutic begins by identifying artifacts of maintenance activities, confirming that women used them, and locating the household space where they were used.

Locating the artifacts means taking into account the basic floor plan of Israelite dwellings. The ground floor usually has two longitudinal rooms

---

24. Published in Beth Alpert Nakhai (ed.), *The World of Women in the Ancient and Classical Near East* (Newcastle upon Tyne: Cambridge Scholars Publishing, 2008).

25. See, e.g., Richard R. Wilk and William L. Rathje, 'Household Archaeology', *American Behavioral Scientist* 25 (1982), pp. 617-39 (618).

26. See Carol Meyers, '"To Her Mother's House": Considering a Counterpart to the Israelite *Bêt 'āb*', in David Jobling, Peggy L. Day and Gerald T. Sheppard (eds.), *The Bible and the Politics of Exegesis: Essays in Honor of Norman K. Gottwald on His Sixty-Fifth Birthday* (Cleveland: Pilgrim, 1991), pp. 39-51, 304-307.

27. The scholarship on this house type, also called 'four-room house', is summarized in Holladay, 'House'. See also Carol Meyers, 'Domestic Architecture, Ancient Israel', in *Oxford Bibliographies Online: Biblical Studies*, available at http://www.oxfordbibliographies.com/view/document/obo-9780195393361/obo-9780195393361-0096.xml (accessed January 27, 2015).

28. Margarita Sanchez Romero, 'Women, Maintenance Activities, and Space', in Georgina Muskett, Aikaterini Kolisida, and Mercourios Georgiadis (eds.), *Symposium on Mediterranean Archaeology 2001* (BAR International Series, 1040; Oxford: Archaeopress, 2002), pp. 178-82 (178).

(one probably for stabling animals) flanking a central rectangular space (likely an interior courtyard) and a transverse room across the back for storage and perhaps for some food consumption. A row of pillars typically divides the central area from one or both of the side longitudinal spaces, hence the name 'pillared' dwelling; and the main entrance was typically through the courtyard area.[29] This arrangement of space served the needs of self-sufficient farm families, and important maintenance activities— including bread making,[30] beer brewing,[31] and textile production[32]—were carried out in or near the dwelling.

Cereal crops were the mainstay of the Israelite diet, supplying over 70 percent of a person's daily caloric intake, and transforming raw grains into edible forms required a number of steps, one of which was grinding grains to produce flour. The most common artifacts of bread production are thus grinding stones. Large slabs (or querns) and smaller handstones correspond to sets of lower and upper grinding stones probably represented by the Hebrew dual *rēḥāyim*. Both biblical texts (e.g., Judg. 9.53; Isa. 47.2) and ethnographic materials indicate that women (not men) carried out this time-consuming (about two to three hours per day) and laborious process. When the number of these tools in a single dwelling and their original usage locations can be determined, an interesting pattern emerges: Israelite households often have multiple sets of grinding stones, indicating that several women, probably from neighboring households, processed grain at the same time. A New Testament passage about two women grinding together (Mt. 24.41) surely reflects a practice going back many millennia. Called *simple task simultaneity*, this strategy organizes labor especially when the

---

29. This is a general description. Archaeologists disagree on the use of these spaces and on the size of the family inhabiting a dwelling. See Rainer Albertz, 'Methodological Reflections', in Rainer Albertz and Rüdiger Schmitt, *Family and Household Religion in the Levant* (Winona Lake, IN: Eisenbrauns, 2012), pp. 21-56 (26-45).

30. Information below about grinding is from Carol Meyers, 'Having Their Space and Eating There Too: Bread Production and Female Power in Ancient Israelite Households', *Nashim* 5 (2002), pp. 14-44; about baking (ovens) from Aubrey Baadsgaard, 'A Taste of Women's Sociality: Cooking as Cooperative Labor in Iron Age Syria-Palestine', in Nakhai (ed.), *World of Women*, pp. 13-44.

31. See Jennie R. Ebeling and Michael M. Homan, 'Baking and Brewing in the Israelite Household: A Study of Women's Cooking Technology', in Beth Alpert Nakhai (ed.), *World of Women*, pp. 45-62.

32. See Deborah Cassuto, 'Bringing Home the Artifacts: A Social Interpretation of Loom Weights in Context', in Beth Alpert Nakhai (ed.), *World of Women*, pp. 63-78; Carol Meyers, 'Material Remains and Social Relations: Women's Culture in Agrarian Households of the Iron Age', in William G. Dever and Seymour Gitin (eds.), *Symbiosis, Symbolism, and the Power of the Past: Canaan, Ancient Israel, and Their Neighbors from the Late Bronze Age through Roman Palestina* (Winona Lake, IN: Eisenbrauns, 2003), pp. 425-44 (432-34).

work is tedious.³³ The grinding tools tend to be found in one of the longitudinal spaces of the dwelling and not in the more remote transverse room at the back.

Baking bread was also a woman's task according to biblical (e.g., Gen. 27.17; 1 Sam. 8.13) and ethnographic evidence. Its archaeological correlates are 'ovens': the remains of small circular, beehive-shaped ovens are sometimes found in interior rooms but were probably used only in inclement weather. Larger ovens are often located near the entrances to pillared houses and accessible to several dwellings, in outdoor spaces between dwellings, or in other open areas. The size of these examples and their location in common space suggest that women from several households shared a single oven. A talmudic text (P.T. Pesaḥim 3, 30b) referring to three women preparing dough together and using only one oven indicates that this ecologically sound practice in areas lacking abundant fuel continued into the post-biblical period. Indeed, communal ovens have long been the norm in small Mediterranean villages, where as many as ten women might use one oven.³⁴ Women gathering at their shared oven gave baking a social dimension.

Beer production in the ancient world was quite different from today's methods, for it depended on the use of baked malt cakes. Probably because it was linked to baking, household beer production was primarily a woman's task. Moreover, the archaeological correlates of beer production—small grinding tools, so-called 'beer jugs' (side-spouted sieve jugs for filtering beer), and ceramic fermentation stoppers—are typically found near the artifacts of bread production in the longitudinal rooms of the pillared dwellings.

The archaeological correlates of textile production, also a woman's activity (see, e.g., Exod. 35.25-26; Judg. 16.13-14; 2 Kgs 23.7; 1 Sam. 2.19; Prov. 31.13, 19, 22, 24) include stone spindle whorls for spinning fibers into yarn or thread, bone weaving shuttles, bone or ivory needles for sewing garments or other items, and ceramic or stone weights to hold warp threads taut on the vertical looms used in the Iron Age. This loom type a priori signifies the work of several women, for setting the threads in the looms is done most effectively by more than one woman. Also, concentrations of loom weights representing two or three looms in one dwelling, often found near food-production tools, have been found at several sites and attest to women weaving together.

---

33. Wilk and Rathje, 'Household Archaeology', p. 622.

34. Alison McQuitty, 'Ovens in Town and Country', *Berytus Archaeological Studies* 41 (1993–1994), pp. 53-76 (70). In Lev. 26.26, ten women share an oven, albeit in a time of scarcity.

The archaeological correlates of several different maintenance tasks are consistently found in central areas of Israelite dwellings and are often near each other. The main rooms of the dwelling were multi-functional, with women's economic activities dominating the use of space and with women often working together.

Women and Household Religion

Because large sections of the Pentateuch present the activities of male priests at a central shrine, the Bible gives the impression that Israelite religious life centered on the male-dominated national sacrificial cult. But that was hardly the only form of Israelite religious activity. People everywhere experience religious life in their own households and communities, and it is inconceivable that those unable to travel to a major shrine had no religious life.

A recent exhaustive analysis of household religious activities shows that ritual objects are consistently found in household contexts at dozens of Iron Age sites.[35] These objects include explicitly religious items (e.g., incense altars and terracotta figurines) and also ordinary objects (e.g., ceramic food and drink vessels), which are considered ritual objects when they are found in assemblages containing one or more explicitly religious items.[36] Judging from the nature of the vessels in these groups, ritual activities usually involved food and drink offerings. For example, most ritual assemblages dating to the tenth–sixth centuries BCE (Iron IIA–C) included ceramic vessels used for preparing and consuming food and drink; libations and grain or bread offerings were arguably the main ritual practices.[37] Indeed, the household foodways represented in domestic offerings were probably the model for the sacrificial regimes of temples and shrines, not vice versa.[38]

Just as important as the presence of ritual objects in household assemblages is their location in areas used for food preparation and consumption. The objects themselves don't specify who set aside pieces of bread for ancestors or a deity in the hope of securing family well-being.[39] How-

---

35. Rüdiger Schmitt, 'Elements of Domestic Cult in Ancient Israel', in Rainer Albertz and Rüdiger Schmitt, *Family and Household Religion in the Levant* (Winona Lake, IN: Eisenbrauns, 2012), pp. 57-219 and 496-504, Tables 3.6-3.9.

36. See Schmitt, 'Elements of Domestic Cult', pp. 60-75, for descriptions of explicitly religious artifacts and non-cultic ones used in ritual contexts.

37. Schmitt, 'Elements of Domestic Cult', pp. 174-75.

38. Stanley Stowers, 'Theorizing Household Religion', in John Bodel and Saul M. Olyan (eds.), *Household and Family Religion in Antiquity* (Malden, MA: Blackwell, 2008), pp. 5-19 (12). Mary Douglas famously declared that 'a very strong analogy between table and altar stares us in the face'; see Mary Douglas, 'Deciphering a Meal', *Daedalus* 101 (Winter 1972), pp. 61-81 (71).

39. Offerings to the dead are implied by the prohibition in Deut. 26.14; see also

ever, the preparation of bread was a female-gendered activity, as was the preparation of most other foodstuffs.[40] This strong association of ritual acts with women's maintenance activities means that women as well as men were actors in household religious activities.

The same would be true for the weekly, monthly, and annual festivals in which households participated, whether in their own communities or at regional or even national shrines, as well as life-cycle celebrations.[41] These festivals and celebrations were sacrificial events, as biblical texts attest, that were also were marked by feasting. Note that Deuteronomy commands everyone to bring offerings and also 'to eat there' at the shrine (Deut. 12.7). And excavations of local and village shrines and also regional and supra-regional sanctuaries provide evidence of food and drink offerings, with animal sacrifice indicated at the larger cult structures.[42] Across cultures, food is a prominent feature of both regular festivals and occasional festivities. Again, as the household members responsible for most food preparation, women had indispensable roles in these religious events.

Religious rituals were also integrated into basic aspects of women's everyday food preparation activities according to both biblical and ethnography evidence. Removing a piece of bread dough as a gift or donation before bread is baked (Num. 15.17-21) so that the household will be blessed (Ezek. 44.30b) resonates with practices of Middle Eastern women striving to protect flour from evil spirits that might cause it to spoil; bread-baking was a sacred activity, and performing it improperly was sacrilegious.[43] Also, women collected, dried, and pulverized herbs in the mortars and pestles found in household space. Their familiarity with herbs used to flavor food meant that women would know how to use them as *materia medica* to treat a sick or injured member of the household; and applying these substances was likely accompanied by chants or incantations, for evil spirits or divine

---

Rainer Albertz, 'Family Religion in Ancient Israel and Its Surroundings', in John Bodel and Saul M. Olyan (eds.), *Household and Family Religion in Antiquity* (Malden, MA: Blackwell, 2008), pp. 89-112 (98-99).

40. For women's role in producing other components of the daily diet, see Meyers, *Rediscovering Eve*, p. 132.

41. Carol Meyers, 'Feast Days and Food Ways: Religious Dimensions of Household Life', in Rainer Albertz, Beth Alpert Nakhai, Saul M. Olyan, and Rüdiger Schmitt (eds.), *Family and Household Religion: Toward a Synthesis of Old Testament Studies, Archaeology, Epigraphy, and Cultural Studies* (Winona Lake, IN: Eisenbrauns, 2014), pp. 225-50 (229-35).

42. Rüdiger Schmitt, 'A Typology of Iron Age Cult Places', in Rainer Albertz, Beth Alpert Nakhai, Saul M. Olyan and Rüdiger Schmitt (eds.), *Family and Household Religion: Toward a Synthesis of Old Testament Studies, Archaeology, Epigraphy, and Cultural Studies* (Winona Lake, IN: Eisenbrauns, 2014), pp. 265-86 (270-77).

43. See Meyers, *Rediscovering Eve*, p. 166.

acts were thought to cause maladies. In their role as household healers, women performed another religious function.

In addition to these food-related events and practices, women's religiosity was manifest in their efforts to achieve reproductive success. Procreation was fraught with difficulty and danger. Infertility was a recurring problem, as seen in the 'barren woman' narratives (about Sarah, Rachel, Hannah, and Samson's mother) and other texts (e.g., Isa. 54.1; Ps. 113.9). Miscarriages and death in childbirth were all too common (Gen. 35.1-19; 1 Sam. 4.19-20), and many newborns did not survive (e.g., 2 Sam. 12.15-18). Women in ancient Israel, as in traditional societies everywhere, used a variety of rituals and apotropaic practices as they sought to conceive, sustain pregnancy, deliver safely, and have healthy offspring. Some of those practices have archaeological correlates—amulets, lamps, terracotta figurines, even knives—all meant to protect women and their newborns.[44]

Personal and Social Correlates of Women's Roles

The identification of women's economic and religious activities does not directly reveal their significance for the women and also their communities. Further ethnohistorical inquiry, by consulting ethnological evidence, is necessary.

Women's economic tasks—providing food and clothing for their households—were carried out in the main activity areas of Israelite dwellings. Women were not sequestered nor cut off from the comings and goings of other household members, an indication that they were part of the suprahousehold life of their communities.[45] Moreover, the discovery of multiple sets of household equipment in individual dwellings meant that women worked together, often for hours at a time. Or they gathered at communal ovens. In traditional societies these joint maintenance activities are 'an active component of social relations.'[46] The regular interaction of women

---

44. The archaeological, textual, and ethnographic evidence for the reproductive rituals of Israelite women is collected in Carol Meyers, *Households and Holiness: The Religious Culture of Israelite Women* (Facet Books; Minneapolis: Fortress Press, 2005). Judean Pillar Figurines are among the artifacts discussed in *Households and Holiness*, but their function in reproductive rituals has since been contested. It now seems that they had more general apotropaic and healing functions and were not gender-specific objects. See Erin Darby, *Interpreting Judean Pillar Figurines: Gender and Empire in Judean apotropaic Ritual* (Forschumgen zum Alten Testament 2, Reihe 69; Tübingen: Mohr Siebeck, 2014).

45. See Meyers, *Rediscovering Eve*, pp. 143-46.

46. Julia Ann Hendon, 'Archaeological Approaches to the Organization of Domestic Labor: Household Practice and Domestic Relations', *Annual Review of Anthropology* 25 (1996), pp. 45-61 (56).

for extended periods created informal social networks that helped transform onerous and tedious processes into enjoyable social experiences. These informal networks also served vital community functions; they constituted mutual aid and support systems when inevitable problems arose. If a nearby household suffered food shortages or if it had labor needs because of the illness or death of a household member, women knew about it and could deploy labor or resources to help others weather the crisis. They thus contributed to the viability of their communities.[47] They helped form what Gottwald calls a 'protective association of families', providing social and economic aid to component households.[48] Male lineages were not the only force binding households together. Women's networks were avenues of communication that functioned politically as well as socially and economically: they regulated many interactions among households and contributed knowledge that impacted local decision-making.[49]

Women's control of the technologies of food and textile production also entailed a little recognized but nonetheless significant amount of social power. The ability to make important household decisions and to function as household managers accrues to women—especially the senior woman in a compound family—in premodern agrarian societies when they control the production of essential commodities that cannot be obtained elsewhere.[50] This informal and less visible form of power is just as important for the dynamics of daily life as are the visible and formal male-dominated power structures.[51] Power should not be viewed as a fixed commodity held by certain people; rather, it is the product of social relations.[52]

---

47. See Carol Meyers, '"Women of the Neighborhood" (Ruth 4:17): Informal Female Networks in Ancient Israel', in Athalya Brenner (ed.), *Ruth and Esther* (FCB, 3, Second Series; Sheffield: Sheffield Academic Press, 1999), pp. 110-27.

48. Norman K. Gottwald, *The Tribes of Yahweh: A Sociology of the Religion of Liberated Israel, 1250–1050 BCE* (Maryknoll, NY: Orbis Books, 1979), pp. 257-67. Military protection may also have been a function of these household groupings, at least in the premonarchic period.

49. See Mary Elaine Hegland, 'Political Roles of Aliabad Women: The Public-Private Dichotomy Transcended', in Nikki R. Keddie and Beth Baron (eds.), *Women in Middle Eastern History: Shifting Boundaries in Sex and Gender* (New Haven: Yale University Press, 1991), pp. 215-30. Hegland notes (p. 223) that 'where social relations and political alliances are one and the same, women's social activities are also political activities'.

50. See Carole M. Counihan, 'Introduction—Food and Gender: Identity and Power', in Carole M. Counihan and Stephen L. Kaplan (eds.), *Food and Gender: Identity and Power* (Amsterdam: Harwood Academic Publishers, 1998), pp. 1-10 (2; 4).

51. See the studies in Tracy L. Sweely (ed.), *Manifesting Power: Gender and the Interpretation of Power in Archaeology* (London: Routledge, 1999).

52. Julia A. Hendon, 'Living and Working at Home: The Social Archaeology of Household Production', in Lynn Meskell and Robert W. Preucel (eds.), *A Companion to Social Archaeology* (Malden, MA: Blackwell, 2004), pp. 272-96 (278).

As for the religious culture of Israelite households—it was long thought to be the domain of the male head of household. Ethnohistorical analysis, however, provides evidence to the contrary. Women's maintenance activities included religious aspects of daily meals, regular and occasional feasting, and health care; and women's childbearing role had ritual dimensions.

Women's religious activities served both individual and group interests. As participants in and facilitators of events that provided a sense of household continuity and fostered community identity and cohesion, women would have experienced the pleasure of these celebratory interludes in the often bleak tedium of daily life. Moreover, preparing special foods—a hallmark of festivals—gave women a chance to serve as ritual experts for their families and communities. Food preparation for both daily offerings and festal events, rather than being considered drudgery, can be conceptualized as ritualized behavior imbued with religious meaning for its practitioners.[53] Providing food for sacral contexts and also safeguarding food supplies were for women the 'giving of self, revealing their knowledge and control over food-producing technology and procedures and their ability to nourish important household-based and community-wide relationships'.[54] Women's religious lives were thus enriched in ways not often recognized.

Ritual practices related to health care entailed the satisfaction of helping ill or injured family members. This kind of ritual behavior assumed the function that modern medicine does today, as did the reproductive rituals that helped women negotiate their gendered identities and expectations.[55] Practices surrounding procreation had the psychological benefit of giving women some relief from the anxiety surely caused by the difficulties of reproduction. Whether efficacious or not, these rituals were believed essential for the creation of new life, which in turn was critical for household and, by extension, community life. Children were not simply the joy of their parents. In an ancient agricultural society, they were important for essential utilitarian reasons: household survival depended upon the labor of children; the transmission of a household's 'inheritance' (*naḥalah*) to the next generation required heirs; and the care of the elderly was the duty of offspring. Women surely derived personal satisfaction in bearing children and thus helping to sustain their household and their kin group, for having viable offspring was important for the larger social units linked by kinship. Women

---

53. See Susan Starr Sered, 'Food and Holiness: Cooking as a Sacred Act among Middle Eastern Jewish Women', *Anthropological Quarterly* 61 (1988), pp. 129-39.

54. Baadsgaard, 'A Taste of Women's Sociality', p. 43.

55. See Diane Bolger, *Gender in Ancient Cyprus: Narratives of Social Change on a Mediterranean Island* (Gender and Archaeology Series; Walnut Creek, CA: AltaMira, 2003).

and men were 'deeply embedded' in their social context and 'enmeshed in the obligations of kinship'.[56]

An important dimension of both economic and religious activities is that they provided opportunities for women to earn status in their communities. Both kinds of activities involved technologies and techniques that women learned from other women—from older relatives and neighbors who were expert in the requisite skills. Technology is a set of social as well as material processes.[57] The informal mentoring involved in the transmission of skills typically creates an informal hierarchy in women's relationships, and the experts acquire prestige because of their proficiency. Similarly, women in informal networks who are adept in organizing aid for others acquire prominence.

Conclusion

Engendering certain discoveries at Israelite sites is a complex process better termed ethnohistory than archaeology. This multidisciplinary approach allows us to foreground features of women's lives that would otherwise go unnoticed. Although it is a recent and little known development, its significance is already clear. A feminist ethnohistorical approach, which means interrogating archaeologically derived data for information about women's lives, shows women to have been significant actors in their households and communities, with senior women functioning as household managers with considerable agency in organizing household life.

Ethnohistorical analysis thus problematizes the biblically-based supposition of female subservience. By using all available resources, it indicates that the idea of male power pervading all aspects of Israelite life cannot be sustained. The notion of male dominance in ancient Israel is based on biblical texts, especially but not only legal ones, and applies to elites and to larger sociopolitical structures, the ones most visible in the Hebrew Bible. There is indeed a disjunction between women in biblical literature and women in Israelite life.[58] There was hardly gender equality, but gender inequality is not the same as absolute male dominance; male dominance in one area of

---

56. Robert A. Di Vito, 'Old Testament Anthropology and the Construction of Personal Identity', *CBQ* 61 (1999), pp. 221, 223. Ancient Israel was 'an aggregate of groups rather than a collection of individuals'; so John W. Rogerson, 'Anthropology of the Old Testament', in Ronald E. Clements (ed.), *The World of Ancient Israel: Sociological, Anthropological and Political Perspectives* (New York: Cambridge University Press, 1989), pp. 17-38 (5).

57. Hendon, 'Living and Working', p. 277.

58. See Carol Meyers, 'Double Vision: Women in Biblical Texts and in Archaeological Contexts', *Hebrew Bible and Ancient Israel* 5.2 (2016), pp. 112-31.

life does not mean male dominance in all areas. Ethnoarchaeological analysis indicates women's agency in significant arenas of everyday life.[59]

Challenging the notion of women's subordination means confronting the patriarchy model that has been applied to ancient Israel since the nineteenth century, when the concept of patriarchy emerged in anthropological research based on rediscovered texts from the classical world and was subsequently applied to Israelite society by biblical scholars.[60] The patriarchy paradigm continues to appear in biblical scholarship, although classicists, anthropologists, and third-wave feminists have critiqued its legitimacy and value.[61] A far more complex model is needed to accommodate the mutable dynamics of daily life.[62]

Archaeology within an ethnohistorical hermeneutic is in its infancy. As the potential for engendering Syro-Palestinian archaeology becomes better known and as ethnohistorical inquiries become more common, our knowledge about Israelite women will surely increase. This in turn will expand our understanding of the interface between biblical text and lived reality. Looking beyond the Bible will enable us to see the Bible more clearly.

---

59. Several biblical texts provide similar evidence; women make household decisions in the narratives about Abigail (1 Samuel 22) and the Shunammite (2 Kgs 4.8-37; 8.1-6) and the Proverbs passage (31.10-31) about the 'strong woman' ('ēšet–ḥayil, NRSV 'capable wife').

60. For a summary of these developments, see Carol L. Meyers, 'Was Ancient Israel a Patriarchal Society?', *JBL* 13 (2014), pp. 8-27 (9-12).

61. Meyers, 'Was Ancient Israel a Patriarchal Society?', pp. 12-18, 24-26.

62. 'Heterarchy' may be a better heuristic model; see Carol Meyers, 'Heterarchy or Hierarchy? Archaeology and the Theorizing of Israelite Society', in Seymour Gitin, J.P. Dessel, and J. Edward Wright (eds.), *Confronting the Past: Archaeological and Historical Essays on Ancient Israel in Honor of William G. Dever* (Winona Lake, IN: Eisenbrauns, 2006), pp. 245-54 (249-51).

5

ADVANTAGES AND CHALLENGES: COMPARATIVE HISTORICAL CRITICISM AND FEMINIST BIBLICAL STUDIES

Rebecca Hancock

Feminist biblical scholars have both engaged in the methods, and simultaneously challenged the assumptions of historical critical scholarship. On the one hand, feminist scholars have contested claims to objectivity that characterized traditional historical critical work. In addition, feminists have objected to the way in which early historical critics focused particularly on males, as well as public institutions, which often served to exclude women and others who were not represented in official religious, political or social roles.[1]

At the same time, historical criticism, and in particular the comparative method, has offered significant opportunity for feminist scholars, and provided a lens through which to challenge uses of the biblical text that serve to subordinate women. As Phyllis Bird notes: 'Feminist critique joins historical-critical analysis in insisting that texts that carry the sacred message are human, historically and culturally conditioned vehicles. Feminist analysis of patriarchy is essentially a historical-critical understanding. It needs to be sharped as a hermeneutical tool, not blunted or discarded.'[2] In addition, attention to the broader cultural context of the Bible provides

---

1. For a discussion of the relationship between historical criticism and feminist/gender-critical scholarship, see Davina C. Lopez and Todd Penner, 'Historical-Critical Approaches', in Julia M. O'Brien (ed.), *The Oxford Encyclopedia of the Bible and Gender Studies* (Oxford: Oxford University Press, 2014), pp. 327-36 (327-28). Their comments at the beginning of the article describe the complicated relationship the two. They state: 'Modern feminist and gender-critical interpretation is intricately bound up with various approaches to biblical interpretation falling under an umbrella called "historical criticism". Often considered the "traditional" paradigm over against which the "innovation" of feminist and/or gender-critical studies of biblical literature are positioned, a more nuanced view reveals an interdependence of "tradition" and "innovation", or at least adaptations of tradition toward innovative ends.'

2. Phyllis Bird, 'What Makes a Feminist Reading Feminist? A Qualified Answer', in Susanne Scholz (ed.), *Biblical Studies Alternatively: An Introductory Reader* (Upper Saddle River, NJ: Prentice Hall, 2003), pp. 67-72 (70 n. 7).

resources for examining women's experiences, even when they were underrepresented in the biblical text itself.

In what follows, I will examine the origins of a comparative method in biblical scholarship, as well as the specific advantages that a feminist hermeneutic contributes to this enterprise. It is the argument of this essay that when scholars employ a feminist hermeneutic to comparative historical work, it serves as an important corrective against generalizations about women's lives in ancient Israel. The comparative method facilitates a sophisticated historical understanding about women and nuanced perspectives about women's status in correlation to Israelite and ancient Near Eastern political and social realities. The historical reconstructions based on this method teach that Israelite women's experiences were varied and conditioned by specific social and political realities. Women in ancient Israel were never merely victims, but even when their status and authority was limited by patriarchal structures, they always enjoyed some level of agency. In addition, feminist comparative historical criticism demonstrates the problematic ways that gendered language constructs and reinforces power dynamics within a culture.

Comparative Historical Criticism in Biblical Studies

Throughout the nineteenth century, interest in comparative materials from the ancient Near East was influenced significantly by a desire to prove the historicity of the biblical text, and the stories within it.[3] Illustrative of this approach is William Harris Rule's anthology, *Oriental Records: Monumental Confirmatory of the Old Testament Scriptures*, whose title underscores the goal of the work.[4] Although interest in parallels to the biblical materials predated the nineteenth century,[5] it was at that time that a host of new

---

3. A number of scholars offer perspectives on the relationship between the field of biblical studies and study of the ancient Near East during the nineteenth century, such as Steven W. Holloway, 'Introduction: Orientalism, Assyriology and the Bible', in Steven W. Holloway (ed.), *Orientalism, Assyriology and the Bible* (Hebrew Bible Monographs, 10; Sheffield: Sheffield Phoenix Press, 2007), pp. 1-41; P.R.S. Moorey, *A Century of Biblical Archaeology* (Louisville, KY: Westminster/John Knox Press, 1992); Mark Chavalas, 'Assyriology and Biblical Studies: A Century of Tension', in Mark W. Chavalas and K. Lawson Younger, Jr. (eds.), *Mesopotamia and the Bible: Comparative Explorations* (Grand Rapids: Baker Academic, 2002), pp. 21-67.

4. See K. Lawson Younger, Jr, 'The Production of Ancient Near Eastern Text Anthologies from the Earliest to the Latest', in Steven W. Holloway (ed.), *Orientalism, Assyriology and the Bible* (Hebrew Bible Monographs, 10; Sheffield: Sheffield Phoenix Press, 2006), pp. 199-219 (207).

5. William W. Hallo, 'Ancient Near Eastern Texts and Their Relevance for Biblical Exegesis', in William W. Hallo (ed.), *The Context of Scripture: Canonical Compositions from the Biblical World* (Leiden: Brill, 2003), pp. xxiii-xxviii (xxiii).

excavations, often fueled by imperialist aims, contributed significantly to archaeological discoveries at that time. New findings, along with the decipherment of hieroglyphic script and Akkadian, created not only scholarly enthusiasm but also new materials for comparative historical work. The possibility of new sources proving the historicity of the Bible and elucidating little-understood biblical figures[6] led to the development of comparative historical work, although some scholars were also concerned that such comparisons might undermine biblical authority.[7]

In the early twentieth century, the reliance on ancient Near Eastern materials to help verify the biblical text was challenged by Friedrich Delitzsch. In fact, his Babel-Bibel lectures in 1902 and 1903 inverted the dominant trend. Many earlier scholars had viewed Assyriology as a discipline that worked primarily in the service of biblical studies. Delitzsch instead suggested that Babylonian materials took precedence over the Bible; to him, they were not only the source for the Bible but superior to it.[8] For instance, Delitzsch argued that Abrahamic monotheism was rooted in Babylonian religious thought.[9] His lectures had played a significant role in the emerging and later widely known notion of 'Pan-Babylonianism', held by several Assyriologists—including Hugo Winckler and Peter Jensen[10]—at the time; it recognized that Babylonian religion influenced all religious traditions. Yet Delitzsch, as well as other scholars associated with Pan-Babylonianism, also emphasized the non-Semitic origins of the biblical materials, in fact reinforcing underlying anti-Jewish assumptions in their approach.[11] Delitzsch's view that biblical materials were derivative created controversy. Ultimately, the ideas of Delitzsch and other Pan-Babylonians did not convince most biblical scholars and Assyriologists although their research did take into account the study of the relationship between biblical and other ancient Near Eastern texts and artifacts.[12]

While the comparative method was at times met with skepticism, new twentieth-century discoveries allowed for numerous additional scholarly

---

6. An example is Pul in 2 Kgs 15.19-20. For a discussion about the use of comparative materials to identify Pul, see Steven W. Holloway, 'The Quest for Sargon, Pul, and Tiglath-Pileser in the 19th Century', in Mark W. Chavalas and K. Lawson Younger (eds.), *Mesopotamia and the Bible: Comparative Explorations* (Grand Rapids: Baker Academic, 2002), pp. 68-87.

7. Chavalas, 'Assyriology and Biblical Studies', pp. 24-45.

8. Holloway, 'Introduction', p. 19.

9. Holloway, 'Introduction', p. 19.

10. Holloway 'Introduction', p. 19, especially n. 45.

11. Holloway, 'Introduction', p. 19. For further discussion of the Delitzsch and the Bibel-Babel controversy, see Chavalas, 'Assyriology and Biblical Studies', pp. 32-35.

12. Chavalas, 'Assyriology and Biblical Studies', pp. 34-35.

works to be produced on the basis of the comparative approach.[13] Still, in 1962, Samuel Sandmel, arguing for continued use of comparative materials, cautioned against 'extravagance' and against 'parallelomania'. He recognized the existence of parallels, and encouraged the use of comparative materials as important to the task of biblical interpretation, but he urged scholars to be judicious. He warned against 'exaggerations about the parallels and about source and derivation'.[14]

During the mid-1970s and 1980s, concern about the need for rigor in the use of the comparative method grew. Younger describes the tension succinctly in this comment:

> Within biblical studies there was a growing opposition that felt that many of the comparative studies of the period were flawed because: (1) they overstated the evidence, (2) they were frequently agenda-driven (trying to 'prove the Bible'), and (3) they simply lacked methodological controls'.[15]

In other words, during the early decades the need to define the comparative historical method became obvious. This development was not unique to the comparative study of the Bible but it mirrored broader trends in scholarship, 'moving away from author-oriented readings toward, at first, text-oriented readings, and then toward reader-oriented reading'.[16] As a consequence, many scholars began addressing the question of methodology in comparative historical criticism.

For instance, in 1978, Talmon explained how comparative materials should be applied to the biblical text. He reminded scholars that comparative biblical studies does not develop on its own, but is impacted by other fields of research.[17] In his view, biblical scholarship was methodologically less rigorous than research in other fields. In biblical studies scholars often identified specific parallels without articulating the broader framework within which they made the comparison. Moreover, he observed a lacking clarity about whether similarities or differences should be highlighted. In other words, he did not criticize the use of comparative materials but the lack of rigorous principles guiding the comparative analysis with

---

13. For a discussion of the various sources discovered in the twentieth century, see Chavalas, 'Assyriology and Biblical Studies', pp. 35-42; K. Lawson Younger, Jr, 'The "Contextual Method": Some West Semitic Reflections', in William W. Hallo (ed.), *The Context of Scripture: Archival Documents from the Biblical World* (Leiden: Brill, 2003), pp. xxxv-xlii.

14. Sandmel, 'Parallelomania', *JBL* 81 (1962), pp. 1-13 (1).

15. Sandmel, 'Parallelomania', p. 201.

16. Sandmel, 'Parallelomania', p. 202.

17. Shemaryahu Talmon, 'The "Comparative Method" in Biblical Interpretation: Principles and Problems', in John A. Emerton (ed.), *Congress Volume: Göttingen 1977* (VTSup, 29; Leiden: E.J. Brill, 1978), pp. 320-56 (321).

ancient Near Eastern sources. Thus, he also proposed a set of guidelines for doing comparative work,[18] which helped to situate comparative work and to evaluate biblical texts within their ancient Near Eastern contexts. According to Talmon, for instance, comparative materials from ancient Near Eastern cultures should not take precedence over inner-biblical parallels, and thus texts should be viewed holistically. Scholars should also attend to both geographic and temporal distances between the compared texts and consider their social functions.[19]

William Hallo made another proposal that recognized the possible problems when scholars interpret ancient Near Eastern materials. Although he acknowledged the potential limitations, Hallo upholds the use of the comparative approach. In his preface to Volume 1 of the *Context of Scripture*, he explains:

> [T]he combination of an intertextual and a contextual approach to biblical literature holds out the promise that this millennial corpus will continue to yield new meanings on all levels: the meaning that it holds for ourselves in our contemporary context, the meanings it has held for readers, worshippers, artists and others in the two millennia and more since the close of the canon; the meaning that it held for its own authors and the audiences of their times; and finally the meanings that it held when it was part of an earlier literary corpus.[20]

Hallo describes two dimensions that ought to be considered when doing comparative work. One dimension is a 'horizontal dimension—the geographical, historical, religious, political and literary setting'; it provides 'the "context" of a given text'. The other dimension is 'on a vertical axis between the earlier texts that helped inspire it and the later texts that reacted to it'.[21] Attention to both the vertical and horizontal axis, then, indicates when materials are in parallel and can be compared productively.

In short, since its early nineteenth-century emergence, the comparative approach in biblical studies has changed significantly. Most importantly, it is no longer regarded as a vehicle to confirm biblical accounts. Many scholars accept the importance of this method, especially when appropriate

---

18. See Talmon, 'The "Comparative Method" in Biblical Interpretation'. Using Talmon's principles in his comparative work, Richard Averbeck summarizes Talmon's four principles with the following phrase: 'proximity in time and place, the priority of inner biblical parallels, correspondence of social function, and the holistic approach to text and comparisons'; see Richard E. Averbeck, 'Sumer, the Bible, and Comparative Method: Historiography and Temple Building', in Mark W. Chavalas and K. Lawson Younger, Jr (eds.), *Mesopotamia and the Bible: Comparative Explorations* (Grand Rapids: Baker Academic, 2002), pp. 88-125 (89).
19. Talmon, 'The Comparative Method', pp. 320-56.
20. William W. Hallo, 'Introduction', p. xxviii.
21. Hallo, 'Introduction', pp. xxv-xxvi.

attention is given to methodological controls.²² To them, the comparative approach helps in understanding the historical settings of biblical texts. The method thus enriches the historical reconstruction of matters pertaining to philology, social roles and customs in ancient Israel, historical changes, literary genres and symbols, and legal traditions.

Feminist Exegesis and the Comparative Historical Method

When feminist scholars have approached comparative historical critical work, they have been interested in a variety of topics related to women's lives, representations of women, and cultural constructions of gender and identity. They investigate nearby cultures to reconstruct women's diverse experiences, and to evaluate the social constructions of gender in biblical texts, including diachronic developments. Among the topics that scholars have explored are: the relationship between goddesses and women's experiences,²³ the role of queen mothers and royal women,²⁴ and a variety of social institutions and roles.

More significant, however, than the subject matter considered in feminist comparative historical work are methodological and hermeneutical concerns attending this enterprise. Certain features that characterize feminist scholarship as a whole are also applied when feminist scholars

---

22. In addition to those listed above, see also Michael Barré, 'The Extrabiblical Literature', *Listening* 19 (1984), pp. 53-72; James K. Hoffmeier, 'Understanding Hebrew and Egyptian Military Texts: A Contextual Approach', in William W. Hallo (ed.), *The Context of Scripture: Archival Documents from the Biblical World* (Leiden: Brill, 2003), pp. xxi-xxvii.

23. There have been several studies on this topic with various perspectives on the relationship between goddesses and Israelite religious practice, and the degree to which it impacted women's status. For a review of the scholarship, see Peggy L. Day, 'Hebrew Bible Goddesses and Modern Feminist Scholarship', *Religion Compass* 6 (2012), pp. 298-308. For other works, see Jo Ann Hackett, 'Can a Sexist Model Liberate Us? Ancient Near Eastern "Fertility" Goddesses', *JFSR* 5 (1989), pp. 65-76; Tikvah Frymer-Kensky, *In the Wake of Goddesses: Women, Culture, and the Biblical Transformation of Pagan Myth* (New York: The Free Press, 1992); Judith Hadley, *The Cult of Asherah in Ancient Israel and Judah: Evidence for a Hebrew Goddess* (Cambridge: Cambridge University Press, 2000); Phyllis Bird, 'Women in the Ancient Mediterranean World: Ancient Israel', *BibRes* 39 (1994), pp. 31-45.

24. See, e.g., Monika Müller, 'The Households of the Queen and Queen Mother in Neo-Assyrian and Biblical Sources', in *My Spirit is at Rest in the North Country (Zechariah 6.8)* (Frankfurt: Peter Lang, 2011), pp. 241-63; Susan Ackerman, 'The Queen Mother and the Cult in Ancient Israel', *JBL* 112 (1993), pp. 385-401; Ktziah Spanier, 'The Queen Mother in the Judaean Royal Court: Maacah: A Case Study', in Athalya Brenner (ed.), *A Feminist Companion to Samuel and Kings* (Sheffield: Sheffield Academic Press, 1994), pp. 186-97.

engage in comparative historical work. One notable feminist scholar, Elisabeth Schüssler Fiorenza, defines a feminist hermeneutic as an orientation that recognizes gender as 'socially constructed, not innate'. To her, gender is a cultural construction, and so she emphasizes that feminists 'insist on the specific historical-cultural contexts and subjectivity, as well as on the plurality of "women"'.[25] Feminists employ various tools, reject claims to objectivity, and investigate how the particularities of context impact cultural representations of gender in biblical texts and their interpretations. Accordingly, two important aspects of Schüssler Fiorenza's feminist hermeneutic hold that neither reading of texts nor material artifacts are neutral or disinterested enterprises[26] and essentialist categories with regard to gender demonstrate androcentric bias and must be rejected.

Applying a feminist hermeneutic to the comparative historical method offers two distinct advantages. First, by providing a variety of new sources for women's lives, feminist comparative historical scholars demonstrate that the lives of women during the biblical period were impacted by a variety of temporal, spatial, and social realities. Thus, their work offers a better understanding of the diverse experiences of women than conventional-androcentric historical reconstructions. The second advantage of this approach, which builds on the first, is that it demonstrates the inadequacy and problematic nature of relying on essentialist categories, suggesting that simple binaries are insufficient not only in describing women's lives, but also various other social dynamics.

Comparative Historical Scholarship Demonstrates Diversity in Women's Experiences

The importance of extra-biblical texts for understanding women's lives and experiences cannot be overstated. Feminist historians have long recognized that biblical texts, produced by a group of elite and urban men, obscure Israelite women's lives.[27] When the texts describe women's experiences,

---

25. Elisabeth Schüssler Fiorenza, 'Feminist Hermeneutics', *ABD* 2 (1992), pp. 783-91 (784). For additional articulations about the characterization of feminist readings, see Bird, 'What Makes a Feminist Reading Feminist?', in Scholz (ed.), *Biblical Studies Alternatively*, pp. 67-72; Pamela Thimmes, 'What Makes a Feminist Reading Feminist? Another Perspective', in Scholz (ed.), *Biblical Studies Alternatively*, pp. 72-79.

26. In addition to the dispute over objectivity, feminist scholars have gone even further. Some question whether such objectivity, even if possible, would be advantageous or desirable; see, e.g., Carol Smith, 'Challenged by the Text: Interpreting Two Stories of Incest in the Hebrew Bible', in Athalya Brenner and Carole Fontaine (eds.), *A Feminist Companion to Reading the Bible: Approaches, Methods, and Strategies* (Sheffield: Sheffield Academic Press, 1997), pp. 114-35.

27. I do not suggest that comparative materials do not have limitations or biases.

they do not necessarily represent the realities of ordinary women. Carol Meyers' description of this dynamic is illustrative. She explains: 'The Israelite woman is largely unseen in the pages of the Hebrews Bible. To presume to locate her in biblical narrative would be to commit a fundamental methodological error. To assume we see nameless women in the named ones is to believe we can see the entire structure when only a fragment is visible'.[28] Athalya Brenner and others also notice that women often 'serve as metaphors or symbols',[29] and they may be entirely invented for literary purposes rather than relate to women's historical and social conditions.

The fact that women's experiences are not accurately depicted in biblical texts means that historians need to access additional sources of information. Even when the patriarchal rhetoric of the Bible describes women as having little authority or power, this language may belie a much more complicated reality.[30] Susanne Scholz summarizes the picture when she states:

> Since biblical writers and editors were mostly men coming from the elite strata of Israelite society, women have tried to determine the reliability of biblical prose and poetry for the historical reconstruction of women's life in ancient Israelite society. Since there is a difference between what people say they do and what they actually do, this incongruence should be assumed for the Hebrew Bible. Biblical texts, then, do not necessarily serve

---

For a discussion regarding the limits of cuneiform and hieroglyphic sources, see, e.g., Carole Fontaine, 'A Heifer from Thy Stable: On Goddesses and the Status of Women in the Ancient Near East', *UQR* 43 (1989), pp. 67-91; Phyllis Bird, 'Women in the Ancient Near Mediterranean World: Ancient Israel', *BibRes* 39 (1994), pp. 31-45 (34).

28. Carol Meyers, *Discovering Eve: Ancient Israelite Women in Context* (Oxford: Oxford University Press, 1988), p. 5.

29. Athalya Brenner, 'Introduction', in Athalya Brenner (ed.), *A Feminist Companion to Esther, Judith and Susanna* (Sheffield: Sheffield Academic Press, 1995), pp. 11-24 (13). About women functioning as metaphors, see Tivkah Frymer-Kensky, 'Introduction', in *Reading the Women of the Bible: A New Interpretation of Their Stories* (New York: Schocken Books, 2002), pp. xiii-xxvii.

30. The observation that gaps exist between a textual rhetoric and lived experience is not exclusive to biblical studies. Feminist scholars in a number of fields recognize that despite the rhetoric endorsed in culture, everyday realities may in fact be very different. For a discussion on the gap between the ideology of the 'cult of domesticity' and women's lived experiences in Deerfield, Massachusetts in late nineteenth and early twentieth centuries, see Deborah Rotman, 'Separate Spheres? Beyond the Dichotomies of Domesticity', *Current Anthropology* 47 (2006), pp. 666-74. However, feminist historians are not the only ones arguing that texts may say more about authorial perspectives than about historical realities. For instance, Mario Liverani explains: 'The thing to do should be to view the document not as a "source of information", but as information itself; not as an opening on a reality laying beyond but as an element which makes up that reality. Or, in keeping with the ethnological comparison made above: not as an informer, but as a member of the community under study'; see Mario Liverani, 'Memorandum on the Approach to Historiographic Texts', *Orientalia* 42 (1973), pp. 178-94 (179).

as evidence for what ancient Israelites actually did. Exterior evidence is needed, such as archaeological data and ancient Near Eastern documents, as well as anthropological and sociological theories, to create a historically reliable picture about women's lives.[31]

One way of filling the gaps in biblical texts is to turn to ancient Near Eastern textual and material artifacts.

One of the most influential feminist Hebrew Bible historians, Carol Meyers has long maintained the importance of social history to biblical studies and feminist studies of the Bible. The understanding of the specific social conditions and shifts in Israelite culture, however, also requires knowledge of 'the Near Eastern cultures from which Israel emerged'.[32] A focus on social history and the broader cultural world of the Bible gives understanding of the diachronic developments in women's experiences. Meyers explains:

> Some three thousand years of male dominance in western civilization, and in particular in religious institutions have clouded our vision of the prebiblical past and have led to the belief that the exclusion of females from regular leadership, at least in public and/or religious life, has been the norm for human history... Yet, as more and more material from the ancient world becomes available to us, the realities of the status of women in ancient societies, including their role in religious life, are becoming invisible behind the double veils of time and misapprehension'.[33]

Meyers thus proposes to uncover how women lived in ancient Israel, undeterred by preconceived notions about gender as they have been shaped by an uncritical historical reading of the Bible for hundreds of years. In her view, a comparative approach offers a better understanding of their lives and the social and historical developments in Israelite society over time. Meyers makes two significant claims related to feminist methods. First, she asserts that women's experiences are not universal and timeless, and second, she maintains that the assumption of women's experiences as universal goes back to patriarchal assumptions. According to Meyers, the social role and the relative status of women in ancient Israel correlate negatively to centralized authority. Accordingly, women in Iron Age I in Israel (1200–550 BCE) had a relatively high status. Only during the era of the Israelite monarchy were women's roles dichotomized between the public and the private realms, which impacted women's authority, particularly in urban settings, negatively. Further changes, related to women's roles, occurred even later, namely when Greco-Roman thought and its 'dualistic way of thinking'

---

31. Susanne Scholz, *Introducing the Women's Hebrew Bible* (New York: T. & T. Clark, 2007), p. 62.
32. Carol Meyers, 'Roots of Restriction', *BA* 41 (1978), pp. 91-103 (92).
33. Meyers, 'Roots of Restriction'.

emerged.³⁴ Traditional scholarly interpretations that view women's experiences as embedded within a patriarchal system that is consistent and immutable reflect more a scholar's historiography than actual women's lives in ancient Israel.

Not all feminist scholars agree with Meyers's specific argument on the diachronic developments of women's social status over time.³⁵ Yet her argument to use ancient Near Eastern sources to contextualize women's history is widely accepted, as is her assertion that social and political realities impacted women's status. Meyers underscores the importance of using extra-biblical texts and artifacts in the reconstruction of women's lives when she contends that too often 'feminist biblical study has not been successful in separating itself from the perspective of biblical authors'.³⁶ When exegetes rely exclusively on biblical literature, their interpretations are in danger of merely reinscribing patriarchal perspectives of the original authors. A narrow reliance on the Bible limits how exegetes formulate their research questions. They may identify with biblical viewpoints that privilege certain religious practices over others, and thus they often obscure women's participation in 'religious culture'.³⁷ Yet when feminist exegetes engage multiple sources, including archaeological and ethnographic data, as well as biblical and non-biblical texts, they approach the question of women's role in Israelite religion differently than in a limited Bible-only approach. Meyers' methodological plea for the comparative historical method is thus not only interested in discovering more information about previously unexamined topics. Rather, comparative historiography done from a feminist hermeneutic uncovers potential liabilities for reconstructing women's lives in ancient Israel that a literary approach alone is unable to identify.

Other feminist scholars, too, rely on the study of nonbiblical materials to understand women's lives in ancient Israel. They, too, want to counter essentialist categories about Israelite women and demonstrate the diversity of women's experiences in terms of geography and social status. One of them is Susan Ackerman who draws on ancient Near Eastern texts to argue that the Judean queen mother (Heb. *gĕbîrîâ*) had an 'official position within the palace', particularly as a 'lady counsellor'. This position linked her to the cultic function that she performed as a representative of Asherah.³⁸

---

34. Meyers, *Discovering Eve*, p. 196.
35. For a different perspective on diachronic developments regarding women's social status, see, e.g., Silvia Schroer, 'Diachronic Section', in Luise Schottroff, Silvia Schroer and Marie-Theres Wacker (eds.), *Feminist Interpretation: The Bible in Women's Perspective* (Minneapolis: Fortress Press, 1998), pp. 102-46.
36. Carol Meyers, *Households and Holiness: The Religious Culture of Israelite Women* (Minneapolis: Fortress, 2005), p. 6.
37. Meyers, *Households and Holiness*, p. 11.
38. Susan Ackerman, 'The Queen Mother and the Cult in Ancient Israel', *JBL* 112

Ackerman, resisting historical generalities about Israelite women's roles, focuses on the specific roles of women living in the Judean royal court as well as women's cultic roles. Using ancient Near Eastern evidence and biblical texts, she maintains that the queen mother may have had a corresponding role to the king. In ancient Judah, the king was revered as the deity's adopted son, and so, according to Ackerman, 'if the queen mother is considered the human representative of Asherah in the royal court, she should be able to legitimate her son's claim to be the adopted son of Yahweh. Indeed, the queen mother, assuming that she speaks as the goddess and thus as Yahweh's consort, is uniquely qualified to attest to her sons' divine adoption'.[39] Implicitly, then, Ackerman challenges simplistic gendered categories often used for Israelite women. They presume that Israelite women were categorically excluded from political and religious leadership. Ackerman does not suggest that women's status was equal to men, but she highlights that women's experiences varied in religious and legal practices.

Another feminist historian, Elna Solvang, argues that ancient Near Eastern evidence, including texts from Ebla, Ugarit, Mari, and Assyria, sheds light on the role of Judean royal women's lives during the eighth and seventh centuries BCE. More specifically, Solvang examines the role of the queen mother and several other roles of royal women. In her view, the biblical narratives, viewed together with ancient Near Eastern texts, indicate that women's involvement in political life was both an integral and consistent feature of palace life.[40] Solvang also provides a framework for a reading of the biblical references in light of the comparative material. She explains:

> Knowledge of the variety of actors, symbols, responsibilities and networks of power in the ancient Near Eastern monarchies *directs* the reader's *close attention to details and characters* in the biblical text. The real, necessary and legitimate activity of royal women within the monarchies of ancient history *requires* the reader's *serious consideration of the royal women of Judah*, viewing them not as outsiders to the monarchy but as valid participants in and representatives of it. Since the realities of monarchy in the ancient Near East factor royal women into their functioning, that will be the starting point of the reading of the biblical texts. The texts themselves will amend or correct that perception as necessary.[41]

(1993), pp. 385-401 (400-401). Ackerman challenges and nuances the views of two other scholars writing on the status of queen mothers; see Zafrira Ben-Barak, 'The Status and Right of the *Gebîrâ*', *JBL* 110 (1991), pp. 23-34; Niels Erik Andreasen, 'The Role of the Queen Mother in Israelite Society', *CQB* 45 (1983), pp. 179-84.

39. Ackerman, 'The Queen Mother', p. 401.

40. Elna Solvang, *A Woman's Place is in the House: Royal Women of Judah and Their Involvement in the House of David* (London: Sheffield Academic Press, 2003).

41. Solvang, *A Woman's Place*, p. 69 [emphasis in the original].

To Solvang, ancient Near Eastern texts about royal women are more trustworthy than biblical depictions, and so the former inform her reading of the latter. Solvang also discusses the challenges of comparative historiography, and she warns that scholars should be cautious in drawing comparisons between different kingdoms and different historical periods.[42] For example, in comparing her conclusions to that of Maria Brosius with regard to Persian royal woman, she notes some similarities, but warns that these 'should not lead to overgeneralisations about the participation of women—or men—in monarchies'.[43] Both of these works dismantle a 'problem in scholarly work that cuts across historical periods: the prevailing and unexamined assumption that women did not participate in significant ways in ancient monarchies'.[44] In contrast, she posits that women participated in Israelite life in the palace and elsewhere and that the original authors of the Bible wrote women out of the text. Thus, indirectly, then, ancient Near Eastern texts give evidence of the androcentric bias in biblical literature. Ultimately, Solvang's use of ancient Near Eastern materials shows that women were integral actors, playing important and diverse roles within Judah's royal court.[45]

The contributions of Meyers, Ackerman, and Solvang demonstrate the importance of extra-biblical sources for better understanding women's lives. Not only do each of these scholars provide strong evidence that women might have had significant status within their communities, and in so doing challenge previously held assumptions. These scholars also contend that women's status and access to power was contingent on a wide range of variables. Carol Meyers maintains that women had greater authority during the decentralized pre-monarchic period, while Ackerman and Solvang argue for religious and political status among royal women. Meyers' argument focuses on temporal aspects, suggesting that changing political realities during the course of Israel's history impacted women's lives. Ackerman and Solvang both emphasize the social and geo-political dimensions that shape women's everyday experiences. In focusing their studies on the lives of royal women, both scholars explore the unique ways that elite, urban women function within the royal households. With regard to geo-political realities, both Ackerman and Solvang examine the impact that Judah's political dynamics and royal ideology might play in determining the religious and political roles that women might access. What all three scholars implicitly challenge, then, is the view that ancient Israelite women's experiences were universal.

---

42. Solvang, *A Woman's Place*, p. 68.
43. Solvang, *A Woman's Place*, p. 68.
44. Solvang, *A Woman's Place*, p. 68.
45. Solvang, *A Woman's Place*, p. 68.

Comparative Historical Scholarship Challenges Essentialist Categories
Evidence from comparative studies that women's social status and access to power varied contributes to the idea that gender is a construct and not inherent. This perspective also suggests, however, that if women's experiences are diverse, not universal, that essentialist discourse correlated to gender binaries is inherently problematic.[46]

Eleanor Ferris Beach demonstrates the way in which gender binaries, and the value systems upon which they rely, have contributed to bias in the type of sources scholars use more frequently. Beach, who employs the comparative historical method, relies on ancient Near Eastern visual representations of women to evaluate the historical accuracy of the historical accuracy of biblical depictions of women. Beach maintains that 'ancient Near Eastern iconographic materials are among those underrepresented elements that can be used as effective, if non-traditional, resources for exegeting texts and investigating dynamics of power and gender in biblical literature'.[47] Analyzing Genesis 38, she suggests that visual analysis has a 'subversive' effect that 'may challenge, if not turn upside down, too simplistic understandings of the word and the authority claimed for it'.[48] Similar to Meyers, Beach's approach that integrates visual analysis and feminist inquiry is not only about finding new sources of information. Rather, she observes that the scholarly habit of overlooking images in favor of texts reflects a broader cultural bias rooted in gendered dualisms. Western thought has a long history of relying on a gendered dichotomization, a way of thinking that privileges one gender over the other. Beach states that the binaries contrasting 'man, mind, and culture to woman, body, and nature', have a parallel in the privileging of word over image.[49] Thus, her comparative work incorporates images and iconography to expose and challenge traditional dualism that values male over female and so further cements the binary structures

---

46. This perspective has especially characterized third wave feminism. Surekha Nelavala describes the shift in feminist discourse thus: 'Nonetheless, third-wave feminism critiques second-wave feminism for assuming that women's experiences are universal, and it questions essentialism of any sort. Considering each experience of each woman to be unique and authentic, third-wave feminism affirms multivocalism and seeks to liberate subjects from frameworks prescribed or defined by others'; see Surekha Nelavla, 'Third-Wave Feminism', in Julia M. O'Brien (ed.), *The Oxford Encyclopedia of the Bible and Gender Studies* (Oxford: Oxford University Press, 2014), pp. 251-55 (252).

47. Eleanor Ferris Beach, 'An Iconographic Approach to Genesis 38', in Athalya Brenner and Carole Fontaine (eds.), *A Feminist Companion to Reading the Bible: Approaches, Methods, and Strategies* (Sheffield: Sheffield Academic Press, 1997), pp. 285-305 (285).

48. Beach, 'An Iconographic Approach', p. 303.

49. Beach, 'An Iconographic Approach', p. 303.

in society, including gender hierarchies.[50] Beach's argument is provocative because it produces a more nuanced understanding of the depictions of women and it also indicates their historical implications. Most importantly, when the comparative historical approach is paired with Beach's feminist inquiry, it uncovers a methodological bias that privileges written over visual sources.

Beach's work demonstrates one problem of binary constructions, that is, the inherent valuing of one aspect of the binary construct over another. Jo Ann Hackett goes even further, maintaining that there is something more fundamental at stake. Her arguments is an important corollary to Beach's critique about dichotomies in cultural-written conventions in which textual binaries reinforce social, political, economic, and religious hierarchies.[51] She examines the publications on ancient Near Eastern 'fertility' goddesses of androcentric scholars and feminist writers who develop positive images for contemporary spirituality. Hackett observes that biblical scholars oversimplify the connections between ancient Near Eastern female deities and fertility and ignore the 'many-sided personalities' of the goddesses. This reductionist portrayal 'conveniently reinforces the reduction of *all* women to the nature side of the nature/culture dichotomy'.[52] Hackett argues that when faced with essentialist discourse that reifies two ideas into opposites, it is not enough simply to reverse how the two are valued with regard to one another. Thus, scholarship that attempts to revalue goddess traditions in a more positive way without challenging the underlying assumption that goddesses are associated only with fertility is problematic. To do so, Hackett contends, merely reinforces patriarchal assumptions. Thus, in her view, 'the most painful alternative, however, is to swallow, and then embrace, a dichotomy that is, I would argue, constructed precisely of the sexist categories we are trying to transcend'.[53] The problem with essentialist language

---

50. Elsewhere Beach makes similar arguments about the relationship between text and image, and the importance of this relationship for feminist analysis. For instance, she contends in her analysis of the Samaria ivories: 'This line of inquiry demonstrates Hebrew biblical texts were in dialogue with, drew upon, and in some cases, were intentionally shaped in relationship to powerful visual symbols, to be understood as an integral element in the signification. The dis-appearance of the visual context has made it difficult for us to see these meanings. Re-vision of exegetical methods to include the visual also has implications for feminist biblical scholarship, since, in these cases and probably others, a feminine component has become invisible'; see Eleanor Ferris Beach, 'The Samaria Ivories, *Marzeaḥ*, and Biblical Text', *Biblical Archaeologist* 56 (1993), pp. 94-104 (103).

51. Jo Ann Hackett, 'Can a Sexist Model Liberate Us? Ancient Near Eastern "Fertility" Goddesses', *JFSR* 5 (1989), pp. 65-76.

52. Hackett, 'Can a Sexist Model Liberate Us?', p. 75.

53. Hackett, 'Can a Sexist Model Liberate Us?', p. 76.

is not only that it values one side over the other (male over female, culture over nature, word over text, etc.), so that the correction of the problem requires the creation of new values systems. The more troubling issue is that when the binaries are maintained, they not only obfuscate complicated social dynamics but work to affirm patriarchal privilege.

The recognition by feminist scholars that gender binaries are not inherent but cultural constructions has important implications, not only for the historical study of women's lives in ancient Israel and the critical analysis of women's biblical representations. As we have seen, gender binaries have cultivated bias in the use of sources and reinforced hierarchies. In the past several decades, scholars have examined how masculinity is 'represented, constructed, or performed in specific cultural contexts'.[54] According to Stephen Moore, scholars working on masculinity maintain that 'masculinity—or masculinities—are not innate, invariable, or inevitable'. Rather, a particular ideal of masculinity is elevated within a culture, which "emerges against *subordinated* masculinities... Masculinity is plural, then, not just across cultures (many cultures, many masculinities) but also within cultures (many masculinities within a single culture).'[55] This suggests a fundamental shift in what gender binaries, and their attendant constructions of masculine and feminine ideals, reveal about particular cultures. Rather than using constructs of gender as evidence for men's and women's historical experiences, gendered discourse demonstrates particular ideologies of power.

Cynthia Chapman's study about the use of gendered language in Israelite and Assyrian warfare is especially significant in demonstrating how masculinity is enacted in Assyria and Israel, particularly with regard to warfare.[56] Chapman's work begins with a careful discussion about the comparative historical method, as well as theories about gender and metaphor.[57] Her work highlights how gendered language does not represent historical realities of men's and women's lives. Rather, it is an ideological construct that reinforces power hierarchies. Chapman describes the construction and performance of gender as outlined in biblical texts and Assyrian royal sources from the ninth to seventh centuries BCE. Her study asks who stands to gain from such a portrayal since gendered language does not necessarily reflect the dynamics between an individual man and an individual woman in a particular culture. Rather, such language makes general

---

54. Stephen D. Moore, 'Masculinity Studies', in Julia M. O'Brien (ed.), *The Oxford Encyclopedia of the Bible and Gender Studies* (Oxford: Oxford University Press, 2014), pp. 540-47 (540).

55. Stephen D. Moore, 'Masculinity Studies', p. 540.

56. Cynthia Chapman, *The Gendered Language of Warfare in the Israelite-Assyrian Encounter* (Harvard Semitic Monographs, 62; Winona Lake, IN: Eisenbrauns, 2004).

57. Chapman, *The Gendered Language*, pp. 1-19.

ideological claims with a vested interest in the demonstration and maintenance of power. Accordingly, gendered language may serve imperialist aims or shape visions of an ethnic 'Other'.

Susan Haddox builds on Chapman's work in several of her publications that examine masculinity and draw on comparative materials.[58] In her analysis of the Gideon narrative, for example, she describes the disjuncture that often exists between a dominant cultural construct of masculinity and everyday experiences. She states: 'Often in a society, one expression of masculinity becomes dominant and is the standard against which all other masculinities are judged. This is known as hegemonic masculinity. Hegemonic masculinity propagates through the institutions and power structures of society, becoming entrenched in the social structure and reproduced, even if it is not an accurate picture of how most men live.'[59] The hegemonic masculinity that is at work within a culture provides a productive framework within which to examine narrative representations. Haddox finds that the Gideon narrative presents a complex picture. Gideon 'downplays his masculinity' in almost every instance, and only when he 'diverges from the divine plan with a more typically masculine figure emerges.'[60] To Haddox, this depiction of Gideon indicates a similar dynamic to the patriarchal narratives in which less masculine characters are selected to carry out divine plans.[61] Her work demonstrates that gender binaries are not only cultural constructs and thus mutable, but they can also be manipulated and adapted for literary or theological purposes.

Each of these studies uses comparative sources from the ancient Near East to showcase significant problems that the reliance on gender essentialism implies. As Beach asserts, this approach has led to an overreliance on certain types of sources, including the preference for textual over visual sources for understanding historical and social dynamics. Furthermore, as Hackett shows, the values attached to gender dualisms prove problematic as well as the way in which those values reinforce a particular ideology of power. Finally, both Chapman's and Haddox's investigations on masculinity

---

58. See, e.g., Susan Haddox, *Metaphor and Masculinity in Hosea* (Studies in Biblical Literature, 141; New York: Peter Lang, 2011); '"The Lord is With You, You Mighty Warrior": The Questions of Gideon's Masculinity', in *Proceedings: Eastern Great Lakes Biblical Society and Midwest Region Society of Biblical Literature* 30 (2010), pp. 70-87; and 'Favoured Sons and Subordinate Masculinities', in Ovidiu Creanga (ed.), *Men and Masculinities in the Hebrew Bible and Beyond* (Sheffield: Sheffield Phoenix Press, 2010), pp. 2-19.

59. Susan Haddox, 'The Lord is With You, You Mighty Warrior': The Questions of Gideon's Masculinity', *Proceedings: Eastern Great Lakes Biblical Society and Midwest Region Society of Biblical Literature* 30 (2010), pp. 70-87 (71).

60. Haddox, 'The Lord is With You, You Mighty Warrior', p. 86.

61. Haddox, 'The Lord is With You, You Mighty Warrior', p. 86.

indicate that gendered binaries are just as problematic in describing historical realities of men as of women. Moreover, gendered language is highly symbolic. It is used to describe a wide range of social features within a culture, including perspectives on warfare, the ethnic 'Other', and the divine choice of individuals. Feminist comparative historical work draws on extra biblical material and textual data to reject essentialist notions of gendered binaries. Such work also questions the rhetoric implicit within the ancient texts.

Methodological Challenges in Feminist Comparative Historiography
Feminist comparative historical work is, however, not without its challenges, a fact that feminist Bible historians readily acknowledge. Similar to the Bible, ancient Near Eastern texts provide limited data on women's lives. Carole Fontaine acknowledges that often ancient Near Eastern texts do not depict women's perspectives. They, too, are the product of 'elite males whose ideological interests were served by the "disappearing" of the voices of women and other subject peoples'.[62] In other words, comparative materials offer significant resources for feminist inquiry, but they also contain an androcentric bias.

Phyllis Bird raises the problem that ancient Near Eastern sources are often 'concentrated in particular find spots, determined by the chances of archaeological discovery'.[63] It is thus difficult to draw generalizations from ancient Near Eastern materials about an entire region, much less to draw conclusions about the lives of women in biblical Israel.[64] Despite these limitations, Bird emphasizes that ancient Near Eastern materials consist of a much greater range of genres than biblical texts. Among them are 'administrative records, contracts, records of legal disputes, letters, omens, edicts, annals, ritual texts, myths, fables, law codes, maxims, school exercises'.[65] They provide important information about women and gender that is unavailable in biblical texts. Fontaine suggests that the various types of ancient Near Eastern sources are catalogued according to their degree of 'verisimilitude' to social realities. In her view, some genres of writing are less rhetorically charged than others in their depictions of social dynamics.[66]

---

62. Fontaine, 'A Heifer from Thy Stable', pp. 68-91 (68). For a similar perspective, see Phyllis Bird, 'Women in the Ancient Mediterranean World: Ancient Israel', *BibRes* 39 (1994), pp. 31-45 (34-35).
63. Bird, 'Women in the Ancient Mediterranean World', p. 34.
64. Bird, 'Women in the Ancient Mediterranean World', p. 34.
65. Bird, 'Women in the Ancient Mediterranean World', p. 34.
66. Fontaine, 'A Heifer from Thy Stable', p. 70. Fontaine states it thus: 'Texts both *respond* to social reality and help shape it. Texts may be classed along a continuum of those which are based in purely referential discourse (high degree of verisimilitude) to those which are highly symbolic and expressive (small degree of verisimilitude), i.e.,

But even if comparative texts, such as legal documents, represent more closely historical and social realities and are less ideologically-driven than the Bible, the problem would not be fully solved. In short, Bird and Fontaine point to an important methodological challenge when feminists rely on ancient Near Eastern texts.

Another word of caution comes from Julia Asher-Greve in a study on the appropriation of Mesopotamian texts.[67] Asher-Greve addresses the considerable level of specialization required for the translation and interpretation of Akkadian texts. She advises that such work include 'an in-depth knowledge of the discipline, its methodology and historiography'.[68] Her advice is not limited to feminist scholarship although she focuses on it. She worries that some scholars have interpreted Akkadian sources with an agenda, such as 'advocat[ing] "matriarchy", "great goddess theory" and the theory of origin and development of patriarchy'. The various agendas advance readings that are based on inaccurate data or they are problematic because 'sources are quoted out of context'.[69] Asher-Greve's concern echoes Hallo's observation that comparative work needs to attend to the 'horizontal dimension' of a text and belong to the same 'the geographical, historical, religious, political and literary setting' to provide 'the "context" of a given text'.[70] What is thus required is strong competency in knowing which comparative texts can appropriately be compared to which biblical texts. This skill also pertains to comparisons between biblical literature and Hittite, Ugaritic, Egyptian, Greek, Persian, Roman, and Aramaic texts. Making textual-historical comparisons requires much more skill than the ability to translate a text and to recognize visual symbols; it takes much training and experience to make appropriate correlations.

Hallo's argument about the need to pay close attention to the relationships between various texts on both the vertical and horizontal axes applies is echoed in the work of feminist comparative-historical scholars. For instance, Solvang cautions against overdrawing parallels between her work and Maria Brosius's study on Persian women; Chapman's work is limited to a particular timeframe when Israel and Assyria were in direct contact with each other. The studies demonstrate conscious choices to delimit the materials used in their comparative analysis.

---

those which are mapped on combinative, syntagmatic axis of language as opposed to those whose nature is more related to the associative, paradigmatic axis.

67. Her comments relate to Mesopotamian sources, but they could also be applied to other types of materials, such as Egyptian or Ugaritic sources.

68. Julia Asher-Greve, 'Feminist Research and Ancient Mesopotamia: Problems and Prospects', pp. 218-37 (219).

69. Julia Asher-Greve, 'Feminist Research and Ancient Mesopotamia: Problems and Prospects', p. 219.

70. Hallo, 'Introduction: Ancient Near Eastern Texts', p. xxviii.

These and other feminist historical-comparative publications remind us that ancient Near Eastern texts are also not free from bias, even if they have sometimes been used to adjust or correct false assumptions about biblical texts. In addition, the concentration of archaeological finds in limited geographic regions presents challenges about whether or not generalizations might be drawn from such limited evidence.[71] Finally, working outside of one's academic specialization presents an ongoing challenge to any scholar working with the comparative-historical method.

Conclusion

Using the comparative historical method during the past decades, feminist scholars have come a long way. Interestingly, their studies share some of the same concerns and challenges that characterize the methodological discussions of this method in general. The concerns relate to the translation of non-biblical texts, the appropriate use of comparative materials, and the establishment of relationships between the different materials. At the same time, feminist historians have also advanced the understanding of the social and political dynamics related to Israelite women's lives, as well as the consistency of androcentric assumptions within the Bible and in biblical interpretation histories. With the discovery and translations of new texts and artifacts, feminist scholars will gain additional opportunities to contextualize women's lives in the ancient Near East and to collaborate with other feminist and non-feminist historians in the shared task of reconstructing the ancient world in the various lands and different eras referenced in the Hebrew Bible.

The past several decades of work by feminist comparative historians have provided important historic and historiographic implications. Comparative materials give new information about the variety and complexity of women's experiences in the ancient world. The studies have also underscored how gendered language serves as a rhetorical function in reinforcing the status quo of social hierarchies. As feminist scholars look forward to the future of comparative historical criticism, it is becoming increasingly clear that gender cannot be studied in a vacuum. Rather, scholars must consider how various social dynamics overlap, challenge, and interact with

71. For instance, a large number of tablets dating to the early second millennium were found at the Anatolian city of Kanesh. Women wrote and received letters, and the contents of the letters indicate that trade was a family business in which women were integral participants. The evidence for women's participation in this particular context is clear, but it is more difficult to determine how such evidence might be used to better understand women's role in economic affairs more broadly. For a translation of these letters into French, see Cécile Michel, *Correspondance des marchands de Kanish* (Paris: Les Editions du Cerf, 2001).

one another. Work in intersectional studies, which has only recently been explored by biblical scholars, provides a framework for exploring gender in connection to other cultural phenomena.[72] Marianne Bjelland Kartzow describes this approach: 'Instead of examining gender, sexuality, race, ethnicity, class, disability, and age as separate categories of oppression, intersectionality explores how to reinforce each other. Every person belongs to more than category, and faced with discrimination it might be difficult to articulate which correlative system of oppression is at work'.[73] Intersectional scholarship, then, highlights that both women and men negotiate complex identities in a variety of contexts vis-à-vis social hierarchies rather than within a rigid binary.

Furthermore, comparative sources from the ancient Near East offer substantial resources for examining intersections and identity negotiation, particularly in the field of Hebrew Bible. Both texts and material culture provide a broad range of sources available for understanding social, political and cultural dynamics than can be found in biblical texts. For instance, texts written by women about trade or devotion to goddesses, as well as legal and economic documents about adoption, marriage, and land sale, supply additional context for understanding complex power dynamics in the ancient world. Feminist scholars, looking to the intersections of aspects of social identity, however, must at the same time continue to resist reification of social categories. Suggesting an intersection between ethnicity, gender, and class need not imply that each of these aspects is a fixed social reality.[74] Rather, overlap and interplay between various dimensions of identity not only challenge simplistic categorization, but also present a lens through which to examine the historiographic perspective of any given text.

---

72. Marianne Bjelland Kartzow, 'Intersectional Studies', in Julia M. O'Brien (ed.), *The Oxford Encyclopedia of the Bible and Gender Studies* (Oxford: Oxford University Press, 2014), pp. 383-89 (383).

73. Bjelland Kartzow, 'Intersectional Studies', p. 383.

74. Bjelland Kartzow, 'Intersectional Studies', p. 383.

6

WITHIN AND WITHOUT PURITY, DANGER, HONOUR, AND SHAME: ANTHROPOLOGICAL APPROACHES IN FEMINIST HEBREW BIBLE STUDIES

Johanna Stiebert

This essay explores intersections between cultural anthropology and feminist Hebrew Bible studies. The approaches highlighted here incorporate empirical data obtained from participant observation in human communities and their impact on textual study. As part of a wider social-scientific endeavour such data inform understanding of social structures, behaviours and interrelations, as reflected in and by the Hebrew Bible. Coexistent with this is an emphasis on the role and contribution of gender but, as will become clear, feminist advocacy is evident in these approaches to various degrees.

Four sections outline this interdisciplinary methodological development in biblical studies. First is a brief and general discussion of feminism in the academic discipline of anthropology. I next turn to the encounter of Hebrew Bible studies with cultural anthropology during the past few decades, focusing particularly on two seminal anthropologists, Mary Douglas and Julian Pitt-Rivers, whose explorations have ventured into the Hebrew Bible. Then follows the most substantial portion: a discussion and illustration of how feminist Hebrew Bible scholars have appropriated anthropological concepts, models, and methods. Their areas of focus range from purity and pollution to the honour-shame value complex and body adornment, but with a new emphasis on women's roles and concerns. Some feminist Bible scholars, moreover, draw less on anthropological data and more on the distinctive cultural-anthropological technique of fieldwork, even if these feminist exegetes do not always explicitly identify their indebtedness to anthropological methodology. Finally, a conclusion asserts the still somewhat underexplored possibilities for dynamism and creativity when feminist Hebrew Bible scholars use anthropological theories and techniques in the interpretation of biblical texts.

Feminism and the Academic Discipline of Anthropology

The social science of anthropology divides into two major fields: physical and social-cultural anthropology. Physical anthropology is the study of biological and behavioural variation of human beings, non-human primates, and extinct ancestors of humans. There have been significant female scholars in this discipline, notably palaeoanthropologist Mary Leakey (1913–1996) and the triumvirs of primatology, Dian Fossey (1932–1985), Jane Goodall (b. 1934), and Birutė Galdikas (b. 1946). Feminist purpose, however, is not in the foreground of their research, and political advocacy among the primatologists has been focused primarily on conservation and animal welfare.

The designations of social and cultural anthropology are sometimes used interchangeably. Cultural anthropology emphasizes cultural diversity whereas social anthropology stresses the continuity of cultural expressions, such as rituals and symbolic actions, and defines them as different subsets of a human social constant.[1] Both social and cultural anthropology focus on human social behaviour and interaction, including customs, social organizations, laws, patterns of kinship and trade, gender relations, and religious rituals. Both also extend beyond strictly social phenomena and include manifestations of culture, such as art, or clothing. The distinctive research method of both is long-term, qualitative, and empirical ethnography; this is also called participant observation or fieldwork. Originally, this approach consisted of micro-studies that focused on the direct observation of small-scale and non-Western[2] communities. Feminist anthropologists,[3] such as Ruth Benedict (1887–1948), Hortense Powdermaker (1896–1970), and Margaret Mead (1901–1978), made significant contributions to the field of early social-cultural anthropology.

Synergies between anthropological and feminist studies[4] extend over several decades. One clear indication of fertile collaboration is that feminist

---

1. For a fuller explanation, see Peter Just, *Social and Cultural Anthropology: A Very Short Introduction* (Oxford: Oxford University Press, 2000).

2. I use 'West' and 'Western' as convenient terms to refer to dominant European and North American contexts. The designation is, admittedly, ethnocentric and problematic. Alternative designations, however, are likely to be verbose and to detract from the central purpose of this essay.

3. Unless otherwise specified, where 'anthropology' is unqualified, I refer to cultural anthropology.

4. The word 'anthropology' refers to 'the study or science of human beings' and has exceedingly wide application. I use the designation in its social-scientific sense. Consequently, I will not discuss feminist theological anthropology, a branch of systematic theology, which explores feminist ideals alongside the relationship between humans and between humans and God. For a full discussion and exposition, with particular reference to Gen. 1.27, see Michelle A. Gonzalez, *Created in God's Image: An Introduction to Feminist Theological Anthropology* (Maryknoll, NY: Orbis Books, 2007). For an anthropologist's assessment of the fusion of anthropology and theology, see Joel Robbins, 'Anthropology and Theology: An Awkward Relationship?', *Anthropological Quarterly* 79.2 (2006), pp. 285-94.

anthropology[5] has been a formally recognized and thriving discipline since the 1970s.[6] Its feminist purpose is evident in various ways, but above all in an endeavour to reduce male bias in the scholarly production of knowledge and in research findings. This goal of challenging androcentrism is widely advocated across the feminist social sciences and characterized by 'placing women at the centre, as subjects of inquiry and as active agents in the gathering of knowledge'.[7] Feminist anthropologists, therefore, seek to expose, confront, and redress the tendencies of researchers in male-dominated academic centres finding, privileging, and describing the activities and affairs of men to the virtual exclusion of women and women's experiences.[8]

But alliance between anthropology and academic feminism has not gone unchallenged. Objections have been raised both on the grounds of disciplinary irreconcilables and concerning the shortcomings in both fields effectively to facilitate minority representation. Regarding the former, cultural anthropologist Marilyn Strathern avers that the relationship between 'feminism' on the one hand and 'anthropology' on the other is at best awkward and at worst dissonant.[9] The two fields, she argues, are not isomorphic partners because feminist scholarship works across disciplines whereas anthropology has distinct and circumscribed subject matters and practices. Above all, for Strathern, tensions stem from cross-purposes. Hence, she identifies feminist purpose as focused on exposing and detoxifying the authority

---

5. Feminist anthropology divides into four branches: archaeological, physical, cultural, and linguistic. My focus here is on cultural anthropology and its intersection with feminist Hebrew Bible studies. Feminist archaeology in Hebrew Bible studies is another significant area discussed by Carol Meyers in a separate chapter in this volume. Sometimes feminist biblical archaeology incorporates also cultural anthropology, giving rise to multidisciplinary interpretations, such as Ebeling's research, which draws on the observations of Hilma Granqvist who, in the first half of the twentieth century documented the lives of the villagers of Artas, a small settlement near Bethlehem. Ebeling argues that for all the many differences that doubtlessly exist between Iron Age I (the archaeological period of her focus) and life in 1920s and 1930s Artas, the small-scale, rural communities of both and equivalence in terms of climatic and terrestrial conditions invite comparison and analogy; see Jennie R. Ebeling, *Women's Lives in Biblical Times* (London: T. & T. Clark, 2010), p. 46.

6. The Association for Feminist Anthropology (AFA) was founded in 1988, but the formation of the discipline predates it by about twenty years. For a full account, see Rachel Nuzman, 'Twenty-Five Years of Feminist Anthropology: A History of the Association for Feminist Anthropology' (2014), available at http://www.aaanet.org/sections/afa/wp-content/uploads/2014/01/AFAHistory25years.pdf.

7. Judith Stacey and Barrie Thorne, 'The Missing Feminist Revolution in Sociology', *Social Problems* 32.4 (1985), pp. 301-16 (303).

8. Sarah Milledge Nelson, *Gender in Archaeology: Analyzing Power and Prestige* (Walnut Creek, CA: Alta Mira Press, 1997), *passim*.

9. Marilyn Strathern, 'An Awkward Relationship: The Case of Feminism and Anthropology', *Signs* 12.2 (1987), pp. 276-92.

of those who determine women's experience as 'Other', an authority often conceived as 'patriarchy' (or, sometimes, a more nuanced kyriarchy). An ethnographer's focus on experience, however, 'remain[s] open to people's emotional and personal lives' and translates findings into written studies, without any predetermined (feminist or other) agenda. As Strathern elaborates, '[a]nthropology here constitutes itself in relation to an Other, vis-à-vis the alien culture/society under study. Its distance and foreignness are deliberately sustained. But the Other is not under attack. On the contrary the effort is to create a relation with the Other...'.[10] Strathern, therefore, is sceptical as to the possibility of combining feminist scholarship and anthropology to good effect unless, she adds, feminist anthropology were to pertain to little more than 'to "women" as its practitioners, as well as its subject matter'.[11]

Further tension arises from the reality that the majority of both second-wave feminists and anthropologists are white, middle-class, and university-educated academics. While feminist anthropologists have engaged widely with feminists from manifold traditions, the perspectives of non-white (especially non-Western), lower socio-economic or non-tertiary-educated feminists have historically been sidelined. Feminist anthropologists claim that their research takes steps towards correcting systemic biases, but they usually come from positions of comparative privilege in the West and not from the cultures under investigation. Consequently, their studies are likely to contain Western-specific assumptions that do not apply to the observed cultures.[12]

What this very brief assessment of feminist anthropology demonstrates is that the combination of feminism and anthropology has been established for several decades. It also highlights, however, that such a combination

---

10. Strathern, 'An Awkward Relationship', p. 289.
11. Strathern, 'An Awkward Relationship', p. 281. For all the complexities summarized here, feminist anthropology continues to thrive. For an excellent source of examples, see Ellen Lewin (ed.), *Feminist Anthropology: A Reader* (Blackwell Anthologies in Social and Cultural Anthropology; Malden, MA: Blackwell, 2006). With Bible scholars applying anthropological approaches to subjects pertinent to gender, or women in particular, feminist orientation is not always unequivocal. As we will see, the degree or even presence of feminist advocacy in the work of Bechtel, for instance, can be questioned.
12. See Michelle Z. Rosaldo, 'The Use and Abuse of Anthropology: Reflections on Feminism and Cross-cultural Understanding', *Signs* 5.3 (1980), pp. 389-417. The considerable imbalance in terms of minority representation is beginning to be addressed; see, e.g., Irma McClaurin (ed.), *Black Feminist Anthropology: Theory, Politics, Praxis, and Poetics* (New Brunswick, NJ: Rutgers, 2001). Within biblical studies, too, womanist and LGBT criticism in particular have thrown a light on intersectionality and the failures of earlier second-wave feminist criticism to resist explicitly discrimination on the grounds of not just gender, but also race, ethnicity, social class, sexual orientation, and gender identity.

is not only a source of creative potential but also of friction. Next, I will explore the encounter of Hebrew Bible studies with anthropology and then the blending of feminist Hebrew Bible studies with cultural anthropological methods and techniques.

Anthropology and Hebrew Bible Studies

A rich and two-directional influence between anthropology and biblical studies is firmly established. The presence of anthropology in Hebrew Bible studies goes back even further than W. Robertson Smith (1846–1894)[13] and a substantial contingent of biblical scholars rely on ethnographic data to illuminate or explain biblical narratives and laws.[14] Conversely, especially since the 1960s and 70s, there are also cultural anthropologists who use the Hebrew Bible.[15] These anthropologists supplement their fieldwork data to understand more fully the historical foundations of small-scale face-to-face societies, particularly in the countries of the circum-Mediterranean region.

The two most influential anthropologists to interpret Hebrew Bible texts are Mary Douglas (1921–2007) and Julian Pitt-Rivers (1919–2001), neither of whose work reflects overt feminism. Douglas was an anthropologist who conducted fieldwork among the Congolese Lele people. Her highly influential book *Purity and Danger*, first published in 1966, combines insights on the topic of ritual purity and pollution from empirical research in different societies and times and contains a chapter on the book of Leviticus in the Hebrew Bible. It also marks the beginning of Douglas' sustained fascination with the Hebrew Bible.[16] The aim of this chapter is to defend the notion

---

13. For a full discussion on the diachronic development of anthropological Hebrew Bible studies, see John W. Rogerson, *Anthropology and the Old Testament* (Oxford: Basil Blackwell, 1978), pp. 1-21. This publication predates the additional infusion of feminist criticism into anthropological approaches to Hebrew Bible texts.

14. See Rogerson, *Anthropology and the Old Testament*, and also David J. Chalcraft (ed.), *Social-Scientific Old Testament Criticism: A Sheffield Reader* (Sheffield: Sheffield Academic Press, 1997).

15. While there is precedent for biblical scholars using data from physical anthropology (see below), I am not aware of (and would be surprised by) *physical* anthropologists turning to the Hebrew Bible for research purposes. This is because the methodology of physical anthropology is closer to that of the natural sciences, whereas social scientists, including cultural anthropologists, have more reason to turn to the Hebrew Bible. For a full account of the relationships and affinities between social sciences and Hebrew Bible studies see Johanna Stiebert, 'Social-Scientific Approaches', in Julia M. O'Brien (ed.), *The Oxford Encyclopedia of the Bible and Gender Studies* (vol. 2; Oxford/New York: Oxford University Press, 2014), pp. 411-20.

16. Mary Douglas, 'The Abominations of Leviticus', in *Purity and Danger: An Analysis of Concepts of Pollution and Taboo* (London: Routledge and Kegan Paul, 1984), pp. 42-58. According to Douglas, concepts derived from anthropology are best placed

that phenomena observable in communities sensitive to concepts of purity and pollution are ossified in the ancient text. Moreover, Douglas argues that in all human societies there exist efforts to create order and avoid anomaly, with a division into sacred and profane spheres constituting one prominent binary of such ordering.

The second anthropologist, Pitt-Rivers conducted fieldwork in Andalusia. He belonged to a group of anthropologists who developed the honour-shame value complex,[17] which went on to become exceptionally significant in Hebrew Bible studies. According to this value complex traditional Mediterranean societies practise rigid gender differentiation. In brief, this makes men publicly vie for honour in zero-sum competitions while women show considerable modesty and restraint in an effort to guard the female variant of honour, which is shame. If a woman's shame is lost (above all through sexual immodesty, the most extreme forms being loss of virginity prior to marriage or incontinence subsequent to marriage), it causes considerable damage and humiliation (also called shame)[18] not only for herself but also for her entire family. In some cases shame can transpire in honour killings of women in order to restore male reputation. Pitt-Rivers turned his attention to the book of Genesis to establish a precedent for his observations about the centrality of honour and shame in the field.[19] In time, the work of both Douglas and Pitt-Rivers received vigorous responses from biblical exegetes,[20] though it took time for the biblical work to acquire a feminist dimension.

---

to solve the 'hoary old puzzle' posed by the odd assortment of dietary prohibitions contained in Leviticus (p. 42). Douglas's other studies on the Hebrew Bible combine anthropological and, increasingly, literary analyses. These include *Leviticus as Literature* (Oxford: Oxford University Press, 1999); *In the Wilderness: The Doctrine of Defilement in the Book of Numbers* (Oxford: Oxford University Press, rev. edn, 2001); *Jacob's Tears: The Priestly Work of Reconciliation* (Oxford: Oxford University Press, 2006).

17. See Julian Pitt-Rivers, 'Honour and Social Status' (pp. 19-77), and also other chapters in J.G. Peristiany (ed.), *Honour and Shame: The Values of Mediterranean Society* (London: Weidenfeld & Nicolson, 1965).

18. Claudia V. Camp distinguishes helpfully between the two opposite meanings of 'shame' as follows: 'the shame-by-which-one-must-be-bound in order to avoid the shame-that-destroys'; see her 'Understanding a Patriarchy: Women in Second Century Jerusalem through the Eyes of Ben Sira', in Amy-Jill Levine (ed.), *'Women Like This': New Perspectives on Jewish Women in the Greco-Roman World* (Atlanta: Scholars Press, 1991), pp. 1-39 (5).

19. Julian Pitt-Rivers, *The Fate of Shechem or the Politics of Sex: Essays in the Anthropology of the Mediterranean* (Cambridge: Cambridge University Press, 1977).

20. Engagement with Douglas's work in biblical studies includes the following examples (alongside those discussed below): Michael P. Carroll, 'One More Time: Leviticus Revisited', *Archives européennes de sociologie* 19 (1978), pp. 339-46; Walter Houston, *Purity and Monotheism: Clean and Unclean Animals in Biblical Law* (JSOTSup, 140; Sheffield: JSOT Press, 1993); John F. Sawyer (ed.), *Reading Leviticus: Responses to*

The honour-shame model, in particular, was widely and often rather uncritically adopted in biblical studies.[21] The apex of the model's application was in the 1990s. Among a glut of publications in this area,[22] there appeared a handbook on biblical social values by John J. Pilch and Bruce J. Malina,[23] which strongly affirmed the pivotal nature of honour and shame, as well as a dedicated anthology edited by Victor H. Matthews and Don C. Benjamin, entitled *Honor and Shame in the World of the Bible*.[24] The latter publication includes applications of the honour-shame model to all of Song

---

Mary Douglas (The Library of Hebrew Bible/Old Testament, 227; Sheffield: Bloomsbury T. & T. Clark, 1996). The latter comprises papers presented at a colloquium on Douglas and Leviticus held at the University of Lancaster in 1995.

21. An example to illustrate this uncritical adoption from New Testament studies is the sweeping claim that '[i]t is truly an understatement to say that the whole of Luke's Gospel, almost every piece of social interaction, should be viewed through the lens of honor and shame' and 'seeing [Jesus's] life through the lens of honor and shame, we begin to view it from the native's perspective and to appreciate the social dynamic as natives see it'; see Jerome H. Neyrey, *The Social World of Luke–Acts* (Peabody, MA: Hendrickson), p. 64. Also see Bruce J. Malina, *The New Testament World: Insights from Cultural Anthropology* (Louisville, KY: Westminster/John Knox Press, rev. edn, 1993), p. 45. If honour and shame function as pivotal core values in the comprehensive way, asserted by Neyrey and Malina, then their meanings are actually rendered little more than 'honour' is everything positively construed and 'shame' everything negatively construed in 'the Bible'; it lacks acknowledging the complexity and internal diversity of social backgrounds in the Hebrew Bible and New Testament. For additional examples and a critical assessment of the model's application to biblical texts, see Johanna Stiebert, *The Construction of Shame in the Hebrew Bible: The Prophetic Contribution* (JSOTSup, 346; Sheffield: Sheffield Academic Press, 2002), pp. 59-75.

22. These include W.R. Domeris, 'Shame and Honour in Proverbs: Wise Women and Foolish Men', *Old Testament Essays* 8 (1995), pp. 86-102; Ken Stone, 'Gender and Homosexuality in Judges 19: Subject-Honor, Object-Shame?', *JSOT* 67 (1995), pp. 87-107; Saul M. Olyan, 'Honor, Shame, and Covenant Relations in Ancient Israel and Its Environment', *JBL* 115.2 (1996), pp. 201-18; T.R. Hobbs, 'Reflections on Honor, Shame, and Covenant Relations', *JBL* 116.3 (1997), pp. 501-503 and Timothy S. Laniak, *Shame and Honor in the Book of Esther* (SBL Dissertation Series, 165; Atlanta: Scholars Press, 1998). Also to be mentioned here are the multiple works on honour-shame by David A. de Silva; see, e.g., his *Despising Shame: Honor Discourse and Community Maintenance in the Epistle to the Hebrews* (SBL Dissertation Series, 152; Atlanta: Scholars Press, 1995). Only Stone's article comes close to a feminist-critical application of anthropological data to biblical texts. Stone explains that male-male rape is constructed as feminizing the raped male. This view of male rape is humiliating for several reasons as females are regarded as socially inferior to males. Accordingly, male rape denotes a feminization of the raped man.

23. John J. Pilch and Bruce J. Malina (eds.), *Biblical Social Values and their Meaning: A Handbook* (Peabody, MA: Hendrickson, 1993), pp. 95-104.

24. Victor H. Matthews and Don C. Benjamin (eds.), *Honor and Shame in the World of the Bible* (Semeia, 68; Atlanta: Society of Biblical Literature, 1994).

of Songs, Joel, and the David narratives, and several New Testament texts. Well before this time, however, cautionary calls had already been raised both within anthropology, including by feminist anthropologists, urging that any adoption of the honour-shame model must be carefully specified and qualified,[25] and among Hebrew Bible scholars, who pointed to the complexities and possible stumbling blocks of applying field data to ancient texts.[26]

Robert R. Wilson makes an important contribution to the debate on the reliance of anthropological concepts in biblical interpretation and again his recommendations long predate the often over-enthusiastic flourish of the honour-shame model in biblical studies. Wilson proposes six guidelines stating that, first, any ethnographic data used by biblical scholars must come from properly trained anthropologists; second, such material must be carefully interpreted in its own context prior to application to any biblical text; third, biblical scholars must, before making comparisons, conduct a wide-ranging survey of societies rather than seizing on just one isolated case study from one discrete society; fourth, biblical scholars should try to avoid the 'interpretive schemata', i.e. the possibly essentializing interpretive patterns, into which anthropologists organize data; fifth, biblical scholars must be careful in determining whether anthropological data are truly comparable to accounts in biblical texts; and sixth, the biblical text, i.e. biblical

---

25. More than a decade before the model appeared so prominently in biblical studies anthropologist Michael Herzfeld argued that the designations 'honour' and 'shame' over time came to encompass such a wide range of local-social, sexual, performative and economic values that they were in effect rendered little more than 'inefficient glosses'; see his 'Honour and Shame: Problems in the Comparative Analysis of Moral Systems', *Man* 15 (1980), pp. 339-51 (339). In the face of this situation, Herzfeld called for careful ethnographic specificity. Unni Wikan's fieldwork in Egypt (*Life Among the Poor in Cairo* [London: Tavistock, 1980]); and Oman (*Behind the Veil in Arabia: Women in Oman* [Baltimore, Maryland: The Johns Hopkins University Press, 1982]) foregrounds the lives and experiences of women. Her article, 'Shame and Honour: A Contestable Pair', *Man* 19 (1984), pp. 635-52, looks more squarely at the perspectives of women than the contributions in Peristiany (1965). Wikan explains that women of the communities of central Cairo (in sharp contrast to the women described in Peristiany's volume) did *not* talk constantly of honour. Moreover, women neighbours did not condemn a woman who committed adultery as shameful. Rather they refrained from telling her husband and considered her a likable person. In this way Wikan, focusing especially on the gender dimension of shame, exposes what she calls 'the illusory generality and abstraction which the anthropologist's concept of "honour" and "shame" provide' (p. 648).

26. Some anthropologists have also expressed reservation alongside enthusiasm with regard to applying the honour-shame model to the Hebrew Bible; see, e.g., Gideon M. Kressel, 'An Anthropologist's Response to the Use of Social Science Models in Biblical Studies', *Semeia* 68 (1994), pp. 153-61.

scholars' area of expertise, must remain the dominant and driving factor in the process of interpretation.[27] These guidelines indicate that anthropological fieldwork-data are valuable to biblical interpretation, and that anthropology must also be respected as a separate specialization. Without some relatively high-level understanding of *both* anthropology *and* biblical studies, the appropriation of data from one discipline into another can result in inaccurate or over-simplistic interpretations of biblical literature.[28] Again, these notes of caution are important to consider as we see how feminist and anthropological methods combine within Hebrew Bible studies.

Feminist Hebrew Bible Scholars Using Anthropological Concepts or Models

The impact of physical anthropology on feminist biblical studies is not pronounced. Indeed, human fossils yield clues about the movements of peoples, and studies on primate behaviour can illuminate human social behaviour, particularly, perhaps, of the distant human ancestral past. Hence, physical anthropological research could be of value to Hebrew Bible studies.[29] The merging of physical anthropology with feminism, however, poses an obstacle due to a fundamental dissonance. Hence, feminism leans toward a constructivist position, which usually asserts that gender (e.g. femininity, masculinity) is *socially constructed* rather than integral to biological sex (i.e. femaleness, maleness, intersex). Moreover, feminism is a political

---

27. Robert R. Wilson, *Prophecy and Society in Ancient Israel* (Philadelphia: Fortress Press, 1980), pp. 15-16.

28. This is demonstrated by David Fiensy, 'Using the Nuer Culture of Africa in Understanding the Old Testament: An Evaluation', *JSOT* 38 (1987), pp. 73-83. Fiensy urges that biblical scholars using anthropological data must remain 'sensitive to anthropologists' ongoing evaluation of ethnological and ethnographic material' (p. 73). He points out that with the enthusiastic appropriation by biblical scholars of field studies among the Sudanese Nuer, anthropologists problematized and sometimes rejected segmentary political and lineage theory just as these enjoyed popularity among biblical scholars as a means for illuminating ancient Israelite society (p. 83). Similarly, biblical scholars embraced the anthropological honour shame value-complex as anthropologists contested and dismantled it; see, e.g., Herzfeld, 'Honour and Shame'; Wikan, *Life Among the Poor in Cairo*.

29. One topic that combines physical anthropological approaches and the study of the Hebrew Bible is incest/incest taboos. The volume by Arthur P. Wolf and William H. Durham (eds.), *Inbreeding, Incest, and the Incest Taboo* (Stanford, CA: Stanford University Press, 2005), contains contributions from primatology (see Anne Pusey, 'Inbreeding Avoidance in Primates', pp. 61-75) and palaeo-anthropology (see Mark T. Erickson, 'Evolutionary Thought and the Current Clinical Understanding of Incest', pp. 161-89). I use these essays to read biblical incest texts; see Johanna Stiebert, *Fathers and Daughters in the Hebrew Bible* (Oxford: Oxford University Press, 2013), pp. 102-65.

movement that promotes *advocacy*, primarily of gender equality. In contrast, physical anthropology often assumes an *essentialist* position that regards both physical and behavioural characteristics as inherent to biological sex. In addition, its method is *descriptive* although advocacy for conservation, for instance, may arise from primatology.

The adoption of cultural anthropological concepts by feminist Hebrew Bible scholars came to prominence in the 1990s. The purity-pollution concept of Douglas and the honour-shame value complex advanced by Pitt-Rivers were popular also with certain feminist exegetes. They applied these concepts to illuminate particularly women's social roles as depicted in biblical texts. Three scholars representing this approach are Lyn M. Bechtel, Claudia V. Camp, and Kathleen O'Grady.

Bechtel is a biblical scholar who applies anthropological data, including the honour-shame model, prominently in her interpretations. Bechtel, like Mediterranean anthropologists, stresses the significance of shame as a pivotal emotion and sanction of behaviour and sees this reflected in ancient Israelite society and in biblical texts. She characterizes Israelite society as group-oriented and thus particularly susceptible to shame. Incorporating psychoanalytic theory into social anthropological concepts,[30] Bechtel examines shame alongside both honour and guilt.[31] In her view, it is important to recognize that most Western Bible scholars live in individual-oriented or 'grid' societies that accentuate guilt-sensitivity. In contrast, she argues, biblical texts come from strongly bonded 'group' societies that nurtured shame sensitivity, where 'the group is capable of exerting great pressure on people, in order to control their behaviour'.[32] In a group society a person's reputation or standing in the community is crucial and usually stratified in terms of an honour hierarchy: Bechtel explains that '[h]onour increases status, while shame decreases honour and lowers status'.[33] While, on the one hand, drawing on the findings of anthropologists, Bechtel, on the other, closely scrutinizes biblical texts. This method substitutes for empirical study of ancient

---

30. Bechtel is explicit about her multidisciplinary approach; see Lyn M. Bechtel, 'Shame as a Sanction of Social Control in Biblical Israel: Judicial, Political, and Social Shaming', *JSOT* 49 (1991), pp. 47-76 (47).

31. Bechtel explains that the early anthropological distinction between 'shame cultures' and 'guilt cultures' depicted shame cultures as amoral and populated by people who only responded to external sanctions without any developed capacity for internal pressures from either conscience or feelings of guilt. Resisting this notion, she explains that 'both shame and guilt arise from external pressure and internal pressure'; see Bechtel, 'Shame as a Sanction', p. 51.

32. Bechtel, 'Shame as a Sanction', p. 51; see Lyn M. Bechtel, 'What if Dinah is not Raped? (Genesis 34)', *JSOT* 62 (1994), pp. 19-36 (19).

33. Bechtel, 'Shame as a Sanction', p. 53. Bechtel also refers explicitly to 'a shame-honour society' in 'What if Dinah is not Raped?', p. 29.

Israelite society, which is, of course, impossible. Bechtel thus analyzes linguistic evidence and points out abundant shame vocabulary. She also asserts that shame vocabulary is unconnected to guilt vocabulary, which legitimates her 'prima facie case for investigating shame as a separate, distinctive emotional experience and as separate means of social control'.[34]

Bechtel does not always highlight gender aspects in her work. Hence, her anthropological approach does not necessarily or in every case qualify as feminist. For instance, in her work on shame in the judicial system in Deuteronomy and in biblical political and military contexts,[35] Bechtel describes male characters as both executers and recipients of shaming. Although she acknowledges that a public shaming ceremony is more acutely shameful if performed by a woman on a man,[36] Bechtel does not expand on this observation. In her study on group-orientation and shame in Genesis 34, Bechtel's emphasis shifts somewhat. Investigating the events surrounding Jacob's daughter Dinah, Bechtel references anthropological ideas *and* discusses and challenges feminist interpretations that depict Dinah as rape victim.[37] While Bechtel's application of anthropological data and models is clear, her feminist purpose is more equivocal. Indeed, the case might be made that her interpretations are only tenuously feminist, as in the sense raised by Strathern: namely, that her anthropological feminism is only 'feminist' insofar as being of a woman and about a woman (Dinah).

Quite different is Claudia Camp's article on honour-shame,[38] which applies the anthropological model to the apocryphal book of Ben Sira but which includes also wider references to the Hebrew Bible. Camp's location as feminist interpreter and her focus on women is clear from the outset. She articulates her aims as, 'recovering aspects of women's lives' and as gaining 'understanding of women's lives and their place in a man's world—and in a man's symbol system'.[39] Like the above-cited Bible scholars of

---

34. Bechtel, 'Shame as a Sanction', p. 55. For her analysis of the Hebrew root *'nh* to establish that shame is in the forefront of Genesis 34; see Bechtel, 'What if Dinah is Not Raped?', pp. 23-27. She uses linguistic analysis in conjunction with anthropological data to illuminate social values behind the biblical text.

35. Bechtel, 'Shame as a Sanction', pp. 63-67.

36. Bechtel, 'Shame as a Sanction', p. 61.

37. Bechtel, 'What if Dinah is not Raped?', p. 20.

38. Camp, 'Understanding a Patriarchy'. The aim of the volume in which Camp's essay appears is to shed light on the 'literary images and social situations' of women in antiquity (Preface, p. xi). Literary investigation, however, outweighs social-scientific investigation overall; see Claudia Camp, 'Understanding a Patriarchy: Women in Second-Century Jerusalem through the Eyes of Ben Sira', in Amy-Jill Levine (ed.), *'Women Like This': New Perspectives on Jewish Women in the Greco-Roman World* (Atlanta: Scholars Press, 1991), pp. 1-40.

39. Camp, 'Understanding a Patriarchy', pp. 1-2.

the 1990s, Camp assumes that Second Temple Period texts were embedded within patriarchal cultural contexts in which honour and shame functioned as pivotal social values. She subscribes to the legitimacy of cultural continuity and accepts the claim of Mediterranean cultural anthropologists (like Pitt-Rivers) that behaviour, observed in small-scale, group-oriented contemporary communities, changed little for centuries.[40] As Camp is dealing with ancient literature, the empirical method of participant observation that is characteristic of cultural anthropology is closed to her. Instead, she examines meticulously the biblical text, pointing out evidence for the centrality of honour and shame and drawing parallels with societies in Mediterranean field studies. She discovers that Ben Sira has a nineteen percent higher concentration of shame vocabulary than other biblical books, vindicating the notion of a preoccupation with this value, as asserted also of modern honour-shame communities.[41] She also finds parallel connections between shame and women's sexuality. Camp observes that the text of Ben Sira witnesses a near-neurotic preoccupation with women's dangerous sexuality precisely because it is typical for Mediterranean men to fear the consequences of women's shame-conferring sexuality. This, in turn, then, justifies the text's expression of men's suspicion and of their need to control women.

Camp's feminist purpose is unambiguous and much of her analysis is devoted to demonstrating how, just like that of modern honour-shame societies, the world behind the words of Ben Sira severely restricts women's lives. Camp comments on Ben Sira's 'rather extreme commentary on controlling the sexuality of one's daughters'[42] and this observation leads her to reinterpret the common understanding of Ben Sira 7.24. The verse reads: 'Do not let your face shine towards [your daughters]'. It is widely interpreted as advising against paternal forbearance or lenience. But Camp, instead, argues that due to the rigid spatial separation of the sexes in Mediterranean honour-shame societies, '[t]here would have been little opportunity for such paternal indulgence'. Consequently, she suggests an alternative interpretation: 'Since the actions of children, virtuous or otherwise, advert to their parents, we should probably read our present stich to mean something like "do not count on your daughters' capacity to bring you honor".'[43]

---

40. Camp, 'Understanding a Patriarchy', p. 2. Camp states that 'the recent work in cultural anthropology that focusses *[sic]* on social-psychological patterns in the circum-Mediterranean area' is critical to her analysis (p. 2).

41. Camp, 'Understanding a Patriarchy', p. 5 n. 16.

42. Camp, 'Understanding a Patriarchy', p. 34.

43. Camp, 'Understanding a Patriarchy', p. 34. Similarly, again because Camp accepts that the emphasis of honour-shame societies on female continence holds validity for Ben Sira, she also recommends that the term translated 'sensible' and used of a

The Mediterranean studies, thus, provide evidence for the acute shame that males experience when their female relatives act in sexually inappropriate ways. Reading Ben Sira in the light of this shame propensity, Camp shows that again and again Ben Sira refers to daughters as inciting anxiety and fear of shame in their fathers (Ben Sira 7.25; 42.9-10). In Ben Sira, so Camp argues, women and daughters act as 'over-determined symbols of male honor'.[44] Camp's essay illustrates persuasively how anthropological findings can be effectively combined with feminist criticism to illuminate social values pertaining to women of ancient literature. Moreover, Camp sees male anxiety about women and the male effort to restrict female movement as social developments that become increasingly pronounced during the Second Temple Period.[45] As a feminist, she is openly troubled by these historical developments as they manifest in the book of Ben Sira.[46]

O'Grady is another feminist scholar who integrates anthropological concepts into her exegesis. She works with anthropological notions of purity, pollution and taboo[47] and focuses her analysis particularly on the binary of

---

daughter (Ben Sira 22.4) has 'the perversely narrow sense of "faithful to her husband"' (p. 34).

44. Camp, 'Understanding a Patriarchy', p. 38.

45. Camp argues that Ben Sira reflects more oppressive and more restrictive attitudes to women than (particularly) early Hebrew Bible texts; see Camp, 'Understanding a Patriarchy', p. 34. This has also been an observation of social historians; see Leonie J. Archer, 'The Role of Jewish Women in the Religion, Ritual and Cult of Graeco-Roman Palestine', in Averil Cameron and Amélie Kuhrt (eds.), *Images of Women in Antiquity* (London: Routledge, 2nd edn, 1983), pp. 273-87.

46. Other feminist biblical scholars have also utilized the honour-shame value complex in their investigations, e.g., J. Cheryl Exum, *Fragmented Women: Feminist (Sub) versions of Biblical Narratives* (JSOTSup, 163; Sheffield: Sheffield Academic Press, 1993), pp. 150-51, 166. For a more extensive study, see Gale A. Yee, *Poor Banished Children of Eve: Woman as Evil in the Hebrew Bible* (Minneapolis: Fortress Press, 2003), pp. 40-48. This again tends to take the form of consolidating the picture of a firmly patriarchal social and ideological context.

47. Kathleen O'Grady, 'The Semantics of Taboo: Menstrual Prohibitions in the Hebrew Bible', in Kristin De Troyer *et al.* (eds.), *Wholly Woman Holy Blood: A Feminist Critique of Purity and Impurity* (Studies in Antiquity and Christianity; Harrisburg, PA: Trinity Press International, 2001), pp. 1-28. The same volume contains two additional feminist readings of purity texts in the Hebrew Bible: Deborah Ellens, 'Menstrual Impurity and Innovation in Leviticus 15', pp. 29-43; Kristin De Troyer, 'Blood: A Threat to Holiness or toward (Another) Holiness?', pp. 45-64. The latter chapter focuses on Leviticus 12. There are earlier interpretations of Douglas's work paying attention to women and gender; see, e.g., Adriana Destro, 'The Witness of Times: An Anthropological Reading of *Niddah*', in Sawyer (ed.), *Reading Leviticus*, pp. 124-43; Jonathan Magonet, '"But If It Is A Girl, She Is Unclean For Twice Seven Days": The Riddle of Leviticus 12.5', in Sawyer (ed.), *Reading Leviticus*, pp. 144-52. However, these pieces are not feminist in orientation. Another example is David Biale, 'Does Blood Have Gender in Jewish

female sanctity and female impurity in biblical texts. The apparent coexistence of sanctity and impurity is central to taboo and particularly relevant to women whose menstrual blood, in terms of its depiction in the Hebrew Bible, has associations with *both* sacred life-giving and profound pollution. O'Grady asserts in explicitly feminist rhetoric that it is 'not likely incidental that the body of a woman "engenders" the sacred since in a patriarchal-defined society her body necessarily exceeds the boundaries and borders established by the (male) normative order'.[48] As O'Grady explains, the notion that menstrual bleeding is a source of impurity is expressed particularly by the Hebrew word *niddah*, which is indicative of profound pollution and almost always associated with menstruation. In her investigation O'Grady considers the idea proposed by some feminists that menstruation is not prohibitive but occasion for celebration and a time of rest from chores and sexual 'duties'.[49] But she rejects this positive reading just as she rejects very negative interpretations of menstruation in Leviticus, instead utilizing anthropological data to defend a more nuanced and complex depiction.[50]

In her work, O'Grady refers to several anthropologists: Mary Douglas, James G. Frazer, and Franz Steiner. Steeped in their anthropological discussions on taboo with its confluences of sacred and polluted, O'Grady explains that all things taboo require separation.[51] In line with this explanation, Leviticus 15 refers to the separation of the impure *niddah* and includes the root *hzr*, a word also used for the consecrated *nazir*, or Nazirite (Numbers 6). Both Leviticus 15 and Numbers 6, so O'Grady, hint at an overarching conceptual ordering system, as proposed by Douglas. According to this system, *both* the polluted (menstruant) and the sacred (*nazir*) are set aside or separated, allowing for the possibility that both can fulfil religious or ceremonial purposes.[52] O'Grady explains:

Culture?', in Barbara Baert (ed.), *The Woman with the Blood Flow (Mark 5:24-34): Narrative, Iconic, and Anthropological Spaces* (Leuven: Peeters, 2006), pp. 335-55. Biale refers to Douglas. Although the chapter appears in a section entitled 'Anthropological Space', the emphasis is literary. Biale pays close attention to gender, but he does not self-identify as a feminist.

48. O'Grady, 'The Semantics of Taboo', p. 28.

49. O'Grady's explicitly feminist critique of feminist interpretations brings home the important point that 'feminist interpretation' is no univocal phenomenon. As mentioned above, Bechtel also refutes some feminist interpretations of Genesis 34. As already alluded to, however, Bechtel's feminism is less easy to defend than Camp's or O'Grady's.

50. O'Grady, 'The Semantics of Taboo', p. 22. O'Grady characterizes such a proposal as 'noble in its intent', but as no more than 'a simplistic inversion of the standard biblical reading of menstruation as a state of defilement', failing, like its opposite, to capture 'the logic of separation inherent in both [sanctity and impurity]' (p. 22).

51. O'Grady, 'The Semantics of Taboo', pp. 15-17.

52. O'Grady, 'The Semantics of Taboo', p. 17.

The specific 'religious' valence of division is lost in the English translation, which simply offers the word 'separate'. Further, and importantly, the verb form is linked to *n-z-r*, from which the word *nazir* or *nazirite*, that is, 'holy person', derives. Here, *h-z-r* is applied directly to the menstruant; yet this verb form is used in only one other place in the entirety of the Hebrew Scriptures, where it is traditionally understood and translated as '*sacred separation*', since it is applied directly to the *nazir*, that is, the holy person of Numbers (Num. 6.2-3, 5-6, 12).[53]

This linguistic observation can be traced back to Douglas's notion of contingent relationships underlying every cultural order and determining who or what is expelled, thereby helping to establish societal cohesion. Famously, Douglas states that nothing is sacred or defiled in or of itself. She elaborates: 'Uncleanness is matter out of place, we must approach it through order. Uncleanness or dirt is that which must not be included if a pattern is to be maintained. The recognition of a pattern is a first step toward insight into pollution. It involves us in no clear-cut distinction between sacred and secular'.[54] Derived from this is the dictum that a rose is a flower in a garden but a weed in a vegetable patch because the system determines status and boundaries. O'Grady uses Douglas's conceptual categories of purity and pollution alongside textual analysis to make holistic sense of apparently divergent ideas in Leviticus 15 and Numbers 6. In this way for O'Grady, following Douglas, it is not the case that 'impure' and 'holy' are the same but, instead, 'they are constructed from the same (and not oppositional) logic and thereby are inscribed within one another'.[55] O'Grady, then, applies anthropological concepts pertaining to purity and pollution to explore the depiction of menstruation and the status of women. Her position is that menstruants are not unequivocally defiled any more than that they are unequivocally holy. Rather, both notions are inscribed in the biblical text. O'Grady's nuanced analysis of biblical texts, incorporating anthropological notions, transpires in a feminist essay that, first, brings a widely marginalized experience common to women (namely menstruation) to the fore and, second, redeems menstruation from being regarded as only a major pollution.

Bechtel, Camp, and O'Grady, then, have adopted anthropological concepts popular among biblical scholars more generally. They reconstruct biblical texts as a plausible cultural backdrop of values that pertain particularly to women. Bechtel's feminist orientation could be questioned, whereas Camp and O'Grady self-identify as feminist. Two more biblical scholars to mention briefly are Tikva Frymer-Kensky and Heather A. McKay.

---

53. O'Grady, 'The Semantics of Taboo', p. 17.
54. Douglas, *Purity and Danger*, p. 41.
55. O'Grady, 'The Semantics of Taboo', p. 27.

Frymer-Kensky had a prolific career publishing in ancient Near Eastern, Hebrew Bible, and Jewish studies. She experimented with a range of methods as is aptly illustrated in a collection of her essays, categorized under the three headings of 'Comparative Culture', 'Feminist Perspectives', and 'Theologies'.[56] Given her astonishing breadth of expertise, Frymer-Kensky focused on biblical women and law in particular, integrating these themes into a wider and comparative ancient Near Eastern scheme. In this way, her work contributes to a rich understanding of the human communities and their social values that gave rise to the texts of the Hebrew Bible.[57] Frymer-Kensky's inspiration, however, is drawn in the first instance from ancient *texts*, not from modern anthropological studies. Also, while some of her earlier work is firmly culturally-comparative in focus, her later and more firmly and explicitly feminist work demonstrates primarily close *literary* analysis.[58]

McKay's publications on the Hebrew Bible are characterized, first, by her consistent self-identification as a feminist and, second, by a diversity of creative and experimental approaches. In the course of a vibrant career, McKay has also incorporated findings from anthropological studies, focusing particularly on the area of clothing and bodily adornment.[59] McKay maintains that abundant cultural anthropological studies confirm clothing as a 'specialised form of human communication' that reinforces a 'society's traditional beliefs, customs and values—including, particularly, gender and status'.[60] Consequently, she argues, '[b]ecause dress and insignia are referred to and described in the text [of the Hebrew Bible], they provide

56. See Tikva Frymer-Kensky, *Studies in Bible and Feminist Criticism* (JPS Scholar of Distinction Series; Philadelphia: Jewish Publication Society, 2006).

57. See especially Tikva Frymer-Kensky, 'Pollution, Purification, and Purgation in Biblical Israel', in Carol L. Meyers and Michael P. O'Connor (eds.), *The Word of the Lord Shall Go Forth: Essays in Honor of D.N. Freedman* (Winona Lake, IN: Eisenbrauns, 1983), pp. 399-414; 'Virginity in the Bible', in Victor H. Matthews, Bernard M. Levinson and Tikva Frymer-Kensky (eds.), *Gender and Law in the Hebrew Bible and the Ancient Near East* (JSOTSup, 262; Sheffield: Sheffield Academic Press, 1998), pp. 79-96.

58. The two above-cited essays illustrate this distinction.

59. Heather A. McKay, 'The Gendering of Display in the Hebrew Bible', in Bob Becking and Meindert Dijkstra (eds.), *On Reading Prophetic Texts: Gender-Specific and Related Studies in Memory of Fokkelien van Dijk-Hemmes* (Leiden: E.J. Brill, 1996), pp. 169-99; 'Gendering the Body: Clothes Maketh the (Wo)Man', in Robert Hannaford and Jan Jobling (eds.), *Theology and the Body* (Leominster: Gracewing, Fowler, Wright, 1999), pp. 84-104.

60. McKay, 'Gendering the Body', pp. 85, 171. McKay lists numerous examples from the biblical text of garments that represent the granting of honour and removal of garments the conferral of shame, alongside analogues from cultural anthropological studies; see McKay, 'The Gendering of Display', pp. 181-83.

actual evidence about life in the narrative worlds depicted'.[61] McKay, moreover, acknowledges being in solidarity with other feminists in her endeavour 'to search for contrived female silences in the biblical texts'.[62] Focusing on descriptions of women's garments, such as Tamar's torn robe and Rizpah's spreading out of mourning sackcloth, she observes that women are often marginalized and silenced whereas '[t]he garments speak silently, but speak they do',[63] not only of women and their lives and roles but also of 'the symbolic universe of the male controllers of society'.[64] McKay thus draws from anthropology to reclaim those parts of biblical women's lives and roles that are expressed if only peripherally and non-vocally in descriptions of the garments they wear. In various ways, then, Bechtel, Camp, O'Grady, and McKay deploy anthropological data to fill and bring resonance to the silences and gaps surrounding women in the Hebrew Bible.

Feminist Hebrew Bible Scholars Using an Anthropological Technique

Other feminist Bible scholars rely less on anthropological concepts but employ distinctive anthropological techniques in their study of biblical texts and readers. More precisely, these scholars use qualitative research methods that are reminiscent of anthropological fieldwork. Admittedly, the few Bible scholars who engage in such approaches do not explicitly classify their work as being anthropological. One example is South African biblical scholar Gerald O. West who is probably better classified as a liberationist rather than a feminist exegete.[65] West coins the phrases 'reading with' and 'ordinary readers' to describe his method of contextual criticism.[66] Using this method, West reads with sometimes non-literate Christians in his native South Africa, especially with those whose voices are not usually heard in the academy and who come from socio-economically disadvantaged, disempowered, and marginalized communities. He calls these co-readers who are always untrained in biblical studies 'ordinary readers'. West characterizes this approach as contextually-specific liberation theology, and he

61. McKay, 'Gendering the Body', p. 93.
62. McKay, 'The Gendering of Display', p. 69 n. 1.
63. McKay, 'Gendering the Body', p. 93.
64. McKay, 'Gendering the Body', p. 99.
65. Gerald West is a founding and central figure of both the Contextual Bible Study project and the Ujamaa Centre of the University of KwaZulu-Natal. Both are committed to a wide range of South African social justice concerns. One of these, the Tamar Campaign, central to which is the shared reading of 2 Samuel 13, is particularly devoted to redressing gender-based injustice; see http://ujamaa.ukzn.ac.za/WhatUJAMAAdoes/campaigns_copy1.aspx#../Libraries/20150528_Worker_Sunday_Launch/15.sflb.ashx.
66. Gerald O. West, *The Academy of the Poor: Towards a Dialogical Reading of the Bible* (Sheffield: Sheffield Academic Press, 1999).

strongly emphasizes both direct encounter and dialogue. His assertion is that when socially-engaged biblical scholars read with ordinary readers, the interpretations and voices of ordinary readers are validated and included in the academy. While West does not state that his method is influenced by anthropology, his approach has some affinity with Strathern's above-cited recommendation that an ethnographic researcher must 'remain open to people's emotional and personal lives' and then translate findings into written studies.[67]

Interestingly, West's method has influenced a few feminist exegetes, notably Avaren Ipsen. Ipsen's book, in which she acknowledges her indebtedness to West,[68] presents the results of her interviews and collaborative interpretations of biblical texts with members of the Sex Worker Outreach Project (SWOP). Ipsen states that her book aims to benefit the 'self-defined struggle' of the SWOP members, which is comparable with West's aims to benefit ordinary readers.[69] She asks: 'How would the interpretations [of these texts] differ if done from the standpoint of sex worker activists?'[70] Her study blends biblical scholarship with empirical research by juxtaposing scholarly interpretations of Joshua 2 and 6, the story of Rahab, and 1 Kgs 3.16-28, the story of Solomon and the two prostitutes, with the readings of the SWOP members, as they emerged in interviews, reading groups, and conversations. In accordance with the anthropological principles of qualitative research methods, Ipsen conducts her own direct empirical investigation. Like West, she instigates the situations in which she shares her expertise in biblical scholarship with a select community of readers. In anthropology, it is more typical for the empirical investigator to integrate, observe, and conduct interviews but not to construct situations comparable to the collaborative reading workshops of West and Ipsen.[71] Ipsen thus creates a forum for the sex workers' perspectives and records and publishes the results in an academically respected forum.

---

67. Strathern, 'An Awkward Relationship', p. 289.
68. Avaren Ipsen, *Sex Working and the Bible* (London: Equinox, 2009), p. 90.
69. Ipsen, *Sex Working*, p. 34.
70. Ipsen, *Sex Working*, p. 2.
71. Arguably, the distinction is not as profound as it may appear. West's and Ipsen's method, like that of anthropologists, also involves extensive incorporation into the community of the subjects they are researching while also remaining distinct from them. Accordingly, West is not an ordinary reader and Ipsen not a sex worker. Also, while anthropologists may claim to be objective observers, their presence is likely to affect the situations of the human communities being observed. While anthropologists may not create the kinds of collaborative reading workshops constructed by West and Ipsen, they frequently conduct interviews. Hence, there is no equivalence of method, but there is affinity.

Ipsen's investigation demonstrates the significant differences between the interpretations of the SWOP members and those of scholars. The SWOP members read the story of Solomon and the two prostitutes in fresh and provocative ways that challenge long-established scholarly assumptions and biases about the meaning of this narrative. Most scholarly readings, for example, downplay the women's profession and emphasize instead their role as mothers. They designate one prostitute as a 'good' and the other as a 'bad' mother. They also emphasize 'Solomon's virtuoso display of wisdom'[72] and the idea that this tale addresses 'a situation where [even] two prostitutes have equal access to the law'.[73] The SWOP members drastically overturn these points of emphasis, redefining the female characters as prostitutes *because they are mothers* who try to support their children. Ipsen enhances this sympathetic view of the two women by proposing that they are like 'biblical widows needing justice, economic or otherwise, [because they are] among the very types of women who might resort to prostitution to survive economically'.[74] The SWOP members also have a different opinion about the legal system as it is depicted in the narrative. According to the sex workers' experience, the legal system is prone to characterize them as 'criminals' and 'unfit mothers'. It regards them as 'risky, corrupt'.[75] Thus, the SWOP members consider the women's rivalry as atypical but the 'element of violent abusive treatment by the legal establishment', namely threatening the child with death, as familiar.[76]

Most importantly, so Ipsen notes, the SWOP members regard 'Solomon's court a toxic justice system for prostitutes'.[77] According to this interpretation, sympathy and solidarity is extended to *both* mothers and not only the 'good' mother. The SWOP members identify the legal system as villainous, as personified by Solomon. Hence, one respondent, Veronica, states that 'he is allowed to even suggest murdering a baby without being a bad guy but if she calls his bluff she is an evil mother'.[78] Ipsen's project is thus inclusive of sex workers and positions their interpretations alongside those of biblical scholars. As Ipsen points out, the inclusion of these lay readers redresses their exclusion and discrimination in the meaning-making process of the Bible. Her study fulfils a liberationist-feminist purpose,[79] and it

---

72. Ipsen, *Sex Workers*, p. 91.
73. Ipsen, *Sex Workers*, p. 100.
74. Ipsen, *Sex Workers*, p. 92.
75. Ipsen, *Sex Workers*, p. 97.
76. Ipsen, *Sex Workers*, p. 97.
77. Ipsen, *Sex Workers*, p. 98.
78. Ipsen, *Sex Workers*, pp. 101-102.
79. Ipsen, *Sex Workers*, p. 206.

utilizes successfully a popular research tool of anthropological studies, even though Ipsen does not explicitly make this connection.[80]

Let me mention briefly another feminist Bible scholar who combines feminist biblical scholarship with qualitative research. Pamela J. Milne is explicit about her feminist research interest and her efforts towards transformation of society toward justice, stating that she wants to 'make life better for women and other marginalised groups' in a context where 'the lived experiences of some women [are] the experiences of subordination in male-dominated societies'.[81] Milne argues that feminist advocacy is essential but also lamentably under-developed even in places in which it would be expected, such as among students in university women's studies programmes. Milne identifies her method as being part of reader-response and audience criticism, as well as fitting firmly within the social sciences.[82] She also identifies her research as involving human subjects and thus as a qualitative study.[83]

Milne defines her research as an endeavour to discover whether feminist studies and gender theory have made any demonstrable impact among lay student readers of the Bible. She characterizes her method as listening to a selected group of female and male, religious and non-religious students as they interpret Judges 11, the narrative of Jephthah's daughter. Her study demonstrates empirically that the students do not apply categories from gender and feminist studies to the interpretation of this biblical tale. Her findings disappoint her but they also legitimate her advocacy for a continuing need for feminism. As with West and Ipsen, Milne's research method imbues the biblical text with a refreshingly purposeful relevance even when the findings are disappointing.

---

80. The method of 'reading with' continues to be practiced by feminist Bible interpreters and is moving back into non-Western contexts. Two examples are, first, Musa W. Dube's publication on Bible readings of ordinary readers in Botswana; see her 'Readings of *Semoya*: Batswana Women's Interpretations of Matt 15:21-28', *Semeia* 73 (1996), pp. 111-30; and, second, a paper delivered by Nancy Tan and Lai Kwen Hui, entitled 'Hong Kong Sex Workers: Mothers Reading 1 Kings 3:16-28', delivered during the International Congress of Ethnic Chinese Biblical Scholars (ICECBS) on August 20, 2014. It is available at http://www.icebshongkong2014.wix.com/icebs#schedule/c/enr. This paper replicates Ipsen's qualitative research method but in a subcultural context in Hong Kong.

81. Pamela J. Milne, 'Son of a Prostitute and Daughter of a Warrior: What Do You Think the Story in Judges 11 Means?', *Lectio Difficilior* 2 (2009): 1-26 (6); available at http://www.lectio.unibe.ch/09_2/pdf/milne_son_of_a_prostitute.pdf. Milne does not refer to West but does use the designation 'ordinary readers' particularly associated with his method (1).

82. Milne, 'Son of a Prostitute', pp. 1-2.

83. Milne, 'Son of a Prostitute', pp. 5-6. Milne provides a full set of questions given to her human research subjects (Appendix, pp. 23-24).

Concluding Comments

Anthropology is a broad designation encompassing a plethora of sub-disciplines. This essay has focused on cultural anthropology, which is characterized by its distinctive method of empirical research, or fieldwork, in a wide range of human communities. The discipline evidences long-standing intersections with academic feminism and even more sustained ones with biblical studies. The adoption by feminist Hebrew Bible scholars of anthropological data, or concepts or techniques, is still relatively isolated by comparison.

I have focused here particularly on feminist biblical scholars who use anthropological data to illuminate either the social world reflected in biblical texts or particular readers of biblical texts. Interest in women's lives, which includes social worlds, is, of course, ubiquitous to feminist Bible scholarship. Yet relatively few feminist Bible scholars emphasize studies or methods from anthropology. Bechtel, whose utilization of anthropological data is clear, occasionally focuses on biblical women (e.g. Dinah) and on how feminist interpretations may be enhanced with recourse to anthropological models.[84] Arguably, however, feminist advocacy is not especially foregrounded by Bechtel. Frymer-Kensky, on the other hand, applies both culturally-comparative and feminist approaches but not often in combination. A number of biblical scholars, however, do apply anthropological research with a distinctly feminist purpose. These include Camp, O'Grady, and McKay.

A smaller group of feminist interpreters, including Ipsen and Milne, has applied an experimental technique of incorporating data obtained directly from discrete and specific groups into the analysis of biblical texts. Their approach has some affinity with direct observation, or fieldwork, which is acknowledged obliquely by Milne but not by Ipsen who attributes indebtedness to West's method. Whether this technique can be credited directly to the discipline of anthropology has to remain speculative since it is not being explicitly acknowledged. Yet it strikes me as highly likely.[85]

The contributions of feminist biblical scholars are manifold. First, the works of Camp and McKay demonstrate that although women in biblical

---

84. Bechtel, 'What If Dinah is Not Raped?'

85. I also suggest that the recent influx of culturally particularizing approaches in feminist biblical criticism draws from anthropology. Examples of culturally particularizing approaches include the contributions to a section on 'African Feminist/Gender-Based Biblical Interpretations', in Musa W. Dube, Andrew M. Mbuvi and Dora R. Mbuwayesango (eds.), *Postcolonial Perspectives in African Biblical Interpretations* (Atlanta: SBL, 2012); Gale A. Yee, '"She Stood in Tears Amid the Alien Corn": Ruth, the Perpetual Foreigner and Model Minority', in Randall C. Bailey, Tat-siong Benny Liew and Fernando F. Segovia (eds.), *They Were All Together in One Place? Toward Minority Biblical Criticism* (Atlanta: SBL, 2009), pp. 119-40.

texts are marginal and often without a voice, the tools of anthropology and parallels drawn from somewhat comparable contemporary societies provide helpful information. Hence, especially Camp, but also Bechtel point to the abundance of shame terminology to legitimate the claim that the text under investigation is from an honour-shame society. As Camp notes, a similar persistence of verbally alluding to shame has been documented in contemporary honour-shame societies. This, in turn, gives her a platform to explain other features of the text, particularly the negative articulations concerning daughters. By bringing in anthropological data, she illuminates the world *behind* the text of Ben Sira and makes visible the male obsession with honour that accounts in large part for men's repression of women. It is informative about women in antiquity whose voices may not be represented directly, but some information about their lives, roles, and status can be uncovered.

Probing different data but with a similar purpose, McKay, too, is resigned about the marginal status of women in biblical texts that are in the first instance for, by, and about men. Again, however, by taking note of descriptions of women's garments and by once more drawing parallels with comparable functions of garments in a wide variety of contemporary cultural contexts, McKay gives voice and substance to women in biblical narratives. In this way Camp's and McKay's applications of anthropological data aid the imagination and give rise to plausible images of women in antiquity. The solid data of anthropology thus conveys some semblance of solidity to the world from which the biblical texts emerged.

O'Grady's contribution, meanwhile, focuses on theoretical concepts derived from anthropological studies. These pertain to the tendency in human societies to order the world on the basis of binary categories, including sacred/profane, and to the discomfort aroused by an ambiguous concept such as taboo, which appears to combine sacred and profane. O'Grady explores a topic pertaining to women, namely menstruation. Her reading is illuminating because it makes sense of the co-existence of divergent associations with menstruation. In this way, with recourse to Douglas in particular, O'Grady succeeds in explaining difficult texts. Again, she does so by opening up the possibility of catching a glimpse of a worldview from antiquity.

Of course, while these works offer possibilities for better understanding social and even cognitive structures of the past, some legitimate questions arise. For instance, can and should biblical texts be treated like windows into the ancient world? This has been called the 'referential fallacy', alerting to the erroneous idea that any text can be neutral or objective, or free from conscious and unconscious ideologies.[86] To put it differently, how

---

86. Tina Pippin, 'Ideology, Ideological Criticism, and the Bible', *CRBS* 4 (1996), pp. 51-78 (52).

well can texts stand in for fieldwork? While Bechtel, Camp, O'Grady, and McKay read the texts under investigation very closely, with careful attention to Hebrew vocabulary, it is worth asking how reliable these ancient texts truly are in terms of capturing and, therefore, for reconstructing, sociocultural contexts. In addition, how legitimately can findings from recent field studies be applied to ancient text? Can any case be made for continuity between communities of antiquity and modernity? After all, on account of the possibility that ethnographic research in small-scale, face-to-face societies captures values akin to those reflected in ancient texts, anthropological studies have had a considerable impact on biblical studies. This ought to be balanced, however, with some reservations and acknowledgment of limitations, as to significant cultural discontinuity, not least because the existing biblical texts are only those that have survived. As has been widely pointed out, surviving texts from antiquity may not necessarily describe social practices that correspond to what actually took place. Moreover, what they contain might provide at best 'access to the privileged conception of reality of a literate stratum of society',[87] as opposed to access to the wider, less privileged (including female) populace.[88]

In addition to these problems of biblical (and other textual) scholars, there is another layer of questions pertaining to anthropological, including feminist-anthropological, data and methods. For instance, how well can anthropologists, as outsiders, represent the communities they research? Do anthropologists project their own, most often Western-centric, assumptions and biases? Are they inappropriately universalizing feminist ideas and agendas? Such questions pertain also to biblical scholars, such as Ipsen and Milne, who use techniques of empirical investigation, and read with, observe, and interview members of distinct groups. Ipsen and Milne focus less on the world *behind* and more squarely at the world *in front of* the biblical text. On the one hand, their interpretations of biblical texts are fresh and interesting, very much distinct from those more typical of the academy. On the other, the reports of alternative readings are nonetheless filtered and represented and possibly distorted by them—even if unconsciously. An analogous criticism has been levelled at second-wave feminists by feminists of

---

87. Keith W. Whitelam, 'The Social World of the Bible', in John Barton (ed.), *The Cambridge Companion to Biblical Interpretation* (Cambridge: Cambridge University Press, 1998), pp. 35-49 (41).

88. Feminist scholars have often pointed to the dearth of female-authored ancient written sources. Ross Shepard Kraemer laments that 'there is virtually no first-hand, direct data (in the sense of trustworthy first-person accounts comparable to the wealth of those available for elite, educated men)'; see her seminal *Unreliable Witnesses: Religion, Gender and History in the Greco-Roman Mediterranean* (Oxford: Oxford University Press, 2011), p. 5.

minority groups, which has given rise to intersectional feminist criticism, such as womanism.

Many of these red flags regarding either the referential fallacy or the limitation of representing readers of a different socio-cultural location than one's own have been raised. The cautionary notes raised by anthropologists with regard to the unqualified application of models to diverse cultural contexts (Herzfeld; Wikan), or to the application of anthropological concepts to biblical texts (Wilson), as discussed above, make clear that any interdisciplinary endeavour requires considerable range and agility of expertise. Is it likely to give rise to (particularly) territorial resistance from scholars of the discipline being appropriated? Yes. Is it not the case that most feminist readings will generate some resistance from some quarters? Yes again. It is also the case, however, that anthropological approaches to feminist Bible studies generate highly creative and persuasively illuminating readings of texts that are particularly perplexing and inaccessible, including with regard to women.

Another striking point about this overview is that anthropological approaches to feminist Bible study are not very prevalent. A similar point about the dearth has been made about feminist biblical archaeology. I agree with Susan Ackerman's assessment that the overwhelming majority of feminist Hebrew Bible scholars have tended to focus on literary-critical rather than on what she calls historically-oriented analysis. The dominant thrust, so Ackerman, probes 'the role literary-critical methodologies might play in illuminating issues concerning women and gender, describing especially the means and techniques by which biblical stories are told and the impact of these means and techniques upon the stories' depictions of women'. A much less developed branch, meanwhile, probes 'what we can ascertain from Hebrew Bible texts regarding the actual lives and experiences of ancient Israelite women'.[89]

Ackerman's case goes some way towards explaining why anthropological approaches, like archaeological ones, are less well represented in feminist Hebrew Bible studies than approaches with a purely literary focus. Given the long and strong establishment of cultural anthropology in Hebrew Bible studies, however, alongside the growth of feminist anthropology as a discrete discipline, especially since the late 1980s,[90] there is reason for optimism that anthropological approaches in feminist Hebrew Bible studies are likely to take a cue from feminist archaeology, which already incorporates sociological and ethnographical data in order to make fuller sense of ancient human cultural remains, and go from strength to strength.

---

89. Susan Ackerman, 'Recent Hebrew Bible Scholarship on Gender and the Contribution of Archaeology', *Near Eastern Archaeology* 6.4 (2003), pp. 172-84 (172).

90. Nuzman, 'Twenty-Five Years of Feminist Anthropology'.

What may be next? There is some need for in-depth synthetic studies of feminist anthropological work on gender and biblical texts; that is, for some equivalent to Sarah Milledge Nelson's monograph on archaeology and gender.[91] Likewise, there is considerable scope for more intersectional approaches: such as, for feminist African biblical scholars to adapt or reclaim anthropological data from African contexts, or to conduct qualitative research.[92] In the current climate that threatens the academic humanities significantly and with biblical studies continually reinventing itself with new interdisciplinary and multidisciplinary configurations, anthropological approaches in feminist Hebrew Bible studies are likely to gather increased momentum in future years.

---

91. Nelson, *Gender in Archaeology*.
92. See, e.g., Dube, 'Readings of *Semoya*'.

7

THE GOD OF THE FATHERS ENCOUNTERS FEMINISM: OVERTURE FOR A FEMINIST OLD TESTAMENT THEOLOGY[1]

Phyllis A. Bird

I understand theology to *describe* reflection on the meaning of religious experience and efforts to articulate systems of religious belief. It seeks patterns of coherence and is concerned with norms and truth claims. The qualifier *Old Testament* orients this activity to the Hebrew scriptures—and places it within a tradition of Christian theological reflection. I use the traditional Christian terminology to identify the avenue by which I approach the subject of biblical theology.[2] This theology cannot be Christian and Christian theology cannot be biblical without the witness of the Hebrew scriptures. And although that witness, for a Christian interpreter, is necessarily bound to the canonical witness of the early Church and read through the lens of Christian faith, I believe it is compromised and distorted when it is not first received as Israel's witness.[3] The responsibility of Old Testament

---

1. This chapter is a shortened and considerably modified version of my previously published essay entitled 'Old Testament Theology and the God of the Fathers: Reflections on Biblical Theology from a North American Feminist Perspective', in Paul Hanson, Bernd Janowsky and Michael Welker (eds.), *Biblische Theologie: Beiträge des Symposiums Das Alte Testament und die Kultur der Moderne anlässlich des 100. Geburtstags Gerhard von Rad (1901–1971) Heidelberg, 19-21 Oktober 2001* (Münster: LIT Verlag, 2005), pp. 69-107. I wish to acknowledge the editor of this volume, Susanne Scholz, who was helped by her research assistant, David A. Schones, for the editorial modifications of this essay.

2. I make explicit acknowledgment of my Christian identity, because I do not think that biblical theology must be a Christian enterprise, despite its origins and history. Referring to the subject as an academic discipline within the field of biblical studies, I use the non-confessional qualifier Hebrew Bible (HB) or, to acknowledge multiple perspectives and users, the dual form OT/HB. There is no common term or conception for the body of literature shared by Christians and Jews when considered from the perspective of its religious meaning and use.

3. The meaning and grounding of this assertion cannot be laid out here. See, e.g., Rolf Rendtorff, 'Approaches to Old Testament Theology', in Henry T.C. Sun and Keith L. Eades (eds.), *Problems in Biblical Theology* (Grand Rapids: Eerdmans, 1977), pp. 13-26 (26); Bernd Janowski, 'The One God of the Two Testaments: Basic Questions of a Biblical Theology', *Theology Today* 57 (2000), pp. 301-306.

scholars is to ensure that that witness is heard as accurately and empathetically as possible.

Old Testament theology, conceived either in descriptive or normative terms, points to a constructive enterprise, concerned with formulations of faith which invite, if not compel, connections and comparisons with contemporary belief. In contrast, *the God of the fathers* suggests an approach to the texts that accents the historical particularity of the witness and the cultural framing, and content, of its theological affirmations. While this particular formation highlights gender, and more particularly patriarchy, as an aspect of the conception—an aspect seen by many today as one of the most problematic features of the biblical legacy—it points to a more general problem. A fundamental problem for all theology, but particularly for theologies with a scriptural base, is the question of how the faith of the ancestors can become the faith of the present generation in a manner that does justice both to the tradition and to the intellectual and spiritual demands of the present. Patriarchy and gendered images of the divine are simply two particularly visible features of the biblical legacy that have become morally and intellectually problematic for contemporary faith and theology.

My work on developing a feminist biblical theology has convinced me that the silence of feminist voices points to critical problems in the conception and practice of biblical theology today. What has emerged from that study is the recognition that the fundamental terms need to be rethought: Whom does this enterprise serve? Who needs it? How is it to be conceived? Where is it to be situated—in relation to biblical and theological scholarship, the teaching of Bible and theology, and the needs of the church? What form(s) should it take? The recitation of the history of the discipline that typically prefaces each new treatment of the subject traces a tradition that remains essentially unbroken in German-speaking Europe,[4] despite major shifts and vigorous internal debate. Some scholars also recognize a 'widened sense' of the term 'Biblical Theology',[5] which it traces to the United States. In this line, others speak of a 'shift toward contestatory diversity played out on leveled fields, at least in North America',[6] and an Australian proposal views the discipline as inherently pluralistic.[7]

---

4. See, e.g., Reiner Albertz, 'Religionsgeschichte Israels statt Theologie des Alten Testaments! Pläoyer für eine forschungsgeschichtliche Umorientierung', *JBTh* 10 (1995), pp. 3-24.

5. See, e.g., H.G. Reventlow, 'Modern Approaches to Old Testament Theology', in L.G. Perdue (ed.), *The Blackwell Companion to the Hebrew Bible* (Oxford: Oxford University Press, 2001), pp, 221-40 (221).

6. See, e.g., B.O. Long, 'Letting Rival Gods Be Rivals: Biblical Theology in a Postmodern Age', in Henry T.C. Sun and Keith L. Eades (eds.), *Problems in Biblical Theology* (Grand Rapids: Eerdmans, 1977), p. 233.

7. See, e.g., M.G. Brett, 'The Future of Old Testament Theology', in André. Lemaire

This essay makes a constructive contribution to the development of feminist biblical theology from a North American feminist Christian perspective. I begin my discussions by tracing briefly the developments of biblical theology in North America and then by talking about the feminist reticence of engaging the discipline of biblical theology before I develop an alternative vision for a feminist biblical theology, historically defined and in rejection of an earlier normatively identified approach by Phyllis Trible. Methodologically, I suggest that such a theology be indispensably grounded in a history-of-religion and cultural approach. A focus on the women in the text or female images of God is insufficient in comprehensively and historically describing the theology of the Old Testament. Awareness of the Bible's androcentric bias means that none of the language and images of the Hebrew Bible may be appropriated uncritically for contemporary affirmations of faith. I thus assert that the God of the fathers must remain part of the retained symbolic-historical language even today.

Tracing Biblical Theology in North America

Biblical theology arose as a response to a particular set of needs. The major shifts in the conception of the discipline reflect changes in these conditions and needs. The one point in the history of the discipline in which significant American involvement is evident is in the 'Biblical Theology Movement' of the post-World War II era, when, under the influence of Karl Barth, interest in theological interpretation of the Bible enjoyed a brief renaissance in some academic settings. Without further analysis of the movement or its demise, I would simply emphasize that it too was a child of its day—and related to particular features of biblical study in the United States. When Brevard Childs proclaimed the failure of the movement and began to articulate his canonical approach to interpretation, it was with the intention of restoring an explicitly theological perspective to the study of scripture in a time and place in which biblical studies had not only declared its independence from ecclesiastical and dogmatic constraints, but was also claiming the status of a secular discipline. While Childs's debt to Barth is considerable, his program was shaped by features unique to the North American religious and academic situation. It is characterized by religious pluralism; the separation of church and state (accompanied at times by strong suspicion of religion); an increasing secularization of culture—with significant resistance from various quarters; and the establishment of departments of religious studies, including biblical studies, in secular universities.

and Magne Sæbø (eds.), *Congress Volume Oslo 1998* (VTS, 80; Leiden: Brill, 2000), pp. 465-88.

By the late 1960s, scholarly interpretation without theological presuppositions or aims had become the accepted norm in the Society of Biblical Literature (SBL) at least at the rhetorical and organizational level. Suspicion or rejection of theological interests continued to define the general ethos of the SBL during most of the following decades. Resistance to this trend may be seen in the establishment of an Old Testament Theology Section in 1971. The fact that no such group had existed previously in the SBL suggests that Old Testament theology, as a distinct discipline of specialization, had remained an essentially German interest after the demise of the Biblical Theology Movement. It may also suggest a continuing covert theological interest that did not seek formal recognition until it could no longer find expression in other forums. Interest in biblical theology, broadly understood, was never completely dead, as Bernhard Anderson demonstrated in his presidential address at the 1980 centennial.[8] Thus Old Testament theology had a special role to play in maintaining conversation with theology, and in claiming the Old Testament for the church, an apologetic aim that has required rethinking of the subject in conversation with Jewish scholars. The Old Testament Theology Section seems to have experienced a low point in the late 1970s and early 1980s, with the result that Bruce Birch, who assumed the chair in 1982, was advised that his term might be the last. A panel that year on 'The Future of Old Testament Theology' seems to have stimulated, or caught, an awakening interest in the subject and it was followed in 1983 by a program on 'The Task of Old Testament Theology'.

New developments in the 1980s and 1990s brought a widening of interest in theology under the banner of hermeneutics, as well as renewed vigor in the 'classical' field of Old Testament theology. Increasing numbers of women in the SBL and a small African American presence led to the formation of program units concerned with the particular hermeneutical interests of these groups. These units gave recognition to the role of experience and religious tradition as well as culture in the interpretation of the Bible. The growing force of postmodernism, with its rejection of the ideals of 'objectivity' and distance associated with historical criticism, fostered interest in the subjectivity and social location of the interpreter, while increasing 'globalization' encouraged efforts of 'contextual interpretation'. Religious identity could resurface in this pluralistic milieu at the same time that the theological imperialism of supposedly neutral historical scholarship was denounced.

---

8. It should be noted that no comparable group existed on the NT side, where theology appears to have remained far more integrally related to the discourse of the field and where hermeneutical theory has a prominent place. Conversation between NT scholars and systematic theologians seems to have been maintained at a significant level.

Despite the broadened hermeneutical activities, it was in relation to Jewish-Christian dialogue that the discipline of biblical theology began to break out of its inherited tradition and engage a wider constituency. The conversations initiated in the aftermath of the Shoah and the increasing Jewish presence in departments of biblical studies and seminaries brought new sensitivity to Jewish perspectives within the SBL, with corresponding changes in nomenclature. Thus the Old Testament Theology Section became the Theology of the Hebrew Scriptures Section in 1985 and determined to encourage Jewish participation. The question of Jewish Bible theology was raised in the late 1980s by a number of authors as part of a broader discussion of Jewish and Christian approaches to biblical interpretation. In 1996, the section featured a panel discussion with two Jewish and two Christian speakers, and in 1998 it added a Jewish co-chair.[9] A newly formed group on 'Biblical Theology' constituted itself as a Consultation in 2000.

Feminism as a Context in North American Developments on Biblical Theology

What is not yet visible in this broadened constituency and debate on biblical theology is significant female presence and feminist perspectives, either in the SBL or in the broader arena of publication. The underrepresentation of women in the Theology of the Hebrew Bible Section during most of the 1990s occurred despite the efforts of a female chair, Alice Ogden Bellis, to encourage women's participation. Bellis was recruited for the Steering Committee as the section's first woman in 1993, and she served as the Chair from 1995 until 2000. Her work increased women's participation on the Steering Committee and the inclusion of women in a Section-related publication.[10] Yet the section did not address feminist concerns during that period.

---

9. Several influential books were the result; see, e.g., M. Tsevat, 'Theology of the Old Testament: A Jewish View', *HBT* 8 (1986), pp. 33-50; Jon Levenson, 'Why Jews Are Not Interested in Biblical Theology', in Jacob Neusner, Baruch A. Levine and Ernest S. Frerichs (eds.), *Judaic Perspectives on Ancient Israel* (Philadelphia: Fortress Press, 1987), pp. 281-307; M.H. Goshen-Gottstein, 'Tanakh Theology: The Religion of the Old Testament and the Place of Jewish Biblical Theology', in Patrick D. Miller, Paul D. Hanson and S. Dean McBride (eds.), *Ancient Israelite Religion: Festschrift Frank M. Cross* (Philadelphia: Fortress Press, 1987), pp. 617-44; Rolf Rendtorff, 'Must "Biblical Theology" be Christian Theology', *BiRe* 4 (1988), pp. 40-43; M.A. Sweeney, 'Tanak versus Old Testament: Concerning the Foundation for the Jewish Theology of the Bible', in Henry T.C. Sun and Keith L. Eades (eds.), *Problems in Biblical Theology* (Grand Rapids: Eerdmans, 1977), pp. 353-72; A.O. Bellis and J.S. Kaminsky (eds.), *Jews, Christians, and the Theology of the Hebrew Scriptures* (SBL Symposium Series, 8; Atlanta: SBL, 2000).

10. Tikva Fryer-Kensky, 'The Emergence of Jewish Biblical Theologies', in Alice

Why did her seven-year effort find so little response? And what does this mean for the discipline? I focus on the organization of North American biblical scholars in the SBL as a way of identifying trends and interests within the field of biblical studies, and because the SBL unites biblical scholars of diverse backgrounds and commitments working in a variety of secular and religious settings although an increasingly large membership from outside North America must qualify any effort to identify the SBL with North American interests. My primary concern has been the place of theology in the study of the Bible because I believe that the future of Old Testament theology in the American context is closely related to this broader issue. But it is also critical for understanding feminist responses because the theological claims made by or for the Hebrew Bible have been particularly problematic for feminists. Some feminists, responding to the theological legacy of biblical patriarchy, want to cut theology free from the (Hebrew) Bible while others want to cut the Bible free from theology.

Before I attempt further analysis, I must extend my documentation of women's silence beyond the SBL section on the Theology of the Hebrew Scriptures. The fact that none of the more than sixty Old Testament Theologies produced during the past century were authored by women is easily explained by the relatively recent entry of women into the field of Old Testament scholarship, as well as the nature of the task. Few, if any, feminist Old Testament scholars have the range and depth of exegetical experience to attempt a comprehensive treatment of the type required, or traditionally assumed, by the genre. Less obvious are the reasons for their absence from other forms and forums of discussion involving less comprehensive demands.

The pattern of women's silence in the field identified as Old Testament theology is clear, but what does it mean? First, I think, it does not mean that feminist scholarship is inconsequential for biblical theology. Feminist are, in fact, engaged in doing biblical theology, in a variety of forms and contexts, and their studies of individual texts, images, and themes, the language and forms of the writings, and the world in which they arose, have greatly enriched and challenged our understanding of the theology of the Old Testament. But these contributions have yet to be registered in any significant degree in comprehensive and synthetic works on the subject.

One of the reasons, I think, that so few women have been involved in the SBL Theology of the Hebrew Scriptures Section is that other demands, from inside and outside the academy, laid prior claims on our energies, and other subjects or sections had greater urgency or offered a more inviting forum for feminist ideas. For women trying to gain a foothold in the

---

Ogden Bellis and Joel S. Kaminsky (eds.), *Jews, Christians, and the Theology of the Hebrew Scriptures* (Atlanta, GA: SBL, 2000).

profession, and sharing the perceptions and concerns of sisters outside the academy, programs on feminist hermeneutics and women in scripture and the biblical world offered needed contexts in which to explore the interface of those concerns with the traditions of the discipline and forge new directions in biblical interpretation. The Consultations, Groups, and Symposia on issues relating directly to women, and the formal and informal associations between women and program units of the SBL and the American Academy of Religion (AAR), served to energize and support feminist scholars and scholarship. But these same structures and dynamics have also isolated feminist discussion from the larger debate, especially in the 'traditional' and 'classic' subjects, such as Old Testament Theology. In light of this pattern, one must ask: What will it take for feminist contributions to move from the ghetto of feminist studies into the 'mainstream', or for the 'mainstream' to realize that it is only a current in the turbulent waters of the discipline?

Feminist engagement with biblical theology has been largely hermeneutical, and limited to the interpretation of selected texts or corpora, or analysis of particular themes, concepts, and images. It has also involved forms of reading 'against the text' and has dared to accuse the God of the tradition on behalf of the victims of patriarchy. In contrast to these piecemeal approaches, 'salvage operations', and counter-readings, Old Testament theology as a summarizing and synthesizing discipline, and genre, aimed at articulating the essential theological content of the whole Old Testament, requires a different kind of engagement and investment with the Bible as a whole, that accords authority to the whole. Here, I think, is the fundamental problem for feminists. The presupposition or demand that the whole of the Old Testament be understood as authoritative is deeply problematic for many women. For many, it would require accepting the claims of normativity made on behalf of Israel's patriarchal God in 'his' role as author and defender of Israel's patriarchal social and religious order. Feminists who reject this androcentric construct of divinity and humanity have little incentive to articulate a theology of the Old Testament or engage in discussion of the subject. That is why a 'feminist Old Testament theology' might be viewed as an oxymoron. The fundamental issue, of course, is the question of normativity, or the nature of the truth claims that are made by and for the portrait offered by the Hebrew scriptures and more broadly, the nature of biblical authority.[11]

---

11. See Phyllis A. Bird, 'The Authority of the Bible', *New Interpreter's Bible* (vol. 1; Nashville: Abingdon Press, 1994), pp. 33-64; also see Phyllis A. Bird, 'Biblical Authority in the Light of Feminist Critique', in *Missing Persons and Mistaken Identities: Women and Gender in Ancient Israel* (Minneapolis: Augsburg Fortress Press, 1997), pp. 248-64.

Another observation about the silence of women in Old Testament theology is in order. It has to do with the fundamental ambivalence that characterizes most women's approaches to the Hebrew scriptures in general. No woman who claims a feminist consciousness can read these texts without experiencing some sense of pain and alienation, unlike most male readers and scholars. Deep and unproblematized love of the Bible is impossible for most feminist biblical scholars and conscienticized readers. Feminists who love these texts also know them as toxic, as dangerous to women's physical and mental health. They know that women's lives have been constricted, warped, and violated by these texts and their interpreters. Some have experienced denial of their vocation on the basis of these texts, others roadblocks to personal and professional fulfillment, while still others simply feel the weight of the absence or silence of women in the text. So even if feminists believe that the poison is in the interpretation rather than the text itself, or that the text supplies an antidote, they cannot approach the scriptures unaware of their potential to harm. That is what distinguishes feminist approaches, however varied. And until all readers acknowledge this dangerous legacy and share the pain of exclusion or estrangement, there can be no gender-inclusive reading or theology.

Overtures for a Feminist Biblical Theology

In 1989, Phyllis Trible published an article entitled 'Five Loaves and Two Fishes: Feminist Hermeneutics and Biblical Theology',[12] the sole work by a woman included in the anthology of twentieth-century contributions to Old Testament theology noted above. I find it necessary to set my own views in relation to Trible's because she addresses Old Testament theology in explicitly feminist terms. While I share many of her values and concerns, I differ in my understanding of the task and aims of biblical theology and the nature of biblical authority as well as the way in which the Bible functions as a source for contemporary theology.

In her 1989 essay, Trible declared that although it was not yet the season to write a feminist biblical theology, it was time to make overtures. She reiterated this position in 1993.[13] She begins with a history of the discipline, whose climax she finds in the period, from 1933 to 1960, a period framed by

---

12. Phyllis Trible, 'Five Loaves and Two Fishes: Feminist Hermeneutics and Biblical Theology', *TS* 50 (1989), pp. 279-95. The essay is reprinted as 'Feminist Hermeneutics and Biblical Theology', in Elmer A. Martens, Ben C. Ollenburger and Gerhard Hasel (eds.), *The Flowering of Old Testament Theology* (Warsaw, IN: Eisenbrauns, 1991), pp. 448-64. Major sections are incorporated into Phyllis Trible, 'Treasures Old and New: Biblical Theology and the Challenge of Feminism', in Francis Watson (ed.), *The Open Text: New Directions for Biblical Studies?* (London: SCM Press, 1993), pp. 32-56.

13. Trible, *Treasures Old and New*, p. 41.

the works of Eichrodt and von Rad.[14] With the fall of the 'great consensus' in the early 1960s, she sees the discipline in a period of decline extending to the time of her writing with few new biblical theologies and none dominating the field.[15] Yet she maintains that the subject has 'grown through experimentation', identifying 'conversation between sociology and theology, discussion of canon, and development of bipolar categories for encompassing scriptural diversity' as elements of this growth. 'More broadly', she concluded, 'biblical theology [had] begun to converse with the world'.[16] It is in this expanded conversation with the world that she situates her feminist approach to the subject, setting it over against a 200 year history whose characteristics she summarizes as follows:

> First, biblical theology (more often OT theology) has sought identity, but with no resolution. Over time the discussion has acquired the status of *déja dit*: proposals and counterproposals only repeat themselves. Second, guardians of the discipline have fit a standard profile. They have been white Christian males of European or North American extraction, educated in seminaries, divinity schools, or theological faculties. Third, overall, their interpretations have skewed or neglected matters not congenial to a patriarchal point of view. Fourth, they have fashioned the discipline in a past separated from the present. *Biblical theology has been kept apart from biblical hermeneutics.*[17]

Trible's emphasis is on the final point. It is the separation of biblical theology from hermeneutics that she wishes to challenge as a feminist, joining feminist critique to challenges coming from many other directions. Among these she identifies 'liberation theologies [which] foster redefinition and application', 'issues such as ecology, medical ethics, creationism, and spirituality [which] press for dialogue', 'racial, religious, and sexual perspectives', and 'African-Americans, Asians, and Jews [who] shape the discipline differently from traditional proponents'.[18]

I think Trible is right in insisting that the circle of the debate on the subject must be widened and include voices not previously heard or even raised; and I think she is right in asserting that this is already taking place. But as she also notes, it is not taking place in the circles perpetuating the 'great tradition' symbolized by the production of volumes entitled 'Old Testament Biblical Theology', or examining the concept of biblical theology. I share Trible's concern for hermeneutics, as well as her identification of the

---

14. Trible, *Treasures Old and New*, p. 34.
15. Trible, *Treasures Old and New*, pp. 34-35.
16. Trible, *Feminist Hermeneutics and Biblical Theology*, p. 453. See also Trible, *Treasures Old and New*, p. 35.
17. Trible, *Feminist Hermeneutics and Biblical Theology*, p. 454 (emphasis added). See also Trible, *Treasures Old and New*, p. 35.
18. Trible, *Feminist Hermeneutics and Biblical Theology*, p. 454.

issues pressing for dialogue, but I do not want to abolish the separation of biblical theology from hermeneutics. I want to preserve the dialogical character of the encounter between ancient text and contemporary context(s) by maintaining the distinction between historical statements of belief and contemporary affirmations of faith. I believe there is need for a biblical theology understood as a historical discipline without thereby rejecting the legitimacy or value of a biblical theology understood primarily as a constructive enterprise oriented by contemporary issues of faith.[19] Thus I want to argue for an alternative to Trible's understanding as a feminist alternative that will also serve the interests and needs of others in the North American context.

A Question of Identity

I have begun with the question of the identity and aims of the discipline, because I believe this is the fundamental question and because this is where I part company with Trible. Trible emphasizes the unresolved nature of the debate over identity of biblical theology as a problem that has characterized the history of the discipline, suggesting that it signals the need for a new approach.[20] I am not troubled by the lack of consensus. It belongs to the nature of the subject or discipline as uniting subject matter and interests belonging to two fields of specialization with distinct, and in part incompatible, methods and aims.[21] And it is dictated by the Bible's dual identity as both ancient writings and contemporary book: historical testimony to the faith of ancient Israel and early Judaism and contemporary guide to belief and practice. How is the integrity of this dual nature to be maintained and honored within the field of Old Testament studies? How does one do justice to these differing perceptions of text and canon? Whose theology does

---

19. Trible, *Feminist Hermeneutics and Biblical Theology*, p. 464. I use 'constructive' as a term of contrast to 'historical', recognizing, however, that historical theology, as every work of historical writing, is also a constructive effort.

20. Trible, *Feminist Hermeneutics and Biblical Theology*, pp. 451, 454.

21. The problem is illustrated by the need for a two-part article on the subject in the new RGG; see Bern Janowski, '*Biblische Theologie: I. Exegetisch*', *RGG*[4] 1 (Tübingen: Mohr Siebeck, 1998), cols. 1544-49; Michael Welker, '*Biblische Theology: II. Fundamentaltheologisch*', *RGG*[4] 1 (Tübingen: Mohr Siebeck, 1998), cols. 1549-53, for helpful overviews and typologies of different construals of the subject. The lack of consensus is recognized by all who have treated the subject, but with differing assessments and responses. Some have attempted to limit its legitimate task, form, and/or method in quite different ways. See, e.g., Rolf P. Knierim, 'The Task of Old Testament Theology', *HBT* 6.1 (1963), pp. 5-57; John J. Collins, 'Is a Critical Biblical Theology Possible?', in William H. Propp, Baruch Halpern and David N. Freedman (eds.), *The Hebrew Bible and Its Interpreters* (Warsaw, IN: Eisenbrauns, 1990), pp. 37-62; and James Barr, *The Concept of Biblical Theology* (Minneapolis: Augsburg Fortress Press, 1999).

the biblical scholar seek to articulate? For whom? What is the relationship between the descriptive-historical and the normative-constructive tasks of theology? I am convinced that debate about the nature of biblical theology needs to continue, and feminists need to be a part of it. Trible's proposal for a feminist biblical theology elaborates one answer to these questions, but it does not close the debate concerning either the nature of biblical theology or the form of feminist engagement with it.

Trible positions herself on the constructive side of biblical theology by her definition of the subject and by her explicit disavowal of the historical tradition whose demise she correlates with the new movements of theology that began in the 1960s. Asking whether feminism and biblical theology can meet, she elaborates: 'After all, feminists do not move in the world of Gabler, Eichrodt, von Rad, and their heirs'. 'Yet', she continues, 'feminists who love the Bible insist that the text and its interpreters provide more excellent ways'.[22] These remarks call for further analysis, but here it must suffice to say that they do not represent the views of all feminists, or even 'feminists who love the Bible' although I do believe they do reflect a widely shared sense of alienation or distance from a tradition of Old Testament scholarship that dominated most of the past century. Trible's disavowal of the heritage of Gabler is evidenced in her definition of biblical theology, which removes it from any historical (or ecclesial/religious) context or constraint. For Trible, biblical theology is simply 'an articulation of faith as disclosed in Scripture'. This 'open' definition corresponds to her understanding of the Bible as 'pilgrim, wandering through history, engaging in new settings, and ever refusing to be locked in the past'.[23] Trible accents the power of the reader to alter the meaning and force of the text,[24] describing the task of a feminist biblical theology as that of 'redeem[ing] the past (an ancient treasure called the Bible) and the present (its continuing use) from the confines of patriarchy'.[25] While she accords an essential role to descriptive and historical study, she views the primary task as constructive and hermeneutical, aiming to 'wrestle from the text a theology that subverts patriarchy'.[26]

I would welcome the theology Trible envisions in her 'overtures', which would focus on the 'phenomenon of gender and sex in the articulation of faith' as the key to its content and contours.[27] A theology of the Hebrew scrip-

---

22. Trible, *Feminist Hermeneutics and Biblical Theology*, p. 458.
23. Trible, *Feminist Hermeneutics and Biblical Theology*, p. 458.
24. Trible, *Treasures Old and New*, p. 49.
25. Trible, *Treasures Old and New*, pp. 38, 49.
26. Trible, *Feminist Hermeneutics and Biblical Theology*, p. 464.
27. Trible, *Feminist Hermeneutics and Biblical Theology*, pp. 461-62. The work would be grounded in exegesis, highlighting neglected texts and reinterpreting familiar ones to recover forgotten women and accent female depictions of God. It would expose

tures systematically informed by feminist concerns and focused on texts and ideas of importance to feminists would call attention to the inadequacies and biases of existing theologies and suggest alternative paradigms and readings. I think there is need for such a work, both by those who have experienced biblical patriarchy as an obstacle to faith, and by those who have not yet recognized the distorting effects of patriarchal androcentrism in biblical theology. Nevertheless, I remain ambivalent about the concept of feminist biblical theology and find Trible's proposal problematic in a number of ways.

I am ambivalent about the concept, because it suggests a special theology for a special audience, which would reinforce the present separation of feminist voices within the discipline. On the other hand, such a targeted work may be what is needed to open conversation and lead to the integration of feminist insights into 'general' Old Testament theologies. Trible herself clearly envisions a broader audience, and her aim is nothing less than the articulation of a 'constructive theology for female and male... for the redemption of humankind'.[28] I share her view of the goal and horizons of feminist theology, as a constructive enterprise, but I cannot follow the moves she makes from the Old Testament to normative theological statements, and my own view of the theology of the Old Testament, both in its historical context and as a source for contemporary theology, is substantially different from hers.

A Question of Norms

Trible's rejection of historical theology as a vehicle for feminist theological interpretation and her proposal for a constructive feminist biblical theology raise a number of questions for me concerning the criteria of assessment and the relationship of historical to constructive theology. Although I recognize a range of options between the strictly historical (which always has a contemporary orientation and involves value judgments) and the normative-constructive (which always involves historical judgments) approaches, I am uncertain what to make of Trible's proposal. How does the theology she envisions relate to other forms of theology, on the one hand, and the Bible's full theological witness on the other? And by what criteria of adequacy or truth is it to be assessed? At times Trible seems to suggest that feminist biblical theology is simply feminist theology that takes the Bible as its primary source. But the theology she proposes is inadequate as an articulation of Christian faith. It offers no hint of how the New Testament, or any other source of faith besides

---

and denounce patriarchal bias and memorialize its victims. It would begin, as the Bible itself, with Genesis 1–3 and find its base in creation theology. And it would expose and denounce idolatry in the scriptures, from within the scriptures (pp. 461-63).

28. Trible, *Treasures Old and New*, p. 49.

feminism, might relate to this 'articulation of faith as disclosed in scripture'. At the same time, it appears to neglect much of the theological content of the Hebrew Bible and, in my view, distorts some of its witness.

Such limitations and 'failings' seem, however, to be inherent in the genre. Any theology (historical or constructive) that attempts to treat the Old Testament as a whole will have to be highly selective, both with respect to the biblical sources and to the range of contemporary issues engaged. One might argue that the use of gender and sex as an organizing theme is compatible to the use of such concepts as *covenant, reign of God*, or *divine presence*, with the same drawbacks. Unlike covenant, however, or reign of God, gender introduces a distinctly contemporary concept of awareness; and despite the fact that the choice of such concepts as covenant undoubtedly reflects theological interests of the scholars' own times, these concepts are thematized in the Hebrew scriptures in a way that gender is not.[29] To make gender the focus of an Old Testament theology is to give it a status it does not have in the biblical writings. While I believe this is a justifiable move in a theology concerned to address the primary stumbling block of many contemporary readers and a source of distortion in traditional Old Testament theologies, I prefer to treat the subject of gender historically, as part of the cultural world of the biblical writings. I see it as a more pervasive influence than Trible's analysis suggests, but as a distorting element that should not be allowed to obscure the fundamental theological ideas of the Old Testament.[30] So while I would not make gender the focus of a theology of the Old Testament, I believe that no theology today (historical or constructive) is adequate if it fails to incorporate a gender analysis.

This brings me again to the question of evaluation or judgment, the area in which I feel the greatest uncertainty in considering Trible's proposal, or any other conception of biblical theology that subordinates the historical to the normative-constructive task. What canons of assessment apply to such a work? For me, biblical interpretation that is oriented toward contemporary issues falls into the same general category as the exegetical sermon and the hermeneutical essay, both of which I would judge by the dual criteria of fidelity to the biblical sources and theological adequacy (judged by the canons of my theological tradition) as a response to the particular contemporary problem(s) or situation(s) it addresses. My training as a biblical scholar

---

29. Trible attempts to find a thematizing statement in Gen. 1.27 by constructing the phrase 'image of God male and female' as a 'topical clue' that authorizes a focus on gender and female images of God; see Phyllis Trible, *God and the Rhetoric of Sexuality* (Philadelphia: Fortress Press, 1978), pp. 12-23.

30. This may appear very similar to Trible's aim of 'liberating the Bible from the confines of patriarchy', but it differs in its emphasis on historical meaning, as distinct from contemporary belief, and on the manner of assessing and responding to gender bias.

makes me more secure in the former task, but as a Christian believer I accept responsibility for the latter, despite the inadequacies of my theological training. Yet even my ability to judge fidelity to the biblical text, which for me requires historical contextualization, is challenged by Trible's view of reader-determined meaning.[31] Thus the problem of assessment that confronts me in her conception of the subject is not simply a matter of relative weight of the normative-constructive component in relation to the descriptive-historical, but the dissolution of the historical by the constructive.

Alternatives

I have lifted up Trible's proposal, because it offers a clear articulation of a feminist approach to biblical theology and because it differs from my own. Critique of her proposal has helped me clarify my own understanding of the problems and issues. What I want to do now is sketch out an alternative, or alternatives, admitting that I am still uncertain about the form or forms of biblical theology that will meet the demands of the text and the needs of readers in the several religious and cultural contexts in which I find myself and exercise my vocation as a biblical scholar. By way of transition, I want to characterize my view of the biblical text and the task of interpretation in relation to Trible's. I begin with her statement of aims, cited above. Trible's aim to 'redeem' the Bible as an 'ancient treasure' and in its continuing use from the 'confines of patriarchy' suggests a cultural captivity that must be broken in order for the Bible to be restored or reclaimed as a theological source. The idea of 'redemption' is appealing but also problematic because patriarchy is an integral aspect of the language and world of the text. It is only through this distorted medium that we encounter (in scripture) the God who transcends and judges the conditions of this historical witness. The Bible cannot escape the confines of history. Whether the God to which it testifies is so bound is another matter, which cannot be tested or confirmed by literary or historical means. Shifting metaphors, Trible speaks of 'wrestling' a theology from the text that will subvert patriarchy. Although I find this metaphor more apt as a description of the hermeneutical process, it also suggests that the Bible contains all that is needed for contemporary belief, requiring only the effort of the reader to release it. I find similar problems with Trible's metaphors of treasure house (from which to seek out treasures that will serve feminist theological needs) and remnant (a theology to be recovered by lifting up neglected or suppressed traditions).[32] Such scripturally charged metaphors command rhetorical authority and suggest a recov-

---

31. Trible, *Feminist Hermeneutics and Biblical Theology*, p. 463.
32. Trible, *Feminist Hermeneutics and Biblical Theology*, pp. 458, 464; see also Trible, *Treasures Old and New*, pp. 32, 49.

ery operation that minimizes or denies the radical disjunction between the biblical world and our own.

In contrast to this 'treasure hunt', I want to hold on to the whole theological testimony of the Old Testament, in its patriarchal form, as a source for a contemporary feminist theology. Instead of seeking a remnant, I want to explore the ancient conversations in which the biblical texts participate within the religio-cultural world of the ancient Near East and within the canon of scripture in order to apprehend the theological issues at stake therein and extend and transform those conversations into contemporary speech in encounter with contemporary problems and questions. I see a more complex interaction with the biblical texts, in which the ancient context and the religio-cultural dynamics operative there play a more critical role in shaping contemporary theological responses.

'Special' and 'General' Theologies in the North American Context

A defining feature of the North American context and global context is an irreducible pluralism that makes 'special' theologies both necessary and problematic. If emphasis in biblical theology is placed on meaning for today, then it would appear that there can only be 'special' or particular theologies that are shaped by the traditions and needs of particular groups of readers. But this creates a new set of challenges for the discipline and the church. Although none of us today can do justice to the full range of experience and perspective represented in our field of study, all of us, especially in North America, work in situations that require us to reach beyond the group or culture in which we were socialized. 'Special' theologies expose the hidden boundaries and biases of 'general' theologies, revealing them to be likewise governed by special interests, albeit of the dominant group(s). But by targeting distinct groups and interests outside the old area of consensus they leave open the question concerning the ground and impetus for conversation across these boundaries of religious, cultural, and class identity. This makes the question of 'center' or essential content all the more urgent, and historical inquiry essential. Fresh attempts to formulate the fundamental theological content of shared texts as an historical task in an ecumenical context should serve to enhance interreligious dialog and invite critical appraisal of traditional understandings and new readings.

Historical Theology as a Feminist Option

I affirm the concept of biblical theology as an historical and descriptive discipline within the field of biblical studies.[33] I understand it as a comple-

---

33. The location of the subject is critical for determining appropriate methods and

ment to the history of the religion of Israel and early Judaism, focusing on religious ideas with attention to how they cohere, change, and interact with other ideas in response to new experience. As a descriptive, historical study, biblical theology invites participation by scholars of different faiths or none, and it demands no assent to the beliefs described. It also demands a willingness to enter the belief-world of the text and a disciplined effort to comprehend the testimonies of faith encountered there without imposition of personal values and judgments. This ideal is never fully realized, but it is nonetheless essential.[34] Because such a theology is determined first of all by the contours and confessions of the historical text, it cannot be feminist, or liberationist, or Christian, or Jewish. But every version (and there can only be versions, never definitive statements) will be a distinctly individual creation, shaped by the peculiar sensitivities and biases of the author, including feminist sensitivities and biases.

The effort to comprehend the faith of biblical authors and editors in their world(s), and articulate it for contemporary readers in their world(s), does not require suspension of a scholar's faith or judgment any more than any other form of historical scholarship or effort of cross-cultural understanding and interpretation. It requires respect for the otherness of the testimony, which allows ancient views and values to be heard as potential critique of the reader's. It also demands evaluative judgment. How that judgment is registered in the interpretive work of presenting the theology of the Hebrew scriptures will depend on the reader, as will the criteria that guide the judgment.

My advocacy of an historical approach is not a retreat from hermeneutics. As a Christian and a feminist, I am committed to a theology that will meet the moral and intellectual demands of the world in which I live: a world of poverty, violence, and oppression; of unimaginable wealth and technological miracles; of sterile earth and polluted seas and mass extinction of species; of racial-ethnic, sexual, and ideological conflicts rending the human

---

aims. Thus Collins, *Is a Critical Biblical Theology Possible*, pp. 8-9, who places it within the field of historical theology, is concerned with the kind of theological statements that are compatible with its historical character and the critical methodologies that history demands. By placing it in the field of biblical studies, I want to assert the legitimacy, and necessity of theological interpretation in a field that no longer understands itself (at least in the United States) as a subfield of theology, but continues to be essential to theology, in both its critical and confessional forms.

34. The ideal is not a caricatured 'objectivity', but a sympathetic hearing that attempts to assure the text's point of view before assessing the message. It does not preclude judgment, and it recognizes the subjectivity of readers as a tool of understanding. But it attempts to avoid imposition of alien values, enlisting the aid of other readers and other ancient texts. Thus comparative literary and socio-historical analysis is essential to the effort; see, e.g., Barr, *The Concept of Biblical Theology*, pp. 15-16, 205-208.

family. I believe that the Hebrew scriptures are an indispensable source for such a theology. But the means by which I appropriate those resources are dialogical in nature and context-specific. And the theology that would meet the contemporary demands of faith, including feminist demands, will not be a biblical theology, but a theology in which the biblical witness is joined to the testimonies of history, experience, and reason in a fresh articulation of faith.[35] If the Bible is the indispensable source of all Christian theology, it is not the only source, and its own testimony presses readers to look beyond it for signs of divine presence and activity.

I have argued that an historical approach to biblical theology does not involve an abdication of judgment or rejection of ethical demands upon the interpreter. But the genre of the Old Testament theology, as a summarizing work, necessarily limits the type and amount of interaction between texts and a reader's context. That is why I prefer to locate the primary work of theological interpretation and judgment of scripture elsewhere, namely in the encounter with specific problems and needs of contemporary faith and life: in sermons, in lectures, in essays addressing particular problems or issues arising in the text and its history of interpretation or arising in the world of the reader,[36] and in teaching and counseling. My choice of the historical method as the primary mode of encounter with the text is dictated by personal experience, desire to converse with a wider audience, and ethical considerations. I believe ancient authors should receive the same respect as contemporary readers and students or colleagues in face-to-face communication. This means that I seek to discern the intention of the other as expressed in and through the words, gestures, and tone of the utterance. The fact that many of the needed clues are lacking in ancient texts does not alter the goal or process in any fundamental way, except to place greater emphasis on the contextual clues and analogy. I recognize that texts, released from an author's control, are multivalent, having as many meanings as readers. And I also recognize that meanings are shaped by communities of interpreters. But I choose to honor an author (and redactor and collectors, insofar as they have left discernable imprints on the text) over a reader, precisely because the author's intention has traditionally been subordinated to that of interpreters who would use the words for their own purposes. For me, this is a feminist issue. As women's words have been suppressed or made

---

35. I betray my Wesleyan heritage with this 'quadrilateral'.
36. See e.g., Phyllis Bird, 'Genesis 1–3 as a Source for a Contemporary Theology of Sexuality', in *Missing Persons and Mistaken Identities*, pp. 123-73; see also Phyllis Bird, 'Genesis 3 in Modern Biblical Scholarship', pp. 174-93; 'The Bible in Christian Ethical Deliberation Concerning Homosexuality: Old Testament Contributions', in David L. Balch (ed.), *Homosexuality, Science, and the 'Plain Sense' of Scripture* (Grand Rapids/Cambridge: Eerdmans, 2000), pp. 142-76.

to serve men's interests, so the words of biblical authors have been made to serve religious and political agendas of churches and synagogues, states and societies. I remain convinced that an historical approach to the theology of the Hebrew scriptures best serves feminist interests, as well as the needs of other biblical scholars and theologians, while protecting the text from arbitrary use.

Rethinking the Discipline and the Genre

With this confession I return to the question of whose interests an Old Testament theology is intended to serve. Who needs it? For what purpose? Or, why is it necessary or desirable, at all? It is not sufficient to carry on the tradition descended from Gabler because it has established itself as an academic specialty.[37] In particular, the genre of the Old Testament theology needs to be rethought in relation to contemporary needs and audiences that are now multiple and varied. In my view, the primary audience of said theology are students of the Old Testament, pastors, or biblical scholars, rather than systematic theologians. While a traditionally stated goal of biblical theology has been to serve the theological needs of the church as a foundation for dogmatics, or as an alternative, it is not clear to me that it has actually functioned in this way,[38] nor is it clear how it might best serve church theology or theologians today.[39] The Protestant principle of the primacy of scripture requires any theology claiming the name Christian to be 'biblical'. What then is the need for a distinct biblical theology, and how do the two relate to one another? The fact that few contemporary theologians can command the full theological resources of the canon, and especially the Hebrew scriptures, points to the need for some sort of interpretive filter or bridge between exegesis and confessional theology, but it is not clear to me that a comprehensive and synthetic work, with its own distinctive theological stamp, is the logical or best form for such mediation.

I am inclined to think that targeted studies are the most useful form of biblical theology for those outside the field. The most productive interchanges

---

37. Here I share Trible's concern, though not her solution.

38. In practice, the direction of influence has seemed to be from dogmatics to biblical theology, with categories of the former imposing themselves on the latter—a threat that von Rad attempted to counter with his concept of Old Testament theology as 'Nacherzählung'.

39. Although Collins criticizes various attempts to make biblical theology serve doctrinal ends, he sees the discipline as a form of historical theology, and as such 'one source among others for contemporary theology'; See Collins, *Is a Critical Biblical Theology Possible*, p. 9. Cf. Barr, *The Concept of Biblical Theology*, pp. 62-76, 240-52; who speaks of biblical theology as a 'participant' in the considerations of doctrinal theology.

between theology and biblical studies may be those that take place in consideration of particular problems, texts, or themes or build on personal relationships between individual theologians and biblical scholars. An advantage of limited and focused studies is that they allow for closer interaction with particular audiences and their particular interests and needs.

Theology of the Old Testament as a Comprehensive and Synthetic Work

I have argued that much of the work of biblical theology might be carried out in limited studies, but I have come to believe that there is also a need for comprehensive and synthetic works of Old Testament theology not primarily as a service to theologians, but to biblical scholars, teachers, students, and pastors. In fact, I maintain that it is necessary for every student of the Old Testament, including those with no theological interest or religious commitment, because of the nature of the texts as theological literature, whether or not they make explicit theological statements. It is needed first to make sense of the intellectual world of the texts, and hence of the texts themselves, and second to draw out and clarify the truth claims made or implied by those texts. A descriptive-historical theology that renounces efforts to formulate meaning for today is still a theology, one concerned with the question of ultimate meaning and truth, and not a mere reporting and cataloging of beliefs. It should enable contemporary readers to understand what is at stake in the Old Testament's portraits of God and statements of divine nature and will, so that they are not dismissed prematurely as anthropomorphic caricatures or superficial 'biography'.

My argument here is that Old Testament theology can no longer be tied to the confessional needs of a particular religious community. It must engage the wider world to which the Bible belongs. Theology is too fundamental to the biblical writings to be claimed, or dismissed, as the exclusive province of believers, and theology is too important to be left to theologians. On September 11, 2001, we saw the devastating consequences of theology in the service of demonic aims, and the roots of that theology as well as evidence of similar perversions are in the Old Testament itself. I think it is both necessary and desirable to envision an Old Testament theology designed for a multireligious and secular audience, one that might be used as a part of an introductory course, or as a separate study. Moreover, I believe that a work that enables readers to enter as fully as possible into the thought world of the text and engage in the battles of belief fought out there will serve the needs of Christian believers and the needs of others. The form that such a theology would take will depend on the particular audience and scholar.

I have argued for a form of Old Testament theology that is not tied to a particular trajectory of faith. At the same time, I think there is also a need within communities of faith that read these texts as scripture to trace the lines between biblical faith and contemporary belief more explicitly. This may take a variety of forms, proceeding either from biblical or contemporary starting points, but the effort will need to come primarily from biblical scholars, who have the requisite knowledge of the texts. As an activity of biblical scholars, dependent on their primary competence with the biblical text, this requires recognition in the field of biblical studies, but it must be understood as a constructive theological activity and a contribution to the field of theology. It thus requires recognition as a legitimate form of theology.

The risks are considerable: on the one hand, the risk of compromising the literary-historical analysis with the confessional demands or theological agendas, and on the other hand, the risk of theological naïveté or 'biblicism' that isolates the Bible as a source and fails to integrate the results into a larger theological system. Despite the risks of violating the canons of both fields in their present academic autonomy, and the attendant risks of being disowned by both fields, I am not willing to declare this activity illegitimate.[40] But I do think that this form of biblical theology needs a descriptive-historical theology as a foundation to guard against unwarranted construals. And it is to this historical task that I prefer to devote my energies as a theologian.

Features of an Historical and Descriptive Theology of the Old Testament

An historical and descriptive theology of the Old Testament also ought to be limited to the data of the Hebrew Bible itself, read in the context of extra-biblical evidence for religious belief and practice of the time. It would be both historical and canonical, giving attention to the religio-cultural contexts of individual traditions and larger literary complexes, from the earliest tradition unit to the latest redactional levels. Thus, for instance, it would treat the God of the fathers as representing both a stage in the development of Israelite religion (relating to the clan, in which the patriarch held religious authority) and a continuing affirmation of God's special relationship to the community (notions of election, promise, and providence), an affirmation whose claim is both tested (by the exile) and contested (by notions of universalism and by skepticism).

---

40. While I agree with Collins' analysis of the inherent conflict between confessional faith as a dogmatic system and historical critical method (see Collins, *Is a Critical Biblical Theology Possible*, pp. 7-9), I think there is a practical need for combining confessional and historical modes of knowing which must open the 'assured results' of both to reformulation. Thus I am willing to grant legitimacy to a wide range of mediating forms of biblical theology, including Trible's.

Such a theology would attempt to comprehend the diverse testimony as parts of a whole, defined by a canon that channels connections and conversations among the text, but also by processes of theological reflection that stand behind the canon, determining the selection of canonical texts. It will be, necessarily, systematic; whether the drive for coherence is understood to inhere in the scriptural testimony itself or to derive from the needs of the contemporary theologian-historian.[41] Whatever the structure chosen to present the fundamental religious ideas, the theology must have a chronological dimension. Time/history in the Hebrew scriptures is both a condition of the data and a subject of theological reflection. An attempt to give an integrated account of the whole theological testimony of the Hebrew scriptures is not in fundamental conflict with the recognition of multiple and conflicting theologies within that corpus. Conflicting views only make sense within a shared universe of thought and discourse.[42] To do justice to the diverse theological data of the Hebrew Bible, a theology of the Hebrew scriptures must be both historically specific and systematic.[43] And it must deal with the relationship of theological ideas to social and political realia.

Feminist Contributions to a Descriptive Historical Theology of the Old Testament: A Preliminary Conclusion

What I have described has very close connections with a history of the religion of Israel, but it is not the same thing. Its primary data are the statements of the Hebrew Bible, understood as a limited corpus constituted by a process of composition and selection that has imposed certain value judgments on the data of religious experience and expression in ancient Israel. Here feminism can make an essential contribution. Contemporary awareness of

---

41. So Rolf P. Knierim, *The Task of Old Testament Theology: Substance, Method, and Cases* (Grand Rapids: Eerdmans, 1995), pp. 30-31, 47-48; Rolf P. Knierim, 'On the Task of Old Testament Theology: A Response to W. Harrelson, S. Towner, and R.E. Murphy', *HBT* 6 (1964), pp. 108-27. It is clear that the drive to comprehend ever greater complexes of evidence is a feature of the redactional/canonical process itself and not simply a contemporary imposition.

42. The attempt to articulate the underlying system of beliefs reveals the shifting boundaries of the area of shared belief, which expands and contracts, at times simultaneously. At times in Israel's history, the competing theologies lie within the realm of Israelite Yahwism; at other times they lie in a shared religious universe that links Israel and/or Yahwism with surrounding nations or religions.

43. Different theologies will handle this dual demand in different ways. One might argue, for example, that creation is the fundamental concept of Old Testament theology, giving this priority in structuring the work. But it is clear from the total evidence that while creation may be logically and canonically prior, it is not historically or experientially first, and this tension between historical and canonical priority has theological significance.

the social location and identity of all authors and literature requires attention to these same factors in the literature of ancient Israel. This means that the theological statements of the Hebrew Bible, which constitute the data for any Old Testament theology, are partial and skewed, not only by the elite status of the authors (a presupposition of all early writing) or by the particular historical and political factors that assured the survival and dominance of certain theological views, but because they represent the theological insights and experience of only half the population. To that extent they are a deficient, and distorted, testimony.[44] The silence of women is of a different order than the silence of particular social classes, ethnic groups, or political parties, because it runs through every class and social category. It is a matter of the most basic of all human distinctions linked to biological markers and endowed with social meanings and consequences in every society. It is also a distinction that is given explicit recognition in the Old Testament and invested with religious significance and theological interpretation.[45] What then is the meaning and what the truth value of a theology that claims to speak about the ultimate nature and meaning of life, but speaks only in a male voice? And how shall we respond to this fundamental distortion in our sources?

There is no single or simple answer to this question. We are only beginning to explore ways to move beyond a patriarchal past into a future shaped by full participation of women with men, a future that would appear to be well beyond our present horizons. In the meantime, however, I think it is at least reasonable to expect that gender analysis and recognition of the fundamentally skewed nature of our data find a place in every new effort to formulate a theology of the Old Testament. I also think that the recognition of this skewing needs to be registered throughout the work, not simply in a prefatory statement or a chapter or section on female deities or attributes of the deity. The whole of the Hebrew scriptures is formulated in gendered language and concepts derived from gendered experience. Every theological idea and expression needs to be examined for implications of this gender bias. A theology today that universalizes concepts presented in the Old Testament in gender-specific language and contexts is not telling the truth about the Old Testament's theology.[46]

---

44. The underlying assumption of this statement is that men cannot speak for women and that men's religious experience cannot provide a fully adequate description of the nature of God and God's relationship to humanity and the world.

45. This statement is not in conflict with my earlier insistence that gender is a contemporary concept. Gender is a contemporary analytical term that is used to interpret phenomena recognized under various terms and categories by all cultures.

46. Consideration of gender bias might begin, by way of example, with the concept of *covenant*, a political metaphor derived from the realm of male experience and transformed into a theological construct in the realm of male religious activity. It is not a

To return to the God of the fathers, symbol of a patriarchal religion and theology and symbol of the patriarchal tradition through which we have received this legacy: I believe we must retain this symbol within our repertoire of theological images, not only in an historical theology, with its multiple meanings, but also in a contemporary feminist theology. It is a necessary reminder of the cultural conditioning of all religious language and experience of the divine, and a reminder of the historical character of all theological constructions. It serves to validate the search for new theological language appropriate to new religious experience and underscores the never-ending need to interpret the images of the past afresh, lest they become empty, or deceptive, idols.

gender-neutral concept. And when marriage is presented as an alternative metaphor for the relationship between God and Israel, it is filled with specific gendered experience of marriage in which the male experience is projected onto God. The 'pornographic' development of this metaphor, which has occasioned so much feminist rage, is simply one vivid example of the way in which the normally hidden assumptions of male authors and audience determine the form and content of theological expression. But covenant is a relatively obvious example of gendered categories being treated as though they were neutral and 'natural' concepts. Concepts such as *justice, righteousness, liberation,* and *love* need to be examined for gender implications as well. How are these terms actually used in the Old Testament? To what situations in life do they refer? From whose perspective are they formulated? For some initial efforts in this direction, see Susan Ackerman, 'The Personal is Political: Covenental and Affectionate Love (aheb, ahaba) in the Hebrew Bible', *VT* (2002), pp. 437-58; Phyllis A. Bird, 'Poor Man or Poor Woman? Gendering the Poor in Prophetic Texts', in *Missing Persons and Mistaken Identities*, pp. 67-78; Fokkelien van Dijk-Hemmes and Athalya Brenner, *On Gendering Texts: Female and Male Voices in the Hebrew Bible* (BI, 1; Leiden: E.J. Brill, 1993); Fokkelien van Dijk-Hemmes and Athalya Brenner (eds.), *Reflections on Theology and Gender* (Leuven: Peeters, 1994); Bob Becking and Meindert Dijkstra (eds.), *On Reading Prophetic Texts: Gender-Specific and Related Studies in Memory of Fokkelien van Dijk-Hemmens* (Biblical Interpretation, 18, Leiden: E.J. Brill, 1996).

Part II
FEMINIST READINGS WITHIN THE TEXT

8

Discovering Her Story in the Text:
Literary Criticism In Feminist Hebrew Bible Studies

Beth LaNeel Tanner

Any act of reading is literary criticism. Such criticism can be as informal as the quick answer to the question, 'Did you like the book?', and as formal as a scholar's life work on the collected works of Shakespeare. Likewise, any approach to the study of the Bible is a literary enterprise, even when it is done with a stated historical or theological purpose. However, within biblical studies, different understandings of literary criticism exist. Therefore, this essay concentrates on the development that began in the 1960s and was named 'new' literary criticism.[1] For the purposes of this essay, new literary criticism will be defined as those studies that focus on issues and questions within the text, often called the world of the text, instead of the world behind the text or its historical setting.

As with any new avenue of research, the influences for this development came both from inside and outside the academy. From the inside, scholars sought to move beyond the historical quest dominating biblical studies since the seventeenth century CE. From the outside, a wealth of vital and growing work occurred in all types of literary studies in Europe and North America. Change, however, did not come without controversy. New literary criticism and one of its major branches, feminist study, were slow to be accepted by traditional biblical scholars. These 'traditional' objections centered on the perception that new literary methods focus on the text and the reader and not on the world behind the text. Yet despite these objections, the cross-fertilization between literary criticism and biblical studies has proven methodologically liberating and productive. It has also enabled creativity and innovation in the development of feminist literary readings of the Bible. In fact, many feminist Bible scholars engage literary criticism because it centers on the text. It invites interpretations examining plot lines and all characters in the narrative. It also looks at the cultural norms within

---

1. J. Cheryl Exum and David J.A. Clines, 'The New Literary Criticism', in J. Cheryl Exum and David J.A. Clines (eds.), *The New Literary Criticism and the Hebrew Bible* (Valley Forge, PA: Trinity Press International, 1993), pp. 11-25 (13).

biblical texts and sees these as just as important as any historical information the text imparts. Finally, it investigates how texts and different readers interact and how those interactions are varied as readers come from different cultures, genders, and social standing.

This chapter begins with comments on literary criticism in general, specifically with the development of literary methods in North America since the 1950s. It thendiscusses the integration of these methods into Hebrew Bible studies. Finally, it turns to literary criticism in feminist Hebrew Bible scholarship, elaborating on some of the works of feminist scholars who made creative and productive use of literary methods. A conclusion outlines possible directions for feminist literary approaches of the Bible.

Literary Criticism in the Twentieth Century

In the mid-twentieth century, New Criticism emerged in English departments as a reaction to the limitations of the historical study of texts. Literary critics wanted to read literature as 'literature' and they developed 'close readings' of the final form of the texts. They did not want to go behind a text but proposed to read 'within' it, ignoring questions about original context and authorship.

In a seminal article of this new school, W.K. Wimsatt, Jr and Monroe Beardsley explain that the study of a literary work is greater than the quest for textual origins or authorship:[2]

> The poem is not the critic's own and not the author's (it is detached from the author at birth and goes about the world beyond his power to intend about it or control it). The poem belongs to the public. It is embodied in language, the peculiar possession of the public, and it is about the human being, an object of public knowledge. What is said about the poem is subject to the same scrutiny as any statement in linguistics or in the general science of psychology.[3]

They also maintain that a literary work does not begin or end with individual critics and their reactions. Rather, the work itself captures a moment and offers that moment again and again to subsequent generations: 'Poetry

---

2. This method is the primary methodological focus against which they reacted.
3. W.K Wimsatt, Jr and Monroe Beardsley, 'The Intentional Fallacy', in W.K. Wimsatt, Jr and Monroe C. Beardsley (eds.), *The Verbal Icon: Studies in the Meaning of Poetry* (Lexington: University of Kentucky Press, 1954), pp. 21-40 (5). Eagleton notes that several of the New Critics were Christians concerned with dogma; see Terry Eagleton, *Literary Theory: An Introduction* (Minneapolis: University of Minnesota Press, 3rd edn, 2008), p. 42. One can see that this was a reaction to the earlier historical and form criticisms.

is a way of fixing emotions or making them more permanently perceptible when objects have undergone a functional change from culture to culture, or when as simple facts of history they have lost emotive value with loss of immediacy'.[4] While Wimsatt and Beardsley dealt with poetry, their statements became the foundation of new literary criticism for all forms of literature. A literary work is a piece of art, belonging not to its author or any individual. It is a place of preserved memory and emotion created with words and syntax—a word picture in its totality. It has its own integrity without dissection. For instance, even without extensive historical knowledge, *Les Misérables* by Victor Hugo creates the mood and tensions of early nineteenth-century France, preserving them for future generations. Indeed, new critics believe so strongly in the integrity of a literary work that, to some of them, it 'could not be paraphrased, expressed in any other language other than itself; each of its parts was folded in on the others in a complex organic unity which it would be a kind of blasphemy to violate'.[5]

While Wimsatt and Beardsley described literature on a macro scale, another lion of the new critics, I.A. Richards worked on the micro level, by developing his model of a close reading of texts.[6] He revived the ancient art of rhetoric because he regarded it as broader than Aristotle's category of persuasion. In *Practical Criticism*, Richards outlined this rhetorical method[7] in which a word's meaning is broader than captured in a dictionary: 'For the very reason a word is *not* like its meaning, it can represent an enormously wide range of different things'.[8] Richards established four categories of meaning for words that relied on the context and the characteristics of sentences, grammar structures, and metaphors.[9] A close study of these structures, in turn, aids readers in their understanding of society and the world, as well as, the development of critical thought. In other words, Richards suggested that a close study of literature impacts and shapes people's view of society. They do not only learn about literature as an object lesson, they also gain skills and morality by reading literature closely. Literature does not only offer content, but it teaches about culture, emotion, and morality. The technique of close reading thus remains a basic element

---

4. W.K. Wimsatt and Monroe Beardsley, 'The Affective Fallacy', in W.K. Wimsatt and Monroe C. Beardsley (eds.), *The Verbal Icon: Studies in the Meaning of Poetry* (Lexington: University of Kentucky Press, 1954), pp. 21-40 (38).

5. Eagleton, *Literary Theory*, pp. 40-41.

6. I.A. Richards, *The Philosophy of Rhetoric* (Oxford: Oxford University Press, 1936).

7. I.A. Richards, *Practical Criticism: A Study of Literary Judgment* (New York: Harcourt & Brace, 1929).

8. Richards, *Practical Criticism*, p. 364.

9. Richards, *Practical Criticism*, pp. 180-82, 357-64. The categories are sense, feeling, tone, and intention.

of all literary criticism to this day. As a methodological approach, New Criticism is, however, limited to investigating individual texts as a unit without any consideration for their original contexts or their interpretation histories.

The work of Northrop Frye addresses this limitation of New Criticism. In his seminal work, *Anatomy of Criticism,* Frye argues that literary criticism must be considered its own discipline. He states: 'It is generally accepted that a critic is a better judge of the *value* of a poem than its creator, but there is still a lingering notion that it is somehow ridiculous to regard the critic as the final judge of meaning, even though in practice it is clear that he must be'.[10] Frye thus aims to develop a 'conceptual framework'[11] that focuses on specific elements present in all literature. A critic evaluates each of these elements individually and in the relationship to other textual elements. Further, a critic may also evaluate individual elements, such as genre, in relationship to other contemporary texts and other texts throughout history.[12] This procedure ensures that critics study the rhetorical elements articulated in Richards's work both systematically and chronologically. To Frye, this methodology distinguishes a critic from a casual reader.

Eagleton notes that Frye cannot be called a structuralist[13] in a strict sense. However, he brings a sense of structure to the study of texts with a focus on a text's genre and sub-genres, and so his work has led to a renewed focus on form criticism and the mapping of genres.[14] His work also led to structuralist interpretation of texts although structuralism is not a literary method *per se*. Discipline-specific structuralist methods have been developed by various scholars, such as Claude Lévi-Strauss in anthropology, Roland Barthes and Gérard Genette in literary studies, Jacques Lacan in psychoanalysis, and Michel Foucault in intellectual history. These works, later labeled under 'structuralism', were 'imported and read in England, the United States, and elsewhere'.[15] Structuralism 'seeks not to produce new interpretations of works but to understand how they have the meaning and effects that they do'.[16] This type of approach also requires a close reading of texts but with different results. In the example above of *Les Misérables*, a structural study would observe how plot line, metaphors, character development, dialogue, and the narrator work together to create the message of

10. Northrop Frye, *Anatomy of Criticism: Four Essays* (Princeton, NJ: Princeton University Press, 1957), p. 5.

11. Frye, *Anatomy*, p. 9.

12. Frye, *Anatomy*. The evaluation is complex and involves evaluating a text's modes, symbols, myths, and genre.

13. Structuralism was a movement primarily in France in the 1960s (see below).

14. Eagleton, *Literary Theory*, p. 82.

15. Jonathan Culler, *Literary Theory: A Very Short Introduction* (Oxford: Oxford University Press, 2000), p. 138.

16. Culler, *Literary Theory*, p. 138.

the book. The critic would seek to understand how this text and its meaning relate to other texts.

As noted from the list of scholars, structuralism is an interdisciplinary method in which literature is only part of a larger entity. Accordingly, the structures found in literature reflect the culture where and when a work was written. For instance, *Les Misérables* reflects class conflict, but it also mirrors patriarchy and hierarchical structures of nineteenth-century France. Literature not only captures the emotional import of a culture but also its moral views and values. For instance, it is debatable whether the depiction of patriarchy in *Les Misérables* is an intended subplot or part of the cultural 'plot' within which the story appears.

The study of 'how' a text is embedded in culture is called semiotics or structural linguistics.[17] Broadly, semiotics concentrates on the level of language or the building blocks of literature. A word is not just a word; it is a 'signifier' for a concept, the 'signified'. To understand the word 'dog' (signifier) as anything other than a sound, a reader must associate it with the concept of a canine animal (signified).[18] If a reader does not know French, the word '*chien*' will mean nothing. The signifier (dog, *chien*) varies from language to language, but the signified remains the same. Yet, even the 'signified' is adaptable to a degree because each reader will have a different image of the concept 'dog'. This difference makes language malleable to a point because the signified can vary within certain parameters. For instance, a 'dog' may be large or small, black or brown, but it will always be a type of canine. Our experience will impact what we see and understand. Thus, a narrative is constantly in flux because the signified is different for different readers and it also changes in a single reader over time.

In short, both New Criticism and structuralism focus on the text as the place of meaning. The text carries 'how' meaning is made. The development of post-structuralism has moved literary criticism to focus on readers, maintaining that readers, not texts, create meaning. This tension between texts and readers as the site of meaning is an ongoing debate in literary studies. Currently, a balanced view is prominent in which texts and readers join a partnership of sorts. For instance, while there are strong women characters in *Les Misérables*, the text was written in a time when women did not control their own destiny and a poor woman was at risk of sexual exploitation

---

17. For texts only, the field is linguistics. Semiotics is the field in which signs are not limited to the written word, i.e. a tornado siren is a familiar sign to persons in the Midwest with a specific meaning, namely danger. To an African tourist, it would not signal danger.

18. Charles Sanders Peirce, 'Pragmatism', in Nathan Houser *et al.* (eds.), *The Essential Peirce Volume 2 (1893–1914)* (Bloomington, IN: Indiana University Press, 1998), pp. 398-431 (411).

in the workplace without any recourse. In other words, women are confined to predictable places by in the narrative, yet within those parameters, readers can 'create' images of women although they cannot be liberated from the gendered limitations of their culture.

Structural linguistics reminds critics of the limits of language. It is meant to communicate, but the meaning of words and the grammar system are arbitrary. For instance, each language has a word for 'dog'. Yet these words are unrelated to each other and have no association with the object that the word represents. Likewise, the grammatical order of a sentence is dictated by the language with a great variety between languages. David Chandler explains this dynamic when he states: 'The Saussurean model, with its emphasis on internal structures within a sign system, can be seen as supporting the notion that language does not "reflect" reality but rather *constructs* it. We can use language to say what isn't in the world, as well as what is. And since we come to know the world through whatever language we have been born into the midst of, it is legitimate to argue that our language determines reality, rather than reality our language.'[19] In other words, both writers and readers are limited by the language in which they work and think, as well as by the grammatical structures that restrict expression to certain forms. One's language constructs reality and shapes one's ability to reason and process information. For instance, egalitarian writing is more difficult in most European languages because the pronoun is gendered, forcing a gendered choice in the singular. However, Turkish uses a genderless pronoun, and so it allows for more inclusion in its language.[20]

The coming of age of literary criticism in the second half of the twentieth century had a major impact on the academy and brought with it seismic shifts in the study of texts. The author ceases to be the central focus, and famously Barthes declares 'him' dead in 1967.[21] The idea of an objective and single meaning also has died a slow death. It has been replaced with a more nuanced methodology that posits texts and readers as both being engaged in textual meanings. Depending on the philosophy of a critic, one or the other exert dominance. Literary criticism has given new life to ancient texts and, in turn, has invited innovative interpretations. The experiences of gender, race, and culture of the interpreters matter and diverse readings are preferred because they offer richer understandings. Engagement with this plurality of interpretations strengthens the next generation of

---

19. David Chandler, 'Semiotics for Beginners'; available at http://visualmemory.co.uk/daniel/Documents/S4B/sem02.html (accessed July 2, 2015).

20. More egalitarian language does not necessarily produce an equivalent change in culture because culture is more complex than language.

21. Roland Barthes, 'The Death of the Author', in *Image, Music, and Text* (trans. S. Heath; New York: Hill and Wang, 1977), pp. 142-48.

readers so that they turn into thinkers rather than mere consumers of someone else's opinion.

Literary Criticism in Biblical Studies

Literary theorists have engaged the Hebrew Bible as an important text of Western culture.[22] Yet the field of biblical studies has remained a discipline apart from these developments. For the most part, biblical scholars argued for the uniqueness of the Bible, declaring its authority as God-inspired. For them, truth has not been plural, and so the standard academic interpretation relies on historical and form criticism.[23] Placed in its most concrete terms, G.E. Wright states: 'In biblical faith everything depends upon whether the events actually occurred'.[24] Mark Powell summarizes how Christian scholars and pastors have viewed biblical texts. He states: '[T]he Bible has been read as a record of significant history, a compendium of revealed truth, or a guidebook for daily living'.[25]

In 1968, James Muilenburg gave his presidential address before the Society of Biblical Literature calling on the academy to move beyond historical criticism and toward literary criticism.[26] He explained:

> Persistent and painstaking attention to the modes of Hebrew literary composition will reveal that the pericopes exhibit linguistic patterns, word formations ordered or arranged in particular ways, verbal sequences which move in fixed structures from beginning to end. It is clear that they have been skillfully wrought in many different ways, often with consummate skill and artistry.[27]

Muilenburg worked hard to convince his colleagues that literary critical readings of the Bible were necessary. Since literary interpretations center on the interaction between texts and readers, some Bible scholars feared it

---

22. See, e.g., Roland Barthes, *Structural Analysis and Biblical Exegesis: Interpretational Essays* (trans. A. Johnson; Pittsburgh: Pickwick Publications, 1974).

23. At first glance, form criticism focuses on genres and appears to have much in common with rhetorical and structural studies. The difference is in what a critic does with the results of such an approach. In biblical studies, scholars use these 'forms' of literature to study the history behind the texts, not for what the texts teach about cultures norms or meaning.

24. G.E. Wright, *The God who Acts: Biblical Theology as Recital* (SBT, 8; London: SCM Press, 1952), p. 126.

25. Mark Allen Powell, *What Is Narrative Criticism?* (Minneapolis: Augsburg Press, 1991), p. 1.

26. James Muilenburg, 'Form Criticism and Beyond', *JBL* 88 (1969), pp. 1-18. Muilenburg uses this literary method prior to his address but he called it rhetorical criticism.

27. Muilenburg, 'Form Criticism', p. 18. See also Michael Fox, 'The Rhetoric of Ezekiel's Vision of the Valley of the Dry Bones', *HUCA* 51 (1980), pp. 1-2.

would represent a move away from God and traditional biblical authority.[28] Interestingly, literary criticism has often resulted in a nuanced understanding of biblical authority that takes the text, tradition, and readers into account. Muilenburg must be regarded as a pioneering scholar who introduced 'rhetorical criticism' as an exegetical method. He explained it as 'understanding the nature of Hebrew composition, in exhibiting the structural patterns that are employed for the fashioning of a literary unit, whether in prose or poetry, and in discerning the many and various devices by which the predications are formulated and ordered into a unified whole'.[29] Muilenburg relied on Richards's work in rhetoric and adapted it for biblical exegesis. It is clear that this and related literary studies in Hebrew Bible maintained the status quo in the field. They made the text an object to be studied and dissected. More importantly, like structural linguists, rhetorical critics centered on 'how' a text creates meaning, and they addressed readers as objective critics.

Yet, soon younger colleagues began to use rhetorical criticism to study biblical prose and poetry. For instance, Cheryl Exum explored the Song of Songs in her 1973 article in which she acknowledges her debt to Muilenburg and the overt exclusion of traditional historical critical scholarship in her work:

> The present study owes much to Muilenburg's observations on style and rhetorical criticism. It proposes to examine in detail the poetic form of the Song and to pay particular attention to its literary and stylistic aspects. A formal analysis being our specific purpose, questions regarding date, authorship, provenance, and *Sitz im Leben*, as well as consideration of textual matters, will not be discussed. Nevertheless, we hope that, if our study is successful, the results gained from literary and structural analysis may be utilized in order to shed light on numerous exegetical problems and interpretations connected with the Song.[30]

While Muilenburg and Exum developed their approach for poetic texts, Yehoshua Gitay, Richard Clifford, and Michael Fox explored the literary structure of persuasion in prophetic literature.[31] In the early 1990s, rhetorical

---

28. Phyllis Trible notes that 'author-ity is authorial power' and it was traditionally attributed to God; see her 'Authority of the Bible', in Walter J. Harrelson, Donald Senior, Abraham Smith, Phyllis Trible and James C. VanderKam (eds.), *The New Interpreter's Study Bible* (Nashville: Abingdon Press, 2003), pp. 2248-54 (2248).

29. Muilenburg, *Form Criticism*, p. 8.

30. J. Cheryl Exum, 'Literary and Structural Analysis of the Song of Songs', *ZAW* 85 (1973), pp. 47-48.

31. Yehoshua Gitay, *Prophecy and Persuasion: A Study of Isaiah 40–48* (Bonn: Linguistica Biblica, 1981); Richard Clifford, *Fair Spoken and Persuading: An Interpretation of Second Isaiah* (New York: Paulist Press, 1984); Michael Fox, 'The Rhetoric of Ezekiel's Vision of the Valley of the Dry Bones', *HUCA* 51 (1980), pp. 1-2.

criticism reached its pinnacle in Phyllis Trible's work in which she explains the method in careful detail, applying it to the book of Jonah.[32] In conversation with of all of these scholars, she presented the history, rationale, and principles of rhetorical criticism as a literary method, and her book teaches how to read biblical texts with this literary approach. She had first begun her explorations into Jonah and rhetorical criticism during her doctoral dissertation work guided by Muilenburg, her doctoral advisor.[33]

In 1975, J.P. Fokkelman published his work on Genesis grounded in literary criticism. He examined the interaction between author and reader in a synchronic reading of the biblical text.[34] Traditional interpretations rely on diachronic approaches that examine the historical development of the biblical book.[35] In contrast to them, Fokkelman introduced a focus on the readers while also asserting the significance of authorial intention. His work demonstrates that these early biblical literary critics integrated concepts from literary criticism into the field of biblical studies by attempting to combine them with the traditional historical critical approaches.

The next major development came from Brevard Childs and James Sanders. Both scholars developed comprehensive literary explanations for the final form of the biblical text which is today called 'canonical criticism'. Yet the two scholars developed two distinctive approaches. To Childs, the text in its final form is Scripture, and canonical readings are synchronic and focused on the theological meanings of the biblical texts.[36] It is difficult to overestimate the impact of Child's work on the development of literary criticism in biblical studies. Childs challenged standard biblical scholarship that assumed a neutral descriptive stance to the exegesis of the biblical text. To Childs, this type of interpreter came to the text and treated it as an object from a neutral or disinterested perspective.[37] Childs argued that this neutrality should be suspended and the interpreter should adopt a self-claimed theological perspective: 'We are arguing that the genuine theological task can be carried on successfully only when it begins from within an explicit

---

32. Phyllis Trible, *Rhetorical Criticism: Context, Methods, and the Book of Jonah* (Minneapolis: Fortress Press, 1994).

33. Phyllis Trible, 'Studies in the Book of Jonah' (PhD thesis, Columbia University, New York, 1963).

34. J.P. Fokkelman, *Narrative Art in Genesis: Specimens of Stylistic and Structural Analysis* (Assen, The Netherlands: Van Gorcum, 1975).

35. Phyllis Trible notes that 'his synchronic method of close reading approximated New Criticism and his overall approach resembled biblical rhetorical criticism'; see Trible, *Rhetorical Criticism*, p. 75.

36. Brevard Childs, *Introduction to the Old Testament as Scripture* (Philadelphia: Fortress Press, 1979).

37. Brevard Childs, 'Interpretation in Faith: The Theological Responsibility of an Old Testament Commentary', *Interpretation* 18 (1962), pp. 432-49 (433).

framework of faith'.[38] Childs challenged readers of biblical texts to clearly state their perspectives and how their views impact their readings.

In contrast, James Sanders developed a specifically diachronic approach that explored how the final form of the biblical canon came into existence and how this canon has functioned within believing communities. He states:

> Canon owes its life to dialogue with those believing communities; and in the believing communities owe their life to their dialogue with it. The kinds of repetition of the text and tradition in ever-changing contexts, the evidence of its multivalency or pregnant ambiguity, the evidence of its adaptability-stability factor and the power of hermeneutics that helped shape and reshape its traditions are all still operative in believing communities today.[39]

Sanders was not that much interested in current interpreters, but in the tradition of biblical interpretation as it had developed over thousands of years. His perspective offers a balance to the readerly perspective of Childs. Their efforts demonstrate that at the time biblical scholars developed various literary-oriented methods of reading the Hebrew Bible that created rich and nuanced meanings, and they declared that current interpreters and the long tradition of interpreters are important factors in the exegetical process.

An important development in the integration of literary criticism into Hebrew Bible studies occurred when two literary scholars published extensively on the Bible as literature. One of them is Robert Alter who published an influential book on characters, plot, and the role of the narrator in biblical literature. On the basis of literary criteria, Alter also isolated type-scenes in biblical texts, classifying them as literary conventions in biblical storytelling.[40] Alter explained his approach in the following statement:

> This instance may suggest that in many cases a literary student of the Bible has more to learn from the traditional commentaries than from modern scholarship. The difference between the two is ultimately the difference between assuming that the text is an intricately interconnected unity, as the midrashic exegetes did, and assuming it is patchwork of frequently disparate documents, as modern scholars have supposed.[41]

Rejecting the centrality of the contemporary field of biblical studies, he asserted the significance of the Jewish exegetical tradition, such as in

---

38. Childs, 'Interpretation', p. 438.
39. James Sanders, *From Sacred Story to Sacred Text* (Philadelphia: Fortress Press, 1987), p. 172.
40. Robert Alter, *The Art of Biblical Narrative* (New York: Basic Books, 1981). This volume is followed by his *the Art of Biblical Poetry* (New York: Basic Books, 1985).
41. Alter, *Biblical Narrative*, p. 11.

Midrash, which constituted a drastic reversal of the scholarly conventions at the time. The text of the Bible with its unevenness and contradictions is not a problem to be solved by modern interpreters but to be appreciated and contemplated as is.

Another literary critic who made a central contribution to the literary investigation of the Hebrew Bible is Meir Sternberg. His work entitled, *The Poetics of Biblical Narrative*, is extensive and complex. Yet two of its aspects changed how biblical texts are read today. One aspect relates to his discussions on the 'omniscient narrator' in which he notes that the omniscient perspective is a consistent thread in all biblical narratives, except in Ezra and Nehemiah. This method, then, is not the creation of one biblical author but of many authors. The narrator knows all of the information throughout time and serves as a guide. Sternberg saw a long standing pattern and suggested that God guides the characters in the text just as the biblical narrator guides the reading experience of the readers.[42] One could argue that the narrator is actually the author, but, according to Sternberg, the narrator and the author are not the same because the narrator is embedded in the text, always traveling within it. Sternberg's second contribution is that any reader of the biblical text

> must answer a series of questions: What is happening or has happened, and why? What connects the present event or situation to what went before, and how do both relate to what will probably come after? What are the features, motives, and designs of this or that character? How does he [*sic*] view his fellow characters? And what norms govern the existence and conduct of all? It is the set of answers given that enables the reader to reconstruct the field of reality devised by the text, to make sense of the represented world. Yet a closer look at the text will reveal how few of the answers to these questions have been explicitly provided there: it is the reader himself who has supplied them, some temporarily, some partially, or tentatively, and some wholly and finally'.[43]

In other words, the narrator provides the structure of ambiguities, gaps, and connections from which a reader creates the narrative. Ultimately, Sternberg did not merge the narrator with God, but he simply invited others to contemplate the narrator's place in the matrix between God, the narrative, and the reader, as well as to realize that even the omniscient narrator remains a teacher who is a guide for readers and not a master providing one single meaning to the text.

These significant publications illustrate how literary approaches to the Bible moved exegetical methods from a focus on authorship and historical questions to the text itself. By the early 1990s, close readings of the text,

---

42. Meir Sternberg, *The Poetics of Biblical Narrative: Ideological Literature and the Drama of Reading* (Bloomington, IN: Indiana University Press, 1987), p. 141.

43. Sternberg, *Poetics*, p. 186.

including its rhetorical and structural elements, were common, at least in the North American scholarly context. Today, the debate between the merits of literary and historical criticism is still ongoing. Also, within literary circles, the debate continues on how texts and readers interact and how much of the meaning comes from textual structures and how much comes from the readers. Yet undoubtedly, biblical exegesis has opened up to literary methods, which has moved the field far beyond historical criticism.

Since historical critical readings are technically a form of literary criticism, this development has been classified as 'new literary criticism'. However, this general term is found only in biblical studies and should not be confused with the 'New Criticism' in literary studies.[44] For instance, J. Cheryl Exum and David Clines relate new literary criticism to biblical publications that are post-structuralist. Yet they also recognize the eclectic nature of exegesis done with new literary methods, which makes such a categorization difficult. They explain:

> The first thing that strikes one is how eclectic the new literary criticism is… Most of them move freely from one critical approach to another, combining materialist with reader-response criticism, psychoanalytic with ideological criticism, and so on.
>
> In their diversity, these [biblical studies]…reflect the multidisciplinary nature of these new criticisms, their resistance to tidy classification (for example, in positing a woman reader, feminist criticism is also reader-response criticism, and in reading against the grain, it works like deconstruction).[45]

Today, literary criticism is still an eclectic approach that includes various sub-methods. A summary of these criticism appears in two anthologies. One is *To Each Its Own Meaning* and the other is *New Meanings for Ancient Texts*.[46] Both volumes include methods as they have been developed by scholars throughout the world.

Feminist Literary Criticism

Feminist literary criticism of the Hebrew Bible is multifaceted with a philosophical foundation that is both ideological and deconstructionist. It is ideological because feminist work aims for women's and other underrepresented groups' equality and liberation. Feminist criticism is also deconstructionist

---

44. Exum and Clines, 'New Criticism', p. 12.
45. Exum and Clines, 'New Criticism', pp. 12-13.
46. Steven McKenzie and Stephan Haynes (eds.), *To Each Its Own Meaning, Revised and Expanded: An Introduction to Biblical Criticisms and Their Application* (Louisville, KY: Westminster/John Knox Press, 1999); Steven McKenzie and John Kaltner (eds.), *New Meanings for Ancient Texts: Recent Approaches to Biblical Criticisms and Their Applications* (Louisville, KY: Westminster/John Knox Press, 2013).

because it names the patriarchal bias in biblical texts and interpretations. To achieve these goals, feminist scholars use rhetorical, intertextual, canonical, and many other literary methods. Thus, feminist literary criticism does not consist of a single method and it also does not produce a single meaning. Rather, it is a philosophy of reading that is openly named and cultivated.[47]

An important purpose of feminist literary criticism is to uncover and emphasize female characters in biblical texts and to expose patriarchal interpretations for neglecting and even burying them. Biblical scholars have used various literary methods, and a hallmark of feminist literary theory has been this multifaceted approach toward this goal. Thus, feminist literary criticism of the Hebrew Bible has attracted many scholars, and the following discussion references only a small number of influential works.[48]

Often, feminist literary scholars have turned their attention to the Pentateuch. For instance, in androcentric exegesis the women of Exodus are usually overlooked characters in contrast to the central role attributed to Moses. J. Cheryl Exum and Renita Weems examined Exodus 1–2 with literary methods to offer interpretations that consider the various women in the narrative. They highlight the women and their roles in saving infants, emphasizing that the women's saving actions save the people of Israel as a whole.[49] Exum and Weems maintain that the women use the 'ways of women' to thwart off the diabolical plans of the powerful Pharaoh. They are not afraid to commit acts of social disobedience. As the opening scene in Exodus 1–2 has always been part of the Bible, it is curious that androcentric readers overlooked these two chapters until feminist critics pointed out the women's central role in Israel's salvation story. In a similar fashion, yet another feminist literary interpreter elevated Miriam from 'sister of Moses and Aaron' to a leader in the wilderness. Rita Burns studied carefully the seven narratives about Miriam in the Pentateuch demonstrating the prominent role of this important female leader in the early narrated history of ancient Israel.[50] These and many other feminist writers found lost women

---

47. All critical readings operate via the critic's philosophy of reading provided by both culture and education whether the critic states the philosophy or not. Feminist work openly declares its philosophy so others can clearly see its objectives and prejudices.

48. It is impossible to discuss all of the accomplishments of feminist exegetes working with literary method. In addition, my survey leaves out many of the feminist writers and is illustrative only.

49. Cheryl Exum, '"You shall let every daughter live": A Study of Exodus 1:8–2:10', *Semeia* 28 (1983), pp. 63-82; Renita Weems, 'The Hebrew Women Are Not Like the Egyptian Women: The Ideology of Race, Gender and Sexual Reproduction in Exodus 1', *Semeia* 59 (1992), pp. 25-34.

50. Rita Burns, *Has the Lord Spoken Only Through Moses? A Study of the Biblical Portrait of Miriam* (SBLDS, 84; Atlanta: Scholar's Press, 1987), p. 121.

in the Hebrew Bible that traditional androcentric interpretation had ignored for centuries.

Other scholars demonstrate that biblical women are not only overlooked but are also minimized in their complexity as characters depicted in biblical narratives. Androcentric exegetes stereotype them as wives and mothers, muting their actual storylines. Thus, for instance, excellent feminist literary studies engage the complex and problematic relationship between Sarah and Hagar, showing that they are not one-dimensional characters. Sarah is both oppressed and oppressor whereas Hagar is both enslaved and one who speaks directly with God.[51] Both women have great strength and their relationship is painful and realistically portrayed, teaching much about women of different social class status even today.[52] In her work on Abigail, Alice Bach explains what this type of literary reading accomplishes: 'Instead of evaluating and praising Abigail as a suitable partner for David, reading the text as it has been controlled by codes of male dominance, I adopt a revisionary approach, in order to explore female influence in a male-authored work…. Thus, even though the story appears to be about male authority, female presence shines through'.[53] Because of Bach's work, Abigail has become more than a minor footnote in David's narrative. Bach's approach encapsulates what feminist exegetes often do: they recover, refocus, and retell often terrifying narratives of biblical women. They show that Sarah, Hagar, Abigail, and many other biblical women appear in stories that present them beyond traditional androcentric roles and expectations.

Another venue in feminist literary criticism relates to the use of literary methods to de-romanticize biblical stories and to place them next to the struggles of contemporary women. For instance, Athalya Brenner offers a close reading of the book of Ruth, which includes contemporary statistics on migrant women in contemporary Israel. The literary technique is

---

51. Some studies include Sharon Pace Jeansonne, *The Women of Genesis: From Sarah to Potiphar's Wife* (Minneapolis: Fortress Press, 1990), pp. 14-30, 43-42; Kathryn Pfisterer Darr, *Far More Precious Than Jewels: Perspectives on Biblical Women* (Louisville, KY: Westminster/John Knox Press, 1991), pp. 85-163.

52. Katherine Doob Sakenfeld, 'Sarah and Hagar: Power and Privileges', *Just Wives? Stories of Power and Survival in the Old Testament and Today* (Louisville, KY: Westminster/John Knox Press, 2003), pp. 7-26; Beth LaNeel Tanner, 'My Sister Sarah: On Being a Woman in the First World', in Linda Day and Carolyn Pressler (eds.), *Engaging the Bible in an Gendered World: An Introduction to Feminist Biblical Interpretation:* in Honor of Katharine Doob Sakenfeld (Louisville, KY: Westminster/John Knox Press, 2006), pp. 60-72; Renita Weems, 'A Mistress, A Maid, and No Mercy (Sarah and Hagar)', in *Just a Sister Away: Understanding the Timeless Connection Between Women of Today and Women in the Bible* (New York: Hatchette, 1988), pp. 1-21.

53. Alice Bach, 'The Pleasure of Her Text', *Union Seminary Quarterly Review* 43 (1989), pp. 41-58 (41).

akin to intertextuality in which two narratives are read together in an effort to see aspects of both that would not have been seen without the shared contexts.[54] It also enables Brenner to provide a practical, survival oriented reading of Ruth. She relies on statistics and legal information on women migrants to give readers new insights into Ruth's decision to go to Israel. This type of literary work accomplishes two goals. It challenges romanticized interpretations of Ruth, which are often told 'in favor of finding spiritual motives over practical ones.'[55] It also helps Brenner to emphasize that for at-risk poor women not much has changed since the Ruth story was first heard and 'there is nothing romantic about being a fugitive, or about seeking economic asylum',[56] then or now. Likewise, Mmadipoane (Ngwana 'Mphahlele) Masenya presents an interpretation of Prov. 31.10-31 that reads the poem of the valiant woman within her contemporary South African Sotho context. Masenya challenges standard readings that equate the woman of this poem with Wisdom personified, successfully turning her into a metaphor.[57] Yet by reading the poem within the context of an African woman who has a parallel function in the day-to-day operations of the household, Masenya reads the poem as a description of African women's daily reality.[58] These two intertexual readings demonstrate that the placement of biblical texts next to the real lives of contemporary women creates innovative and de-romanticized understandings of biblical literature. It proves that what is read in concert with biblical texts impacts the interpretation. By bridging the gap between ancient and modern women, feminist interpreters demonstrate that biblical texts indicate how little has changed for some women even in today's world.

These are only a few examples of feminist literary readings. Many of the other forgotten women in the Hebrew Bible appear in the contributions of the other two volumes of *Feminist Interpretation of the Hebrew Bible in Retrospect*. Feminist literary approaches often recover female characters, highlighting overlooked characters in various biblical texts and in androcentric interpretations. Feminist scholars use close literary readings connecting them to gender, race, and class in ways not previously seen in the field of biblical studies.

Next to literary explorations of female characters in particular biblical narratives, other works engage the patriarchal nature of biblical texts and

---

54. Athalya Brenner, 'From Ruth to the "Global Woman": Social and Legal Aspects', *Interpretation* 64 (2010), pp. 162-68 (162).

55. Brenner, 'From Ruth', p. 168.

56. Brenner, 'From Ruth', p. 168.

57. Mmadipoane (Ngwana 'Mphahlele) Masenya, 'A *Bosadi* (Womanhood) Reading of Proverbs 31:10-31', in Musa W. Dube (ed.), *Other Ways of Reading: African Women and the Bible* (Atlanta: Society of Biblical Literature, 2001), pp. 145-57 (146).

58. Masenya, 'A *Bosadi* (Womanhood) Reading', p. 152.

traditional scholarship. The first Hebrew Bible monograph with a clearly stated feminist perspective is Phyllis Trible's *God and The Rhetoric of Sexuality*.[59] This work, based in rhetorical criticism, highlights feminine images for God and also points to a diverse set of biblical texts in which female and male interact on a level plain field. Trible notes: 'Clearly, the patriarchal stamp of scripture is permanent. But just as clearly, interpretation of its content is forever changing, since new occasions teach new duties and contexts alter texts, liberating them from frozen constructions. Moving across cultures and centuries, then, the Bible informed a feminist perspective and correspondingly, a feminist perspective enlightened the Bible'.[60] A hallmark of feminist literary approaches is the honest evaluation of Scripture and the history of its androcentric interpretation. Trible's second book, *Texts of Terror*, features four narratives in which women appear as victims. Employing a combination of literary and intertextual readings, referencing the so-called Servant songs in Second Isaiah, the passion narratives in the New Testament, and Eucharistic sections of the New Testament Epistles, she writes: 'Women, not men, are suffering servants and Christ figures… Scripture thus interpreting Scripture undercuts triumphalism and raises disturbing questions of faith'.[61] In other words, by not side-stepping the violent ways women were treated in biblical narratives and prophetic texts, Trible and others questioned biblical authority. In particular, Trible pushed the edge of that authority by demonstrating biblical women bear the pain and sins of androcentric culture. It makes them Christ-like figures.

Another feminist literary critic works very differently, and yet her interpretations also illuminate the feminist effort to deal honestly with biblical androcentrism and to overcome the androcentric interpretation history. Focusing primarily on the so-called love songs and women's stories in the book of Judges, Mieke Bal[62] relies on structuralism to understand gender, moral, and religious codes in biblical texts and their interpretations. She asserts that interpreters see only those parts of a text that embedded codes reveal to readers when readers privilege one code over others. For instance, if a reader privileges an androcentric assumptions about women and men, this reader will find it in the text.[63] Bal illustrates this point by using various

---

59. Phyllis Trible, *God and the Rhetoric of Sexuality* (Overtures to Biblical Theology; Philadelphia: Fortress Press, 1978).

60. Trible, *God and Rhetoric*, p. 202.

61. Phyllis Trible, *Texts of Terror: Literary-Feminist Readings of Biblical Narratives* (Philadelphia: Fortress Press, 1984), p. 3.

62. Not a traditionally trained biblical scholar, Mieke Bal is a literary critic of note whose *Narratology: Introduction to the Theory of Narrative* (trans. C. van Boheemen; Toronto: University of Toronto Press, 1985) is a standard textbook in religion departments and seminaries globally.

63. Mieke Bal, *Lethal Love: Feminist Literary Readings of Biblical Love Stories*

codes. Hers is thus not only a feminist enterprise but one that aims to challenge long-held prejudices and assumptions about reading the Bible in general. She demonstrates that readerly biases impact what one sees and interprets in the biblical corpus.

Yet a third example of a feminist literary approach comes from Dana Nolan Fewell and David Gunn. They combine literary criticism and semiotics to understand how gender with power appear in biblical narratives. They state: 'Because of this instability [of language] the meaning of crucially important social terms like "feminine" and "masculine", "female" and "male", "woman" and "man" are always open to challenge and redefinition which shifts power relations within which language functions'.[64] By reading biblical texts as 'other', Fewell and Gunn challenge conventional understandings about gender and power.

Several other examples of feminist literary interpretations need to be mentioned. Ilana Pardes is concerned with the 'unexpected ways in which antipatriarchal perspectives have been partially preserved, against all odds, in the canon'.[65] She notes the influence of Bakthin and his work to understand the text as a diverse entity, or, as she calls it, as heteroglot. She explored mostly texts that are 'antipatriarchal'. Renita Weems produced literary feminist readings that focus on the so-called marriage metaphor and the promiscuous relationships depicted in the prophetic books such as Hosea 2, Jeremiah 13, and Ezekiel 16 and 23. She alleges that the original audiences for these texts were male and that 'imaging Israel as the promiscuous wife and God as the dishonored, outraged husband became a way for the prophet and audience to contemplate and explain Israel's experience with God whom people perceived at times as actively engaged in their history and at other times to be deadly silent to their pleas'.[66] These and other literary feminist readers investigate biblical language and culture to expose androcentric qualities of the biblical texts within their Israelite settings.

By the 1990s, feminist literary critics produced anthologies on every biblical book. The *Women's Biblical Commentary*[67] in the United States

---

(Bloomington, IN: Indiana University Press, 1987), pp. 5-6. Also *Murder and Difference: Gender, Genre, and Scholarship on Sisera's Death* (Bloomington, IN: Indiana University Press, 1988) and *Death and Dissymmetry: The Politics of Coherence in the Book of Judges* (Chicago: University of Chicago Press, 1989).

64. Dana Nolan Fewell and David Gunn, *Gender, Power, and Promise: The Subjects of the Bible's First Story* (Nashville: Abingdon Press, 1993), p. 17.

65. Ilana Paedes, *Countertraditions in the Bible: A Feminist Approach* (Cambridge: Harvard University Press, 1992).

66. Renita Weems, *Battered Love: Marriage, Sex and Violence in the Hebrew Prophets* (Minneapolis: Fortress Press, 1995), p. 70.

67. Carol A. Newson and Sharon H. Ringe (eds.), *Women's Bible Commentary* (Louisville, KY: Westminster/John Knox Press, 1992). For the most recent edition, see Carol

and the *Kompendium Feministische Bibelauslegung*[68] in German-speaking countries in Europe combined historical criticism with literary methods to highlight female characters and gender aspects of the various biblical texts. These publications represent an important step in feminist literary studies of the Bible because they demonstrate that literary feminist work enhances and broadens exegetical research. In addition, the series called *The Feminist Companion to the Bible*, edited by Athalya Brenner, contains articles on individual biblical books. The Series does not aim to be comprehensive but it showcases the feminist-exegetical work available at the time.[69] The nineteen volumes include a wide range of feminist literary scholarship based on every method used in the field. They invite readers to study biblical literature in creatively feminist ways and with literary methods.

A. Newsom, Sharon H. Ringe and Jacqueline E. Lapsley (eds.), *Women's Bible Commentary* (Louisville, KY: Westminster John Knox, 3rd rev. and updated edn, 2012).

68. Luise Schottroff and Marie-Theres Wacker (eds.), *Kompendium Feministische Bibelauslegung* (Gütersloh: Gütersloher Verlagshaus, 1998). For the translation into English, see Luise Schottroff and Marie-Theres Wacker (eds.), *Feminist Biblical Interpretation: A Compendium of Critical Commentary on the Books of the Bible and Related Literature* (trans. from the German by Martin Rumscheidt; Grand Rapids, MI: Eerdmans, 2012). For a critical review of the translation, see Susanne Scholz (ed.), 'Feminist Commentary upon Feminist Commentary: A Report from the Feminist Biblical Trenches', *lectio difficilior: European Feminist Journal for Feminist Exegesis* 1 (June 2014): http://www.lectio.unibe.ch.

69. The first series was edited by Athalya Brenner from 1993–2001 (with the exception of one co-edited volume) and published by Sheffield Academic Press: *A Feminist Companion to the Genesis* (1993); *A Feminist Companion to Judges* (1993); *A Feminist Companion to the Song of Songs* (1993); *A Feminist Companion to the Ruth* (1993); *A Feminist Companion to the Samuel to Kings* (1994); *A Feminist Companion to the Wisdom* (1995); *A Feminist Companion to the Esther, Judith and Susannah* (1995); *A Feminist Companion to the Latter Prophets* (Sheffield: Sheffield Academic Press, 1995); A *Feminist Companion to the Hebrew Bible in the New Testament* (Sheffield: Sheffield Academic Press, 1996); Athalya Brenner and Carole Fontaine (eds.), *A Feminist Companion to Reading of the Bible* (Sheffield: Sheffield Academic Press, 2001). The second series was also published by Athalya Brenner from 1998-2002 (with the exception of one co-edited volume) and published with Sheffield Academic Press: *Genesis: A Feminist Companion to the Bible (Second Series)* (1998); Athalya Brenner and Carole Fontaine (eds.), *Wisdom and Psalms: A Feminist Companion to the Bible (Second Series)* (1998); *Judges: A Feminist Companion to the Bible (Second Series)* (1999); *Ruth and Esther: A Feminist Companion to the Bible (Second Series)* (1999); *Samuel and Kings: A Feminist Companion to the Bible (Second Series)* (2000); *Exodus and Deuteronomy: A Feminist Companion to the Bible (Second Series)* (1998); *The Song of Songs: A Feminist Companion to the Bible (Second Series)* (2000); *Prophets and Daniel: A Feminist Companion to the Bible (Second Series)* (2002). The editor of the New Testament series is Amy-Jill Levine who has edited a growing series since 2000 with T. &T. Clark. The current publisher of Brenner's edited volumes is Bloomsbury T. & T. Clark.

A serious critique of the feminist literary enterprise, especially in its early states, has been that many feminist women in biblical studies have been white, Christian and mostly Protestant, and of European descent. Thus, both womanists and Jewish scholars stress that this kind of feminist perspective is not shared by *all* women but representative of only a small minority of women.[70] They also emphasize that every reader comes from a particular context defined by gender, race, and class paradigms of that context, and thus many different voices from many different cultures and faiths are needed to offer the wide spectrum of women's perspectives.

Concluding Remarks

So the question is what benefit literary criticism provides for biblical studies in general and feminist studies in particular? Three possible answers come to mind. First, literary studies challenges the status quo of historical and form criticism, and despite controversy it maintains that there is more to be learned by studying the world within the text than behind the text. Literary critics teach biblical scholars how to read and assess prose and poem as works of that art, contain messages far beyond historical kernels. Second, literary critics demonstrate that the text has a life of its own. It is not grounded only in the culture in which it was written but it also has an integrity in and of itself. Third, literary critics demonstrate that interpreters and their culture, gender, and social status matter to the interpretation of biblical texts. Readers come to biblical literature, identifying in it what our cultural codes allow us to see, and so we need many different readers interpreting with different parameters to expose what has been overlooked, neglected, and marginalized.

What has feminist literary criticism added to biblical studies? For sure, it has produced innovate and new readings of traditional texts. It has also demonstrated that interpreters and their perspectives matter. Feminist literary criticism brings honesty to the interpretation process by unmasking androcentric biases in traditional interpretations. Accordingly, the narratives of the patriarchs in the book of Genesis turn into narratives of patriarchs and matriarchs. Feminist literary criticism has thus made biblical interpretations more inclusive of the characters contained in biblical literature. It demonstrates that textual meaning is as important as the historical issues embedded in the text. Feminist literary criticism, along with literary criticism in general, has changed biblical studies for the better.

---

70. Judith Plaskow, 'Christian Feminism and Anti-Judaism', *Cross Currents* 28 (1978), pp. 306-309; Clarice Martin, 'Womanist Interpretations of the New Testament: The Quest for Holistic and Inclusive Translation and Interpretation', *JFSR* 6 (1990), pp. 41-61 (51).

The question then is whether there is a future for feminist literary criticism or whether everything that needs to be changed, emphasized, and uplifted has been done by now. If multi-voiced criticism has taught us anything, it is that importance is not vested in the conclusions but in the very process of study. Each new generation must engage in the interpretative process because their perspectives will be different from the ones already in print. In addition, feminist literary criticism must respond to its critics, as for instance, to the challenge articulated by Musa Dube when she states:

> The implication of the postcolonial era is that the Christian Bible no longer coexists with Jewish texts alone…. The Bible no longer belongs to Western Christians alone; rather, Two-Thirds World people, including the natives of North America, Canada and Australia, have had the Bible ever since the days when their lands were taken during a prayer. We therefore need a model of reading that takes serious the presence of both imperialism and patriarchy, and seeks for liberating interdependence between genders, races, nations, economies, cultures, political structures, and so on.[71]

Feminist literary critics must be honest about who we are and that our realities are not everyone's reality. Thus, feminist literary critics, too, need to be more proactive because they continue to write in a world in which women are at risk, paid less than men for the same work, and worship in churches that do not often accept feminist interpretations. The last forty years have seen great strides in biblical studies, but there remains still much to be done.

---

71. Musa Dube, *Postcolonial Feminist Interpretation of the Bible* (St. Louis: Chalice Press, 2000), p. 39.

9

Patriarch on the Couch:
Psychology in Feminist Exegesis[1]

Serge Frolov

Even by the standards of the twentieth century, with its explosive across-the-board expansion of human knowledge, the rise of psychology was nothing short of spectacular. As recently as the late 1800s, it simply did not exist as a field in its own right: those who were later recognized as its pioneers, such as Sigmund Freud, Carl Jung, Alfred Adler, and Otto Rank, initially saw themselves as neurologists or psychiatrists developing new techniques of therapy.[2] Today, slightly more than a century later, it is a full-fledged scholarly discipline with a wide range of subfields, such as developmental, occupational, organizational, and abnormal psychology. It has accumulated a wealth of experimental data, to say nothing of informal empirical observations and clinical experience, and it developed a rich array of theoretical frameworks aiming to account for them. The psychoanalytical theory of Freud and his followers came to be supplemented and to a great extent supplanted by such approaches as analytical psychology, individual psychology, behaviorism, *Gestalt* psychology, humanistic psychology, cognitive behavioral psychology, and reality psychology. Practical recommendations and techniques stemming from these theories are broadly applied in a variety of areas, such as education, industrial organization and corporate management, advertisement, politics, entertainment, and the military, not to mention counseling and psychotherapy, and so 'psychological language, concepts, and categories have become the everyday vocabulary of Western culture'.[3] With all that in mind, Peter Homans' characterization of the

---

1. I would like to thank my wife Elena Frolov, M.A., LPC, for her invaluable help with psychological concepts and literature.
2. Ira Progoff, *The Death and Rebirth of Psychology: An Integrative Evaluation of Freud, Adler, Jung and Rank and the Impact of Their Insights on Modern Man* (New York: McGraw-Hill, 1973), pp. 16-18.
3. D. Andrew Kille, 'Reading the Bible in Three Dimensions: Psychological Biblical Interpretation', in J. Harold Ellens and Wayne G. Rollins (eds.), *Psychology and the Bible: A New Way to Read the Scriptures*. I. *From Freud to Kohut* (Psychology, Religion, and Spirituality; Westport, CT: Praeger, 2004), pp. 17-32 (20).

contemporary Western individual as a 'psychological man' is not much of an exaggeration; if anything, the term (coined in 1979) has never rung truer than it does now.[4]

Dealing with how humans perceive and respond to each other and the surrounding world, how they form their ideas and emotions, and how they act (or refrain from acting) upon them, psychology seems to offer potentially powerful, and in many respects irreplaceable, tools for the study of religion on the one hand and literature on the other. The Bible in general and the Hebrew Bible in particular, lying on the intersection of the two, can thus be expected to be especially receptive to psychological analysis. As explained by Harold Ellens and Wayne Rollins, the emergence of such analysis was initially hampered by the grossly reductionist nature of early Freudian studies that antagonized both academics and Judeo-Christian believers by seeking to debunk religion rather than to understand it, and it was then brought to a standstill for several decades by behaviorist aversion to the subject.[5] The dominance of historical-critical approaches in biblical scholarship doubtlessly was another major damper. However, with the control of behaviorism in psychology and historical criticism in biblical studies coming to an end in the closing decades of the twentieth century the situation began to change, with major monographs and collective volumes as well as numerous articles and chapters firmly placing psychology on the increasingly diverse map of approaches to the Bible.[6]

It would appear that feminist interpreters of the Hebrew Bible could particularly benefit from the insights offered by psychological research. After all, gender issues have loomed large in modern psychology since its inception, and hardly any major theory or technique in the field has managed to avoid grappling with them, both directly and in conjunction with other aspects of human mind. It is hardly accidental that in one of the earliest

---

4. Cited in Kille, 'Reading the Bible in Three Dimensions', p. 20. Given the parlance of the day, there is little doubt that by 'man' Homans meant all humans.

5. J. Harold Ellens and Wayne G. Rollins, 'Introduction', in Ellens and Rollins (eds.), *Psychology and the Bible*, vol. 1, pp. 1-2.

6. Particularly notable (in the chronological order of appearance) are Wayne J. Rollins, *Jung and the Bible* (Atlanta: John Knox Press, 1983); David L. Miller (ed.), *Jung and the Interpretation of the Bible* (New York: Continuum, 1995); Rollins, *Soul and Psyche: The Bible in Psychological Perspective* (Minneapolis: Fortress Press, 1999); Kille, *Psychological Biblical Criticism* (Minneapolis: Fortress Press, 2001); Ellens and Rollins (eds.), *Psychology and the Bible: A New Way to Read the Scriptures* (4 vols.; Westport, CT: Praeger, 2004); Ellens and Kille (eds.), *Psychological Insight into the Bible: Texts and Readings* (Grand Rapids: Eerdmans, 2007); Barbara M. Leung Lai, *Through the 'I'-Window: The Inner Life of Characters in the Hebrew Bible* (Hebrew Bible Monographs, 34; Sheffield: Sheffield Phoenix Press, 2011); J. Harold Ellens (ed.), *Psychological Hermeneutics for Biblical Themes and Texts: A Festschrift in Honor of Wayne G. Rollins* (London: T. & T. Clark, 2012).

introductions to postmodern methodologies of biblical studies about a third of the chapter on 'psychoanalytic criticism' is devoted to its interaction with feminist approaches.[7] What is more, psychology appears positioned uniquely well to serve the unique task of feminist exegesis, trying to make sense of an ancient document with an eye on today's issues. Since patriarchy and misogyny are known to have existed, and still to exist, in a variety of extremely different societies, its primary locus must be not in socioeconomic systems, institutions, or culture, but rather in the inner workings of human psyche. In what follows, I will review a sample of publications by feminist biblical scholars seeking (with a broadly varying degree of intensity) to realize the promise that psychology holds for them, and then summarize my findings.

Authority or Subtext? Psychology in the Biblical Exegesis of Mieke Bal

Although occasional feminist treatments of the Bible indirectly informed by Freudian psychoanalysis—mostly as mediated by Jacques Lacan—can be found already in the writings of Julia Kristeva, Mieke Bal (also a literary and cultural critic rather than a biblical scholar) was the first to use this theory for the purposes of sustained feminist exegesis of Hebrew scriptures.[8] In her first book on the subject, *Lethal Love*, the overarching approach is narratological but in dealing with specific subjects she repeatedly invokes psychological concepts and ideas. Three examples will suffice. Trying to make sense of the seemingly apposite but in fact profoundly incongruous reference in 2 Sam. 11.20-21 to Abimelech's death as reported in Judg. 9.52-54, Bal claims—without citing any specific sources—that a within a 'psychoanalytical framework' this reference expresses 'the unconscious complex of the fear of woman'. If so, it 'can be understood to say something like this: one dies a shameful death as soon as one is so foolish as to fight a woman when she is defending her wall/entrance from her mighty position as the feared other'.[9] By placing this reference in David's mouth, Joab implicitly fingers Bathsheba as the agent of trouble that embroiled Uriah, David, and him. Thus, 'his anger with David about the bad strategy and the death of an innocent man imposed on him, an anger that, as a subordinate "servant

---

7. The Bible and Culture Collective, 'Psychoanalytic Criticism', in *The Postmodern Bible* (New Haven: Yale University Press, 1995), pp. 211-22. On the tendency to subsume psychology under psychoanalysis as a major pitfall, see the concluding section of the present chapter.

8. See, e.g., Julia Kristeva, *Powers of Horror: An Essay on Abjection* (trans. Leon S. Roudiez; New York: Columbia University Press, 1982), pp. 56-132.

9. Mieke Bal, *Lethal Love: Feminist Literary Readings of Biblical Love Stories* (Indiana Studies in Biblical Literature; Bloomington: Indiana University Press, 1987), p. 33.

of the king", he cannot afford, is directed against the intuitively appropriate scapegoat, woman in general'.[10]

Likewise, Bal purports to build upon psychoanalysis—again, without referring to any of the school's numerous publications—when she addresses the fraught relationship between Samson and another (supposedly) lethal woman, Delilah. Taking note of the hair leitmotif in Judges 16, Bal points out that 'according to Freud, the cutting of hair is a symbol of castration', so that 'the Nazirite vow relates the growing of hair to abstinence. In that vow, fear of castration receives symbolic expression'.[11] She also interprets Samson's deceptive statement in v. 13 that he will lose his strength if seven of his locks are woven into a web by treating the latter as a metonymy for Delilah's (supposedly) long hair and then bringing up Freud's comparison of women's long hair 'via pubic hair, to the vagina as a representation of the dangers of too committed a love: the *vagina dentata*, that phantasmagoric horror for men who fear to lose the penis and, synechdochically, the self'.[12] Freudian theory—this time, as represented by two individual articles of his—is invoked again in Bal's exegesis of Genesis 38. Stressing that Tamar disguises herself as a ritual prostitute, whose role 'is probably to help men overcome their fear of defloration', Bal argues that her 'transformations all point to the taboo of virginity, so well described by Freud (1918), and the subsequent taboo of sex with a respectable woman, to which Freud devoted another essay (1912)'.[13]

In *Murder and Difference*, Bal explicitly declines to read the Hebrew Bible in terms of what she calls 'psychoanalytic code' despite its being 'highly relevant to the present case'. The reason she gives is that this 'code' is the subject of 'greater dissent...which would give rise to the kind of debate that could only hinder the progress of our present discussion'.[14] The import, and importance, of this cryptic statement will become apparent in the concluding section of my chapter. It should, however, be mentioned right away that the profound ambivalence towards Freud that Bal expresses here—and that is largely absent from *Lethal Love*—is amply reflected in the third installment of her 'biblical suite', *Death and Dissymmetry*, which just like *Murder and Difference*, focuses on Judges.[15] As we have just seen, in

10. Bal, *Lethal Love*, pp. 34-35.
11. Bal, *Lethal Love*, p. 55.
12. Bal, *Lethal Love*, pp. 54-55.
13. Bal, *Lethal Love*, p. 101. Freud's publications that she refers to here are 'The Taboo of Virginity' and 'On the Universal Tendency to Debasement in the Sphere of Love'.
14. Bal, *Murder and Difference: Gender, Genre, and Scholarship on Sisera's Death* (Indiana Studies in Biblical Literature; trans. Matthew Gumpert; Bloomington: Indiana University Press, 1988), p. 13.
15. Bal, *Death and Dissymmetry: The Politics of Coherence in the Book of Judges*

Lethal Love, Bal employs psychoanalytical ideas, sporadically but strategically, as hermeneutical tools. A similar trajectory can be seen in chapter 6 of *Death and Dissymmetry*, where she builds the discussion of the gang rape-murder narrative in Judges 19 to a considerable extent upon Freud's concept of the 'uncanny'.[16] Playing upon his original German term, *Unheimlich* (literally, 'unhomely'), she maintains that in terms of the patriarchal worldview, fully shared by the chapter's (presumably) male author, the woman's violent death was a logical consequence of her stepping, both literally and figuratively, out of the proper—and therefore safe—enclosed space of the husband's or father's home. Yet, while commending this concept as 'insightful', Bal at the same breath characterizes it as 'particularly male-oriented' and then proceeds to expose it as such.[17]

The latter trend reigns supreme in the book's second chapter, where Bal brings back Freud's above-mentioned article on virginity in conjunction with her feminist reading of the famous 'Jephthah's daughter' narrative in Judg. 11.30-40.[18] The article receives close attention; an entire section of the chapter deals with it rather than with the biblical text, but explicitly not as a source of authority on the workings of human psyche, or, for that matter, on anything else.[19] Rather, Bal uses Freud, as well as a much more recent psychoanalytic study of the story by Robert Seidenberg, 'as *subtexts*, as texts that can shed some light on the ancient text, mediated by [her] reading of both, in that their discourse resembles the discourse of Judges. The result [is not] a master-discourse in which the ancient text is the object and the scholarly text a tool. A dialogue between three discourses, which mutually illuminates and criticizes each other, would be a more appropriate image.'[20] In essence, Freud and (to a much lesser extent) Seidenberg serve here as proxies for the (presumably male) ancient author of Judg. 11.30-40. Bal hypothesizes that 'the culture of Judges, different as it is from our own, struggles with [the] same problems'.[21] Accordingly, the notion of female virginity found in the works of twentieth-century male authors can illuminate the conceptuality of gender that is operative in the biblical text and that otherwise could hardly be reconstructed with any degree of certainty because the story is short (under 200 words) and idiosyncratic and because the narrator never comments on the reported events. After carefully reading and

(Chicago Studies in the History of Judaism; Chicago: University of Chicago Press, 1988).

16. Bal, *Death and Dissymmetry*, pp. 169-96 (186-96).
17. Bal, *Death and Dissymmetry*, pp. 192-94 (192).
18. Bal, *Death and Dissymmetry*, pp. 41-68.
19. Bal, *Death and Dissymmetry*, pp. 52-59.
20. Bal, *Death and Dissymmetry*, p. 19 (italics hers); cf. Robert Seidenberg, 'Sacrificing the First You See', *The Psychoanalytic Review* 53 (1966), pp. 49-62.
21. Bal, *Death and Dissymmetry*, p. 59.

critiquing Freud, Bal concludes that his understanding of 'the taboo of virginity' is a 'complex of confusions, aggressions, entanglements, and projections', and while denying the universality of this phenomenon she proceeds to interpret the narrative in Judges 11 on the assumption that the same was the case with whoever wrote it.[22] As we shall see in the following sections of the present article, Bal's conflicted pattern of building upon Freud and his ideas while also exposing them as androcentric is typical in feminist-psychological interpretation of the Hebrew Bible.

Who Is on the Couch? Psychology in the Works of Ilona Rashkow

Rashkow is doubtlessly the 'poster child' for the use of psychological theory in feminist exegesis: she is the only scholar to have published two volumes of Hebrew Bible exegesis that are both explicitly feminist and explicitly informed in their totality by (mainly Freudian) psychology. Rashkow is also the only feminist scholar represented—by three chapters, no less—in *Psychology and the Bible*.[23] For the sake of brevity and clarity, I will concentrate here on Rashkow's book-length publications, especially since many of her articles and chapters either revise these publications or overlap with them.

Rashkow begins her first book by grappling with a question that Bal largely eludes: what exactly is the object of psychoanalysis as a tool of biblical hermeneutics?[24] She dismisses as inherently speculative the once-popular approach to literary texts, the Hebrew Bible included, as clues to their authors' psyche and notes that attempts to psychoanalyze the biblical characters—or, for that matter, those of any other narrative—fail because literary characterization may be shaped to a considerable, perhaps decisive, extent by rhetorical considerations or conventions of the genre. Having argued that, she invokes reader-response criticism and draws parallels between the process of reading and that of psychoanalysis to imply (without saying it in so many words) that for her, Freudian psychology is a way

---

22. Bal, *Death and Dissymmetry*, pp. 58-68 (citation on p. 59).

23. Ilona Rashkow, 'Sexuality in the Hebrew Bible: Freud's Lens', in Ellens and Rollins (eds.), *Psychology and the Bible*, vol. 1, pp. 33-74; Rashkow, 'What Is Wrong with This Picture? Daughters and Fathers in Genesis', in Ellens and Rollins (eds.), *Psychology and the Bible: A New Way to Read the Scripture. II. From Genesis to Apocalyptic Vision* (Westport, CT: Praeger, 2004), pp. 41-63; Rashkow, '"What's in a Name? That Which We Call a Rose by Any Other Name Would Smell as Sweet": God's Name, Lacan, and the Ultimate Phallus', in Ellens and Rollins (eds.), *Psychology and the Bible, Vol. 2*, pp. 237-65.

24. Rashkow, *The Phallacy of Genesis: A Feminist-Psychoanalytic Approach* (Literary Currents in Biblical Interpretation; Louisville, KY: Westminster/John Knox Press, 1993), pp. 15-25.

of understanding the routes she takes as a reader of the Hebrew Bible as well as the effect that this reading has on her.

In accordance with this penetrating epistemological discussion, Rashkow proceeds to employ the notion of 'transference', first formulated by Freud and still commonly used (although evaluated in a vastly different way) in contemporary psychology, in explaining why her reading of the 'wife-sister' stories in Genesis 12 and 20 tends to identify with Sarah and the foreign rulers rather than Abraham.[25] Just as the patient may be 'triggered' to unconsciously project his or her issues upon the therapist, Sarah's blatant silencing in the stories and the passionate reactions of the Pharaoh and King Abimelech to Abraham's ruse 'trigger' Rashkow's sympathy. Yet already the next chapter, focused on Gen. 20.1-18 and even more specifically on Abimelech's dream (vv. 3-7), starts to move away from her programmatic hermeneutical pattern.[26] On the one hand, she remains attentive to her role as a reader. On the other, while Freudian theory of 'night dreams' as manifestations of the individual unconscious that she uses here as a hermeneutical clue is certainly applicable to Abimelech (imagined for that purpose as an actual person) and, somewhat less so, to the text's author this is not the case with the reader. The content of the dream is something the latter reads or hears about (much as a therapist would), not an artifact of her mind.[27] The contrast remains despite Rashkow's attempt to stay on track by ingeniously positing that only v. 3 reports the actual dream, whereas the remainder of the scene (vv. 4-7) represents Abimelech's attempt to make sense of it. Even granting that this would make him a counterpart of the exegete trying to make sense of both the dream and the story as a whole, in terms of a therapeutic encounter Abimelech is still the patient, and the exegete, the counselor—a crucial distinction to which I will return in the last section of my essay.

In the remaining two chapters of her book, Rashkow firmly switches to the path blazed by Bal and discussed above. Addressing what she sees as ambiguous status of 'the biblical daughter' who 'can be seen as locked into a conflicted text of desire and prohibition', she draws a parallel between the Hebrew Bible's reluctance to explore father-daughter relationships, fraught with the possibility of incest, and Freud's abandonment of his early 'seduction theory' that pointed in the same direction.[28] In a twist that brings to

---

25. Rashkow, *The Phallacy of Genesis*, pp. 26-48.
26. Rashkow, *The Phallacy of Genesis*, pp. 49-64.
27. It is possible to argue, of course, that according to the plain meaning of the text Abimelech's dream was induced by the deity rather than produced by his unconscious. Yet in such case Freudian dream interpretation is entirely unsuitable for the reading of the story.
28. Rashkow, *The Phallacy of Genesis*, pp. 65-75 (68).

mind the overall pattern of *Death and Dissymmetry* with regard to Freud, Rashkow builds her interpretation of Genesis 3 on both Freud and his feminist critics, such as Luce Irigaray.[29] In other words, just like Bal, Rashkow uses Freud as a 'subtext', leaving little place for the reader's self-(psycho) analysis, which largely fades from the picture. The pattern remains in place (while becoming considerably more explicit) in the book's last chapter. Its stated goal is to 'juxtapose some of Freud's writings which deal with female sexuality and biblical narratives with the same theme', and predictably, Rashkow concludes that 'in biblical narratives, as in Freud, female sexuality is explicitly subordinated to and subsumed by the male'.[30]

In the introductory chapter of her second volume, Rashkow seems to oscillate (or should I say vacillate?) between employing Freudian theory as a hermeneutical tool and as a 'subtext' in Bal's sense.[31] After introducing the basics of Freudian theory and its Lacanian revisions, she rejects the relationship between literature and psychoanalysis in which 'the literary text is considered as a body of language to *be* interpreted, while psychoanalysis is a body of knowledge used *to* interpret'. Accordingly, the book's stated procedure 'is to read psychoanalytic literary theory and the Bible concurrently rather than to provide a hierarchical positioning'. Yet at the same breath Rashkow describes her theoretical approach as 'literary, albeit *influenced* by psychoanalytic theory' and claims to 'appropriate…psychoanalytic *approaches* as tools for biblical interpretation'.[32] How this is antonymous to using psychoanalysis as a body of knowledge with which to unlock the body of language that is the Hebrew Bible—and synonymous to reading the biblical and Freudian-Lacanian texts concurrently—remains unexplained.

When it comes to actual exegesis, Rashkow predominantly follows the former trajectory, more or less straightforwardly viewing the Hebrew Bible through the psychoanalytical lens. Freudian presence is especially strong in the book's third chapter, where she revisits the Garden of Eden story.[33] After a broad cross-cultural overview, meant to demonstrate that mother goddesses usually play a central role in creation mythology, Rashkow asks why there is no such figure in Genesis—despite the ample archeological and textual evidence of goddess worship in ancient Israel. The answer, coming straight from Freud's famous concept of the Oedipal complex, is that since the mother, as a demonstrably sexual female, is the object

---

29. Rashkow, *The Phallacy of Genesis*, pp. 75-80.
30. Rashkow, *The Phallacy of Genesis*, pp. 85-109 (85, 108).
31. Rashkow, *Taboo or Not Taboo: Sexuality and Family in the Hebrew Bible* (Minneapolis: Fortress Press, 2000).
32. Rashkow, *Taboo or Not Taboo*, pp. 1-14 (9; emphasis in the original).
33. Rashkow, *Taboo or Not Taboo*, pp. 43-73.

of rivalry between the father (here represented by the deity) and the son, she needs to be excluded from the narrative in order to forestall the conflict and guarantee the power of the male parent. Eve's rebellion against this power is likewise seen in Freudian terms, this time with regard to daughter-father relationship. Here, Rashkow retreads much of the ground she covered in her first book.

The Oedipal theory and especially the concept of castration fear remains the dominant interpretive framework in the next three chapters of the book. Rashkow repeatedly and massively applies both when dealing with circumcision, the homosexual and heterosexual father-child incest as represented by the account of Noah's drunkenness in Gen. 9.18-27 and the narrative of Lot and his daughters in Genesis 19, and male sibling rivalry as represented by Jacob and Esau in Genesis 27 and Cain and Abel in Genesis 4.[34] Rashkow also brings up Freud's ideas about the meaning and significance of dreams in her discussion of Jacob's 'staircase' vision in Gen. 28.12-15 and his nocturnal wrestling match with a supernatural adversary in Genesis 32, which she assumes, without substantiation, to be a nightmare of sorts.[35] Remarkably, throughout all these chapters that constitute the bulk of the book, Rashkow hardly ever applies Freudian theory to the exegetical process.[36] Instead, she psychoanalyzes the biblical characters as actual individuals and to some extent, especially when she addresses circumcision and the Garden of Eden story, the author or the culture that created the Hebrew Bible—seemingly oblivious of the fact that her earlier book exposes both *modi operandi* as epistemologically vulnerable.

Only two examples of a 'concurrent' reading of the biblical and Freudian texts *à la* Bal's *Death and Dissymmetry* can be found in this book. Moreover, one of these examples is a paragraph-length critique of Freud's views on female virginity that largely reprises the arguments made by Bal.[37] Another makes its appearance as an equally brief afterthought to the book's first chapter that offers a predominantly cross-cultural overview of sexual prohibitions in the Hebrew Bible with an admixture of anthropology and reception history and mentions Freud and psychoanalysis only in the opening and closing paragraphs (there is also one reference to Lacan).[38] What

---

34. Rashkow, *Taboo or Not Taboo*, pp. 75-92, 93-113, and 115-38 respectively.

35. Rashkow, *Taboo or Not Taboo*, pp. 132-38.

36. Contrary to her claim in the concluding paragraph of the afterword that 'what [she has] tried to do throughout this book...is to show that we *also* invest Scriptures with our own characteristic clusters of wishes—our fantasies—and transform these fantasies into the kind of significance we find meaningful: intellectual, social, moral, and/or aesthetic'; see Rashkow, *Taboo or Not Taboo*, pp. 159-60 (emphasis hers).

37. Rashkow, *Taboo or Not Taboo*, p. 108; cf. Bal, *Death and Dissymmetry*, pp. 52-59.

38. Rashkow, *Taboo or Not Taboo*, pp. 15-42.

is more, the Freudian pronouncement that 'sexuality...is of a wholly masculine character'—compared by Rashkow to the alleged tendency of the biblical commandments to suppress female sexuality and subordinate it to men—is cited already in *The Phallacy of Genesis*.[39]

Indeed, while Rashkow may occasionally revel in demonstrating that when it comes to gender the characters and readers of the Bible often think and behave as predicted by Freud (witness the asides like 'anything Freudian there, do you suppose' or 'sound Freudian?'), at other times there is an almost perfunctory feel to her psychoanalytical references.[40] In particular, the book's opening and closing chapters both devote disproportionate attention to cross-cultural parallels and the Bible's reception, especially in art and rabbinic midrash.[41] A similar tendency appears in some of the publications that are reviewed in the next section of the present chapter.

Divergent Trajectories: Psychology in the Feminist Biblical Interpretations of Cheryl Exum, Lyn Bechtel, Mayer Gruber, Bernhard Lang, and Julia O'Brien

In the introduction to her *Fragmented Women*, Cheryl Exum states that it 'draws on contemporary feminist literary theory, in particular certain aspects of deconstruction and psychoanalytic literary theory', creating thereby an impression that both approaches are more or less equally important to the exegesis that she offers here.[42] In fact, the latter approach is employed in only one out of the book's six chapters, titled 'Who's Afraid of "the Endangered Ancestress"' and devoted to the 'wife-sister' episodes in Genesis 12, 20, and 26.[43] Almost from the outset, Exum categorically states that she is 'not proposing to psychoanalyze the characters...in a story as if they were real people with real neuroses'. Instead, the object of her Freudian (or, more precisely, Freud-inspired) investigation is 'a kind of collective androcentric unconscious' whose vehicle is the biblical text.[44] She brings up Freud's concept of repetition compulsion (*Wiederholungszwang*), 'the impulse to work over an experience in the mind until one becomes the master of it', to argue that as far as Genesis is concerned a major aspect of this unconscious is the fantasy 'that the wife has sex with another man', which is

---

39. Rashkow, *Taboo or Not Taboo*, p. 42; cf. Rashkow, *The Phallacy of Genesis*, p. 108.
40. Rashkow, *Taboo or Not Taboo*, pp. 110, 138.
41. Rashkow, *Taboo or Not Taboo*, pp. 139-57.
42. J. Cheryl Exum, *Fragmented Women: Feminist (Sub)versions of Biblical Narratives* (JSOTSup, 163; Sheffield: Sheffield Academic Press, 1993), p. 9.
43. Exum, *Fragmented Women*, pp. 148-69.
44. Exum, *Fragmented Women*, p. 155.

simultaneously entertained and feared.[45] Exum proceeds then to examine the idiosyncratic trio of narratives as a continuous 'working out of a neurosis', in which the male ancestor acts similarly to Freudian id (the locus of the forbidden desire) and the foreign ruler to super-ego, blocking this desire and expressing moral outrage based on patriarchal social norms and endorsed by the deity.[46]

Article-length publications appear even more liable than monographs to employ psychological theory in a desultory fashion (if at all). Mayer Gruber cites several fairly recent (especially at the time of the essay's appearance) studies of marital relations to argue that Hos. 4.10-19 'castigates men who are unfaithful to their wives, seeking intimacy elsewhere, instead of seeking help to create true intimacy in their marriages' and even—in a supposedly feminist fashion—suggests that women would be justified in imitating this behavior.[47] Yet most of his study is philological and to a somewhat lesser extent comparative.[48] Early on in his discussion of the female Wisdom figure in Proverbs 1–9, Bernhard Lang engages the ideas of Carl Jung, Freud's one-time disciple and later his bitter opponent.[49] He compares the chapters' configuration of characters—a creator deity and a father, who are indistinguishable as the source of instruction, Lady Wisdom, and Lady Folly—with Jungian description of archetypal human persona as consisting of a Wise Old Man and his daughter Anima, a female representing the irrational and the wild but also associated with secret knowledge.[50] Yet this comparison plays almost no role in the bulk of the article, whose main point—that Wisdom functioned as a personal and corporate goddess of ancient Israelite scribes, similarly to female polytheistic deities of the ancient Near East—has much more to do with history of religion than psychology.[51] Arguably the most striking example is Julia O'Brien's otherwise stimulating log of

---

45. Exum, *Fragmented Women*, pp. 154, 158.

46. Exum, *Fragmented Women*, pp. 160-69. She claims to use Freudian terms as a metaphor, 'without applying them in a strictly Freudian sense' (p. 160).

47. Mayer I. Gruber, 'Marital Fidelity and Intimacy: A View from Hosea 4', in Athalya Brenner (ed.), *A Feminist Companion to The Latter Prophets* (The Feminist Companion to the Bible, 8; Sheffield: Sheffield Academic Press, 1995), pp. 169-79 (179).

48. Gruber, 'Marital Fidelity', pp. 172-79.

49. Bernhard Lang, 'Lady Wisdom: A Polytheistic and Psychological Interpretation of a Biblical Goddess', in Athalya Brenner and Carole Fontaine (eds.), *A Feminist Companion to Reading the Bible: Approaches, Methods and Strategies* (Sheffield: Sheffield Academic Press, 1997), pp. 400-23.

50. Lang, 'Lady Wisdom', pp. 402-406. Jung believed that this component of psyche is female in men and male (called Animus) in women. However, since the scribes who created Proverbs 1–9 and whose beliefs it reflects according to Lang were most likely men, it is logical for the book's character allegedly corresponding to this component to be female rather than male.

51. Lang, 'Lady Wisdom', pp. 406-21.

her personal struggles with gender issues in the Book of Malachi.[52] She apparently believes that a single reference to Exum's citation of Freud is sufficient to couch these struggles in psychoanalytic terms of 'repetition compulsion'.[53] One notable exception to the tendency is Lyn Bechtel's detailed study of Genesis 2–3 whose intention is to demonstrate that this text should not be understood in terms of 'sin and fall', with their almost inevitably misogynistic implications, but rather in those of 'movement toward the emergence of human consciousness, maturity, socialization, and the realization of identity in relation to the group'.[54] Since developmental psychology views individuation and differentiation as fundamental to human maturation, Bechtel consistently looks for indications of these processes in the narrative's symbolic texture.

It is also worth noting that while O'Brien, as the discussion above makes abundantly clear, briefly follows Rashkow (in parts of *The Phallacy of Genesis*) in making herself as a reader the object of psychological examination, Bechtel, Gruber, and Lang take a path that we have not yet seen. In essence, they imply, although never claim explicitly, that the biblical fragments they work with anticipate the findings of modern psychological research. In Bechtel's case, the author(s) of Genesis 2–3 could express humanity's alleged maturation in these chapters through individuation and differentiation only if they knew—moreover, could reasonably expect their audience to know—that the latter are indispensable for the former. Likewise, Gruber reads Hosea 4 as displaying awareness of the gap between sexuality and intimacy, as stressed in recent manuals on couples therapy, and Lang's Jungian parallels appear to suggest in the larger context of his article that what looks like a bold twentieth-century idea is in fact just a rediscovery of ancient truths.[55] Preposterous as these implications may be, I will argue further that the three studies in question point toward the most methodologically sound and exegetically profitable ways of incorporating psychology into feminist biblical exegesis.

---

52. Julia M. O'Brien, 'On Saying "No" to a Prophet', in Brenner (ed.), *Prophets and Daniel* (A Feminist Companion to the Bible, Second Series 8; Sheffield: Sheffield Academic Press, 2001), pp. 206-17.

53. O'Brien, 'On Saying "No" to a Prophet', p. 212, citing Exum's article that was also published as chapter 5 of her *Fragmented Women* (see above).

54. Lyn M. Bechtel, 'Rethinking the Interpretation of Genesis 2.4b–3.24', in Athalya Brenner (ed.), *A Feminist Companion to Genesis* (The Feminist Companion to the Bible, 2; Sheffield: Sheffield Academic Press, 1993), pp. 77-117 (85).

55. In fact, it may be worth its while to place these parallels on their head by checking whether Jung's quasi-mythological concepts of the Wise Old Man and Anima/Animus—formulated, after the manner of biblical prophets, as a dream report—could be influenced by the Bible, Gnostic literature, and the Kabbalah.

Realizing the Promise: Synopsis and Reflection

While by no means comprehensive, this overview makes it possible to conclude that psychology's potential as a powerful hermeneutical tool of feminist exegetes remains largely unrealized. Most scholars (even Rashkow, by far the most invested of them) seem to be wary about deploying it. Hence, psychology is used only sporadically and for the most part inconsistently or desultorily. The attitude in question is understandable given that the actual readings emerging at the nexus of feminism, biblical interpretation, and psychological theory have so far been methodologically vulnerable in three major aspects, two of them uniquely associated with this specific theory and the third having to do with the broader notion of 'theory' in postmodern approaches to the Hebrew Bible.

One of these pitfalls is the object of psychological, or psychologically informed, analysis of the Hebrew Bible—or, for that matter, of any other text. As mentioned above, in the introduction to her first book Rashkow cogently explains that a psychological examination of a literary character would be an exercise in futility. It is never obvious—and in the case of ancient writings, not even likely—that his or her characterization is meant to present how actual people think and act rather than make a rhetorical point while following conventions of a genre.[56] It can also be added that while Freud was presumptuous enough to psychoanalyze Moses and his followers, today no serious therapist would venture a professional judgment based solely on a sketchy report of the person's life, without at least talking to her.[57] From this perspective, not only all psychological evaluations in Bal's *Lethal Love* (such as the 'diagnosis' of castration fear in Samson) but also many of those in Rashkow's very own *Taboo or Not Taboo* (for example, her application of the Oedipal theory to several biblical characters) are premature at best.

Problems of a somewhat different if related kind beset application of psychological theory to the creator(s) of the biblical texts. Since in the heavily oral culture of ancient Israel the very notion of individual authorship was largely non-existent, the identity of biblical writers cannot be established with any degree of certainty and even their sociohistorical background is subject to debate. Under such conditions, for the purposes of psychological investigation they inevitably become stand-ins for the entire culture they belonged to, as Exum explicitly acknowledges when she describes the 'wife-sister' stories of Genesis as 'collective androcentric unconscious'. This shift, subtle as it is, opens a whole new can of worms. If the biblical

---

56. Rashkow, *The Phallacy of Genesis*, pp. 17-19.
57. Sigmund Freud, *Moses and Monotheism* (trans. Katherine Jones; New York: A.A. Knopf, 1939).

requirement of circumcision has to do (as per Rashkow) with the supposedly universal Oedipal complex and castration fear, why did the equally, if differently, patriarchal Greek and Hellenistic cultures place a premium on long, bushy foreskin?[58] Is it conceivable that ancient Israelite men were uniquely prone to share their wives—as it would seem to follow from Exum's analysis of the trio of 'wife-sister' narratives, unparalleled in world literature? Indeed, given that the descendants of these men are still identifiable in today's world, do feminist exegetes who apply psychological theory to biblical interpretation in such a way inadvertently open the door to racial anti-Semitism?[59]

That leaves the reader as the object of study, but since the only reader whose experiences an exegete can realistically access is herself such a procedure runs afoul of the therapist-patient (or analyst-analysand, in Freudian parlance) dichotomy that is foundational to all schools and sub-fields of psychological theory and practice. Simply put, psychological self-analysis is an impossibility; the proverbial 'physician, heal thyself' does not apply to mental conditions. By overlooking this principle, Rashkow commits a major epistemological fallacy (not phallacy!) when she describes the responses that the biblical text 'triggers' in her in terms of transference. The standard definition of the latter—'the client's unconscious shifting to the analyst of feelings and fantasies that are reactions to significant others in the client's past'—makes it clear that it is a form of interaction between two involved parties.[60] While Rashkow may project her feelings upon the Bible, it is not her therapist; she may feel being in a relationship with a story or its characters but they are not and cannot be in a relationship with her. Likewise, after reading O'Brien's piece (and most likely following up with a conversation), a psychologist may discern in it an attempt to resolve a neurosis by semiotic means, but this determination is not the author's to make. In addition, while self-reflection is essential in postmodern exegesis, a reading that is predominantly self-reflection is difficult to maintain for long. As suggested by the

---

58. Frederick M. Hodges, 'The Ideal Prepuce in Ancient Greece and Rome: Male Genital Aesthetics and Their Relation to *Lipodermos*, Circumcision, Foreskin Restoration, and the *Kynodesmē*', *Bulletin of the History of Medicine* 75 (2001), pp. 375-405.

59. When Reinhold Krause, speaking in November 1933 at the Berlin rally of Nazi-inspired *Glaubensbewegung 'Deutsche Christen'*, dismissed the Old Testament as 'tales of cattle-traders and pimps' he most likely had the ancestral narratives of Genesis in mind. See Richard L. Rubenstein and John K. Roth, *Approaches to Auschwitz: The Holocaust and Its Legacy* (Louisville, KY: Westminster/John Knox Press, 2nd rev. edn, 2003), p. 256.

60. Gerald Corey, *Theory and Practice of Counseling and Psychotherapy* (Belmont: Thomson Brooks/Cole, 8th edn, 2009), p. 71. Cf. Heinrich Racker, *Transference and Counter-Transference* (London: Karnac Books, 1982).

examples of O'Brien and Rashkow, it can sustain an article but not even a relatively short monograph.

With all this in mind, it would appear that the only methodologically sound niche for psychology in feminist exegesis is a juxtaposition of the ideas formulated by the former with those discovered by the latter in the Bible. One way of doing so is represented by Bal's and Rashkow's critique of Freud as sharing the gender biases if not misogynistic attitudes of the biblical texts. Yet the profitability of this approach, fitting as it is into the broader stream of critically inclined feminist biblical scholarship, seems to be limited (which may be one reason why neither Bal nor Rashkow follows it consistently). It replaces the Bible as the object of study with the modern psychologist – a cultural icon of much lesser stature, and one that has already been subjected to withering feminist criticism, to which biblical parallels add very little.[61]

More promising, then, is the trajectory taken by Bechtel, Gruber, and Lang. The examples of Gruber and especially Bechtel suggest that reading the Bible as though it is informed by recent psychological concepts can go a long way in reclaiming the texts that have long been, in Bechtel's words, 'a misogynist's playground'.[62] The actual studies discussed here fall short of attaining the goal, mainly because of their historical tack, implicit in Gruber and explicit in Bechtel (who sees Genesis 2–3 as 'a myth that reinforces the values and concerns of monarchical society') and especially Lang. It is highly implausible that ancient writers could anticipate, even unconsciously, the developments in twentieth-century scholarship with its vastly different frames of reference and research techniques.[63] Yet a reader-response readjustment would easily resolve the issue. To use Gruber's study as an example, there would be nothing inherently flawed about arguing that by approaching Hosea from the standpoint of current literature on relationships, a modern audience may discover advocacy of monogamy for men.

Another major weakness of feminist biblical exegesis as far as psychology is concerned is the questionable choice of theoretical frameworks. As the overview above makes amply clear, for the most part feminist scholars tend to subsume modern psychological theory under Freudian psychoanalysis. Only two of the reviewed publications, both of them article-length, eschew references to Freud or his immediate disciples, such as Jung and

---

61. See n. 67 below.
62. Bechtel, 'Rethinking the Interpretation of Genesis 2.4b–3.24', p. 77.
63. The claim that the findings of modern science have all along been encoded in religious texts, such as the Bible, is typical for traditionalists (and neo-traditionalists, such as Westerners discovering the religions of South and East Asia) in the postmodern age. One of its less sophisticated incarnations is the meme, making rounds on the Internet, that biblical dietary rules fully comport with current ideas about healthy nutrition.

Otto Rank (whose 'trauma of birth' concept is mentioned once in Bal's *Lethal Love*). Bechtel builds upon the studies of Erich Fromm and Erik Erikson, and Gruber relies upon recent marriage counseling manuals.[64] This is not just about a nearly total disregard for almost a century worth of empirical data and conceptual advancement, which is bad enough in its own right when dealing with such a burgeoning, highly dynamic discipline. A much greater issue is that Freudian theory has not been simply subsumed or even superseded by subsequent developments; over the last few decades, it has been increasingly exposed as specious and even unscientific, on account of having never been confirmed by a legitimate observation or experiment or of even being unfalsifiable in principle.[65] In other words, citing Freud as the only authority on the human mind is not even like citing Newton as the only authority on physics, without ever mentioning Einstein or Heisenberg—it is more like citing Hermes Trismegistus as such.

The matter is not merely that of being behind the curve. To be sure, biblical scholars do not usually receive sustained training in psychology for the simple reason that such training is nearly impossible to fit into already busy curricula of doctoral programs. Yet the examples of Bechtel and Gruber show that the obstacle is by no means insurmountable. While their knowledge of the field may not be extensive, it is clearly adequate for their purposes. And although attacks on Freud have intensified in the last two decades, cogent (and lay-reader friendly) critique of his psychoanalysis (such as Eysenck's book) was available already to Bal, to say nothing of Exum and Rashkow. It stands to reason then that Freudian psychoanalysis has proven especially attractive for feminist exegetes precisely because of its non-scientific (and, as far as its current admirers and practitioners are concerned, even counter-scientific) nature. More specifically, since the point of departure for feminist interpreters is the reader's identity, it would appear that their personal rootedness in the twentieth-century Western world that has been in part shaped by Freud far outweighs the hard data obtained by research (of which the

---

64. See Bal, *Lethal Love*, pp. 59-60; Bechtel, 'Rethinking the Interpretation of Genesis 2.4b–3.24', p. 85; Gruber, 'Marital Fidelity', pp. 170-71.

65. See, e.g., Hans Eysenck, *Decline and Fall of the Freudian Empire* (London: Penguin Books, 1986), which also cites earlier publications critical of Freud; Frank Cioffi, *Freud and the Question of Pseudoscience* (Chicago: Open Court, 1998); Frederick Crews (ed.), *Unauthorized Freud: Doubters Confront a Legend* (London: Penguin Books, 1999); Jacques Benesteau, *Mensonges freudiens: Histoire d'une désinformation séculaire* (Sprimont: Mardaga, 2002); Richard Webster, *Why Freud Was Wrong: Sin, Science and Psychoanalysis* (Oxford: Orwell Press, 2005); René Pommier, *Sigmund est fou et Freud a tout faux: Essai sur la théorie freudienne du rêve* (Paris: Fallois, 2008); Catherine Meyer (ed.), *Le livre noir de la psychanalyse: Vivre, penser et aller mieux sans Freud* (Paris: Arènes, 2005).

broader culture may become aware only much later, if ever).⁶⁶ Yet *qua* cultural phenomenon psychoanalysis has been thoroughly exposed by feminist critics as profoundly androcentric. This insight has led, as we have seen, to the paradox of its most intensive users among feminist biblical exegetes, Bal and Rashkow, both critiquing psychoanalysis and employing it as an exegetical framework.⁶⁷ In addition, readers might appreciate a disclaimer to the effect that Freud cited by feminist exegetes is a cultural rather than scientific figure.⁶⁸

Finally, there is the perennial question of the relationship between hermeneutics and the exegete's individual creativity. Reader-oriented literary interpretation, especially of the identity-based kind, is heavy on 'theory', and feminist psychological exegesis is no exception in this respect. Yet in too many cases it is less than obvious that the 'theory' expounded at length in the beginning of a publication is indeed indispensable in generating the

66. In this respect, it is important to keep in mind that Freud was, among other things, an outstanding popularizer who not only wrote and spoke powerfully, published prolifically, and lectured extensively but also put together an organization that to all practical purposes functioned as a non-theistic cult, propagating his ideas, massively recruiting acolytes, and working hard to keep them in line. In Eysenck's opinion, Freud 'was, without doubt, a genius, not of science, but of propaganda, not of rigorous proof, but of persuasion, not of the design of experiments, but of literary art' (*Decline and Fall of the Freudian Empire*, p. 208). Eysenck makes a careful distinction between Freudian psychology as *Naturwissenschaft* (natural science) and *Geisteswissenschaft* ([cultural] hermeneutics) but argues that it fails on both counts (pp. 193-208).

67. See, e.g., Karen Horney, *Feminine Psychology* (The Norton Library; ed. Harold Kelman; New York: Norton, 1973); Luce Irigaray, *Speculum de l'autre femme* (Paris: Minuit, 1974); Hélène Cixous and Catherine Clément, *The Newly Born Woman* (Theory and History of Literature, 24; trans. Betsy Wing; Minneapolis: University of Minnesota Press, 1986 [first published 1975]); Carol Gilligan, *In a Different Voice: Psychological Theory and Women's Development* (Cambridge: Harvard University Press, 1982). While defending psychoanalysis as indispensable to feminism, Nancy Chodorow admits that 'Freud does give us a prime example of an *ad hominem*, distorted ideology about women and women's inferiority'; see her *Feminism and Psychoanalytic Theory* (New Haven: Yale University Press, 1989), pp. 165-98 (176). It is, most likely, this 'dissent'—and not that represented by Eysenck, Cioffi, *et al.*—that Bal opaquely cites in declining to use the 'psychoanalytic code' in her *Murder and Difference* (p. 13). Among biblical scholars, Brenner, 'On Incest', in Brenner (ed.), *A Feminist Companion to Exodus to Deuteronomy* (The Feminist Companion to the Bible, 6; Sheffield: Sheffield Academic Press, 1994), pp. 113-38 (125), notably discounts psychoanalysis as a clue to incest, and prohibitions thereof, in the Hebrew Bible.

68. Exum makes a step in this direction by frankly admitting that she uses 'psychoanalytic criticism' in full knowledge that both it and psychoanalysis proper are 'neither externally verifiable nor falsifiable'; see her *Fragmented Women*, pp. 153-54. A similar intent may be operative in the unanimous insistence of Bal, Rashkow, and Exum that they draw on 'psychoanalytic literary theory' rather than psychoanalysis per se but in such case, an explanation of the difference between the two would be in order.

reading that this publication offers or at least in validating it. Is Freud's (rather convoluted) concept of the 'uncanny' requisite in recognizing the sheer horror exuded by Judges 19, especially for women?[69] Does a feminist interpreter need to invoke transference (as shown above, in a highly imprecise way) in order to justify her identifying with Sarah rather than Abraham when reading 'wife-sister' stories?[70] Do these enigmatic stories start to make any sense when Abraham is identified with the Freudian id and the foreign rulers with the super-ego?[71] There is no arguing that theory may be instrumental in giving rise to an interpretation, sustaining, or at least enhancing it, but theory for theory's sake is nothing but a distraction.[72] Thus, what needs to be done is developing theoretically astute, detailed, and extensive feminist exegetical engagement with the wide varieties of psychological concepts, theories, and ideas, yet without succumbing to the temptation of empty theorizing. Such engagement with psychological scholarship, as it emerges today, would go a long way in deepening the feminist study of the Bible.

---

69. Bal, *Death and Dissymmetry*, pp. 186-96. She admits that when it comes to the picture of a gang-raped woman lying at the threshold of the house sheltering her husband (Judg. 19.26-27), 'we hardly need a Freudian perspective for this concrete bodily image of the social conflict about the female body' (p. 196).

70. Rashkow, *The Phallacy of Genesis*, pp. 26-48.

71. Exum, *Fragmented Women*, pp. 160-65.

72. Again, Bechtel's and Gruber's articles stand out positively in this respect: for their readings, psychological theory is undeniably indispensable.

10

Tracing Differance, Power, and the Discourse of Gender: Deconstruction in Feminist Hebrew Bible Studies

Susanne Scholz

The founding parent of deconstruction, Jacques Derrida (1930–2004), would be rather unhappy to see deconstruction included in a book on method. He stated explicitly that 'deconstruction is not a method, and cannot be transformed into one. Especially if the technical and procedural significations of the word are stressed'.[1] In fact, Derrida explained that deconstruction is not only not a method but it is also neither an analysis nor a critique. His apophatic descriptions of deconstruction are famous, and so critics wonder what deconstruction is if it is neither method, analysis, nor critique. Many positive definitions exist. One of them, coming from the Bible and Culture Collective, explains that deconstruction 'was a dismantling of structures (philosophical, cultural, political, institutional, and above all and from the start textual) that was designed to show how they were put together in the first place'.[2] Stating it in a more tongue-in-cheek fashion, religion scholar John D. Caputo sums it up in this way: 'One might even say that cracking nutshells is what deconstruction *is*. In a nutshell'.[3] Or as Jennifer L. Koosed affirms breezily: '[D]econstruction is at play in the spaces between the points' of nihilism and absolutism.[4] William A. Beardslee explains: 'Deconstruction...means dismantling the seeming coherence of the text and reading it in a way that resists "closure"'.[5] Edward L. Greenstein hits the nail on

---

1. Jacques Derrida [1983], 'Letter to A Japanese Friend', in David Wood and Robert Bernasconi (eds.), *Derrida and Différance* (Warwick: Parousia, 1985), pp. 1-5 (3).
2. Bible and Culture Collective, 'Post-Structuralist Criticism', in *The Postmodern Bible* (New Haven, CT: Yale University Press, 1995), pp. 119-48 (120).
3. John D. Caputo (ed.), *Deconstruction in a Nutshell: A Conversation with Jacques Derrida* (New York: Fordham University Press), 1997, p. 32.
4. Jennifer L. Koosed, 'Nine Reflections on the Book: Poststructuralism and the Hebrew Bible', *Religion Compass* 2.4 (2008), pp. 499-512 (501).
5. William A. Beardless, 'Poststructuralist Criticism', in Steven L. McKenzie and Stephen R. Haynes (eds.), *To Each Its Own Meaning: An Introduction to Biblical Criticisms and Their Application* (Louisville, KY: Westminster/John Knox Press, rev. and exp. edn, 1999), pp. 253-67 (256).

the head when he classifies deconstruction '[a]s one of the most radical and difficult expressions of postpositivist thinking...'; it 'takes apart the system it reads'.[6]

Once Derrida chose this word to circumvent the terminology he had inherited, namely 'destruction' (or, in German: *Abbau*), the noun and associated readerly practices of deconstruction have been built upon, adapted, and expanded to all kinds of thought, analysis, and interpretation. Thus, undoubtedly, deconstructive approaches to feminist biblical exegesis have been significant and momentous. In light of the emerging epistemological and hermeneutical deconstructions of the hegemonic ways of living in the world and in the mind since the late 1960s, some feminist biblical critics turned to deconstructing androcentric reading habits of biblical literature. The pervasiveness of textual ambiguities and incoherence of the Bible, the multitude of narrative gaps, the ongoing illusiveness of authorial intent, and a tradition of exegetical 'proto-deconstructors'[7] have aided feminist interpreters to challenge and to undermine the scientific-empiricist and androcentric foundations of biblical studies.

This essay reviews, analyzes, and evaluates these developments in three sections. The first section summarizes the emergence of deconstruction as a hermeneutical enterprise since the late 1960s to provide a context for the second and third sections. They present overviews of deconstruction in Hebrew Bible studies and in feminist Hebrew Bible interpretations. A conclusion offers comments about the future of deconstructive reading strategies at this post-postmodern moment in time.

The Emergence of Deconstruction as a Philosophical Enterprise

Without structuralism there would not have been any deconstruction, and so Derrida's work must be understood as a response to structuralism. Derrida was always clear on this fact, as, for instance, when he explained:

> To deconstruct was also a structuralist gesture or in any case a gesture that assumed a certain need for the structuralist problematic. But it was also an antistructuralist gesture, and its fortune rests in part on this ambiguity. Structures were to be undone, decomposed, desedimented (all types of structures, linguistic, 'logocentric', 'phonocentric'—structuralism being especially at that time dominated by linguistic models and by a so-called structural linguistics that was also called Saussurian—socio-institutional, political, cultural, and above all and from the start philosophical).[8]

---

6. Edward L. Greenstein, 'Deconstruction and Biblical Narrative', *Prooftexts* 9.1 (January 1989), pp. 43-71 (43, 54).
7. For this term, see Greenstein, 'Deconstruction', p. 55.
8. Jacques Derrida, 'Letter to a Japanese Friend. (Prof. Izutsu)', in David Wood

Derrida regarded his deconstructive moves as 'a structuralist gesture' as much as 'an antistructuralist gesture' because he assumed structuralism as the conversation partner or context that needed to be deconstructed. Without structuralism, he would not have been able to invent deconstruction or poststructuralism. Deconstructional readings posit an oppositional stance questioning hegemonic ways of thought; they challenge explicit and implicit hierarchies of binary thinking, as assumed in structuralism.

In other words, deconstruction adopts some of the same ideas that are also assumed in structuralism. Both are text-centered approaches and both do not merely read texts on the surface level but, digging deeper, they look for the meanings between the lines and on the sidelines. Both structuralism and post-structuralism question implicit, normalized, and accepted meanings. Yet while structuralism, as taught by Ferdinand de Saussure in linguistics, Claude Lévi-Strauss in anthropology, or Vladimir Propp in folklore studies, aims to uncover the unconscious and embedded structures of communication, deconstruction fosters suspicion toward all systems of meaning. As Derrida explained, all systems are based on 'différance', a homophonous and artificial word with the French 'différence', playing on its double meaning of deference and difference. Gayatri Chakravorty Spivak elaborates on this dynamic: 'This difference—being the structure (a structure never quite there, never by us perceived, itself deferred and different) of our psyche— is also the structure of "presence", a term itself under erasure. For difference, producing the differential structure of our hold on "presence", never produces presence as such.'[9] She continues:

> The structure of 'presence' is thus constituted by difference and deferment. But since the 'subject' that 'perceives' presence is also constituted similarly, differance is neither active nor passive. The '-ance' ending is the mark of that suspended status. Since the difference between 'difference' and 'differance' is inaudible, this 'neographism' reminds us of the importance of writing as a structure. The 'a' serves to remind us that, even within the graphic structure, the perfectly spelled word is always absent, constituted through an endless series of spelling mistakes.[10]

In the concept of 'differance', then, Derrida argued against the structuralist delusion of any foundational concept being embedded in any structure.

In poststructuralism, meaning is always already displaced in the moment when it appears to be present. It is elusive, ambiguous, suspended,

and Robert Bernasconi (eds.), *Derrida and Différance* (Coventry, UK: Parousia Press, 1985), pp. 1-5 (2).

9. Gayatri Chakravorty Spivak, 'Translator's Preface', in Jacques Derrida, *Of Grammatology* (trans. Gayatri Chakravorty Spivak; Baltimore/London: The Johns Hopkins University Press, 1974), pp. ix-xc (xliii).

10. Spivak, 'Translator's Preface', p. xliii.

suppressed, and it is easily repressed by words. Deconstruction 'seeks to undo both a given order of priorities and the very system of conceptual opposition that makes that order possible' [emphasis in original].[11] Thus, Derrida looked for a new grammar, a new way of thinking and interpretation that is not stuck in the assumptions of Western metaphysics. To him, meaning is always different from and endlessly deferrable to something else; it is never fixed, stable, or definable. Greenstein explains it in two words: 'Meaning flickers'.[12] Deconstruction 'exposes the exclusions, seeks the moment when the system falters and thus demonstrates the instability of the system'.[13] Deconstruction looks for contradictions, incoherences, and inconsistencies. It 'denies the objectivity of order', and it denounces 'technocractic, predictive, or authoritarian formulas'. It denies 'given centers and structures, favors the roads not taken, the margins, even the unthinkable, or more precisely, the unthought. To get a better look, it likes to invert'.[14] Above all, it never settles.

Much more could be said about Derrida, but he is not the only theorist who has played a major role in the intellectual and cultural development known as deconstruction or post-structuralism. Another important thinker is his countryman, Michel Foucault (1926–1984). His notions about the genealogy and archaeology of power have been widely influential. Foucault maintained that knowledge and power are always intertwined and that any system of thought— also known as 'episteme' or 'discursive formation'— is infused by power regimes. Everyone adheres to them as they shape the intellectual boundaries in any given place and time. Outlining his view about 'discourses' of knowledge, Foucault notes:

> Discourses are not once and for all subservient to power or raised up against it… We must make allowances for the complex and unstable process whereby a discourse can be both an instrument and an effect of power, but also a hindrance, a stumbling point of resistance and a starting point for an opposing strategy. Discourse transmits and produces power; it reinforces it, but also undermines and exposes it, renders it fragile and makes it possible to thwart.[15]

As 'regimes of truth', such 'discourses' of knowledge are forms of social control that are practiced in various social institutions. Individual people and groups do not create, uphold, or change these all-pervasive power

---

11. Christopher Norris, *Deconstruction: Theory and Practice* (London/New York: Routledge, rev. edn, 1991), p. 31.
12. Greenstein, 'Deconstruction and Biblical Narrative', p. 48.
13. Koosed, 'Nine Reflections on the Book', p. 500.
14. Greenstein, 'Deconstruction and Biblical Narrative', p. 57, 55.
15. Michel Foucault, *The History of Sexuality: The Will to Knowledge* (London: Penguin, 1998), pp. 100-101.

formations. Instead, they pervade the entire system which they rule. Power represses and enables simultaneously. It is positive and negative, producing and censoring, enabling and masking. It is constituted through normalized, that is unconsciously held, ideas of knowledge. Power is negotiated and in constant flux. To Foucault, power can be traced historically by excavating its genealogies in textual artifacts. Power is everywhere and it comes from everywhere. It defines what is called 'truth' and it changes regimes of truth.

Foucault unearthed modern discourses of power in psychology, medicine, and criminology. For instance, in *The History of Sexuality* he noted that discourses on sexuality were not so much repressed as proliferating since the seventeenth century CE. Scientific terminologies about sexuality were invented at that time and implemented as regimes of disciplinary power in prisons, schools, and mental hospitals. So-called experts developed classification systems about people's feelings and actions to learn the 'truth' about sex. For instance, in regard to the 'repression hypothesis' Foucault maintains:

> We must therefore abandon the hypothesis that modern industrial societies ushered in an age of increased sexual repression. We have not only witnessed a visible explosion of unorthodox sexualities; but—and this is the important point—a deployment quite different from the law, even if it is locally dependent on procedures of prohibition, has ensured, through a network of interconnecting mechanisms, the proliferation of specific pleasures and the multiplication of disparate sexualities.[16]

In this sense, then, Foucault's work contributes to an understanding of deconstruction as a project that excavates, traces, and makes visible networks of power embedded in past and present discursive practices. As David A. Kaden explains, Foucault's 'archaeological method is not essentialist, and does not examine the contradictions in discourse for a reality outside the statement itself'.[17] Rather it is about the study of power formations in discourses of knowledge to show the embeddedness of power in the functioning of society. It has been debated whether Foucault's proposal is ultimately nihilistic in the sense that 'resistance is futile'. Does Foucault suggest that resistance is always already part of the game and thus always already implicated in the power structure? Or does his concept of resistance support various forms of political actions that circumvent the status quo of power? Foucault scholars have identified both positions in his work.[18]

---

16. Foucault, *The History of Sexuality*, p. 49.
17. David A. Kaden, 'Foucault, Feminism, and Liberationist Religion: Discourse, Power, and the Politics of Interpretation in the Feminist Emancipatory Project of Elisabeth Schüssler Fiorenza', *Neotestamentica* 46.1 (2012), pp. 83-104 (97).
18. For a general discussion, see Kevin Jon Heller, 'Power, Subjectification and

Among other influential deconstructionist and poststructuralist thinkers are Roland Barthes, Jean-François Lyotard, Giles Deleuze, Julia Kristeva, Luce Irigary, Hélène Cixous, Judith Butler, Homi Bhabba, Gayatri Chakravorty Spivak, and Emmanuel Levinas. Each developed critiques of metanarratives, difference, hybridity, multiplicity, ambiguity, rupture, intertextuality, and undecidability in their numerous scholarly writings since the late 1960s and 1970s, offering theoretical insights and argumentations of great influence to the many fields of the humanities, social sciences, the arts, and architecture. It has included the field of Hebrew Bible studies.

Deconstruction Making It as a 'Method' in Hebrew Bible Studies

D'une certaine manière, in a certain way, deconstruction à la Derrida has made it into biblical studies. This poststructuralist biblical criticism has not led to the destruction or an end of biblical studies, but to the reading of the Bible in a certain way.[19] As Herbert N. Schneidau articulates it in one of the first publications on deconstruction in biblical studies, Derrida's deconstruction has much to offer biblical scholarship. Its emphasis on the priority of texts over against Western metaphysical logocentrism and its critical stance toward notions of '"ordinary language", "literal language", and "common sense" thinking invite us to see the illusory metaphysics'.[20] The undecideability about the difference between history and fiction, since deconstructionists regard fiction as a constitutive element of all writing,[21] has also angered many Bible scholar invested in historical explorations of biblical literature. The note by Robert Detweiler that there is 'curiosity about Jacques Derrida's writing and the more than occasional cycnicism and hostility toward it by American academics, including biblical scholars and theologicans',[22] hints at the resistance and opposition from the scholarly mainstream in 1982. Yet deconstructionist Bible scholars insist on the need to press on. In 1986, David Jobling acknowledges his interest in the new approach when he states:

Resistance in Foucault', *SubStance* 25.1.79 (1996), pp. 78-110. For the latter position, see, e.g., Brent L. Pickett, 'Foucault and the Poltics of Resistance', *Polity* 28.4 (Summer 1996), pp. 445-66. For brief online explanations on key Foucauldian concepts, created by Foucault scholar Clare O'Farrell, see http://www.michel-foucault.com/concepts/.

19. For an elaboration on this idea in Derrida's work, see John P. Leavey, Jr, 'Four Protocols: Derrida, His Deconstruction', *Semeia* 23 (1982), pp. 43-57 (43).

20. Herbert N. Schneidau, 'The Word Against the Word: Derrida on Textuality', *Semeia* 23 (1982), pp. 5-28 (5).

21. Schneidau, 'The Word Against the Word', p. 23.

22. Robert Detweiler, 'Introduction (Derrida and Biblical Studies)', *Semeia* 23 (1982), pp. 1-2 (1).

> I find my present work taking two new directions, following two trends which are both well-established in recent scholarship, but which, at least in biblical studies, have remained separate. The first, indeed, has made little impact on biblical studies at all; this is the critical approach most often indicated by the term 'deconstruction' (though other terms, especially the 'indeterminacy' of texts, indicate something similar). Despite the fashionable term 'post-structuralism', deconstruction does not claim simply to supersede structuralism—it *assumes* structuralism, and subverts it from within. The most characteristic move in Derrida is to subvert/cancel/reverse binary oppositions; one can deconstruct only where one has posited structure... Deconstruction depends, then, on structural analysis, and structural analysis tends towards deconstruction.[23]

After this brief statement about deconstruction as a possible new influence in biblical studies, Jobling elaborates on liberation theologies, including feminist exegesis, as the other significant trend. For instance, in a chapter on the 'Myth and Limits in Genesis 2.4b–3.24',[24] he highlights the manifold patriarchal features within the famous story infused with 'the bad conscience that goes along with trying to make sense of patriarchalism'. Jobling's interpretation points to inexplicable configurations, such as the garden that stands in spatial distinction to the earth as a whole, the ambiguity and incoherence of God, the oppositional logic of human existence, and the existence of a dominant and a 'recessive' narrative. Although Jobling's approach is very much indebted to structuralist and especially Greimasian models of analysis, his discussions on Genesis 2–3 and other biblical texts (related to pro- and anti-monarchical parts mostly in 1 Samuel 1–12 and biblical traditions on the Israelites living east of the river Jordan) expose countless textual oppositions, contradictions, and ambiguities.

In the mid-1980s, biblical studies was still relatively untouched by deconstruction in contrast to the raging debates it had instigated in such fields as philosophy and literary criticism. Consequently, Edward L. Greenstein's 1989 article, entitled 'Deconstruction and Biblical Narrative', must have seemed quite bold at the time. Greenstein indicates that much in his opening comments when he observes that the 1987 anthology by Robert Alter and Frank Kermode, *The Literary Guide to the Bible*, 'specifically excludes the bugaboo deconstruction, along with Marxism and feminism, as an unsympathetic approach to reading biblical literature'.[25] He also states

---

23. David Jobling, 'Introduction', in *The Sense of Biblical Narrative. II. Structural Analysis in the Hebrew Bible* (JSOTSup, 39; Sheffield: Sheffield Academic Press, 1986), pp. 9-16 (12).

24. David Jobling, 'Myth and Its Limits in Genesis 2.4–3.24', in *The Sense of Biblical Narrative. II. Structural Analysis in the Hebrew Bible* (JSOTSup, 39; Sheffield: Sheffield Academic Press, 1986), pp. 17-43.

25. Greenstein, 'Deconstruction and Biblical Narrative', p. 43. For an even earlier

that '[l]ittle has been published as yet on the application of deconstruction to the Hebrew Bible, and I have seen virtually no purely deconstructive reading of it'.[26] Greenstein's essay is meant to familiarize his colleagues with the new approach, to make it palpable, and perhaps even attractive.

After outlining some general ideas and principles of deconstructive philosophy, Greenstein interprets Lev. 10.1-5 based on the deconstructionist notions of ambiguity, the indeterminacy of meaning, the denial of the objectivity of order presented in the text, and the multiplicity of meaning. These concepts enable him to offer an intriguing reading of this biblical passage that has long been recognized even in mainstream scholarship as opaque and puzzling. As Greenstein grasps for deconstructive clues, he proposes that the 'possible irrationality or disorderliness' of the biblical text is 'a means of remystifying the text, insisting on the unknown as we grope for the known'.[27] In this way, the biblical passage teaches 'the limits/borders of human understanding as a consequence of the instability of linguistic sense', and so it 'paradoxically facilitate[s] a God-belief'.[28] The unorthodox approach of deconstruction assists Greenstein to remind Bible readers that in Lev. 10.1-5 God is non-normative, unpredictable, and transcendent. The difficult biblical passage turns into theological orthodoxy as 'Yhwh breaks up the orderliness to show he [*sic*] is above/beyond the cultic order. A God worthy of the name cannot be trammeled by rules, any more than an infinite God can be contained by names, by language.'[29] Who can resist such a theological conclusion even when it comes with the help of deconstruction?

Other journal collections on deconstruction in biblical studies appeared shortly thereafter in *Semeia*, which from 1972 to 2002 functioned as 'an experimental [SBL] journal devoted to the exploration of new and emergent areas and methods of biblical criticism'.[30] In 1990 and 1991, two volumes were devoted to poststructuralism in biblical studies, indicating perhaps that deconstruction had finally arrived at the doorsteps of the biblical guild. The Semeia articles reflect the stony but joyous road taken by scholars who labor within the wide spectrum of the Christian canon of the Bible and engage deconstruction in biblical interpretation. Their works illustrate how to navigate Derridean, Foucauldian, and other poststructuralist thought and how to evaluate its impact on biblical exegesis. For instance, in a theoretically comprehensive essay, Jobling sought to develop 'a broad framework'

---

deconstructive interpretation, this one of Psalm 23, see David Paul McCarthy, 'A Not-So-Bad Derridean Approach to Psalm 23', *Proceedings (Grand Rapids, MI)* 8 (1988), pp. 177-91.

26. Greenstein, 'Deconstruction and Biblical Narrative', p. 44.
27. Greenstein, 'Deconstruction and Biblical Narrative', p. 62.
28. Greenstein, 'Deconstruction and Biblical Narrative', p. 62.
29. Greenstein, 'Deconstruction and Biblical Narrative', p. 64.
30. See http://www.sbl-site.org/publications/books_semeiaj.aspx.

within which to analyze 'the world of [textual] discourse' in relationship to power.³¹ He proposed to study '[h]ow...the methods applied to the Bible as "valid" [have] been determined by the social location of the guardians of validity' and thus to investigate 'what has been the political context for the ascendancy of historical criticism'.³² In Jobling's judgment, deconstruction ought to be seen as an ally in liberation and feminist exegetical work because deconstruction understands that '[a]s we seek systemic change, we are so much part of the system (or it of us) that we cannot determine in advance what it is we are after; any "program" we follow will simply encode the dominant assumptions we are locked into'.³³ Deconstruction, then, helps us to avoid repeating 'gestures of power' prevalent in orthodoxy. In his paradigmatic discussion, Jobling also suggests that deconstruction 'give[s] up the ultra-critical habit of mind, and the methodological superiority complex, to which it is prone'.³⁴ In his view, liberationist and feminist deconstructionists of the Bible need to work 'on two fronts simultaneously': 'exuberant celebration of freedom and methodological plurality' on the one hand and 'the desire to be a coherent paradigm which can challenge the dominant paradigm within the politics of biblical studies'³⁵ on the other. Thanks to Jobling and the other deconstructionist Bible scholars, the quest for methodological plurality and alternative interpretative viewpoints has characterized deconstructionist readings in biblical studies ever since.

Other contributors in the two *Semeia* volumes also celebrated the arrival of a new era in biblical studies. It seemed in 1990 as if the field was finally poised to become part of the larger academic world again. The following statement of Gary A. Phillips communicates this mood about the possibilities that the arrival of deconstruction promised to bring to biblical studies:

> In short, the present debate over literary critical theory and its ideological consequences announces a discursive transformation not simply in the way biblical critics or academicians and religious leaders perform their disciplinary or professional tasks but, more broadly, in the way we as modern selves have come to understand our collective social and intellectual history, our ideological and metaphysical commitments, and the changing role ascribed to the critics of religion and culture in the late twentieth century West... Spotlighted here is the changing status, then, of modern discourse itself which has exercised its rule over (and given definition to) 'modernity' with its associated common-sense for better than two centuries, and which

31. David Jobling, 'Writing the Wrongs of the World: The Deconstruction of the Biblical Text in the Context of Liberation Theology, *Semeia* 51 (1990), pp. 81-118 (99).
32. Jobling, 'Writing the Wrongs of the World', p. 100.
33. Jobling, 'Writing the Wrongs of the World', p. 103.
34. Jobling, 'Writing the Wrongs of the World', p. 104.
35. Jobling, 'Writing the Wrongs of the World', p. 106.

has provided us as exegetes with the critical means for understanding history, our methods of interpreting texts, and our professional identities as modern, critical selves.[36]

Enthusiastically, Phillips announces that postmodernism arrives in biblical studies with powerful cultural forces transforming modern biblical studies and its preferred method, historical criticism. This development, according to Phillips, will reenergize the field. In the same volume, Fred W. Burnett predicts that poststructuralist ways of reading biblical literature will 'require an *ontological* rethinking' [emphasis in original][37] of historical critical discourse, requiring biblical exegetes 'to be "voice-reflective" as participant-critics'.[38] The postmodern, poststructural, and deconstructionist challenges to modern biblical discourse will change the field's stance toward history, text, authorship, and its basic commitments to method and epistemology.

The following year gave rise to yet another *Semeia* issue on deconstruction in 1991. One of the contributors, Robert Detweiler observes poignantly that the volume's editors, David Jobling and Stephen D. Moore, 'achieved a brilliant stroke' in demonstrating that 'the sacred texts of the West, the Hebrew Bible and the Christian New Testament, need new interpretations in our age to assure their survival, their overliving, so that we will somehow survive'.[39] Containing essays by Jacques Derrida, Regina M. Schwartz, David Jobling, Mieke Bal, Peter D. Miscall, Fred W. Burnett, Susan Lochrie Graham, Stephen D. Moore, Elizabeth A. Castelli, Kirk T. Hughes, and Detweiler, this *Semeia* volume puts deconstruction squarely into the center of the exegetical attention although Stephen D. Moore acknowledges that deconstruction 'has been oddly neglected by biblical literary critics'.[40]

Both the 1990 and 1991 *Semeia* volumes helped legitimize deconstruction as an exegetical approach. They encouraged the development of this approach and indirectly enabled various scholarly monographs in the field, written by the next generation of biblical exegetes, among them Hugh Pyper, Yvonne Sherwood, Timothy K. Beal, Erin Runions, Tod Linafelt, Jennifer L. Koosed, Fiona C. Black, and others.[41]

---

36. Gary A. Phillips, 'Exegesis as Critical Praxis: Reclaiming History and Text from a Postmodern Perspective', *Semeia* 51 (1990), pp. 7-49 (14).

37. Fred W. Burnett, 'Postmodern Biblical Exegesis: The Eve of Historical Criticism', *Semeia* 51 (1990), pp. 51-80 (51).

38. Burnett, 'Postmodern Biblical Exegesis', p. 70.

39. Robert Detweiler, 'Outliving', *Semeia* 54 (1991), pp. 239-55 (240).

40. Stephen D. Moore, 'Introduction', *Semeia* 54 (1991), pp. 1-2 (2).

41. Hugh S. Pyper, *David as Reader: 2 Samuel 2–11 and the Poetic of Fatherhood* (New York: E.J. Brill, 1996); Yvonne Sherwood, *The Prostitute and the Prophet: Hosea's Marriage in Literary-Theoretical Perspective* (Sheffield: Sheffield Academic Press, 1996); Timothy K. Beal, *The Book of Hiding: Gender, Ethnicity, Annihilation, and Esther* (New York: Routledge, 1997); Todd Linafelt, *Surviving Lamentations:*

Another anthology, published in 2004, needs to be highlighted here because it demonstrates that deconstruction had matured in biblical studies. Edited by Yvonne Sherwood and entitled *Derrida's Bible (Reading a Page of Scripture with a Little Help from Derrida)*, this book contains eighteen essays from various Bible scholars.[42] In her introduction, Sherwood explains that the origins of the collection go back to the 2002 annual meeting of the SBL in Toronto which Derrida attended. According to Sherwood, the time had come 'to combat the nullification that came from two fronts: the reification of "deconstructionism" as a complex machine, and the domestication of "deconstruction" as a mere synonym for critical business as usual'.[43] The invitation of Derrida to the event aimed to make him 'real' and to shake the field 'out of some ossified image of Derrida'.[44] Much had changed during the past decade. Derrida had become a household name, even in biblical studies, and 'institutionalized misreadings of vintage Derrida' needed to be fought off.[45] The goal was to create some 'pause for thought into the increasingly atomized sphere of contemporary biblical studies' and to take a second look at the resources offered by Derrida's extensive bibliography, even on a number of biblical texts.[46]

The book illustrates an ambitious and comprehensive agenda. Detailed and specific text studies characterize the contributions gathered in the volume that go far beyond the pragmatic and introductory essays of the 1990 and 1991 *Semeia* volumes. Regardless of whether the contributors deal with Qoh. 12.1-8, Genesis 14, or Judges 12, each engages in 'Derridean Bible study',[47] positioning themselves as 'inheritors', readers, and negotiators of biblical texts by filtering, selecting, criticizing, and sorting out the multiple,

---

Catastrophe, Lament, and Protest in the Afterlife of a Biblical Book (Chicago: University of Chicago, 2000); Yvonne Sherwood, *A Biblical Text and Its Afterlife: The Survival of Jonah in Western Culture* (Cambridge: Cambridge University Press, 2000); Erin Runions, *Changing Subjects: Gender, Nation, and Future in Micah* (New York: Continuum, 2001); Jennifer L. Koosed, *(Per)mutations of Qohelet: Reading the Body in the Book* (New York: Continuum, 2006); Fiona C. Black, *Artifice of Love: Grotesque Bodies and the Song of Song*s (New York: Continuum, 2007).

42. Yvonne Sherwood (ed.), *Derrida's Bible (Reading a Page of Scripture with a Little Help from Derrida* (New York: Palgrave, 2004). For Derrida's works on the Bible, see, e.g., Jacques Derrida, 'Des Tour de Babel (in French, 1980; in English, 1985)', in *Acts of Religion* (ed. and with an introduction by Gil Anidjar; New York/London: Routledge, 2002), pp. 102-34.

43. Yvonne Sherwood, 'Introduction', in Yvonne Sherwood (ed.), *Derrida's Bible (Reading a Page of Scripture with a Little Help from Derrida* (New York: Palgrave, 2004), pp. 1-20 (7).

44. Sherwood, 'Introduction', in Sherwood (ed.), *Derrida's Bible*, p. 7.
45. Sherwood, 'Introduction', in Sherwood (ed.), *Derrida's Bible*, p. 7.
46. Sherwood, 'Introduction', in Sherwood (ed.), *Derrida's Bible*, p. 9.
47. Sherwood, 'Introduction', in Sherwood (ed.), *Derrida's Bible*, p. 11.

ambiguous, contradictory, and possible meanings. As Sherwood expresses it so well, Derridean Bible study teaches to practice 'a mode of interpretation that, instead of dividing the world into those who accept or reject a given religious inheritance…, implicates us all in little acts of micro-choosing and micro-decision'.[48] Derridean Bible study turns us into readers and inheritors of incomplete writings to be read nonetheless. The book documents that in the year of Derrida's death, deconstruction in biblical studies had moved from introductory and generalizing explanations about origins, purpose, and goals of deconstruction to exegetical and meditative ruminations about biblical literature as inherited texts, to be read over and over again, because presence, whether divine or not, can only be found in the never ending re-reading process.

Feminist, (Feminist), or ~~Feminist~~ Deconstructionist Approaches to the Hebrew Bible

Perhaps unsurprisingly, feminist deconstructionist Bible exegetes have an ambiguous and indeterminate opinion about feminist exegesis. Mostly sympathetic toward the feminist call for biblical reinterpretation, they often question the exegetical viability of feminist meanings based on historical, literary, or epistemological observations. Further, they often characterize existing feminist appropriations as 'revisionism'. Feminist biblical interpretations that tend to assume essentializing notions about women and gender in the Bible appear too singular, monolithic, and fixed to them. It is therefore not always certain whether deconstructionist engagement with feminist exegetical work is indeed 'feminist', especially when such engagement is not explicitly identified as feminist work and instead stresses the ambiguity of all biblical meanings, feminist or not. Thus, feminist deconstructionist scholars do not unanimously endorse feminist-political positionalities, and they often deconstruct early feminist works.[49]

---

48. Sherwood, 'Introduction', in Sherwood (ed.), *Derrida's Bible*, p. 14. For other works on deconstruction in Hebrew Bible Studies, see, e.g., Jacob D. Myers, 'Before the Gaze Ineffable: Intersubjective Poiesis and the Song of Songs', *Theology & Sexuality* 17.2 (2011), pp. 139-60; Alissa Jones Nelson, *Power and Responsibility in Biblical Interpretation: Reading the Book of Job with Edward Said* (Sheffield: Equinox, 2012).

49. David Jobling, 'The Myth Semantics of Gen. 2:4b–3:24', *Semeia* 18 (1980), pp. 41-49; David Jobling, 'Myth and its Limits in Gen. 2:4b–3:24', in *The Sense of Biblical Narrative*. II. *Structural Analysis in the Hebrew Bible* (JSOTSup, 39; Sheffield: JSOT Press, 1986), pp. 17-43; Pamela J. Milne, 'Eve and Adam: Is a Feminist Reading Possible?', *Bible Review* 4 (1988), pp. 12-21, 39; Ellen Van Wolde, *A Semiotic Analysis of Genesis 2–3: A Semiotic Theory and Method of Analysis Applied to the Story of the Garden of Eden* (Studia semitica neerlandica; Maastricht: Assen, 1989); David J.A. Clines, 'What Does Eve Do to Help? And Other Irredeemably Androcentric Orientations

One example of this analysis can be seen in the work of the literary-cultural scholar Mieke Bal, who in the mid-1980s offered a forceful critique that characterizes feminist and androcentric readings as 'equally false'.[50] Bal herself does not aim for a feminist interpretation because she considers such a goal impossible; nevertheless, her work is often classified as feminist.[51] She explains in her work on Genesis 2–3: 'If my interpretation of Eve's position shows her in a more favorable light than do the common uses of the text, I do not want to suggest that this is a feminist, feminine, or female-oriented text'.[52] To Bal, the androcentric text uses both negative and positive gender markers that serve 'to limit repression to acceptable, viable proportions' and to make the domination bearable to both the dominators and the dominated.[53] Bal understands that 'dominators have, first, to establish their position, then to safeguard it. They must make both the dominated *and* themselves believe in it'.[54] Thus Bal considers the Bible as neither 'a feminist resource [n]or a sexist manifesto',[55] but as literature that includes 'traces of problematization of the represented ideology'.[56]

Bal views Genesis 2–3 as 'a patriarchal myth that is related to an ideology that cannot be monolithic'.[57] The patriarchal bias of the text is complex because it is not blatantly hostile to the 'other'. Apparent tolerance of the 'other'—here 'woman'—does not make Genesis 2–3 woman-friendly

in Genesis 1–3', in *What Does Eve Do to Help? And Other Readerly Questions to the Old Testament* (JSOTSup, 94; Sheffield: JSOT Press, 1990), pp. 25-48; David M. Carr, 'The Politics of Textual Subversion: A Diachronic Perspective on the Garden of Eden Story', *JBL* 112.4 (1993), pp. 577-95; John Goldingay, 'Postmodernizing Eve and Adam (Can I Have My Apricot as Well as Eating It?)', in P.R. Davies and D.J.A. Clines (eds.), *World of Genesis: Persons, Places, Perspectives* (JSOTSup, 257; Sheffield: Sheffield Academic Press, 1998), pp. 50-59; Deborah F. Sawyer, *God, Gender and the Bible* (London: Routledge, 2002).

50. Mieke Bal, 'Sexuality, Sin, and Sorrow: The Emergence of the Female Character', in *Lethal Love: Feminist Literary Readings of Biblical Love Stories* (Bloomington: Indiana University Press, 1987), pp. 104-30 (110); orig. in *Poetics Today* 6 (1985), pp. 1-2, 21-42.

51. See, e.g., Edward L. Greenstein, review of *Lethal Love: Feminist Literary Readings of Biblical Love Stories* (Bloomington: Indiana University Press, 1987), by Mieke Bal, in *JR* 69.3 (July 1989), pp. 395-96; Joseph Abraham, *Eve: Accused or Acquitted? An Analysis of Feminist Readings of the Creation Narrative Texts in Genesis 1–3* (Eugene, OR: Wipf & Stopf, 2002).

52. Bal, 'Sexuality, Sin, and Sorrow', p. 110.

53. Bal, 'Sexuality, Sin, and Sorrow', p. 110.

54. Bal, 'Sexuality, Sin, and Sorrow', p. 110 (emphasis in original).

55. Mieke Bal, 'Introduction', in *Lethal Love: Feminist Literary Readings of Biblical Love Stories* (Bloomington: Indiana University Press, 1987), pp. 1-9 (1).

56. Bal, 'Sexuality, Sin, and Sorrow', p. 110.

57. Bal, 'Sexuality, Sin, and Sorrow', p. 110.

or feminist, Bal contends, but it is an essential strategy to androcentric ideology. Woman-friendly elements obfuscate gender bias, and invite both men and women to believe in the Bible. This complex and 'heterogeneous' strategy works and made the Bible 'one of the most influential mythical and literary documents of our culture',[58] endorsed both by women and men. Bal analyzes the strategies that help both feminist and androcentric interpretations to suppress the heterogeneity of the text and to gain 'coherence and authority'. She seeks to expose the domination model and to understand the biblical narrative's contributions to 'the possibility of dominance itself'.[59]

Bal's analysis gained considerable renown because it proposes that both feminist and androcentric interpretations share the same hermeneutical convictions. Both attempt to streamline the Bible's heterogeneous ideology, and both reach for monolithic explanations. To do so, both also have to commit to what Bal calls the 'retrospective fallacy'. This strategy requires that readers project a character's fully developed identity from the end to the beginning of the story. In the case of Genesis 2–3, readers have to assume that Eve, as depicted at the story's end, is already a fully developed character at the narrative's beginning. They must ignore the literary stages, the 'semiotic chronology', in which 'Eve' appears only in Genesis 3.[60] They have to forget that '[w]hat existed before was an earth creature, then a woman, next an actant, then a mother, and finally, a being named "Eve"'.[61]

Committing the retrospective fallacy, readers—both feminist and androcentric—do not recognize that Genesis 2–3 contains two stories, an early one that presents a 'myth of creation' and a later story that presents a 'myth of Eve'. When readers collapse both narratives into one, they read the story from its end. According to Bal, this strategy has led to a fundamental problem in the history of interpretation: 'What went wrong in the history of reception…is precisely the repression of the problem… (namely) the heterogeneous ideology of the text, which had to be turned into a monolithic one'.[62] The consequences of the hermeneutical collapse are significant, as they contributed to 'dominance itself'. Feminist and androcentric interpretations could certainly have avoided this hermeneutical problem had they recognized Eve's and Adam's gradual literary development:

> First its [the character of *ha-adam*] existence was posited, but then it was not yet a sexual being. Then it was sexually differentiated, addressed, and

---

58. Bal, 'Introduction', p. 1
59. Bal, 'Introduction', p. 3.
60. Bal, 'Sexuality, Sin, and Sorrow', p. 107.
61. Bal, 'Sexuality, Sin, and Sorrow', pp. 107-108.
62. Mieke Bal, 'Afterword', in *Lethal Love: Feminist Literary Readings of Biblical Love Stories* (Bloomington: Indiana University Press, 1987), pp. 131-32 (131).

successively endowed with different aspects of subjectivity. It became the
subject of awareness, hence of focalization; of speech; of possible action;
of choice; and of actual actions. It was characterized by description. Then,
and only then, it was named: Adam the man, Eve the woman.[63]

Yet feminist and androcentric readers have ignored this literary development, reducing the biblical text to a monolithic meaning, and denying the possibility of heterogeneous meaning. Consequently, both kind of readings have contributed to the domination model, Bal maintains, preventing readers from seeing the heterogeneous ideology of the biblical text.

Another feminist deconstructionist approach that challenges other feminist readings of Genesis 2–3 comes from Susan Lanser. In her 1998 article '(Feminist) Criticism in the Garden', Lanser critiques feminist exegetes for relying on a formalistic 'theory of language' that defines communication as 'a process of encoding and decoding sentences'.[64] Focusing her review on the exegetical work of Phyllis Trible and Mieke Bal and classifying Bal's work as feminist, Lanser charges that feminist interpreters reduce Genesis 2–3 to 'a function of semantic, grammatical, and phonological or orthographical properties'.[65] The problem of these 'surface' readings is that they ignore the significance of 'context' in the meaning-making process, and underestimate that 'every act of understanding relies (unconsciously and sometimes also consciously) on complex rules and assumptions about social and cultural behavior and language use'.[66] Basing her assessment on the philosophical and literary-theoretical convictions of Jacques Derrida and Stanley Fish, Lanser criticizes feminist approaches for failing to recognize that '*every* reading creates and is created by its context; no uncontextual reading is possible'.[67] Accordingly, she finds that interpretative differences consist 'both in the degree to which context is brought explicitly to bear and in the kind of context the reading creates'.[68] Yet feminist interpretations, grounded in formalist assumptions, separate literary observations from social and linguistic contexts, and so they explain insufficiently 'the social custom, grammatical principles, cultural attitudes and common experience'.[69] They ignore the significance of 'inference', how readers infer meaning depending on the reading contexts.

---

63. Bal, 'Sexuality, Sin, and Sorrow', p. 130.
64. Susan S. Lanser, '(Feminist) Criticism in the Garden: Inferring Genesis 2–3', *Semeia* 41 (1988), pp. 67-84 (70).
65. Lanser, '(Feminist) Criticism in the Garden', p. 70.
66. Lanser, '(Feminist) Criticism in the Garden', pp. 70-71.
67. Lanser, '(Feminist) Criticism in the Garden', p. 77 (emphasis in original).
68. Lanser, '(Feminist) Criticism in the Garden', p. 77.
69. Lanser, '(Feminist) Criticism in the Garden', p. 77.

Other feminist deconstructionist Bible scholars have taken still other routes, for instance, grounding their biblical exegesis in the ideas of French feminist deconstructionist Julia Kristeva, Hélène Cixous, or Luce Irigaray.[70] Harold C. Washington presents such an approach in his reading of Ezra 9–10, a passage generally known as a postexilic prohibition against intermarriage and the expulsion of the 'foreign women'. Proposing to read this text 'as the tragic narrative of a fragile, emerging Judean subjectivity',[71] Washington finds Kristeva's psychoanalytical observation central for his discussion. Kristeva asserts that the abjection of the maternal, feminine body is always necessary for the development of human subjectivity. This dynamic defines the symbolic order of human societies, including the biblical worldview, as, for instance, outlined in the Levitical purity and holiness system. It, too, 'reinscribes this primordial repudiation of the feminine'.[72]

In alignment with Kristeva's claim, Washington maintains that this fundamental principle about the abjection of the feminine also appears in the imaginary order of the Ezra-Nehemiah corpus. There, women are classified as the unclean that needs to be expelled in order for Judean identity to emerge. As women are disproportionately held to the designed 'purity strictures',[73] the biblical texts record the initial trauma of the collective identity while also attempting to repress it. Washington is aware of the difficult interpretation history of Ezra 9–10 that have fostered considerable anti-Jewish sentiments throughout Christian history. Even so, his reliance on the deconstructionist principles in Kristeva's psychoanalytical study of the symbolic order as the unconscious enable him to emphasize textual ambiguities and multiplicities in these texts. He also stresses that the texts never mention the women's expulsion although they include 'peculiarly gendered vocabulary', which clearly stigmatizes 'women as signifiers of the stranger within'.[74] Thus, the women's predicament becomes inevitable within the

---

70. See, e.g., Timothy K. Beal, 'The System and the Speaking Subject in the Hebrew Bible: Reading for Divine Abjection', *BibInt* 2.2 (1994), pp. 172-89; S. Brent Plate and Edna M. Rodríguez Mangual, 'The Gift That Stops Giving: Hélène Cixous's "Gift" and the Shunammite Woman', *BibInt* 7.2 (1999), pp. 113-32; Deborah F. Sawyer, 'Dressing Up/Dressing Down: Power, Performance and Identity in the Book of Judith', *Theology & Sexuality* 15 (2001), pp. 23-31; Hugh S. Pyper, '"Job the Dog": Hélène Cixous on Wounds, Scars and the Biblical Text', *BibInt* 11.3/4 (2003), pp. 438-48; Deborah F. Sawyer, 'Hidden Subjects: Rereading Eve and Mary', *Theology & Sexuality* 14.3 (2008), pp. 305-20.

71. Harold C. Washington, 'Israel's Holy Seed and the Foreign Women of Ezra-Nehemiah: A Kristevan Reading', *BibInt* 11.3/4 (2003), pp. 427-37 (428).

72. Washington, 'Israel's Holy Seed', p. 428.

73. Washington, 'Israel's Holy Seed', p. 429.

74. Washington, 'Israel's Holy Seed', p. 431.

rhetorical logic of the text although it does not describe the implementation of the women's inevitable fate.

In line with Kristeva's theory that 'subjectivity is always provisional, contested, in process',[75] Washington observes that 'in the final words of the book of Ezra, the foreign women and their children are still present, and they remain visible through the book of Nehemiah'.[76] Although their expulsion is repetitively announced, it is never reported as completed. To Washington, who reads 'the troubling narrative' of Ezra 9–10 in accordance with Kristeva's psychoanalytical model, readers of any kind of religious or nonreligious persuasion could learn that it is always 'we' who 'are therefore heterogeneous, pure and impure, and as such always potentially condemnable', as outlined in Kristeva's reading of the Levitical laws. There is no 'other' out there but it is 'we' who need to learn to live with the other, 'the subject's hidden contradictions'.[77] With the help of Kristeva, Washington turns a biblical text filed 'under the rubric of Ezra-Nehemiah's "exclusivism"'[78] into an opportunity for individual and collective therapy. An interesting move indeed, but is it a 'feminist' one?

For some interpretations, the question can be answered unambiguously. They are not 'feminist' *per se* although these exegetes converse with feminist deconstructionist theorists. For instance, Roland Boer offers a sophisticated and compelling engagement with Kristeva on the issue of (biblical) motherhood, making abundant comments about Kristeva's references to the taboo laws in Leviticus and her views as a (Marxist) psychoanalytical philosopher. Boer's discussion teases out Kristeva's conviction that gender needs to be understood within 'political economics' based on a 'communitarian rather than individual feminism'.[79] Boer also lays out that, according to Kristeva, the Levitical incest taboos are grounded in the taboo of the mother or 'the abhorrence of the fertile female body'.[80] Yet he also challenges her 'mono-causal explanations' in which the taboo of the mother becomes 'overarching'. In classic Marxist fashion he plays out gender against economic explanations:

> Rather than the prime cause of the system as whole, the taboo of the mother is but one element in a wider concern of fertility, a concern that includes those of animals and land... For it turns out that the taboo is merely part of a wider socio-economic system.[81]

---

75. Washington, 'Israel's Holy Seed', p. 436.
76. Washington, 'Israel's Holy Seed', p. 436.
77. Washington, 'Israel's Holy Seed', p. 437.
78. Washington, 'Israel's Holy Seed', p. 437.
79. Roland Boer, 'The Forgetfulness of Julia Kristeva: Psychoanalysis, Marxism and the Taboo of the Mother', *JSOT* 33.3 (2009), pp. 259-76 (271).
80. Boer, 'The Forgetfulness of Julia Kristeva', p. 271.
81. Boer, 'The Forgetfulness of Julia Kristeva', p. 274.

Boer offers a very stimulating engagement with the work of this French feminist poststructural theorist in his biblical ruminations. However, when push comes to shove, he places economics above feminism to explain the 'sacred economy' of the Hebrew Bible. This is fine and important in itself, but it is not feminist despite Boer's considerable sympathies with feminist theories, causes, and explanations.

Yet another exegete, Roland J. De Vries, also relies on a feminist deconstructionist thinker, in this instance Luce Irigaray, but ultimately his interpretation, too, ought not to be confused as a feminist deconstructionist approach. Rather, he aims to create cohesion in the evangelical-conservative Christian world of biblical exegesis, most specifically between egalitarian and complementarian readings.[82] De Vries considers Gen. 2.23 which he reads with Irigaray's emphasis on 'wonder' and 'astonished recognition'.[83] De Vries argues that 'the astonished declaration of the first man, when confronted with the first woman..., may be construed as a declaration of wonder, along Irigarayan lines'.[84] His work elaborates on the details, but suffice it to quote the following point of his reading: '[N]ot only should the relationship between woman and man in the garden be construed as an egalitarian one (they, together, are in the image of God), but their equality must be construed in terms of an equality and unity in difference (A + B = One) along lines suggested by Irigaray. Each can only wonder before the face of the other'.[85] The creation of sexual difference in Gen. 1.27 and 2.23 helps De Vries to define the biblical notion of human gender as coming 'as irreducibly two'.[86]

French feminism in general and Irigaray in particular have always been suspiciously examined for charges of essentialism, as De Vries notes,[87] and

---

82. For more information on Christian conservative approaches to biblical literature, see, e.g., Susanne Scholz, 'The Christian Right's Discourse on Gender and the Bible', *JFSR* 21.1 (Spring 2005), pp. 83-104; Karen Strand Winslow, 'Recovering Redemption for Women: Feminist Exegesis in North American Evangelicalism', in Susanne Scholz (ed.), *Feminist Interpretation of the Hebrew Bible in Retrospect: Social Location (vol. II)* (Sheffield: Sheffield Phoenix Press, 2014), pp. 269-89.

83. Roland J. De Vries, 'Wonder Between Two: An Irigaryan Reading of Genesis 2:23', *Modern Theology* 24.1 (January 2008), pp. 51-74 (53-54, 55, 57-64). For a more extensive presentation of his argument in which he engages not only Irigaray's theories but also Kierkegaard's, see his *Becoming Two in Love: Kierkegaard, Irigaray, and the Ethics of Sexual Difference* (Eugene, OR: Pickwick Publications, 2013).

84. De Vries, 'Wonder Between Two', p. 63.

85. De Vries, 'Wonder Between Two', pp. 63-64.

86. De Vries, 'Wonder Between Two', p. 60.

87. He states: '[S]exual difference does not imply that she [Irigaray] is an essentialist (as is frequently charged), since her theory of sexual difference advances an account of woman and man in which each is perpetually in a process of becoming'; see De Vries, 'Wonder Between Two', p. 56.

so it is interesting that this explicitly 'Christian'-evangelical approach never questions the binary of female and male. On the contrary, De Vries notices that 'Irigaray's insistence on the human as two (and not as one)—as both woman and man—resonates with the insistence of the classical Christian tradition that God created the human as male and female, together'. However, he then asks whether 'the novel claims of Irigaray, concerning the nature of sexual difference and of mediation between the sexes, are consistent with the epistemic primacy of Jesus Christ, and might be incorporated within the Church's convictions and beliefs about the nature of human being in the world'.[88] Much could be said about this statement and De Vries's appropriation of Irigaray's work in his Christian-evangelical theological work, but it is obvious that he does not make a 'feminist' biblical argument despite his cherished engagement with the French feminist thinker. In fact, in the end it is not clear that De Vries's approach could even be called deconstructionist. Such are the ambiguities and complexities in feminist deconstructionist interpretations of the Hebrew Bible; some interpreters engage French feminist deconstructionist ideas in ways that make them neither feminist nor deconstructionist.

Yet not all is lost in the prolific arena of feminist deconstructionist exegesis. In 2009, Ken Stone elaborates on the merits of Foucault for a queer biblical hermeneutics suggesting 'that we conceptualize biblical interpretation as one component of what Foucault calls the "technology of the self"'.[89] According to Stone, Foucault developed this idea toward the end of his life with which he described the production of the subject as coming into existence 'through processes of self-formation' and not so much 'through its subjugation to relations of power'.[90] This 'different mode of self-constitution'[91] that comes from the inner willingness to transform oneself according to one's own ideas about how to be in the world, 'to the constitution of *new* forms of existence'.[92] Since '[b]iblical interpretation...is a technology of the self inasmuch as it is one route by which new experiences of self are created and recreated',[93] Stone advises to articulate interpretations that counter 'the traditional negative evaluation of gay men by religious authorities', and to 'encourage resistance to those evaluations', as

---

88. De Vries, *Becoming Two in Love*, pp. xvii-xviii.

89. Ken Stone, 'Biblical Interpretation as a Technology of the Self: Gay Men and the Ethics of Reading', in Björn Krondorfer (ed.), *Men and Masculinities in Christianity and Judaism: A Critical Reader* (London: SCM Press, 2009), pp. 203-15 (207).

90. Stone, 'Biblical Interpretation as a Technology of the Self', p. 207.

91. Stone, 'Biblical Interpretation as a Technology of the Self', p. 208.

92. Stone, 'Biblical Interpretation as a Technology of the Self', p. 209 [emphasis in original].

93. Stone, 'Biblical Interpretation as a Technology of the Self', p. 210.

done in the field.[94] Stone also suggests that such biblical readings be evaluated for their ability to not only side with marginalized peoples, such as gay men, but also to 'open up possibilities for new experiences, new relationship (including new relationships to our religious traditions…), and new forms of cultural existence, or, as Foucault might have put it, a new ethos'.[95] Such exegetical work ought to nurture the invention and living of 'modes of being' that have been repressed, denied, and persecuted for far too long. Stone's rather programmatic essay encourages queer biblical readings as an ethical practice, indirectly welcoming feminist exegesis to join in working toward this aim.

Last but not least, this discussion of feminist deconstructionist interpretations of the Hebrew Bible warrants a discussion of the work by Yvonne Sherwood on Hosea 1–3, as it is openly and consistently grounded in Derridean theories of deconstruction.[96] The prophetic text, centering Sherwood's analysis, has played a significant role in feminist and general biblical interpretation and Sherwood sets herself the task to investigate 'the complexities in the relationship between the text and readers', especially in light of the fact that readers have so often considered this text to be highly 'disturbing and disorienting'.[97] The book's four chapters examine the 'metacommentary' or the interpretation history of this biblical passage; they consider the text's 'sign language' or semiotics; they examine the texts with strategies of deconstruction, especially as proposed by Derrida; and finally they present a feminist deconstructionist reading of the prophetic text, drawing from both feminist methodology and deconstructionist theory.

Sherwood is a feminist exegete who grounds her work in the theories of a male-performing thinker. Even so, her reliance on Derrida does not entail giving up her integrity as a feminist reader. She emphasizes what the biblical text represses; she inverts the meaning of Hosea 1–3 and its interpretation history, and she does not consider the female character as the problem, as assumed by countless patriarchal interpreters. Instead, she takes 'the woman as the standard of judgment' and explores 'how the premises of patriarchy are a problem for her'.[98] Sherwood's deconstructionist feminist

---

94. Stone, 'Biblical Interpretation as a Technology of the Self', p. 210.

95. Stone, 'Biblical Interpretation as a Technology of the Self', p. 211. For a plethora of interpretations grounded in deconstructionist notions, often less explicitly connected to this or that deconstructionist theorist, see also Deryn Guest, Robert E. Goss, Mona West and Thomas Bohache (eds.), *Queer Bible Commentary* (London: SCM Press, 2006).

96. Yvonne Sherwood, *The Prostitute and the Prophet: Hosea's Marriage in Literary-Theoretical Perspective* (JSOTSup, 212; Gender, Culture, Theory, 2; Sheffield: Sheffield Academic Press, 1996).

97. Sherwood, *The Prostitute and the Prophet*, p. 12.

98. Sherwood, *The Prostitute and the Prophet*, p. 255.

hermeneutic challenges the notion that '[t]he male is the standard and the woman the deviant; the man possesses the text and the woman is banished or strays beyond/outside it'.[99] At the same time she worries about feminist interpretations affirming this hierarchy, thereby being unable to challenge the oppositional logic inherent in androcentric reading practices. To Sherwoord, every reading always comes from the commentator, the interpreter, the reader, who is the 'henchman, carrying out the threats of the text'.[100] In short, Sherwood argues that, in the process of reading, 'objectivity is an illusion'.[101] This also means that '[n]either feminist nor androcentric readings diligently follow all textual detail, and both types of readers are forced by the text's sparseness to read between the lines'.[102]

Thus, a feminist reading is needed that follows 'stubbornly' the letters of the text, resisting the description of the female character and forming an 'alliance' with her.[103] In other words, Sherwood's 'strategy of resistance' promises a different view of what is going on in Hosea 1–3.[104] As it turns out, at the heart of the problem is the marriage metaphor, which depicts the relationship between the prophetic husband and his wife as 'assymetrical'. In Hosea 1–3, the metaphor is certainly '"extended in the technical sense, but also pushed to its most extreme limits when the punishment of the land is expressed in threats of physical violence against the female'.[105] After detailed studies of past and present androcentric and feminist interpretations, Sherwood reads the biblical poem as an ambiguous seduction. She states: 'The text begins with a woman, a "wife of harlotry", who presumably plays a seductive role, and ends with a fantasy of a pliant woman who is the object of her husband's seduction'.[106] Nothing is clear or certain about this wife: the seduction of the woman may be ideal but it may not even be one after all; the wife is urged to submit but it is unclear if she will accept; female readers may take her point of view but they may not. Textual and readerly ambiguities determine the indeterminate meanings of the biblical poem. The discomfort about this textual situation that 'violates' not only feminist sensibilities but also 'principles which society has been growing accustomed to over the last century'.[107] Sherwood asserts '[a] conflict between reader and text' as the

---

99. Sherwood, *The Prostitute and the Prophet*, p. 256.
100. Sherwood, *The Prostitute and the Prophet*, p. 261.
101. Sherwood, *The Prostitute and the Prophet*, p. 257.
102. Sherwood, *The Prostitute and the Prophet*, p. 264.
103. Sherwood, *The Prostitute and the Prophet*, p. 265.
104. Sherwood, *The Prostitute and the Prophet*, p. 265.
105. Sherwood, *The Prostitute and the Prophet*, p. 266.
106. Sherwood, *The Prostitute and the Prophet*, p. 291.
107. Sherwood, *The Prostitute and the Prophet*, pp. 301-302.

latter 'causes embarrassment' for even androcentric interpreters.[108] She lists the variously embarrassed readers, non-feminist and feminist, and eventually identifies the textual tension as a reflection of the androcentric author's fear of losing power:

> The violent hierarchies in Hosea 1–3 are, and are not, like the hierarchies described by Derrida. The violence of their formation is not merely metaphorical but is often graphically visible, and unlike the assimilated hierarchies of Derrida's 'Western metaphysics', they seem to lay bare the struggle of their formation. The impression is of patriarchy in process rather than patriarchy as an established and unassailable system, as if the dominant voice is aware of a countervoice that, if listened to, threatens to relativize and jeopardize the main/male perspective.[109]

In short, this feminist deconstructionist approach to Hosea 1–3 emphasizes the ambiguous, multiple, and even contradictory possibilities of reading an amorphous piece of biblical text, urging readers not to get stuck in androcentric claims of objectivity, essentializing notions about the binaries of female and male, or the intentional fallacy as a solution to the problems of uncertain biblical meanings. This and the other varieties of feminist-deconstructionist readings of biblical texts indicate the rich possibilities of this approach for feminist biblical exegesis to this very day.

Concluding Remarks at This Post-Postmodernist Moment of Time

Many biblical texts, characters, and topics await feminist exegesis grounded in deconstructionist notions of interpretation. Although the foregoing survey indicates the rich and diverse spectrum of deconstructionist approaches in feminist exegesis, it also demonstrates that much more exploration needs to develop in the future. Almost any part of the Hebrew Bible canon awaits such further engagement and the wide range of deconstructionist theories have yet to be brought into direct conversation with the field of biblical studies, no less feminist biblical studies in its diverse scope of hermeneutical and methodological expressions. The general reluctance of bringing in feminist theoretical discourse into biblical exegesis means that almost any exploratory direction is open and available. Why not investigate Foucault's discourse theory together with biblical genealogies that have long been bemoaned as androcentric expressions of socio-linguistic power? Or how about a systematic look at French deconstructionist feminist engagement with the Bible and how it could be related to feminist biblical scholarship? And why not correlate the rise of essentializing exegetical publications on 'women in the Bible' with the critique of French feminism as potential

---

108. Sherwood, *The Prostitute and the Prophet*, p. 302.
109. Sherwood, *The Prostitute and the Prophet*, p. 308.

enablers of such a dynamic? The possibilities for future scholarship on deconstruction in feminist Hebrew Bible studies seem almost endless.

Yet I also want to mention a concern that should not be misunderstood as diminishing the great need and opportunities for feminist deconstructionist exegesis. Rather, this concern is a cautionary remark about the wider implications of deconstructionist notions about ambiguity, multiplicity, and the dismantling of any kind of structure. In the beginning it was obvious, and Derrida always acknowledged this fact, that deconstruction assumes structuralism and thus stable, fixed, and monolithic forms of understanding the world. However, times have changed in this regard, and the cultural logic of capitalism is different than it was forty years ago. It is not accidental or to be neglected that nowadays we have begun speaking about 'post-postmodernism', regardless of whether this word is 'ugly'.[110] Jeffrey T. Nealon observes poignantly that the double prefix of 'post-post' indicates that certain tendencies and developments of the time of 'postmodernity' have been intensified, mutating to another level of what came before. He explains it so clearly that it is worthwhile to quote him:

> So the initial 'post' in the word is less a marker of postmodernism's having fully used up its shelf life at the theory store than it is a marker of postmodernism's having mutated, passed beyond a certain tipping point to become something recognizably different in its contours and working; but in any case, it's not something that's absolutely foreign to whatever it was before.[111]

More specifically, what he sees as intensified, mutated, and thus ultimately as having shifted cultural sensibilities has to do with what is called 'neoliberalism'.[112] Other analysts prefer different terminologies, such as 'digimodernism' or 'altermodernity'.[113] After all, this is the 'post-Derridean' era, the post-9/11 era, and the era of the so-called 'War on Terror'.

We live in the era of the '"new economics" (post-Fordism, globalization, the centrality of market economics, the new surveillance techniques of the war on terrorism, etc.) and their complex relations to cultural production

---

110. Jeffrey T. Nealon begins his book with this statement: 'Post-postmodernism is an ugly word'; see his *Post-Postmodernism or, The Cultural Logic of Just-In-Time Capitalism* (Stanford, CA: Stanford University Press, 2012), p. viiii.

111. Nealon, *Post-Postmodernism*, p. xviiii.

112. For important discussions on neoliberalism, see, e.g., Henry A. Giroux, *Neoliberalism's War on Higher Education* (Chicago: Haymarket Books, 2014). For an analysis on the economic shifts of contemporary capitalism, see, e.g., Sheldon S. Wolin, *Democracy Incorporated: Managed Democracy and the Specter of Inverted Totalitarianism* (Princeton, NJ: Princeton University Press, 2008).

113. See, e.g., Alan Kirby, *Digimodernism: How New Technologies Dismantle the Postmodern and Reconfigure Our Culture* (New York/London: Continuum, 2009); Nicolas Bouriaud, *The Radicant* (New York: Lukas & Sternberg, 2009).

in the present moment, where capitalism seems nowhere near the point of its exhaustion'.[114] This era's key words are efficiency, flexibility, privatization, globalization, and diversification. In other words, fluidity, hybridity, and instability rule not only in the labor market but increasingly also everywhere else. How shall resistance to the gambling logic of the contemporary financial systems, 'the new global casino capitalism',[115] look like when any kind of 'traditional' structure or code is easily undermined by even faster computer programs that create money out of nano-second delays on somebody else's computer? There are no more structures to be assumed and, at best, all 'traditional' institutions have been weakened. So the question is how to talk about ambiguity, multiplicity, and flexibility without simultaneously reinforcing neo-colonial, financialized structures of domination that exist today? In my view, this is the question that needs to be raised when anyone relies on deconstruction as an approach to the interpretation of any kind of text, including biblical literature. It will take feminist deconstructionist readings of the Bible from the present into the future.

---

114. Nealon, *Post-Postmodernism*, p. 15.
115. Nealon, *Post-Postmodernism*, p. 29. For the problem of the contemporary financialization of the economic system, see Costas Lapavitsas, *Profiting Without Producing: How Finance Exploits Us All* (London/Brooklyn, NY: Verso, 2013).

Part III
FEMINIST READINGS IN FRONT OF THE TEXT

11

SEEKING OUR SURVIVAL, OUR QUALITY OF LIFE, AND WISDOM:
WOMANIST APPROACHES TO THE HEBREW BIBLE

Karen Baker-Fletcher

Womanist concepts of the Bible as canon are not limited to a predominant, androcentric Western understanding of biblical canon formation, historical-criticism, archaeological findings, and cultural studies of 'Near Eastern Civilization'. Instead, womanists challenge Western notions of biblical canonical formation and hermeneutical norms. They emphasize that scholars and communities from diverse cultures always bring a particular and distinctive set of so-called 'norms' to the interpretations of the Bible. Womanists are especially interested in Black appropriations and interpretations of biblical texts in the African diaspora with attention to Black women's historical hermeneutics and real-lived experiences. The word 'womanist' is a signifier of a radical and revolutionary movement in Back women's scholarship since the early 1980s.

Being and Writing 'Womanist':
A Signifier of Embodied Womanist Epistemology

A womanist is a Black woman who employs hermeneutical lenses and tools from Black women's real-lived, social-historical, and economic experience to interpret written texts and oral traditions with attention to a survival ethics, quality of life and liberating praxis. A womanist is concerned with healing and wholeness of entire communities, female and male. After Alice Walker coined the term 'womanist' in her 1983 work, *In Search of Our Mothers' Gardens: Womanist Prose*,[1] many Black women scholars and activists in the United States have committed to both women's and Black survival and liberation. They began using the term 'womanist' to describe their approaches in a variety of theological disciplines.[2] The appeal of the term 'womanist' is

---

1. Alice Walker, *In Search of Our Mothers' Gardens: Womanist Prose* (Orlando, FL: Harcourt Brace Jovanovich Publishers, 1983), pp. xi-xii.
2. This phenomenon also occurred in a diversity of academic fields, including sociology, literature, theater and film, media studies, psychology, history and anthropology. A helpful resource for a sense of the breadth of womanist scholarship in disciplines

that it is one wholistic term. Even so, some Black women scholars, such as Cheryl Anderson, prefer the term 'Black feminist' and others, such as Traci West, challenge the distinctions between 'Black feminist' and 'womanist'.[3]

While Alice Walker is given credit for 'coining' the term 'womanist', the word is derived from the Black US cultural expression 'acting womanish'. The saying 'acting womanist' is part of a longer oral tradition and a written canon among Black women across generations. Thus, womanist scholars both use and move beyond Walker's four-part description of the term in which she includes a description of a 'womanist' as a 'black feminist or feminist of color'.[4] As womanist scholarship began to grow in the study of religion after 1985, Walker's four-part description became one of several canonical sources from Black women's culture for researching Black women's traditions and approaches for survival, liberation and emancipatory hope.[5]

---

outside the study of religion and theological education is Layli Phillips, *The Womanist Reader: The First Quarter Century of Womanist Thought* (New York/Oxford: Routledge, 2006).

3. Traci West emphasizes that womanist theology needs to give greater attention to its significance for the wellness of all women in 'Is a Womanist a Black Feminist? Marking the Distinctions and Defying Them: A Black Feminist Response', in Stacey Floyd-Thomas (ed.), *Deeper Shades of Purple: Religion, Race and Ethnicity* (New York: New York University Press, 2006), pp. 291-95. West argues that 'women's wholeness takes priority for her'. She finds that 'some womanists have engaged feminism with the assumption Whiteness and feminism are indistinguishable, problematically erasing the contributions of a generation of Black feminist foremothers' (p. 295). Others are committed to womanist scholarship and praxis as particularly focusing on Black women's contexts globally in the African diaspora. Some encourage greater engagement with US feminists and global feminists on issues of sexuality in scripture, the fluidity of gender and economic analysis in relation to Western empire.

4. Alice Walker, *In Search of Our Mothers' Gardens*, p. xi. Like Stacey Floyd-Thomas and some other womanist scholars I have chosen to write 'Black' with a capital 'B' to be consistent with the style several womanists discussed in this essay employ. This spelling also renders Blackness visible. In contrast I spell 'white' in all lower case letters. The social-historical construction of whiteness renders Blackness invisible. Alice Walker writes 'black feminist' and 'white' in all lower case letters. Here I use 'Black' and 'white' to visually signify the irony and paradox of racialized ontologies. My particular understanding of 'Blackness' is different from 'ontological Blackness', as articulated by James Cone and some womanists. I emphasize *becoming* rather than *being*. While 'Blackness' and 'womanist' are not essentialism, strategic essentialism in womanist biblical hermeneutics is a necessary activity for survival, quality of life and liberation of Black women and entire communities, male and female.

5. Nyasha Junior offers a discussion about 'womanist' that includes similar observations regarding the term 'womanist', but it is largely derivative of what senior womanist scholars like Katie Cannon, Delores Williams, Jacquelyn Grant, Kelly Brown Douglas, Emilie Townes, M. Shawn Copeland, Marcia Riggs, Karen Baker-Fletcher,

Womanist Hebrew Bible scholars employ various methods in biblical hermeneutics, including sociological, cultural, economic, historical-critical, political and literary approaches. Womanist biblical scholars, like womanists in general, are diverse in specific areas of study and praxis as well as in method. They tend to hold in common attention to interlocking systems of oppression in religious social practices and theories.[6] In other words, since the beginning of their engagement with religion, womanist scholars have given strong attention to what many feminist scholars call 'intersectionality' today. Like feminist bible scholars and some feminist theologians, womanist biblical interpreters usually view the Hebrew Bible as a largely androcentric collection of sacred texts from which one may tease out strands that hold wisdom for survival and liberation.

In the 1970s and 1980s, Black women began entering Christian seminaries. They found it difficult to gain full access to the field of Hebrew

---

and many other womanists have said in their manifold publications long before her 2013 essay on womanist biblical interpretation. Moreover, she includes Clenora Hudson Weems who uses 'Africana womanism' to avoid Alice Walker's description of a womanist as loving 'other women sexually and/or nonsexually'. She does not note that the copyright permissions for publishing Alice Walker's full definition is very expensive. Womanists rarely cite Walker's full description of 'womanist' for economic reasons and in accordance with their editors and publishing houses. Another weakness is that Junior infers that womanist theologian Monica Coleman was the first to discuss heterosexism in publication when, in fact, Delores Williams, Traci West, and Kelly Brown Douglas published books that clearly addressed sexuality issues and the problem of heterosexism. It is true that Coleman offers an extensive discussion of LGBQT womanist thought and practice in *Making a Way out of No Way* (Minneapolis, Minnesota: Fortress Press, 2008), but the publications by Williams, Douglas, and West precede Coleman's work. See Delores Williams, *Sisters in the Wilderness: Womanist God-Talk* (Maryknoll, NY: Orbis Books: 1993), pp. 183-84, 208, 213; Kelly Brown Douglas, *Sexuality and the Black Church: A Womanist Perspective* (Maryknoll, NY: Orbis Books, 1999), pp. 87-144; Kelly Brown Douglas, *What's Faith Got to Do With It? Black Bodies/Christian Souls* (Maryknoll, NY: Orbis Books, 2005), pp. 39-222; Traci West, *Disruptive Christian Ethics: When Racism and Black Women's Lives Matters* (Louisville, KY: Westminster/John Knox Press, 2006), pp. 141-80. The primary weakness of Junior's essay is her derivative description of 'womanist' in womanist scholarship of religion. Junior employs an either/or approach that separates womanist method from embodied womanist praxis and embodied self-naming from within womanist bodies. The strength of her essay is her excellent discussion of womanist biblical interpretation, which I will discuss below. See Nyasha Junior, 'Womanist Interpretation', in Steven L. McKenzie (ed.), *The Oxford Encyclopedia of Biblical Interpretation* (New York: Oxford University Press, 2013), pp. 448-56.

6. Paula Treichler and Cheris Kramarae, 'Feminism', in Wendy K. Kolmar and Frances Bartkowski (eds.), *Feminist Theory: A Reader* (New York: McGraw Hill, 4th edn, 2013), pp. 2-10; Patricia Collins, *Black Feminist Thought* (New York: HarperCollins, 1990), p. 44.

Bible without conceding to the dominant, Western-European, androcentric normative understanding of the historical-critical paradigm. Black women scholars, such as Katie Cannon and Delores Williams, found the fields of Christian Ethics and Theology more welcoming of new approaches that were advanced by Black scholars, White feminist scholars, and Black feminist scholars. Feminist scholars Beverly Wildung Harrison at Union Theological Seminary in New York City and Letty Russell at Yale Divinity School actively supported this new scholarship that was necessarily and intentionally interdisciplinary, as the works of Cannon and Williams illustrate. Renita Weems was the only formally recognized womanist within the discipline of Hebrew Bible scholar for several years. As Nyasha Junior observes, however, 'despite her various discussions of womanist approaches', Weems does not use a womanist method in *Battered Love: Marriage, Sex, and Violence in the Hebrew Prophets*. Junior would like to see Weems offer 'more technical discussions of what womanist' scholarship, method, and hermeneutics has to offer to Hebrew biblical scholarship.[7]

The Womanist Approaches to Religion and Society Group voted and agreed some years ago that we would not fragment over discussions of what is essentially womanist, as white feminists did in the 1990s. The womanist *praxis* of offering collective support and criticism is more important to womanists. There are too few womanists in the Academy, so it would be Machavellian—in this case dividing and killing an embodied school of thought—to do so. Therefore, womanists intentionally have decided to avoid womanist fundamentalism regarding the term 'womanist', which is neither a definition nor even simply a description, but rather an embodiment of commitment to the survival, quality of life and liberation of Black women. This decision for this group was a collective matter, rather than the decision of an individual womanist.

An understanding of 'womanist' includes the body[8] and this group is a body that supports, criticizes and constructs together. The body includes the

---

7. Nyasha Junior, 'Womanist Interpretation', p. 452. She states that Weems 'resists the historical/critical method as well as the gender focused analysis of feminist criticism. She advocates for a womanist approach that addresses multiple oppressions and suggests that womanists, having been victimized by these multiple oppressions, can bring their experiences to bear within womanist scholarship.' She discusses Renita Weems, *Battered Love: Marriage, Sex, and Violence in the Hebrew Prophets* (Minneapolis, MN: Fortress Press, 1995), pp. 1-11.

8. On womanist embodiment I recommend the following books: Douglas, *Sexuality and the Black Church* and *What's Faith Got to Do With It?*; M. Shawn Copeland, *Enfleshing Freedom: Body, Race, and Freedom* (Minneapolis, MN: Fortress Press, 2009); Eboni Marshall Turman, *Toward a Womanist Ethic of Incarnation: Black Bodies, the Black Church and the Council of Chalcedon* (New York: Palgrave Macmillan, 2013). While these books are not specifically on womanist Hebrew biblical hermeneutics, they

intellect and the 'spirit' that are part of the body. As Junior observes, there is not a womanist program unit in the Society for Biblical Literature (SBL) even today. In her view, this may be so because there are so few womanist scholars who specialize in biblical interpretation as defined by the Western academic guild.[9] The numbers of womanist biblical scholars, she argues, have been too few to warrant such a unit. Hopefully, one day the number of womanist biblical scholars will constitute a sufficient critical mass to have a womanist program unit in the SBL, which seems to be what Junior is vying for. May that day come sooner rather than later! The SBL needs its own group of womanist scholars to challenge and expand the general discipline of biblical studies. This would also be helpful to the Womanist Approaches to Religion and Society Group for its ongoing interdisciplinary understandings of womanist method, hermeneutics and epistemology.

When the word 'womanist' emerged in Alice Walker's clear, yet multivalent, poetic description, several Black women were engaged in doctoral research at Union Theological Seminary in New York. Jacquelyn Grant, Delores Williams, and Katie Cannon quickly adopted the term to describe their approaches in the study of religion. Within a couple of years of Walker's publication, the use of the term 'womanist' spread across the Northeast of the United States and soon became popular among Black women scholars across the nation.[10] In the mid-1980s, the 'Womanist Approaches to

---

discuss womanist culture and womanism as an *embodied* reality. Womanist Hebrew biblical hermeneutics is more complete when it attends to questions and lenses of womanist embodiment.

9. Junior, 'Womanist Interpretation', p. 454.

10. Katie Cannon was an important influence in the Boston and Cambridge, Massachusetts region in 1983–1984 when she taught, researched, and lectured as a Women's Studies Research Associate at Harvard Divinity School. Cannon then taught at the Episcopal Divinity School in Cambridge for several years before taking a position at Temple University in Philadelphia and later at Union Theological Seminary, Virginia. Through the American Academy of Religion along with other professional organizations, Cannon came to have national and global influence. Delores Williams, a theologian of culture, and Cheryl Townsend Gilkes, a sociologist of religion, also taught as Women's Studies Research Associates at the Harvard Divinity School Women's Studies in Religion Program at Harvard Divinity School in 1980–81 and 1981–82 respectively. Each of these scholars, along with Kelly Brown Douglas, Emilie Townes, and others had a major role in organizing and developing the Womanist Approaches to Religion and Society Group in the American Academy of Religion (AAR). Both Cannon and Williams used Black women's literature in their work and both were pioneers in early womanist biblical interpretation. Renita Weems is a pioneer in womanist biblical interpretation who broke through some of the barriers in the field of Old Testament and the Society of Biblical Literature (SBL). See Stacey Floyd-Thomas, 'Welcome to the BSRG's Congregational Initiative'; available at the Black Religious Studies Group Website, http://womanistinstitute.org/welcome/

Religion and Society Group' institutionalized itself at the American Academy of Religion (AAR). According to womanist theological ethicist Stacey Floyd-Thomas, Katie Cannon was the first Black woman scholar of religion who used the term 'womanist' in her essay 'The Emergence of Black Feminist Consciousness'.[11] Cannon also introduced the term 'womanist' to the AAR and SBL at the time. She was instrumental in setting up the AAR section on womanist thought.

The most important value of the term 'womanist' is that it is *one* word describing Black women's hermeneutics of liberation and survival. As Stacey Floyd-Thomas puts it, the term 'womanist' represents a 'revolutionary epistemology' regarding Black women's knowledge and the power to write about our knowing. To Floyd-Thomas, '[w]omanism is revolutionary. Womanism is a paradigm shift wherein Black women no longer look to others for their liberation, but instead look to themselves... Black women are engaged in the process of knowledge production that is most necessary for their own flourishing rather than being exploited for the enlightenment and entertainment of male egos.'[12] As Black women, the ability to name ourselves is an act of resistance to being named by others. Black women, writing our own knowing, become not 'them' or 'they' but 'us' and 'we'. Self-naming rejects Western imperialist, white supremacist, and androcentric norms that violate Black women's bodies and minds. The word 'womanist' signifies an epistemology that values both-and thinking rather than either-or thinking. For some Black women scholars, the term 'black feminist' emphasizes the relationship of Black feminism to a diversity of feminisms, including postcolonial feminists in more recent research. Still others use both terminologies interchangeably.[13]

We, Too, Are Hebrew Bible Interpreters:
Womanist Mothers in Hebrew Bible Scholarship

The first published work in the field of religious studies using the term 'womanist' was Cannon's work on biblical interpretation, published in Letty Russell's *Feminist Interpretation of the Bible*. In her chapter, Cannon concludes her historical overview of Black US women's epistemology

---

11. See Katie Cannon, 'The Emergence of Black Feminist Consciousness', in Letty Russell (ed.), *Feminist Interpretation of the Bible* (Louisville, KY: Westminster, 1985), pp. 30-40; Stacey Floyd-Thomas, 'Introduction: Writing for Our Lives: Womanism as an Epistemological Revolution', in Floyd-Thomas (ed.), *Deeper Shades of Purple: Religion, Race and Ethnicity*, pp. 1-5, 13.

12. Stacey Floyd-Thomas, 'Introduction: Writing for Our Lives', pp. 1-2.

13. For further discussion of the multiplicity of womanists, see my book, *Dancing with God: A Womanist Perspective on the Trinity* (St. Louis, MO: Chalice Press, 2006), pp. ix-xi.

and hermeneutics with a section entitled 'Black Womanist Consciousness'.[14] Here Cannon writes that 'Black Feminist consciousness may be more accurately identified as Black womanist consciousness, drawing from Alice Walker's concept and definition. As an interpretive principle, the Black womanist tradition provides the incentive to chip away at oppressive structures, bit by bit. It identifies those texts which help Black womanists to celebrate and rename the innumerable incidents of unpredictability in empowering ways'.[15] Cannon stresses that renaming is an important aspect of the womanist epistemological and hermeneutical task and of womanist ways. Moreover, Cannon articulates which biblical texts are significant for womanist scholarship. In her view, not all biblical texts are equally important but only those that empower Black women. As she explains: 'The Black womanist identifies with those biblical characters who hold on to life in the face of formidable oppression.... Black womanists search the scriptures to learn how to dispel the threat of death in order to seize the present life'.[16] Cannon employs the qualifier 'Black' before 'womanist' during this period. Her first book is the revised version of her dissertation, entitled *Black Womanist Ethics*.[17] When she published her second book, her transition from 'Black' to 'womanist' was complete. Cannon then used the term 'womanist' without a qualifier or adjective, and so her second book is entitled: *Katie's Canon: Womanism and the Soul of the Black Community*.[18]

One of the most intriguing contributions Cannon makes in *Black Womanist Ethics* appears in the chapter, 'Resources for a Constructive Ethic in the Work of Zora Neale Hurston'. There she discusses Hurston's *Moses, Man of the Mountain* (1939) by observing that this novel, 'the longest fiction in Hurston's canon, serves as an allegorical satire about the affinities between Voodoo and Christianity...retelling the biblical legend of Moses in the Black esthetic tradition. Moses, associated with the god Damballah, is 'the finest hoodoo man in the world'.[19] While any number of womanist, Black feminist, and Black male scholars consider the significance of the book of Exodus, the prophetic work of Moses and Miriam, and themes of freedom in Black cultural interpretations of scripture, Cannon's work stands out in its attention to Hurston as an anthropologist who studied 'voodoo' and 'hoodoo' practices in Black religion and culture in Florida and the Caribbean. Moreover, as an anthropologist Hurston was familiar with syncretic

---

14. Katie G. Cannon, 'The Emergence of Black Feminist Consciousness', in Russell (ed.), *Feminist Interpretation of the Bible*, p. 39.
15. Cannon, 'Black Feminist Consciousness', p. 41.
16. Cannon, 'Black Feminist Consciousness', p. 41.
17. Katie G. Cannon, *Black Womanist Ethics* (Atlanta, GA: Scholars Press, 1988).
18. Katie G. Cannon, *Katie's Canon: Womanism and the Soul of the Black Community* (New York: Continuum, 1995).
19. Cannon, *Black Womanist Ethics*, p. 136.

hermeneutical principles in the traditions she observed. For instance, she researched the speech patterns in the field before using them in her novel.

Cannon explains: 'Hurston used Black speech, to codify into written form, the subtle dynamics of the metaphorical and proverbial connections between the exodus of the Hebrews and the African-American trek from slavery to freedom. She deflated the rigid seriousness of biblical rhetoric. Just below the surface of this drama is the collective wisdom revealed in the Black community related to the discrepancy between professing Christian learnings and practicing a religious faith.'[20] Cannon also observes that, to Hurston, the biblical account of Moses is 'a mythical concoction of Miriam, the daughter of a Hebrew couple, Jochebed and Amram'.[21] So to Cannon, Hurston's Moses is a conjuror taught by Jethro in Midian. The characters are all Black, and they reflect not only the culture and many of the syncretic beliefs in the Floridian and Caribbean cultures, but an approach to biblical texts that was compatible with African retentions in these cultures.

In Hurston's retelling, Cannon finds that Miriam concocts an alibi for her role in Moses' disappearance. Miriam has not intentionally sent Moses down the Nile, but rather she fell asleep after Jochebed made a basket for Moses and put it into the Nile River. Jochebed asked Miriam, her daughter, to keep an eye on her brother Moses. In other words, Miriam was supposed to babysit. When she wakes up, Miriam does not know where Moses is. In the novel, she hides that she fell asleep and does not know where Moses is by offering an alibi. Once the community hears Miriam's alibi, the story becomes a legend.[22] As a legend, it becomes significant for a communal vision of freedom-fighting and the power of survival. While Hurston interprets scripture in relation to Black folk culture and religion, Cannon examines Hurston's interpretation with attention to the roles of the women characters. She writes: 'The women in this novel illustrate quiet grace as the search for truth in much subtler forms than Moses'.[23] In the wake of Hurston, Cannon emphasizes the subtle grace of Miriam's, Jochebed's, and Zipporah's moral agency.

Cannon also offers a thickly layered interpretation of the Exodus account of Jochebed, Miriam, Zipporah, Moses, and Pharaoh. No longer is scripture in the hands of what Cannon calls 'the canonical boys'.[24] Cannon thus describes the usual process of Black women trying to be accepted as

---

20. Cannon, *Black Womanist Ethics*, p. 137.
21. Cannon, *Black Womanist Ethics*, p. 137.
22. Cannon, *Black Womanist Ethics*, p. 138.
23. Cannon, *Black Womanist Ethics*, p. 140.
24. Cannon, 'Hitting a Straight Lick with a Crooked Stick: The Womanist Dilemma in the Development of a Black Liberation Ethic', in *Katie's Cannon*, pp. 122-24. Cannon notes that 'this chapter was first published in the *Annual Society of Christian Ethics*, 1987'. Also see Katie G. Cannon, 'Hitting a Straight Lick with a Crooked Stick: The

scholars. She explains that 'to prove that she is sufficiently intelligent' a Black woman scholar 'must discount the particularities of her lived experiences and instead focus on the validity of generalizable external analytical data. The dilemma she faces in joining the canonical boys is that of succumbing to the temptation of mastering only the historically specified perspective of the Euro-American masculine preserve.'[25] This limits not simply time but 'opportunity to expand her creative energy in the direction of liberation ethics' or liberation biblical hermeneutics.[26] For Cannon, the task of transforming a context that marginalizes Black women scholars as 'noncanonical others' is to 'change the imbalance caused by an androcentric view, wherein it is presumed that only men's activities have theological value'.[27] In short, Cannon performs the task of 'unmasking'[28] androcentric privilege. She resists the norms of the canonical boys, by instead uncovering how deeply Hurston knew Black women's and men's bible reading practices in Black religion, culture, preaching,[29] and storytelling. Cannon shows that Hurston was aware of the presence of African peoples in the Hebrew Bible, whether they were mentioned as being part of Egypt or Midian.

While *Black Womanist Ethics* is Cannon's most significant publication in 1988, her collaborative work with white feminist Letty Russell is also important. Cannon published a chapter called 'Surviving the Blight' in Letty Russell's *Inheriting Our Mothers' Gardens* in 1988.[30] Her essay, focuses on prayer and the spirituals based in the Black women's oral tradition of biblical interpretation. Cannon writes: 'While waiting for the ongoing storm to subside, my mother invites the family to join her in singing Afro-American spirituals. Among these spirituals are those that include lines such as: 'Oh,

Womanist Dilemma in the Development of a Black Liberation Ethic', *The Annual of the Society of Christian Ethics* (1987), pp. 165-77.

25. Cannon, 'Hitting a Straight Lick with a Crooked Stick', p. 123.
26. Cannon, 'Hitting a Straight Lick with a Crooked Stick', p. 123.
27. Cannon, 'Hitting a Straight Lick with a Crooked Stick', p. 127.
28. Cannon, 'Hitting a Straight Lick with a Crooked Stick', p. 127.
29. Cannon, *Black Womanist Ethics*, pp. 128-31. Here Cannon exegetes Zora Neale Hurston's *Jonah's Gourd Vine*, which includes a sermon by the character John Buddy Pearson that Hurston recorded in her anthropological research. The novel ostensibly is about the philandering preacher John Buddy Pearson, but as Cannon notes, his wife 'Lucy is the strongest character in the novel, "teaching John how to dispel the church members" discontent with his behavior'. She advises him to preach a sermon about himself and some of his good practices, without lying about the bad. John may be a preacher, but Lucy reveals the secret of good biblical story telling. A good story or 'lie' must say something truthful to become a story with perennial staying power and meaning.
30. See Katie G. Cannon, Ada Maria Isasi-Diaz, Kwok Pui Lan and Letty Russell, *Inheriting Our Mothers' Gardens* (Louisville, KY: Westminster Press, 1988), pp. 75-90; Katie G. Cannon, *Katie's Canon: Womanism and the Soul of the Black Community* (New York: Continuum, 1995), pp. 27-37.

my soul got happy when I come out the wilderness'.³¹ Womanist theologian Cheryl Kirk-Duggan carries this line of thought further in a book about womanist prophecies on the spirituals.³² Kirk-Duggan explains that '[t]he Hebraic worldview provided immediacy between creators of Spirituals and creators of biblical texts, sowing intimacy between son and singer. Though the differences between Spirituals and Psalms concern cultural development, historical background, and modes of retaliation, these Hebraic and African chanted narratives recreate and confront myths and rituals to give meaning to the singers' worlds and to understand and communicate differences in those worlds.'³³ Thus, Kirk-Duggan's work reinforces Cannon's brief discussion on the spirituals and their connections to biblical texts, characters, and themes.

Cannon's early work makes another important contribution to womanist biblical hermeneutics. She examines the white supremacist ideology in Hebrew Bible interpretations that affirm slavery.³⁴ Cannon mentions 'three intellectual, hierarchical constructs that lie at the center of the Christian antebellum society'.³⁵ The three constructs are first, the historical era and 'conditions in which Americans of African descent lost their status as members of the moral universe', second, 'the ethical grounds' for 'a formula for "heathen conversion"', and, third, 'the hermeneutical distortions that shaped the slavocracy's polemical patterns of biblical propaganda'.³⁶ With attention to racism and sexism, Cannon states that the so-called ethical grounds and distortions of biblical interpretation 'that make the formula for heathen conversion' are 'intrinsically wrong'.³⁷ Cannon discusses that pro-slavery white Christians are engaged in 'remythologizing divine will'. They argued that 'slavery was constantly spoken of in the Bible without any direct prohibition of it, no special law against it'.³⁸ Cannon suggests that advocates of modern slavery found no prohibitions against slavery in the Bible and thus claimed that slavery was not a sin.³⁹ She writes: 'Slave apologists were successful

---

31. Cannon, *Katie's Canon*, p. 34.
32. See Cheryl Kirk-Duggan, *Exorcising Evil: A Womanist Perspective on the Spirituals* (Maryknoll, NY: Orbis Books, 1997), pp. 57-70.
33. Kirk-Duggan, *Exorcising Evil*, p. 69.
34. Cannon, 'Slave Ideology and Biblical Interpretation', *Semeia* 47 (1989), pp. 9-22. The essay is reprinted in Cannon, *Katie's Canon*, pp. 39-46. The discussion is not exclusively about white supremacist interpretations of pro-slavery advocates during modern transatlantic slavery, but it also includes references to Greek Christian biblical texts that pro-slavery activists employed.
35. Cannon, *Katie's Canon*, p. 39.
36. Cannon, *Katie's Canon*, p. 39.
37. Cannon, *Katie's Canon*, pp. 39, 43-45.
38. Cannon, *Katie's Canon*, p. 43.
39. Cannon, *Katie's Canon*, p. 43.

in convincing at least five generations of White citizens that slavery, an essential and constitutionally protected institution, was consistent with the impulse of Christian charity'.[40] In other words, Cannon exposes that slave apologists employed scripture to support a capitalist system dependent on the institution of slavery. They 'spiritualized Scripture to justify capitalism' and they biblically authorized 'the exploitation of Black people'.[41] Cannon also argues that Black women's notion of sacred texts from the authorized white, androcentric, capitalist distortions of Hebrew and Greek scriptures must be expanded and include the real-lived experiences of Black women as they are inscribed in Black women's writings.[42]

Another womanist scholar in theo-ethical studies is important for the development of womanist Hebrew Bible studies. Delores Williams, a theologian of culture, grounds her work in a womanist exegesis of Gen. 16.1-16 and Gen. 21.9-21. Williams' project focuses on the biblical character Hagar, a figure who has played a prominent role in black women's interpretation of the Bible. Williams explains: 'The African-American community has taken Hagar's story unto itself. Hagar has "spoken" to generation after generation of black women because her story has been validated as true by suffering black people... Hagar, like many black women, goes into the wide world to make a living for herself and her child, with only God by her side.'[43] Williams emphasizes that Hagar is the only woman in the Bible to name God—'El Roi'—God of seeing or God who sees (Gen. 16.1-16). Hagar's problems begin when Sarai gives her to Abram. As a result of the encounter with Abram, Hagar becomes pregnant with Ishmael. Hurt by Sarai's treatment, she flees into the wilderness, only to be given a promise by God and told to return to Abram and Sarai. Williams states: 'The word used in Genesis 16 to describe Hagar is *sipha*, meaning "a virgin, dependent maid who serves the mistress of the house". This means that Hagar was a virgin when she was made to lie down with Abram.'[44] 'Could it be', Williams asks, 'that Hagar, because of her Egyptian heritage and her protection against rape by Sarai, had status among other female slaves? Did she lose pride and status because of Sarai's betrayal of her virginity?'[45]

Williams also observes that Hagar is the first woman in the Bible to liberate herself. In the wilderness God cares for Hagar, directing her to return to Abram and Sarai to raise her child under their care. Moreover, in Gen.

---

40. Cannon, *Katie's Cannon*, p. 46.
41. Cannon, *Katie's Cannon*, p. 46.
42. Cannon, *Katie's Cannon*, pp. 69-90.
43. Delores Williams, *Sisters in the Wilderness: The Challenge of Womanist God-Talk* (New York: Orbis Books, 1993), p. 33.
44. Williams, *Sisters in the Wilderness*, p. 17.
45. Williams, *Sisters in the Wilderness*, p. 17.

16.11-12 God promises that 'Yahweh has heard your cries of distress' and the son will become a strong man 'in defiance of all his kinsmen'.[46] Williams highlights Hagar's authority in naming God 'El Roi' and interprets Gen. 16.13-14 to read: 'Did I not go on seeing here, after him who sees me?'[47] Williams also relates the Genesis narratives to Black women's historical tradition that identify with Hagar's wilderness experience and Hagar's power to name God. Although Hagar liberates herself in Genesis 16, Williams finds that 'God does not always liberate'. After all, God sends Hagar back to Abram and Sarai where she can survive and receive quality of life. Williams finds black women's historical and contemporary identification with Hagar helpful for womanist biblical hermeneutics. She recognizes that God provides Hagar with a vision for 'survival' and 'quality of life' so that she survives her 'wilderness experience'.[48] For Williams' womanist hermeneutics the phrase, 'wilderness experience', depicts an important value.[49]

Williams offers a womanist critical analysis on the abuse of power in any era regardless of the religion and ethnicity of the slaveholders. Hagar is Egyptian. She is taken from Egypt, possibly given as a gift. As a foreigner, she stands in an outsider-within position. Abram has more power than Sarai. Sarai has more power than Hagar. Sarai and Abram force Hagar to conceive a son by Abram, and Hagar bears this son. Williams argues that as one who possesses less power than Sarai and Abram, Hagar is a survivor of rape. Similarly Susanne Scholz,[50] relying on womanist biblical interpretations in her research on rape, agrees with Williams that Abram rapes Hagar. During the time of slavery in the United States, Black women were raped by white masters and their relatives, often to impregnate the women and to cheaply produce more slaves.

Williams's work shows that Black women, particularly in the United States, have historically identified with Hagar because of modern, transAtlantic slavery's rape of Black women. These hermeneutical connections resonate with Cannon's discussion about Black women's status as 'brood sows' and 'breeders'.[51] Historically, Black women have found truths in the Bible about servitude and sexual violence because they have resonated with their own experiences. The significance of Hagar's story in Black women's social-historical experience is that God is a God of seeing who provides survival resources. Williams' womanist biblical contribution is that God does not always liberate, but God provides us with survival resources.

    46. Williams, *Sisters in the Wilderness*, p. 22.
    47. Williams, *Sisters in the Wilderness*, p. 23.
    48. Williams, *Sisters in the Wilderness*, pp. 17-22.
    49. Williams, *Sisters in the Wilderness*, pp. 144-46, 149-50, 153-61, 175-77.
    50. Susanne Scholz, *Sacred Witness: Rape in the Hebrew Bible* (Minneapolis: Fortress Press, 2010), pp. 57-62.
    51. Cannon, *Katie's Canon*, p. 29.

Cannon and Williams are two womanists who resist androcentric, Western Eurocentric biases regarding epistemological and hermeneutical norms in Hebrew Bible interpretation. Although they write outside the mainstream of Hebrew Bible studies with its very restrictive academic institutional structures, faculty positions, and exegetical curricula, they are Hebrew Bible scholars.[52] They have employed the marginalization of Black women in biblical studies as a constructive opportunity to create an interdisciplinary field with other womanists, called 'Womanist Approaches to Religion and Society'. In doing so, they acknowledge the particularities of womanist biblical hermeneutics, and they also challenge Western-European, androcentric, and hegemonic scholars to admit their cultural biases.

Academy and Church:
Audiences for Womanist Hebrew Biblical Scholarship

Another pioneer of womanist Hebrew Bible interpretation is Renita Weems who has written for both the church and the academy. Her primary audience is ordinary Black women, particularly Black church women. Her first book, *Just a Sister Away*,[53] examines sex, sexuality, intimate violence, and marital metaphors in biblical literature. It has been helpful for laity and seminarians alike by raising questions about agency and accountability and by loving self and community. Womanist clergy, laity, and seminarians have found this volume helpful because it addresses issues of health, violence, sexism, racism, classism, and wisdom in Black women's real-lived experience.

In a book primarily written for academic audiences, *Battered Love*, Weems analyzes biblical metaphors on sexual violence. Her exegesis explores 'marriage as a controlling metaphor', 'male prestige in the marriage metaphor', the rhetoric of 'is she not my wife' in Hosea, romance rhetoric in Hosea and Jeremiah. Womanist Hebrew Bible hermeneutics includes social-ethical criteria regarding the wholeness, survival, quality of life and liberation of Black women. Weems' social-ethical aim in *Battered Love* is 'resisting rape and romance rhetoric', understanding how metaphors hurt, and engaging the

---

52. Junior makes a similar observation regarding the Western and North American guild's treatment of womanist biblical hermeneutics; see Junior, 'Womanist Interpretation', pp. 452-54. It is important to further note that the general consensus of womanist and Black male scholars of religion is that much of the guild has treated Weems's work in a biased and oppressive manner that is sexist, racist, and classist. Much of the guild fails to adequately appreciate her commitments to womanist praxis. It is also important to note, however, that some academic institutions encourage more scholarly outreach to lay communities, aiming to bridge church, academia, and society.

53. Renita Weems, *Just a Sister Away: A Womanist Vision of Women's Relationships in the Bible* (Philadelphia: Innisfree Press, 1988).

metaphor of the broken-hearted.⁵⁴ Weems encourages readers to critically engage these texts to understand their metaphorical and rhetorical significance for the Israelite people. While such texts were ostensibly about returning to God and moving away from idolatry, they also reflect the problem of reinforcing patriarchy and violence against women. Weems discourages uncritically appropriating such texts. Her interest '[a]dmittedly has had a lot to do with my identity as a woman—an African American woman', but she is also interested in studying these metaphors to give attention to 'ethically responsible exegesis'.⁵⁵ The volume does not rely on a womanist method, yet it contributes to understandings of survival, quality of life, and loving oneself 'regardless', as Alice Walker puts it. It is not, however, a book about Black women's social-historical context and experience.

Weems explains her position with the following words: 'I have always identified myself as a biblical scholar who not only traffics in the intellectual world making enterprise of scholarship and academy. But I have also been eager to make my mark as a public intellectual, a woman in the academy who tries to make work accessible and available to the non-specialists and grassroots activists working for liberation in ecclesial and non-ecclesial contexts'.⁵⁶ As Junior observes, to Weems, 'womanist biblical hermeneutics does not begin with the Bible; instead it comes from African American women's experience, in particular as survivors of slavery and as survivors of various forms of oppression.' 'For Weems', Junior writes, 'womanist biblical interpretation begins with the notion that "people have power, not texts"'.⁵⁷ Weems recognizes that since modern slavery, African American women and men have generally chosen to interpret the Bible for themselves in relation to their own social-historical experiences. They have not accepted the biblical interpretations of their slave masters.⁵⁸

Another Hebrew Bible scholar who refers to her approach as 'womanist or feminist depending on the context' is Wil Gafney. In her works, Gafney prioritizes attention to 'multidimensionality, women's experience, eradicating human oppression, and making biblical scholarship accessible to ordinary worshipping communities'.⁵⁹ This description of a womanist

---

54. Renita Weems, *Battered Love: Overtures to Biblical Theology* (Minneapolis, MN: Fortress Press, 1995), pp. 1-4, 45-67, 92-115.

55. Weems, *Battered Love*, p. 9.

56. Renita Weems, 'Re-Reading for Liberation: African American Women and the Bible', in Mitzi J. Smith (ed.), *I Found God in Me: A Womanist Biblical Hermeneutics Reader* (Eugene, OR: Cascade/Wipf & Stock Books, 2015), pp. 42-55 (44).

57. Weems, 'Re-Reading for Liberation'. See also Sylvia Schroer and Sophia Bietenhard (eds.), *Feminist Interpretation of the Bible* (London: T. & T. Clark, 2003), p. 26.

58. Weems, 'Re-reading for Liberation', pp. 47-49.

59. Junior, 'Womanist Interpretation', p. 453. See also Wil Gafney, 'A Black Feminist Approach to Biblical Studies', *Encounter* 67.4 (2006), pp. 391-403.

approach is consistent with Weems' *praxis* of producing books on Hebrew biblical scholarship that bridge church and academy, as well as reach out to ordinary people of faith.

Gafney offers a constructive womanist interpretation of the Hebrew Bible in her essay entitled 'A Womanist Midrash on Zipporah'. She looks at Moses' wife, interprets the name Zipporah as meaning 'songbird', and describes Zipporah as 'a motherless daughter, a sister, a shepherd, a survivor, a wife, a clergy spouse, a mother, a woman who struggles with God... with her own spiritual knowledge and power, abandoned by that same (ungrateful!) man, divorced, a single mother, and a biblical matriarch'.[60] Moreover, Moses would not have known the God of the Mountain without his relationship to Zipporah and her father, 'whose name is Jethro, *Yitro* and *Yether)* or *Reuel, depending on whether we are reading Ex 2.1-22 Reuel)* or the bulk of Exodus in which he is called *Yitro*'.[61] In other words, Gafney emphasizes Zipporah's moral agency and the various background texts that inform a readerly understanding of Miriam's and her father's relationship with the God. To Gafney, as for Cannon and Hurston, Moses does not know his God well until he meets Zipporah who, according to Gafney's reading, is a Black woman and 'sainted mother'.[62]

The works of these womanist Bible scholars raise the following questions: What makes a biblical hermeneutic womanist? Moreover, are some contexts more appropriate for the term 'womanist' than others? If so, why? Junior believes that more continuity in the definition and description of womanist biblical hermeneutics would be beneficial to the future of womanism in the academic study of the Hebrew Bible.

Reading Womanist Biblical Hermeneutics into the Future

The future of womanist biblical hermeneutics looks bright, as indicated by recent publications. For instance, Mitzi J. Smith's anthology, *I Found God in Me: A Womanist Biblical Hermeneutics Readers*,[63] includes essays by various womanist biblical interpreters who work inside and outside mainstream biblical studies. The book features Katie Cannon's prophetic work in womanist biblical interpretation.[64] She writes there that '[a] womanist critique of

---

60. Wil Gafney, 'A Womanist Midrash on Zipporah', in Smith (ed.), *I Found God in Me*, pp. 131-57 (131).

61. Gafney, 'A Womanist Midrash on Zipporah', in Smith (ed.), *I Found God in Me*, p. 131.

62. Gafney, 'A Womanist Midrash on Zipporah', in Smith (ed.), *I Found God in Me*, pp. 156-57.

63. Smith (ed.), *I Found God in Me*, pp. 42-55.

64. Katie G. Cannon, 'Womanist Interpretation and Preaching', in Smith (ed.), *I Found God in Me*, pp. 56-67.

homiletics challenges conventional biblical interpretations that characterize African American women as "sin-bringing Eve", "wilderness-whimpering Hagar", "henpecking Jezebel", "whoring Gomer", "prostituting Mary Magdalene", and "conspiring Saphira'".[65] She emphasizes 'radically rethinking' epistemologies regarding gendered duties and roles 'in the black church community' to move womanist scholarship further.[66]

To expand and move womanist Hebrew biblical interpretation forward, it is important for womanists to practice the courage and audacity of senior scholars like Cannon and Williams. A strength of Smith's anthology is that it includes senior, mid-career, and emerging womanist biblical interpreters. One voice from the emerging generation is Kimberly Russaw. She argues that 'the work of womanist biblical interpretation is subversive', because it 'disrupts tightly held images of God and God's relationship to humanity'.[67] Like Cannon, she includes economic concerns in her description of a womanist hermeneutic; an approach that 'unsettles images that privilege the concerns of males who possess social economic, and political capital'.[68] In a world in which neoliberal economics reign globally, even going so far as threatening academic freedom and innovation through the corporatization of universities, the courage to do subversive work is necessary. Younger womanist scholars need the support of other radical and subversive scholars in the field, much like the first and second generation of womanist scholars who worked with liberationist and progressive feminists, forming meetings and conferences with other womanists. Working with global and postcolonial feminists is also important given our common experiences of conquest and colonization from the modern period well into the twenty-first century.

Another issue relates to the definition of womanism. One of the strengths of Nyasha Junior's description of 'womanist' is that she refers to Nigerian womanism in the work of Chikwenye Okonyo Ogunyemi 'who claims she developed the term 'womanist' independently of Walker'. Obunyemi asserts that her definition features a more communal and nonindividualistic approach than Walker's. It emphasizes global African women's concerns more ably than African American womanism.[69] Although womanists have worked with theologian Mercy Amba Oduyoye of Ghana since the early days of womanist studies, in the future we need to expand this practice and converse more with other African women that we have in the past.

---

65. Weems, 'Re-Reading for Liberation', in Smith (ed.), *I Found God in Me*, p. 57.
66. Weems, 'Re-Reading for Liberation', in Smith (ed.), *I Found God in Me*, p. 57.
67. Kimberly Dawn Russaw, 'Wisdom in the Garden: The Woman of Genesis 3 and Alice Walker's *Sophia*', in Smith, *I Found God in Me*, pp. 223-35 (223, 231-33).
68. Russaw, 'Wisdom in the Garden', pp. 222-23.
69. Junior, 'Womanist Interpretation', p. 450.

Emerging global womanist scholars should thus be on our collective womanist agenda. In *I Found God in Me*, Smith seems to anticipate concerns for womanist Hebrew biblical scholarship. Her volume includes scholars from African countries, such as Madipoane J. Masenya. Her essay on 'An African Methodology for South African Biblical Sciences: Revisiting the Bosadi'[70] outlines the characteristics of her '*bosadi* biblical hermeneutics'.[71] It begins with 'the experiences of the marginalized' South African women and 'not the contexts that produced the Bible'.[72] By working together, we will create common ground and also learn about the differences among African American, African, Caribbean, and other global womanists. In order for womanist biblical hermeneutics to avoid the twentieth century problem of being limited to Western and US norms, more engagement with global womanists, Black feminists, and feminists will be necessary.

The words 'colonial' and 'postcolonial' appear in some womanist biblical hermeneutics, particularly in the field of New Testament. Why do we not see more of this in Hebrew womanist biblical scholarship? We ought to pay more attention to the writings of postcolonial feminist biblical scholars, such as Musa W. Dube, to enhance our comparative, critical, and constructive analyses. Such work need not be limited to womanists and feminists of African descent, as for instance, Kwok Pui-lan honors womanist work in her writing by discussing the significance of womanist work for the postcolonial feminist imagination.[73]

Finally, as Junior observes, some womanist biblical interpreters address the problems of homophobia and heterosexism, while others do not. Katie Cannon specifically addresses issues of heterosexism and homophobia in androcentric biblical interpretations in 'Sexing Black Women: Liberation from the Prisonhouse of Anatomical Authority'.[74] Cannon writes that '[t]o begin with, powerbrokers in the Black church, all too often subject women to a litany of verbal abuse, known as lezzy-baiting. To a large degree, antilesbian hysteria consists of assaultive speech, wherein the word lesbian is used as a weapon, as a defiant verbal punch, teetering on the edge of physical violence in order to terrorize women who refuse to acquiesce to the

---

70. Madipoane J. Masenya, 'An African Methodology for South African Biblical Sciences: Revisiting the *Bosadi*', in Smith (ed.), *I Found God in Myself*, pp. 68-79 (68).

71. Madipoane J. Masenya, 'Marginalized People, Liberating Perspectives', *Anglican Theological Review* 83 (2001), pp. 41-47 (**75**).

72. Masenya, 'Marginalized People, Liberating Perspectives', p. 75.

73. Kwok Pui-lan, *Postcolonial Imagination & Feminist Theology* (Louisville, KY: Westminster/John Knox Press, 2005).

74. Katie G. Cannon, 'Sexing Black Women: Liberation from the Prisonhouse of Anatomical Authority', in Anthony B. Pinn and Dwight N. Hopkins (eds.), *Loving the Body: Black Religious Studies and the Erotic* (New York: Palgrave Macmillan, 2004), pp. 11-26.

so-called supremacy of the mama-papa, missionary position as the solo, dominant pattern for love making.'[75] Of course, such powerbrokers assert to proclaim the 'Word of God'. As systematic theologian M. Shawn Copeland states, black women's bodies are a matter of life and death.[76] Indeed, then, womanist biblical hermeneutics is a matter of life, and death for all those who are committed to the survival, quality of life and liberation of entire communities through subversive biblical hermeneutics. Womanist Bible scholars need to develop a womanist biblical hermeneutic that addresses problematic texts and the ways in which they have been used to oppress Black women's bodies. While Weems has produced work that is related to this concern, we also need to produce highly academic works to gain academic credibility and respect.

Cannon and other womanists advanced many of these issues during the pioneering years of the 1980s. For instance, Elisabeth Schüssler Fiorenza and Letty Russell included womanist studies in their respective anthologies.[77] We womanists will always need time and energy to do our own work because no one in the guild seems to love black women's bodies as much as black women called womanists. Our collaboration is important for forging relationships of solidarity and to envision quality of life and wisdom for Black women, their families, and, in fact, the entire Earth.

75. Cannon, 'Sexing Black Women', p. 14.
76. Copeland, *Enfleshing Freedom*.
77. Karen Baker-Fletcher, 'Anna Julia Cooper and Sojourner Truth: Two Nineteenth-Century Black Feminist Interpreters of Scripture', in Elisabeth Schüssler Fiorenza (ed.), *Searching the Scriptures: A Feminist Introduction, Volume One* (New York: Crossroad, 1993), pp. 41-51; Karen Baker-Fletcher, 'Difference' and 'Womanist Voice', in Letty Russell and J. Shannon Clarkson (eds.), *Dictionary of Feminist Theologies* (Louisville, KY: Westminster/John Knox Press, 1996), pp. 68-69, 316-17.

12

WHEN WOMEN AREN'T ENOUGH:
GENDER CRITICISM IN FEMINIST HEBREW BIBLE INTERPRETATION

Nicole J. Ruane

At first glance, the term 'gender' may seem so intrinsic to the enterprise of feminist Hebrew Bible interpretation that gender criticism should not need its own entry. A survey of publications in biblical studies indicates that 'gender' analysis has long been a part of the field. Yet what do biblical scholars mean when they use the term 'gender'? In the context of critical methodology, 'gender criticism' is a distinct form of analysis that stems largely from the early work of the philosopher Judith Butler. She defined gender as performative action that is taught by society to achieve heteronormative reproductive goals. Variously called 'gender criticism', 'gender theory', or 'gender analysis', this approach is heavily influenced by queer and trans* theory and masculinity studies. It focuses on gender in all of its manifestations, it uncovers heteronormative structures and ideologies, and it exposes the constructed nature of gender by calling attention to areas in which gender norms are subverted or undermined. It reveals the fragile and inessential quality of gender itself.

This essay centers on gender criticism as a method, discussing its background, goals, and presentations in Hebrew Bible studies. Importantly, gender criticism is not uniformly defined in biblical studies. Some exegetes use 'gender' as an alternate term for 'women' without engaging gender theory. Their interpretations raise the question whether gender criticism is a form of feminist criticism or if it is a separate approach. At stake is whether exegetes who conflate gender with 'women' adhere to an earlier understanding of feminist criticism that limits itself to the study of women, even when it uses the term 'gender'. Does any reference to 'gender' signify that the interpreter relies on gender criticism? If not, why not, and what is at stake when we differentiate between the two approaches? Further, do exegetes who use the term 'gender' in the sense of 'women' avoid classifying their work as 'feminist' because they fear the charge of advancing an explicitly political perspective? Is gender criticism inherently a-political?

This essay tackles these and related issues as they relate to gender criticism. The following sections present key issues in gender theory, survey how biblical critics use gender theories effectively and prominently, and assess exegetical works that conflate gender with 'women' while refraining from engagement with gender theoretical theory. A conclusion discusses the future of gender criticism in feminist Hebrew Bible studies.

Key Issues in Gender Theory

Although the field of gender studies, also called 'gender theory', relates directly to critical and deconstructive theory, it originates primarily from feminist theory. Advocating on behalf of women, feminist theorists examine the oppression of women and the power structures working against them. At the same time, gender theory includes insights from LGBQTI and queer theory, masculinity studies, and intersectional analyses related to race, geopolitics, class, or physical ability. As a result of these varied influences, gender studies has expanded the analysis of power structures, social status, and the role of gender beyond the status of women. Five key concerns have extended gender criticism beyond early feminist perspectives. One concern questions the view that women are a monolithic group. A second concern challenges essentialist notions of gender. A third concern critiques binary assumptions about gender. A fourth concern exposes ideologies of compulsory heterosexuality, and a fifth concern focuses on 'men' and the 'male' in the emerging field of masculinity studies. The following discussion elaborates on these five key issues, as they have contributed to the development of gender criticism.

First, gender theorists challenge the idea that women are a monolithic group with universal characteristics independent of place and time. Early feminist work did not always recognize that women's experiences vary depending on location and time period, as well as on the social categories of race, class, age, ability, or geopolitics. Women of color especially criticized totalizing assumptions about 'women' and called attention to the unrecognized privilege of white theorists.[1] Some women of color have thus rejected the term 'feminism' and named their school of thought 'womanism'.[2] Similarly, even though many prominent and influential women in the second wave US-American women's movement have been lesbians, the movement

---

1. See, e.g., Audrey Lorde, *Sister/Outsider: Essays and Speeches* (Berkeley, CA: Crossing Press, 1984); bell hooks, *Ain't I a Woman: Black Women and Feminism* (Brooklyn, NY: South End Press, 1981); Angela Davis, *Women, Race and Class* (New York: Vintage Press, 1983).

2. The term was coined by author and poet Alice Walker; see her short story 'Coming Apart: By Way of Introduction to Lorde, Teish and Gardner', in Laura Lederer (ed.), *Take Back the Night: Women on Pornography* (New York: William Morrow, 1980), pp. 84-93. Walker develops the concept more fully in her work *In Search of Our Mothers' Gardens: Womanist Prose* (New York: Harcourt Brace, 1983), pp. xi-xii.

often marginalized specifically lesbian perspectives. Accordingly, lesbian feminists have criticized straight feminist theorists for promoting an overtly heteronormative agenda.

Since these voices have asserted that women's experiences are always connected to ideologies of race and sexuality, as well as to class, geopolitics, age, or physical abilities, feminist theorists expanded their analyses to address the complex phenomena of gender. This expanded critique has led to important questions about the nature of feminism: Does feminism seek to secure women's equality with men, or does it examine inequities of power and affiliated hierarchies related to the many other intersectional structures of domination? In other words, is the work of 'feminism' defined by its subject—women, or is it a method that analyzes power structures that includes but goes far beyond the category of women? In the field of biblical studies, a basic question is whether feminist interpretations focus on women only or whether they also need to critique intersectional power dynamics. Conversely, one must also ask whether exegetical works about women are inherently feminist, and whether 'feminist' scholarship must have an activist political agenda, including LGBTQI concerns, at its core. Most feminist theorists would probably agree that an exclusive focus on women is insufficient as it ignores other oppressive regimes of gender and their intersectional hierarchies. Yet others might fear that a focus on other structures of domination distracts from specific concerns about women.

Second, another key issue in gender theoretical concerns relates to essentializing notions of gender. Gender theorists reject essentialism because it promotes biological, 'naturalized' notions about gender. They oppose the early feminist assumption that women have the same 'essential' nature located in their shared biology.[3] Second-wave feminists have sometimes asserted that women's experience of 'womanhood' is universal and that, for example, all women are compassionate, spiritual, and emotional. Yet feminist theorists from various racial, sexual, and class locations have challenged this idea, including the French deconstructionist philosophers Hélène Cixous, Luce Irigaray, and Julia Kristeva. They criticize second-wave feminist thought for advancing essentializing notions about 'woman' because such notions are built upon ideas about women constructed by men. To androcentric culture, 'woman' is the 'other'. Cixous, Irigaray and

---

3. Two scholars accused of 'essentialist' thinking are the feminist philosopher Mary Daly (as in her work *Gyn/Ecology: The Metaethics of Radical Feminism* [Boston: Beacon Press, 1990]) and the psychologist Carol Gilligan, best known for her book *In a Different Voice: Psychological Theory and Women's Development* (Cambridge, MA: Harvard University Press, 1982). Elizabeth V. Spelman forcefully argued against essentializing gender in her work *Inessential Woman: Problems of Exclusion in Feminist Thought* (Boston: Beacon Press, 1990).

Kristeva argue that women may indeed have a shared essence but it is currently unknown because 'women' are known only through male representations. Thus women need to embark on self-discovery and write about their experiences, thoughts, and reflections about life so that women gain autonomous knowledge of themselves. Although other feminist thinkers disagree that there could be some distinctively female essence, waiting to be discovered, Cixous, Irigaray, and Kristeva recognize that attributes about women, thought to be 'natural' and based on biology, are socially produced constructs by men who benefit from such ideas.

The recognition of 'woman' as a social construct was already articulated by the mid-twentieth century philosopher Simone de Beauvoir who observed: 'One is not born, but rather becomes, a woman'.[4] De Beauvoir's famous statement articulates the fundamental feminist conviction that biological sex is not identical to social gender. While sex and sexual difference are physical facts, 'gender' is a social construct that is interrelated with socio-political, cultural, economic, and even religious traditions and practices. Since gender is not 'natural', not biological, not inherent, and not universal, gender roles and gender relations can and do change over time.

In the last few decades, the philosopher and queer activist Judith Butler has articulated some of the most important challenges to essentialist thought. In the early 1990s, she published two important works that advanced the notion of gender as a social construct.[5] According to Butler, gender is always 'performed' to conform to social 'scripts'. For instance, in Western culture, women perform femininity by wearing dresses. Since prevailing gender norms prescribe that only women should wear dresses, the wearing of a dress performs the 'script' of femininity. Constant repetition of this kind of gender performance defines gender, and so gender itself depends on repetition. In other words, gender is a performative act, even when it does not appear to be so. Butler illustrates this dynamic in a discussion about the phenomenon of 'drag'. When a man wears a dress, he performs femininity like a woman when she wears a dress. Even when his performance is not entirely convincing, it nevertheless demonstrates that gender is created through the performance of wearing a dress. Thus, to Butler, 'drag' is an exaggerated instance that exemplifies what we already know: we show ourselves to others (and ourselves) according to generally accepted or unaccepted gender norms because there are no inherently 'natural' or 'normative' ways of performing gender. Furthermore, 'drag' illustrates the gaps between successful and unsuccessful attempts of gender performance.

    4. Simone de Beauvoir, *The Second Sex* (New York: Vintage Books, 1973), p. 301.
    5. Judith Butler, *Gender Trouble: Feminism and the Subversion of Identity* (London: Routledge, 1990); Judith Butler, *Bodies that Matter: On the Discursive Limits of Sex* (London: Routledge, 1993).

Some men make convincing women while others do not. The gap illustrates the constructed nature of the performance, as there are always gaps in any gender performance even when they are not as dramatic as in 'drag'. Gaps thus expose, undermine, and sometimes even sabotage gender performance. When gender critics focus on the gaps in gender performance, they call attention to the constructed nature of gender to signify the unstable and changeable characteristics of any existing gender norms.

Third, gender critics also challenge binary assumptions about gender. Many past and present societies divide gender into two (acceptable) forms: female and male. Often gender critics examine this binary view in the context of LGBQTI theory to highlight the instability and untenability of the gender binary. In fact, gender appears on a spectrum, as does biological sex. Butler shows in various ways that biological sex is much more diverse than suggested by the rigid binary of female and male. The experiences of intersex and trans* people indicate a whole range of biological possibilities for sexual identity that go far beyond the conventional binary of female and male. The emerging field of transgender and intersex studies has built upon this challenge of the gender binary.[6]

Fourth, gender critics also expose ideologies of compulsory heterosexuality. Their works are often grounded in LGBQTI and queer theory because it convincingly and forcefully deconstructs heteronormativity.[7] Gender critics maintain that the primary reason for the restriction of gender to the female-male binary relates to society's need for sexual reproduction. Throughout human history, political and economic forces in society have compelled people to reproduce within traditional kinship relations. They have integrated compulsory heterosexuality into social life so pervasively that even nowadays it seems 'natural', mandatory, and essential. However, gender critics argue that the existence of LGBQTI people undermines the notion of heterosexuality as 'natural,' just as 'drag' exposes the constructed and 'unnatural' state of gender. Thus, gender criticism usually includes discussions about heteronormativity, as prescribed, advanced, and practiced in political, cultural, and social ideologies, traditions, and institutions. It denaturalizes compulsory heterosexuality and exposes it as a construct of social control.

---

6. For scholarly reviews of these developments, see, e.g., Anne Fausto-Sterling, *Sexing the Body: Gender Politics and the Construction of Sexuality* (New York: Basic Books, 2000); Emi Koyama, 'The Transfeminist Manifesto', in Rory Dicker and Alison Piepmeier (eds.), *Catching a Wave: Reclaiming Feminism for the Twenty-First Century* (Boston: Northeastern University Press, 2003), pp. 244-62.

7. Certainly, Butler is not the first theorist to articulate this idea. Perhaps one of the most famous articulations comes from Adrienne Rich, 'Compulsory Heterosexuality and Lesbian Existence', *Signs* 5 (1980), pp. 631-60.

Fifth, another emerging theoretical area of study increasingly shapes gender criticism. It is the research area of masculinity studies, arising from feminist theory and LGBQTI and queer theory. It deconstructs 'men' and 'the male' similar to early feminist investigations of 'women' and 'the feminine'. Since it evaluates the connections between maleness and socio-political power, masculinity studies are part of gender criticism. Various works on masculinity and religion have provided the impetus for biblical scholars to investigate depictions of male characters such as David, Samson, or even Jesus.[8]

In sum, gender theory has built upon feminist theory, LGBQTI, and intersectional analysis to comprehensively investigate gender beyond 'women' and 'the feminine'. Gender criticism challenges structures of power in text and society as they relate to gender broadly defined. It does not limit itself to issues of 'women' or 'womanhood' and rejects essentializing, binary, and heteronormative constructs of gender. While feminist theorists have, to varying degrees, also investigated these topics since the 1970s, 'gender criticism' reflects a widened scope of topics and analytical perspectives that feminist scholarship of the second-wave movement has not usually included. Expanded notions about gender have also made feminist work more complicated, challenging, and complex. The development has broadened the scope from a narrow concern about 'women' to concerns about gender in its varied expressions and practices. Nevertheless, gender criticism is inherently a feminist approach. However, important questions remain. Foremost among them is whether gender criticism has different aims and purposes than feminist criticism. Some feminist theorists worry that the broadened notion of gender dodges feminism's main purpose, which is to better women's lives in an androcentric world.[9] They fear that women's experiences of patriarchal oppression will disappear from the theoretical and political agenda if gender criticism no longer recognizes women as a distinct group. Who will stand for women if the very category of 'female' no longer exists? Yet other feminist thinkers embrace gender criticism because they recognize gender-based systems as devaluing not only one group—women—but as a systemic problem in need of general transformation. Many feminist and gender critics also agree that the elimination of sexism and the oppression

---

8. For a detailed analysis of masculinity studies, see Katherine Low's essay 'Space for Women and Men: Masculinity Studies in Feminist Biblical Interpretation' in this volume.

9. See, e.g., J. De Groot and M. Maynard, 'Facing the 1990s: Problems and Possibilities for Women's Studies', in J. De Groot and M. Maynard (eds.), *Women's Studies in the 1990s: Doing Things Differently?* (Basingstoke: Palgrave Press, 1993), pp. 149-78; Mary Evans, 'The Problem of Gender for Women's Studies', *Women's Studies International Forum* 13.5 (1990), pp. 457-62. Both sources are cited in Guest, *Beyond Feminist Biblical Studies*, pp. 33-35.

of women must include a critique of heteronormativity, gender binaries, and other structures of domination, such as race, class, physical abilities, or geopolitics, because the analysis of 'women' alone cannot accomplish this formidable goal.

Gender Theory in Hebrew Bible Interpretations

Although many works in biblical studies include the term 'gender' in their titles, there are relatively few that address gender theory, as described above, as a distinct interpretive method. Bible scholars who have used Butler's work have done so mostly in the context of queer interpretation.[10] While there is an overlap between feminist and queer interpretation, studies that use gender theory to focus on gender are less common. Following is a discussion of some of the most helpful publications that use elements of Butler's work or an explicitly 'gender critical' approach to the interpretation of biblical texts.[11]

One of the earliest publications in biblical studies that relies on gender theory as articulated by Butler is Dorothea Erbele's article 'Gender Trouble in the Old Testament: Three Models of the Relation between Sex and Gender'.[12] Erbele examines four Hebrew terms for inner body parts that relate to procreation: *baśar*, *beṭen*, *me'îm*, and *reḥem*. She finds that the terms express culturally specific understandings of procreation and biological organs. For instance, while the noun *reḥem* ('womb', 'uterus') refers to female reproductive organs, males, including the biblical deity, are sometimes described with the attribute of *raḥamîm* ('compassion'; perhaps literally 'wombishness') that contains the same root, *rḥm*, as the singular term. In other words, in biblical Hebrew the term 'womb' does not convey the

---

10. See, e.g., Teresa J. Hornsby and Ken Stone (eds.), *Bible Trouble: Queer Reading at the Boundaries of Biblical Scholarship* (Atlanta: SBL Press, 2011).

11. Publications not discussed in this article include, e.g., Harold C. Washington, 'Violence and the Construction of Gender in the Hebrew Bible: A New Historicist Approach', *BibInt* 5.4 (1997), pp. 324-63; Stuart Macwilliam, 'The Prophet and His Patsy: Gender Performativity', in Christl M. Maier and Carolyn J. Sharp (eds.), *Jeremiah in Prophecy and Power: Jeremiah in Feminist and Postcolonial Perspective* (London: Bloomsbury, 2014), pp. 173-88; Christl M. Maier, *Daughter Zion, Mother Zion: Gender, Space and the Sacred in Ancient Israel* (Minneapolis: Fortress Press, 2008); Nicole J. Ruane, *Sacrifice and Gender in Biblical Law* (New York: Cambridge University Press, 2013); Danna Nolan Fewell and David M. Gunn, *Gender, Power and Promise: The Subject of the Bible's First Story* (Nashville: Abingdon Press, 1992); Angela Bauer, *Gender in the Book of Jeremiah: A Feminist-Literary Reading* (Oxford: Peter Lang, 1999); Cheryl Kirk-Duggan (ed.), *Pregnant Passion: Gender, Sex and Violence in the Bible* (Semeia Studies; Leiden: Brill, 2004).

12. Dorothea Erbele, 'Gender Trouble in the Old Testament: Three Models of the Relation between Sex and Gender', *SJOT* 13 (1999), pp. 131-41.

same meaning as in English. Rather, it reflects a different view of biological organs. The term includes a sense of emotional empathy ('compassion') that in English is never associated with the female uterus. Erbele also explains that the term *beṭen* ('womb', 'inner part') refers to an internal reproductive organ possessed by both women and men. This connotation is radically different from other Western languages in which women and men are not thought of as having the same reproductive organs. In fact, men are not even thought of as having an internal reproductive organ at all. The culturally different terminology for procreation and the body illustrates that even those aspects of sex and sexuality that seem 'natural' and obvious are always socially constructed, even linguistically. Thus, even the most basic understandings of sex distinction and procreation are not objective, universal, or grounded in biology.

Another scholar who has written extensively about and with gender studies is Deborah F. Sawyer. In her various publications, she regards gender criticism as a distinct method that is a new and improved version of feminist criticism.[13] In her view, the works of the French feminist philosophers Cixous, Irigary, and Kristeva, along with the US-American philosopher Butler, have enabled the intellectual move from the second-wave feminist focus on 'women' to the expanded notion of 'gender'.[14] Sawyer stresses the constructed nature of both the female and male gender, and she emphasizes how gender construction undermines itself, thereby revealing its fragile and inessential nature. She does not, however, address some of the other vital aspects of gender theory, such as heteronormativity and the gender binary.

Sawyer offers a gender critical reading of the Eden story, largely following Cixous and Irigaray. She depicts Eve's story as one that 'presents a competing and subversive counter discourse'[15] of autonomous maturing in which Yahweh creates the first woman endowed with the ability to be liberated from divine control. This reading contrasts with the more traditional understanding of Eve as sinful and as made by a deity who sees her as defective rather than with the autonomous ability to empower herself. Unfortunately, Sawyer does not use gender criticism to its full advantage in her reading of Genesis 2–3; the story of Eden begs for criticism of its insistence on compulsory heterosexuality and the gender binary. Nevertheless, the implicit answer to the question posed in Sawyer's title is that, indeed, gender criticism is a form of feminist criticism. It stretches and expands the

---

13. Deborah F. Sawyer, 'Gender Criticism: A New Discipline in Biblical Studies or Feminism in Disguise?', in Deborah Rooke (ed.), *A Question of Sex? Gender and Difference in Ancient Israel and Beyond* (Sheffield: Sheffield Phoenix Press, 2007), pp. 2-19.

14. See also Deborah F. Sawyer, 'Gender', in John F.A. Sawyer (ed.), *Blackwell Companion to the Bible and Culture* (West Sussex: Wiley-Blackwell, 2006), pp. 464-79.

15. Sawyer, 'Gender Criticism', p. 14.

range of questions to be asked and the range of analyses to be performed on biblical texts. As Sawyer puts it, gender criticism considers the feminist questions of power and patriarchy 'more profoundly'.[16] In her opinion, gender criticism goes deeper than feminist exegesis.

Sawyer uses Butler's gender theories, French feminist thought, and queer theory to analyze various biblical and apocryphal texts. For instance, she examines the character of Judith to argue that Judith is not only permitted to violate gender norms—thereby subverting them and illustrating their constructed nature, but she is also supported by God who enables her to challenge gender norms of her era.[17] Yet it is always God's power that undoes and transgresses gender distinctions in the book of Judith. In a discussion of Jer. 31.22b, Sawyer stresses that this verse depicts Yahweh's 'anarchic' presentation of future gender relations in the world.[18] It illustrates the constructed nature of gender and the possibility of its undoing in various biblical texts. This concept is also featured in her monograph entitled *God, Gender and the Bible*.[19] There she maintains that, like Judith, other biblical women are often given the ability to destabilize the masculinity of powerful men so that Yahweh is enabled to assert 'his' power as the ultimate patriarch. In biblical literature, to Sawyer, human gender contrasts with the eternal and ultimate power of God even though human gender is always depicted as a relative and changeable cultural construct.

Still other exegetes offer guidance for using gender theory in biblical studies. Beatrice Lawrence surveys the method and illustrates its productive use in an essay on 'Gender Analysis: Gender and Method in Biblical Studies'.[20] She explains that gender criticism is a hermeneutical stance rather than a discrete method. Thus, any gender critical analysis requires other methods in service of this stance. For instance, literary criticism lends itself easily to gender criticism. Lawrence also lists basic questions that gender critics seek to answer: 'How is gender presented in this text? How are males and females identified, and what do they do? What do they want,

---

16. Sawyer, 'Gender Criticism', p. 3.

17. Sawyer, 'Gender Strategies in Antiquity: Judith's Performance', *FemTh* 10 (2001), pp. 9-26.

18. Sawyer, 'Gender Play and Sacred Text: A Scene from Jeremiah', *JSOT* 83 (1999), pp. 99-111.

19. Deborah Sawyer, *God, Gender and the Bible* (London: Routledge, 2002). Also see Sawyer, 'Biblical Gender Strategies: The Case of Abraham's Masculinity', in Ursula King and Tina Beattie (eds.), *Gender, Religion and Diversity: Cross-Cultural Perspectives* (London and New York: Bloomsbury Academic, 2005), pp. 162-74.

20. Beatrice Lawrence, 'Gender Analysis: Gender and Method in Biblical Studies', in Joel M. LeMon and Kent Harold Richards (eds.), *Method Matters: Essays on the Interpretation of the Hebrew Bible* (Festschrift in Honor of David L. Petersen; Atlanta: SBL Press, 2009), pp. 333-45.

and how do they achieve their goals? ... Who 'fits' the models of femininity and masculinity presented in the text? What about those characters who do not fit? ... Who has power over whom? How is this power expressed?'[21] Moreover, she describes some of the difficulties that arise in gender critical exegesis. She explains:

> (1) The text itself is not a clear pane of glass, affording easy access to its notions of gender; (2) the text is from a time and place about which we know relatively little; (3) we do not know if the text is representing an ideal (construction) or a reflection of reality; and (4) every presentation of gender is obscured to some extent, as part of a culture that most likely does not name in an outright fashion what it is saying or doing with gender'.[22]

Her discussion emphasizes the ambiguity of biblical texts, their historical locatedness, and the difficulties of reading them as historical.

Lawrence illustrates her theoretical explanations with a 'gender critical' analysis of Prov. 31.10-31, the poem praising the 'woman of valor', traditionally recited on the Jewish Sabbath. Lawrence shows that the poem uses gender playfully and flexibly. The poem praises the ideal woman by employing several words normally associated with masculinity. The noun *ḥayil* ('valor') normally refers to male warriors. The woman is also said to give her husband *šalal* ('booty', 'spoils') like a victorious warrior. At the same time, the poem confines the woman's abilities to the domestic sphere, so that her husband is free to engage in public life, which he could not do otherwise were his house in disorder. Lawrence thus argues that the poem presents a gendered model for Jewish women, as it is read on the Sabbath, but this model is harmful because it is unattainable and sets up unrealistic expectations for women. Nevertheless, the poem presents only one constructed view of femininity that may encourage readers to create other more useful models about women and femininity. Like Sawyer, then, Lawrence stresses the constructedness of gender. However, and again like Sawyer, she does not extend the analysis of gender as far as it could go. For instance, the poem's use of traditionally masculine terms for the woman offers an opportunity to criticize the binary view of gender, as it undermines the concept of essential female roles altogether. Yet Lawrence does not comment on this possibility.

Another proponent of gender criticism is Ken Stone, who describes the history and purpose of gender criticism as a method.[23] He focuses particularly on the distinction between sex and gender and discusses Butler's

---

21. Lawrence, 'Gender Analysis: Gender and Method in Biblical Studies', pp. 335-36.
22. Lawrence, 'Gender Analysis: Gender and Method in Biblical Studies', p. 337.
23. Ken Stone, 'Gender Criticism: The Un-manning of Abimelech', in Gale Yee (ed.), *Judges and Method: New Approaches in Biblical Studies* (Minneapolis: Fortress Press, 2nd edn, 2007), pp. 183-201.

theory of gender performance. Stone then relates the method to biblical studies. Like Lawrence, he lists central questions that gender critics ask when they interpret biblical texts:

> What norms or conventions of gender seem to be presupposed by this text? ... How are assumptions about gender used in the structure of a particular plot, or manipulated for purposes of characterization? How is gender symbolism related to other types of symbolism used in the text? How does the manipulation of gender assumptions in a text relate to other textual dynamics, including not only literary but also theological or ideological dynamics? Which characters embody cultural gender norms successfully, and which characters fall short of such norms or embody them in unexpected ways? Might a character's success or failure at embodying gender norms result from a strategy to cast that character in a particular light, whether positive or negative? Is the text itself always successful at manipulating gender assumptions? Do biblical texts, like persons, sometimes fail to 'cite' gender conventions in expected ways or according to dominant norms? How does our attention to these and other questions contribute to our understanding of both gender and the Bible?[24]

The questions provide a good starting point for reading biblical texts with gender criticism. They also teach how biblical constructs of gender relate to other dynamics, such as power, symbolic language, and overall textual purpose.

Stone illustrates his theoretical explanations about gender criticism with a reading of Abimelech in Judges 9. Abimelech, like Saul and other men in the Deuteronomistic History, is depicted as performing manhood in inferior ways. Stone shows how the text relates inferiority and powerlessness to femininity and the loss of masculinity. Accordingly, Abimelech is feminized not only by his death at the hands of a woman, but also by being inferior to his half-brothers. His mother is a *pilegeš*, a woman whose relationship to a man is legitimate but inferior to a 'regular' wife. Abimelech's feminization occurs through his secondary status, submission, shame and subordination to other men who perform their gender more successfully than he does. Abimelech's feminization contributes to the portrayal of his leadership as illegitimate, a situation that aligns him with Saul and Jonathan, the other feminized characters against whom the Deuteronomistic historians polemicize.

Finally, the scholar who has most thoroughly and directly advocated for biblical gender criticism is Deryn Guest. Although she regards gender criticism as different from feminist criticism, she finds both compatible with each other. Yet she favors superseding feminist analysis with gender criticism. Her various publications elaborate on the elements of gender analysis,

---

24. Stone, 'Gender Criticism', p. 192.

critique feminist criticism, and give examples of gender analysis as an extension of feminist interpretation.[25] For example, Guest contrasts her gender critical reading with feminist readings of the biblical woman, Jael, as she appears in Judges 4. To several feminist interpreters, Jael exhibits non-normative gender behavior: she has 'masculine' attributes and takes 'masculine' actions, especially in killing Sisera, which Guest describes as a 'rape'. Feminist interpreters have also classified Jael's non-normative behavior as 'gender reversal' or 'gender transgression'. She acts like a 'man'. Yet despite her unusual activity, she is described as 'most blessed of women' in Judg. 5.24.

To feminist interpreters, however, these gender reversals or transgressions are only temporary. Guest challenges this kind of reading, arguing that Jael's characterization illustrates the flexible nature of gender. When feminist readers advance the notion of 'transgression' or 'reversal', they affirm the binary view of gender. Guest thus proposes an alternative reading that she calls a 'genderfuck' reading. It views Jael as entering a space of gender confusion in which she is both a woman and a warrior/rapist. Jael is a character who is beyond the gender binary, perhaps even a character whose gender cannot be pinpointed, and who cannot be contained within the concept of 'woman'. Guest criticizes the existing feminist assumptions of gender, which keep Jael's essential nature as a woman intact even though Jael's behavior and the verbal imperative directed at her in Judg. 4.20 do not limit her to only one gender category. Guest explains: 'Jael is a figure who unsettles and destabilizes, whose performativity provides one of those unintelligible genders which give the lie to ideas of sex as abiding substance'.[26]

Guest expands on these ideas in a book on gender analysis, its history, its potential for biblical studies, and its possible conflict with feminist analysis.[27] She explains in detail why she wants to go beyond a narrowly defined feminist biblical hermeneutic and discusses key issues of gender theory. She criticizes feminist interpreters, including this one,[28] for offering analyses that confirm binary notions about gender and operate within it instead of subverting it. A key element in her proposal is her 'genderfuck' interpretive stance with which she questions and problematizes gender categories as they are depicted in biblical literature. Guest offers an interpretation

---

25. Deryn Guest, 'From Gender Reversal to Genderfuck: Reading Jael through a Lesbian Lens', in Teresa J. Hornsby and Ken Stone (eds.), *Bible Trouble: Queer Reading at the Boundaries of Biblical Scholarship* (Semeia Studies, 67; Atlanta: SBL Press, 2011), pp. 9-44.

26. Guest, 'From Gender Reversal to Genderfuck', p. 18.

27. Guest, *Beyond Feminist Biblical Studies*.

28. In her book *Beyond Feminist Biblical Studies*, pp. 20-21, Guest critiques my article entitled 'Bathing, Status and Gender in Priestly Ritual', in Rooke (ed.), *A Question of Sex*, pp. 66-83.

of the 'pornoprophetic debate' from a genderqueer perspective that questions heteronormativity and allows for the exploration of homoeroticism in prophetic texts. Perhaps most importantly, she suggests that the 'sexual economy' and violence, depicted in the marriage metaphor, reinforce heteronormative views of marriage and stereotypical images of masculinity including that of the divine character. In a nutshell, Guest proposes that biblical scholars, straight or queer, adopt a genderqueer perspective in a genuine way.

Guest also addresses the significance of gender criticism for feminist exegesis. She asks what feminist criticism might lose if it were overtaken by gender criticism. Would feminist exegetical readings disappear from gender critical readings? Would the incorporation of masculinity studies and the recognition of multiple sexualities detract from 'women' and diminish advocacy for women's issues? Would men be seen as an equally oppressed category as women? If 'men' and 'women' are socially constructed and not natural categories, will women, who have been harmed by these ideas, not lose the benefit that comes from basing feminist analysis on them? Other questions relate to the political effects of such a move within academia. Would switching to gender criticism be regarded as less political? Or, as Guest raises, would the feminist study of the Bible lose some of its 'political edge' and 'transformative power' if it became known as 'gender study'?[29] Would gender criticism become a means of 'camouflaging the abandonment of a stigmatized and overtly political "F-word" [feminist], in favor of a more neutral, "respectable" and sweeter sounding G-spot [gender]'.[30] In other words, would scholars speak about 'gender' rather than 'feminism' in order to please university departments, promotion committees, and other powerful entities that see 'feminism' as too political or even unsavory? Yet, Guest recognizes, these concerns and worries might be exaggerated. Most scholars who prefer gender critical readings are often the most politically engaged scholars in the field, interested in changing unjust power imbalances wherever they find them.

In sum, there have been few exegetical studies of the Hebrew Bible that actively engage comprehensive gender criticism in the form described in this chapter. Many studies have used Butler's understanding of gender constructs and gender performativity in fruitful ways, while feminist critics have been slow to engage with the critique of compulsory heterosexuality or the gender binary. To date, gender criticism has been engaged more by LGBTQI critics than by scholars concerned with the status of 'women'. However, Guest's extensive plea in 2012 to move more fully from feminist studies to gender studies is recent, and it seems likely that her work, as

29. Guest, *Beyond Feminist Biblical Studies*, p. 7.
30. Guest, *Beyond Feminist Biblical Studies*, p. 4.

well as the others described here, will influence self-described feminists as it becomes more well-known than it is currently.

'Gender' as 'Women' in Hebrew Bible Scholarship

In contrast to the more complicated and broader views of gender, as employed in gender theory, feminist exegetes have also used the term 'gender' in the sense of 'women'. Some of them have conflated references to 'gender' with 'women' because the female has been the marked sex in Western society. Men have seen themselves as the primary and dominant representations of the human, and so the male gender has not been remarkable but the assumed and dominant norm. 'Man' is the standard whereas 'woman' is the variation, the 'other,' the one marking the difference. To think about gender has thus meant to think about women because women as a group have called attention to sex and gender.

This phenomenon of understanding 'gender' as identical to 'woman' appears in several important early and recent anthologies in feminist biblical studies.[31] One of the earliest is edited by Peggy L. Day and it is entitled *Gender and Difference in Ancient Israel*.[32] The volume contains some essays that describe historical experiences and literary presentations of women. For example, one contributor, Paula S. Hiebert, describes the social and legal situations of widows in biblical and ancient Near Eastern texts. Another contributor, Susan Ackerman, discusses the worship of the 'Queen of Heaven' described in Jeremiah as an illustration of women's religious practice in ancient Israel. Although biblical texts denounce these ritual practices, Ackerman argues that people involved saw them as legitimate. Such practices are also examples of female-led religious rituals. Both exegetes emphasize that biblical authors depict women in different ways, depending on their particular circumstances, but both scholars focus mainly on women.

Other contributors in Day's anthology recognize the constructed discourse about women in biblical literature. For instance, Phyllis Bird outlines the relationship of gendered biblical language and rhetoric to social

---

31. Guest, *Beyond Feminist Biblical* Studies, p. 13, refers to this use of 'gender' as 'weak'. She describes Peggy L. Day's volume (see my discussion below) in this way, and she also mentions two other important volumes that purport to be about 'gender' when they are really about women. The two books are: Phyllis Bird, *Missing Persons and Mistaken Identities: Women and Gender in Ancient Israel* (Minneapolis: Fortress Press, 1997); Victor Matthews, Bernard M. Levinson and Tikva Frymer-Kensky (eds.), *Gender and Law in the Ancient Near East* (JSOTSup, 262; Sheffield: Sheffield Academic Press, 1998).

32. Peggy L. Day (ed.), *Gender and Difference in Ancient Israel* (Minneapolis: Augsburg Fortress Press, 1989).

power by highlighting the rhetorical use of non-standard gendered language. More specifically, she shows that the prophet Hosea refers to men with a verb that is usually reserved for women. The verb, *znh*, is usually translated as 'to play the harlot', 'to fornicate', or 'to be adulterous'. According to Bird, Hosea employs this verb to insult and to belittle idolatrous Israelite men. Her argument illustrates the relationship of gendered biblical vocabulary to male power. This gender-transgressive use of Hebrew roots also occurs when Hosea calls his male Israelite audience 'whores'. By describing men as literary women, biblical authors use gender terminology in non-biological ways. Similarly, Carol Newsom shows that the male author of Proverbs 1–9 creates images of proper and improper females in order to persuade his male audience to behave in a certain way. Yet while the author creates 'discourse' about wisdom and folly, the poetry also threatens to undermine itself, as gender terminology is flexibly employed.

Day's volume was published in 1989, one year before Butler's *Gender Trouble* appeared on the feminist theoretical scene. Yet clearly, Day's contributors understood the socially constructed nature of gender, and they assumed that gender is flexible, inessential, and related to other social dynamics. Still, they did not question heteronormative ideas, and they also did not critique the gender binary or the very category of women. The volume might thus be classified as an example of a 'proto' gender critical approach in feminist biblical studies.

More recent collections exhibit a similar mixed recognition of gender theoretical concerns as they have emerged since the 1990s. Two books, edited by Deborah W. Rooke, stand out, as they feature the term 'gender'.[33] A few of these essays mention gender theoretical concepts. Rooke's essay on gender construction in the sex laws of Leviticus 18 and 20 is one of them. She shows that female relatives turn into a new gendered category of 'pseudo-men' because these women were regarded as unavailable for sexual intercourse with certain men.[34] Rooke understands the constructed nature of gender categories and posits possibilities for gender categories beyond the gender binary. Other essays are more traditionally focused on women. For instance, Tal Ilan investigates the depiction of female characters in the Apocrypha and Pseudepigrapha without grounding her work in any discussion of 'women' as complex, differentiated, and multifaceted

---

33. Deborah W. Rooke (ed.), *A Question of Sex? Gender and Difference in Ancient Israel and Beyond* (Sheffield: Sheffield Phoenix, 2007); Deborah W. Rooke (ed.), *Embroidered Garments: Priests and Gender in Biblical Israel* (Sheffield: Sheffield Phoenix, 2009).

34. Deborah S. Rooke, 'The Bare Facts: Gender and Nakedness in Leviticus 18', in Rooke (ed.), *'A Question of Sex'*, pp. 20-38.

subjects.[35] I single out these works not to challenge their characterization of biblical women but to illustrate that the study of women and the study of gender are not the same because they do not share the same theoretical foundation.

In retrospect, it becomes clear that gender theory offers considerable theoretical insights into universalizing and essentializing views of 'women' or gender. If feminist exegetes ignore gender theory, their works will be too limited, too narrow, and set apart from gender theoretical discussions. It is important that feminist biblical interpreters engage gender theory, recognizing and evaluating assumptions about 'women' and 'men'.

About the Future of Gender Criticism in Feminist Hebrew Bible Studies

The emergence of gender criticism has significantly broadened the inquiry into the nature, purpose, and dynamics of gender. Gender criticism has destabilized the concept of 'women' as a singular, monolithic, or stable category of analysis. Due to the influence of LGBTQI studies, it has also contributed to exposing binary ways of thinking about gender and the prevalence of heteronormative ideologies. Gender analysis takes feminist questions and deconstructs the very categories on which those questions are based. This development has influenced feminist biblical exegetes to varying degrees. Some consider the expanded inquiry into gender as a productive challenge, engaging it despite some reluctance to fully accept gender theoretical concerns. Others use gender criticism to eliminate the notion of 'women' altogether. Still others are entirely untouched by the theoretical debates about gender. In general, then, feminist biblical scholars have both engaged and ignored the extensive theoretical discourse on gender, as it has taken place outside the field of biblical studies.

The emergence of gender criticism presents the opportunity for feminists to reflect on the nature and purpose of their work, to be aware of the problems and possibilities of feminist interpretation, and to clarify their assumptions about sexuality and gender identity. Three areas are especially important for a fruitful encounter with gender theoretical concepts. First, Hebrew Bible exegetes need to become conscious about their use of terminology and references to gender. The emergence of gender criticism has made the nomenclature of gender much more complicated than in the past. Although sometimes the use of 'gender' in biblical publications refers to the social construction of gender, exegetes have far too often conflated it with 'women'. Surely some Bible exegetes will continue to use 'gender' in this limited fashion whereas others are already much more engaged with its

---

35. Tal Ilan, 'Women in the Apocrypha and the Pseudepigrapha', in Rooke (ed.), *'A Question of Sex'*, pp. 126-44.

critical use. Yet, because of the success of gender criticism, biblical exegetes must consider whether their topic is about 'women', 'gender', or sexuality.

Second, as Guest's work suggests, feminist scholars who do not use the term 'gender' in the sense of 'gender criticism' need to be clear about the implicit and explicit politics of their work. Do they study 'gender' instead of 'women' because of the politics of their institution? Do they choose to classify their work as 'gender analysis' rather than 'feminist analysis' because they want to appear less political or perhaps even a-political? Or do they try to avoid engaging theological implications raised by biblical views of gender? These questions pertain to all interpretations, but perhaps they are most crucial for interpretations based on descriptive approaches. On the surface level such readings often do not appear to pursue a political agenda, in contrast to explicitly prescriptive approaches that are more properly called 'feminist'. Yet, to be sure, descriptions of the historical status of Israelite women, of biblical notions of femininity and masculinity, and of the gender of the biblical deity always contain ideological concerns. Usually, however, descriptive studies do not disclose their hermeneutical interests, and they do not make connections with women's lives today. While biblical scholars are certainly not required to disclose their political, theological, or hermeneutical agenda, the lack of openness raises questions about the purpose of their research. It simply cannot be completely divorced from contemporary gender practices, conventions, and inequities. In other words, although descriptive works may seem to avoid political positions, the description itself is a political act. Thus, if scholars use 'gender' in a general way, they must ask why they do so. They also need to consider how their descriptive work relates to contemporary definitions of gender equality and justice for women today, whether in the field of biblical studies or in society at large.

Third, with the influences from LBGTQI and queer studies, the enterprise of 'gender criticism' challenges the assumptions and perspectives of heterosexual feminist interpreters. Gender critics argue that it is insufficient to focus on 'women' or 'gender' without challenging binary notions of gender and the prevalence of heteronormativity. Many feminist exegetes find LGBTQI-informed gender theories helpful and they want to make their research on 'women', 'gender', 'the feminine', and other related topics comprehensive. Yet there are also some feminists who might resist the far-reaching aspects of gender criticism. These feminists may be concerned that the shift from women to 'gender' results in decreased attention to 'women,' especially when their goal has been to restore women to the historical or literary record. Moreover, since women have historically been marginalized as 'women', some feminists may be reluctant to abandon the category of 'women'. They might feel that it would be disingenuous to the experiences of women who were marginalized on the basis of being women. These are legitimate concerns. A combination of both positions might offer a way out of the impasse. Feminist exegetes of all persuasions might agree that it is a good idea to avoid essentializing, binary, and heteronormative assumptions about gender, as well as to keep the focus on 'women'.

Ultimately, another fundamental, more complicated, and more personal concern may underlie the reluctance of some feminist interpreters to embrace gender criticism. Guest maintains that interpreters must adopt a 'genderqueer' perspective, informed by LGBQTI theory, in order to properly do 'gender analysis'. She describes how to make this kind of move, but perhaps it is not as easy as she suggests. Some straight feminists might not agree that LGBQTI concerns relate to their exegetical interests. Others might be reluctant to let go of heteronormative assumptions prescribed by cultural traditions and religious beliefs. Perhaps their reluctance might be due to personal beliefs. Still others might be uncomfortable questioning the gender binary and locating gender identity on a spectrum. Taking on a 'genderqueer' perspective in biblical interpretation involves questioning one's own sexuality and gender identity in ways that some feminists might want to avoid. Thus, they might decide to avoid these aspects of gender criticism in ways that could be unfortunate for both feminist and gender analysis.

In conclusion, biblical exegetes working in the field of gender criticism have sought to clarify whether and how this approach is a form of feminist criticism. To some degree, the answer to those questions will depend upon what one means by 'feminism'. If feminism means, in part, valuing LGBQTI insights, understanding the full range of gendered experiences, and working toward the dismantling and transformation of all oppressive systems, then indeed gender criticism is feminist criticism.

13

Biblical Women as Ideological Constructs Toward Justice: Ideological Criticism as a Feminist/Womanist Method

Tina Pippin

> Ideology…is not a set of deliberate distortions imposed on us from above, but a complex and contradictory system of representations (discourse, image and myth) through which we experience ourselves in relation to each other and to the social structures in which we live.[1]

'Ideology' is a slippery term, at once difficult to define and politically charged. Anyone doing 'ideological criticism' of the Bible is suspected of bringing their own political opinions and commitments to the interpretive process. An ideology runs the risk of being imposed, of smothering a text, or of piling on agendas. Ideological criticism is about exposing either existent or imagined value systems in texts. Ideological criticism hints at its roots in Marxist philosophy, thus bringing ancient texts forward in time and place in ways that cease to be objective and mess up with the authoritative voices of normative historical critical methods. Of course, feminist and womanist interpreters have ideological baggage, stepping out of the normative spaces of biblical scholarship into uncharted territory. These feminists and womanists join with the 'Others' on the margins of the academy to acknowledge social location, politics, and the history of oppressions. All of these groups together bring a thick fog of ideologies as if to hinder the goal of finding the meaning or truth of biblical texts. In this essay I will briefly trace the development of ideological criticism in philosophy and literary theory (and in particular, Marxist feminist theory), and then show the intersections with biblical studies and feminist and womanist readings of the Hebrew Bible. Lastly, I will introduce two newer directions of ideological criticism in reception theory and new materialism.

Negative evaluations of ideological criticism historically derive from Marx, who considered ideology to be a false consciousness upheld as dominant ideology by the ruling classes. Even so, Marx also thought of ideology

---

1. Judith Newton and Deborah Rosenfelt, 'Introduction: Toward a Materialist Feminist Criticism', in Judith Newton and Deborah Rosenfelt (eds.), *Feminist Criticism and Social Change* (New York: Methuen, 1985), pp. xv-xxxix (xix).

in different ways, and used the discussion of ideology in more positive ways to mean the exposure unjust hegemonic relationships. The most basic definition of ideology Marx offers is, 'the production of ideas, of conception, of consciousness' through economics, politics, religion, etc.[2] Ideological critics in biblical studies enter through these debates and societal critiques of texts. Further, as Fredric Jameson notes, ideology can also refer to the unconscious, or political unconscious, of texts.[3] Jameson's definition operates from Louis Althusser's definition of ideology as 'the lived relation between men and their world'.[4] Ideology can be visible and invisible at once, like Schrödinger's cat, alive and dead at the same time, in an indeterminate state. The Ideological Criticism section of the Society of Biblical Literature took up Jameson's approach in the early 1990s.[5]

Defining Ideology

This paradox of ideology as both false consciousness and also uncovering false consciousness is taken further by Gilles Deleuze and Felix Guattari when they say: 'There is no ideology and never has been'.[6] Ideology is uncertainty at the quantum level of a text. Slavoj Žižek pushes the traditional Althusserian understanding. For Žižek, ideology is both interior and exterior to a text. He understands ideology in both Marxist and psychoanalytic (Lacanian) terms. Ideology is both concrete (class struggle) and spectral. In addition, ideology can designate anything from a contemplative attitude that misrecognizes its dependence on social reality to an action-oriented set of beliefs, from the indispensable medium in which individuals live out their relations to a social structure to false ideas which legitimate a dominant political power. It seems to pop up precisely when we attempt to avoid it, while it fails to appear where one would clearly expect it to dwell'.[7] Definitions of ideology go across a continuum of negative to positive connotations.[8] In biblical scholarship, ideology has roots in Marxist

---

2. Karl Marx and Friedrich Engels, *The German Ideology Part One* (New York: International Publications, 2001), p. 47.

3. Fredric Jameson, *The Political Unconscious: Narrative as a Socially Symbolic Act* (Cornell, NY: Cornell University Press, 1982).

4. Louis Althusser, *For Marx* (trans. Ben Brewster; New York: Pantheon, 1970), p. 213.

5. See the essays, along with and interview with Jameson, in David Jobling and Tina Pippin (eds.), 'Ideological Criticism of the Bible', *Semeia* 59 (1992).

6. Gilles Deleuze and Felix Guattari, *A Thousand Plateaus: Capitalism and Schizophrenia* (Minneapolis, MN: University of Minnesota Press, 1987), p. 4.

7. Slavoj Žižek, 'The Spectre of Ideology', in Slavoj Žižek (ed.), *Mapping Ideology* (London: Verso, 1994), pp. 1-33 (3-4).

8. In the critical theory world, some of the main overviews of ideology and ideo-

literary theory but expands to include feminist, womanist, liberation, and postcolonial hermeneutics.⁹ Biblical ideological critics struggle with the

---

logical criticism include: Pierre Macherey, *A Theory of Literary Production* (London: Routledge, 2006); Michel Foucault, *Discipline and Punish: The Birth of the Prison* (trans. Alan Sheridan; New York: Vintage, 1995); Terry Eagleton, *Criticism and Ideology: A Study in Marxist Literary Theory* (London: Verso, 1996); Eagleton, *Ideology: An Introduction* (London: Verso, 1991); Eagleton, *Marxism and Literary Criticism* (London: Routledge, 2003); Fredric Jameson, *The Political Unconscious: Narrative as a Socially Symbolic Act* (Ithaca, NY: Cornell University Press, 1981); Nannerl O. Keohane, Michelle Z. Rosaldo, and Barbara C. Gelpi (eds.), *Feminist Theory: A Critique of Ideology* (Chicago, IL: University of Chicago Press, 1983); Michèle Barrett, *The Politics of Truth: From Marx to Foucault* (Stanford, CA: Stanford University Press, 1991); W.J.T. Mitchell, *Iconology: Image, Text, and Ideology* (Chicago, IL: University of Chicago Press, 1988).

9. Jobling and Pippin (ed.), 'Ideological Criticism'; Christopher Rowland, 'Ideological Criticism', in Stephen L. McKenzie (ed.), *Oxford Encyclopedia of Biblical Interpretation: Volume 1* (New York: Oxford University Press, 2013), pp. 95-96; Itumeleng Mosala, 'The Implications of the Text of Esther for African Women's Struggle for Liberation in South Africa', *Semeia* 59 (1992), pp. 129-37; Gerald West, 'Africa's Liberation Theologies: An Historical Hermeneutical Analysis', in S.D. Brunn (ed.), *The Changing World Religions Map* (Dordrecht: Springer Science+Business Media, 2015), pp. 1971-85; Fernando F. Segovia, 'Reading the Bible Ideologically: Socioeconomic Criticism', in Segovia and Tolbert (eds.), *To Each Its Own*, pp. 283-306; David Penchansky, 'Up for Grabs: A Tentative Proposal for Doing Ideological Criticism', *Semeia* 59 (1992), pp. 35-41; Tina Pippin, 'Ideological Criticism and the Bible', *CRBS* 4 (1996), pp, 51-78; Beverly Straton, 'Ideology', in A.K.M. Adam (ed.), *Handbook of Postmodern Biblical Interpretation* (St. Louis, MO: Chalice Press, 2000), pp. 120-27; The Bible and Culture Collective, 'Ideological Criticism', in *The Postmodern Bible* (New Haven, CT: Yale University Press, 1995), pp. 272-310; Gail Yee, 'Ideological Criticism', in John Hayes (ed.), *Dictionary of Biblical Interpretation* (Nashville, TN: Abingdon Press, 1999), pp. 534-37; Robert P. Carrol, 'On Representation in the Bible: An *Ideologiekritik* Approach', *JNSL* 20 (1994), pp. 1-15; Elsa Tamez, *The Bible of the Oppressed* (trans. M.J. O'Connell; Maryknoll, NY: Orbis Books, 1982); Timothy K. Beal, 'Ideology and Intertextuality: Surplus of Meaning and Controlling the Means of Production', in Danna Nolan Fewell (ed.), *Reading Between Texts: Intertextuality and the Hebrew Bible* (Louisville, KY: Westminster/John Knox Press, 1992), pp. 27-40; Juan Luis Segundo, 'Faith and Ideologies in Biblical Revelation', in Norman K. Gottwald and Richard A. Horsley (eds.) *The Bible and Liberation: Political and Social Hermeneutics* (Maryknoll, NY: Orbis Books, 1993), pp. 92-115; Norman K. Gottwald, 'Social Class and Ideology in Isaiah 40–55: An Eagletonian Reading', in Norman K. Gottwald and Richard A. Horsley (eds.), *The Bible and Liberation: Political and Social Hermeneutics* (Maryknoll, NY: Orbis Books, 1993), pp. 329-42; Itumeleng J. Mosala, 'Biblical Hermeneutics and Black Theology in South Africa', in Norman K. Gottwald and Richard A. Horsley (eds.), *The Bible and Liberation: Political and Social Hermeneutics* (Maryknoll, NY: Orbis Books, 1993), pp. 51-73; Itumeleng J. Mosala, 'A Materialist Reading of Micah', in Norman K. Gottwald and Richard A. Horsley (eds.), *The Bible and Liberation: Political and Social Hermeneutics* (Maryknoll, NY: Orbis Books, 1993), pp. 264-95; Fredric

ambivalence of the text and the ways it has been used to validate and support oppression. Ideological criticism tells stories on the stories or speaks out of turn about sacred texts. All of this can sometimes lead to disparaging the Bible. Even though it takes an interpreter to wield a textual weapon, such texts are not neutral and thus bear part of the responsibility for harm. Walter Benjamin's famous quote sets the stage:

> There has never been a document of culture, which is not simultaneously one of barbarism. And just as it is itself not free from barbarism, neither is it free from the process of transmission, in which it falls from one set of hands into another. The historical materialist thus moves as far away from this as measurably possible. He regards it as his task to brush history against the grain.[10]

Reading against the grain is the primary act of the ideological critic. These acts of rough reading most often occur on the margins and not in mainstream critical circles. Armin Siedlecki explains: 'Ideological criticism is suspicious of any totalizing hermeneutical paradigm, because it is chiefly concerned with the critique of closed systems. As a result, ideology is most often negotiated at the margins—of society or of the text.'[11] Thus, in the field of biblical studies, ideological criticism has direct connections to liberation theologies and hermeneutics.

The definition of ideology takes on further forms in feminist theory. For instance, in materialist-feminist circles Rosemary Hennessey offers a useful

---

Jameson, *The Political Unconscious: Narrative as a Socially Symbolic Act* (Ithaca, NY: Cornell University Press, 1981); Roland Boer, *Marxist Criticism of the Bible* (London: Continuum, 2003); Ken Stone and Teresa J. Hornsby (eds.), *Bible Trouble: Queer Reading at the Boundaries of Biblical Scholarship* (Semeia Studies; Atlanta, GA: Society of Biblical Literature, 2011); Elaine M. Wainwright, David J. Neville, and Jione Havea (eds.), *Bible, Borders, Belonging(s): Engaging Readings from Oceana* (Semeia Studies; Atlanta, GA: Society of Biblical Literature, 2014); Michel Clévenot, *Materialist Approaches to the Bible* (Maryknoll, NY: Orbis Books, 1985); Eryl W. Davies, 'Ideological Criticism', *Biblical Criticism: A Guide for the Perplexed* (New York: Bloomsbury, 2013); David Jobling, *1 Samuel* (Collegeville, MN: Liturgical Press, 1998); Marcina L. Grossman, 'Is Ancient Jewish Studies (Still) Postmodern (Yet)?', *Currents in Biblical Research* 13.2 (2015), pp. 245-83; Laurel Dykstra and Ched Myers (ed.), *Liberating Biblical Study: Scholarship, Art and Action in Honor of the Center and Library for the Bible and Social Justice (vol. 1)* (Eugene, OR: Cascade Books, 2011); Leo G. Perdue and Warren Carter, *Israel and Empire: A Postcolonial History of Israel and Early Judaism* (ed. Coleman A. Baker; New York: Bloomsbury, 2015).

10. Walter Benjamin, *Illuminations: Essays and Reflections* (ed. Hannah Arendt; New York: Schocken Book, 1969), pp. 256-57.

11. Armin Siedlecki, 'The Bible, David Jobling and Ideological Criticism', in Wesley J. Bergen and Armin Siedlecki (eds.), *Voyages in Uncharted Waters: Essays on the Theory and Practice of Biblical Interpretation in Honor of David Jobling* (Sheffield: Sheffield Phoenix Press, 2006), pp. 80-86 (84).

definition of ideology as 'the array of sense-making practices which constitute what counts as "the way things are" in any historical moment'.[12] Here ideology is political and social. Hennessy elaborates on the theory and practice of ideology critique:

> [I]deology critique is a mode of reading that recognizes the contesting interests at stake in discursive constructions of the social. It does so from a committed position within a social analytic whose legitimacy is argued for not on the grounds of its scientific Truth but on the basis of its explanatory power and its commitment to emancipatory social change.[13]

Discourse, and thus text, is a material act, grounded in lived experience. For feminist interpreters ideological criticism forefronts the experiences of women in the complexities and specificities of social locations.

The connection with Marxism and Marxist feminism can be problematic. As Roland Boer and Jorunn Økland explain, Marxism 'provides us with a toolbox that helps us address the contradictions, power issues and veiling ideologies in which we are also trapped, as scholars living and working within "Western", Anglophone contexts'.[14] Together with feminist criticism, Marxist interpretation examines the underlying power structures in both texts and interpretation. Boer and Økland use both a negative understanding of ideology—as something that veils, rather than reveals—and a positive definition of ideology as embedded in a web of social relations. They summarize that 'the various texts of the Bible are inescapably ideological, not because they express certain opinions or positions, but because they are part of the web of human existence'.[15] Using Louis Althusser's explanation of Marxism, they look at the connectedness of the term ideology: '[I]deology is tied up with the Marxist problem of base and superstructure—the base designates economic structures, whereas superstructure refers to areas such as culture, religion, politics, law, and of course, ideology, and both realms relate to one another by means of social relations (class)'.[16] Topics such as, gender, effects, mode of production, divisions of labor, household, sex, ideology, exploitation, and liberation are part of Marxist ideological criticism.

---

12. Rosemary Hennessy, *Materialist Feminism and the Politics of Discourse* (New York: Routledge, 1992), p. 14.
13. Hennessy, *Materialist Feminism*, p. 15.
14. Roland Boer and Jorunn Økland, 'Towards Marxist Feminist Biblical Criticism', in Roland Boer and Jorunn Økland (eds.), *Marxist Feminist Criticism of the Bible* (Sheffield: Sheffield Phoenix Press, 2008), pp. 1-25 (2).
15. Boer and Økland, 'Towards Marxist', p. 16.
16. Boer and Økland, 'Towards Marxist', p. 15.

The inner workings of story, text, canon, and interpretation are not objective sites of Truth, but rather complex spaces of power and oppression and liberation. The Bible and Culture Collective elaborates on this idea:

> As signifying *practice*, the ideology of a text is tied structurally to the ethical push and pull of interpretation... Ideological criticism...has to do with the ethical character of and response to the text and to those lived relations that are represented and reproduced in the act of reading... [I]t demands a high level of self-consciousness and makes an explicit, unabashed appeal to justice.[17]

This concern for justice is intersectional and risk-taking in its intense focus on the connection of reading texts to real existence. The desire for Truth is forever thwarted in ideological criticism, as there are multiple truths that need inclusion in the conversation. These other voices often change the course or question the commitments of ideological readings.

Ideological Criticism in Feminist Hebrew Bible Studies

In biblical studies, ideological criticism had several beginning points, one of which serves as an example of the power of these marginal voices in ideological criticism. Norman Gottwald's *The Tribes of Yahweh* provided a central space for discussion of political rereadings of the history in Joshua and Judges.[18] Robert Allen Warrior then critiqued this whole debate over Exodus and Conquest and how the Israelites settled into the land of Canaan from the point of view of Native Americans and the ideology of the Exodus story as biblical grounds for the conquest of the Americas.[19] Liberation hermeneutics provides a different starting point, examining how a 'text' is always plural or 'texts' and depends on a reader's social location. These reader-centered approaches reveal both the liberative and oppressive histories of biblical texts. Such a concept as 'the ethics of the text' becomes complicated because there is no pure interpretation; all reading is tainted by systemic violence, whether in the story world or in human communities. Andrea Smith follows Warrior's lead with a further indictment: '[C]an any church escape complicity in Christian imperialism?... Hence, all Christian theology, even liberation theology, remains complicit in the missionization and genocide of Native peoples of the Americas'.[20]

---

17. The Bible and Culture Collective, *The Postmodern Bible* (New Haven, CT: Yale University Press, 1995), p. 275.

18. Norman Gottwald, *The Tribes of Yahweh: A Sociology of Liberated Israel 1050–1250 BCE* (Sheffield: Sheffield Academic Press, 1999).

19. Robert Allen Warrior, 'Canaanites, Cowboys, and Indians: Deliverance, Conquest, and Liberation Theology Today', *Christianity and Crisis* 49.12 (September 1989), pp. 261-65.

20. Andrea Smith, 'Dismantling the Master's Tools with the Master's House: Native

Feminist and womanist biblical scholars offer different ways of defining ideology and of doing ideological criticism.[21] For example, Esther Fuchs notes that feminist biblical hermeneutics is, in general, about power: 'the relationship between the production of feminist biblical knowledge and the politics of its guiding theories'.[22] She clarifies that 'feminist epistemology is not only a criticism of ideology, that is, a questioning of the cultural inscriptions of gender hierarchies—it is also a critique of conventional norms and procedures in any given discipline a field of study'.[23] The relationship of feminist and ideological criticisms consists of unmasking power relations and unjust hierarchies, even within a non-dominant group. Fuchs calls for 'a feminist politics of solidarity' as a strategy of critique and as positive change in the discipline of biblical studies.

Fuchs also notes the ever-present ideology of male supremacy and patriarchy. She offers a definition to show how these power relations work: 'Patriarchal ideology does not differ from other hegemonic ideologies in its dependence on the control of the production and consumption of signs, or

---

Feminist Liberation Theologies', *JFSR* (Fall 2006), pp. 85-97 (87). The Bible and Culture Collective asks: 'How can biblical critics read the Bible ideologically without being coopted', see The Bible and Culture Collective, *The Postmodern Bible*, p. 277. They state: 'Ideological criticism, to repeat, must ever be concerned with exposing the discourse-power relations wherever they may be found, especially those at work in their own readings' (p. 282).

21. Athalya Brenner and Carole Fontaine (eds.), *A Feminist Companion to Reading the Bible: Approaches, Methods and Strategies* (Sheffield: Sheffield Academic Press, 1997); Dana Nolan Fewell, 'Reading the Bible Ideologically—Feminist Criticism', in Steven L. McKenzie and Stephen R. Haynes (eds.), *To Each Its Own Meaning* (Louisville, KY: Westminster/John Knox Press, 1999), pp. 268-82; Kathleen Nadeau, 'Asian Liberation Theologies: An Eco-Feminist Approach for a More Equitable and Justice Oriented World', in Stanley D. Brunn (ed.), *World Religion Map: Sacred Places, Identities, Practices and Politics* (Dordrecht: Springer, 2015), pp. 1987-97; Sandra Schneiders, 'Feminist Ideological criticism and Biblical Hermeneutics', *BTB* 19 (1989), pp. 3-10; J. Cheryl Exum, *Fragmented Women: Feminist (Sub)versions of Biblical Narratives* (Valley Forge, PA: Trinity Press International, 1993); David Jobling, 'Feminism and 'Mode of Production' in Ancient Israel: Search for a Method', in David Jobling, Peggy L. Day and Gerald T. Sheppard (eds.), *The Bible and the Politics of Exegesis: Essays in Honor of Norman K. Gottwald on His Sixty-Fifth Birthday* (Cleveland, OH: Pilgrim Press, 1991), pp. 239-51; Katie G. Cannon, *Katie's Canon: Womanism and the Soul of the Black Community* (New York: Bloomsbury Academic, 1998); Jennifer L. Koosed, *The Bible and Posthumanism* (Semeia Studies; Atlanta, GA: Society of Biblical Literature, 2014); Esther Fuchs, 'Biblical Feminisms: Knowledge, Theory and Politics in the Study of Women in the Hebrew Bible', *BibInt* 16 (2008), pp. 205-26; Julye Bidmean, *Introduction to Women in the Near East* (Sheffield: Equinox, 2015).

22. Fuchs, 'Biblical Feminisms', p. 206.

23. Fuchs, 'Biblical Feminisms', p. 209.

what we might call the semiotic economy'.[24] Fuchs investigates the relationship of women and language in the Hebrew Bible, especially in relation to scenes of lying and reception, and the patriarchal representation of women characters, like Rachel in Genesis 31. She calls out traditional patriarchal readings: 'A failure to deal with the political aspect of female deceptiveness in the biblical narrative is both an academic and a political failure'.[25] In another example of the elevation of the biblical bridegroom over the bride, patriarchal ideology has the effect of making women subordinate to men. Fuchs call this characterization 'a literary strategy of biblical patriarchal ideology, the purpose of which is to neutralize, legitimate and promote the legally subordinate position of women'.[26] Thus women characters in the Hebrew Bible are ideological signifiers, and in the hands of patriarchal biblical interpretation are made subordinate to men—by both the biblical text and the contemporary patriarchal interpreters.

Elisabeth Schüssler Fiorenza also provides a context to feminist ideological criticism:

> The new and emerging paradigm of biblical studies...must be named and recognized as engaging in 'emancipatory rhetoric', rather than simply being 'ideological', 'postcolonial', or 'cultural'. This is because, like malestream historical criticism, so also ideology criticism as well as postcolonial and cultural biblical criticism have for the most part not made *wo/men* subjects of interpretation, connected intellectuals, or historical agents central to their theoretical frameworks. Neither have they sufficiently recognized the importance of gender analysis for biblical studies or developed an ethics of interpretation that always takes wo/men's experience into account when analyzing social location and the operations of power within discourse.[27]

Schüssler Fiorenza pulls away from the term 'ideology', noting its patriarchal roots and lack of inclusion of women's voices. Yet in the 1990s, a new generation of feminist and womanist biblical scholars embraced the term ideology, along with a critique of these patriarchal, philosophical roots.

Carol Newsom concurs with her linking of ideological and postcritical readings; both share a postmodern approach to reading the biblical text. Newsom traces the definition of ideology beginning in the nineteenth

---

24. Esther Fuchs, '"For I Have the Way of Women": Deception, Gender, and Ideology in Biblical Narrative', *Semeia* 42 (1988), pp. 68-83 (82).

25. Fuchs, 'Deception, Gender, and Ideology', p. 82. For a discussion of 'the political subtext of a text, or such a text's interpreter', see also Johanna Stiebert, *Fathers and Daughters in the Hebrew Bible* (New York: Oxford University Press, 2013).

26. Esther Fuchs, 'Structure, Ideology and Politics in the Biblical Betrothal Type-Scene', in Athalya Brenner (ed.), *A Feminist Companion to Genesis* (London: T. & T. Clark, 1993), pp. 273-381 (273).

27. Elisabeth Schüssler Fiorenza, *Wisdom Ways: Introducing Feminist Biblical Interpretation* (Maryknoll, NY: Orbis Books, 2001), p. 5.

century and the beginnings of Marxist philosophy. Here ideology meant a type of false consciousness—a way of obfuscating the 'real' world with propaganda: '[T]he task of ideological criticism is to unmask the falsification of reality by ideology... There is no "real". Rather, all that there "is" is representation. It is ideology, all the way down'.[28] In this way Newsom exposes the connection with postmodernism. There is no Truth, only truths. These truths are held by both dominant and marginal interpreters of the Bible. Those on the margins wield ideological criticism to expose power relations. Newsom describes how ideology works:

> Ideology is a term for the symbolic structures of meaning by means of which a society constructs its understanding of the meaningful nature of things...one of the primary functions of ideology is to naturalize a particular state of power and economic relations. Ideology in this sense functions as a kind of theodicy (either secular or religious), allowing both those who benefit from the given social arrangements and those who are disadvantaged by them to see the state of affairs as just or natural or simply inevitable. Ideology provides persuasive explanations for what is experienced, and in this way it continually reproduces the reality that it justifies.[29]

As Newsom points out, different constituencies experience the world from their position in these power arrangements. In other words, biblical readers are socially located in intersectional ways. Mainstream biblical scholarship has a history of being centered in oppressive patriarchal structures. There are no neutral or objective readings, since all readings adhere to certain ideological commitments.[30]

Thus the connections to social-scientific and literary approaches to the text are an integral part of ideological criticism. Cultural critic Mieke Bal's concept of 'ideo-stories' helps describe the roles of women in biblical narratives. Michele Tapp observes: 'Ideo-stories propagate ideologies. If narrated well, these ideologies become so integrated with the narrative that it is impossible to distinguish one from the other without dissecting the text'.[31]

---

28. Carol A. Newsom, 'Reflections on Ideological Criticism and Postcritical Perspective', in Joel M. LeMon and Kent Harold Richards (eds.), *Method Matters: Essays on the Interpretation of the Hebrew Bible in Honor of David L. Petersen* (Atlanta, GA: Society of Biblical Literature, 2009), pp. 541-60 (543).

29. Newsom, 'Reflections on Ideological Criticism', p. 544.

30. See also Carol A. Newsom, 'Woman and the Discourse of Patriarchal Wisdom: A Study of Proverbs', in Peggy L. Day (ed.), *Gender and Difference in Ancient Israel* (Philadelphia: Fortress Press, 1993), pp. 142-60; David J.A. Clines, *Interested Parties: The Ideology of Writers and Readers of the Hebrew Bible* (Sheffield: Sheffield University Press, 1989).

31. Anne Michele Tapp, 'An Ideology of Expendability: Virgin Daughter Sacrifice', in Mieke Bal (ed.), *Anti-Covenant: Counter Reading Women's Lives in the Hebrew Bible* (Sheffield: Sheffield Academic Press, 1989), pp. 157-74 (171).

Ideological criticism is a tool to encounter the nameless and silent (and not so silent) women of the Hebrew Bible. In this same volume Jane Shaw uses Bal's concept of ideo-story to describe the story of Deborah in Judges. She concludes, 'Ideology plays an important part in the cultural construction of gender and the subsequent presentation of such constructions as natural... Ideology does not function independently of the systems in which we are positioned and thus we all, unconsciously or consciously, play a part in its workings'.[32] 'Deborah' is a signifier of multiple meanings, all revolving around her position as 'woman' in the text. She becomes subject and/or object, depending on the location and ideology of the reader. And she remains embedded in a patriarchal text.

Ideological criticism also exposes the hegemonic use of 'woman' as a singular signifier. The struggle against essentializing 'woman' to mean dominant white, western, heterosexual, economically privileged 'woman' continues in feminist biblical interpretation. As a counter narrative, Renita Weems offered one of the first womanist ideology critiques. Her reading of the Hebrew midwives in Exod. 1.8-22 shows the conflicts of interests (slaves and slave-owners) in the text.[33] The midwives, Shiphrah and Puah, refuse to obey Pharaoh, and expose the hegemonic relationships of slave and master and of female and male. They overturn the power structure to save the children and to claim Hebrew superiority over the Egyptians.[34] Also in her work on Gomer, Weems uncovers the complicated ideologies in the marriage metaphor in Hosea and the use of sexual violence as a way of talking about the covenant.[35] Thus, Weems shows that ideological criticism illuminates the multiple vectors in biblical texts from the overlapping and conflicting power relations to the cracks in the dominant structures that allow for liberating actions.

Similarly, Gale Yee uses Judges 17–21 and women's bodies as the platform for exploring ideological criticism. She explains that ideological readings are both intrinsic (what the text says) and extrinsic (the historical,

---

32. Jane Shaw, 'Constructions of Woman in Readings of the Story of Deborah', in Mieke Bal (ed.), *Anti-Covenant: Counter Reading Women's Lives in the Hebrew Bible* (Sheffield: Sheffield University Press, 1989), pp. 113-32 (116-17).

33. Renita J. Weems, 'The Hebrew Women Are Not Like the Egyptian Women: The Ideology of Race, Gender and Sexual Reproduction in Exodus 1', *Semeia* 59 (1992), pp. 25-34.

34. Weems, 'Hebrew Women', p. 32.

35. Renita Weems, 'Gomer: Victim of Violence or Victim of Metaphor?', *Semeia* 47 (1989), pp. 87-104. See also, Renita J. Weems, 'Reading *Her Way* through the Struggle: African American Women and the Bible', in Norman K. Gottwald and Richard A. Horsley (eds.), *The Bible and Liberation: Political and Social Hermeneutics* (Maryknoll, NY: Orbis Books, 1993), pp. 31-50.

social, and political worlds of the text).³⁶ In other words, '[i]deological criticism entails, then, an extrinsic analysis that uncovers the circumstances under which the text was produced and an intrinsic analysis that investigates the text's reproduction of ideology in the text's rhetoric.³⁷ Using sociological and literary methods, ideological critics determine the world of the production of the text. She notes the relationship with Marxist criticism and the move of ideological theorists to 'redefine Marx's relationship between *base* (socioeconomic relations) and *superstructure* (culture, ideology, politics, and legal system), the core insight remains that literature is grounded in historical, real-life power relations. Literature is regarded as an ideological production of social practices'.³⁸ Yee explains: 'The woman's fractured body becomes an ideological symbol of tribal disintegration. As the Levite literally mutilates the body of his wife, the Deuteronomist narratively dismembers the "body" of the tribes.'³⁹

Yee advances her use of ideological criticism in her materialist-feminist investigation of Genesis 2–3, Hosea 1–2, Ezekiel 23 and Proverbs 7.⁴⁰ She includes race/ethnicity, class, gender, sexuality, and postcolonial perspectives so that her interpretation reflects 'a systemic analysis of interlocking oppressions'.⁴¹ More specifically, Yee examines the ideology of woman as evil in the Hebrew Bible, and her study produces a 'double absence' of the mostly silent women in the texts.⁴² She also exposes the history of interpretation that relies on gender stereotypes and ignores the economic and political relations underlying the text.⁴³ For Yee, an ideological reading of Genesis 2–3 demonstrates the concerns of a pre-exilic monarchy that is focused on survival and lineage. For instance, the origin story in Genesis 2–3 lends some voice to the chaos of the economic oppression of taxation during the monarchy'.⁴⁴ At the same time, women's status becomes set in the patriarchal hierarchy. The not-said of the text allows for ideological slippage and women's informal networks of power. Feminist and womanist ideological criticisms center on power and politics, as well as on the complex roles of women across identities and differences. The goal is to transform biblical exegesis.

---

36. Gale A. Yee, 'Ideological Criticism: Judges 17–21 and the Dismembered Body', in Gale A. Yee (ed.), *Judges and Method: New Approaches in Biblical Method* (Minneapolis, MN: Fortress Press, 2nd edn, 2007), pp. 138-60 (138, 142-43).
37. Yee, 'Ideological Criticism', p. 141.
38. Yee, 'Ideological Criticism', p. 139.
39. Yee, 'Ideological Criticism', p. 156.
40. Gale A. Yee, *Poor Banished Children of Eve: Woman as Evil in the Hebrew Bible* (Minneapolis, MN: Fortress, 2003).
   41. Yee, *Children of Eve*, p. 4.
   42. Yee, *Children of Eve*, p. 5.
   43. Yee, *Children of Eve*, pp. 9-28.
   44. Yee, *Children of Eve*, p. 63.

The Ideology of Reception

In more recent years two directions of feminist and womanist ideological criticism have taken place. One is influenced by reception history that also incorporates media and popular culture. The other is shaped by new materialism, i.e. Marxist revisionist theory that explores the nature of human and non-human. In both theoretical positions, the textual object has a history and a current life in culture, and the interactions with the text effect bodies and communities. Past, present, and future existence of the Hebrew Bible are spaces of interpretive encounters, and these encounters are about power and voice. At what point does a biblical text limit, exclude, or do violence to women? Where does it provide a liberating space for women in the line of misogynistic interpretations? In reception theory, biblical 'text' includes multiple existences of the text as it appears in art, music, film, advertising, introductory bible textbooks, or preaching.

Some feminist interpreters examine the afterlives of biblical texts in the reception history (*Rezeptionsgeschichte, Nachleben,* or *Wirkungsgeschichte*). The leading feminist scholar of reception theory, J. Cheryl Exum, traces the ideological representations of women in art, film, and literature. She examines the 'gender ideology' of biblical texts. She describes her process as going beyond the surface structure of the text because 'it limits us to describing and thus to reinscribing, the text's gender ideology'.[45] Exum sends a warning to feminist critiques: 'Since as long as we remain within the "androcentric ideology of the text", we can do no more than describe ancient men's views of women, a feminist critique must, of necessity, read against the grain. It must step outside the text's ideology and consider what androcentric agenda these narratives promote.'[46] Exum asserts that questioning both the text and its interpretations is necessary.[47]

Exum explores readings of biblical women in their 'afterlives' of the Bible. For example, she follows Delilah in Judges and into Cecil B. DeMille's 1949 film, *Sampson and Delilah.*[48] DeMille pushes the boundaries of

---

45. J. Cheryl Exum, *Plotted, Shot and Painted: Cultural Representations of Biblical Women* (Sheffield: Sheffield Phoenix Press, 2nd rev. edn, 2012), p. 88. See also her discussion of gender ideology in *Fragmented Women: Feminist (Sub)versions of Biblical Narratives* (London: T. & T. Clark, 2015), pp. 9-10. On the afterlives of a biblical text, see also Yvonne Sherwood, *A Biblical Text and Its Afterlives: The Survival of Jonah in Western Culture* (Cambridge: Cambridge University Press, 2001).

46. Exum, *Painted*, p. 89.

47. Cheryl Anderson gives a similar reminder to adopt—or not—the ideology of the text. She also points out that there is no monolithic or singular 'gender ideology' in the Hebrew Bible. See Cheryl B. Anderson, *Women, Ideology, and Violence: Critical Theory and the Construction of Gender in the Book of the Covenant of the Deuteronomic Law* (London: T. & T. Clark, 2004), pp. 3-4, 116 n. 102.

48. Cecil B. De Mille (dir.), *Sampson and Delilah* (Paramount Pictures, 1949).

the erotic, portraying Delilah as the ultimate *femme fatale*. Exum notes: 'DeMille is simply exaggerating the gender ideology implicit in the biblical story and other versions of the fabula, pushing it to its (il)logical conclusion. "Bring a woman and she'll bring trouble"'.[49] Through the portrayal(s) of Delilah, the dominant ideological reading becomes that she is dangerous and sexually promiscuous and this danger spills onto all women. Exum sees multiple ideological voices in the Delilah story—of gender, but also of politics and the ideology of Israelite over Philistine.[50] Exum encourages biblical readers to question androcentric readings, but in the end, ideological criticism is a lens to examine all afterlives and their interpretations.

In a similar use of reception theory, Katie Edwards takes readers on a journey into the land of advertising and the endless afterlives of Eve.[51] She traces Eve in the biblical world and in contemporary culture. Eve as a 'cultural icon'[52] is a source of pleasure in ads for perfume, computers, and accessories, and pornography. In her postfeminist appearances, Eve is too often a scantily dressed, seductive *femme fatale*.

Edwards provides a range of images to guide our reading of Eve beyond the biblical text and back. One of them is the ultimate photo-op moment in which Eve's hand on the 'apple' in the Garden of Eden with Adam standing sheepishly nearby. This mythic moment has been copied for thousands of years in stories, art, music, and film. Copies upon copies of Eves, the moment repeating itself in a swirl of seduction, shame, and bold assertion. The images morph, at once subverting the gender binaries and then returning them to their decaying prison. Eve is forever just a while longer in the Garden, beckoning men—and women—into this temporary Paradise. Readers are allowed a glimpse of this freshly created world, but we are barred from entry. Yet we are tempted by a taste of the Edenic forbidden fruit that we will never taste. So time goes backwards and forwards at once; creation becomes the moment of apocalypse, and apocalypse becomes the moment of creation. Eve bears witness to all.

Perhaps the Genesis photo is the first misogynistic advertisement featuring Eve, condemning women to the vagrancies of the male gaze and interpretive power base. The first woman, like most, causes tragedy and destruction, the start of an inevitable apocalyptic doomsday. Eve's story is a fairy tale turned to horror; she is so briefly innocent in Genesis, and this theme is what gets exploited in popular culture. Her innocence is really not so innocent, but often only a trick to lure men to their destruction through

---

49. Exum, *Plotted*, p. 90.
50. Exum, *Plotted*, p. 212.
51. Katie B. Edwards, *Admen and Eve: The Bible in Contemporary Advertising* (Sheffield: Sheffield Phoenix Press, 2012).
52. Edwards, *Admen and Eve*, p. 11.

the women who identify with her. Edwards states: 'In popular culture, Eve becomes the signifier for female sexual temptation as a route to achieving social power'.[53] In so many images, Eve carries her snake companion with her; in fact, they are often entwined. This snake can be revitalized as the goddess wisdom—or Satan—it depends on the retelling. But these various versions are also contaminated with misogynistic, heteropatriarchal, and capitalist propaganda. These remakes of the Eden tale show that Eve has always been irresistible and ripe for consumption. Eve is mostly white and one wonders what happened to the African Eve? She does not age and is always dangerous. She is a beautiful monster. Edwards comments that 'one could argue that male dominance is a thread that runs through the biblical text even before the transgression in Genesis 3'.[54] Yet as popular culture teaches, the attempt to control Eve is ultimately futile.

For the most part, popular culture pushes desire at us in a form of perverted mother-love (going back to Eve as 'the mother of all living'). Taken literally, all these 'Eves' are our original ancestor-mother. All women are Eve, but not quite. We can never be as beautiful or desirable unless, of course, we purchase all those goodies she is hawking in the advertisements. The Eve in the garden did not and could not 'have it all'—she was trapped in a paradise, in a prison-house of language, and image. There was no equality of the sexes in Eden, and Eve gets to drag out these injustices into the larger world. She was never *not* an advertisement, abused by ad-men through the centuries. Edwards notes that '[i]n advertising, offering the forbidden fruit, an apple, is a metaphor for offering the woman's body'.[55] Thus, women's bodies become trapped in a misogynist interpretive cycle.

In a turn toward Marxist theory, Robert Myles investigates 'the intersections of texts and capitalism that function beneath the layers of gendered ideology' in his review of Edwards' book.[56] He claims that Eve's 'image and character can be used in a way that supports not only the ideologies of postfeminism, but also the gendered divisions of labour under capitalism, even if these have transformed dramatically over the past fifty or so years'.[57] 'A central question thus emerges: How is biblical imagery utilized in advertising to obfuscate the social relations of the production of commodities?'[58] The buying and selling of a woman's body, leaving open the possibility

---

53. Edwards, *Admen and Eve*, p. 7.
54. Edwards, *Admen and Eve*, p. 20.
55. Edwards, *Admen and Eve*, p. 66.
56. Robert J. Myles, 'The Commodification of Biblical Texts in Advertising and Contemporary Capitalism', *Bible and Critical Theory* 10.2 (2014), pp. 11-21 (11-12); http://novaojs.newcastle.edu.au/ojsbct/index.php/bct/article/view/599
57. Myles, 'Commodification', p. 14.
58. Myles, 'Commodification', p. 16.

for all women's bodies, underlies much of the reception history of the Eve story.

Conclusion: The Future of Ideology

Although ideological criticism in biblical studies had its main activity in the 1980s and 1990s, its connections with materialist and Marxist criticism continues in many forms. Feminist and postcolonial biblical critics and outright Marxist scholars all rely on the legacy of ideological readings anchored not only in the biblical texts but also in Marxist philosophy of the class struggle and power relations. Theory connects with real, lived experience in these approaches. What matters is place, body, gender/sexuality, economy, politics, ecology, and their relationships. Ideological critics remind us that the Bible is not a singular Text, with one strand of ideology throughout. Subjectivity and voice/s rise up in its interpreters. Readers exist with/in texts, and the texts engage readers in conversations about lived relations.

Thus, there is no 'arrival' at the ultimate meaning of a text. Readers enter into a never-ending journey. The trip has different stops: overlooks, treacherous terrain, dangerous roads and towns, along with the poor, diseased, migrant, slave, conquered, conqueror, wealthy, or powerful. A 'walk' through the Bible takes one through gardens, floods, wars, rituals, violence, family dysfunction, birth, death, stories within stories, apocalypse. The Book also has material: paper, vellum, or digital images, and it is also in material worlds, both 'real' and fictional.

This focus on the material, on matter, is the central feature of New Materialism, including materialist feminism. Marxist feminists have sought gender equality within Marxist philosophy and taken material to include capitalist and patriarchal systems. The economy of women, and women's bodies and lives within economies, was the focus of materialist feminists of the 1960s and 1970s.[59] Agency is a key term and especially necessary for women as they fight oppression. What Marxism gives to feminism is the ability to make transparent the structures of oppression and the space to develop theoretical tools to work for liberation.

---

59. The main beginning sources for materialist feminism include: Christine Delphy, 'A Materialist Feminism Is Still Possible', *Feminist Review* 4 (1980), pp. 79-105; Dorothy Smith, *The Everyday World as Problematic* (Milton Keynes: Open University Press, 1987); Michèle Barrett, *The Politics of Truth: From Marx to Foucault* (Stanford, CA: Stanford University Press, 1991; Rosemary Hennessy, *Material Feminism and the Politics of Discourse* (New York: Routledge, 1993); Rosemary Hennessy and Chrys Ingraham (ed.), *Materialist Feminism: A Reader in Class, Difference, and Women's Lives* (New York: Routledge, 1997). See also Sarah Ahmed, 'Open Forum Imaginary Prohibitions: Some Preliminary Remarks on the Founding Gestures of the "new Materialism"', *European Journal of Women's Studies* 15.1 (2008), pp. 23-29.

Marx, grounded in Hegel's philosophy, created the concept of dialectical materialism, positing that matter stands over mind, so that social change evolves out of the forces of politics, economics, and gender. New materialism calls for further evolution of Marxist philosophy. Diana Coole and Samantha Frost explain the different focus of new materialism away from a dualistic ontology: 'For materiality is always something more than "mere" matter: an excess, force, vitality, relationality, or difference that renders matter active, self-creative, productive, unpredictable'.[60] New Materialism draws on the theoretical writings and critiques of Marx, Nietzsche, Freud, Foucault, Althusser, Deleuze, Lefebvre, and modern science, economics, and political theory.

Elizabeth Grosz relates the crux of the turn toward materialism in feminist theory: 'That is, the challenge facing feminism today is no longer only how to give women a more equal place within existing social networks and relations but how to enable women to partake in the creation of a future unlike the present'.[61] Another of the main feminist new materialists, Rosi Braidotti, envisions a focus on 'difference' (Irigaray, Butler, *et al.*), imagination (Diderot), and post-humanism (Haraway) in new ways that address the shifting challenges in women's lives.[62] She takes a 'nomadic' version of the body and the subject in which bodies cross blurred boundaries of desires and contexts. Accordingly, '[t]he body refers to the materialist but also vitalist groundings of human subjectivity and to the specifically human capacity to be both grounded and to flow and thus to transcend the very variables—class, race, sex, gender, age, disability—which structure us'.[63] New materialism is in dialogue with postmodernism, math and science (especially theoretical physics), and virtual reality. The concern for the human and post-human but also the universe drives new materialist theories. Calls for the death of Marxism and/or postmodernism over the last ten or more years are premature. Morphing has occurred and social movements continue to build, even stronger, in this current age of economic and political and gender inequality.

---

60. Diana Coole and Samantha Frost, 'Introducing the New Materialism', in Diana Coole and Samantha Frost (eds.), *New Materialisms: Ontology, Agency, and Politics* (Durham, NC: Duke University Press, 2010), pp. 1-43 (9). See also Stacy Alaimo and Susan Hekman, 'Introduction: Emerging Models of Materiality in Feminist Theory', in Stacy Alaimo, Susan Hekman and Michael Hames-Garcia (eds.), *Material Feminisms* (Bloomington, IN: Indiana University Press, 2008), pp. 1-22.

61. Elizabeth Grosz, 'Feminism, Materialism, and Freedom', in Coole and Frost (eds.), *New Materialsms*, pp. 139-57 (154).

62. Rick Dolphijn and Iris van der Tuin, 'Interview with Rosi Braidotti', in Rick Dolphijn and Iris van der Tuin (eds.), *New Materialism: Interviews and Cartographies* (Ann Arbor, MI: Open Humanities Press, 2012), pp. 19-37 (28).

63. Dolphijn and van der Tuin, 'Braidotti', p. 33.

What all of these philosophical and critical theory happenings have to do with feminist ideological criticism of the Bible is that biblical scholars continue the interdisciplinary conversations that have consequences for subverting white, male, Eurocentric, heteropatriarchal biblical scholarship. Ideological criticism reminds us that reading is an ethical act, and that interpretation has political consequences. Traditional methods of history, archeology, textual, form, or source criticisms still remain conversation partners, and their multiple but often slowly changing hypotheses cannot be ignored. Literary critics, deconstructionists, and postcolonialists share a common schooling in the mainstream before venturing to and/or from the borderlines. These paths are not as sparsely travelled in recent years, and are filled with new voices.[64] Randall C. Bailey points to the need for ideological criticism to be a central part of (teaching) exegesis, 'most notably Afrocentric, Womanist/feminist, and Queer studies'.[65] Bailey draws on Mary Ann Tolbert's seminal article on Protestant women being taught to read like men,[66] and thus calls out the dominance of white supremacist readings of biblical texts. He calls for biblical exegetes to foreground 'the needs of oppressed people living in genocidal conditions in the twenty-first century'.[67]

The 'preferential option' of the oppressed calls for the intersectionality of voices and approaches to biblical interpretation, and ideological criticism provides one theoretical lens to read under the surface of the biblical text. Ideological criticism helps to make transparent the uses and abuses of the Bible, especially as seen by women in their different locations in and out of the text. Biblical women remind us of different ideologies and the ways these ideologies shape our world. Biblical women also call on the reader to question and critique inequality and injustice. They provoke readers to invent new worlds and imagine new ideological stances that embody justice. And with the tools of womanist and feminist ideological criticism, biblical readers continue to hear these textual voices and address the challenges in new ways.

---

64. R.S. Sugirtharajah (ed.), *Voices from the Margins: Interpreting the Bible in the Third World* (Maryknoll, NY: Orbis Books, 2006); R.S. Sugirtharajah (ed.), *The Postcolonial Bible Reader* (Oxford: Blackwell, 2006).

65. Randall C. Bailey, 'Teaching Exegesis Using New Literary and Ideological Criticisms', *Teaching Theology and Religion* 17/2 (April 2014), pp. 150-54 (150).

66. Mary Ann Tolbert, 'Protestant Feminists and the Bible: On the Horns of a Dilemma', in Alice Bach (ed.), *The Pleasure of Her Text: Feminist Readings of the Biblical and Historical Texts* (Peabody, MA: Hendrickson, 1990), pp. 3-23.

67. Bailey, 'Teaching Exegesis', p. 154.

14

DEALING WITH EMPIRE AND NEGOTIATING HEGEMONY:
DEVELOPMENTS IN POSTCOLONIAL
FEMINIST HEBREW BIBLE CRITICISM

Jeremy Punt

Compliance and resistance to imperial powers are evident in the Hebrew Bible, and have nudged feminist scholars increasingly to use postcolonial theory. Steering away from personal proclivities regarding the best use of postcolonial work or what postcolonial work may or may not entail, I start with some general parameters of the postcolonial optic. The essay then traces the intersections between feminist and postcolonial analysis, as well as the use of postcolonial criticism in feminist biblical readings. Amidst a changing biblical interpretation landscape, postcolonial criticism has gained more currency among New Testament than Hebrew Bible scholars.[1] Yet postcolonial feminist interpretation is gaining significant ground in Hebrew Bible studies and the main section of this essay elaborates on the various twists and turns this work has taken so far. The discussion of postcolonial feminist work demonstrates that feminist readings consist of a diverse range of feminist approaches, hermeneutics, and methods. A conclusion outlines future possibilities in the development of postcolonial feminist approaches to the Bible.

Conceptualizing Postcolonialism

The fact that imperialism and patriarchy intersect cannot be ignored, and postcolonial feminist scholars emphasize the complex and intricate

---

1. So e.g. Bradley L. Crowell, 'Postcolonial Studies and the Hebrew Bible', *Currents in Biblical Research* 7 (2009), pp. 217-44 (218); Joerg Rieger, 'Responses to Miles, Perdue, West and Boer', in Roland Boer (ed.), *Postcolonialism and the Hebrew Bible: The Next Step* (Semeia Studies; Atlanta: SBL, 2013), pp. 261-72 (261). However, Roland Boer reckons that 'postcolonial approaches to the Bible were first broached by Hebrew Bible scholars', although acknowledging that the postcolonial analysis 'initiative has clearly been taken up by New Testament scholars'; see his 'Introduction', in Roland Boer (ed.), *Postcolonialism and the Hebrew Bible: The Next Step* (Semeia Studies. Atlanta: SBL, 2013), pp. 1-7 (1).

association and interaction between the two. They assert that the analysis of one without the other is inadequate. As Kwok Pui-lan explains: 'Those male postcolonial critics who leave out gender run the risk of overlooking that colonialism involves the contest of male power and that patriarchal ideology is constantly reshaped and reformulated in the colonial process. On the other hand, those feminist critics who isolate gender from the larger economic and colonial context court the danger of providing a skewed interpretation that tends to reflect the interests of the socially and economically privileged'.[2] In this sense, then, the classification of the first element in 'postcolonial feminist criticism' is appropriate.

The meaning and use of the terms postcolonial, postcoloniality, and postcolonialism—sometimes used in hyphenated form—are contested,[3] and it is thus not easy to agree on their definition. However, a general explanation about the broad parameters helps to orientate the debate. The postcolonial label must be understood as being grounded in both a historical and a political position, as explained by Susan V. Gallagher and Roland Boer in their book on postcolonialism in biblical studies.[4] On the one hand, a chronological marker of a certain form of historical colonialism comes to a messy end in the 1960s that has, however, lingering effects. It is accompanied by neocolonialism in innovative and disastrous new guises. On the other hand, the postcolonial is a critical theoretical stance and analytical approach.[5] Sometimes scholars claim that postcolonial studies addresses 'nations' and political power formations, in general and excludes issues of race, gender, or sexual orientation.[6] Others argue that '[p]ioneers of postcolonial criticism

---

2. Kwok Pui-Lan, 'Making the Connections: Postcolonial Studies and Feminist Biblical Interpretation', in Rasiah S. Sugirtharajah (ed.), *The Postcolonial Biblical Reader* (London: Blackwell, 2006), pp. 45-63 (48).

3. The terminological struggle still prevails on a widespread level, including literary, historical and not only biblical studies. Other ideological critical yet differently oriented hermeneutical approaches have been developed in recent decades, such as feminist studies, decolonizing studies, imperial studies, liberation hermeneutics, and various others; see Gale Yee, 'Postcolonial Biblical Criticism', in T.B. Dozeman (ed.), *Methods for Exodus* (Cambridge: Cambridge University Press. 2010), pp. 193-233 (205).

4. Susan V. Gallagher, 'Introduction', in Susan V. Gallagher (ed.), *Postcolonial Literature and the Biblical Call for Justice* (Jackson: University Press of Mississippi, 1994), pp. 1-33 (2); Boer, 'Introduction', p. 2.

5. The extent to which the distinction between postcolonial criticism ('reading strategies examining economic, cultural, and political relations of domination and subordination between nations, races, and cultures with histories of colonial and neocolonial rule) and postcolonial theory (with 'banal theory, jargonized language infantile radical one-upmanship, tiresome self-obsessiveness, and bloated theory' deriving from French theorists likes Derrida, Lacan, or Foucault) can be sustained, is questionable; see Yee, 'Postcolonial Biblical Criticism', pp. 194-95.

6. Georg M. Gugelberger, 'Postcolonial Cultural Studies', in M. Groden and

are from the outset also seeking to make alliances with those subjected to and seeking liberation from sexual, racial, colonial, and class domination'.[7] Notwithstanding this debate, Kwok is probably correct in claiming that '[a]lthough the works of postcolonial male critics may include some discussion of women's scholarship, gender remains a marginal issue in their overall analysis'.[8]

Postcolonial work concerns itself with social formation and analysis as well as cultural production, and therefore it constitutes an attempt to rewrite history. Postcolonialism also posits a reflective modality that allows for a critical rethinking[9] of historical imbalances and cultural inequalities established by colonialism.[10] Postcolonial work articulates the desire of subjugated people regarding their sense(s) of identity and self-determination, and it also poses a counter-offensive against political, economic and cultural forms of imperialism,[11] without neglecting aspects of gender, sexuality and ethnicity.[12]

M. Kreiswirth (eds.), *The Johns Hopkins Guide to Literary Theory & Criticism* (Baltimore/London: The Johns Hopkins University Press, 1994), pp. 581-85 (582).

7. Richard A. Horsley, 'Introduction: Krister Stendahl's Challenge to Pauline Studies', in Richard A. Horsley (ed.), *Paul and Politics: Ekklesia, Israel, Imperium, Interpretation: Essays in Honor of Krister Stendahl* (Harrisburg, PA: Trinity Press International, 2000), pp. 1-16 (10). Rasiah S. Sugirtharajah also argues that the overlapping issues of race, empire, diaspora and ethnicity have indeed been included in the hermeneutical agenda of postcolonialism; see his essay 'Biblical Studies after the Empire: From a Colonial to a Postcolonial Mode of Interpretation', in Rasiah S. Sugirtharajah (ed.), *The Postcolonial Bible* (Bible and Postcolonialism, 1; Sheffield: Sheffield Academic Press, 1998), pp. 12-22 (15). Also see Musa W. Dube who adds religion, gender, and nation into the mix; see her essay '"Woman, What Have I To Do With You?" A Post-Colonial Feminist Theological Reflection on the Role of Christianity in Development, Peace and Reconstruction in Africa', in Isabel A. Phiri, Kenneth R. Ross and James L. Cox (eds.), *The Role of Christianity in Development, Peace and Reconstruction* (Nairobi: All Africa Conference of Churches, 1996), pp. 244-58 (249). It is interesting that Dube is one of the few voices who includes 'religion' as a hegemonic category.

8. Pui-lan Kwok, 'Making the Connections', p. 47.

9. 'Post' should not conjure up amnesia or repetition, but rather 'a procedure in "ana-", including analysis, anamnesis, anagogy and anamorphosis which elaborates an "initial forgetting"'; see Leela Gandhi, *Postcolonial Theory: A Critical Introduction* (New York: Columbia University Press, 1998), p. 174, referring to Lyotard.

10. Gandhi, *Postcolonial Theory*, p. 176.

11. See Annemarie Carusi, 'Post, Post and Post: Or, Where Is South African Literature in All This?', in Ian Adam and Helen Tiffin (eds.), *Past the Last Post: Theorizing Post-Colonialism and Post-Modernism* (New York: Harvester Wheatsheaf, 1991), pp. 95-108 (95-96).

12. See Jeremy Punt, 'Postcolonial Biblical Criticism in South Africa: Some Mind and Road Mapping', *Neotestamentica* 37 (2003), pp. 59-85. Postcolonial biblical studies is an 'ideological reflection on the discourse and practice of imperialism and colonialism

I argued elsewhere that postcolonial biblical hermeneutics as a multidimensional theoretical approach provides many conspicuous gains.[13] More than other approaches, a postcolonial biblical hermeneutic recognizes inherent tensions identified in texts and the production of meanings without invoking or reverting back to binaries. It thus accounts for complex relationships of power as identified in reading texts and contexts.[14] The postcolonial endeavour goes beyond an accusatory mode and does not insist on the absolution of guilt. Postcolonial work reacts to guilt which result when imperialist or colonialist perpetrators subjugate others. It also reacts to implicated guilt—that is when the previously subjugated re-establish new or replacement structures of privilege and want, apparently oblivious to hegemonic patterns criticized previously. Postcolonial analysis brings into focus relationships built upon unequal power at geo-political and local or subsidiary levels. It emphasizes the complex yet co-constituting interrelationships between the powerful and the marginalized. A postcolonial optic, with ancient or contemporary alignment, focuses on framing and investigating hegemony, construing and analysing power relations in, through, and of texts. In short, postcolonial work is averse to exclusivist binaries and instead highlights mimesis and hybridity in postcolonial settings. It makes theoretical perspectives available with which to address pressing and lingering tensions in and around texts, but without the predisposed tendency to reverse alienation, marginalization, or disenfranchisement.

Important Contributions to Postcolonial Feminist Interpretation

Postcolonial analysis is often found across three important areas of investigation, all of which are legitimate angles of inquiry. Much postcolonial work on the Bible concerns the investigation of biblical texts as artefacts from contexts

from the vantage point of a situation where imperialism and colonialism have come—by and large but by no means altogether so—to a formal end but remain very much at work in practice, as neoimperialism and neocolonialism'; see Fernando F. Segovia, 'Biblical Criticism and Postcolonial Studies: Towards a Postcolonial Optic', in Rasiah S. Sugirtharajah (ed.), *The Postcolonial Bible* (Bible and Postcolonialism, 1; Sheffield: Sheffield Academic Press, 1998), pp. 49-65 (51 n. 3).

13. Jeremy Punt, *Postcolonial Biblical Interpretation: Reframing Paul* (STAR, Leiden: Brill, 2015).

14. So while '[p]ostcolonial biblical criticism…analyzes the factors of economic and cultural expansion, domination, and exploitation as major forces of production of the biblical texts under the colonial rule of different empires in antiquity', is interested in 'Israel's relations with the empires', uncovering 'the subaltern or marginalized lives and voices', foregrounding 'the unequal and exploitative relations between the imperial and the colonial in ancient and modern times'; see Yee, 'Postcolonial Biblical Criticism', p. 195. In other words, postcolonial work is well poised to move beyond the anti-empire stance to address the co-constitutive nature of empires, then and now.

of empire, hegemony, and suppression, and such work is sensitive to struggles and resistance in contexts of unequal power.[15] Similar to other approaches, a postcolonial optic is more profitable in studying certain Hebrew Bible texts than others. For example, as much as a narrative-critical approach may be more feasible, even if not exclusively so, for the historically oriented books of the Hebrew Bible and less so for poetic structures, so too is postcolonial interpretation likely to be more advantageous for texts originating in an environment shaped by power differentials at the geo-political level.[16] At a second level, postcolonial work also addresses how biblical texts have been co-opted and made serviceable to Western imperial interests over many centuries. And finally, a postcolonial optic is useful for framing and making sense of biblical interpretation in the Two Thirds World.[17]

My attention is on postcolonial feminist Hebrew Bible scholars who have focused on the first textual oriented level, although the boundaries

---

15. The neglect of such dimensions are getting more attention: 'The tensions between empire, colonialism, and various forms of resistance are so deeply engrained in many of these texts that one wonders how we were able to interpret them for so long without noticing those tensions'; see Rieger, 'Responses', p. 261.

16. However, space does not allow questions such as the following to be addressed here: What to do when power differentials are considered at less broad than geo-political level? Or is the point of departure rather that power differentials at the micro-level in any case resemble those at macro-level? Can and how would postcolonial interpretation engage a text like Song of Songs?

17. See Kwok, 'Making the Connections', pp. 46-47. Also see Yee, 'Postcolonial Biblical Criticism', pp. 204-209. Although Richard A. Horsley uses a similar threefold typology for framing postcolonial work on biblical texts, his characterization of the first element, namely on the understanding of the biblical texts as colonial, unnecessarily limits the range of investigations undertaken on how biblical texts function in and even reflect their originating socio-historical contexts of empire and/or hegemony; see his essay '"It Is More Complicated": Reflections on Some Suggestive Essays', in Roland Boer (ed.), *Postcolonialism and the Hebrew Bible: The Next Step* (Semeia Studies; Atlanta: SBL, 2013), pp. 241-60 (242). In fact, Horsley, admits elsewhere that postcolonial work is helpful also in showing that biblical texts are or were not what they became in colonial appropriation, and that a postcolonial optic can open up and give voice to submerged histories and the voiceless of the texts; see his essay 'It Is More Complicated', p. 243. Crowell agrees when he claims that postcolonial work investigates the role of empire and its effects on society and literature. He examines how colonial empires interpreted the Bible, how indigenous and colonized populations interpreted it, and how empires and reactions to them shaped their use of the Bible; see Crowell, 'Postcolonial Studies', p. 217. Musa W. Dube makes it simple and clear that the postcolonial '[a]s used in literature… seeks to highlight the role of texts in the power struggles of imperialism between the dominated and the dominators'; see her essay 'Jumping the Fire with Judith: Postcolonial Feminist Hermeneutics of Liberation', in Sylvia Schroer and Sophia Bietenhard (eds.), *Feminist Interpretation of the Bible and the Hermeneutics of Liberation* (JSOTSup, 374; London: Sheffield Academic Press, 2003), pp. 60-76 (64 n. 12).

between the three areas are often blurred. New Testament scholar Musa Dube is one of the earliest postcolonial feminist voices in biblical studies.[18] In her scene-setting monograph on postcolonial feminist interpretation, she explains her interpretive framework. She investigates the literary-rhetorical strategies employed by imperial or colonial powers in their anti-conquest ideologies.[19] Although three other strategies are also important, the use of female gender as an expression of subjugation and oppression is central to Dube. She shows that the Exodus-Joshua narratives are constructed around the notion that the Israelites are God's chosen people and entitled to conquer the land belonging to other peoples, and they do so with divine sanction. Yet within this colonizing strategy, patriarchy constantly intersects with imperialism, to the extent that the colonizer-colonized relationship is ultimately perceived as male-female.[20] Foreign women who represent the status of the land are the biggest threat to the Israelites, to their unity and to purity and entitlement.[21] Dube's work is typical of postcolonial feminism as it has emerged in recent years. The most enduring trait relates to the range(s) of intersectionality between imperialism and patriarchy, as well as among power, gender, and sexuality.[22]

Five approaches characterize the current state of postcolonial feminist approaches to Hebrew Bible. The following provides a brief outline and relevant publications on them.

Approach One:
The Intersection of Colonization and Gender

Colonization has always been heavily invested in scripting gender in terms of roles and identity. A 2012 anthology focused on Africa investigates this

---

18. Musa W. Dube, *Postcolonial Feminist Interpretation of the Bible* (St. Louis: Chalice Press, 2000).

19. Brett argues that biblical narratives were used in the past to authorize and justify colonization but such use inverted biblical narratives that are inherently anti-imperial texts; see Mark G. Brett, *Decolonizing God: The Bible in the Tides of Empire* (Bible in the Modern World; Sheffield: Sheffield Phoenix Press, 2008). For a different explanation, see Jeremy Punt, *Postcolonial Biblical Interpretation*. See also the discussion of ambivalence, mimicry, and hybridity in Yee, 'Postcolonial Biblical Criticism', pp. 196-205.

20. Conversely, the fight against imperialism while leaving patriarchy intact, along the lines of the 'first things first' strategy promoted by African-American males in the civil rights struggle of the 1960s, is detrimental to the cause of liberating interdependence. This position does not entail that patriarchy and imperialism are equated or made interdependent; see Dube, 'Jumping the Fire with Judith', pp. 69-70.

21. Dube, *Postcolonial Feminist Interpretation*, pp. 66-76.

22. These authors and publications are reflective of a broad range of postcolonial feminist perspectives and cannot be fully discussed here.

phenomenon, or what can be called gendered colonization, as one particularly significant focus area in biblical interpretation. An anthology edited by Musa Dube, Andrew M. Mbuvi, and Dora Mbuwayesango signals developments in the feminist and postcolonial intersections. Already in the introduction to the book, Dube points to the notion of gendered colonialization: 'In... extremely gendered colonial language, the African continent was being penetrated by the West, its male subjugator, and inseminated with Western seed to give birth to the Westernized African'.[23]

Yet not all of the contributions are shaped by feminist and gender-focused readings. What holds the book together is the postcolonial optic as the backbone of the discussion that regularly intersects with gender concerns. The editors arranged the different chapters according to categories such as 'African Feminist/Gender-Based Biblical Interpretations', 'Colonized Bible: Re-reading the Colonial Translated Bibles', Scrambling for the Land: Reading the Bible and Land', Afrocentric Biblical Interpretations', Biblical Interpretations for Reconstruction', 'Social Engagement and Biblical Interpretations', and 'Embodiment and Biblical Interpretation in the HIV/AIDS Context'. The categories indicate concerns that encapsulate gender, race, and power issues, and the very identification of these topics and themes shows the extent to which the Bible signifies and is signified in Africa.[24] The volume represents feminist and postcolonial work in its immense diversity rather than the explicit or conscious theorizing of such work. The social locations of the contributors are consciously or unwittingly incorporated and articulated. In other words, gender is an important concern among many but does not stand at the centre of this postcolonial publication in African biblical studies.

Yet some contributions show exactly the importance of gender in postcolonial studies. For instance, Lynne Darden refers to her social location as a feminist as the hermeneutical lens that employs Dube's notion of Rahab's prism to negotiate a conversation between the African continent and diasporic people of African descent.[25] It is Rahab's middle position, being both inside and outside, 'living in-between continuity and discontinuity,

---

23. Musa W. Dube, 'Introduction', in Musa W. Dube, Andrew M. Mbuvi, and Dora Mbuwayesango (eds.), *Postcolonial Perspectives in African Biblical Interpretations* (Global Perspectives on Biblical Scholarship, 13; Atlanta: Society of Biblical Literature, 2012), pp. 1-26 (2). Dube even states that 'Africa, surrounded by suitors, did not have the choice to choose a suitor nor to refuse one', which means that 'it was indeed a gang rape'; see Dube, 'Introduction', p. 3.

24. See, e. g., Vincent L. Wimbush (ed.), *Theorizing Scriptures: New Critical Orientations to a Cultural Phenomenon* (New Brunswick, NJ; London: Rutgers University Press, 2008).

25. Dube identifies her reading lens as 'Rahab's prism'; see Dube, 'Jumping the Fire with Judith', pp. 73-74.

acceptance and rejection, life and death, and dream and nightmare'[26] that appeals to Darden. Furthermore, Rahab's prism allows the privileging of marginal social locations, and so Darden uses the self-same prism to read back to Rahab. She interprets Rahab's request of the Israelites as showing mercy to her family in Josh. 2.13 and as an indication of Rahab's less than marginalized status. 'She schemes like an elitist who is only interested in preserving her family's wealth and position.'[27] Thus, to Darden, Rahab manipulates people and especially men. As a 'sexual deviant' who morphs into 'ancestor of the king of the Israelite nation',[28] Rahab chooses colonization above annihilation. In other words, Darden depicts Rahab as an embodiment of the postcolonial position; it is a negotiated identity caught between the push and pull of empire.

Uriah Kim uses traditional historical and literary readings to explain how, in Judges the role of women, and of Israelite women in particular, was tied to the identity of men, and of Israelite men in particular.[29] Judges ends with the horrific tales of Israelite men 'subjugating their women in order to give identity to the land and themselves'. However, the ending of Judges does stand somewhat in contrast to the otherwise important role women play in this text. Another reversal of imperial logic in Judges is that instead of portraying the self as strong and the others as weak, incompetent and sinful, the enemies are depicted as intimidating and the Israelites as tricksters. The moral and religious superiority of the Israelites remains in doubt, often acting as immoral and violent as their opponents with the unfaithfulness to Yahweh, epitomized by their chasing after foreign gods and foreign women. All in all, it is women who provide the resolution: 'It is only by subjugating women, either Israelite or foreign, that the sons of Israel can recover their manhood (therefore their identity), which is lost when they

---

26. Lynne Darden, 'Hanging out with Rahab: An Examination of Musa Dube's Hermeneutical Approach with a Postcolonial Touch', in Musa W. Dube, Andrew M. Mbuvi and Dora Mbuwayesango (eds.), *Postcolonial Perspectives in African Biblical Interpretations*, pp. 63-71 (64).

27. Darden, 'Hanging out with Rahab', p. 71.

28. Darden, 'Hanging out with Rahab', p. 71.

29. Uriah Y. Kim, 'Is There an "Anticonquest" Ideology in the Book of Judges?', in Roland Boer (ed.), *Postcolonialism and the Hebrew Bible: The Next Step* (Semeia Studies; Atlanta: SBL, 2013), pp. 109-28 (126-27). Kim follows Dube in identifying four literary-rhetorical depictions of 'anticonquest' ideology, which he characterizes as 'conquest-denial' or 'conquest-masking' ideology that authorizes travel, constructs colonized others, constructs the colonizer-self, and uses female gender to foment domination and subjugation. Dube uses the Exodus narratives to explain her interpretive framework; see Dube, *Postcolonial Feminist Interpretation*, pp. 60-83. It would be a mistake to view these strategies as independent or separate strategies because they intersect with each other.

are dominated by the other men of empires'.[30] The roles accorded to women and the treatment they receive in Judges, is testimony to the connection between imperialism and patriarchy.

Darden's and Kim's interpretation stress the intersection of the power plays between colonization and gendered social structure of patriarchy. They highlight the ambivalence and double-sided nature of life, power, and identity in imperial times and the negotiated nature of life in empire.

Approach Two: Colonial Domination and
Subordination Invoking Divine Agency and Sanction

Postcolonial feminist Bible scholars make another important point. They observe that people living in colonized contexts often invoke God in response to their unjust experiences under empire. The dynamic of invoking divine agency and sanction becomes clear in another book on postcolonial and feminist approaches, edited by Carolyn J. Sharp and Christl M. Maier.[31] The included essays employ either postcolonial or feminist approaches, theorizing about them but not necessarily or consistently interrelating them.[32] Yet, the essays also theorize and illustrate the intersections and various interrogations of the two approaches on a range of historical, literary, and ideological observations. The volume focuses on Jeremiah although women do not feature significantly in this biblical book.[33] Exploring the Bible as a complex cultural production, Maier and Sharp question its androcentric bias as well as the normalization and naturalization of biblical scholarship's phal-

---

30. Kim, 'Is There an "Anticonquest" Ideology in the Book of Judges?', p. 127.

31. Christl M. Maier and Carolyn J. Sharp (eds.), *Prophecy and Power: Jeremiah in Feminist and Postcolonial Perspective* (Library of Hebrew Bible/Old Testament Studies, 577; London: Bloombury, 2013).

32. Feminist scholars use narrative, deconstructive, and reader-response criticism. They also allude to the epistemological and advocacy links between feminist, postcolonial, womanist, and queer criticism and disability; see Christl M. Maier and Carolyn J. Sharp, 'Introduction', in Christl M. Maier and Carolyn J. Sharp (eds.), *Prophecy and Power: Jeremiah in Feminist and Postcolonial Perspective* (Library of Hebrew Bible/ Old Testament Studies, vol. 577; London: Bloomsbury, 2013], pp. 1-18 [9-10]). Kwok Pui-Lan and Musa W. Dube combine feminist and postcolonial insights in their works referenced in various places in my essay.

33. Except for a few metaphors, such as Israel as unfaithful wife or as Daughter of Zion or Rachel weeping for her children (Jeremiah 31), the disapproving portrayal of Judean women's leadership (Jeremiah 44) and the stereotypical gendered shaming of foreigners in the oracles against the nations, Jeremiah shows little interest in women's bodies, cultural and social roles, and spiritual experiences; see Carolyn J. Sharp, 'Mapping Jeremiah as/in a Feminist Landscape: Negotiating Ancient and Contemporary Terrains', in Christl M. Maier and Carolyn J. Sharp (eds.), *Prophecy and Power*, pp. 38-56 (39).

locentric assumptions.³⁴ The editors also emphasize various aspects related to postcolonial and feminist readings. They point to postcolonial resonances in the language of imperialism and resistance, the construction of Jeremiah's identity, and Judah's status as subaltern. It becomes clear that, in the past few decades, feminist exegetes have identified in Jeremiah's gendered imagery both the speaking subject and the Judean body politic, as well as the gendered presentation and treatment of deities in the text.³⁵

Some contributors deliberately sought out intersections between postcolonial and feminist emphases. For instance, Else K. Holt deals with Jeremiah 2–3, which has been a particularly problematic text in feminist exegesis.³⁶ The biblical passage portrays God as an angry, abusive, and violent father who beats his children and abuses his wife. The poem depicts God as a deity whose justice is retributive and whose mercy requires submission. In short, the poem's imperialism shows the gendered nature of hegemony at various levels. For instance, Holt maintains that the abusive and misogynistic images in Jeremiah are not only dangerous to its female readers. They are also 'misandric' by shaming men because the texts originally addressed a male audience.³⁷ Yet Holt does not stop here but also looks for alternatives to deal with a text that portrays God as an abusive father and parent who emasculates male listeners by turning them into sexually insatiable, unfaithful women. She also criticizes the depiction of God as controlling, jealous, abusive, and violent. Holt does not deny the offensive nature of such imagery, and she also does not favour the removal of Jeremiah 2–3 from the canon, as if the poem were irredeemable due to its misanthropical tone and perverted images of God. Rather, Holt appeals to the biblical tradition of critical intra-textual dialogue, suggesting that the Bible as a whole endorses dialogue. She explains: 'The authority of the Bible is

---

34. Maier and Sharp, 'Introduction', pp. 3-10.

35. In a brief but worthwhile and up-to-date-synopsis on the various developments in feminism, the editors signal their interest in pursuing intersectionality in regard to gender, race, and class.

36. Else K. Holt, '"The Stain of your Guilt is Still before me" (Jeremiah 2:22): (Feminist) Approaches to Jeremiah 2 and the Problem of Normativity', in Christl M. Maier and Carolyn J. Sharp (eds.), *Prophecy and Power: Jeremiah in Feminist and Postcolonial Perspective* (Library of Hebrew Bible/Old Testament Studies, 577; London: Bloomsbury), pp. 101-16.

37. Diverging from Van Dijk-Hemmes and Brenner's readings, Holt finds the analysis of Robert Carroll more appealing because he insists upon a distinction between the tenor and vehicle of metaphors. Holt also refers approvingly to Carroll's notion against modern readers imposing meaning upon ancient texts when she states that 'the text has a right to be heard from the outset on its own historical and ideological terms'; see Holt, 'The Stain of your Guilt', p. 111. She views texts as polysemous and capable of accommodating many meanings.

not an authority of permanence, but an authority of dialogue'.[38] She reminds us that the Bible is fallible like any other book, and she recommends critical engagement with Jeremiah's violent texts and with its reception history. Holt's work exposes the fact that most interpreters defend the biblical canon, often paying uncritical allegiance to it.

The book's editors advance another important notion about postcolonial approaches in the interpretation of Jeremiah. By introducing the idea that 'bondage of the colonized and the colonizer [appear] in the same discourse',[39] they avoid the binaries created and maintained by the empire and colony divide, as postcolonial criticism questions these binaries. Maier and Sharp take their cue from Spivak who argues that the voices of the subalterns are muted because the dominant discourse provides the language and conceptual categories through which everyone speaks.[40] They also use Homi Bhabha's notion of mimicry to articulate the ambivalent relationship between colonized and colonizer as a smokescreen for the colonized. The latter adopts the colonizer's language, cultural habits, assumptions, and values, yet in an obfuscating and debilitating way, since mimicry oscillates between imitation and mockery.[41]

Furthermore, Sharp explores the methodological intersection of postcolonialism and feminism when she interprets Jer. 30.5-22. Due to her allegiance to feminist inquiry, she aligns her reading with countering ideologies of subjugation, deconstructing essentialist notions, and promoting *shalom*. Among a range of issues, she points out the ambivalent role of Yahweh in Jer. 30.8-9, which ostensibly portrays Yahweh in opposition to imperialism, as liberation theology has long claimed. Sharp comments: 'With God as ally, the position of subaltern can become a position of strength'.[42] However, she also advises that the position of subalternity should not be romanticized and essentialized although it provides a vantage point.[43] Depicting the bondage between colonizers and colonized, Jer. 30.8-9 locates imperial power positively in the Davidic king and endorses monarchy. The invoca-

38. Holt, 'The Stain of your Guilt', p. 113.
39. Maier and Sharp, 'Introduction', p. 11.
40. Gayatri C. Spivak, 'Can the Subaltern Speak?', in Bill Ashcroft, Gareth Griffiths and Helen Tiffin (eds.), *The Post-Colonial Studies Reader* (London and New York: Routledge, 1995), pp. 24-28.
41. Homi K. Bhabha, *The Location of Culture* (London and New York: Routledge, 1994), pp. 122-29.
42. Sharp, 'Mapping Jeremiah', p. 50.
43. Marginality can be taken up, claimed and become a place of 'radical openness and possibility'; see bell hooks, *Yearning. Race, Gender, and Cultural Politics* (Boston: South End, 1990), p. 153. Also see Rasiah S. Sugirtharajah, 'Introduction: The Margin as Site of Creative Revisioning', in Rasiah S. Sugirtharajah (ed.), *Voices from the Margin: Interpreting the Bible in the Third World* (Maryknoll, NY: Orbis Books, 1995), pp. 1-8.

tion of the king as 'the Lord of hosts' (יְהוָה צְבָאוֹת, Jer. 30.8) and other pro-monarchic statements demonstrates the ambiguity of the text toward empire. Yet Sharp's analysis fails to retain the tensions of the textual ambiguity when she maintains: 'In any case, the resistant reader can see in Jer. 30.8-9 that Yhwh is positioned against all other claims of dominance'.[44] However, not all readers have shown such clarity of vision that Sharp assumes, even when a reader's responsibility is clear and amplified. Moreover, it remains questionable whether the muted subaltern voice, when it speaks, is not so ensconced in imperialist hegemony that it merely succeeds in changing the roles of those dominated and being dominated.

In short, the anthology by Maier and Sharp addresses postcoloniality's intersection with feminism by focusing on life in the colonized/imperial context and the dynamics of invoking divine agency and sanction. This intersection highlights the hybridity which is so typical of the postcolonial condition, but it does not address postcolonial hybridity in all its ambivalence.

Approach Three:
Women and Colonial Hybridity

Some postcolonial feminist Bible scholars focus on yet another element in the relationship between postcolonialism and feminism, namely the move from a binary approach of oppressor and oppressed in textual analysis. They highlight the enduring hybridity of the dominated and the dominators as the key characteristic of life under empire. For instance, Gale A. Yee describes this characteristic as 'the power relations and disparities between empire and colony, between centre and periphery'.[45] Analysing Exodus 1–2 in relationship with Exodus 19–20, she places both textual units within the wider literary context of the Hebrew Bible. In her view, '[t]he stories of the Hebrew Bible narrate Israel enduring the different structures of imperial control in the course of its history, each with its particular brand of oppressive rule'.[46] She views the texts as products of colonial hybridity. They were constructed in the vicissitudes of empire, namely in the Yehud-province of the Persian Empire. The texts are 'products of colonial hybridity' that 'served the interests of the centre and the margins, the empire and the colony'.[47] Yee also points out that the identities of the dominated and the oppressors are mutually constituted, an observation that enables her to dissemble the binaries that the various essays in Maier's and Sharp's volume keep intact.

44. Sharp, 'Mapping Jeremiah', p. 51.
45. Yee, 'Postcolonial Biblical Criticism', p. 205.
46. Yee, 'Postcolonial Biblical Criticism', p. 206.
47. Yee, 'Postcolonial Biblical Criticism', p. 230.

Yee makes another important point. She maintains that Exodus 1–2 centre on the wise/foolish binary. This binary is invoked to portray Egypt, the great enemy and lingering threat to Persia's regional domination in the years of the Persian period (ca. 538–323 BCE), as childish, inept, and foolish. Although notions such as 'Exodus', 'Sinai', and 'Conquest' probably developed early and differently in ancient Israel, their composition in the colonial Yehud bestowed canonical approval and sanction upon them during the Persian period. For instance, Yee indicates that despite stereotypical descriptions of women, and especially colonized women, as stupid and inept, the narrative portrays them in the opposite way.[48] The two midwives who have names outsmart the nameless Pharaoh, as does Pharaoh's daughter and other Israelite women whereas the Pharaoh is depicted as incompetent.[49] Accordingly, Yee theorizes that women 'demarcate national differences among nations' and 'literally and symbolically designate the "porous frontiers" through which nation, ethnicity, and culture can be penetrated'.[50] Women play a double role. On the one hand, they resist the tyranny of empire by circumventing royal decrees. On the other hand, they serve male interests that are embedded in the narrative. For instance, Pharaoh's daughter, whether she is interpreted as a compassionate heroine or a comedic foil, contributes to her father's dim-witted portrayal. She helps Moses to flourish in the royal court, and she is the means through which the Egyptian empire is infiltrated or 'penetrated'.[51]

Yee then moves to her reading of Exodus 19–20, the depiction of Israel covenanting with Yahweh on Sinai.[52] Her exegesis shows that the liberation

---

48. Stereotyping (e.g. through ethnic jokes or slurs) in colonizing endeavors serves the purpose of making the Other knowable while maintaining difference and distance from the colonizer; in the Exodus narratives, the contrasts between Egyptian and Hebrew women manipulate gender and racial differences, and gender differences are advanced also with the distinction between male and female babies; see Yee, 'Postcolonial Biblical Criticism', pp. 197-99; 215-17.

49. 'From a postcolonial perspective, women become a trope for nationalist and ethnic identity, of collusion with empire or of resistance to it'; see Yee, 'Postcolonial Biblical Criticism', p. 221. Or, in the words of Musa W. Dube, 'Toward a Postcolonial Feminist Interpretation of the Bible', *Semeia* 78 (1997), pp. 11-26 (17): 'The colonized are symbolized by their indigenous women, who epitomize all backwardness, evil, and helplessness'.

50. Yee, 'Postcolonial Biblical Criticism', p. 221.

51. With reference to women's stories in Exodus 1–2, Yee states: 'Because women biologically produce members of racial and ethnic groups, control of women and their sexuality is central to national and ethnic polities. In order to preserve racial and national boundaries, male-generated laws and customs define with whom and under what circumstances women and men can marry and have sexual relations'; see Yee, 'Postcolonial Biblical Criticism', p. 220.

52. Yee, 'Postcolonial Biblical Criticism', p. 230. Yee connects the Hittite suzerainty

and related accounts in Exodus and the rest of the Pentateuch depict Israel's resistance to the imperial forces of Egypt. Yet at the editorial level, added when the texts were composed during the Persian period, the Persian authorities and the local Jewish elites revelled in the depiction of an inept, bumbling, and even foolish Pharaoh, as this image reflected negatively on his people. Thus, so Yee argues, Exodus 1–2 and 19–20 are products of colonial hybridity brought about by empire, and the narratives serve the interests of both the centre and the margins, empire and colony. In other words, narratives of Israel's liberation from slavery are intertwined with texts about the Sinai covenant and the conquest narratives. Although all of them serve male interests, the women must also be understood as enabling the national unfolding of Israel's story. This story turns out to be a story of liberation and conquest, submission and domination. Yee's approach to the Hebrew Bible thus explains that the Exodus narratives are tales of gendered colonization. They stand at the intersection of power and gender, illustrating the ever present ambivalences of colonization and imperialism in biblical depictions as featured in the book of Exodus, highlighting colonial hybridity.

Approach Four:
Contrapuntal Reading Strategies

A fourth area of investigation can be identified in postcolonial feminist bible readings, namely the contrapuntal readings of two or more narratives. Since postcolonial feminist approaches cannot really claim a particular methodology, sometimes they employ the inter-alignment of apparently divergent imperial-colonial narratives. This strategy is called a 'contrapuntal' or 'counterpoint' reading. Judith McKinlay's work represents this strategy in a volume entitled *Postcolonialism and the Hebrew Bible*.[53] In her contrapuntal reading she juxtaposes the story about Zelophehad and his daughters in Numbers 27 and 36 with reports about Edward Gibbon Wakefield and his New Zealand Company, specifically about the company's attempts from its base in London to settle Port Nicholson. McKinlay highlights two intersecting issues. First, in both cases land is allocated by outsiders although the

---

treaties and the Israelite Sinai covenant in their underlying imperial ethos of domination and subordination; and at another level, the Pentateuch 'became the civic constitution of the temple community of Yehud' while adherence to Torah is the condition for capturing and keeping the land (Josh. 1.7); see Yee, 'Postcolonial Biblical Criticism', pp. 223, 225-26. Also see Sharp, 'Mapping Jeremiah', p. 53: 'Empire is at heart of the covenant, it would seem'. The ensuing conquests in narratives of the (Former) Prophets show the intertwined nature of the Pentateuch and the prophetic literature.

53. Judith McKinlay, 'Playing an Aotearoa Counterpoint: The Daughters of Zelophehad and Edward Gibbon Wakefield', in Roland Boer (ed.), *Postcolonialism and the Hebrew Bible: The Next Step* (Semeia Studies; Atlanta: SBL, 2013), pp. 11-37.

land did not belong to the distributors, and second, the land redistribution was done from a geographically removed location.[54] McKinlay uses these two key elements to set up a contrapuntal reading.[55] Yet the narrative in Numbers poses challenges. Daringly, the narrative about Zelophad's daughters subverts the daughters' prescribed gender roles by focusing on their insistence to inherit land, a privilege only accorded to sons. However, the problem is also that the daughters demand land that belongs to other people.

In her interpretation, McKinlay opts for a postcolonial optic that reveals the ideological shaping of the skilfully constructed text.[56] Grounded in a postcolonial interventionist strategy, she rejects the dominant interpretive position that sees in the story an uncomplicated reflection of a past event. McKinlay also invokes Sugirtharajah's notion of a lopsided history constructed to reflect present needs and concerns. This idea allows McKinlay to identify a strong ideological element in the biblical narrative that addresses the postexilic Yehud. She finds a similar ideological element articulated in narratives about the colonial endeavours as they occurred in New Zealand. Her comparison shows that those in power invoke carefully crafted narratives to justify the conquest of other peoples' lands. They pre-arrange the conquest from a distance and without the consent from the conquered people.

McKinlay proposes that in the end the position of the story about the daughters of Zelophehad is ambiguous. On the one hand, it emphasizes

---

54. See also the various essays in Musa W. Dube, Andrew M. Mbuvi and Dora Mbuwayesango (eds,), *Postcolonial Perspectives in African Biblical Interpretations*; On the intersection of land and biblical narratives, see, e.g., Robert Wafawanaka relates land in Africa to Lev. 25.23 (pp. 221-34); Temba Mafico uses Psalm 24 to connect the concept of land and tenure in Israel to African tradition (pp. 235-44); and Robert Wafanula considers the quest for land in Africa from the perspective of the stories of Abraham and Lot (pp. 245-56).

55. Edward Said promoted a contrapuntal reading which amounts to 'a simultaneous awareness both of the metropolitan history that is narrated and of those other histories against which (and together with which) the dominating discourse acts'. Said's intention was to avoid univocal or one-sided readings of history, 'as making up a set of what I call intertwined and overlapping histories' and so 'to formulate an alternative both to a politics of blame and to the even more destructive politics of confrontation and hostility'; see Edward Said, *Culture and Imperialism* (New York: Knopf, 1993), pp. 51, 18. Alissa Jones Nelson embarks on an extensive contrapuntal reading of Job in an effort to include vernacular voices in biblical interpretation. Because she does not explicitly opt for a feminist approach in conjunction with her postcolonial slant, her work is not discussed here; see her book, *Power and Responsibility in Biblical Interpretation: Reading the Book of Job with Edward Said* (Sheffield: Equinox, 2012).

56. McKinlay, 'Playing an Aotearoa Counterpoint', p. 18. The compositional history of Numbers is not discussed in detail, but McKinlay cites Sakenfeld's appreciation for it; see McKinlay, 'Playing an Aotearoa Counterpoint', pp. 13-17.

the female characters and their daring challenge of the inheritance rule. On the other hand, the narrative portrays the daughters as demanding the land that belongs to others; they want what does not belong to them. As Dube explains: 'The general picture is that imperialism is a male game with women characters articulating men's power positions in it'.[57] Yet I wonder whether McKinlay should not have further explored the link between land and women. She rightly recognizes that women were like land in ancient times,[58] but land is also gendered. It is taken, expected to produce fruit, manipulated and mapped by men throughout Israelite history, as it is throughout the colonization period of New Zealand.[59] Yet McKinlay has shown that a contrapuntal reading demonstrates the interaction and, in fact, the intersection of imperialism and patriarchy by producing a counterpuntal reading of a biblical text with insights gained from the colonial era of New Zealand.

Approach Five:
Challenging Textual 'Property Rights'

Our focus up to this point has been to explain the intersection between imperialism and feminism in Hebrew Bible texts. Now we take a step back to consider at a meta-theoretical level the *impact* of reading texts with postcolonial and feminist goals in mind. I will consider the bearing of such readerly goals on the texts themselves, as well as the claims of others upon the texts. Such meta-theoretical concerns are not distinct from but strategically aligned with the other two levels of postcolonial investigation noted in the introductory remarks of this section, as they trace imperialist patterns in ancient texts and investigate their use over the course of history.

In a volume on postmodern biblical interpretation, Zahia Pathak discusses the need for a pedagogy in postcolonial feminism as part of the larger concern about the politics of reading.[60] Pathak wants to develop a pedagog-

---

57. Dube, 'Toward a Postcolonial Feminist Interpretation', p. 17.
58. Referring to Delaney, in McKinlay, 'Playing an Aotearoa Counterpoint', p. 15.
59. Dube makes this point in her study of Exodus–Joshua account; see Dube, *Postcolonial Feminist Interpretation*, pp. 57-80. The land of the others can be taken in the same way and especially foreign women are to be taken by men. So, too, in Ezekiel 23, 'the woman was used as a trope for the land and the nation, and sexual images became tropes for colonial dominance'; see Kwok, 'Making the Connections', p. 48. Yee also refers to Said's study on orientalism, in which the Orient is typified as feminine and as available for conquest, domestication, and exploitation; see Yee, 'Postcolonial Biblical Criticism', pp. 196-97.
60. Zahia Pathak, 'A Pedagogy for Postcolonial Feminists', in David Jobling, Tina Pippin and Ronald Schleifer (eds.), *The Postmodern Bible Reader* (Oxford: Blackwell, 2001), pp. 219-32.

ical politics to challenge the property rights of biblical texts as imposed by and through the First-World academy. She regards her approach as a challenge to 'the exertion of proprietorial rights of interpretation as expressed through the determination of interpretive paradigms by canonized criticism, which determines the production of meaning'. Her aim is to use other discursive paradigms when she interprets biblical texts in a process of 'abrogation and appropriation'.[61] Pathak's work on texts about property rights relates to the postcolonial endeavour of 're-placing language' since the colonizing endeavour has always been discursive.[62]

She illustrates her idea in rereading the book of Job that she regards as a discourse of law and not as religious discourse. She asserts that the book of Job is an amalgamation of various epics, folktales, and wisdom poems. It shows the evolution of the Yahweh figure and points toward a particular religion's construction of history through ascribing a determining role to the divine figure. In Pathak's reading, the book Job is a religious text that is constituted by hermeneutical fiats. She introduces the discourse of law in contra-distinction to that of revelation, and she also refers to the role of the Sanhedrin to decide which law was violated. Accordingly, the character of Job is 'that of a subjectivity fractured by contending discourses of revelation and law'.[63]

The significance of her work consists in her pedagogical effort to displace the authority of biblical and imperialist texts and to open up religion to other discourses.[64] She imposes readerly ideologies onto the text to unsettle the use of the Bible in support of 'imperialist heteropatriarchy'.[65] As a side-effect, her approach dissolves the threat of postmodern relativism often levelled at postcolonial work, especially by liberation hermeneutical scholars.[66] Thus, Pathak's essay highlights successfully the discursive nature of

---

61. Pathak, 'A Pedagogy for Postcolonial Feminists', pp. 221-22. Pathak borrowed these ideas from Bill Ashcroft, Gareth Griffiths and Helen Tiffin, *The Empire Writes Back: Theory and Practice in Post-Colonial Literature* (London: Routledge, 2nd edn, 2002), pp. 37-38: 'Abrogation is a refusal of the categories of the imperial culture, its aesthetic, its illusory standard of normative or "correct" usage, and its assumption of a traditional and fixed meaning "inscribed" in the words.'

62. Ashcroft, Griffiths and Tiffin, *The Empire Writes Back*, pp. 37-76. Language includes critical theory, harboring an ideological subtext of 'oppositional thinking where structures of domination are perceived to be oppressive'; see Pathak, 'A Pedagogy for Postcolonial Feminists', p. 230.

63. Pathak, 'A Pedagogy for Postcolonial Feminists', p. 222.

64. David Jobling, Tina Pippin and Ronald Schleifer describe Pathak as 'a subversive gatekeeper within the boundaries of institutional rule/s'; see their 'Introduction', in David Jobling, Tina Pippin and Ronald Schleifer (eds.), *The Postmodern Bible Reader* (Oxford: Blackwell, 2001), pp. 163-76 (172).

65. Jobling, Pippin and Schleifer, 'Introduction', p. 163.

66. Liberation hermeneutics has influenced postcolonial theory. Some scholars assert

colonization as well as the effect of claims about property rights on religious texts.

Trends

After this brief review of five approaches in postcolonial feminist readings of the Hebrew Bible, several trends emerge in postcolonial feminist exegesis. I will consider only two of them, namely the postcolonial feminist interest in matters related to social location and the rejection of essentialism. Postcolonial feminist criticism shares the ideological critical perspective of other socially engaged hermeneutics in which social location plays a central role in biblical interpretation.[67] Yet social location is not a neutral term. As Christopher Rowland explains: 'It becomes essential to understand something of the culture, in the widest sense of that term, out of which the struggle for power comes and in which the biblical interpreter is located. In this she or he is not just a passive observer, but part of that conflict of interests and concerns which engulf the individual in an increasingly global capitalism'.[68] In fact, partly due to the different social locations of Hebrew Bible scholars and partly due to a range of other factors, such as education and training or interpretive choices and purposes, a wide spectrum of approaches and methodologies characterizes postcolonial feminist biblical interpretation.[69]

---

it has given liberation theology renewed impetus; see, e.g., Roland Boer, *Symposia: Dialogues Concerning the History of Biblical Interpretation* (BibleWorld; London: Equinox, 2007), p. 136. Also see Yee, 'Postcolonial Biblical Criticism', p. 205. Kari Latvus writes that '[p]ostcolonial criticism does not imitate liberation hermeneutics but obviously owes a lot to this tradition. Both approaches share a commitment to "the other" (not in power, ignored, marginalized) and both also emphasize empowerment of the oppressed. Liberation theology/hermeneutics was, however, a child of modernity and a battering ram against the fortified castles of traditionalism'; see Latvus, 'Decolonizing Yahweh: A Postcolonial Reading of 2 Kings 24–25', in Rasiah S. Sugirtharajah (ed.), *The Postcolonial Biblical Reader* (London: Blackwell, 2006), pp. 186-92 (187).

67. Rieger writes that '[p]ostcolonial interpretations of ancient biblical texts are welcome and necessary because they also invite an account from the interpreters about the tensions of empire, colonialism, and various forms of resistance in their own contexts'; see Rieger, 'Responses', p. 261.

68. Christopher Rowland, 'Social, Political, and Ideological Criticism', in Jon W. Rogerson and Judith M. Lieu (eds.), *The Oxford Handbook of Biblical Studies* (Oxford and New York: Oxford University Press, 2006), pp. 655-71 (665).

69. For instance, Ashcroft, Griffiths and Tiffin claim: 'As the hey-day of European imperialism recedes further into the past, the theoretical issues raised by postcolonial theory: questions of resistance, power, ethnicity, nationality, language and culture and the transformation of dominant discourses by ordinary people, provide important models for understanding the place of the local in an increasing globalized world'; see Ashcroft, Griffiths and Tiffin, *The Empire Writes Back*, p. 202.

Like feminist inquiry, postcolonial work rejects essentialism.[70] It eschews essentialist notions of people as well as the 'naturalness' and even 'normativity' of the trilogy of the categories of gender, race, and class, all three of which have proven to be so vitally important in scripting the colonialist endeavour and for providing ostensible legitimate categories for prevailing global hegemonic practices. In biblical studies, feminist scholar Elisabeth Schüssler Fiorenza has set the scene by refusing to essentialize women in biblical texts, arguing instead for a strategic and politically destabilizing hermeneutics. Similarly, postcolonial scholars explore the asymmetrical binary opposition between colonizers and colonized, but with a view to show that, uneven as they are, power relationships function reciprocally.

Scholars point out the dangers of essentialism in evaluating and in practicing explorative intersections of feminist and postcolonial discourses, and rightly encourage thinking of gender, race, and class through social construction lenses. But how is the socially, politically, culturally, and geographically inscribed body in play in the feminist-postcolonial interstices, without explicit engagement in the discourse? Is the acknowledgement of corporeal feminism[71] sufficient for feminist scholars to assume it as a scholarly identity rather than to employ it as an analytical key in their work? Can Pathak's neglect of women in her postcolonial feminist approach be justified with the remark that '[f]eminist readings (of the role of Job's wife in particular) are secondary only because of the urgency of the political conflict'?[72] Can the hierarchical scripting and even eliding of Job's still nameless wife be made subordinate to the dominating tendencies of the narrative? More particular, are the suppressive gender tendencies not reflective or even constitutive of the dominant socio-political and religious discourses? Bluntly put, is it even possible to de-acknowledge gender concerns in favour of a politically tuned analysis, as if these two are conflicting goals?

These, and other challenges, face postcolonial feminist criticism, but before entertaining such challenges, briefly attending to some criticism of such work is appropriate. As some scholars explain, the origins of criticism may be other than academic or ethical: 'The fear of critical theory in biblical (and other) studies has been used by the status quo to maintain power in "self-evident" truths. Feminism/womanism, postcolonialism, and poststructuralism have been scapegoated; in other words, theory is blamed for

70. In some feminist circles, however, the debate is still poised around the dissolution of 'essential woman' in favor of 'separate, diverse local genders', and its ill-effects for the political goals of feminism; see Mary-Anne Tolbert, 'Gender', in A.K.M. Adam (ed.), *Handbook of Postmodern Biblical Interpretation* (St Louis: Chalice, 2000), pp. 99-105 (101).

71. Elizabeth Grosz, *Volatile Bodies: Towards a Corporeal Feminism* (Theories of Representation and Difference; St Leonards: Allen & Unwin, 1994), pp. 62-85.

72. Jobling, Pippin and Schleifer 'Introduction', p. 172.

disrupting the dominant power system.'[73] Resisting scapegoating does not mean to sidestep fair criticism, especially as it pertains to accusations of ignoring or even eliding categories of class, imposing authoritarian ambivalence, and supporting anachronism.

Critique

Criticism levelled against postcolonial interpreters includes that they are not socially engaged enough in their work, do not take gender concerns seriously enough, do not consider the Bible's complicity in colonialist endeavours, and that they anachronistically retroject anti-colonial theory into the biblical past. Postcolonialism's reach extends to the global *academic* world and provides 'an ethical paradigm for a systematic critique of institutional suffering'.[74] Yet, liberation and Marxist scholars have levelled criticism against postcolonial work.[75] In such circles, postcolonial work is seen as incapable of dealing with the issue of class in its analysis, as much as with the world of capitalism, largely because of its adoption of Derridean and Foucauldian theories.[76] Postcolonial work is at times accused of not sufficiently accommodating categories of race and class.[77]

---

73. Jobling, Pippin and Schleifer, 'Introduction', p. 173. Postcolonial authors explain that scapegoating is one way in which the colonizer retains power in the form of intellectual hegemony over die colonized; see Albert Memmi, *The Colonizer and the Colonized* (London: Earthscan, 2003). Racism is often instrumental since it is 'the generalized and final assigning of values to real or imaginary differences, to the accuser's benefit and at his victim's expense, in order to justify the former's own privileges or aggression'; see Albert Memmi, *Racism* (Minneapolis: University of Minnesota Press, 2000), p. 180. Memmi's failure to account for colonialism's intersections with gender and race has come under fire in the past; see Maria G. Davidson, 'Albert Memmi and Audre Lorde: Gender, Race, and the Rhetorical Uses of Anger', *Journal of French and Francophone Philosophy* 20 (2012), pp. 87-100. Bhabha explains: 'Stereotyping is not only the setting up of a false image which becomes the scapegoat of discriminatory practices. It is a much more ambivalent text of projection and introjection, metaphoric and metonymic strategies, displacement, guilt, aggressivity; the masking and splitting of "official" and fantasmic knowledges…'; see Homi K. Bhabha, 'The Other Question: Difference, Discrimination and the Discourse of Colonialism', in Franci Barker, Peter Hulme and Margaret Iversen (eds.), *Literature, Politics & Theory* (London: Methuen, 1986), pp. 148-73 (169).

74. Gandhi, *Postcolonial Theory*, p. 174.

75. Fernando F. Segovia, *Decolonizing Biblical Studies: A View from the Margins* (Maryknoll, NY: Orbis, 2000), pp. 136-40.

76. Yee, 'Postcolonial Biblical Criticism', p. 201.

77. See Roland Boer, 'Marx, Postcolonialism, and the Bible', in Stephen D. Moore and Fernando F. Segovia (eds.), *Postcolonial Biblical Criticism: Interdisciplinary Intersections* (The Bible and Postcolonialism; London: T. & T. Clark International, 2005), pp. 166-83; T. Benny Liew, 'Margins and (Cutting-)Edges: On the (Il)Legitimacy and

Postcolonial theorists have also been accused of disregarding gender, apart from the category of class. Ideological representations of colonized women by colonizers demonstrate their two- or threefold subjugation: racism and classicism of colonialism, and sexism of patriarchy.[78] Taking a cue from Lorde's argument that the master's tools will never succeed in bringing down the master's house,[79] some scholars argue that 'Postmodern biblical interpretation, as with any other, is always in danger of creating its own unchanging method of reading or trivializing its insights in their very multiplication'.[80]

Criticism against earlier postcolonial feminist work includes the accusation that the acknowledgment of the Bible's historical complicity with colonial domination in Africa and elsewhere, cannot legitimately see it retained as contemporary foundational text.[81] Can feminism be an ally against religiously sanctioned imperialism, even if it involves some ambiguity? Feminism has been denounced for its implicit Eurocentrism and its accompanying failure to acknowledge and destabilize strategies of covert and strategic rationalization of imperial domination. How will feminism ensure that its gendered focus will not lead to further neglect of intersecting lines of divisions marked out by race, class, or geography?

The criticism that postcolonial work on the Bible anachronistically retrojects theory, developed in modern colonialism into ancient times, is countered by Kwok's statement: 'I would like to point out that history is interpreted according to the mental apparatus and framework we have constructed'.[82] Any contemporary theory reflects modern biases!

Challenges

Related to but also going beyond the above criticisms are five interrelated challenges which postcolonial feminist work still has to address. An evident first challenge for postcolonial feminist criticism is internal, namely the lingering mutual discontent found between postcolonial critics and feminist critics. Postcolonial criticism is sceptical at times about feminism's willingness to let go fully of its tendency to inscribe privilege through prevailing essentialist categories, as well as the identity politics that props up

---

Intersections of Race, Ethnicity, and (Post)Colonialism', in Stephen D. Moore and Fernando F. Segovia (eds.), *Postcolonial Biblical Criticism: Interdisciplinary Intersections* (The Bible and Postcolonialism; London: T. & T. Clark International, 2005), pp. 114-65.

78. Yee, 'Postcolonial Biblical Criticism', pp. 202-203.

79. Audre Lorde, *Sister Outsider: Essays and Speeches* (Crossing Press Feminist Series; Berkeley: Crossing, 1984; 2007), pp. 110-13.

80. Jobling, Pippin and Schleifer, 'Introduction', p. 174.

81. See, e.g., Dube, *Postcolonial Feminist Interpretation*.

82. Kwok, 'Making the Connections', p. 46.

essentialism.⁸³ Conversely, radical feminism continues to questions postcolonial theory's commitment to political action, especially in that it ostensibly fails to address the praxis of women's oppression.⁸⁴ Such divergences do not mean that postcolonial and feminist work do not find natural alliances in one another, as much as they do not make postcolonial feminist *biblical interpretation* self-evident. In fact, their interpretations pose a further challenge.

A second challenge relates to the status of the texts themselves. Does the recognition that the Hebrew Bible narratives neither simply constitute Europe's colonial Bible nor automatically serve as self-justifying ideology for colonial powers and missions⁸⁵ resolve the matter of the Bible's 'guilt' by association? Do Hebrew Bible texts, *sans* the colonial mission, receive a clean bill of health? Is the problem one of simply having to study the texts long enough, postcolonial-feminist enough, and all problems relating to them and oppression will be resolved? Or are the textual relationships with matters imperial more complicated? At times texts render themselves complicit in imperial endeavours by buying into reigning ideology and justifying imperial designs, while at other times texts show signs of resisting and subverting dominance and hegemony. Most of the time, however, texts provide evidence of entanglement in both the push and pull of empire. The textual materials we interpret reflect the ambivalence typical of imperial contexts, which provide a challenge on its own. The context of academia in which the texts are studied further sharpens the challenge.

Postcolonial feminist inquiry confronts, as a third challenge, an academy that often still prides itself on detachment, ostensible objectivity, and even

---

83. Essentialism narrows down the spectrum of human identities, at least as far as gender and to some extent, sex, are concerned.

84. Such critique, levelled against postcolonial work, is akin to the criticism often heard against queer theory. Blaming queer theory's postmodernist focus on language and binaries, its 'anguished introspection', is found to be based on postmodern masters such as Foucault, and its non-essentialism is seen as nothing else but reinvoked individualism and liberalism covered with some intellectual veneer; see Sheila Jeffreys, 'Return to Gender: Post-Modernism and Lesbianandgay Theory', in Diane Bell and Renate Klein (eds.), *Radically Speaking: Feminism Reclaimed* (London: Zed Books, 1996), pp. 359-74 (372). For Jeffreys, the affirmation of essentialism steers away from biological determinism and focuses on 'any similarity amongst a class of people on which political theorizing or action can be based'; see Jeffreys, 'Return to Gender', p. 372. On the other hand, queer theory is seen as an ally of feminism since '[q]ueer theory…enriches and critiques feminist readings by turning attention to the deep constructions and performances of gender that shape texts and interpretations'; see Laurel C. Schneider, 'Queer Theory', in A.K.M. Adam (ed.), *Handbook of Postmodern Biblical Interpretation* (St Louis: Chalice, 2000), pp. 206-12 (211).

85. Kim, 'Is There an "Anticonquest" Ideology in the Book of Judges?'; Horsley, 'It Is More Complicated', p. 252.

professed neutrality. However, the political nature of postcolonial and feminist readings, separately and jointly, engenders a step beyond detached studies of ancient texts relegated to an isolated past. It challenges contemporary interpreters with regard to the complexities of present-day life.[86] Since postcolonial feminist interpretation is a 'reading posture'[87] rather than a methodology, the choice of appropriate analytical tools appropriate to the task remains a subsidiary challenge. Once detached inquiry is set aside and even when a sound hermeneutical method is identified, the identification of the contemporary value of postcolonial feminist readings is no easy task and contains considerable challenges.

A fourth challenge, therefore, relates to the *comparative* frame typical of much postcolonial work. It requires discernment and the ability to engage different historical forms of empire and colonialism in different times. Joerg Rieger expresses this challenge well when he states: 'Merely identifying empires and colonialisms today with empires and colonialisms in the past without a comparative framework is not only inadequate but also misleading'.[88] Postcolonial interpretation cannot become satisfied with only studying biblical texts as colonial, but also need to expand its enquiry to the relationship between colonial practices and the colonial Bible, as well as studying the political-economic and cultural effects of the colonial Bible.[89] Some see great value in using traditional methods alongside postcolonial inquiry. Historical criticism is seen for example as an aid in opening up access to people's histories submerged in texts, and exposing the ideological commitments of textual compositions that found their way into the Bible.[90] However, still greater circumspection may be required.[91]

86. Boer, 'Introduction', p. 3.
87. Rasiah S. Sugirtharajah, 'A Postcolonial Exploration of Collusion and Construction in Biblical Interpretation', in Rasiah S. Sugirtharajah (ed.), *The Postcolonial Bible* (The Bible and Postcolonialism, 1; Sheffield: Sheffield Academic Press, 1998), pp. 91-116 (93).
88. Rieger, 'Responses', p. 261.
89. Horsley, 'It Is More Complicated', p. 242. Unequal relationships of domination and subordination should be investigated with regard to cultural production but also economic conditions since texts develop out of specific social locations; see Fernando F. Segovia, 'Mapping the Postcolonial Optic in Biblical Criticism: Meaning and Scope', in Stephen D. Moore and Fernando F. Segovia (eds.), *Postcolonial Biblical Criticism: Interdisciplinary Intersections* (The Bible and Postcolonialism; London, New York: T. & T. Clark International, 2005), pp. 23-78 (67-68).
90. Horsley, 'It Is More Complicated', pp. 243, 251; Kwok, 'Making the Connections', p. 46.
91. 'It is important to stress that postcolonial criticism does not necessarily reject the insights of historical criticism, because much of the work of the historical critics contributes to the understanding of the "worldliness" of the text, that is, the material and ideological backgrounds from which the texts emerged and to which the texts responded';

A final and fifth challenge relates to normative value bestowed upon historical criticism, and postcolonial feminist critics' relation to it. Postcolonial critics pose new questions and often critique the normativity ascribed to historical criticism. Kwok Pui-lan asserts: 'Once the historical-critical method was established as the norm for studying the Bible, it excluded the validity of other contextual readings and devalued the contributions of non-academic interpretations'.[92] Some scholars even argue that historical criticism is an imperialist tool, particularly for sanctioning authorial intention or validating an author's perspective through claims about historical contexts in order to legitimate an offensive text.[93] To what extent can different analytical approaches be used as part of a multidimensional approach to biblical interpretation? When does the combined use of approaches begin to resemble a promiscuous marriage? Or should biblical scholars simply resign themselves to defaulting to a particular privileged approach to texts, even when such privilege remains unacknowledged?[94] How can such default interpretive stances be identified and described? Is methodological intersectionality an ideal never to be reached or a realistic possibility devoid of disabling compromises?[95]

see Kwok, 'Making the Connections', p. 46. Perhaps at least the distinction between historical criticism and its results need to be made. See also Caroline Vander Stichele and Todd C. Penner who argue for a broader discussion on the relation of other approaches to historical criticism; see their *Her Master's Tools? Feminist and Postcolonial Engagements of Historical-Critical Discourse* (Atlanta: Society of Biblical Literature, 2005).

92. Kwok, 'Making the Connections', p. 47.

93. Susanne Scholz, '"Tandoori Reindeer" and the Limitations of Historical Criticism', in Caroline Vander Stichele and Todd C. Penner (eds.), *Her Master's Tools? Feminist and Postcolonial Engagements of Historical Critical Discourse* (GPBS, 9; Leiden: Brill, 2005), pp. 47-69; cited by Crowell, 'Postcolonial Studies'. Maier and Sharp write that '[t]he flourishing of feminist and postcolonial criticism marks the end of the hegemony of the historical critical model of interpretation'; see Maier and Sharp, 'Introduction', p. 13.

94. The boundary-shaping function of methodologies cannot be denied, or that methods define the insider and outsiders to academic norms, or their role in the construction of the academic guild; how the criterion of challenging oppressive ideas in the text will play out, need some further explanation; see Dora Mbuwayesango and Susanne Scholz, 'Dialogical Beginnings: A Conversation on the Future of Feminist Biblical Studies', *JFSR* 25 (2009), pp. 93-103.

95. Crenshaw sees the value of intersectionality in its ability to challenge identity politics, especially in terms of gender, race and class and how all three in different ways were involved in discrimination. It is in the realization that these notions intersect, both coalesce but also divert from each other that allows for significant crisscrossing reconfigurations of gender, race and class, Kimberle Crenshaw, 'Mapping the Margins: Intersectionality, Identity Politics, and Violence against Women of Color', *Stanford Law Review* 43 (1991), pp. 1241-99.

When it comes to the imperialism inherent in all explanatory theory and practice, to the power exerted by scholarly epistemology and methodology, when do postcolonial and feminist and postcolonial feminist approaches run the risk of the anti-conquest that is always present in colonial and imperial endeavours? When do these approaches become 'strategies of representation whereby European bourgeois subjects seek to secure their innocence in the same moment as they assert European hegemony'?[96]

Concluding Remarks

Postcolonial [feminist] readings are not superfluous.[97] The interpretation of biblical texts has benefited from postcolonial feminist criticism in today's always complex and often tense geo-political world that is characterized by uneven power relations between people, groups, and structures.[98] The litmus test for postcolonial analyses does not so much consist in readings that amount to enchanted depictions of biblical texts as righting all wrongs or as turning injustices into justice, but perhaps rather by admitting that 'it is more complicated'.[99] In fact, postcolonial feminist readings address the problem of the Bible as double-sided literature that readers cherish both as an inspiration for liberation and as a justification for oppression.

In postcolonial feminist work an important tension requires further attention. On the one hand, an advocacy position biased toward women often characterizes feminist analysis. On the other hand, postcolonial critics fear the perpetuation of past regimes through a replaced agency which turns the power tables without affecting the nature of the power regime.[100] No easy solution to the colonizing and androcentric ways of the world exist. However, if mimicking 'the ways of empires for corporate survival is an ambiv-

---

96. Mary Louise Pratt, *Imperial Eyes: Travel Writing and Transculturation* (London and New York: Routledge, 2nd edn, 2008), p. 9. Pratt asks: '[T]he self-effacing protagonist of the anticonquest is often surrounded by an aura not of authority, but of innocence and vulnerability'; see Pratt, *Imperial Eyes*, p. 55.

97. Yee, 'Postcolonial Biblical Criticism'; see also Rieger, 'Responses', p. 261.

98. At least in as far as postcolonial work engages 'the pieties of the powerful'; see Rasiah S. Sugirtharajah, *Exploring Postcolonial Biblical Criticism: History, Method, Practice* (Chichester: Wiley-Blackwell, 2012), p. 27.

99. McKinlay takes her cue from Rasiah S. Sugirtharajah, *The Bible as Empire: Postcolonial Explorations* (Cambridge: Cambridge University Press, 2005), p. 3; see McKinlay, 'Playing an Aotearoa Counterpoint', p. 18. Sugirtharajah argues that a postcolonial optic is 'an interventionist instrument which refuses to take the dominant reading as an uncomplicated representation of the past', p. 3.

100. Yee emphasizes the intersection between postcolonial nationalism and feminist concerns when she states: 'From a postcolonial perspective, women become a trope of nationalist and ethnic identity, of collusion with empire or resistance to it'; see Yee, 'Postcolonial Biblical Criticism', p. 221.

alent strategy',[101] then the mimicking of heteropatriarchy in the pursuit of the structural and epistemological advancement of women is also an ambivalent tactic. Nevertheless, if it is true that, '[a]s long as people believe in the Yahweh of deliverance, the world will not be safe from Yahweh the conqueror',[102] it is also true that as long as people believe in a male God, women will not be safe from men. Postcolonial feminist exegesis of the Hebrew Bible needs to continuously expose and elevate the intersecting power structures that persist in the text, the history of interpretation, and in our minds and practices, with the awareness of the push and pull of past and present empire.

---

101. Kim, 'Is There an "Anticonquest" Ideology in the Book of Judges?', p. 127.
102. Robert A. Warrior, 'Canaanites, Cowboys, and Indians', *USQR* 59 (2005), pp. 1-8 (7-8).

15

SURPASSING THE LOVE OF WOMEN:
FROM FEMINISM TO QUEER THEORY IN BIBLICAL STUDIES

Rhiannon Graybill

Queer theory is a bit like pornography. Those charged with defining it often refuse or resist doing so, even resorting, like Justice Stewart, to 'I know it when I see it'. It is bound up with desire. It takes sex seriously, but also playfully. At other times, it seems to have very little to do with sex at all. It can still cause a start when introduced at the dinner table. And it has a fraught relationship with feminism.

In the field of biblical studies, queer theory and its predecessor/uneasy contemporary, gay and lesbian studies (or more recently, LGBT or LGBTQ studies[1]), maintain a close relationship with feminist theory and feminist hermeneutics. Feminist and queer scholars occupy similar structural locations in the larger academy. They write for similar audiences. They often take up the same texts (for example, Ezekiel 16, Genesis 2–3). They are frequently mistaken for each other—and often, they *are* each other, for there is a significant crossover between fields and scholars. And yet there are also important differences.

Is queer theory a feminist method? Yes, and no. As is fitting for queer theory, given its playfulness and resistance to norms and definitions, the answer is a contradictory one. Both inside and outside of biblical studies, queer theory owes important debts to feminist theory. Many queer projects are explicitly feminist; many more are informed by feminism or feminist theory in subtle or unacknowledged ways. And yet queer theory also has its own commitments, engagements, and politics, which sometimes run against those of feminist and gender studies. This article will trace the relationship between feminist and queer hermeneutics. I will begin with a brief overview of queer theory before taking up in greater detail its practice in biblical studies. Throughout, I will track queer theory's points of contact and points of tension with feminist theory; the final sections offer some

---

1. Trans issues were not a focus of earlier work in lesbian and gay studies, either in biblical studies or more generally. 'LGBT' or 'LGBTQ' studies reflects a partial corrective to this omission. Trans is also sometimes grouped under 'queer'.

more pointed feminist critiques of queer theory in biblical studies, as well as chart out some possible future directions for an intentionally feminist queer theory.

Queer theory has the potential to serve as a powerful feminist method. It may also be used to further the benign neglect of gender issues, or even to perpetrate patriarchy, misogyny, and homonationalism. Queer theory is playful; we must play wisely—or, to adopt the methodological metaphor of Ken Stone, we must 'practice safer texts'.[2] What could be wiser; what could be queerer?

What is Queer Theory?

It is a commonplace in writings on queer theory to begin by protesting against the very project of defining 'queer theory' or even 'queer'. In an introductory article on queer theory and religious studies, Kent Brintnall writes: 'Anyone with a passing familiarity with queer theory should be suspicious of any introductory article on queer studies and religion', noting in particular 'the tension between the demands of an introductory article—order, classify, simplify—and the suspicions of queer theory'.[3] Brintnall's words are a useful reminder for this chapter as well. Queer theory is indeed suspicious of many things, including names and definitions, as well as other forms of normativity. This suspicion is part of what makes pinning down queer theory such a struggle.

Defining queer theory is difficult in part because there is no one single definition for the term 'queer'. 'Queer' was once derogatory, but has been reclaimed by both activists and scholars, though not always for the same purposes. As a discipline, 'Queer theory' emerged as a deliberate alternative to 'lesbian and gay studies'; the name was intended both to provoke and to demarcate a new field of knowledge production. The specific phrase was coined by Teresa de Lauretis in 1991 in a special issue of the journal *differences* entitled 'Queer Theory: Lesbian and Gay Sexualities'. By using 'queer', de Lauretis aimed 'to mark a certain critical distance' from 'lesbian and gay studies', which elided the differences between lesbians and gay men (largely neglecting the former). 'Lesbian and gay studies' likewise neglected, in de Lauretis' view, race, ethnicity, class, and other forms of difference. In this context, 'queer' represented a call to theorize and critically interrogate these categories.

---

2. Ken Stone, *Practicing Safer Texts: Food, Sex and Bible in Queer Perspective* (Queering Theology Series; London: T. & T. Clark International, 2004).

3. Kent L. Brintnall, 'Queer Studies and Religion', *Critical Research on Religion* 1.1 (2013), pp. 51-61 (51).

However, for some scholars, 'queer' quickly became a new name for the same old 'lesbian and gay studies', if one that offered more concise alternative to increasingly lengthy acronyms such as 'LGBT', 'LGBTQ', or 'LGBTQQIA'.[4] This usage persists, in part, because the boundary between lesbian and gay studies and queer theory is not always clear. As Sharon Marcus writes,

> Despite the fanfare that heralded queer theory as an advance over lesbian and gay studies, usage has not affirmed any firm distinction between *queer* and *lesbian and gay*. While *queer* foregrounds the belief that sexual identity is flexible and unstable, *gay* and *lesbian* do not assert the contrary. *Queer* is more capacious than *lesbian and gay*, but it always includes gays and lesbians and often functions as a metonymy for *lesbian and gay*. And while queerness is supposed to signify the instability of all sexual identities, scholars who define queerness as the lability of sexual identity in general almost always do so with reference to gay identity in particular.[5]

Thus while queer theory is positioned as a break with lesbian and gay studies, there are continuities and overlaps both in usage and in practice.

Within the discipline of queer theory, the term 'queer' is often used to describe an oppositional relationship to dominant forms of power. One often-cited definition is that given by David M. Halperin in *Saint Foucault*:

> Queer is by definition *whatever* is at odds with the normal, the legitimate, the dominant. *There is nothing in particular to which it necessarily refers.* It is an identity without an essence. 'Queer' thus describes not specific identities or objects of inquiry, but rather an entire structure of power.[6]

Halperin's definition of queer stresses the importance of power while refusing to link 'queer' to a specific identity. It thus moves queer theory beyond identity politics toward a broad critique of sex, sexuality, and even culture (too broad, some critics have alleged).

Related but not identical to this meaning is the use of the term 'queer' to describe a style of writing, critiquing, and even being in the world. In this usage, 'queer' is closer to an aesthetics or even a stylistics. Queer theorists often describe the practice of textual critique as 'queering' the text. There is no single notion of what such a 'queering' looks like, just as queer theory itself refuses tight definition. However, it generally entails abandoning authorial intention or 'reading with the grain', seeking instead to uncover

---

4. 'LGBTQQIA' refers to lesbian, gay, bisexual, transgender, queer, questioning, intersex, ally or asexual. Sometimes additional identities (and letters) are added.

5. Sharon Marcus, 'Queer Theory for Everyone: A Review Essay', *Signs* 31.1 (September 2005), pp. 191-218 (196).

6. David M. Halperin, *Saint Foucault: Towards a Gay Hagiography* (New York: Oxford University Press, 1995), p. 62. On this definition and its use in religious and biblical studies, see Brintnall, 'Queer Studies and Religion', pp. 52-53.

what queer possibilities may be found in the text. While a queer approach has continuities with a 'hermeneutic of suspicion', it is less interested in exposing the text as problematic then in offering playful new readings. Queer readings can be provocative, even outrageous; playing with style and pushing boundaries are both features that characterize queer reading.

Queer theory has varied theoretical and practical ancestors. The works of Eve Kosofsky Sedgwick and Judith Butler are often cited as foundational, along with Michel Foucault's magisterial three-volume *History of Sexuality*.[7] The 1990s saw the rapid emergence of queer theory as a field of thought and scholarship. In 1995, only four years after de Lauretis coined the term 'queer theory', the *PMLA* published a special issue dedicated to queer theory. In the introduction, Lauren Berlant and Michael Warner, leading figures in the still-new field, expressed a certain shock at the rapid explosion of queer theory, as well as the frequent question, phrased by the title of their essay, 'What Does Queer Theory Teach Us about X?'[8] Despite the warnings of Berlant, Warner, and others—de Lauretis distanced herself from the term as early as 1994, dismissing it as 'a conceptually vacuous creature of the publishing industry'[9]—queer theory continued to grow, spawning books, articles, calls for papers, dictionary entries, courses, and a canon of its own.

Queer Theory and Feminism

From its beginnings, queer theory has been bound up with feminism. Feminist theory played a key role in its emergence, even as the relationship between the two remains fraught. As has been well documented elsewhere, second-wave feminism, though conceived of as a movement for all women, came under increasing criticism for its neglect of race, class, and other forms of difference. Lesbian feminists in particular objected to the heterosexism of mainstream feminism, and lesbian separatist feminism emerged as an

---

7. Eve Kosofsky Sedgwick, *Between Men: English Literature and Male Homosocial Desire* (New York: Columbia University Press, 1985) and *Epistemology of the Closet* (Berkeley: University of California Press, 1990); Judith Butler, *Gender Trouble: Feminism and the Subversion of Identity* (New York: Routledge, 1989) and *Bodies That Matter: On the Discursive Limits of 'Sex'* (New York: Routledge, 1993); Michel Foucault, *The History of Sexuality: An Introduction (vol. 1)* (trans. Robert Hurley; New York: Vintage Books, 1990), *The Use of Pleasure (vol. 2)* (trans. Robert Hurley; New York: Vintage Books, 1990), and *The Care of the Self (vol. 3)* (trans. Robert Hurley; New York: Vintage Books, 1988). On the formation of this canon, see also David M. Halperin, 'The Normalization of Queer Theory', *Journal of Homosexuality* 45.2-4 (2003), pp. 339-43 (241).

8. Lauren Berlant and Michael Warner, 'What Does Queer Theory Teach Us about X?', *Pmla* 110.3 (1995), pp. 343-49.

9. Teresa de Lauretis, 'Habit Changes', *differences: A Journal of Feminist Cultural Studies* 6.2-3 (1994), pp. 296-96 (296).

important movement.¹⁰ This movement was influential in the emergence of both gay and lesbian studies and, subsequently, queer theory. Queer theory also drew from feminist theory, offering, for example, a critique of essentialism that followed the critique already set forth by feminist theory. Annamarie Jagose explains,

> The refusal of normative identity categories, so often taken as queer theory's signature gesture, is not unique to that project. Before there was queer theory—that is, before queer theory became the most recognizable name for anti-identitarian, anti-normative critique—feminist scholarship had already initiated a radically anti-foundationalist interrogation of the category of women.¹¹

The foundational texts of queer theory are likewise in dialogue with feminist theory. Of Sedgwick's and Butler's work, Marcus writes: 'One of the crucial innovations of both *Between Men* and *Gender Trouble* was that they took the encounter between gender and sexuality, previously staged more or less exclusively within feminism, and reoriented it as an encounter between feminism and gay studies'.¹² These works, central to the establishment of queer theory, are themselves positioned in conversation with feminist thought. Queer theory thus engages with feminist theory from the beginning.

Queer theory had political dimensions as well, influenced by both feminist theory and practice. The feminist activism of the 1970s and 1980s offered a model for political engagement around questions of sex, gender, and the body. Equally influential for the emergence of queer theory was LGBT and queer political activism, especially ACT UP, Queer Nation, and other groups that formed in response to the AIDS crisis. Organizing around AIDS helped bring previously separate gay male and lesbian activists and scholars together, even as it created a sense of heightened urgency around sexuality and other issues affecting queer lives.¹³

Yet the relationship between queer theory and feminist theory was not always a friendly one. Feminists accused queer theory of positioning itself as the hipper, more sex-positive successor to feminism, pitting 'renegade sex

---

10. For an overview, see Rosemarie Tong, *Feminist Thought: A More Comprehensive Introduction* (London: Routledge, 2013), pp. 71-72.

11. Annamarie Jagose, 'Feminism's Queer Theory', *Feminism & Psychology* 19.2 (2009), pp. 157-74 (160).

12. Sharon Marcus, 'Queer Theory for Everyone', p. 199; contrast Danielle Clarke, 'Finding the Subject: Queering the Archive', *Feminist Theory* 5.1 (April 2004), pp. 79-83 (79-80).

13. Suzanna Danuta Walters, 'From Here to Queer: Radical Feminism, Postmodernism, and the Lesbian Menace (or, Why Can't a Woman Be More like a Fag?)', *Signs* 21.4 (Summer, 1996), pp. 830-69 (833).

"radicals" against their bad "feminist" mothers'.[14] Already in 1996, a mere five years after the coining of the term 'queer theory', Suzanna Danuta Walters synthesized a number of feminist concerns, writing,

> My main critique of the new popularity of 'queer' (theory and, less so, politics) is that it often (and once again) erases lesbian specificity and the enormous difference that gender makes, evacuates the importance of feminism, and rewrites the history of lesbian feminism and feminism generally.[15]

Her critiques have been echoed by a number of feminist critics. Of particular concern is the threat that queer theory, with its emphasis on gay male sexuality, reinscribes the domination of the masculine, leading to the erasure of lesbians and indeed of women as such. Walters charges: 'Queer discourse sets up a universal (male) subject, or at least a universal gay male subject, as its implicit referent'.[16] Her words are polemical, but also worrisome, and indeed, this worry has persisted in the intersections of feminist and queer scholarship. Responding to these concerns, a number of scholars have offered suggestions on how to craft a more feminist queer theory, and a queerer feminist theory.[17] Important progress has been made. Still, the relationship remains a testy one. I will return to this question, and how it plays out in biblical studies, below.

Origins, Influences, and Interdisciplinary Liaisons

Queer reading does not appear in biblical studies *sui generis*; neither is it simply adopted from queer theory as such. Feminist studies and approaches were instrumental in introducing queer theory to biblical studies. Feminist critique provided a model for critically interrogating categories such as gender, sexual difference, and the body from perspectives other than those provided by the historical-critical method. The first waves of feminist readings had also fought a hard-won battle to establish the legitimacy of such readings. In addition, feminist journals, conference panels, and so forth provided a receptive institutional space for queer readings. LGBT critique, for its part, was intertwined with queer biblical criticism almost from its beginning. While some scholars have called for an LGBT or specifically

---

14. Arlene Stein, 'The Year of the Lustful Lesbian', in Arlene Stein (ed.), *Sisters, Sexperts, Queers: Beyond the Lesbian Nation* (New York: Plume, 1993), p. 19; see also Walters, 'From Here to Queer', p. 857.

15. Walters, 'From Here to Queer', p. 843.

16. Walters, 'From Here to Queer', p. 846.

17. See, e.g., Walters, 'From Here to Queer', pp. 864-65, Clarke, 'Finding the Archive', pp. 79-80, Kathy Rudy, 'Radical Feminism, Lesbian Separatism, and Queer Theory', *Feminist Studies* 27.1 (Summer 2001), pp. 191-222 (219-21).

lesbian and/or gay criticism, most work on LGBT topics or themes is undertaken within, or in conjunction with, queer theory. However, feminist work was not the only historical point of contact between biblical studies and the emerging discipline of queer theory. Instead, its origins are promiscuous. It is thus worth noting other points of interdisciplinary contact that contributed to the emergence of queer biblical criticism.

Queer Theory and Literary Theory
We have already noted the close relationship between queer theory and literary theory. Like other forms of 'theory', especially those influenced by postmodernism and poststructuralism, queer theory found in literary criticism a receptive entry point into biblical studies. From a literary critical perspective, queer theory offered another way of destabilizing the biblical text, in continuity with other postmodern, poststructuralist, and deconstructive methods. In the early years of queer theory in particular, queer literary readings also offered a much-desired point of contact between biblical studies and other disciplines of literary study.[18] The growing interest in queer theory is apparent in theory-oriented literary publications from this time. In 1995, *The Postmodern Bible*, a collection of then-new methods of biblical criticism, contained only scattered references to sexuality and did not mention queer theory explicitly.[19] In contrast, *The Postmodern Bible Reader*, published a few years later, explicitly addressed this lacuna and sought to remedy it.[20]

Queer Theory and Religious Studies
Unlike other literary fields, religious scholars were slow to warm to queer theory. As Melissa Wilcox describes, scholarship on LGBT and queer issues in religion began to emerge in the 1970s.[21] This work took a number of forms, including autobiographical writing, theological work, historical studies, comparative studies, and social science. In its early instantiations, such work often considers sexuality, especially homosexuality, as objects of study without undertaking rigorous theoretical engagements with queer theory or LGBT studies. Wilcox criticizes the lack of scholarly conversation across boundaries of both discipline (religion scholars and queer theorists) and gender (gay male experience and lesbian experience are typically

18. Stephen D. Moore, *God's Beauty Parlor: And Other Queer Spaces In and Around the Bible* (Stanford, CA: Stanford University Press, 2002), pp. 7-18.
19. Bible and Culture Collective, *The Postmodern Bible* (New Haven: Yale University Press, 1995).
20. David Jobling, Tina Pippin and Ronald Schleifer (eds.), *The Postmodern Bible Reader* (Oxford; Malden, MA: Blackwell, 2001).
21. Wilcox, 'Outlaws or In-Laws?', *Journal of Homosexuality* 52.1-2 (2006), pp. 73-100 (74).

treated separately, both in scholarly work and by scholarly organizations such as the American Academy of Religion).[22] In spite of these shortcomings, queer studies in religion have helped advance queer theory as a biblical method. Queer studies of religion also direct attention to ritual, a topic of interest for biblical studies.[23] In addition, the academic location of many biblical scholars in religious studies departments, as well as forms of scholarly collaboration encouraged by the AAR and SBL have helped bringing the queer study of religion to biblical studies.

Queer Theology
Queer theology has been especially influential in introducing queer readings of the Bible. Queer theology overlaps with biblical studies in a number of ways, including shared texts and practitioners. Indeed, many queer readings of the Bible blur the boundaries between theological and non-theological biblical studies. To be sure, the boundaries between forms of reading, including 'theological' and 'secular', have themselves been called into question by postmodernism and its successors. Not all queer theological work is bound up in reconstructing textual realities, however. Instead, Christian and Jewish queer theologians have offered a number of creative, generative, and influential readings of biblical texts and their attendant traditions. Jewish theologians, such as Rebecca Alpert, have reimagined and rewritten rituals to reflect queer Jewish experience.[24] On the Christian side, Marcella Althaus-Reid's work offers a highly influential model of rethinking sexuality and the queer tradition.[25]

Queer Theory, Classics, and Ancient Near Eastern Studies
Biblical studies is also influenced by the disciplines of classics and Near Eastern studies. In the case of classics, a standing interest in Greek sexuality (among both the ancient Greeks and modern scholars) made the field ripe for theoretical work on sex and gender. Foucault's close engagement with Greek and Roman texts in volumes 2 and 3 of *The History of Sexuality* also drew the discipline into the conversation.

---

22. Wilcox, 'Outlaws or In-Laws?', p. 74.
23. Wilcox, 'Outlaws or In-Laws?', Claudia Schippert, 'Implications of Queer Theory for the Study of Religion and Gender: Entering the Third Decade', *Religion and Gender* 1.1 (2011), pp. 66-84 (73).
24. Rebecca T. Alpert, *Like Bread on the Seder Plate: Jewish Lesbians and the Transformation of Tradition* (New York: Columbia University Press, 1998).
25. Marcella Althaus-Reid, *Indecent Theology: Theological Perversions in Sex, Gender, and Politics* (London: Routledge, 2000); *The Queer God* (London: Routledge, 2003). See further Laurel C. Schneider and Carolyn Roncolato, 'Queer Theologies', *Religion Compass* 6.1 (2012), pp. 1-13.

Aside from speculations over the nature of the relationship between Gilgamesh and Enkidu (friends? lovers? homosocial warrior pals?),[26] ancient Near Eastern studies has lagged behind even biblical studies in its approach to sexuality, let alone queer theory. From a Hebrew Bible perspective, one exception is Martti Nissinen, whose work on homoeroticism in the ancient Near East offers a careful comparative consideration with ancient Israel.[27] Equally illuminating from a queer theory perspective is Ken Stone's engagement with Nissinen's work, which critiques Nissinen's narrow focus on 'homosexuality and the Bible' as implicitly heterosexist.[28] As Stone's and Nissinen's work indicates, biblical studies may offer a helpful model for queer theoretical approaches in other ancient Near Eastern contexts.

Queer Theory, Queer Criticism, and the Hebrew Bible

Queer work on the Bible has taken on a number of forms. What was once an uncommon and often risky endeavor—writing 'queer commentary' or 'queering the Bible'—has become a more broadly accepted scholarly practice. This is not to say that queer readings are accepted by all biblical scholars or all institutions at which biblical scholars are employed. However, queer reading asserts itself as having become part of the academic discipline of biblical studies.

The first works of queer biblical studies were often unapologetically political. Inspired both by LGBT activism and by religious organizations (such as the Metropolitan Community Church), their work challenged understandings of the Bible as homophobic and irrelevant to people of Christian and/or Jewish faiths. Often, their projects involved a search for 'queer ancestors' in the pages of the Bible. Nancy Wilson's *Our Tribe: Queer Folks, God, Jesus, and the Bible* is an early and important example of this form of queer reading.[29] Wilson uncovers a number of 'queer folk' in the Bible, among them barren women, eunuchs, and same-sex couples such as David and Jonathan and Ruth and Naomi.[30] A few years later, Robert Goss and Mona West

---

26. David M. Halperin, *One Hundred Years of Homosexuality: And Other Essays on Greek Love* (New York: Routledge, 1989), pp. 75-88.

27. Martti Nissinen, *Homoeroticism in the Biblical World: A Historical Perspective* (Minneapolis: Fortress Press, 1998). See also Martti Nissinen, 'Are There Homosexuals in Mesopotamian Literature?', *JAOS* 130.1 (2010), pp. 73-77.

28. Ken Stone, 'Homosexuality and the Bible or Queer Reading? A Response to Martti Nissinen', *Theology & Sexuality* 14 (2001), pp. 107-18 (114).

29. Nancy L. Wilson, *Our Tribe: Queer Folks, God, Jesus, and the Bible* (San Francisco: HarperSanFrancisco, 1995). From a Jewish perspective, see Gregg Drinkwater, Joshua Lesser, and David Shneer, *Torah Queeries: Weekly Commentaries on the Hebrew Bible* (New York: New York University Press, 2009).

30. Wilson, *Our Tribe*, pp. 120-31, 148-57.

edited *Take Back the Word*, an anthology of queer readings. In many ways, the volume continued the therapeutic or redemptive theological work of early queer readings; the introduction thus promises: 'When queers "take back the Word", we see within the Scriptures visions of hope and dreams of liberation'.[31]

Several years later, Ken Stone edited another collection, *Queer Commentary and the Hebrew Bible*. In the introduction, Stone writes: 'The value of queer intellectual work lies above all in its effects, in the spaces that it opens for voices previously unheard, and in the possibilities that it creates for a transformation of the practices, pleasures, desires and identities associated with sexuality'.[32] The essays that follow live up to Stone's vision in a number of ways, often taking on the playful spirit of certain strands of queer theory. The volume also offers methodological reflections and an increased degree of theoretical sophistication. A mere five years later saw the publication of *The Queer Bible Commentary*, 859 pages devoted to queering every book of the Hebrew Bible and New Testament.[33] While the quality of commentaries is mixed—due, in part, to the varying receptiveness to queer reading of the various books of the Bible, as well as the creativity and skill of the commentators—the very arrival of this anthology signaled the significance of queer theory as a biblical method.

Queer theoretical works on the Bible are not limited to edited volumes or to commentary. Instead, the past fifteen years have seen an increasing number of biblical studies monographs informed by queer theory. Stone's *Practicing Safer Texts: Food, Sex, and Bible in Queer Perspective* offers a reading of a range of biblical texts. The book incorporates queer theoretical work on topics such as public sex, constructions of masculinity, and the boundaries of the body.[34] Stuart Macwilliam's *Queer Theory and the Prophetic Marriage Metaphor* reads the marriage metaphor texts (the subject of frequent feminist commentary) through contemporary queer theory.[35] Theodore Jennings takes up male homoeroticism in the Hebrew Bible.[36] Roland Boer's work frequently touches on queer themes or reading practices; New

---

31. Robert E. Goss and Mona West (eds.), *Take Back the Word: A Queer Reading of the Bible* (Cleveland, OH: The Pilgrim Press, 2000), p. 7.

32. Ken Stone, 'Queer Commentary and Biblical Interpretation: An Introduction', in Ken Stone (ed.), *Queer Commentary and the Hebrew Bible* (JSOTSup, 334; Cleveland, OH: Pilgrim Press, 2001), pp. 11-34 (33).

33. Deryn Guest, Robert E. Goss, Mona West, and Thomas Bohache (eds.), *The Queer Bible Commentary* (London: SCM Press, 2006).

34. Stone, *Practicing Safer Texts*.

35. Stuart Macwilliam, *Queer Theory and the Prophetic Marriage Metaphor in the Hebrew Bible* (Sheffield: Equinox, 2011).

36. Theodore W. Jennings, *Jacob's Wound: Homoerotic Narrative in the Literature of Ancient Israel* (New York: Continuum, 2005).

Testament scholar Stephen D. Moore has also included several queer readings of biblical texts in his works, including a queer reading of the Song of Songs in *God's Beauty Parlor: And Other Queer Spaces in and Around the Bible*.[37] Queer readings are blossoming in biblical studies.

As feminist readers will no doubt recognize, the works listed above share, in addition to their queer reading practices, a pronounced focus on men and masculinities. The texts under discussion feature men and are deeply interested in the category of masculinity. Male sexuality, human or divine, is privileged (sometimes it even figures in autobiographical interludes, as in the work of both Moore and Boer). When women or femininity appear, it is generally in the context of male humiliation. There are, of course, exceptions to this pattern. Deryn Guest's work on a 'lesbian-identified hermeneutic' as well as 'genderqueer criticism' are important examples.[38] There is also scattered work on queer female figures and practices, some of which I discuss below. Still, the field of queer biblical studies remains dominated by masculinity, male sexualities, and male homoeroticisms.

What's Queer? Who's Queer? Reading the Hebrew Bible

As *The Queer Bible Commentary* attests, there are seemingly no biblical texts that cannot be given a queer reading. I want to consider, briefly, a few of the texts that have attracted especially significant or notable attention.

David and Jonathan
In what will surprise no one who has attempted to purchase a greeting card for a gay wedding, the story of David and Jonathan has attracted numerous queer readings. Classifying David and Jonathan's relationship (or, alternately, critiquing the very desire to classify this relationship) has become a minor scholarly industry all its own. Early LGBT and queer readings sought to 'claim' David and Jonathan as queer. More readings, informed by work in queer theory on the historical situatedness of the category of 'homosexuality',[39] have sought instead to understand the relationship as homosociality, warrior homoeroticism, or more generally the politicization

---

37. Roland Boer, *The Earthy Nature of the Bible: Fleshly Readings of Sex, Masculinity, and Carnality* (New York: Palgrave Macmillan, 2012); Stephen D. Moore, *God's Beauty Parlor*.

38. Deryn Guest, *When Deborah Met Jael: Lesbian Biblical Hermeneutics* (London: SCM Press, 2005); *Beyond Feminist Biblical Studies* (The Bible in the Modern World 47, Sheffield: Sheffield Phoenix Press, 2012).

39. Foucault, *The History of Sexuality (vols. 1–3)*; Mark D. Jordan, *The Invention of Sodomy in Christian Theology* (Chicago: University of Chicago Press, 1997).

of sexuality (queer or otherwise).[40] David's relationship with Saul has also come under scrutiny using a queer lens.[41]

Sodom and Gomorrah

The destruction of Sodom and Gomorrah (Genesis 19) has also attracted significant queer attention. Scholarship on Sodom demonstrates the tendency in certain strands of queer interpretation to offer readings that counteract or neutralize 'texts of terror'. These readings pursue a variety of strategies to argue that the problem in Sodom is not sodomy or homosexuality, but something else, such as a failure of hospitality.[42] Both queer and non-queer readings also direct attention to the related story of the Levite's concubine in Judges 19. This intertext, as well as the narrative of Lot's daughters, have sometimes rendered Genesis 19 as a meeting point for queer and feminist reading practices, though not always. The destruction of Sodom and Gomorrah, which also figures occasionally in the prophets, has also been an important text for queer work on the history of interpretation, such as Mark D. Jordan's *The Invention of Sodomy in Christian Theology*.[43]

Yahweh's Marriage

The relationship between Yahweh and the Israelites has been a productive subject for queer readings. Yahweh's relationship with Israel is described in the biblical text as a marriage (for example, Hosea 2, Jeremiah 2–3, Ezekiel 16); the crucial insight of queer theory is that this marriage is a rather queer one. Specifically, the bride of Yahweh, Israel, is really a collective of male believers—hardly a conventional or straight scene of matrimony. This kind of reading already appears in Howard Eilberg-Schwartz's *God's Phallus: And Other Problems for Men and Monotheism* in 1995. It takes the prohibition on images of the divine as a starting point for the male homoeroticisms of the Hebrew Bible.[44] The queer marriage argument reappears across queer scholarship and receives its fullest theoretical articulation in MacWilliam's *Queer Theory and the Prophetic Marriage Metaphor*. But it is not only Yahweh's marriage that has attracted a queer eye. Instead, the divine body, including the phallus according to Eilberg-Schwartz, is also an object

---

40. See, e.g., Jennings, *Jacob's Wound*; Stone, '1 and 2 Samuel', in Guest, Goss, West, and Bohache (eds.), *The Queer Bible Commentary*, pp. 195-221.

41. Jennings, *Jacob's Wound*; Roland Boer, *Knockin' on Heaven's Door* (New York: Routledge, 1999), pp. 13-32.

42. See, e.g., Michael Carden, 'Remembering Pelotit: A Queer Midrash on Calling Down Fire', in Stone (ed.), *Queer Commentary and the Hebrew Bible*, pp. 152-68.

43. Jordan, *The Invention of Sodomy in Christian Theology*.

44. Howard Eilberg-Schwartz, *God's Phallus: And Other Problems for Men and Monotheism* (Boston: Beacon Press, 1995).

of queer interest.[45] Queering God's body has since become a not-uncommon move in queer reading and a resource for conceiving of a queer Bible.

Eunuchs

Long confined to the margins, eunuchs have been accorded significant attention in queer readings of the Bible. In many early works of queer reading, such as Wilson's *Our Tribe,* eunuchs are identified as queer ancestors positioned outside dominant sexual norms and celebrated.[46] However, queer readers have not universally accepted the figure of the eunuch. Many LGBT or queer readers resist being identified with or as eunuchs.[47] A second critique concerns the role of eunuchs in constructing biblical masculinity. Do the eunuchs truly represent an alternate sexuality or are they a figure of 'deficient' masculinity that serves to humiliate Israelite men? If this is the case, then the eunuchs no longer represent any sort of 'outside' to a patriarchal and heterosexist sex-gender system. Alternately, if the eunuchs are taken as points of identification for a trans reading, the narrative risks setting trans and cisgender women against each other.[48] If so, the text is hardly a cause for queer celebration, especially given the relative scarcity of trans readings of the Hebrew Bible.[49]

Lament and Wisdom Literature

Lamentations and other texts of lament have proved surprisingly significant to queer readings of the Bible. These texts have provided a valuable resource for queer communities confronting the AIDS epidemic. Mona West writes: 'The poetry of Lamentations provides those in the Queer community who are in "mute despair" words to order and articulate their experience'.[50] Ken Stone makes a similar argument about the book of Job, particularly Job's vigorous protests.[51] Finally, Deryn Guest maintains that Lamentations and

---

45. Stephen D. Moore, *God's Gym: Divine Male Bodies of the Bible* (New York: Routledge, 1996).
46. Wilson, *Our Tribe*, pp. 281-85, offers a 'Roll Call of Eunuchs'. See also Ron L. Stanley, 'Ezra-Nehemiah', in Guest, Goss, West, and Bohache (eds.), *The Queer Bible Commentary*, pp. 268-77.
47. Timothy R. Koch, 'Cruising as Methodology: Homoeroticism and the Scriptures', in Stone (ed.), *Queer Commentary and the Hebrew Bible*, pp. 169-80 (174).
48. Victoria S. Kolakowski, 'Throwing a Party: Patriarchy, Gender, and the Death of Jezebel', in Gross and West (eds.), *Take Back the Word*, pp. 109-14.
49. See, e.g., Moore, *God's Gym*; Boer, 'Yahweh as Top'.
50. Mona West, 'The Gift of Voice, the Gift of Tears: A Queer Reading of Lamentations in the Context of AIDS', in Stone (ed.), *Queer Commentary and the Hebrew Bible*, pp. 140-51 (141).
51. Ken Stone, 'Job', in Guest, Goss, West, and Bohache (eds.), *The Queer Bible Commentary*, pp. 286-303 (294-95).

lament literature speak to LGBT and queer victims of violence and harassment.[52] These studies offer a model for queer interpretations of poetic and wisdom texts.

Laws Policing Sexual Practice and Gender Identity
It is not only narrative and poetic texts that attract queer readings. Biblical laws concerning sexual practice and gender performance have also attracted the attention of queer readers. Of particular importance are a handful of 'texts of terror', including Lev. 18.20 and 20.13 (prohibitions on male-male anal intercourse) and Deut. 22.5 (the prohibition on cross-dressing). Much ink has been spilled over what, precisely, the prohibitions in Leviticus mean.[53] The debate assumes familiar contours. Some scholars argue for the historical situatedness of the prohibition. Others turn to comparative evidence or the finer points of philology to understand what is 'really' meant, some summon narrative counter-texts, such as David and Jonathan. Still others suggest that the prohibition is part of a general 'othering' of non-Israelites as sexual deviants. Ken Stone's 'The Hermeneutics of Abomination' offers a good summation of, and intervention in, this debate.[54] The question of gender identity, as well as trans and intersex issues, in many ways resemble the ongoing debates about 'the Bible and homosexuality', and seem primed to repeat many of its contours. There are no explicit prohibitions on female-female sexual activity in the Hebrew Bible.

Queer Women?
In this proliferation of queer readings, where are all the women? The neglect of female experience and female eroticism is indeed a major critique that has been levied against queer readings of the Bible. Still, a few female figures have attracted queer readings. Ruth and Naomi have been read as queer lovers, with Ruth's words of dedication taken up as a moving description of same-sex love.[55] However, other readers have

---

52. Deryn Guest, 'Lamentations', in Guest, Goss, West, and Bohache (eds.), *The Queer Bible Commentary*, pp. 394-411 (400).

53. For an introduction, see Ilona N. Rashkow, *Taboo Or Not Taboo: Sexuality and Family in the Hebrew Bible* (Minneapolis, MN: Fortress Press, 2000), pp. 15-42; Martti Nissinen, *Homoeroticism in the Biblical World*; Jerome T. Walsh, 'Leviticus 18:22 and 20:13: Who Is Doing What to Whom?', *JBL* 120.2 (2001), pp. 201-209.

54. Ken Stone, 'The Hermeneutics of Abomination: On Gay Men, Canaanites, and Biblical Interpretation', *BTB* 27.2 (May 1997), pp. 36-41.

55. Mona West, 'Ruth', in Guest, Goss, West and Bohache (eds.), *The Queer Bible Commentary*, pp. 190-94. See as well Rebecca Alpert, 'Finding Our Past: A Lesbian Reading of the Book of Ruth', in Judith A. Kates and Gail Twersky Reimer (eds.), *Reading Ruth: Contemporary Women Reclaim a Sacred Story* (New York: Ballantine Books, 1996), pp. 91-96.

challenged this interpretation, noting Ruth's reintegration into the heterosexual economy as Boaz' wife and David's ancestress. Esther has also attracted queer attention. In her classic *Epistemology of the Closet*, Eve Kosofsky Sedgwick argues that Esther's concealment and eventual revelation of her Jewish identity represent a 'coming out' story and fit the larger pattern Sedgwick terms 'the epistemology of the closet'.[56] Other queer readers have associated Esther (both the queen and the book) with the categories of drag and of camp.[57]

Many of the most famous female characters in biblical narrative have received only limited attention. This reflects both lesbian erasure[58] and the depressingly banal fact that almost no biblical narratives pass the so-called 'Bechdel test' (two women talk to each other, not about a man).[59] This lack of narratives between women facilitates the neglect of female eroticism. Still, the relationships between Rachel and Leah and between Sarah and Hagar have received some attention. Drawing on anthropological and ethnographic accounts of female friendship, companionship, and love, Gale Yee recovers the possibility of reading alternate motifs, such as 'cooperation' and 'solace', into relationships between women in the text. That these relationships are primarily presented as scenes of conflict between women is itself an effect of the androcentric gender economy of the text.[60] Building on Yee's analysis, Guest argues that the subaltern position of women, combined with the prevalence of 'sexually segregated space', facilitated certain forms of female companionship and eroticism, including 'finding support, solace, sexual satisfaction and a sense of solidarity in the arms of female partners'.[61] Yee and Guest offer helpful models. Challenging the assumption that relationships between women are necessarily competitive (as well as the assumption of compulsory heterosexuality) opens the possibility of new forms of relations, including female homoeroticism.

Beyond reconstructing suppressed love and desire between women, scholars have offered multiple queer strategies to respond to the apparent lack of female homoeroticism in the text. Taking as an example Bathsheba, Guest proposes an erotics of reading that positions the female figure in the

---

56. Sedgwick, *Epistemology of the Closet*, pp. 74-81.

57. Mona West, 'Esther', in Guest, Goss, West, and Bohache (eds.), *The Queer Bible Commentary*, pp. 278-85.

58. Guest, *When Deborah Met Jael*, p. 112.

59. Alison Bechdel, *Dykes to Watch Out for* (Ithaca, NY: Firebrand Books, 1986), pp. 22-23. Bechdel does not claim the rule as her own but rather thanks Liz Wallace; however, in popular parlance it has come to be known as the Bechdel (not Wallace) Test.

60. Gale A. Yee, *Poor Banished Children of Eve: Woman as Evil in the Hebrew Bible* (Minneapolis: Augsburg Fortress, 2003), p. 54.

61. Guest, *When Deborah Met Jael,* pp. 145-46.

text in relation to a lesbian-identified reader/spectator.[62] Laurel Schneider, meanwhile, suggests,

> The queerest stories of women in the Hebrew Bible may in fact be those about women who managed to have a voice at all, women who managed to survive and/or overcome with some kind of chutzpah their barrenness, widowhood, slavery, rape, virginity, abandonment, marriage, ugliness, and other signifiers of their male-derivative identity, economic dependency and status.[63]

Indeed, it is in tracing a broad range of '[queer] stories of women in the Hebrew Bible' that feminist and queer methods find many of their most valuable intersections.

Queer Theory and Feminist Critique: Four Challenges

Although queer theory is in many ways indebted to feminist methods, its commitment to feminism remains contested. Four feminist challenges to queer theory are particularly pronounced.

Does Queer Theory Neglect Feminist Critique? The First Challenge

The first and perhaps most dire challenge to queer biblical criticism concerns its basic relationship to feminist critique. As we have already seen, queer readings at present are predominantly concerned with masculinity. At best, women, female sexuality, and female homoeroticism are under-theorized. At worst, queer readings reintroduce old misogyny. Assessing queer theory's feminist credentials, Guest writes: 'There is justifiable concern that queer will turn out to be a critical tool that is insufficiently cognizant of the feminist criticism that precedes it and enabled its birth. At worst, the anxiety is that queer will not be gender neutral but will install a new universal masculinity at its heart.'[64] Queer theory runs the danger of replacing the universal heterosexual subject with a (queer) male subject.

More specifically, queer theory risks forgetting feminist critique in at least two ways: neglecting women and female sexuality as a *subject* and neglecting the methods of feminist critique as *tools* of critical inquiry. While addressing the former is an important step toward a more feminist queer criticism (that is, queer topics should not be synonymous with 'a new universal masculinity), this on its own is not sufficient. Roland Boer, for

---

62. Deryn Guest, 'Looking Lesbian at the Bathing Bathsheba', *BI* 16.3 (May 2008), pp. 227-62.

63. Laurel C. Schneider, 'Yahwist Desires: Imagining Divinity Queerly', in Ken Stone (ed.), *Queer Commentary and the Hebrew Bible*, pp. 210-27 (218).

64. Guest, *When Deborah Met Jael*, p. 46.

example, notes the absence of women in the biblical text through an imagined conversation between the Marquis de Sade and Moses:

> 'What a nice little gathering; a pity there's no women', he [Sade] begins.
> 'The Hebrew Bible is like that', observes Moses.[65]

Noting the absence of women with a wink and a nudge functions as a knowing acknowledgement of the dilemma. It is not enough, however, to compensate for the lack of any sort of critical engagement with 'women' or female sexuality.

There is also a serious concern that feminist and queer methods are, on some level, incommensurable. Clarke writes:

> For many, the largely deconstructive theoretical underpinnings of queer theory represent a real threat to some of the political and intellectual claims that feminist work has been making. To put this a little more precisely, political and ideological radicalism that makes sense within the conceptual boundaries of queer theory does not always travel well, especially where relationships between language and power have traditionally been exceptionally close.[66]

There is a real way in which the deconstructive and even radical positions of queer theory threaten feminist critique, especially when the feminist reading of a text is bound up with women's lived experience as gendered subjects. Responding to queer readings that emphasize Yahweh's masculinity and his homoerotic relationship with the male Israelites, Schneider notes that such readings can lead 'to a further marginalization of women' and 'really can come to suggest a misogynistic strain in the human-divine relationship. This leaves contemporary women exegetes of all kinds, and queer women in particular, in an awkward (and all too familiar) position'.[67] Queer readings thus risks replicating the worst tendencies of pre-feminist critique —hardly something to aspire to. Negotiating the potential elision or even suppression of women and of feminist perspectives remains a crucial task for queer biblical readings.

Does Queer Theory Abandon Its Political Commitments? The Second Challenge

A second critique of queer theory concerns its relationship to activism. Feminist theory and gay and lesbian studies share activist origins, with theoretical work linked to political and other forms of activism. In the early stages of queer readings of the Bible such as *Our Tribe* or *Take Back the Word*, this activist impulse is clear. Even *The Queer Bible Commentary* opens with an

---

65. See, e.g., Boer, 'Yahweh as Top', p. 86.
66. Clarke, 'Finding the Subject', p. 79.
67. Schneider, 'Yahwist Desires', p. 217.

essay entitled 'Disarming Biblically-Based Gay Bashing'.[68] Yet not all queer work in biblical studies shares in this therapeutic or theological impulse. Some queer readers are openly critical of such projects to redeem the text and position their work as an unveiling of the text as dangerous, historically specific, or irrelevant to the contemporary moment; this sort of reading may also constitute a political or theological act. However, other queer readings adopt the playful spirit of queer as a sort of hipper, more modern alternative to poststructuralism, postmodernism, or 'Theory' as such. This usage, however, dilutes the political force of 'queer', including its use by activists such as Queer Nation and ACT UP. As Marcus writes, 'If everyone is queer, no one is'.[69] Similarly, if queer is used only to mark a style of playing with language, it loses any sort of political or critical thrust.

For Guest, the refusal of political commitment is grounds for rejecting queer theory in favor of a lesbian-centered approach. Guest, one of the editors of *The Queer Bible Commentary*, calls for a 'lesbian-identified hermeneutics' that is 'indebted to its feminist roots' and 'committed to liberative engagement, committed to making a difference'.[70] As Guest demonstrates in *When Deborah Met Jael: Lesbian Biblical Interpretation*, a lesbian-identified hermeneutic maintains strong political commitments to equality and human rights for lesbians and others. It likewise stands against the erasure of women that queer reading sometimes perpetuates. Shifting from queer theory to 'a feminist-informed, lesbian-identified hermeneutic' is one way to maintain the political force of critique. It is not the only way, however, and Guest leaves open the possibility that queer theory might also perform this work. In *Beyond Feminist Biblical Criticism*, published in 2012, she goes further, proposing 'genderqueer' criticism as a form of scholarship and practice of liberation. As part of this project, the volume offers a series of strategies for 'queer straight feminists', 'gender traitors', and other 'genderqueer hermeneut[s]' to approach texts and contexts alike.[71] Guest notes, 'Changing the agenda of biblical studies and its heteronormative framework is not only a matter of theory and its application, it is also a practical matter of individual, disparate, situational politics', which occur in classrooms, academic departments, committee meetings, and everyday life.[72]

Guest's genderqueer hermeneut—an identity 'identified not by who one *is,* but by what one *does* with biblical texts' (as a teacher, a scholar, a human

---

68. Ronald E. Long, 'Introduction: Disarming Biblically Based Gay-Bashing', in Guest, Goss, West and Bohache (eds.), *The Queer Bible Commentary*, pp. 1-20. See also Brintnall, 'Queer Studies and Religion', pp. 52-53.
69. Marcus, 'Queer Theory for Everyone', p. 196.
70. Guest, *When Deborah Met Jael*, p. 237.
71. Guest, *Beyond Feminist Biblical Criticism*, pp. 152, 157, 162.
72. Guest, *Beyond Feminist Biblical Criticism*, p. 163.

being)—offers a model of scholarship that brings together scholarship and social justice.[73] Other queer theorists and scholars, however, have resisted such moves, for a range of reasons. It is possible, for example, to argue that efforts at incremental or internal change (in academic, religious, or other institutions) are insufficiently radical and that cooperation with such efforts is naïve or even a form of collusion. Other queer readers are simply uninterested in tying sexualities, textual or otherwise, to politics. The political commitments and activist engagement of queer biblical studies thus remain an open question for scholars.[74]

Does Queer Theory Adequately Address Race, Ethnicity, and Other Forms of Identity? The Third Challenge

It is not only gender that queer theory is accused of neglecting. In addition, critics have challenged queer theory on grounds of race, ethnicity, and class. In his response to *Queer Commentary and the Hebrew Bible*, Tat-siong Benny Liew raises the issue forcefully, charging that the range of essays and contributors 'continue to (dis)miss...how various texts elide nation and culture—and thus race and ethnicity—within sexuality and gender'.[75] Liew's critique remains largely unanswered. In *The Queer Bible Commentary*, ethnicity and race figure only occasionally. There are a few exceptions; Michael Carden, for example, frames his queer reading of Joshua by writing 'The book is about the Other, the othering process, deploying sexuality and gender, together with ethnicity and religion to mark the boundaries of the community and outsider'.[76] Sexuality remains largely divorced from questions of ethnicity and race as well as social class.

It is not only in biblical studies that queer theory operates largely independently of a rigorous critique of other axes of identity. In coining the term 'Queer Theory', de Lauretis sought to introduce race, ethnicity, and gender to the analysis of sexuality and, in Halperin's words, 'to offer a possible escape from the hegemony of white, male, middle-class models of analysis'.[77] Yet her efforts have been largely ignored, and certain structures of privilege have reasserted themselves, subtly or less so. Still, more recent

---

73. Guest, *Beyond Feminist Biblical Criticism*, p. 163.

74. Guest herself raises the question 'What about the politics?' with respect to the practice of queer theory. See further Guest, *Beyond Feminist Biblical Studies*, pp. 68-71.

75. Tat-siong Benny Liew, '(Cor)Responding: A Letter to the Editor', in Ken Stone (ed.), *Queer Commentary and the Hebrew Bible*, pp. 182-92 (186).

76. Michael Carden, 'Joshua', in Guest, Goss, West and Bohache (eds.), *The Queer Bible Commentary*, pp. 144-66 (166). Ken Stone also addresses ethnicity in his interpretation of the books of Samuel and Kings; see Stone, '"1 and 2 Samuel" and "1 and 2 Kings"', in Guest, Goss, West and Bohache (eds.), *The Queer Bible Commentary*, pp. 195-250.

77. Halperin, 'The Normalization of Queer Theory', p. 340.

work in queer theory has sought to address these shortcomings. One tactic has focused on reconstructing alternate genealogies of the field of queer theory that acknowledge the contributions of critical race studies and ethnic studies and the work of scholars and writers such as Gloria Anzaldúa, Cherríe Moraga, and James Baldwin.[78] In addition to reimagining genealogies, other work in queer theory has sought to intentionally integrate race and ethnicity, offering an instructive example for biblical studies. As Schippert writes of queer theory and religious studies:

> The emerging body of queer ethnic and diasporic scholarship challenges many assumptions in conventional—including queer conventional—scholarship regarding kinship or same sex desire. It is producing new perspectives and a reordering of issues concerning identities, nationalism, communities, and material practices. Scholars of religion and gender have a rich emerging body of critical work to engage—to which scholarship attentive to gendered rituals or transformative practices can make important contributions.[79]

Her words hold as true for biblical studies as they do for the study of religion.

Integrating race and ethnicity into the study of sexuality also offers a promising point of contact between queer and feminist studies of biblical texts. This is because feminist biblical criticism, too, has struggled to address the intersections of gender, ethnicity, and class.[80] As for feminisms, so too for queer theory and the Hebrew Bible: race, ethnicity, and other forms of difference are essential and must be addressed.

Is Queer Theory Homonormative and/or Homonationalist? The Fourth Challenge

The final critique I want to consider in relation to queer reading comes from within contemporary queer theory: the charge of homonormativity and, relatedly, homonationalism. 'Homonormativity' was coined by Lisa Duggan to name certain troubling developments in the practice of queer politics and identity. Duggan describes homonormativity as

> a politics that does not contest dominant heteronormative assumptions and institutions but upholds and sustains them while promising the possibility of a demobilized gay constituency and a privatized, depoliticized gay culture anchored in domesticity and consumption.[81]

---

78. Brintnall, 'Queer Studies and Religion', p. 54. De Lauretis mentions Moraga, Anzaldúa, and a number of other gay and lesbian writers of color in her original article; see De Lauretis, 'Queer Theory', pp. viii-xi.

79. Schippert, 'Implications of Queer Theory for the Study of Religion and Gender', p. 76.

80. Esther Fuchs, 'Biblical Feminisms: Knowledge, Theory and Politics in the Study of Women in the Hebrew Bible', *BI* 16.3 (2008), pp. 205-26 (225-26).

81. Lisa Duggan, 'The New Homonormativity: The Sexual Politics of Neoliberalism',

Just as earlier critiques drew attention to queer theory's neglect of gender, race, ethnicity, and class, Duggan's argument calls out certain forms of queer politics that align with neoliberalism.

Building on this argument about homonormativity, Jasbir Puar offers an important theorization of 'homonationalism' in *Terrorist Assemblages: Homonationalism in Queer Times*. Puar argues that certain forms of queerness, particularly queerness under neoliberalism, trade political stability for participation in orientalism, racism, and other forms of state domination.[82] Here 'pinkwashing'—promoting LGBT rights to cover human rights abuses, especially of non-white subjects—is a common example.[83] Joseph Marchal has argued that biblical studies ought to engage critically with homonationalism, writing: 'The task of bringing Puar's work into engagement with ostensibly foundational(ist) religious figures, texts or traditions would be a stimulating, even necessary operation'.[84] Taking homonationalism seriously will bring queer biblical studies in conversation with larger debates about sexuality, security discourses, and imperialism. It also provides a point of continuity with feminist debates over gender, colonialism, and neoliberalism.[85] Here, queer and feminist critiques have the opportunity to benefit from each other's negotiations of gender, sexuality, and the political order.

Conclusions: Feminist and Queer?

Queer theory is no longer a stranger to biblical studies. In particular, it has many overlaps with feminist critique and holds great potential as a feminist method. In taking seriously sexuality, the sexed body, and the critique of essentialism, it continues the work of feminist critique. It also offers new ways of reading texts that have long drawn the attention of feminist readers. Still, there are also risks. In its playfulness, queer theory shakes up categories and calcified modes of thought, but this same playfulness has also been charged with ignoring the lived experience of gender and the high stakes surrounding gender and sexuality alike. Queer theory likewise threatens

---

in Russ Castronovo and Dana D. Nelson (eds.), *Materializing Democracy: Toward a Revitalized Cultural Politics* (Durham, NC: Duke University Press, 2002), pp. 175-94 (179).

82. Jasbir K. Puar, *Terrorist Assemblages: Homonationalism in Queer Times* (Durham, NC: Duke University Press, 2007).

83. Jasbir Puar, 'Rethinking Homonationalism', *International Journal of Middle East Studies* 45.2 (2013), pp. 336-39 (337).

84. Joseph A. Marchal, 'Bio-Necro-Biblio-Politics? Restaging Feminist Intersections and Queer Exceptions', *Culture and Religion* 15.2 (2014), pp. 166-76 (170).

85. For example Charles Hirschkind and Saba Mahmood, 'Feminism, the Taliban, and Politics of Counter-Insurgency', *Anthropological Quarterly* 75.2 (2002), pp. 339-54.

to become a theory of queer men and masculinities only, erasing lesbians and lesbian-oriented hermeneutics. Indeed, queer theory must be vigilant to avoid reinscribing old forms of domination, such as masculine supremacy, or supporting new ones, such as neoliberal homonationalism. There are risks involved in queer theory – but also risks in ignoring it. If feminist theorists do not take queer theory seriously, both disciplines will be the worse for it. Queer theory needs feminist critique, even as feminist readings of the Bible benefit from a queer touch.

16

MODES OF PRODUCTIONS AND READING LABORS ON THE MARGINS:
MARXIST FEMINIST CRITICISM OF THE HEBREW BIBLE

Roland Boer

Of feminist criticism of the Hebrew Bible there is already a rich history; of Marxist criticism there is once again a fluorescence; but of Marxist feminist criticism there is less of a tradition than one might expect. This situation means that a survey of the historical trends in Marxist feminist biblical criticism must focus on the contributions of key individual scholars. Thus, in the first section of the following, I survey the work of Gale Yee, David Jobling, and Avaren Ipsen. This critical survey forms the bulk of the presentation, raising a number of critical issues (second section) and then potential future directions in light of the current situation (third section).

Before proceeding, a couple of introductory matters need to be addressed. To begin with, 'Marxist feminism' relates to the feminist and Marxist traditions in slightly different ways. With respect to feminism, by Marxist feminism I mean all of the versions of radical feminism that owe some debt to the work of Marx and Engels.[1] Thus, Marxist feminism is not another

---

1. For some wider theoretical context, see Christine Delphy, *Close to Home: A Materialist Analysis of Women's Oppression* (Amherst: University of Massachusetts Press, 1984); Rosemary Hennessy, *Materialist Feminism and the Politics of Discourse* (London: Routledge, 1993); Rosemary Hennessy and Chrys Ingraham (eds.), *Materialist Feminism: A Reader in Class, Difference, and Women's Lives* (London: Routledge, 1997); Donna Landry and Gerald MacLean, *Materialist Feminisms* (Cambridge: Blackwell, 1993); Toril Moi and Janice Radway (eds.), *Materialist Feminism* (Durham, NC: Duke University Press, 1994); Michèle Barrett, *Women's Oppression Today: The Marxist/Feminist Encounter* (London: Verso, 2014). Another good scholarly source is *Lies: A Journal of Materialist Feminism*. By contrast, the so-called 'new materialism' studiously avoids the long and detailed tradition of Marxism. The omission may be a leftover from the end of the Cold War, which some regard as a delegitimization of Marxist approaches. For a sample of new materialist feminism, see Stacey Alaimo and Susan Hekman (eds.), *Material Feminisms* (Bloomington: Indiana University Press, 2008). For an insightful Marxist feminist criticism of these developments, see Martha E. Gimenez, 'What's Material About Materialist Feminism? A Marxist Feminist Critique', *Radical Philosophy* 101 (2000), pp. 18-27. This article is also available at http://www.colorado.edu/Sociology/gimenez/work/rphil.html.

faction within the collection of Left feminisms, taking its place alongside radical, anarchist, poststructuralist, postcolonial, transgender, and green feminisms. In regard to Marxism, I mean the dimension that explicitly includes matters of gender within the collection of problems known as Marxism. This assumes that Marxism is less an established template with given answers, but rather a set of problems that are constantly debated and reconfigured. It would be a mistake, however, to see Marxist feminism as a corrective to a blind spot within Marxism concerning gender. This mistake is understandable if one views the history of Marxism through the prism of English-speaking Western Marxism. In this case, Juliet Mitchell's article, 'Women: The Longest Revolution', from the early days of the New Left is often seen as the moment when feminist issues were first addressed within Marxism.[2] The Western New Left may well have neglected women in its agenda, but the perception generated by Mitchell's article is both misleading and implicitly imperialist. It points out that the liberation of women was a core platform for nineteenth and early twentieth-century socialism, but it neglects the first real political achievements for women among the Bolsheviks after the Russian Revolution. Here Alexandra Kollontai is the most important revolutionary, although Clara Zetkin and Rosa Luxemburg were also key participants from the German socialist movement.[3] Indeed, the first substantial achievements for working and peasant women happened in the Soviet Union—in terms of education, economic opportunity, social standing, reproductive rights, and political participation. The achievements took place in the first state-sponsored affirmative action program,[4] although it is usually neglected in Western narratives of the history of feminism, let alone Marxism.

A further preliminary matter concerns the scope of this study. I focus on biblical scholars who make explicit and intelligent use of Marxist feminist approaches. I do not deal with a much wider range of scholars who have

2. Juliett Mitchell, 'Women: The Longest Revolution', *New Left Review* 1.40 (1966), pp. 11-37. The article alludes to the deeply influential book by Raymond Williams, *The Long Revolution* (London: Chatto and Windus, 1961).

3. Alexandra Kollontai, *Selected Writings* (trans. Alix Holt; New York: Norton, 1980); Alexandra Kollontai, *The Essential Alexandra Kollontai* (trans. Alix Holt; Chicago: Haymarket, 2008); Klara Zetkin, *Selected Writings* (New York: International Publishers, 1984); Klara Zetkin, 'Organising Working Women', *International Socialism: A Quarterly Journal of Socialist Theory* 96 (1977 [1922]), pp. 22-24; Rosa Luxemburg, *Ausgewählte Reden und Schriften* (2 vols.; Berlin: Dietz, 1951), pp. 433-41. See also https://www.marxists.org/archive/luxemburg/1912/05/12.htm.

4. Terry Martin, *The Affirmative Action Empire: Nations and Nationalism in the Soviet Union, 1923–1939* (Ithaca, NY: Cornell University Press, 2001); Choi Chatterjee, *Celebrating Women: Gender, Festival Culture, and Bolshevik Ideology, 1910–1939* (Pittsburgh: University of Pittsburgh Press, 2002).

deployed and continue to deploy the approaches of Western European feminists such as Simone de Beauvoir, Julia Kristeva, Luce Irigaray, and Helene Cixous. The reason is not that these philosophers are not Marxist, but that the Marxism with which they struggled has almost invariably been quietly dropped as they were appropriated for English language biblical (and indeed literary) scholarship. To be sure, their relations with Marxism were critical and often 'heretical' (in the best traditions of Marxism), but their theories took root in an intellectual soil that was inescapably socialist and communist. Yet as they have been taken up by biblical scholars, the distinctly Marxist tone of their deliberations has disappeared. It is not my task to restore that dimension of their work, for my agenda is more modest: to present the work of biblical scholars who explicitly deploy Marxist feminist approaches.

Key Contributions

The major contributions to Marxist feminist criticism may be relatively few, but they are nonetheless significant.[5]

Gale A. Yee
In Hebrew Bible studies, the most sustained project is that of Gale A. Yee, to whom I devote considerable space due to the importance of her work. Later, I also outline the main contributions of David Jobling and Avaren Ipsen. Tellingly, in an American context, Yee is usually celebrated as a feminist scholar rather than as a Marxist feminist. Yet she consistently points out that her work draws on historical materialist approaches, as well as on feminism and the social sciences—a combination she calls ideological criticism. Yee combines a robust Marxist economic and political framework, a concern with reading texts from below, and a focus on women comprising the most marginalized and silenced voices of the texts. Yee's major work to date is *Poor Banished Children of Eve: Women as Evil in the Hebrew Bible*.[6] Here she offers studies of Eve in Genesis, Gomer in Hosea, Oholah and Oholibah in Ezekiel, and the 'strange woman' of Proverbs 1–9.[7] Before

---

5. I do not discuss liberation theology directly here, not only because of its wary dealings with Marx. Liberation theology made use of Marxist analysis for socio-economic conditions, but it was much more comfortable with the ambiguous tradition of Roman Catholic social teaching.
6. Gale A. Yee, *Poor Banished Children of Eve: Woman as Evil in the Hebrew Bible* (Minneapolis: Fortress Press, 2003).
7. See also Gale A. Yee, 'The Other Woman in Proverbs: "My Man's Not Home… He Took His Money Bag with Him"', in Roland Boer and Jorunn Økland (eds.), *Marxist Feminist Criticism of the Bible* (Sheffield: Sheffield Phoenix Press, 2008), pp. 98-133.

doing so, she offers a clear explanation of the methodological basis of her approach to biblical texts.

Yee argues that gender cannot be separated from oppression in terms of class, ethnicity, or colonialism. Rather than fall back on 'intersectionality' and its inability to deal effectively with such matters,[8] she draws upon the stronger materialist-feminist tradition for her method. Here material (economic and social) realities connect with ideologies (patterns of meaning-making that conceal their origins in situations of struggle).[9] These two factors form an extrinsic and intrinsic analysis in her work: the former concerns the broader Marxist framework for situating the texts, specifically the economic categories of modes of production and forces of production, or the economic and social forms that produce any given situation; the latter deals with the text itself, especially the rhetorical strategies by which it engages with and reshapes the ideologies produced within social and economic forms, often producing imaginary resolutions of real social and economic contradictions.[10]

In more detail, Yee's extrinsic analysis draws heavily on the work of Norman Gottwald,[11] who distinguished between two modes of production in ancient Israel. The tributary mode of production was characteristic of the city-based ruling class, led by the local despot or aspiring emperor, and extracted various forms of tribute (native and foreign) from the laboring peasantry and other lesser states. By contrast, the communitarian mode of production was peasant-based and relied on the clan-based allocation and reallocation of labor, land, and produce. For Gottwald, early Israel challenged the dominant tributary mode with its communitarian mode, which was based in the Judean hills. Later, with the arrival of the monarchy in 'Israel', a tributary mode was reinstated, although it did not close down the

---

8. Kimberlé Crenshaw, 'Mapping the Margins: Intersectionality, Identity Politics, and Violence against Women of Color', *Stanford Law Review* 43.6 (1991), pp. 1241-99; Leslie McCall, 'The Complexity of Intersectionality', *Signs: Journal of Women in Culture and Society* 30.3 (2005), pp. 1771-1800; Jennifer Nash, 'Rethinking Intersectionality', *Feminist Review* 89.1 (2008), pp. 1-15.

9. Yee offers a detailed exposition of her understanding of the contradictory complexity of ideology, drawing heavily on Terry Eagleton; see Yee, *Poor Banished Children of Eve: Woman as Evil in the Hebrew Bible*, pp. 9-28. The work of Michèle Barrett is also useful outlining the two traditions within Marxism concerning critical and descriptive understandings of ideology; see Michèle Barrett, *The Politics of Truth: From Marx to Foucault* (Stanford: Stanford University Press, 1991), pp. 18-34.

10. This crucial insight comes from her relatively rare references to Fredric Jameson, *The Political Unconscious: Narrative as a Socially Symbolic Act* (Ithaca, NY: Cornell University Press, 1981), pp. 79-80.

11. Norman K. Gottwald, *The Tribes of Yahweh: A Sociology of Liberated Israel 1250–1050 BC* (reprint with new preface; Sheffield: Sheffield Academic Press, 1999 [1979]).

constant challenges posed by the purveyors of the communitarian mode. Even Jesus drew on this communitarian tradition. In taking up and developing Gottwald's proposal, Yee prefers to call the communitarian mode a familial mode of production, emphasizing its patterns of mutual support and its comparatively better situation for women. Like Gottwald, she designates the settlement of the highlands in Judea during the long economic crisis at the turn of the first millennium BCE as such a familial mode.[12] The choice of 'familial' shifts the focus to the role of the clan as the key economic and social unit in the peasant agriculture of the Southern Levant.[13]

Yee argues that this mode of production provided relatively more scope for women, given its mutually supportive nature, levelling of class differences, minimization of division of labor, and the necessity of a greater sharing of roles. I would add here the flexibility and malleability of uses of space and roles that show up in the archaeological record of village life. For instance, in the 'cult corners' it is difficult to distinguish between sacred and profane uses. The same space was constantly reproduced through its usage. What may have been used for cultic purposes was also used for everyday activities, belying a sharp separation between the two. Instead, while the corner was the location for a sheaf of grain, worked animal bone, amulet, figurine, incense, jug of beer, or a representation of food left for the sake of a god of harvest, or perhaps for animal wellbeing, safe birth of a child, or for the rains at the right time, it was also the place to put a cooling cooking

---

12. Gale A. Yee, 'The Creation of Poverty in Ancient Israel', in Ronald Simkins and Thomas Kelly (eds.), *The Bible, the Economy, and the Poor* (Omaha: Creighton University, 2014), pp. 4-19 (6).

13. Other terms, with largely the same understanding of its economic and social practices, include 'domestic' and 'household'; see Marshall Sahlins, *Stone Age Economics* (Chicago: Aldine-Etherton, 1972). See also Carol Meyers, *Discovering Eve: Ancient Israelite Women in Context* (New York: Oxford University Press, 1988); Carol Meyers, 'The Family in Early Israel', in Leo S. Purdue *et al.* (eds.), *Families in Ancient Israel* (Louisville, KY: Westminster/John Knox Press, 1997), pp. 1-47; David Jobling, 'Feminism and "Mode of Production" in Ancient Israel: Search for a Method', in David Jobling, Peggy L. Day, and Gerald T. Sheppard (eds.), *The Bible and the Politics of Exegesis: Essays in Honor of Norman K. Gottwald on His Sixty-Fifth Birthday* (Cleveland: Pilgrim Press, 1991), pp. 239-51; David Jobling, *1 Samuel* (Collegeville, MN: Liturgical Press, 1998); Ronald Simkins, 'Gender Construction in the Yahwist Creation Myth', in Athalya Brenner (ed.), *Genesis: The Feminist Companion to the Bible (Second Series)* (Sheffield: Sheffield Academic Press, 1998), pp. 32-52; Ronald Simkins, 'Patronage and the Political Economy of Ancient Israel', *Semeia* 87 (1999), pp. 123-44; Ronald Simkins, 'Class and Gender in Early Israel', in Mark Sneed (ed.), *Concepts of Class in Ancient Israel* (Atlanta: Scholars Press, 1999), pp. 71-86; Ronald Simkins, 'Family in the Political Economy of Ancient Israel', *The Bible and Critical Theory* 1.1 (2004), http://novaojs.newcastle.edu.au/ojsbct/index.php/bct/article/view/19.

pot, a loaf of bread before a meal, or some clothes needing repair.[14] The flexible use—by both men and women—of these spaces indicates the way the sacred was interwoven with everyday life. Yet Yee is also fully aware that these activities took place under the direction of the clan head who was always a male. Thus, Yee wants to know how women both subverted such a situation, through 'weapons of the weak' and the exercise of informal power, and constituted a world of their own through a 'conspiracy of silence'.[15]

The question emerges how one should read the biblical texts in such a context, which which is twice removed from the lives of peasant women. Not only are the lives of peasants largely absent from texts, but women's lives are doubly absent, both through their own agency and through the studied neglect of the text's producers. Luckily, biblical texts exhibit traces of their lives, albeit in the negative characterizations of women. Ideology, however, is always contradictory, so we cannot expect to find uniform patterns. For instance, in Hosea the ruling class of northern Israel becomes an adulterous wife who runs after her lovers (foreign states). Ezekiel 23 (and 16) gives voice through its violent and misogynist language to the trauma of a ruling class that had been colonized and disempowered. Proverbs 1–9, coming from a postexilic context, expresses the fears of a returning ruling class about its status in relation to those who had done rather well in their absence. The sons of the returning exiles express their economic concern about their sons marrying the 'right' wife, while the text also tries to produce ideological hegemony. By excluding economic matters, it offers a symbolic resolution of the real material conditions of class difference.

For Yee, the image of woman-as-evil functions as what may be called a national allegory. The deception, unfaithfulness, and fickleness of women represent a rival state (Israel in Hosea), the trauma of a dispossessed ruling class (Ezekiel), and an attempt at ideological hegemony by a ruling class (Proverbs). This ideological connection between woman and state provides the crucial link that enables Yee's linking of extrinsic and intrinsic analysis. The socio-economic context provides the framework for and is informed by the ideological production of the texts. The same can be said of Genesis 2–3, again in terms of internal class dynamics. Yee argues that that the text exhibits significant ideological tensions. It is a product of a royal ideology

---

14. Louise A. Hitchcock, 'Cult Corners in the Aegean and the Levant', in Assaf Yasur-Landau, Jennie R. Ebeling, and Laura B. Mazow (eds.), *Household Archaeology in Ancient Israel and Beyond* (Leiden: Brill, 2011), pp. 321-45; Beth Alpert Nakhai, 'Varieties of Religious Expression in the Domestic Setting', in Assaf Yasur-Landau, Jennie R. Ebeling, and Laura B. Mazow (eds.), *Household Archaeology in Ancient Israel and Beyond* (Leiden: Brill, 2011), pp. 347-60.

15. See the excellent discussion in Yee, *Poor Banished Children of Eve*, pp. 48-56.

that seeks to overcome the ties of kinship (familial) in favor of the king (tributary). In other words, the story challenges the primary loyalty to the tribe and the father's house, a loyalty that often leads to resistance and even rebellion in response to efforts to break down such social organization so that the ruling class could exploit the peasantry. The story does so by focusing on gender relations: instead of marriage patterns that strengthened the clan in terms of the extended family, the text of Genesis 2–3 presents the ideal as the conjugal bond of the nuclear family. These family structures weaken the bonds of kinship and redirect loyalties to the king, as nuclear families are far less likely to be sources of rebellion against centralized authority.

At this point a central feature of Yee's analysis appears, as this shift to gender relations obscures the class nature of the struggle. 'Adam' is clearly a peasant, so the real target of the Genesis story is the class solidarity of the peasants which the new monarchy wants to break. Yee expresses her enthusiasm for this discovery because it connects Marxist and feminist analysis. Negative depictions of women become symptoms of class conflict. Indeed, gender conflict functions as a deflected form of class conflict, especially between the small ruling class (symbolized by the despot) and the vast majority of peasants. Thus in biblical texts, class conflicts often appear as clashes between men and women. The question is whether this depiction relegates gender to a secondary status, tying gender into a cover for a primary class conflict. Yee's arguments occasionally show this tendency, but perhaps this preference is a necessary correction in the United States context in which class is often neglected in favor of other forms of oppression. At the same time, Yee's close analysis of the biblical texts reveals that she is as much concerned with class as with gender. To her, the two are inseparably connected.

Since Yee's study was published in 2003, she has modified her approach in some ways, particularly in the development of her current project, *Open Your Hand to the Poor: The Creation of Poverty in Ancient Israel*.[16] Three important features of her new work include the use of Fernand Braudel's distinction between *longue durée*, *histoire conjoncturelle*, and *histoire événementielle*;[17] the use of James Scott's notions of the public and hidden

---

16. Some preliminary studies have appeared: Gale A. Yee, 'Recovering Marginalized Groups in Ancient Israel: Methodological Considerations', in Robert B. Coote and Norman K. Gottwald (eds.), *To Break Every Yoke: Essays in Honor of Marvin L. Chaney* (Sheffield: Sheffield Phoenix, 2007), pp. 10-27; Yee, 'The Creation of Poverty in Ancient Israel'.

17. *Longue durée* emphasises the long-term interaction of human beings with land and geography; *histoire conjoncturelle* concerns the rhythms of economies and societies over decades; *histoire événementielle* deals with the history of individuals and

transcripts;[18] and a model derived from *régulation theory* and called the 'sacred economy'.[19] Since I discuss the matter of mode of production in the following section, I focus on the first two items here.

Concerning Braudel, Yee deploys each of his key categories—*longue durée*, *histoire conjoncturelle*, and *histoire événementielle*—in turn. She begins by stressing the marginal status of early Israel and traces the way variations in soil and geography led to disparities of wealth (what may be called a narrative of differentiation common to many economic histories). From here, she moves to discuss the shorter rhythms of economic fluorescence and downturn, which led to political centralization, economic specialization, and statehood. In particular, the move to states exacerbated the tendencies to economic disparities and stratification, with an emergent and non-laboring wealthy ruling class increasingly exploiting the peasants. The former extracted 'surpluses'—as tax, tribute, and rent—for their own growing desires (food, armies, and building projects), leaving barely sufficient for those working in the village communities. For the third category—*histoire événementielle*—Yee discusses key early individuals: Omri, Ahab, Elijah, and Elisha. In this case, the building projects and costly wars of the first real kings exacerbated class difference and disparities of wealth, with the burden falling on the peasantry who were called on to construct the edifices of power and fill the ranks of the armies. In this new situation prophets arose, not only to provide services to the rulers in terms of divination, sorcery, and healing, but also as voices of resistance to the depredations of the monarchies. These stories are full of the indifference by rulers to the plight of common people, of the devastating effects of famine and war, and of systemic economic oppression (1 and 2 Kings).

As for the use of James Scott, Yee is concerned to recover as far as possible a 'social history of agency for marginalized groups'.[20] The marginalized are, of course, the peasants, the 'unclean and degraded', and the 'expendables'—who together form the majority of the population of the ancient world. Marginalization was therefore a strategy of the ruling class, through economic, androcentric, and ethnocentric strategies, as well as through social

---

events—the focus of so much conventional history Fernand Braudel, *The Mediterranean and the Mediterranean World in the Age of Philip II* (London: Collins, 1972 [1949]).

18. Theoretically and for comparative examples, Yee relies heavily on James C. Scott, *Weapons of the Weak: Everyday Forms of Peasant Resistance* (New Haven: Yale University Press, 1985); James C. Scott, *Domination and the Arts of Resistance: Hidden Transcripts* (New Haven: Yale University Press, 1992).

19. Roland Boer, *The Sacred Economy of Ancient Israel* (Library of Ancient Israel (Louisville, KY: Westminster/John Knox Press, 2015).

20. Yee, 'Recovering Marginalized Groups in Ancient Israel: Methodological Considerations', p. 10.

behavior. Women clearly suffered the most under such strategies. Yee's effort to identify the agency of the marginalized majority plays a double game. On the one hand, the biblical texts largely voice the ideological concerns of the ruling class (the 'public transcript'), so one must look outside and between the texts to find that agency (in the 'hidden transcript'). On the other hand, some voices do seem to speak from the side of the marginalized, at the intersections between the public and hidden transcripts, where subversion by the marginalized appears in disguised form or in outbursts that condemn injustice. Yee is particularly interested in this in-between zone because it enables her to read biblical texts for such moments.[21] This mode of interpretation is part of Yee's wider search for themes of social justice in biblical texts.

David Jobling
Social justice is also an under-riding dimension of the work of David Jobling. His methodological framework, which he also dubs ideological criticism, is highly complex and sophisticated. It employs structuralist (especially Lévi-Strauss), poststructuralist, psychoanalytic, feminist, and Marxist dimensions. My focus is primarily on the Marxist and feminist elements of his work although the others are never far away. The prime text is his commentary (or perhaps anti-commentary) on 1 Samuel[22] but I begin with his key essay, 'Feminism and "Mode of Production" in Ancient Israel'.[23] In it, Jobling proposes a very similar mode of production to that of Yee. Yet he calls it the domestic mode.[24] He too finds the economic and social primacy of the household in early Israel, the dominance of domestic buildings and the absence of fortifications, and the division of labor according to gender: women grow and cook food, make textiles, socialize and educate children, whereas men clear forests, cut cisterns, and build terraces. How does such a domestic mode of production appear in the biblical texts? The tensions between two productions of domestic space are the key,

---

21. Here we find prophecy (and later apocalyptic), a new phenomenon in the context of states. A prophet is 'one who reads the present social situation, analyzes it, and courageously proclaims the dire future consequences of injustice, corruption, and exploitation, if this situation is not rectified'; see Yee, 'The Creation of Poverty in Ancient Israel', p. 13.

22. Jobling, *1 Samuel*. I mention 'anti-commentary' since Jobling wrote the work in a way that seeks to undermine the conventions of biblical commentary and its attention to minutiae.

23. Jobling, 'Feminism and "Mode of Production" in Ancient Israel: Search for a Method'. See also the summary in Jobling, *1 Samuel*, pp. 144-45.

24. This is explicitly derived from Meyers, *Discovering Eve: Ancient Israelite Women in Context*. However, Meyers washes the proposal of its Marxist dimensions, drawing the idea from Sahlins, *Stone Age Economics*.

specifically between virilocal and patrilocal marriage.²⁵ Virilocal (the old patrilocal) means that the woman leaves her household to live in the man's, while patrilocal (the old matrilocal) means that the man leaves his household to live in the household of the woman's father. The shift in terminology is crucial, for it shows more accurately that ultimately a man—the head of the clan—is in charge. However, the two systems are characteristic of different modes of production. Thus, virilocal marriage is typical of the tributary mode of production in the era of kingship, while a domestic mode of production operates with a patrilocal system. For Jobling, many of the stories in the Hebrew Bible exhibit tensions between these two family structures, which in turn are manifestations of the tensions between tributary and domestic modes of production. Once we have this key, other aspects of the tension appear, such male-based versus female-based patterns of kinship, and low-level agriculture controlled by women versus intensive agriculture dominated by men. Jobling argues, like Yee, that in this situation the domestic mode of production was relatively better for women as it minimized class structures and forms of economic exploitation.

In his commentary on 1 Samuel, Jobling organizes his analysis in terms of class, gender, and race. Yet, the distinctions seem initially curious, for the part concerning class has little to say about class at all. Instead, it deals with the political structures imagined for Israel, between judgeship and kingship. We may implicitly read Lenin's observation behind Jobling's argument, namely, that the state is a manifestation of irresolvable class conflict, indeed that the existence of a state is a sure sign that class conflict continues.²⁶ However, class does emerge more clearly when Jobling analyzes gender and race in the following sections. Thus, the profound shifts that take place in the transition from tribal to monarchic Israel (from domestic to tributary modes of production) appear most sharply in the degradation of women. One by one, the women who appear (singularly and in groups) in 1 Samuel—and even the man who is a woman, Jonathan—are co-opted into the narrative goal of the kingship of David. As they do so, their subordinate status becomes ever clearer. In regard to race, the Philistines appear as the ethnic other. Yet this too has a class dimension, particularly in relation to patterns of exploitation: the Philistines seem to own the means of production while they also reveal class fractures within biblical Israel.

---

25. The terms and distinction are drawn from Mieke Bal, *Death and Dissymmetry: The Politics of Coherence in the Book of Judges* (Chicago: University of Chicago Press, 1988).

26. V.I. Lenin, 'The State and Revolution', in *Collected Works* (vol. 25; Moscow: Progress Publishers, 1917 [1964]), pp. 381-492 (387).

Jobling's work contains a wealth of insights, so much so that I can hardly do justice to them here. Yet two have always remained with me. The first concerns egalitarian Israel. For Jobling, this Israel is rather elusive, with the text uncertain as to whether it has been lost, or if it is still to come. The catch with what is lost is that one forgets it, only to find traces appearing at odd moments. Or is it really still to come, an Israel that is yet to achieve justice, egalitarianism, harmony between the sexes and ethnicities, and the overcoming of class difference? This issue runs through Jobling's work,[27] informing both his biblical commentary and Marxist politics. At times, he invokes Derrida's theme of the 'specter' of communism, the ghost that persists before, during, and after communist experiments have come and gone.[28] Yet the specter will not rest, a perpetual presence that demands a world that is far better than the one we have. So also may we understand the trope of 'Jerusalem' in both the biblical text and in the current situation of the Middle East. At other times, this theme of the memory of revolution appears in terms of the 'interregnum', the period in between the petty despots that populate ancient Southwest Asian history. In one of his later pieces, Jobling deploys this theme in a complex and astute way in an analysis of Bertolt Brecht's *The Caucasian Chalk Circle* (not least because Brecht admitted that his main inspiration was the Bible).[29] Not only does the Bible appear in a multilayered fashion, but it does so as Brecht explores participatory communism in a Georgian setting. Here the 'affirmative action'[30] involves women, peasants, and workers as they work out the problem of who should inhabit a certain valley (herders or cultivators). But Jobling is interested in the way the play invokes the theme of an interregnum, a 'power vacuum' that enables ordinary people to exercise a greater degree of freedom and autonomy. The moment in the play is such an interregnum, as is the period between the Babylonian and Persian Empires in ancient Southwest Asia, as is the period of 'collapse' and economic 'crisis' at the end of the second millennium BCE during which the Judean Highlands were first settled. I argue elsewhere that these interregna were actually the stable and normative periods of ancient Southwest Asian socio-economic life, when

---

27. I find a distinct echo in the wonderful work by Dick Boer, *Verlossing uit de Slavernij: Bijbelse Theologie in Dient van Bevrijding* (Amsterdam: Skandalon, 2009).

28. David Jobling, 'Jerusalem and Memory: On a Long Parenthesis in Derrida's *Specters of Marx*', in Yvonne Sherwood (ed.), *Derrida's Bible (Reading a Page of Scripture with a Litte Help from Derrida)* (New York: Palgrave Macmillan, 2004), pp. 99-115; Jacques Derrida, *Spectres of Marx: The State of the Debt, the Work of Mourning and the New International* (trans. Peggy Kamuf; New York: Routledge, 1994).

29. David Jobling, '"Old and New Wisdom Mix Admirably": Bertolt Brecht's *The Caucasian Chalk Circle*', in Roland Boer and Jorunn Økland (eds.), *Marxist Feminist Criticism of the Bible* (Sheffield: Sheffield Phoenix, 2008), pp. 70-97.

30. Martin, *The Affirmative Action Empire*.

the village communities, engaged in subsistence survival economics, were able to return to their tried and tested modes of life.³¹

In the commentary on 1 Samuel, Jobling invokes the theme of interregnum in an insightful reading of the slogan in Judg. 17.6: 'In those days there was no king in Israel; all the people did what was right in their own eyes'. The textual setting suggests that the overarching editorial framework is a negative one: a man called Micah requests a silversmith to construct an 'idol' (*pesel*) from a portion of the silver he had recovered for his mother. He puts the resultant image in a shrine he has made, adds an ephod and teraphim, and makes one of his sons a priest. Later, a passing Levite is invited to become priest, only to join a larger crowd of marauders from the tribe of Dan who also take the image and associated shrine-ware. If we assume the ban on images in the second commandment, as well as the various instances of supposed 'lawlessness' that follow, this story seems to be a negative one, giving voice to ruling class concerns of chaos and crisis, expressed through the pens of the scribal sub-class. By contrast, Jobling suggests that it may also be read as a slogan of freedom.³² The statement that there was no king (see also Judg. 18.1; 19.1; 21.25; 1 Kgs 22.17; 2 Chron. 18.16) and that 'all the people did what was right in their own eyes' is an almost utopian image, a claim and a desire for a society without oppression from some petty potentate seeking to squeeze the peasants once again. Indeed, the text from Judges echoes a rallying-call from one of the Habiru leaders, 'Abdi-Aširta:

> Let us drive out the mayors from the country that the entire country be joined to the 'Apiru... to the entire country. Then will (our) sons and daughters be at peace forever. Should even so the king come out, the entire country will be against him and what will he do to us?³³

Avaren Ipsen

The third major critic who has deployed Marxist feminist approaches is Avaren Ipsen, especially her effort at what may be called 'escort exegesis' in *Sex Working and the Bible*.³⁴ Ipsen engages directly with sex-worker

---

31. Boer, *The Sacred Economy of Ancient Israel*.
32. In the extraordinary final section of his commentary (drawing on psychoanalysis), Jobling argues for a transference of Judg. 17.6 to biblical criticism itself. As early Israel struggled between monarchy and judgeship, between tributary and familial modes of production, so also struggles biblical criticism today between an authorized method and a plethora of approaches that Jobling classifies as polytheistic, Philistine, and even anarchist.
33. William L. Moran, *The Amarna Letters* (Baltimore: The Johns Hopkins University Press, 1992), p. 143. See also Igor M. Diakonoff, 'Syria, Phoenicia, and Palestine in the Third and Second Millennia B.C.', in Igor M. Diakonoff and Philip L. Kohl (eds.), *Early Antiquity* (Chicago: University of Chicago Press, 1991), pp. 286-308 (295).
34. Avaren Ipsen, *Sex Working and the Bible* (London: Equinox, 2009). For her ear-

activists, seeking their insights in reading key biblical texts concerning prostitutes: Rahab (Joshua 2 and 6.22-25), Solomon and the two prostitutes (1 Kgs 3.16-28), the anointing of Jesus (Jn 12.1-8; Lk. 7.36-50; Mk 14.3-9 and Mt. 26.6-13), and the whore Babylon (Rev. 17.1–19.10). Since my study focuses on the Hebrew Bible, I restrict my observations to the first two texts. Other texts might have been included, such as the matter of sacred prostitutes, Judah and Tamar (Genesis 38), Samson and prostitutes (Judg. 16.1, 4), the polemic against Israel and Judah in Ezekiel 16 and 23, Hosea and Gomer (Hosea 1–2), and the gospel accounts of Jesus and the prostitutes. To include these additional texts would have made an already involved book impossibly long, so one hopes for further studies.

Ipsen's method is twofold. Her basic strategy is to interpret these four texts with her collaborators in the Sex Workers Outreach Project (SWOP). This interpretation was only part of the method, for Ipsen also engaged sex worker activism in the Bay Area of San Francisco during the project. The second feature of her method concerns feminist analysis, which is strengthened through liberation theology, especially through the preferential option for the poor (prostitutes) and feminist reworking of Marxist approaches through standpoint theory. Let me say a little more about standpoint theory, which Ipsen follows Sandra Harding in defining as: '(1) utilising women's experiences as new empirical and theoretical sources, (2) committed to doing research for the explicit benefit of women, and (3) locating the researcher on the same critical plane as the overt subject matter of research rather than keeping her hidden from view'.[35] Standpoint theory is an adaptation of historical materialist analysis that recovers its earlier focus on the experiences of women, particularly those who are multiply marginalized and whose voices are rarely heard in scholarly work. In this light, Ipsen locates prostitutes within the realities of exploitative economic systems: the military prostitute complex, the economies of gross misdistribution and crisis, and exploitative extraction economies.[36]

The structure of each of the studies is similar: a translation of the text (drawn from the NRSV); detailed engagement with scholarly interpretation; counterpointing this interpretation with the hooker hermeneutics of the SWOP activists; brief comparison between the SWOP and scholarly

lier study of the two prostitutes in 1 Kgs 3.16-28, see Avaren Ipsen, 'Solomon and the Two Prostitutes', in Roland Boer and Jorunn Økland (eds.), *Marxist Feminist Criticism of the Bible* (Sheffield: Sheffield Phoenix, 2008), pp. 134-50.

35. Ipsen, *Sex Working and the Bible*, p. 30; Ipsen, 'Solomon and the Two Prostitutes', p. 136.

36. Ipsen, *Sex Working and the Bible*, pp. 68-69, 173-74; Avaren Ipsen, 'Political Economy, Prostitution, and the *Eschaton* of the Whore Babylon: Festschrift für Luise Schottroff zum 70. Geburtstag', in Frank Crüsemann (ed.), *Dem Tod nicht glauben: Sozialgeschichte der Bibel* (Gütersloh: Gütersloher Verlagshaus, 2004), pp, 504-27.

readings; a conclusion that weaves together the various observations of the SWOP readers and Ipsen herself. Here we encounter the borderlines of a new genre of commentary, full of the colloquialisms of the SWOP readers, generated by those who live at the borderlines of conventional society.

As examples of such an approach, I provide a few observations on the interpretations of Rahab and the two prostitutes in the story of Solomon. As for Rahab, any negative reading of her identity as a prostitute is dismissed. Rahab does not need to be excused. She is not a metaphor for erring Israel, blemished Church or repentant sinner, and she is not (as in some feminist readings) a ventriloquist for Deuteronomistic theology. By contrast Rahab is an agent, a sex-positive figure who enables a definition of prostitution as 'sacrifice for one's own survival and the survival of one's family'.[37] This positive identification of Rahab follows two paths: a majority opinion (among the SWOP readers) in which Rahab acts in her own best interests and opts for the 'invaders'; a minority reading in which Rahab becomes a counter-deity, a Goddess, in opposition to an oppressive Yahweh. Both readings resist any hermeneutical desire to dismiss the prostitute and find a more respectable position for her in the text or in interpretation.

The same sex-positive perspective is applied to the interpretation of 1 Kgs 3.16-28, where readers side with the two prostitutes. Indeed, interpretations of the story tend to neglect the fact that they are, narratively speaking, prostitutes. However, given the story's focus on Solomon, the result is somewhat different. Here Solomon enacts violence against prostitutes, running a corrupt legal system prejudiced against sex workers. In other words, when an interpreter identifies with the story's prostitutes, the experiences of these literary prostitutes are judged in this light: the Israelite spies and the men of the city in Joshua 2 are found to be devious; Solomon's wisdom dissipates and he becomes a cynical, prejudiced, and corrupt wielder of judicial power, given to violence. The life experiences of these activist sex workers clearly intersect with and illumine the texts in question.

Ipsen's studies are politically engaged, more obviously so than those of Yee and Jobling. At one level she shares the political agendas of academic approaches, such as feminism and Marxism. But she goes further: every sentence is full of political passion. Three features may be identified. First, Ipsen's studies opt strongly for the sex-positive side of the debate over prostitution and pornography. Ipsen points out that she began her analysis from the abolitionist position in regards to prostitute politics—like many feminists, conservative politicians, and the religious right. But after engaging in sex-worker political campaigns, she came around to supporting decriminalization, since prostitute activists take this position. Thus

---

37. Ipsen, *Sex Working and the Bible*, pp. 74, 108.

the strongest criticisms in Ipsen's work are directed against abolitionists and sex-negative campaigners.

Second, this opposition between abolition and decriminalization appears in the way Ipsen presents interpretations of the biblical prostitute texts. She notes how prostitutes have been erased, banished, and driven from the texts, similar to the efforts of 'law abiding' citizens and the police to 'rid the streets' of hookers. As noted previously, in the story of Solomon readers often do not realize that the text depicts the two women as prostitutes.

Third, the issue of the mediator—Ipsen—is highlighted. One often finds that an intellectual mediator is quietly effaced, especially in postcolonial readings, but in standpoint theory the researcher herself must be on the same critical plane as the subject matter of research. At times, this approach produces some quandaries for Ipsen. For instance, Ipsen's hesitations over whether to include interpretations about the sacred prostitute run up against the wish of the SWOP readers to find those sacred prostitutes.[38] Ipsen is then caught between the dictates of scholarship and the prostitute readings. At other times, she sides with the latter and critiques the former, but the problem of straddling both occasionally creates problems. Yet this difficulty is the nature of an organic intellectual's struggle (Gramsci). This struggle appears not merely in decisions on what to include or exclude in the analysis, but also in sentence structures and language issues. For instance, the language of sex workers is often at odds with the polite discourse of biblical criticism: 'horseshit', 'cuz', 'motherfucking', and 'ya know' appear frequently; it is the language of everyday working people for whom polite language is a marker of class, corruption, and double standards. These and other expressions appear in the midst of one the extraordinary collages as the end of each chapter, where Ipsen weaves observations, comments, and reactions to the text in a stunning series of commentaries.[39] Perhaps the sharpest appears in the revolutionary statement concerning the whore of Babylon: 'I am not going to find any of this liberating until she says, "Fuck you motherfuckers" and starts fighting'.[40]

Critical Issues

From this survey of the key contributions to Marxist feminist approaches to the Bible, I would like to identify a number of issues: the relations between class and gender; activism and political liberation; and mode of production. The first is really a non-issue, as those working with a Marxist-feminist framework assume the inseparability of gender and class

---

38. Ipsen, *Sex Working and the Bible*, pp. 42-43.
39. Ipsen, *Sex Working and the Bible*, pp. 86-88, 116-19, 161-65, 196-204.
40. Ipsen, *Sex Working and the Bible*, p. 204.

(and indeed socio-economic exploitation). The mono-causal trap—class or gender as the primary category—is simply misleading and reductionist because exploitation is always multi-faceted.[41]

Although it is clear that all approaches to interpreting texts like the Bible are imbued with politics, Marxist feminist methods provide a distinct dimension to such politics. Scientifically 'objective' methods tend to support the status quo; they provide the mechanisms for the Western world to study itself and explain its own functioning to better control what is happening.[42] By contrast, Marxist feminist approaches arise from and feed into political movements that challenge the status quo. For some, the preferred option is reform, tinkering with the system for the sake of improvement. For others, the socio-economic system and its cultural products—of which the Bible is a classical text—is irretrievably geared to exploit workers and women. It is thereby irredeemable, and it calls for another world. Those I have studied above fall into the latter group.[43] But what possible contribution can a biblical critic make to such a project? Here the example of Antonio Negri, one of Italy's leading Marxists, is pertinent. In 1979, Negri was arrested for his involvement in the Autonomy Movement, which was supposed to be the political wing of the Red Brigades (*Brigate Rosse*). Accused of being the mastermind and leader of the Red Brigades, Negri languished in prison, unable to gain access to lawyers or any clarity as to the charges that were to be laid against him.[44] Briefly released from prison in 1983, he fled from Italy to France, where he remained in exile for some two decades. In the end, no evidence of any direct involvement was found, and so he was charged and convicted for writing books and articles that radical political activists read. Upon his return to Italy (with the promise of amnesty for others who languished in prison, which was soon broken), he was placed

---

41. Thus, it should come as no surprise that the *Radical Women Manifesto* deals with law, economics, biology, children, health, education, ethnicity, indigeneity, sexuality, age, disability, poverty, prisons, prostitution, violence, environment, culture, the military, and self-defence. Radical Women, *The Radical Women Manifesto: Socialist Feminist Theory, Program and Organizational Structure* (Seattle: Red Letter Press, 1996).

42. Immanuel Wallerstein, *The Modern World-System IV: Centrist Liberalism Triumphant, 1789–1914* (Berkeley: University of California Press, 2011), p. 264.

43. As Landry and MacLean put it, Marxist feminists wanted to distinguish themselves from radical and liberal feminists 'who contend that women's oppression will end with the achievement of women's power or women's equality, respectively, within existing class societies'. Landry and MacLean, *Materialist Feminisms*, p. 22.

44. While in prison, he was permitted few books, apart from the Bible. So he began to read and then write. The result was his study of the book of Job, eventually completed in Paris. Initially the study of Job was not published because Negri wrote it as a process of self-clarification, a way of dealing with doubt and fear and suffering while in prison. Antonio Negri, *The Labor of Job: The Biblical Text as a Parable of Human Labor* (trans. Matteo Mandarini; Durham, NC: Duke University Press, 2009 [2002]).

under house arrest and had his passport confiscated for a number of years. My point on the role of intellectuals, such as Negri the philosopher or Marxist feminist biblical critics, is not that they need to spend time in prison. Rather, they need to create the cultural climate for thinking about alternative possibilities. They need to write works that radical activists may read.

The third issue concerns the mode of production which is both largely historical and the focus of those studying the Hebrew Bible. Both Gale Yee and David Jobling have maintained, following Norman Gottwald, that the early settlements in the Judean hills (which may or may not be early Israel) developed a distinct mode of production. They call it variously the familial or domestic mode of production, with ultimate debts to Marshall Sahlins. Its features include a focus on the household as the prime economic and social unit, which provided the social determination of economic life; extensive agriculture; optimal rather than maximal use of soil, water, and animals; risk aversion through diversity in crop growing and animal husbandry; the collection of small surpluses for lean years; allocation of land shares, labor, and produce; minimization of the division of labor and class stratification; and thereby a relatively more egalitarian status for women. This mode of production, they propose, stood in contrast to the tributary mode of production characteristic of the aspiring despots of the little and big kingdoms, often called empires.[45]

In this list of features I have actually included more than either Yee or Jobling provides. But I have done so for a specific reason: they are in the end mistaken in speaking of a distinct mode of production. It is better to speak of a socio-economic regime within a mode of production.[46] The regime in question is a subsistence regime, made up of two building blocks or institutional forms known as subsistence survival (focused on agricultural organization) and kinship-household (the social determination of economic life), the combined features of which I have described above. This regime was, and for many still is, a tried method used over millennia in many parts of the world, in which human beings need little rather than wanting much.[47]

---

45. I follow Liverani in using such terms because ancient texts already use them; see Mario Liverani, *Israel's History and the History of Israel* (trans. Chiara Peri and Philip Davies (London: Equinox, 2005), p. 7.

46. I draw this terminology from the *régulation* school of economic theory, a Marxist inspired approach that provides the framework—with appropriate modifications—for reconstructing the economics of the ancient world. What follows is a brief summary of Boer, *The Sacred Economy of Ancient Israel*, pp. 53-109.

47. As Sahlins succinctly observes: 'There are after all two roads to satisfaction, to reducing the gap between means and ends: producing much or desiring little'; see Marshall Sahlins, 'Tribal Economics', in George Dalton (ed.), *Economic Development and Social Change: The Modernization of Village Communities* (New York: Natural History Press, 1971), pp. 43-61 (49).

This regime, characteristic of village communities across ancient Southwest Asia, was primarily allocative rather than extractive in its working. That is, it focused on allocation and reallocation of land, labor, and produce. It struggled with two other regimes in ancient Southwest Asia that were extractive, in which the non-laboring ruling class, based in the towns (few real cities existed), extracted its 'needs' from peasants. These two are the palatine regime, based on palatine and temple estates, which dominated from time to time until the end of the second millennium; the regime of plunder, based on tribute-exchange as variations on tax, tribute, and exchange (long-distance preciosities and local produce), which flourished in the first millennium and provided the basis for the expansion of the Neo-Assyrian, Neo-Babylonian, and Persian empires. This latter period is when Israel finally appeared. Due to its late arrival and marginal economic and political status, Israel (and the southern Levant more generally) tended towards a subsistence regime, preferably out of reach of the great powers whenever possible. Indeed, given the destructive effects on the subsistence regime by the extractive mechanisms of these powers (and their regime of plunder), the peasant laborers of the subsistence regime found the absence of palatine and then plunder regimes highly desirable. They often acted to bring them to an end when the opportunity arose.

This reconstruction draws together earlier insights and proposes a new model for making sense of the social and economic realities of ancient Israel within ancient Southwest Asia. Indeed, Yee has begun to make deployment of this reconstruction for her project on poverty.[48] In her use of this model, we can see how Yee's concern for the production of poverty and agency of marginalized groups may be located within economic structures. Accordingly, palatine and plunder regimes, focused on towns and fostered by the ruling class, exacerbate poverty among peasants. However, the relatively stable subsistence regime constitutes the basis for resistance against such domination. This view is really a modification of Yee's earlier familial mode of production (except that now 'mode of production' is not an appropriate term), where the minimization of division of labor and thereby of class difference provided greater scope for women. To be added is the need for all hands to work the land, especially in light of the constant shortage of labor.

Future Directions

On the issue of economic reconstruction, I turn to potential future directions. While a reasonable amount of work has been done, much of the current economic studies are beholden to neo-classical economic theories,

---

48. Unfortunately, David Jobling is no longer able to engage with such work.

which are particularly inadequate for dealing with the ancient world.[49] In order to understand the situation better in relation to women, class, and exploitation, a more workable model based on alternative economic theories is required. The key is to focus not on the centers of power—temple and palace—but rather on the labor done by 90% of the small populations of ancient Southwest Asia: agriculture, by which I mean both animal husbandry and crop growing. Indeed, the economic modes characteristic of such agriculture, on the borders or outside the wavering range of the power of the petty despots who appeared from time to time in ancient Southwest Asia, are quite different from the modes of palace and temple. Needless to say, the clashes between them became constitutive of the economics of the ancient world.

Second, the question of political emancipation remains central, especially in relation to the reading of biblical texts. Are they so deeply enmeshed within the production of empire and exploitation that even what looks like resistance is actually playing a role in sustaining the status quo? Or can one locate, even in the midst of the ruling class hegemony of texts, traces of resistance, whether in terms of a negative depiction of such resistance or as conflicting voices that inadvertently made their way into the text or as the inevitable inconsistencies and contradictions of that hegemony?

Finally, more work needs to be done in biblical criticism using Marxist feminist approaches. I have discussed three key contributors, which also happen to be the three Hebrew Bible contributors to the edited collection, *Marxist Feminist Criticism of the Bible*.[50] In this work, reading for resistance or the inability of such readings is once again at the forefront. Little, however, is devoted to economic reconstruction, with a preference for the careful reading of texts and engagement with various Marxist feminist philosophical theories. Yet this is to be expected from a collection that was an early foray into a potentially rich area of biblical criticism. Texts needed to be identified and theories developed. Much more remains to be done, especially in terms of sustained economic analysis and more sophisticated approaches to modes of resistance. The collection is in many respects an early foray into expanding such studies and it would now look quite different.

---

49. For instance, see Joseph Gilbert Manning and Ian Morris (eds.), *The Ancient Economy: Evidence and Models* (Stanford: Stanford University Press, 2005); Walter Scheidel, Ian Morris and Richard Saller (eds.), *The Cambridge Economic History of the Greco-Roman World* (Cambridge: Cambridge University Press, 2008).

50. Boer and Økland (eds.), *Marxist Feminist Criticism of the Bible*.

17

SPACE FOR WOMEN AND MEN:
MASCULINITY STUDIES IN FEMINIST BIBLICAL INTERPRETATION

Katherine Low

The method of masculinity studies exists because of ground-breaking efforts of women's studies to examine the roles of gender in society. Those engaged in masculinity studies acknowledge that 'for at least two decades, the women's movement (and also, since 1969, the gay liberation movement) has suggested that the traditional enactments of masculinity were in desperate need of overhaul'.[1] This overhaul came with questioning a 'sex-role paradigm' in which the biological bodies of males and females are socialized to fit into certain sex-roles in society. Gender roles—masculinities and femininities—are historically and socially conditioned, vary over time, and are not static. In other words, the assumption that the biological body acts as a container with which to fill-in appropriate sex-roles ignores the importance of culture in constructing numerous ways that people live out masculinities and femininities in everyday life. Both men and women can step into masculine gender roles in society. When the so-called 'crisis of masculinity' emerged in the late nineteenth-century in the United States, it did so because of the pervasiveness of the feminist model to question traditional sex roles in society.[2] To call masculinity in crisis means different things depending on who uses the term, but, in academia, this idea of crisis evidences that what was once a fixed and stable concept is now under the scrutiny of scholarly analysis.[3]

An influential study from 1985, *Between Men*, by feminist scholar Eve Kosofsky Sedgwick, heralded what would be called 'masculinity studies' by the 1990s. The work calls into question homosocial bonds for constructions of heterosexual desire, making it important for queer studies as well. *Between Men* also attests to the continual impact of feminist thought on

---

1. Michael S. Kimmel, 'Rethinking 'Masculinity': New Directions in Research', in Michael S. Kimmel (ed.), *Changing Men: New Directions in Research on Men and Masculinity* (Newbury Park, CA: Sage Publications, 1987), pp. 9-24 (9).
2. Kimmel, 'Rethinking Masculinity', p. 13.
3. See John Beynon, 'Masculinities and the Notion of Crisis', in *Masculinities and Culture* (Philadelphia, PA: Open University Press, 2002), pp. 75-97.

emerging methods.⁴ So does Judith Butler's influential *Gender Trouble: Feminism and the Subversion of Identity*, published a few years later in 1990.⁵ In her work, Butler introduces the concept of the gender performative, the social reproduction of spectacles of gender in society that makes gender seem like a stable reality.⁶ Both Sedgwick and Butler question the existence of the seeming polarity of gender. They assume gender functions perpendicular on the same plane with constant negotiations of meanings of masculinity and femininity depending on history and culture.

A critical mass of scholarship on masculinities in biblical studies is just now beginning to emerge. At the time of my writing this piece, only a few edited monographs concerning masculinities in the Hebrew Bible have been published, and each essay situates itself differently in terms of its theoretical orientation toward feminism.⁷ Stephen Moore notes that feminist biblical scholarship did not include critical analysis on masculinity in the 1970s or 1980s. The 1990s began to see studies on biblical masculinity, more so in New Testament studies than in Hebrew Bible studies.⁸ Intersecting with many cross-disciplinary approaches, such as women's studies, queer studies, and gender studies, the emerging field known as 'masculinity studies' in religion recognizes women and men as gendered beings, critically destabilizing multiple masculinities as performative roles rather than normative categories. The concept of 'biblical masculinities' investigates what makes a male or a female a 'man'; it investigates the ways religion and the Bible endorse or subvert restrictive social norms for what it means to be

---

4. Eve Kosofsky Sedgwick, *Between Men: English Literature and Male Homosocial Desire* (New York: Columbia University Press, 1985).

5. Judith Butler, *Gender Trouble: Feminism and the Subversion of Identity* (New York: Routledge, 1990). I further discuss the role of these works in gender theory in Katherine Low, *The Bible, Gender, and Reception History: The Case of Job's Wife* (New York: Bloomsbury, 2013), pp. 16-20.

6. Judith Butler, *Undoing Gender* (New York: Routledge, 2004). Eve Kosofsky Sedgwick's later works do not fall completely in line with Butler's performative theory; see, e.g., Eve Kosofsky Sedgwick, *Touching Feeling: Affect, Pedagogy, Performativity* (Durham, NC: Duke University Press, 2003).

7. These include Ovidiu Creangă (ed.), *Men and Masculinity in the Hebrew Bible and Beyond* (Sheffield: Sheffield Phoenix Press, 2010); Ovidiu Creangă and Peter-Ben Smit (eds.), *Biblical Masculinities Foregrounded* (Sheffield: Sheffield Phoenix Press, 2014). Although, the reader will be introduced to several other individual monographs throughout this essay.

8. Stephen D. Moore, '"O Man, Who Art Thou. . . ?" Masculinity Studies and New Testament Studies', in Stephen D. Moore and Janice Capel Anderson (eds.), *New Testament Masculinities* (Atlanta, GA: SBL, 2003), pp. 1-22; Stephen D. Moore, 'Final Reflections on Biblical Masculinity', in Ovidiu Creangă (ed.), *Men and Masculinity in the Hebrew Bible and Beyond* (Sheffield: Sheffield Phoenix Press, 2010), pp. 240-55.

'feminine' and 'masculine'.[9] In many ways, then, it can be seen as a subset of critical gender studies as an analytical perspective.[10]

Several central issues pertaining to the use of masculinity studies in feminist biblical interpretation, particularly within the area of the Hebrew Bible, are outlined below. They include the plurality of masculine expressions in biblical literature, the use of the concept of hegemonic masculinity by biblical scholars, and the complexity of bodily discourse, especially for the deity. These central issues provide a platform for discussing future directions in the study of biblical masculinities.

Multiple Masculinities

One overall early assumption feminist biblical scholars bring to the study of masculinity in the Bible, at least the traditional idea of what it means to be masculine, is that the social world-view of biblical authors ranks masculinity, and therefore men, as superior. In the words of Susan Ackerman: '[T]he Bible is an almost exclusively male-oriented document, it typically tells us only men's perspectives on things and does not concern itself with women's experiences'.[11] Ackerman's statement aligns with feminist concerns about the Bible and a focus on multiple women's experiences in the Bible as a response. Feminists, acutely aware of the multiplicity of women's voices, provide a platform for masculinity studies in the Bible. They maintain that as women's experiences vary, so men's experiences vary as well. Masculinity studies challenges feminism not to constitute what is known as 'man' as 'a homogeneous entity, the "fall-guy" for a one-sided rather than really radical deconstruction'.[12] Furthermore, masculinity studies remains crucial since feminists have pointed out that overwhelmingly elite classes of multiple male authors have embedded assumptions about men and women in biblical texts. Analysis of these assumptions reveals a rich trove of hermeneutical possibilities.

Those engaged in masculinity studies agree that 'masculinity' is not one monolithic entity in the Bible. While masculinity is associated with virility, strength, aggression, rationality, and independence, and the Bible

---

9. Ovidiu Creangă, 'Introduction', in Creangă and Smit (eds.), *Biblical Masculinities Foregrounded*, pp. 3-14.

10. Björn Krondorfer, 'Introduction', in Björn Krondorfer (ed.), *Men and Masculinities in Christianity and Judaism: A Critical Reader* (London: SCM Press, 2009), pp. xi-xxi.

11. Susan Ackerman, 'The Personal is Political: Covenantal and Affectionate Love ('$\bar{A}H\bar{E}B$, '$AH\breve{A}B\hat{A}$) in the Hebrew Bible', *VT* 52 (October 2002), pp. 437-58 (442).

12. Joseph A. Boone, 'Of Me(n) and Feminism: Who(se) Is the Sex That Writes', in Joseph A. Boone and Michael Cadden (eds.), *Engendering Men: The Question of Male Feminist Criticism* (New York: Routledge, 1990), pp. 11-25 (18).

demonstrates concern for men to uphold such associations with masculinity, rich variances and negotiations of masculinities exist. A word of caution emerges at this point, for often scholars will engage the ideas of 'male' and 'female' as two opposite poles rather than as parallel conceptions into which various gender roles are placed. An example is the adaptation of Laura Mulvey's feminist film theory, the 'male gaze', in feminist biblical scholarship. Traditionally, the 'male gaze' gives feminist biblical scholars a method through which to set up a simple act of 'looking' as an activity of gender and sexual difference.[13] In regards to Susanna and the elders, Jennifer Glancy engages Mulvey's male gaze with what she deems 'the gendered polarity of the gaze—in which looking represents masculinity and "to-be-looked-at-ness" represents femininity'.[14] Through the elders' gazing at Susanna bathing, the story puts emphasis on femininity as erotic object for male perception. Glancy is concerned about women readers as spectators of female sexuality; while looking at Susanna's bathing body along with the elders, are women not participating in the male gaze? This question complicates a seemingly simple matter—that masculinity is associated with activity and femininity with passivity. Yet the question still assumes a monolithic kind of gendered polarity functioning in the text. Gender studies, however, advocates that multiple expressions of femininity and masculinity exist on a wide spectrum of negotiations. It is not just one kind of femininity that relates to women and it is not just one kind of masculinity that relates to men. Rather, conflicting masculinities abound and assumptions of heteronormativity should also be examined. Philip Culbertson points this out when he suggests through the lens of Sedgwick that the male gaze must 'objectify for homosociality to work. Ironically, the homosocial system can be maintained only when men avert their gaze from each other; the gaze, however figuratively, must remain focused on women.'[15] Studies in masculinities complicate clear-cut gender activities; masculinity does not just belong to men or ones born with male genitalia. Gender is a social construct in constant maintenance and negotiation; numerous models of masculinity and femininity function in societies at one time.[16] The Hebrew Bible,

---

13. Laura Mulvey, *Visual and Other Pleasures* (Theories of Representation and Difference; Bloomington: Indiana University Press, 1989).

14. Jennifer Glancy, 'The Accused: Susanna and Her Readers', *JSOT* 18.58 (1993), pp. 103-16 (109).

15. Philip L. Culbertson, 'Designing Men: Reading the Male Body as Text', in Björn Krondorfer (ed.), *Men and Masculinities in Christianity and Judaism: A Critical Reader* (London: SCM Press, 2009), pp. 115-24 (117).

16. Maurice Berger, Brian Wallis and Simon Watson, 'Introduction', in Maurice Berger *et al.* (eds.), *Constructing Masculinity* (New York: Routledge, 1995), pp. 1-7.

for instance, constructs gender that 'both supports and undercuts the gender binary of exclusively masculine and exclusively feminine'.[17]

As masculinity studies began to emerge in biblical scholarship in the 1990s, some biblical scholars have subjected biblical (male) characters to gendered analysis. The hallmark of such an analysis comes from David Clines's discussion of a type of masculinity imposed on the David story (1 Samuel 16 to 1 Kings 2) that reflects the cultural norms of the biblical authors, who encourage valor in war and physical strength along with physical desirability. The concept ascribed to David, ruddiness, attests to some kind of physical beauty (1 Sam. 17.42). Furthermore, although David had many wives (2 Sam. 15.16), the biblical authors keep women at a casual distance from their kind of masculinity, which includes the ability to choose sex for political motivation rather than for love and the lack of dependency on women for creating an identity; David does not need to show 'love' to any woman. To Clines, David thus embodies everything his culture wants to propose about masculinity, so much so that even his failures reinforce traditional norms.[18]

Clines has set out what one scholar suggests is a 'measuring rod', or a framework, for analyzing masculinity in the Hebrew Bible. Therefore, other (male) characters have been examined in light of how they measure up to the kind of masculinity set out for David.[19] However, it is important to ask questions about David as an institutionalized literary figure of the Deuteronomist. Could David stand as an idealized figure that carries multiple, and impossible, personality characteristics? Milena Kirova asks a similar question, suggesting that the literary character of David is almost '"beyond-human" and serves well the messianic ideas implicit in his literary presence'.[20] Literary characters and the ideologies that come with them include the complexities of gender.

Samson (Judges 13–16) is another character analyzed by feminist scholars engaging masculinity studies. Samson exhibits aggression and strength

---

17. Sandra L. Gravett, Karla G. Bohmbach, F.V. Greifenhagen, and Donald C. Polaski, *An Introduction to the Hebrew Bible: A Thematic Approach* (Louisville, KY: Westminster/John Knox Press, 2008), p. 133.

18. David J.A. Clines, 'David the Man: The Construction of Masculinity in the Hebrew Bible', in David J.A. Clines (ed.), *Interested Parties: The Ideology of Writers and Readers of the Hebrew Bible* (Sheffield: Sheffield Phoenix Press, 2009), pp. 212-43 (226, 231).

19. Marcel V. Măcelaru, 'Saul in the Company of Men: (De)Constructing Masculinity in 1 Samuel 9–31', in Creangă and Smit (eds.), *Biblical Masculinities Foregrounded*, pp. 51-68.

20. Milena Kirova, 'When Real Men Cry: The Symbolism of Weeping in the Torah and the Deuteronomistic History', in Creangă and Smit (eds.), *Biblical Masculinities Foregrounded*, pp. 35-50 (48).

as a judge of Israel with elements of hypermasculinity, or an exaggeration of the traits usually associated with masculinity.[21] The hypermasculinity portrayed by Samson interplays with his 'weakness' for foreign women. One biblical scholar calls his over-extension of masculinity a display characteristic of that of a 'man-child', one who is boyishly immature.[22] Samson cedes control over his strength when he reveals his source to Delilah, a woman whom he loves (v. 4). The loss of his hair alters his status. His warrior-like strength is symbolized in his hair.[23] Susan Niditch analyzes hair in this case as a gendered symbol operating with particular cultural expectations: 'For Samson, hair is related to strength, dominance as a man, and the activities of a warrior'.[24]

Scholars have more recently begun to analyze male prophets. Clines has approached prophetic masculinities, arguing that the Hebrew prophetic tradition remains sharply gendered toward masculinity. He sets out a paradigm of masculinity present in the prophets, which includes a rhetoric of strength, violence (sexual and otherwise), and holiness, defined only in relation to men. The vivid masculine imagery remains so pervasive, Clines notes, that interpreters have nearly ignored, or taken for granted, such features. Masculinity studies brings such imagery to light.[25]

When it comes to the marital relationships of the prophets, particularly Jeremiah and Ezekiel, Corrine L. Carvalho suggests that performance of masculinity remains central to understanding how men become men through marriage. In Ezekiel the marital agenda, or dismissal/lack thereof (see Ezek. 24.15-27), serves as a theological metaphor for the destruction of the temple and the shameful response of not publicly mourning for the loss because of the iniquities brought on by the people. Jeremiah, on the other hand, remains more marginalized from Jerusalem prophecy than Ezekiel. His character's frustration and ambiguity is also reflected in some gender ambiguity, particularly reflected in 16.1-5 when God disallows Jeremiah an honorable family through marriage.[26]

---

21. Gravett *et al.*, *Introduction to the Hebrew Bible*, pp. 135-40.

22. Stephen M. Wilson, 'Samson the Man-Child: Failing to Come of Age in the Deuteronomistic History', *JBL* 133.1 (2014), pp. 43-60.

23. Ela Lazarewicz-Wyrzykowska, 'Samson: Masculinity Lost (and Regained?)', in Ovidiu Creangă (ed.), *Men and Masculinity in the Hebrew Bible and Beyond* (Sheffield: Sheffield Phoenix Press, 2010), pp. 171-88.

24. Susan Niditch, *'My Brother Esau is a Hairy Man': Hair and Identity in Ancient Israel* (Oxford: Oxford University Press, 2008), p. 67.

25. David J.A. Clines, 'He-Prophets: Masculinity as a Problem for the Hebrew Prophets and their Interpreters', in Alastair G. Hunter and Philip R. Davies (eds.), *Sense and Sensitivity: Essays on Reading the Bible in Memory of Robert Carroll* (Sheffield: Sheffield Academic Press, 2002), pp. 311-28.

26. Corrine L. Carvalho, 'Sex and the Single Prophet: Marital Status and Gender in

Hegemonic Masculinity

One critique about feminists engaging masculinity studies is that it elevates men to a privileged status while feminists have worked hard for woman-centered approaches and challenged androcentrism and patriarchal systems.[27] Indeed, feminist biblical scholarship in the past several decades has uncovered the patriarchal nature of biblical texts. Yet it is an oversimplification to suggest that those engaged in the critical study of masculinity are hijacking feminist analysis or positioning themselves against feminism. The question is how masculinity studies positions itself in relation to feminism.[28] Deborah Sawyer, for instance, calls for gender critique as a 'wider lens' of feminism, particularly in order to further engage with concepts of power and patriarchy: 'The manner in which masculinity is presented is an additional vital issue'.[29] In contrast, Deryn Guest warns against simply adding men to the mix of feminist agendas without concern for how gender categories are constructed, and even how heterosexuality is an assumed frame-of-reference. Guest asserts that 'the analysis of masculinities within feminist biblical scholarship has been undertaken in the service of a prioritized focus upon women, and this is *not* on a par with the critical study of masculinities that is such an important element within gender criticism'.[30] Ovidiu Creangă suggests that the field of masculinity studies aids feminists in the deconstruction of male-dominated systems, ideologies of patriarchy, and androcentrism because it engages an entire spectrum of masculinities and challenges the idea of the existence of one normative expression of what it means to be a man.[31]

When feminists engage masculinity not as synonymous with maleness, men, or manhood, they can appeal to masculinity studies to deconstruct dominant ideologies, especially because masculinity is often equated with

---

Jeremiah and Ezekiel', in Jonathan Stökl and Corrine L. Carvalho (eds.), *Prophets Male and Female: Gender and Prophecy in the Hebrew Bible, the Eastern Mediterranean, and the Ancient Near East* (Atlanta: Society of Biblical Literature, 2013), pp. 237-67.

27. Therefore, Björn Krondorfer suggests calling the field 'critical men's studies' as a way to raise the level of inquiry beyond just 'another way to talk about privileged men'; see his 'Introduction', in *Men and Masculinities in Christianity and Judaism*, pp. xi-xxi (xiv).

28. Moore, 'Masculinity Studies and New Testament Studies', p. 5.

29. Deborah F. Sawyer, 'Gender Criticism: A New Discipline in Biblical Studies or Feminism in Disguise', in Deborah W. Rooke (ed.), *A Question of Sex? Gender and Difference in the Hebrew Bible and Beyond* (Sheffield: Sheffield Phoenix Press, 2007), pp. 1-17 (5).

30. Deryn Guest, *Beyond Feminist Biblical Studies* (Sheffield: Sheffield Phoenix Press, 2012), p. 26.

31. Ovidiu Creangă, 'Introduction', in Creangă and Smit (eds.), *Biblical Masculinities Foregrounded*, pp. 3-14.

maleness to socially legitimate men. Masculinity is a category of gender, a construction of performance; it is a role that cannot, or should not, be reduced to the male body or an imitation of maleness. Masculinity comes with notions of power and privilege, and therefore, feminists employ masculinity studies as a way to challenge the maintenance of dominant systems. Judith Halberstam's *Female Masculinity*, a first full-length study on the matter, challenges the notion of male masculinity as a dominant form and expression of masculinity—masculinity functions independent of men.[32]

Halberstam's study is nearly contemporary with R.W. Connell's work on masculinities first published in 1995. Connell builds on Antonio Gramsci's research on class relations and how dominant groups sustain power in society. He also introduces the concept of 'hegemonic masculinity', which naturalizes the appearance that a strong relationship between men and power exists in society. Connell states: 'Hegemonic masculinity can be defined as the configuration of gender practice which embodies the currently accepted answer to the problem of legitimacy of patriarchy, which guarantees (or is taken to guarantee) the dominant position of men and the subordination of women'.[33] Given Connell's definition, it is fitting that feminists would engage masculinity studies to gain insight about hegemonic masculinity's effort to sustain rigid forms of gender in order to impose and maintain power, even as a constant negotiation takes place between groups that challenge clearly delineated constructions of gender in society.[34]

Hegemonic masculinity is a major idea invoked by feminist biblical scholars because it represents a dominant ideology of masculinity existent in textual traditions. It is supported by dominant discourse in biblical traditions. For instance, Roland Boer approaches Chronicles through masculine hegemony, claiming that a queer or unstable hegemonic view of the text creates an artificial world built upon the temple as the locus of ideology and politics of gender.[35] Colleen Conway points out that a dominant ideology is maintained by a small group of people but the ideology of masculinity is consistently threatened and unstable.[36] Through the connection between metaphor and masculinity, Susan Haddox introduces hegemonic masculinity as a concept for interpreting Hosea. She shows that hegemonic masculinity represents a construct about men seeking to maintain its power

---

32. Judith Halberstam, *Female Masculinity* (London: Duke University Press, 1998).

33. R.W. Connell, *Masculinities* (Berkeley: University of California Press, 2nd edn, 2005), p. 77.

34. R.W. Connell and James W. Messerschmidt, 'Hegemonic Masculinity: Rethinking the Concept', *Gender & Society* 19 (2005), pp. 829-59.

35. Roland Boer, *The Earthy Nature of the Bible: Fleshly Readings of Sex, Masculinity, and Carnality* (New York: Palgrave Macmillan, 2012), pp. 71-80.

36. Colleen M. Conway, *Behold the Man: Jesus and Greco-Roman Masculinity* (New York: Oxford University Press, 2008), p. 10.

by pitting itself against constructs of alternative masculinity and of femininity as weakness. Since hegemonic masculinity defines femininity as its complete opposite, Haddox refers to femininity as 'straw-woman femininity'. In her view, a focus on masculinity illuminates that Hosea orients itself around concerns driven by male desires and audiences. Thus, the femininity depicted in the book is limited to its masculine perspective, and masculinity studies uncovers the gendered interplay of rhetoric in biblical texts.[37] By using predetermined categories for 'femininity', namely of weakness, impotency, and subordination, the author of this prophetic book criticizes Ephraim with the rhetoric of masculinity. For instance, Hosea 7 contains imagery of dough and bread, particularly an unturned cake (7.8) to connect to Ephraim's lack of political potency.[38] The metaphor relates Ephraim to a seemingly viable country that has support from its neighbors, such as Egypt, but its 'raw and doughy' side implicates that it remains impotent in light of Assyria's strength.[39]

Scholars of gender studies have not overlooked baking imagery as an area of constant gender interplays. For instance, Lot's food presentation in Gen. 19.3 seems less impressive than that of Abraham's (18.6). Abraham, after all, orders Sarah to provide provisions for heavenly guests while Lot prepares his own. Ken Stone notes that 'the representation of Lot as a man who "bakes" is part of a textual strategy that calls into question Lot's manhood'.[40] In fact, Stone brings attention to a process that focuses on the unmanliness of certain biblical characters in light of political polemics. Abimelech, for instance, is remembered for dying at the hands of a woman who throws a millstone on his head even though he tried to cover up the event by asking a young armor-bearer to slay him (Judg. 9.53-54; 2 Sam. 11.21).[41] Stone notes that 'manliness' is not something a 'male biblical character either inhabits or fails to inhabit by virtue of that character's sex', which means that, in the words of Connell, '[h]egemonic masculinity is not a fixed character type, always and everywhere the same. It is, rather,

---

37. Susan E. Haddox, *Metaphor and Masculinity in Hosea* (New York: Peter Lang, 2011).

38. Susan E. Haddox, '(E)Masculinity in Hosea's Political Rhetoric', in Brad E. Kelle and Megan Bishop Moore (eds.), *Israel's Prophets and Israel's Past* (New York: T. & T. Clark, 2006), pp. 174-200 (195).

39. Susan E. Haddox, *Metaphor and Masculinity in Hosea*, p. 81.

40. Ken Stone, *Practicing Safer Texts: Food, Sex, and Bible in Queer Perspective* (New York: T. & T. Clark, 2005), p. 97.

41. Ken Stone, 'Gender Criticism: The Un-Manning of Abimelech', in Gale A. Yee (ed.), *Judges and Method: New Approaches to Biblical Studies* (Minneapolis: Fortress Press, 2nd edn, 2007), pp. 183-201.

the masculinity that occupies the hegemonic position in a given pattern of gender relations, a position always contestable'.[42]

The concept of hegemonic masculinity remains a helpful touchstone for masculinity studies, as Haddox states: '[T]he play between the hegemonic and subordinate variants of masculinity is particularly active in the biblical texts'.[43] Hilary Lipka proposes a helpful hegemonic model in light of the book of Proverbs, that of complicity, subordination, or marginalization. Biblical texts uphold the notion of strength, on the battlefield or in the production of progeny and long-life, as the ideal masculine performance. Examining masculine performance with an emphasis on wisdom, inner strength, and the performance of virtues as superior to physical strength in Proverbs, Lipka suggests that the book negotiates 'an alternative ideal of masculine performance for at least a sub-group or a sub-culture within the population'.[44]

Scholars have noted that this interplay of masculinities is strongly depicted with hierarchal claims regarding God's masculinity. Haddox demonstrates in her study that male imagery negotiates various forms of masculinity, especially in terms of social scaffolding, self-initiated behaviors and potencies, and power dynamics, but the masculinity of God remains solid. While God's actions may hint at feminine imagery at times, God is 'consistently portrayed as the über-male'.[45] The next section deals with this idea of divine masculinity.

The (Male and Military) Body

In light of analyzing the claims of hegemonic masculinity, another area of focus in masculinity studies and the Hebrew Bible is the constructed male body and the body of God, or, the masculine-constructed body of God in textual descriptions. Feminists have long been interested in God's gender, especially in terms of gendered god-language, and specifically in terms of claiming feminine imagery for the deity in light of an almost exclusively male and explicitly androcentric platform.[46] For instance, Danna Nolan Fewell and David Gunn want biblical scholars to take seriously that God

---

42. Connell, *Masculinities*, p. 76.

43. Susan E. Haddox, 'Favoured Sons and Subordinate Masculinities', in Creangă (ed.), *Men and Masculinity in the Hebrew Bible and Beyond*, p. 3.

44. Hilary Lipka, 'Masculinities in Proverbs: An Alternative to the Hegemonic Ideal', in Creangă and Smit (eds.), *Biblical Masculinities Foregrounded*, pp. 86-103 (99).

45. Susan E. Haddox, *Metaphor and Masculinity in Hosea*, pp. 155-56.

46. For an overview of such interests, Hanne Løland's slightly revised doctoral dissertation contains a scholarly review in chapter 1; see Hanne Løland, *Silent or Salient Gender? The Interpretation of Gendered God-Language in the Hebrew Bible, Exemplified in Isaiah 42, 46 and 49* (Tübingen: Mohr Siebeck, 2008), pp. 6-20.

functions as a male character in biblical stories because God is 'a key manifestation of the male Subject'.[47]

The contribution of critical gender studies, especially masculinity studies, to the question of god-language is slowly emerging. The work by Howard Eilberg-Schwartz in the early 1990s certainly paved the way for investigating masculinities in light of the God of Israel. According to his work, the biblical complementary model of two sexes in light of the deity—God/Israelite man/Israelite woman—consistently threatens Israelite masculinity in light of God who is imagined as male. Israelite cultic activity supports and legitimizes a social order that validates the male as a mirror of the Israelite God. Yet a complementary model could potentially make Israelite male masculinity unnecessary because in this model female Israelites and their femininity would complement an Israelite male god's masculinity, leaving no room for the place of Israelite men and their masculinity to complement Israelite femininity. Therefore, Israelite men subject Israelite women to cultic impurity, for instance, so that they remain excluded and non-challenging of the connection the Israelite male has with God.[48] Deborah Sawyer suggests that the Hebrew Bible establishes a hierarchy of the divine over human, even at the expense of male autonomy. Masculinity is constructed through the divine, as the top embodiment of masculinity.[49]

The question remains how to apply gender/sex categories to Yhwh: Does the dominant masculine-centered language and imagery for God assume a male-sexed body for God? Hanne Løland notes that the Hebrew Bible depicts Yhwh with body parts excluding descriptions of sexual organs (Isaiah 40–55 as an example), and biblical literature does not remain gender-neutral in its concepts of the body; it assumes differences between male and female bodies.[50] Feminism has called attention to imagery such as Yhwh 'like a woman in labor' (Isa. 42.14) but Løland also points out that the same passage depicts Yhwh 'like a man of war' (Isa. 42.13). Both similes revolve around power, pain, and struggle, and both similes include assumptions concerning the sexed body. A female body has a womb from which it gives birth while a male body engages in battle. Does the existence of such imagery indicate that despite the male pronoun ascribed to God, an equally constructed concept of God as both feminine and masculine can be achieved? Claudia Bergmann argues that in the Hebrew Bible giving

---

47. Danna Nolan Fewell and David M. Gunn, *Gender, Power, and Promise: The Subject of the Bible's First Story* (Nashville: Abingdon Press, 1993), p. 19.
48. Howard Eilberg-Schwartz, *God's Phallus: And Other Problems for Men and Monotheism* (Boston: Beacon Press, 1994).
49. Deborah F. Sawyer, *God, Gender, and the Bible* (New York: Routledge, 2002).
50. The closest term in the Hebrew Bible for 'body' is 'flesh'; see Hanne Løland, *Silent or Salient Gender?*, pp. 71-74.

birth does not necessarily negate the presence of the masculine expectation of strenuous activity; the figure of speech 'like a woman giving birth' can apply to warrior-like situations similar to gaining a badge of honor. Thus biblical authors assume that giving birth is the essential feminine activity and mastery of war is the essential masculine activity. To apply both expressions to Yhwh, a man of war and a woman giving birth, is to show the deity's ultimate mastery over human crisis and over human death and life.[51]

Biblical authors use gendered bodily metaphors for God's actions, and so investigations of the bodily implications for the deity in light of biblical masculinities becomes necessary. An insecurity about a gendered deity is apparent as are explorations about political contexts of domination shaping portrayals of Yhwh. For instance, Stephen Moore asks if the God of Israel has a body and finds the answers of the Hebrew Bible ambivalent. Yet after a discussion of biblical imagery in conjunction with rabbinical texts, Moore concludes that 'Yahweh is a God who, from all eternity, has been intent on amassing the defensive trappings of hegemonic hypermasculinity, pre-eminently an awe-inspiring physique'.[52] Even the metaphor of Yhwh as a jealous violent husband lends itself to this image. Accordingly, the passage in Ezekiel 23 that characterizes Jerusalem of whoring around with Egyptians, 'whose members were like those of donkeys, and whose emissions was like that of stallions' (v. 21), reveals an anxiety that Egyptian and Mesopotamian gods dwarf the physique of Yhwh, so the prophet exaggerates the masculinity of God as that of an 'ultra-virile male'.[53] Incidentally, through the lens of disability studies, Jeremy Schipper shows that the presentation of Mosaic authority by Deuteronomistic History sets up Moses as a hyper-virile and non-disabled body of the ultimate male leader superior to any subsequent post-Mosaic leader.[54] At the end of his days, Moses' 'sight was unimpaired and his vigor had not abated' (Deut. 34.7).

---

51. Claudia Bergmann, 'Like a Warrior and Like a Woman Giving Birth: Expressing Divine Immanence and Transcendence in Isaiah 42:10-17', in S. Tamar Kamionkowski and Wonil Kim (eds.), *Bodies, Embodiment, and Theology of the Hebrew Bible* (New York: T. & T. Clark, 2010), pp. 38-56.

52. Stephen D. Moore, 'Gigantic God: Yahweh's Body', *JSOT* 70 (1996), pp. 87-115 (112). This article is contemporary to Stephen D. Moore, *God's Gym: Divine Male Bodies of the Bible* (New York: Routledge, 1996).

53. Stephen D. Moore, 'Gigantic God', p. 113. Moore also maintains that the attempt at ultimate masculine virility allows for God's body to take on feminine characteristics, such as removal of body hair, concern about weight and body image, and possible shrinking of testicles and pubescent breast development if steroids are involved.

54. Jeremy Schipper, 'Disabling Israelite Leadership: 2 Samuel 6:23 and Other Images of Disability in the Deuteronomistic History', in Hector Avalos, Sarah J. Melcher and Jeremy Schipper (eds.) *This Abled Body: Rethinking Disabilities in Biblical Studies* (Atlanta: Society of Biblical Literature), pp. 103-113.

Interestingly, masculinity studies plays an important role in disability studies, especially when it comes to biblical presentations of able-bodied male characters. They are the carriers of God's representation on earth.[55] For instance, in regard to priestly garments, Deborah Rooke notes the various visible gendered markers in priestly garments that stem from social customs. Clothing marks social hierarchies as well as gender and social status. The tunic described only for Aaron and his sons marks their male bodies with particular cultic functions that other non-priestly male bodies do not embody.[56] Multiple masculinities come into play here once again. Leviticus 21 offers a prime example because it excludes any physically flawed male body from offering food to the deity. God requires a 'perfect' and physically pure male body, creating a hierarchy between the blemished and unblemished priests, the latter having access to God.[57] The clear boundaries have consequences which, as Deborah Sawyer explains, are vulnerable masculinities. Thus, an 'overriding theology' exists that 'affirms the deity largely at the expense of the autonomy of the male audience'.[58]

A word here about Colleen Conway's study on masculinity in the Greco-Roman world highlights continuing concern for the role of the deity in gender and social hierarchies. In the Greco-Roman world, physical anatomy determined one's existence as a 'male' but that did not guarantee a natural masculine achievement. The body was regarded as being unstable in itself, and so one had to prove being 'a man' (*vir*) through performance, most importantly mastery.[59] The relationship between body and manliness implies precarious interchanges especially pertaining to social hierarchy. For instance, male children and slaves are not necessarily considered 'men'. The notion of hierarchy applies to both the Hebrew Bible and the New Testament when it comes to divine-human representations. Conway thus observes that 'if masculinity is equated with perfection, unity, rationality, order, and completeness, as it was in the ancient world, God would necessarily be masculine, even while incorporeal and asexual'.[60]

---

55. For a Christological perspective in light of masculinity in the Greco-Roman world, see Conway, *Behold the Man*.

56. Deborah W. Rooke, 'Breeches of the Covenant: Gender, Garments and the Priesthood', in Deborah W. Rooke (ed.), *Embroidered Garments: Priests and Gender in Biblical Israel* (Sheffield: Sheffield Phoenix Press, 2009), pp. 19-37.

57. For a general discussion, see Thomas Hentrich, 'Masculinity and Disability in the Bible', in Hector Avalos, Sarah J. Melcher and Jeremy Schipper (eds.), *This Abled Body: Rethinking Disabilities in Biblical Studies* (Atlanta: Society of Biblical Literature), pp. 73-87.

58. Sawyer, *God, Gender and the Bible*, p. 64.

59. Conway, *Behold the Man*, pp. 17-29.

60. Conway, *Behold the Man*, p. 36.

In the Hebrew Bible, the battlefield becomes what Cynthia Chapman calls 'the performance venue for achieving masculinity'.[61] Jeremiah images Yhwh as a 'strong warrior' (20.11) and this warrior God demonstrates magnificent masculinity in the continual battle with the forces of creation chaos (Job 40.19; 41.1).[62] The participation in warfare is a masculine expectation and, if the deity performs in such a way, biblical literature legitimizes participation in war as a major expression of masculinity. The body becomes a primary conceptual space on which this idea of warfare plays out. For example, Deuteronomy 21 explains the shaving of the heads of women captives. Elsewhere, I note that girding the loins (*motnayim* and *halatsayim*) denotes preparation for battle or strenuous activity, and it applies to all bodies under gendered and political negotiation.[63] Political interplays remain a critical component of biblical masculinities and warfare. Chapman refers to Assyrian inscriptions and reliefs to demonstrate an ideological presentation of the Assyrian King as the ideal male through the use of 'failed masculinity and feminization to present the enemy as one who forfeited or failed the masculine contest'.[64] The demotion of other men's masculinity is done by engaging several motifs against adversaries, such as the surrendering king, the failure to provide for people, and, in visual representations, the depiction of naked and dismembered members of the rival army. In light of this presentation, Susan Niditch points to 2 Samuel 10, in which Hanun of the Ammonites takes David's Israelite men and shaves off half the beard of each (10.4). David sends word that the men are not to return for battle until their beards have grown. Such humiliation points to an 'unmanning' of the enemy through the removal of facial hair.[65]

Carole Fontaine analyzes gender and disabilities when it comes to male bodies through the public art from ancient Near Eastern source materials that depict the shaming of male war victims.[66] They show them as sexually exploited by animals, unable to tame the natural predator let alone the

---

61. Cynthia R. Chapman, *The Gendered Language of Warfare in the Israelite-Assyrian Encounter* (Winona Lake, IN: Eisenbrauns, 2004), p. 20.

62. These ideas are developed in my doctoral dissertation, Katherine Low, 'Domestic Disputations at the Dung Heap: A Reception History of Job and his Wife in Christianity of the West' (PhD dissertation, Brite Divinity School, Texas Christian University, Fort Worth, TX, December 2010), pp. 55-69.

63. Katherine Low, 'Implications Surrounding Girding the Loins in Light of Gender, Body, and Power', *JSOT* 36 (2011), pp. 3-30. See also Boer, 'The Patriarch's Nuts: Concerning the Testicular Logic of Biblical Hebrew', in *The Earthy Nature of the Bible*, pp. 49-58.

64. Chapman, *Gendered Language of Warfare*, p. 20.

65. Niditch, *'My Brother Esau is a Hairy Man'*, p. 98.

66. Carole R. Fontaine, *With Eyes of the Flesh: The Bible, Gender and Human Rights* (Sheffield: Sheffield Phoenix Press, 2008), pp. 31-77.

ruler who often images himself as a mighty hunter who captures the wild beast. Another common visual display, as noted by Chapman, are the naked and dismembered male bodies of the rival army. Fontaine notes that females are rampantly missing from these visual displays; reliefs show female captives walking. Fontaine finds no depiction of the wide-scale rape of enemy women that accompanied realities of the battlefield or aftermath of warfare.[67] Chapman suggests, from the point of view of Assyrian material culture, that by showing clothed, unmolested foreign women, the conquering king assumes the role of their new protector, thus shaming the enemy men who could not protect their property.[68]

Current Context for Future Work

The central issues of multiple masculine expressions, even beyond heterosexual normativity, masculine hegemony, and Israelite bodies in contexts of war especially in light of a male deity, are only touchstones for the various ways feminist Hebrew Bible scholars have recently begun to incorporate masculinity studies into their work. A variety of multidisciplinary arrangements between feminism and biblical masculinities exists from within a vast array of orientations toward gender studies. The very idea of 'masculinity studies', however, suggests that masculinity is the object of study and that even the term 'masculinity' holds complexity.

As pointed out above, if masculinity is a performative role, then it need not become reduced to acts only ascribed upon the male body. Yet much of the research highlighted in the previous sections focuses on male bodily experience and masculinity. For instance, a lacking area of analysis is female expressions of masculine performance. In fact, only one essay in the most recent monograph on masculinity in the Hebrew Bible focuses on a female character.[69] The next question is, of course, how an analysis of female masculinity would differ, if at all, from a gendered analysis of the interplays between masculinity and femininity. To exemplify the latter, Cheryl Exum maintains that Deborah and Jael (Judges 4–5) are meant to 'advocate the male ideology of war', suggesting that 'men go to war in order to steal and plunder for their women, and that this is something women want'.[70] In other words, Jael, for instance, 'plays the man' better than Sisera by successfully

---

67. Fontaine, *With Eyes of the Flesh*, pp. 63-66.
68. Chapman, *The Gendered Language of Warfare*, p. 47.
69. Stuart Macwilliam, 'Athaliah: A Case of Illicit Masculinity', in Creangă and Smit (eds.), *Biblical Masculinities Foregrounded*, pp. 69-85.
70. J. Cheryl Exum, 'Judges: Encoded Messages to Women', in Luise Schottroff and Marie-Theres Wacker (eds.), *Feminist Biblical Interpretation: A Compendium of Critical Commentary on the Books of the Bible and Related Literature* (Grand Rapids: Eerdmans, 2012), pp. 112-27 (117).

engaging in an act of war, but she does so as a seducer, a mother-figure, and as a form of a rapist. Thus, the narrator creates a gender reversal through the character of Jael, a female embodying male traits in order to reflect the narrator's male ideology of war. In contrast, Deryn Guest disagrees with feminist scholars approaching female and male characters through the binary of masculine/feminine. She presents Jael not as a female embodiment of masculinity or a woman warrior but simply as a warrior. Does having a penis necessarily qualify one as a warrior (*geber*) in the Hebrew Bible? Guest suggests that the idea of 'gender reversal' reinforces a two-gender binary, and she holds Jael up as an example of a character occupying indeterminant gendered space.[71] Guest also advocates for the use of queer theory to resist and deconstruct gender binaries and that those queer theorists who engage 'masculinity studies would look at examples of female masculinity as part of it remit and subvert the all-too-easy connection between masculinity studies and men'.[72] A foundation has been established within biblical masculinities to take on female masculinity as a serious area of inquiry and this area holds promise for the future.

As evident, masculinity studies operates among various other areas of study, including gender, queer, and disability studies. As masculinity is not monolithic, neither is feminist criticism. According to Mary Ann Tolbert, when 'racially and ethnically marginalized women and lesbians' began to protest a universalization of womanhood, beginning particularly in the 1980s, they brought to light the 'realization concerning the interwoven nature of gender with other social markers to the contemporary situation of racially and ethnically marginalized women'.[73] A parallel experience could benefit masculinity studies by bringing race and ethnicity into the conversation about multiple masculinities, especially with marginalized peoples. As an example of racial difference impacting masculine constructs in contemporary US culture, 'men of color are constructed as criminal, violent, lascivious, irresponsible, and not particularly smart'.[74] What would an analysis of ethnicity bring to biblical masculinities? Willa Johnson's study on identity and interethnic marriage in Ezra 9–10 does not engage masculinity studies, but it illustrates the connection of biblical literature with

---

71. Deryn Guest, 'From Gender Reversal to Genderfuck: Reading Jael through a Lesbian Lens', in Teresa J. Hornsby and Ken Stone (eds.), *Bible Trouble: Queer Reading at the Boundaries of Biblical Scholarship* (Atlanta: Society of Biblical Literature, 2011), pp. 12-20.

72. Guest, *Beyond Feminist Biblical Studies*, p. 142.

73. Mary Ann Tolbert, 'Gender', in A.K.M. Adam (ed.), in *Handbook of Postmodern Biblical Interpretation* (St. Louis, MI: Chalice Press), pp. 99-105 (100).

74. Richard Delgado and Jean Stefancic, 'Minority Men, Misery, and the Marketplace of Ideas', in Maurice Berger, Brian Wallis and Simon Watson (eds.), *Constructing Masculinity* (New York: Routledge, 1995), pp. 211-20 (211).

economics and ethnicity. Biblical masculinities could further her analysis, which claims that ideas about landowning, inheritance, ethnocentrism, and sexism emerge through the problems raised in Ezra-Nehemiah. In her view, the biblical passage fits a pattern for those returning to postexilic Yehud that forces them to redefine the 'in-group'. Marriage is a major metaphorical vehicle through which to establish such boundaries,[75] but marriage is also related to other political, social, and gendered factors. When scholars focus on biblical masculinities, they need to consider these other factors as well.

Feminist Hebrew Bible interpreters have used masculinity studies, especially the idea of hegemonic masculinity, to highlight patriarchal constructions in biblical literature. At this point, the theory of hegemonic masculinity remains a helpful starting point because it is unstable and some biblical texts undermine or challenge it. It is also a multivalent concept, as Susanna Asikainen explains when she states: '[S]everal [biblical] hegemonic masculinities' seem to 'compete for hegemonic position'.[76] Such instability and multivalency allows feminist scholars to connect with subordinated groups from within the hegemonic model.

The question of whether or not hegemonic masculinity can always be engaged in terms of a patriarchal system remains noteworthy for biblical studies. In later research, Connell raises the issue of assuming that the function of the hegemonic masculinity model is centrally defined against a history of subordination of women; rather the model can be open to the equality of women because it remains 'possible that a more humane, less oppressive, means of being a man might become hegemonic, as part of a process leading toward an abolition of gender hierarchies'.[77] Connell's statement holds significance for future work with feminist biblical studies and masculinity studies in the identification of intersections between patriarchy and hegemonic masculinity in biblical texts, just as some feminists have already raised concerns about the usefulness of the model of patriarchy in biblical interpretation.[78] Also, Connell rejects 'those usages [of the model] that imply a fixed character type, or an assemblage of toxic traits. These usages are not trivial—they are trying to name significant issues about gender such as the persistence of violence or the consequences of

---

75. Willa M. Johnson, *The Holy Seed Has Been Defiled: The Interethnic Marriage Dilemma in Ezra 9–10* (Sheffield: Sheffield Phoenix Press, 2011).

76. Susanna Asikainen, '"Eunuchs for the Kingdom of Heaven": Matthew and Subordinated Masculinities', in Creangă and Smit (eds.), *Biblical Masculinities Foregrounded*, pp. 156-88 (159).

77. R.W. Connell and James W. Messerschmidt, 'Hegemonic Masculinity: Rethinking the Concept', *Gender & Society* 19 (2005), pp. 829-59 (833).

78. Carol L. Meyers, 'Was Ancient Israel a Patriarchal Society?', *JBL* 133.1 (2014), pp. 8-27.

domination'.[79] The hegemonic masculinity model is understood not as a fixed position that justifies the subordination and oppression of women but as a socially acceptable, yet adjustable, strategy that keeps men in positions of power. Therefore, it is not always assumed that the model is functioning in all gendered constructions of biblical texts. The model should not function as a catch-all model or a single dimension of gender but as a working theory about a forceful element in cultural process that may not hold up as a wide net cast over biblical texts without consideration of specialized and unique versions of masculinity and femininity functioning in the texts. Future scholarship with feminist biblical studies and masculinity studies can reveal how biblical texts, as gendered constructions, embody, defy, or negotiate hegemonic masculinity in light of women's experiences and power dynamics.

Further Elaborations of Power Relations: Concluding Comments

The engagement of masculinity studies by feminist biblical interpreters is a new enterprise that has only emerged since the late 1990s. Given the fledgling status of the approach, much remains to be seen. No major debate is occurring at this time about the engagement of masculinity studies in feminist scholarship. However, as the method continues to make its way into biblical studies, and as more and more feminist scholars deal with it, discussions may arise about the critical study of masculinity within feminism and gender studies.

This new research area has come with many mutual benefits. First, many male-performing exegetes engaging masculinity studies have made strong contributions to gender and sexuality in the Bible in light of feminist biblical interpretation. For instance, Clines entered into masculinity studies through a conversation with feminist exegete J. Cheryl Exum.[80] She encourages the collaboration between masculinity studies and feminist studies. In her view, such collaboration does not exclude women's experiences but it enriches the understanding about maleness, often so central to feminist critiques.[81] The emerging dialogue is already leading to many results in both feminist and masculinity studies. In short, masculinity studies aids feminist exegetes in the exploration of power relations and patriarchal systems

---

79. R.W. Connell and James W. Messerschmidt, 'Hegemonic Masculinity: Rethinking the Concept', *Gender & Society* 19 (2005), pp. 829-59 (854).

80. David J.A. Clines, 'Ecce Vir, or, Gendering the Son of Man', in J.C. Exum and S.D. Moore (eds.), *Biblical Studies/Cultural Studies* (Sheffield: Sheffield Phoenix Press, 1998), pp. 352-75 (353).

81. J.C. Exum, 'Feminist Study of the Old Testament', in A.D.H. Mayes (ed.), *Text in Context: Essays by Members of the Society for Old Testament Study* (Oxford: Oxford University Press, 2000), pp. 86-115.

as they function in biblical texts. As part of a larger field of gender studies, masculinity studies is unstable and offers space for all kinds of gendered exegetes, including those performing as female and male. Masculinity is just as unnatural and cultural as femininity, not belonging into any kind of heteronormative framework. As such, the field of masculinity studies belongs in the field of Hebrew Bible studies and it will continue to broaden the critical analysis of gender and sexuality in the Bible.

18

ENGAGING WITH CULTURAL DISCOURSES:
CULTURAL FEMINIST CRITICISM IN HEBREW BIBLE STUDIES

Caroline Blyth

As a methodological approach to feminist biblical studies, cultural studies is a relatively new kid on the block. Yet its youthfulness should not deter us from acknowledging the important role it has played and will continue to play in feminist engagements with the Bible. This essay begins by offering a brief history of cultural studies and the primary aims of this approach within the Arts, followed by a review of cultural studies within biblical studies and especially feminist biblical interpretation.

A Brief History of Cultural Studies

Cultural studies developed in Great Britain during the 1950s and 1960s as a response to the disillusionment with modernity that soaked through British cultural consciousness in the aftermath of World War II. The social realities of gender inequality, immigration, poverty, and the continuing threat of war fuelled public anxieties, which were in turn increasingly articulated within the ever-expanding fields of mass media and consumer culture.[1] Cultural studies was a response to this social crisis, a way for post-war academics to think seriously and deeply about the cultures in which they lived and the impact that master discourses of nationalism, patriarchy, capitalism, and imperialism had upon these cultures and upon those who lived their everyday lives within them.[2] It was a political endeavour, which grew less out of the carefully nurtured nursery beds of the university than from the guerrilla gardening adventures of extramural adult education and the New Left political landscape of Britain in the 1950s.[3] As Stuart Hall explains, the initial aim of cultural studies was 'to engage with some real problems out there in the dirty world, and to use the enormous advantage given to a tiny handful

---

1. John Hartley, *A Short History of Cultural Studies* (London: Sage, 2003), pp. 2-3; Stuart Hall, 'The Emergence of Cultural Studies and the Crisis of the Humanities', *October* 53 (1990), pp. 11-23 (12).
2. John Hartley, *Short History*, p. 2.
3. Hall, 'Emergence of Cultural Studies', p. 12.

of us in the British educational system who had the opportunity to go into universities and reflect on these problems, to spend that time usefully to try to understand how the world worked'.[4]

The academic pursuit of cultural studies first bloomed in the Centre for Contemporary Cultural Studies (CCCS), set up by Richard Hoggart and Stuart Hall in the English Department at the University of Birmingham in 1964. As it developed through the 1960s and 1970s, it drew political and theoretical inspiration first from the Frankfurt School of critical theory and the Marxist ideologies of Louis Althusser and Antonio Gramsci, and later, in the 1980s, from the writings of poststructuralists such as Michel Foucault and literary theorist Roland Barthes.[5] Moreover, while the CCCS had begun within the University's English Department, cultural studies was, from the outset, radically interdisciplinary in its pedagogical and theoretical approaches.[6] Like magpies around a trinket box, scholars and students 'raided'[7] other disciplines to see what methods, hermeneutics, and theoretical models they could use, including those from anthropology, sociology, literary studies, philosophy, film and media studies, political studies, and art history.[8]

Moreover, cultural studies also caused a bit of a stir rejecting conventional distinctions between high culture and popular culture. While the former (which included fine art, classical music, and the western canon of English literature) had until then been considered the only cultural texts worth exploring within academic circles, cultural studies practitioners insisted that popular culture was also a valuable source of scholarly analysis. They pored over TV soap operas, advertising, women's magazines, popular fashion trends, and rock music. University curricula began to include artefacts and texts from working-class culture, queer culture, trans culture, youth culture, postcolonial culture, and all the everyday cultures and identities that had hitherto been regarded as too marginal for serious academic attention.[9]

---

4. Hall, 'Emergence of Cultural Studies', p. 17.

5. J. Cheryl Exum and Stephen D. Moore, 'Biblical Studies/Cultural Studies', in J. Cheryl Exum and Stephen D. Moore (eds.), *Biblical Studies/Cultural Studies: The Third Sheffield Colloquium* (Gender, Culture, Theory, 7; Sheffield: Sheffield Academic Press, 1998), pp. 19-45 (23).

6. Stuart Hall, 'Race, Culture, and Communications: Looking Backward and Forward at Cultural Studies', *Rethinking Marxism* 5 (1992), pp. 10-18 (11).

7. The term used by Hall, 'Emergence of Cultural Studies', p. 16. I am indebted to Graeme Turner, *What Becomes of Cultural Studies?* (London: Sage, 2012), pp. 25-26, for the magpie allusion.

8. Hall, 'Emergence of Cultural Studies', p. 16. For examples of this ongoing interdisciplinarity within cultural studies, see the essays in Toby Miller (ed.), *A Companion to Cultural Studies* (Malden: Blackwell, 2001).

9. Hartley, *Short History*, pp. 3, 10.

According to Hall, cultural studies was the 'dirty crossroads' where popular culture and high culture finally met.[10]

Since the 1980s, cultural studies has become increasingly popular within Arts programs, not only in Britain, but also internationally, exploding into 'a highly visible global phenomenon'.[11] Perhaps part of such recent popularity lies in the fact that cultural studies has always been recognized as a project whose goals extend beyond the traditional academic concerns of theory and pedagogy. Instead, it impels scholars to confront the *impact* of their scholarship—its political bearing and practical influence on the 'dirty world' in which it unfolds.[12] Particularly, cultural studies has as its focus the significance of popular culture in everyday life—how it shapes, coerces, and contests people's political and social experiences within their own communities and cultures.[13] Practitioners of cultural studies believe that a scholarly exploration of these phenomena provides opportunities to make 'bold and important' changes to the everyday lives of people situated within these communities and cultures.[14] As one of the early pioneers of cultural studies Lawrence Grossberg asserts: 'Cultural studies matters because it is about the future, and about some of the work it will take, in the present, to shape the future'.[15] In today's age of 'impact-driven' research demands and funding opportunities, perhaps academics and program coordinators within the Arts realize that the theoretical *and* practical goals of cultural studies may remind their STEM-obsessed critics that Arts disciplines continue to have a crucial relevance within today's ever-troubled and ever-messy world.

Definitions of Cultural Studies

After this brief description of the origins of cultural studies, it is time to explain how the methodology is practiced. When it comes to definitions, cultural studies is a slippery fellow to pin down. With a notoriously broad remit, its subject matter, its theoretical approaches and its relevance—in other words what it does, how, and why—can vary widely. Even scholars who were foundational in inaugurating cultural studies as an academic

---

10. Hall, 'Race, Culture, and Communications', p. 10.
11. Gilbert B. Rodman, *Why Cultural Studies?* (Hoboken: Wiley, 2014), p. vii. Although, ironically, the University of Birmingham closed the CCCS in 2002, despite high undergraduate demand and exemplary teaching scores. See Hartley, *Short History*, p. 10.
12. Rodman, *Why Cultural Studies?*, pp. 40-41.
13. Hall, 'Emergence of Cultural Studies', p. 17; Turner, *What Becomes of Cultural Studies?*, p. 15.
14. Rodman, *Why Cultural Studies?*, p. vii.
15. Lawrence Grossberg, *Cultural Studies in the Future Tense* (Durham, NC: Duke University Press, 2010), p. 1.

pursuit disagree about the specifics of this methodological approach. As Stuart Hall insists: 'Cultural studies is not one thing; it has never been one thing'.[16] Or to quote Chris Barker: 'Cultural studies does not speak with one voice, it cannot be spoken with one voice'.[17] But for the purpose of this essay I will sketch out a definition of cultural studies that reflects the particular use of this methodology within the discipline of biblical interpretation. There it refers to the exploration of the Bible in light of popular culture texts that include music, literature, popular media, and the visual arts.

Simply put, practitioners of cultural studies travel along two paths: first, they investigate how cultural 'texts', including literature, films, music, TV programs, art, advertising, and other cultural 'products', are sites in which cultural ideologies and power structures are articulated, authenticated, resisted, and promulgated.[18] These ideologies and power structures may pertain to gender, sexuality, class, economy, politics, race, and other trajectories that construct and shape people's cultural realities and everyday lives.[19] The books we read, the movies we watch, the music we listen to, and the social media sites we haunt—all of these cultural texts offer us, as consumers, a way of looking at the world and a sort of reality 'cheat sheet' that invites us to understand our experiences in a particular light. Rarely non-partisan, they present us with their creators' viewpoints and summon us, either implicitly or explicitly, to embrace these viewpoints. As such, they are locations where *existing* constructions of power can be either strengthened *or* contested. For example, a crime novel or TV police procedural may champion dominant (white) social ideations of the police as upholders of law and social justice, while a protest song, TV interview, or Instagram image arising from the #BlackLivesMatter movement may instead highlight common cultural concerns about police brutality and the inherent racism of the judiciary.

In essence, cultural studies examines how people's everyday lives may be shaped *and* articulated by the cultures and contexts in which cultural texts are immersed and the cultural texts they consume. As Stuart Hall explains, when approaching a popular culture text, the question that should 'haunt' cultural studies scholars is: 'What does this have to do with everything else?'[20] Drawing on a chosen set of critical theories, scholars interrogate

---

16. Hall, 'Emergence of Cultural Studies', p. 11.

17. Chris Barker, *Cultural Studies: Theory and Practice* (London: Sage, 2nd edn, 2005), p. 4.

18. See, for example, Rodman, *Why Cultural Studies?*, pp. 39-40; Hall, 'Race, Culture, and Communications', p. 10.

19. Grossberg, *Cultural Studies in the Future Tense*, p. 8.

20. Stuart Hall, 'That moment and this', presented as part of a plenary panel at the 'Cultural Studies Now' conference, University of East London, 20 July, 2007. Cited by Rodman, *Why Cultural Studies?*, p. 4.

these texts, asking 'central, urgent, and disturbing questions' about them and trying to understand how they intersect with cultural ideologies, values, and discourses of social power.[21] Crucial to this process is the scholarly conviction that such an exercise is worth doing, not only in an academic or pedagogical sense, but also for social, ethical, and political reasons. This is the second 'path' along which scholars engaged in cultural studies travel. As I mentioned above, they firmly believe that cultural studies *matters*, that the study of popular culture *matters*, because popular culture texts and phenomena carry immense power. They share power with those who conform to their ideological claims, but they may likewise withhold that power from anyone who resists. Cultural studies is thus always an intellectual *and* a political project—and neither is optional,[22] using theoretical resources to gain better understandings of how culture both empowers and disempowers those within its borders. It interrogates prevailing power structures and seeks new possibilities of political resistance and change, not only in the lecture room or the academic conference hall, but also in the 'real world'.[23] As Lawrence Grossberg insists, the academic study of popular culture provides 'a vital component of the struggle to change the world and to make it more humane and just'.[24]

Cultural Studies and Biblical Studies

In the past few decades, cultural studies has ensconced itself within biblical studies as a form of reception history, exploring how biblical texts are received and reinterpreted within cultural texts, including music, literature, and the visual arts, across space and time. Setting aside biblical studies' characteristic 'obsession' with the 'original' meaning of the text and its traditional leaning towards devotional or homiletic reading strategies,[25] biblical scholars engaging with cultural studies methodologies have their eyes fixed firmly upon the continued cultural significances of biblical texts. They investigate how these significances are negotiated within contemporary cultures and communities in which biblical traditions are read, retold, and re-visioned. Retellings of these traditions within cultural texts are extolled as accessible and valuable acts of interpretation, expressed by their creators in visual, musical, dramatic, or written form, thereby offering a window

---

21. Hall, 'Race, Culture, and Communications', p. 11. See also Chris Rojek, *Cultural Studies* (Cambridge: Polity Press, 2007), p. 6.
22. Rodman, *Why Cultural Studies?*, pp. 40-41, 50-58.
23. Grossberg, *Cultural Studies in the Future Tense*, p. 8; Hall, 'Emergence of Cultural Studies', p. 17; Rojek, *Cultural Studies*, pp. 7, 28.
24. Grossberg, *Cultural Studies in the Future Tense*, pp. 5-6 (see also pp. 54-55).
25. Stephen D. Moore, 'Preface', in Stephen D. Moore (ed.), *In Search of the Present: The Bible through Cultural Studies* (Semeia, 82; Atlanta: SBL, 1998), pp. vii-viii (viii).

into their understandings of the biblical text. Like a biblical commentary or exegetical essay, these cultural retellings thus serve as interpretive tools, inviting audiences to contemplate biblical traditions from novel perspectives and to consider how these creative retellings have invariably been shaped by their creators' historical, geographical, sociocultural, and theological milieus.

Moreover, cultural studies also highlights the fact that biblical texts lend themselves to multiple readings and interpretations. Rather than being monologic, cultural representations and retellings reveal a wealth of meanings that texts convey within different temporal and spatial locations.[26] Just as there are many ways to translate texts from one language to another, cultural retellings of biblical texts, whether as images, music, performances, or literary works, offer any number of interpretations.[27] While some cultural retellings promote sympathetic readings of the biblical traditions, others refuse to leave these traditions unchallenged, inviting audiences to critically scrutinize them.[28] Cultural studies thus draws biblical scholars into fascinating conversations with biblical texts, to consider and to debate their multiple meanings, and to re-view the ancient traditions, often in surprising and at times troubling lights.[29]

Cultural studies in biblical scholarship, similar to cultural studies undertaken in other disciplinary areas, also dissolves the boundaries traditionally erected between cultural texts considered 'high culture' and those deemed 'popular culture'. Searching through recent publications in this area, we discover monographs, journals, and edited volumes dedicated to scholarly discussions of biblical themes in cultural genres as diverse as fine art, classical music, English literature, popular cinema and television, dance, hip hop, rap, comic books, and even advertising. While some of these scholarly outputs focus on particular genres of cultural text,[30] others consider biblical

---

26. John Harvey, *The Bible as Visual Culture: When Text Becomes Image* (Bible in the Modern World, 57; Sheffield: Sheffield Phoenix Press, 2013), p. 10.

27. Harvey, *Bible as Visual Culture*, p. 10.

28. Peter S. Hawkins, 'Lost and Found: The Bible and its Literary Afterlives', *Religion and Literature* 36 (2004), pp. 1-14 (8).

29. Hugh Pyper, *The Unchained Bible: Cultural Appropriations of Biblical Texts* (London: Bloomsbury, 2012), p. 1.

30. To offer just some examples, Erin Runions, *How Hysterical: Identification and Resistance in the Bible and Film* (New York: Palgrave McMillan, 2003); Adele Reinhartz, *Scripture on the Silver Screen* (Louisville, KY: Westminster/John Knox Press, 2003); Martin O'Kane, *Painting the Text: The Artist as Biblical Interpreter* (Bible in the Modern World, 8; Sheffield: Sheffield Phoenix Press, 2009); Alison M. Jack, *The Bible and Literature* (SCM Core Text; Norwich: SCM Press, 2012); Robert Glen Howard, *Network Apocalypse: Visions of the End in an Age of Internet Media* (Bible in the Modern World, 36; Sheffield: Sheffield Phoenix Press, 2011); Caroline Vander Stichele

themes, characters, or traditions as they are retold and represented across a spectrum of cultural creations.³¹ Edited volumes and monographs, meanwhile, offer hungry readers a smörgåsbord of encounters between popular culture and biblical studies,³² while a number of journals, annuals, and encyclopaedias have likewise dedicated themselves to enriching the field of biblical studies.³³ From Rembrandt to street art, Wagner to Kanye West, Milton to manga comics—cultural studies breathes into biblical studies a warm wealth of engagements between the Bible and culture, vivifying a discipline that can, at times, appear awfully distant from the lived experiences of everyday life.

Despite the growing popularity of culture studies among some biblical scholars, the established academy of biblical studies has yet to embrace fully this area of reception history. Regardless of the fact that it fuels fascinating research, fills classrooms, engages public debate and often ticks the 'impact' box favoured by funding providers, cultural studies is not always considered as *bona fide* biblical scholarship. Rather, it is scowled at suspiciously as something radical, even as iconoclastic, challenging the

and Hugh S. Pyper (eds.), *Text, Image, and Otherness in Children's Bibles: What Is In the Picture?* (Atlanta: SBL, 2012).

31. See, e.g., Tina Pippin, *Apocalyptic Bodies: The Biblical End of the World in Text and Image* (London: Routledge, 1999); Paul C. Burns, *Jesus in Twentieth Century Literature, Art and Movies* (New York: Continuum, 2007); Linda S. Schearing and Valarie H. Ziegler, *Enticed by Eden: How Western Culture Uses, Confuses (and sometimes Abuses) Adam and Eve* (Waco, TX: Baylor University Press, 2013); William Goodman, *Yearning for You: Psalms and the Song of Songs in Conversation with Rock and Worship Songs* (Bible in the Modern World, 46; Sheffield: Sheffield Phoenix Press, 2012); Yvonne Sherwood, *A Literary Text and its Afterlives: The Survival of Jonah in Western Culture* (Cambridge: Cambridge University Press, 2001).

32. See, e.g., Fiona C. Black (ed.), *The Recycled Bible: Autobiography, Culture, and the Space Between* (Atlanta: SBL, 2006); Helen Leneman and Harry Dov Walfish (eds.), *The Bible Retold by Jewish Artists, Composers, Writers and Filmmakers* (Bible in the Modern World, 71; Sheffield: Sheffield Phoenix Press, 2015); Philip Culbertson and Elaine M. Wainwright (eds.), *The Bible in/and Popular Culture: A Creative Encounter* (Semeia Studies, 65; Atlanta: SBL, 2010); J. Cheryl Exum (ed.), *Retellings: The Bible in Literature, Music, Art and Film* (Leiden: Brill, 2007); George Aichele, *Culture, Entertainment and the Bible* (London: Bloomsbury, 1997); Pyper, *Unchained Bible;* Roland Boer, *Knockin' on Heaven's Door: The Bible and Popular Culture* (London: Routledge, 1999).

33. See, e.g., Dale C. Allison *et al.* (eds.), *Encyclopedia of the Bible and its Reception* (Berlin: W. de Gruyter, 2009–); *Journal of the Bible and its Reception*; *Relegere: Studies in Religion and Reception*; *Biblical Reception.* The Semeia series has also published several volumes focused on cultural studies approaches to biblical interpretation, including Alice Bach (ed.), *Biblical Glamour and Hollywood Glitz* (Semeia, 74; Atlanta: Scholars Press, 1996) and Moore (ed.), *In Search of the Present: The Bible through Cultural Studies*.

'privileged space' within the academy that is preserved for more traditional methodological pursuits.[34] I have heard stories of cultural studies enthusiasts who were challenged by academic peers about the legitimacy or relevance of their work. At the SBL annual conference a few years ago, one of the speakers at the Bible and Visual Arts panel recounted how a colleague had asked if she was taking a 'holiday' from her research to write the paper she presented. When I gave a conference paper a short while ago on biblical allusions in Stieg Larssen's *The Girl with the Dragon Tattoo*, a fellow biblical scholar who was in the audience asked me afterwards what my 'real' research area was. There is a sense in biblical studies, as Katie B. Edwards notes, that popular culture is not 'appropriate' for academic study.[35] I would add that the study of biblical reception in 'high culture' is likewise regarded by some members of the guild as a less valuable method than historical, textual, and theological approaches so beloved within traditional western scholarship.

Furthermore, I concur with Edwards that attempts within the guild of biblical studies to ascribe higher 'value' to certain methodologies than others not only smack of 'intellectual snobbery'[36] but they are also shortsighted *and* potentially fatal to the future of the discipline. By my reckoning, cultural studies research *is* 'real' research; it *is* relevant and it has the potential to strengthen the heartbeat of biblical scholarship, making a case for its ongoing importance within the increasingly impact-driven world of academia.

Cultural Studies and Feminist Interpretation of the Hebrew Bible

When Stuart Hall writes about feminism's entry into British cultural studies, he describes it as a 'thief in the night', which 'broke in' to the predominantly masculine domain of cultural studies and then 'interrupted, made an unseemly noise, seized the time, [and] crapped on the table'.[37] While feminist biblical scholarship may not have made quite such a dramatic entrance into biblically-focused cultural studies, it has, nevertheless, impacted significantly upon this methodological approach. To a degree, at least, this is

---

34. Fiona C. Black, 'The Recycled Bible: Autobiography, Culture, and the Space Between', in Black (ed.), *Recycled Bible*, pp. 1-10 (3 n. 7).

35. Katie B. Edwards, *Admen and Eve: The Bible in Contemporary Advertising* (Bible in the Modern World, 48; Sheffield: Sheffield Phoenix Press, 2012), p. ix.

36. Edwards, *Admen and Eve*, p. ix.

37. Stuart Hall, 'Cultural Studies and its Theoretical Legacies', in Lawrence Grossberg, Cary Nelson, and Paula A. Treichler (eds.), *Cultural Studies* (New York: Routledge, 1992), pp. 277-94 (282). Hall is highly self-critical about the inherent androcentrism of cultural studies in the 1960s and 1970s, which feminism brought to light with an uncomfortable honesty.

not surprising. Feminist biblical interpretation has found a suitable bedfellow in feminist cultural studies, both methodologies sharing an awareness of the rhetorical power of cultural texts to act on the world by conveying and promoting gendered ideologies to their audiences, ideologies that inevitably affect the beliefs, behaviours, politics, privileges, and power relations that intersect and intrude within women's everyday lived experiences.[38]

Feminist scholars working in the field of cultural studies focus their attention on *two* sets of cultural texts: the Bible on the one hand and its cultural retellings and afterlives on the other. As 'one of the most influential mythical and literary documents of our culture',[39] the Bible continues to be appropriated in religious, social, popular, and political discourses to serve ideological ends. Cultural studies acknowledges and highlights this biblical power and influence within contemporary culture, recognizing it as a 'multifaceted icon',[40] a cultural 'prop',[41] which may be used to validate, guide, or challenge its readers' ideological stances, political choices, and personal responses to gender concerns within their own cultures, communities, and beyond.

Moreover, feminist biblical scholars also recognize that those cultural texts which depict retellings and afterlives of the biblical traditions may *likewise* serve as an influential 'prop' with which to articulate the gendered ideologies and power relations that their creators identify within the biblical material. Readers often make sense of biblical traditions, not from close and careful examinations of the texts themselves, but rather by drawing on the various presentations of these texts within popular culture as a means of locating biblical meaning.[42] Such retellings of the biblical material invariably embody rhetorical power of their own. The artists shape the cultural, political, and theological ideologies of the biblical retellings with which the audience is then invited to engage.[43] These ideologically-laden interpretations are valuable for feminist biblical scholars, as they interrogate and explore how cultural texts endorse *and* challenge various discourses about gender, culture, and power.

---

38. Hartley, *Short History*, pp. 124-25.
39. Mieke Bal, *Lethal Love: Feminist Literary Readings of Biblical Love Stories* (Bloomington: Indiana University Press, 1987), p. 1.
40. Moore, 'Preface', p. vii.
41. Joel Baden uses this term in 'What Use is the Bible?', a Nantucket Project lecture delivered in 2014, in which he describes how the Bible functions in contemporary culture as a 'symbol of power and authority' that people wield like a 'sledgehammer' to drive home their own cultural and ideological beliefs. For further details, see https://www.nantucketproject.com/joel-baden (accessed 24 June 2015).
42. J. Cheryl Exum, *Plotted, Shot, and Painted: Cultural Representations of Biblical Women* (Sheffield: Sheffield Phoenix Press, 2nd edn, 2012), p. 14.
43. Exum and Moore, 'Biblical Studies/Cultural Studies', p. 39.

In the following sections, I will offer several examples to illustrate how feminist interpreters working with the Hebrew Bible traditions have incorporated cultural studies into their work. Owing to space limitations, this discussion is not exhaustive but presents a 'tasting tray' of feminist cultural analysis. It highlights this method's significance within the current academy of biblical studies, aiming to whet readers' appetites to sample more of this fascinating research area.

Making the Implicit Explicit
One of the most common uses of cultural studies within feminist biblical interpretation involves considering how cultural texts bring to the forefront of our attention those gendered themes and ideologies that often lie hidden beneath the surface of biblical texts. Biblical writers do not always make explicit the ideological tenets that they endorse, leaving it to readers to eke out textual ideologies through careful reading and reflection. Some readers also turn to cultural texts and retellings to aid them in their interpretations, as these texts can present implicit biblical ideologies more *explicitly*, lifting them to the surface and conveying them clearly through visual, aural, or written media.

An excellent example of the explicit ideological stances communicated by cultural texts appears in cultural retellings of Genesis 2–3, especially in the many afterlives of Eve. Of all biblical women and of all biblical texts, Eve's characterization in the biblical account is one of the most ubiquitous biblical traditions to weave its way into the cultural imagination. Elevated to the status of a cultural icon, Eve graces countless canvases, inspires numerous poetic works, and is the muse behind cultural products as diverse as songs, advertising campaigns, jokes, sex toys, and dating websites.

And yet, as a number of feminist biblical scholars have noted, Eve's cultural afterlives are less likely to valorise than vilify this biblical figure, casting her as a dangerous temptress and sexual seductress, a *femme fatale*, whose legacy lives on, embodied by women even today. These afterlives are thus far from harmless, for Genesis 2–3 remains 'arguably the most influential cultural document for gender relations in Western society'.[44] Both the text and its cultural retellings have had significant influence on the experiences of women and girls living in societies where cultural and religious traditions are deeply rooted in Genesis 2–3. As Mary Daly notes, Genesis 2–3 'has projected a malignant image of the male-female relationship and the "nature" of women that is still deeply embedded in the modern psyche... As long as the myth of feminine evil is allowed to dominate

---

44. Edwards, *Admen and Eve*, p. 9. See also Shelly Colette, 'Eroticizing Eve: A Narrative Analysis of Eve Images in Fashion Magazine Advertising', *JFSR* 31.2 (Fall 2015), pp. 5-24.

human consciousness and social arrangements, it provides the setting for women's victimization, by both men and women.'[45]

In other words, cultural texts that portray Eve as the embodiment of feminine weakness and sexual temptation commonly reinscribe the same misogynistic understandings of women and gender relations that, according to some biblical scholars, are voiced, albeit implicitly, within the biblical text itself.[46] As Edwards explains, visual images of Eve are omnipresent. In both art and advertising she is a flame-haired woman pressing a juicy red apple into a reluctant Adam's hand; *sans* Adam, she flirts coquettishly with the serpent, her body blending sensuously with the serpent's coils until the two become one flesh. These visual depictions portray Eve as a dangerous temptress, while at the same time exonerating the blame from Adam and validating God's decision to place women under their husband's containment and control (Gen. 3.16).[47]

Another biblical tradition that conveys a similarly implicit message about women's problematic sexuality is 2 Samuel 11, David's disastrous encounter with Bathsheba. Within this narrative, Bathsheba is a passive object of (hetero)sexual desire and abuse. She is a sexualized body who is gazed-upon, penetrated, and then dismissed, at least initially, by David.[48] Nevertheless, there are also hints in the text that Bathsheba is in some sense complicit in this illicit sexual encounter with David. Her bathing in close proximity to the royal palace may be read as a deliberate attempt on her part to attract the king's attention and as nothing less than an act of female 'provocation' or 'flirtation' designed to arouse his lust and ultimately to cause his ruin.[49]

The problematics of such a text have been a popular source of discussion among feminist biblical scholars, not least of all those scholars who adopt a cultural studies approach. Considering Bathsheba's cultural afterlives in

---

45. Mary Daly, *Beyond God the Father: Toward a Philosophy of Women's Liberation* (Boston: Beacon Press, 1973), p. 45.

46. See Edwards' discussion in *Admen and Eve*, pp. 12-34. Some feminist biblical scholars argue that Genesis 2–3 might be read in a more redeeming and less patriarchal light: see for example Phyllis Trible, *God and the Rhetoric of Sexuality* (Philadelphia: Fortress Press, 1978), pp. 72-143; Deborah W. Rooke, 'Feminist Criticism of the Bible: Why Bother?', *Feminist Theology* 15 (2007), pp. 160-74.

47. Edwards, *Admen and Eve*; see also J. Cheryl Exum, 'Notorious Biblical Women in Manchester: Spencer Stanhope's Eve and Frederick Pickersgill's Delilah', in Martin O'Kane (ed.), *Bible, Art, Gallery* (Bible in the Modern World, 21; Sheffield: Sheffield Phoenix Press, 2011), pp. 69-96.

48. Exum, *Plotted, Shot, and Painted*, pp. 27-59.

49. Exum, *Plotted, Shot, and Painted*, pp. 32-33, surveys previous biblical scholarship that identifies Bathsheba as a 'temptress' who orchestrated an encounter with David for her own gain.

music, film, and art, such exegetes raises concerns about the biblical ideologies highlighted by these afterlives that present the female body as a desired but dangerous commodity, which 'innocent' men find simply too hard to resist. Helen Leneman, for instance, notes that contemporary popular musicians portray Bathsheba as a temptress, like Eve, whose sexual allure was the ruin of David. The songwriters appropriate her depiction within the biblical narrative as a 'vehicle to warn men of the dangers of women's charms'.[50]

Meanwhile, Exum examines this biblical woman's status in visual texts, including film and art, presenting her as the creation, possession, and object of the (male) gaze. Using Laura Mulvey's theory of female *to-be-looked-at-ness* in visual culture, Exum explores visual texts that plot, shoot, and paint Bathsheba as a passive body to be observed and as a body complicit in allowing spectators to gaze upon her with desire, lust, and voyeuristic pleasure.[51] Similarly, Mieke Bal discusses Rembrandt's well-known painting, *Bathsheba at her Bath* (1654), noting that Rembrandt's Bathsheba 'colludes' with David's voyeurism by displaying her body to viewers. Yet at the same time, the painting reminds viewers of the artificiality of Bathsheba's existence as she refuses to meet our gaze and and poses awkwardly, distorted by the artist's *trompe l'oeil*.[52] Bathsheba seems at once to be an object of desire and an object of anxiety. As in the biblical narrative, her vulnerability is eclipsed within cultural texts in favour of an explicit androcentric vision of her dangerous power to enthral and entice. As with cultural images of Eve, visual portrayals of the sexualized and naked Bathsheba draw out implicit and explicit ideologies about female sexuality that lie hidden within the biblical tradition. Cultural studies enables feminist biblical scholars to explore the potency of these ideologies and to lay bare their pervasive presence in ancient and modern societies.

Filling in Textual Gaps
Biblical narratives are rarely comprehensive in their storytelling or their characterization. Rather, they contain gaps and absences that require readers to fill them in with their own knowledge, assumptions, and ideologies. Similarly, producers of cultural texts fill in these gaps and absences as they construct the afterlives of biblical characters, often in ways that exhibit their views about the biblical traditions. Feminist cultural studies, digging into these 'fillings', explores and interrogates the gendered ideologies expressed therein.

50. Helen Leneman, 'Portrayals of Power in the Stories of Delilah and Bathsheba: Seduction in Song', in Aichele, *Culture, Entertainment, and the Bible*, pp. 139-55 (154).
51. Exum, *Plotted, Shot, and Painted*, pp. 37-53.
52. Mieke Bal, *Reading 'Rembrandt': Beyond the Word Image Opposition* (New York: Cambridge University Press, 1991), p. 244.

One particular biblical character whose afterlives typically involve much gap filling is Delilah, Samson's love interest, and the catalyst of his grisly demise in Judges 16. In her excellent discussion of Delilah's cultural afterlives, Exum probes the cultural fillings at length.[53] She observes that the narrator of Judges 16 reveals very little about Delilah. Yet, like Eve, Delilah is typically presented as a *femme fatale*, and, even worse, as a foreign *femme fatale* in her innumerable afterlives on stage, screen, and canvas. Through her treachery and seduction, she is portrayed as luring an unsuspecting Samson towards destruction and ultimately death.[54] Cultural presentations of Delilah drip with the decadent sexual excess of the fatal woman. This is a Delilah with shimmering lips, dark smoky eyes, sensuous curves and a schizophrenic personality that terrifies and thrills. Such a Delilah does not exist explicitly within the biblical text of Judges 16. Rather, her cultural afterlives testify to the troubling and equally schizophrenic ideologies and attitudes dominant within patriarchal cultures that problematize and pathologize women's sexuality, validating women's policing and containment.

But is this important? Does it really matter whether these cultural texts have 'accurately' captured Delilah as depicted in Judges 16? As a feminist biblical scholar who is engaged in cultural studies research, I argue that yes, it *does* matter. Like Eve's and Bathsheba's cultural reputation as dangerous temptresses, Delilah's influential afterlives are similarly problematic. They bring into sharp relief those malignant stereotypes about women's sexual, social, and ethnic identities within ancient and contemporary cultures.[55] The lethally sexualized Philistine Delilah ceases to be merely a character in an old Bible story and instead becomes a signifier for the danger of *all* sexualized women, particularly foreign women, thus validating the othering and marginalization of these women within contemporary contexts.

Nevertheless, not all cultural texts portray biblical women in a censorious or misogynist light. On the contrary, some cultural appropriations fill in the gaps surrounding female characters to highlight a reading of their personas that biblical texts neglect and suppress. For instance, various visual afterlives depict Hagar, Sarah's Egyptian slave, who was used as a 'surrogate' by Sarah to bear Abraham a son (Genesis 16, 21). Textual gaps surround Hagar's character in the biblical text, preventing readers from accessing her point of view and thereby making it difficult to sympathize with her. Yet

---

53. Exum, *Plotted, Shot, and Painted*, pp. 209-75.
54. Exum, *Plotted, Shot, and Painted*, p. 210. See also Bal, *Lethal Love*, p. 38.
55. Dan Clanton, *Daring, Disreputable, and Devout: Interpreting the Bible's Women in the Arts and Music* (New York: T. & T. Clark International, 2009), pp. 66-77; Caroline Blyth and Teguh Wijaya Mulya, 'The Delilah Monologues', in *Sexuality, Ideology and the Bible: Antipodean Engagements* (Bible in the Modern World, 70; Sheffield: Sheffield Phoenix Press, 2015), pp. 144-62.

as Exum notes,[56] artistic portrayals may redress this textual ambiguity by bringing her subjectivity to the fore. They focus on her experiences to invite sympathy for her. Examining Hagar's artistic portrayal across the centuries, Exum articulates how the various images depict a family torn asunder, a woman and her son excluded and abjected, and a father who could have prevented this exclusion but fails to do so and grieves for his loss. While the biblical traditions silence and objectify Hagar, some artists give her a voice, inviting viewers to recognize her subjectivity and the intolerable space she occupies within the biblical text. Some cultural afterlives thus grant female characters an attentiveness and centrality that is absent from their biblical portrayal. Through engagement with these afterlives, feminist cultural interpreters look beyond the silenced and marginalized female figures in biblical literature and ponder them in new, and at times empowering, lights.

Final Thoughts and Future Directions

The discussion above provides a tempting taster of what is involved in cultural studies, and its value as an accessible and engaging feminist methodology for biblical exegesis. It allows researchers to delve into popular culture that infuses past and present everyday societies, highlighting the value and relevance of feminist biblical studies as a means of engaging with the lived experiences of many women and girls. It recognizes the Bible as a potent cultural location for a myriad of ideologies and attitudes about gender and sexuality, a textual space where gendered power, privilege, and patriarchy intersect, creating cultural landscapes in which women and men can co-exist. Feminist cultural investigators turn a critical eye toward these locations and intersections, holding them up for scrutiny and critical evaluation. They interrogate them, respond to them, and explore their potential for advancing or hindering socio-political and cultural change.

Finally some thoughts about future goals and directions of cultural studies are in order to outline the vitality and vibrancy of this method for feminist Hebrew Bible studies. First, in terms of participation, feminist biblical studies would benefit from including producers of cultural texts, such as artists, filmmakers, musicians, performers, and poets, for collaboration on research projects. As a methodology, cultural studies has never been restricted to the corridors of the academy, but it engages participants both inside and outside academia in cultural analysis and critique.[57] In doing so, cultural studies remains relevant and fresh, compelling scholars to talk *with*, rather than about, cultural producers. It also encourages scholars to venture

---

56. J. Cheryl Exum, 'The Accusing Look: The Abjection of Hagar in Art', *Religion and the Arts* (2007), pp. 143-71.

57. Rodman, *Why Cultural Studies?*, pp. 60-61.

out of the cloistered world of academia and to recognize the 'radical context', or *situatedness*, of cultural texts under investigation.[58]

Additionally, such collaboration across scholarly and cultural fields invites cultural critics to present their research using media other than the more customary written texts. Rather than publish monographs or articles, scholars should also collaborate with cultural producers to present their works in diverse cultural genres, such as film, music, or theatre performances, thus exhibiting their research in the medium that both scholars and the public can experience and explore together. A recent example of such a joint venture is the 'Garden of Eden: Bible Burlesque' cabaret and variety show organized in 2014 by Hidden Perspectives, a public outreach project organized by the Sheffield Institute for Interdisciplinary Biblical Studies at the University of Sheffield.[59] Through the media of dance and song, the show's performers interpreted various biblical traditions to challenge conventional understandings of sexuality and gender in the Bible. Attracting scholars, students, and the public, the show inspired enthusiastic responses from the audience that appreciated the accessibility of this kind of biblical interpretation and the power of performance to shed new light and significance on these ancient traditions.

Furthermore, it is also time for feminist cultural critics of the Bible to recall the centrality of politics and praxis that this academic methodology initially inspired. In the 1990s, Stuart Hall reflects on the AIDS epidemic when he poses the following question: 'Against the urgency of people dying in the streets, what in God's name is the point of cultural studies?'[60] At the same time, he also notes that while cultural studies cannot do everything, it can achieve *something*. In its 'privileged capacity' within the cloisters of academia, it can provoke and unsettle cultural and political discourses within the public sphere. It can disrupt established power structures that silence and harm. It can offer new understandings and propose alternative and less harmful ways of making sense of the world.[61] In a similar fashion, Lawrence Grossberg emphasizes:

> Cultural studies is not going to save the world, or even the university; rather, it is a modest proposal for a flexible and radically contextual intellectual-political practice. It attempts to produce the best knowledge possible in the service of making a better world. And as such, it may help us get a little further toward our goal of making the world a more just and equitable place for all people.[62]

58. For further discussion of 'radical contextuality' in cultural studies, see Grossberg, *Cultural Studies in the Future Tense*, pp. 9, 20-40.
59. For further information on this show, see http://www.hiddenperspectives.org (accessed 29 September 2015).
60. Hall, 'Cultural Studies and its Theoretical Legacies', p. 284.
61. Hall, 'Cultural Studies and its Theoretical Legacies', p. 285.
62. Grossberg, *Cultural Studies in the Future Tense*, p. 55. Also Rodman, *Why Cultural Studies?*, pp. ix, 55-58.

Grossberg's understanding of cultural studies as an academic endeavour in the service of 'making a better world' lies at the heart of this method. It exemplifies the goal of cultural studies as it has been practiced by feminist biblical exegetes and indeed *all* biblical interpreters. Were it to fail in this endeavour, cultural studies would offer nothing more than an impotent, introspective approach to popular culture and would become increasingly inconsequential both academically and politically.[63] While such an ambition may appear idealistic, it coheres with theoretical and practical imperatives that, as Annette Kolodny asserts, have always been central to feminist scholarship:

> Ideology, however, only truly manifests its power by ordering the sum of our actions. If feminist criticism calls anything into question, it must be that dog-eared myth of intellectual neutrality. For, what I take to be the underlying spirit, or message, of any consciously ideologically premised criticism—that is, that ideas are important *because* they determine the way we live, or want to live, in the world—is vitiated by confining those ideas to the study, the classroom, or the pages of our books.[64]

In short, cultural studies, including feminist cultural studies, is an intellectual exercise firmly anchored in the realities of everyday life. It constructs a bridge between the academic world and the world 'out there'.[65] It is committed to being critic and conscience of *both* these worlds. For many people, living the experiences of oppression, racism, sexism, homophobia, silencing, and marginalization, and for women living in the perpetual shadows of rape culture, economic inequality, and limited reproductive rights, these are unquestionable realities that can appear near nigh unchallengeable. Cultural studies reminds everyone that these harmful cultural discourses are neither eternal nor beyond our critique. To challenge them requires intellectual engagement *and* commitment by both the academy and beyond. As a method of feminist biblical interpretation, cultural studies offers a valuable and accessible resource for engaging with biblical and cultural ideologies about women, gender, and sexuality. Through such engagements, feminist biblical scholars can, as Grossberg insists, 'produce the best knowledge possible in the service of making a better world'.[66]

---

63. Rodman, *Why Cultural Studies?*, pp. xi-xii, 2.
64. Annette Kolodny, 'Dancing through the Minefield: Some Observations on the Theory, Practice, and Politics of a Feminist Literary Criticism', in Robyn R. Warhol and Diane Price Herndl, *Feminisms: An Anthology of Literary Theory and Criticism* (New Brunswick: Rutgers University Press, rev. edn, 1997), pp. 171-90 (186). Original italics.
65. Ien Ang, 'Who Needs Cultural Research?', in Pepi Leistyna (ed.), *Cultural Studies: From Theory to Action* (Maldon: Blackwell, 2005), pp. 477-83 (478).
66. Grossberg, *Cultural Studies in the Future Tense*, p. 55.

INDEXES

INDEX OF REFERENCES

OLD TESTAMENT

Genesis		20.4-7	187	5.22	43
1–3	147	21	376	6	124, 125
1.1–2.4	57	21.9-21	235	6.2-3	125
1.26-28	56	25.22-26	72	6.5-6	125
1.27	56, 112,	26	190	6.12	125
	148, 216	27	189	15.17-21	85
2–3	15, 26-28,	27.17	83	27	291
	60, 192,	28.12-15	189	36	291
	195, 205,	29–30	72		
	211-13,	31	268	Deuteronomy	
	250, 271,	32	189	7.5	68
	304, 331,	34	33, 34,	12.3	68
	332, 373,		121, 124	12.7	85
	374	35.1-19	86	16.21	68
2	27			21	358
2.23	216	Exodus		22.5	317
3	188, 212,	1–2	173, 289-	25.5-10	65
	274		91	26.14	84
3.2-3	27	1.8-22	270	34.7	356
3.6-8	27	2.1-22	239		
3.16	374	19–20	289-91	Joshua	
4	189	20–23	65	1.7	291
9.18-27	189	35.26	83	2	128, 338,
12–36	72				339
12	187, 190	Leviticus		2.1	44
14	209	10.1-5	206	2.8-12	44
16	235, 236,	15	124, 125	2.13	44, 285
	376	18.20	317	6	128
16.1-16	235	18.24-28	40	6.22-25	338
16.11-12	236	20.13	317	15.16-18	43
16.13-14	236	21	357	15.16	43
18.6	353	25.23	292	15.19	44
19	189, 315	26.26	83		
19.3	353			Judges	
20	187, 190	Numbers		1.12-15	43
20.1-18	187	5.11-31	41	3.7	68
20.3-7	187	5.14	42	4–5	359
20.3	187	5.21	42		

Index of References

4	254	13	127	31.13	83
4.18	45	13.12-13	47	31.19	83
4.20	254	15.16	349	31.22	83
5.24	254			31.24	83
5.27	45	*1 Kings*			
9	253	2	349	*Ecclesiastes*	
9.52-54	183	3.16-28	128, 338, 339	12.1-8	209
9.53-54	353				
9.53	82	11.1	47	*Isaiah*	
11	28-31, 46, 130, 186	15.13	68	8.3	49
		18.19	68	40–55	355
11.30-40	185	19.2	47	42.13	355
12	209	21	48	42.14	355
13–16	349	22.17	337	47.2	82
14.4	46			54.1	86
16	184, 376	*2 Kings*			
16.1	338	4.8-37	47, 89	*Jeremiah*	
16.4-5	46	8.1-6	89	2–3	287, 315
16.4	338, 350	15.19-20	93	13	177
16.13-14	83	21.7	68	16.1-5	350
16.13	184	23.4	68	20.11	358
16.18-22	46	23.7	83	30.5-22	288
17–21	270	30–37	48	30.8-9	288, 289
17.6	337			30.8	289
18.1	337	*2 Chronicles*		31.22	251
19	46, 185, 198, 315	18.16	337		
				Ezekiel	
19.1	337	*Ezra*		13.17-22	49
19.26-27	198	9–10	71, 214, 215, 360	16	177, 304, 315, 331
21.25	337			23	177, 271, 293, 331, 356
1 Samuel		*Nehemiah*			
1–12	205	13	71		
1–2	47			23.21	356
2.19	83	*Job*		24.15-27	350
4.19-20	86	40.19	358	44.30	85
8.13	83	41.1	358		
16	349			*Hosea*	
17.42	349	*Psalms*		1–3	48, 218-20
22	89	23	206	1–2	271, 338
		24	292	2	177, 315
2 Samuel		113.9	86	4	192
10	358			4.10-19	191
10.4	358	*Proverbs*		7	353
11–12	47	1–9	191, 328, 331	7.8	353
11	374				
11.20-21	183	7	271		
11.21	353	31.10-31	89, 175, 252		
12.15-18	86				

NEW TESTAMENT			*John*		22.4	123
Matthew			12.1-8	338	42.9-10	123
24.41	82					
26.6-13	338		*Revelation*		PALESTINIAN TALMUD	
			17.1–19.10	338	*Pesaḥim*	
Mark					3, 30b	83
14.3-9	338		APOCRYPHA			
			Ecclesiasticus			
Luke			7.24	122		
7.36-50	338		7.25	123		

INDEX OF AUTHORS

Abraham, J. 211
Ackerman, S. 45, 48, 62, 96, 100, 101, 134, 158, 347
Ahmed, S. 275
Aichele, G. 370
Alaimo, S. 276, 326
Albertz, R. 82, 85, 137
Allison, D.C. 370
Allison, P.M. 78
Almond, P.C. 15
Alpert, R.T. 311, 317
Alter, R. 170
Althus-Reid, M. 311
Althusser, L. 262
Anderson, B. 37
Anderson, C.B. 40, 272
Andreasen, N.E. 101
Ang, I. 379
Archer, L.J. 123
Ashcroft, B. 294, 295
Asher-Greve, J. 108
Asikainen, S. 361
Averbeck, R.E. 95

Baadsgaard, A. 82, 88
Bach, A. 42, 67, 68, 174, 370
Baden, J. 372
Bailey, M.A. 277
Bal, M. 46, 176, 177, 183-86, 196-98, 211-13, 335, 372, 375, 376
Barker, C. 367
Barr, J. 145, 151, 153
Barré, M. 96
Barrett, M. 263, 275, 326, 329
Barthes, R. 166, 167
Barton, J. 14
Bauer, A. 249
Beach, E.F. 103, 104
Beal, T.K. 208, 214, 263
Beardless, W.A. 199
Beardsley, M. 162, 163

Beauvoir, S. de 246
Bechdel, A. 318
Bechtel, L.M. 34, 120, 121, 131, 192, 195
Becking, B. 158
Bellis, A.O. 140
Ben-Barak, Z. 101
Benesteau, J. 196
Benjamin, D.C. 117
Benjamin, W. 264
Berger, M. 348
Bergmann, C. 356
Berlant, L. 307
Beynon, J. 345
Bhabha, H.K. 37, 288, 297
Biale, D. 123, 124
Bietenhard, S. 238
Bird, P.A. 3, 5, 26, 44, 57, 66, 91, 96-98, 107, 136, 142, 152, 158, 256
Bjelland Kartzow, M. 110
Black, F.C. 209, 370, 371
Blyth, C. 376
Boer, D. 336
Boer, R. 71, 215, 264, 265, 278, 279, 295, 297, 300, 314, 315, 320, 333, 337, 342, 344, 352, 358, 370
Bohache, T. 218, 313
Bohmbach, K.G. 349, 350
Bolger, D. 88
Boone, J.A. 347
Bouriand, N. 221
Braudel, F. 333
Brayford, S. 11, 12
Brecht, B. 336
Brenner, A. 49, 98, 158, 175, 178, 197, 267
Brett, M.G. 137, 138, 283
Brettler, M.Z. 45
Brintnall, K.L. 305, 306, 323
Bryson, V. 12
Burnett, F.W. 208
Burns, P.C. 370

Burns, R. 173
Butler, J. 36, 246, 307, 346

Camp, C.V. 35, 116, 121-23
Cannon, K. 230-35, 239, 241, 242, 267
Caputo, J.D. 199
Carden, M. 315, 322
Carmack, R.M. 79, 80
Carr, D.M. 211
Carroll, M.P. 116, 263
Carter, C.E. 78
Carter, W. 264
Carusi, A. 280
Carvalho, C.L. 350, 351
Cassuto, D. 82
Chalcraft, D.J. 115
Chandler, D. 166
Chapman, C. 105, 359
Chapman, C.R. 358
Chatterjee, C. 327
Chavalas, M. 92-94
Chaves, K.K. 80
Childs, B.S. 169, 170
Chodorow, N. 197
Cioffi, F. 196
Cixous, H. 197
Clanton, D. 376
Clarke, D. 308, 309, 320
Clément, C. 197
Clévenot, M. 264
Clifford, R. 168
Clines, D.J.A. 161, 172, 210, 211, 269, 350, 362
Coleman, M. 227
Colette, S. 373
Collins, J.J. 145, 151, 153, 155
Collins, P. 227
Conkey, M.W. 77
Connell, R.W. 352, 354, 361, 362
Conway, C.M. 352, 357
Cook, S.L. 68
Coole, D. 276
Copeland, M.S. 228, 242
Corey, G. 194
Counihan, C.M. 87
Creang², O. 346, 347, 351
Crenshaw, K. 301, 329
Crews, F. 196
Crowell, B.L. 278, 282, 301
Culbertson, P. 370

Culbertson, P.L. 348
Culler, J. 164

Daly, M. 245, 374
Darby, E. 86
Darden, L. 285
Darr, K.P. 174
Davidson, M.G. 297
Davies, E.W. 264
Davis, A. 244
Day, P.L. 2, 58, 74, 75, 96, 256
De Groot, J. 248
De Troyer, K. 66, 71, 123
De Vries, R.J. 216, 217
DeVault, M. 10
Deleuze, G. 262
Delgado, R. 360
Delphy, C. 275, 326
Derrida, J. 199-201, 209, 210, 221, 336
Descartes, R. 1
deSilva, D.A. 117
Destro, A. 123
Detweiler, R. 204, 208
Dever, W.G. 74
Di Vito, R.A. 89
Diakonoff, I.M. 337
Dijk-Hemmes, F. 158
Dijkstra, M. 158
Dolphijn, R. 276
Domeris, W.R. 117
Douglas, K.B. 227, 228
Douglas, M. 84, 115, 116, 125
Drinkwater, G. 312
Dube, M.S. 35, 44, 130, 135, 180, 280, 282-84, 290, 292, 293, 298
Duggan, L. 323, 324
Durham, W.H. 119
Dykstra, L. 264

Eagleton, T. 162-64, 263
Ebeling, J.R. 61, 82, 113
Edwards, K.B. 273, 274, 371, 373, 374
Eilberg-Schwartz, H. 40, 315, 355
Ellens, D. 66, 123
Ellens, J.H. 182
Engels, F. 262
Erbele, D. 249
Erickson, M.T. 119
Eskenazi, T. 64
Evans, M. 248

Index of Authors

Exum, J.C. 3, 11, 46, 123, 161, 168, 172, 173, 190, 191, 197, 198, 267, 272, 273, 359, 362, 365, 370, 372, 374-77
Eysenck, H. 196, 197

Fander, M. 69
Fausto-Sterling, A. 247
Feinstein, E.L. 67
Fewell, D.N. 35, 43, 177, 249, 267, 355
Fiensy, D. 119
Fischer, I. 72
Fletcher, K. 230, 242
Floyd-Thomas, S. 230
Fokkelman, J.P. 169
Fontaine, C.R. 58, 98, 107, 178, 267, 358, 359
Foucault, M. 202, 203, 263, 307, 314
Fox, M. 167, 168
Freud, S. 193
Frost, S. 276
Frye, N. 164
Frymer-Kensky, T. 41, 67, 96, 98, 126, 140, 141, 256
Fuchs, E. 3, 4, 29-31, 38, 39, 48, 267, 268, 323

Gafney, W. 238, 239
Gallagher, S.V. 279
Gandhi, L. 36, 37, 280, 297
García Bachman, M.L. 64
Gelpi, B.C. 263
George, R.M. 36
Gero, J.M. 77
Gilchrist, R. 75
Gilligan, C. 197, 245
Gimenez, M.E. 326
Giroux, H.A. 221
Gitay, Y. 168
Glancy, J. 348
Gnuse, R.K. 68
Goldingay, J. 211
Gonzalez, M.A. 112
Goodman, W. 370
Goshen-Gottstein, M.H. 140
Goss, R.E. 218, 313
Gottwald, N.K. 87, 263, 266, 329
Gravett, S.L. 349, 350
Greaves, L. 23
Greenstein, E.L. 200, 202, 205, 206, 211
Greifenhagen, F.V. 349, 350

Griffiths, G. 294, 295
Grossberg, L. 366, 368, 378, 379
Grossman, M.L. 264
Grosz, E. 276, 296
Gruber, M.I. 66, 191, 196
Guattari, F. 262
Guest, D. 218, 254-56, 313, 314, 317-19, 321, 322, 351, 360
Gugelberger, G.M. 279, 280
Gunn, D.M. 35, 177, 249, 355

Hackett, J.A. 62, 68, 96, 104
Haddox, S. 106, 353, 354
Hadley, J. 96
Halberstam, J. 352
Hall, S. 38, 364-68, 371, 378
Hallo, W.W. 92, 95, 108
Halperin, D.M. 306, 307, 312, 322
Hardin, J.W. 77
Harding, S. 6, 23
Harris, M. 80
Hartley, J. 364-66, 372
Harvey, J. 369
Havea, J. 264
Hawkins, P.S. 369
Haynes, S. 172
Hegland, M.E. 87
Hekman, S. 276, 326
Heller, K.J. 203, 204
Hendon, J.A. 86, 87, 89
Hennessy, R. 265, 275, 326
Hentrich, T. 357
Herzfeld, M. 118, 119
Hesse-Biber, S.N. 6, 7, 24
Hirshkind, C. 324
Hitchcock, L.A. 331
Hobbs, T.R. 117
Hodges, F.M. 194
Hoffmeier, J.K. 96
Holladay, J.S., Jr 79
Holland, J. 7, 10
Holloway, S.W. 92, 93
Holt, E.K. 287, 288
Homan, M.M. 82
hooks, b. 244, 288
Hopkins, K. 75
Horney, K. 197
Hornsby, T.J. 249, 264
Horsley, R.A. 280, 282, 299, 300
Houston, W. 116

Howard, R.G. 369
Hui, L.K. 130

Ilan, T. 258
Ingraham, C. 326
Ipsen, A. 128, 129, 337-40
Irigaray, L. 41, 197
Isasi-Diaz, A.M. 233

Jack, A.M. 369
Jagose, A. 308
Jameson, F. 262-64, 329
Janowski, B. 136, 145
Jeansonne, S.P. 174
Jeffreys, S. 299
Jennings, T.W. 313, 315
Jobling, D. 65, 205, 207, 210, 262-64, 267, 294, 296-98, 310, 330, 334, 336
Johnson, W.M. 361
Jordan, M.D. 314
Junior, N. 227-29, 237, 238, 240
Just, P. 112

Kaden, D.A. 203
Kaltner, J. 172
Kaminsky, J.S. 140
Keddie, N.R. 75
Keefe, A.A. 50
Keohane, N.O. 263
Kille, D.A. 181, 182
Kim, U.Y. 285, 286, 299, 303
Kimmel, M.S. 345
Kirby, A. 221
Kirby, S. 23
Kirk-Duggan, C. 234, 249
Kirova, M. 349
Knierim, R.P. 145, 156
Knoppers, G.N. 66
Koch, T.R. 316
Kolakowski, V.S. 316
Kollontai, A. 327
Kolodny, A. 379
Koosed, J.L. 199, 202, 209, 267
Koyama, E. 247
Kraemer, R.S. 133
Kramarae, C. 227
Kramer, C. 78
Krech, S. 80
Kressel, G.M. 118

Kristeva, J. 40, 183
Krondorfer, B. 347, 351
Kwok, P.-L. 233, 241, 279, 282, 293, 298, 300, 301

Lai, B.M. 182
Landry, D. 326, 341
Lang, B. 191
Laniak, T.S. 117
Lanser, S.S. 213
Lapavitsas, C. 222
Lapsley, J.E. 178
Latvus, K. 295
Lauretis, T. de 307, 323
Lawrence, B. 251, 252
Lazarewicz-Wyrzykowska, E. 350
Leavey, J.P., Jr 204
Lemos, T.M. 63, 64
Leneman, H. 370, 375
Lenin, V.I. 335
Lentin, R. 38
Lesser, J. 312
Letherby, G. 24
Levenson, J. 140
Levenson, J.D. 36, 38
Levinson, B.M. 66, 256
Lewin, E. 114
Liew, T.B. 297, 298, 322
Linafelt, T. 208, 209
Lipka, H. 354
Liverani, M. 98, 342
Løland, H. 354, 355
Long, B.O. 137
Long, R.E. 321
Lopez, D.C. 91
Lorde, A. 244, 298
Low, K. 248, 346, 358
Luxemburg, R. 327

MacKinnon, C. 22
MacLean, G. 326, 341
Măcelaru, M.V. 349
Macherey, P. 263
Macwilliam, S. 249, 313, 359
Magonet, J. 123
Mahmood, S. 324
Maier, C.M. 249, 286-88
Malina, B.J. 117
Mangual, E.M.R. 214

Manning, J.G. 344
Marchal, J.A. 324
Marcus, S. 306, 308, 321
Marsman, H.J. 62, 63, 68
Martin, C. 179
Martin, T. 327, 336
Marx, K. 262
Masenya, M. 175, 241
Matthews, V.H. 117, 256
Mayer, T. 39
Maynard, M. 248
Mazar, A. 77
Mbuvi, A. 292
Mbuwayesango, D. 292, 301
McCall, L. 329
McCarthy, D.P. 206
McClaurin, I. 114
McClintock, A. 39
McKay, H.A. 126, 127
McKenzie, S. 172
McKinlay, J.E. 35, 48, 291-93, 302
McQuitty, A. 83
Memmi, A. 297
Messerschmidt, J.W. 352, 361, 362
Meyer, C. 196
Meyers, C. 59, 60, 67, 75-77, 80-82, 85-87, 89, 90, 98-100, 330, 334, 361
Michel, C. 109
Miller, D.L. 182
Miller, T. 365
Milne, P.J. 31, 130, 210
Mitchell, J. 327
Mitchell, W.J.T. 263
Moi, T. 37, 326
Monhanty, C.T. 36
Moore, S.D. 2, 14, 15, 105, 208, 310, 314, 316, 346, 351, 356, 365, 368, 370, 372
Moorey, P.R.S. 92
Moran, W.L. 337
Morris, I. 344
Mosala, I. 263
Muilenburg, J. 167, 168
Müller, M. 96
Mulvey, L. 348
Mulya, T.W. 376
Murdock, G.P. 79
Myers, C. 264
Myers, J.D. 210
Myles, R.J. 274

Nadeau, K. 267
Nakhai, B.A. 81, 331
Naples, N.A. 8, 9
Nealon, J.T. 15, 221, 222
Negri, A. 341
Nelavla, S. 103
Nelson, A.J. 210, 292
Nelson, S.M. 79, 113, 135
Neville, D.J. 264
Newsom, C.A. 177, 178, 269
Newton, J. 261
Neyrey, J.H. 117
Niditch, S. 56, 61, 62, 350, 358
Nissinen, M. 312, 317
Norris, C. 202
Nuzman, R. 113, 134

O'Brien, J.M. 192
O'Grady, K. 123-25
O'Kane, M. 369
Økland, J. 265, 344
Olyan, S.M. 117
Otto, E. 65

Paedes, I. 177
Pathak, Z. 293, 294
Peirce, C.S. 165
Penchansky, D. 263
Penner, T. 35, 70, 91, 301
Perdue, L.G. 264
Philip, T. 67
Phillips, G.A. 208
Phillips, L. 226
Piatelli, D. 6, 7
Pickett, B.L. 204
Pilch, J.J. 117
Pippin, T. 48, 132, 262, 263, 294, 296-98, 310, 370
Pitt-Rivers, J. 116
Plaskow, J. 179
Plate, S.B. 214
Polaski, D.C. 349, 350
Pommier, R. 196
Powell, M.A. 167
Pratt, M.L. 302
Pressler, C. 40, 65
Progoff, I. 181
Provost, C. 79
Puar, J.K. 324
Punt, J. 280, 281, 283

Pusey, A. 119
Pyper, H.S. 208, 214, 369, 370

Racker, H. 194
Radway, J. 326
Ramazanogly, C. 7, 10
Rapoport, A. 81
Rashkow, I. 186, 188-90, 193, 198, 317
Rathje, W.L. 83
Reid, C. 23
Reinhartz, A. 369
Rendtorff, R. 136, 140
Reventlow, H.G. 137
Rich, A. 247
Rich, J. 12
Richards, I.A. 163
Rieger, J. 278, 282, 295, 300, 302
Ringe, S.H. 177, 178
Robbins, J. 112
Rodman, G.B. 366-68, 377-79
Rogers, S.C. 75
Rogerson, J.W. 89, 115
Rojek, C. 368
Rollins, W.G. 182
Romero, M.S. 81
Roncolato, C. 311
Rooke, D.S. 257
Rooke, D.W. 66, 257, 357, 374
Rooney, E. 38
Rosaldo, M.Z. 114, 263
Rosenfelt, D. 261
Roth, J.K. 194
Rotman, D. 98
Rowland, C. 295
Ruane, N.J. 249, 254
Rubenstein, R.L. 194
Rudy, K. 309
Runions, E. 209, 369
Russaw, K.D. 240
Russell, L. 233

Sahlins, M. 330, 342
Said, E. 292
Sakenfeld, K.D. 75, 174
Saller, R. 344
Sanders, J. 170
Sandmel, S. 94
Sawyer, D.F. 211, 250, 251
Sawyer, J.F. 116, 117, 214, 351, 355, 357
Schearing, L.S. 370

Scheidel, W. 344
Schipper, J. 356
Schippert, C. 311, 323
Schleifer, R. 294, 296-98, 310
Schmitt, R. 84, 85
Schneidau, H.N. 204
Schneider, L.C. 299, 311, 319, 320
Schneiders, S. 267
Scholz, S. 5, 19, 20, 32, 33, 57, 99, 178, 216, 236, 301
Schottroff, L. 19, 178
Schroer, S. 13, 14, 100, 238
Schüssler Fiorenza, E. 9, 10, 69-71, 97, 268
Schwartz, R.M. 37, 47
Scott, J.C. 333
Sedgwick, E.K. 307, 318, 346
Segovia, F.F. 263, 281, 297, 300
Segundo, J.L. 263
Seidenberg, R. 185
Sered, S.S. 88
Sharp, C.J. 286-89, 291
Shaw, J. 270
Shectman, S. 55, 63, 64, 72
Sherwood, Y. 2, 14, 15, 49, 208, 209, 218-20, 272, 370
Shneer, D. 312
Siedlecki, A. 264
Simkins, R. 330
Simmons, W.S. 80
Smit, P.-B. 346
Smith, A. 266, 267
Smith, C. 97
Smith, D. 275
Smith, M.J. 239
Solvang, E. 101, 102
Spanier, K. 96
Spelman, E.V. 245
Spinoza, B. de 1
Spivak, G.C. 36, 201, 288
Stacey, J. 113
Stanley, L. 11
Stanley, R.L. 316
Stanton, E.C. 2
Stefancic, J. 360
Stein, A. 309
Steinberg, N. 65
Stenström, H. 70, 71
Sternberg, M. 171
Stiebert, J. 115, 117, 119, 131, 268

Stone, K. 43, 117, 217, 218, 249, 252, 253, 264, 305, 312, 313, 315, 322, 353
Stowers, S. 84
Strathern, M. 113, 114, 128
Straton, B. 263
Sugirtharajah, R.S. 38, 277, 280, 288, 300, 302
Sweely, T.L. 87
Sweeney, M.A. 140

Talmon, S. 94, 95
Tamez, E. 263
Tan, N. 130
Tanner, B.L. 174
Tapp, A.M. 269
Thimmes, P. 5, 26, 97
Thorne, B. 113
Tiffin, H. 294, 295
Tolbert, M.A. 277, 296, 360
Tong, R. 308
Treichler, P. 227
Trible, P. 3, 5, 26-29, 56, 57, 143-49, 168, 169, 176, 374
Tsevat, M. 140
Tuin, I. van der 276
Turman, E.M. 228
Turner, G. 365, 366

Van Wolde, E. 210
Vander Stichele, C. 35, 70, 301, 370

Wacker, M.-T. 19, 57, 58, 80, 178
Wainwright, E.M. 264, 370
Walfist, H.D. 370
Walker, A. 225, 244
Wallerstein, I. 341
Wallis, B. 348
Walsh, J.T. 26, 317
Walters, S.D. 308, 309
Warner, M. 307

Warrior, R.A. 266, 303
Washington, H.C. 40, 214, 215, 249
Watson, P.J. 78, 79
Watson, S. 348
Webster, R. 196
Weems, R. 9, 49, 173, 174, 177, 228, 237, 238, 240, 270
Wegner, J.R. 63
Welker, M. 145
West, G. 263
West, G.O. 127
West, M. 218, 313, 317, 318
West, T. 226, 227
Whitelam, K.W. 133
Wikan, U. 118, 119
Wilcox, M. 310, 311
Wilk, R.R. 83
Williams, D. 227, 235, 236
Williams, R. 327
Wilson, N.L. 312, 316
Wilson, R.R. 119
Wilson, S.M. 350
Wimbush, V.L. 10, 284
Wimsatt, W.K., Jr 162, 163
Winslow, K.S. 216
Wise, S. 11
Wolf, A.P. 119
Wolin, S.S. 221
Wright, G.E. 167

Yasur-Landau, A. 77
Yee, G.A. 35, 50, 123, 131, 263, 271, 279, 282, 289-91, 293, 295, 297, 298, 302, 318, 328-34
Younger, K.L., Jr 92, 94
Yuval-Davis, N. 39

Zetkin, K. 327
Ziegler, V.H. 370
Žižek, S. 262

www.ingramcontent.com/pod-product-compliance
Lightning Source LLC
Chambersburg PA
CBHW070932230426
43666CB00011B/2411